1   *Scratch off security foil (gently).*

2   *Use code to register online.*

STARTED

3   *Start your experience.*

4   *Discover, interact, learn.*

login.cengagebrain.com

Dear Student:

Every day we're bombarded by information, and it's impossible to take it all in. You may have a similar experience when you stare at a textbook page. Do you ever feel confused about what's *essential* to focus on—and perhaps more on your mind, do you wonder what will be on the final exam?

Discovery Series: Introduction to Psychology was created for students who want to do their best in their courses, but sometimes find themselves trying to figure out what's most relevant in their reading material. This book is briefer than many introductory textbooks, without some of the details that can cause information overload. In addition, as you read this text, you'll *always* know what's important because learning objectives throughout each chapter describe exactly what you're expected to learn. As a result, you'll be able to focus your attention on the "must know" topics.

DISCOVER

A NEW WAY OF LEARNING

At the same time, knowing *what* to focus on doesn't mean you'll "get it," or remember it. That's why this textbook is also paired with interactive online resources that reflect methods known to help learners absorb, understand, and retain concepts more effectively. By guiding your active involvement with text discussions, images, videos, animations, and quizzing (sorry, there's no avoiding quizzing), this new approach to learning meets you in your comfort zone—*and* helps you meet the course learning objectives in a way that a textbook alone cannot.

You've invested in this book, so take a minute to check out the next few pages, which introduce you to the learning path you'll follow in every chapter. It's a brief user's guide that will help you take full advantage of your course materials—and do your best in the course.

You're about to discover a new way of learning. Enjoy the journey.

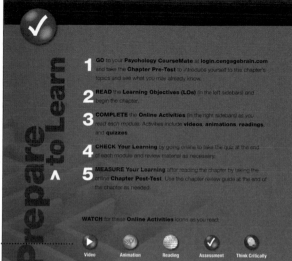

Prepare to Learn

1 **GO** to your **Psychology CourseMate** at **login.cengagebrain.com** and take the **Chapter Pre-Test** to introduce yourself to this chapter's topics and see what you may already know.

2 **READ** the **Learning Objectives (LOs)** (in the left sidebars) and begin the chapter.

3 **COMPLETE** the **Online Activities** (in the right sidebars) as you read each module. Activities include **videos**, **animations**, **readings**, and **quizzes**.

4 **CHECK Your Learning** by going online to take the quiz at the end of each module and review material as necessary.

5 **MEASURE Your Learning** after reading the chapter by taking the online **Chapter Post-Test**. Use the chapter review guide at the end of the chapter as needed.

WATCH for these **Online Activities** icons as you read:

Video   Animation   Reading   Assessment   Think Critically

Prepare to Learn lays out the steps you'll complete as you work through each chapter. This page is the same in every chapter, serving as a reminder that keeps you on track as you complete the chapter's lessons.

Online Activities

Online activities are important to mastering this chapter. As you read each module, access these materials by going to .cengagebrain.com.

Video Explore studies and firsthand accounts of biological and psychological processes:

- How Alzheimer's disease is diagnosed
- Watch the changes a person with Alzheimer's disease gradually begins to exhibit
- Watch and listen to someone with Alzheimer's disease answer questions about himself
- Discover whether or not the brain can grow and make connections in a person who has been living in a minimally conscious state for 20 years
- Watch how fMRI brain scans are used to

Animation Interact with and visualize important processes and concepts:

- See how fertilization takes place
- Explore the probability of developing blue or brown eyes
- Engage with the forces thought responsible for the evolution of the human brain
- Experience the effects of excitatory and inhibitory transmitters
- Practice identifying the overall organization of the brain's nervous systems
- Experience how the sympathetic and parasympathetic nervous systems work
- Identify the location of the major parts of

- Explore how surgeons are able to reattach both of John Thompson's arms and how his arms function post-surgery
- Explore how surgeons are able to transplant a face
- Learn how people can feel sensations and movement from a missing limb
- Learn whether brain size varies among different races and if intelligence is determined by brain size
- Explore how the brains of males and females differ

Assessment Measure your mastery:

- Chapter Pre-Test

Watch for these **icons** as you read. They direct you to go online where videos, animations, additional reading, and quizzes illuminate the text discussion at hand. You'll be quizzed on information covered in these online activities when you take the chapter test, so be sure to complete them.

On the page next to **Prepare to Learn**, check out the resources you'll interact with online. In the chapter shown here, you'll see a video about the female brain, interact with a brain scan, explore how surgeons transplant a face, and much more.

PREPARE

TO LEARN

FIND OUT

WHAT YOU KNOW

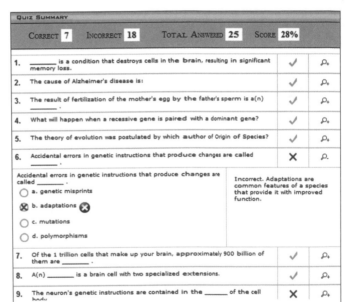

Step 1 when you begin a new chapter is to go to **Psychology CourseMate** at **login.cengagebrain.com** and take the **Chapter Pre-Test** to introduce yourself to the chapter's topics. Seeing your correct and incorrect answers will help you identify topics to pay particular attention to in the chapter—and those that may not require as much attention. You may already know more than you think you do!

Each chapter is divided into several brief learning modules. **Learning Objectives (LOs)** appear in the upper left sidebar throughout each module. They keep you focused by highlighting what you are expected to learn in the pages that immediately follow. Study each objective, and then read the accompanying narrative.

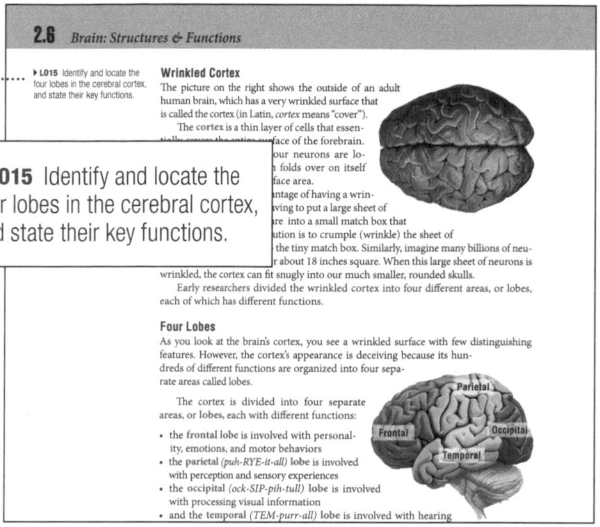

2.6 *Brain: Structures & Functions*

▶ **LO15** Identify and locate the four lobes in the cerebral cortex, and state their key functions.

Wrinkled Cortex

The picture on the right shows the outside of an adult human brain, which has a very wrinkled surface that is called the cortex (in Latin, *cortex* means "cover").

The cortex is a thin layer of cells that essentially covers the entire surface of the forebrain. Almost all our neurons are located in folds over on itself surface area.

The advantage of having a wrinkled cortex is having to put a large sheet of neurons into a small match box that would crumple (wrinkle) the sheet of neurons into the tiny match box. Similarly, imagine many billions of neurons measuring about 18 inches square. When this large sheet of neurons is wrinkled, the cortex can fit snugly into our much smaller, rounded skulls.

Early researchers divided the wrinkled cortex into four different areas, or lobes, each of which has different functions.

Four Lobes

As you look at the brain's cortex, you see a wrinkled surface with few distinguishing features. However, the cortex's appearance is deceiving because its hundreds of different functions are organized into four separate areas called lobes.

The cortex is divided into four separate areas, or lobes, each with different functions:

• the frontal lobe is involved with personality, emotions, and motor behaviors
• the parietal *(puh-RYE-it-all)* lobe is involved with perception and sensory experiences
• the occipital *(ock-SIP-pih-tull)* lobe is involved with processing visual information
• and the temporal *(TEM-purr-all)* lobe is involved with hearing

WANT TO READ ONLINE? READ THE EBOOK!

Psychology CourseMate gives you access to an electronic version of this text. You can read the text, take notes, get one-click access to all of the online resources—and do your homework wherever there's a computer.

② FOCUS ON

THE TEXT

③ INTERACT

A Terrible Accident

Railroad crewmen were about to blast a rock that blocked their way. Foreman Phineas Gage filled a deep, narrow hole in the rock with powder and rammed in an iron rod to tamp down the charge before covering it with sand. But the tamping iron rubbed against the side of the shaft, and a spark ignited the powder.

The massive rod—3½ feet long, 1¼ inches in diameter, and weighing 13 pounds—shot from the hole under the force of the explosion. It struck Phineas just beneath his left eye and tore through his skull. It shot out the top of his head and landed some 50 yards away. The long-term result caused Phineas to have emotional outbursts and problems in making decisions, something he did not experience before the accident.

Cerebral Cortex
Examine what the cerebral cortex of our brain looks like.

Remember the icons on the **Prepare to Learn** page? They always appear in the lower right sidebars throughout each module, prompting you to go online to enhance your understanding of text discussions through videos, animations, and readings.

▶ Video: Cerebral Cortex

Module 2.6 - LO15: Identify and locate the four lobes in the cerebral cortex, and state their key functions.

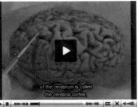

of the cerebrum is called the cerebral cortex

© 2013 Cengage Learning

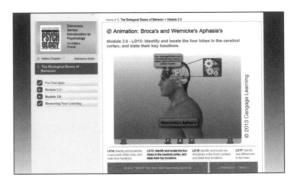

You'll view and interact with online resources many times as you work through each chapter. You may find them so interesting that you won't even know you're studying.

Right Hemisphere

- **Nonverbal** Although usually mute, the right hemisphere has a childlike ability to read, write, spell, and understand speech (Gazzaniga, 1998). For example, the right hemisphere can understand simple sentences and read simple words.
- **Spatial** The right hemisphere is very good at solving spatial problems, such as arranging blocks to match a geometric design. Because the hemispheres control opposite sides of the body, the left hand (right hemisphere) is best at completing spatial tasks.
- **Holistic** The right hemisphere appears to process information by combining parts into a meaningful whole. For example, the right hemisphere is better at recognizing and identifying whole faces (J. Levy et al., 1972).

After comparing the functions of the left and right hemispheres, you see that each hemisphere has specialized skills and is better at performing particular tasks. How-ever specialized they may be, it's important to note that both hemispheres work together to successfully complete many tasks (Zimmer, 2009b).

Right hemisphere

Split-brain Demonstration
Learn how each hemisphere is specialized for performing certain tasks.

✓
Check Your Learning Quiz 2.6
Go to **login.cengagebrain.com** and take the online quiz.

This **Check Your Learning Quiz** icon signifies that you've reached the end of a module.

Go online and take this self-study quiz to make sure you "get it" (in other words, that you can demonstrate your understanding of the module's learning objectives).

For the questions you miss, go back and review the text and related online materials before you move on. Reviewing is also a great way to ensure that what you've just learned "sinks in."

④ **CHECK**

YOUR LEARNING

MEASURE

After reading each chapter, find out how well you've absorbed the material in all of the modules by taking the online **Chapter Post-Test.** Results go to your instructor's gradebook, so take your time and answer carefully. Your results, tied to **Learning Objectives**, will also help you identify areas that require further review so you can overcome weak areas and prepare more effectively for course exams.

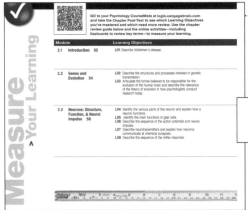

The **Measure Your Learning** chart simplifies study and review by providing an at-a-glance summary of **Learning Objectives**, key terms, important online media resources, and page references to discussions of key topics.

| 2.2 | Genes and Evolution 54 | LO2 | Describe the structures and processes involved in genetic transmission. |
| | | LO3 | Articulate the forces believed to be responsible for the evolution of the human brain and describe the relevance of the theory of evolution in how psychologists conduct research today. |

Let's say your **Post-Test** indicates that should review the material on genes and evolution. In a snap, you can see on the chart that the discussion begins on page 54. If you aced the **Post-Test**, you're done with the chapter.

GET STARTED FOR REAL

Now that you've got the hang of how *Discovery Series: Introduction to Psychology* works, it's time to get started for real. Use the printed card on the inside front cover of this text to register at **login.cengagebrain.com**. Good luck!

We thank the instructors and students who reviewed this project and provided insightful comments:

ACKNOWLEDGMENTS

Reviewers

Jeffrey Baker, *Monroe Community College*
Renee R. Boburka, *East Stroudsburg University*
Pamela Costa, *Tacoma Community College*
Vera Dunwoody, *Chaffey College*
Rebecca R. Escoto, *North Lake College*
Rhiannon Hart, *Rochester Institute of Technology*
Mark Kavanaugh, *Kennebec Valley Community College*
Camille King, *Stetson University*
Juliet Lee, *Cape Fear Community College*
Angela MacKewn, *University of Tennessee at Martin*
Jan Mendoza, *Golden West College*
Lawrence A. Pfaff, *Spring Arbor University*
Hugh Riley, *Baylor University*
Evelyn Schliecker, *Gordon College*
Caitlin Shepherd, *Colorado State University*
Amy Skinner, *Gordon College*
Adam Sturdevant, *College of Menominee Nation*
Holly E. Tatum, *Randolph College*
Jean Wynn, *Manchester Community College*
Christi Young, *Southwestern Michigan College*
Elizabeth Rellinger Zettler, *Illinois College*

Instructor Focus Group Participants

Cheryl Ann Bacheller, *Brevard College— Palm Bay Campus*
Morgan Ann Barnett, *St. Johns River State College*
Andrew Blair, *Palm Beach State College— Lake Worth*
Jennifer T. Blake, *College of Central Florida*
Salena Brody, *Collin College*
Diana L. Ciesko, *Valencia College—East*
Doreen Collins-McHugh, *Seminole State College of Florida*
Richard Dehmer, *Miami-Dade College— Virtual College*

Dora A. Falls, *Eastfield College*
Kenneth Foster, *Texas Woman's University*
Jennifer Gibson, *Tarleton State University*
David Giles, *Tarrant County College— Trinity River*
Jerry Green, *Tarrant County College— Northwest*
Marlene Groomes, *Miami-Dade College— Virtual College*
Lois Herrin, *Brookhaven College*
Patricia Holley, *St. Leo University*
Debra L. Hollister, *Valencia College—Lake Nona*
Regina Marie Hughes, *Collin College*
Sheneice M. Hughes, *Eastfield College*
Alisha Janowsky, *University of Central Florida*
Margaret Jenkins, *Seminole State College of Florida*
Barbara Kennedy, *Brevard College—Palm Bay Campus*
Cheri L. Kittrell, *State College of Florida at Bradenton*
Franz Klutschkowski, *North Central Texas College*
James Matiya, *Florida Gulf Coast University*
Yvonne McCoy, *Tarrant County College— Northeast*
Ticily Medley, *Tarrant County College—South*
Tracy Meyer, *Collin College*
Elizabeth A. Norcross, *North Central Texas College*
Michaelle O'Quin Norman, *Cedar Valley College*
Lois Pasapane, *Palm Beach State College— Lake Worth*
Sheryl S. Peterson, *St. Petersburg College— Seminole*
Cynthia Kay Shinabarger Reed, *Tarrant County College—Northeast*
Karl Robinson, *Tarrant County College— Southeast*
Peggy Ann Russell, *Indian River State College*
Shannon Rich Scott, *Texas Woman's University*

M. Lisa Valentino, *Seminole State College of Florida*
Barbara VanHorn, *Indian River State College*
Linda Wechter-Ashkin, *Palm Beach State College—Boca Raton*

Student Focus Group Participants

Charles Corbitt, *Drexel University*
Kimberly Lorditch, *Bucks County Community College*
Monica Malek, *Bucks County Community College*
Morgan Oechsle, *Chestnut Hill College*
Olivia Stevenson, *Chestnut Hill College*
Diana Washington, *Community College of Philadelphia*

About the Authors

Rod Plotnik earned his Ph.D. as a biological psychologist from University of Florida and a post doctorate at Yale University. Early in his career, he realized the effectiveness of teaching students through visuals to get them excited about the material, a technique he utilizes throughout his other text, ***Introduction to Psychology***, now in its Ninth Edition (Cengage Learning, 2011).

Haig Kouyoumdjian earned his M.A. in psychology from San Diego State University and Ph.D. in clinical psychology from University of Nebraska-Lincoln. Through his classroom teaching, presentations, and publications, Kouyoumdjian has demonstrated a strong commitment to the development and use of innovative teaching methods. Kouyoumdjian is also coauthor of ***Introduction to Psychology***, now in its Ninth Edition (Cengage Learning, 2011).

INTRODUCTION TO PSYCH OLOGY

ROD PLOTNIK
San Diego State University

HAIG KOUYOUMDJIAN
Mott Community College

WADSWORTH
CENGAGE Learning·

Australia • Brazil • Japan • Korea • Mexico • Singapore • Spain • United Kingdom • United States

WADSWORTH
CENGAGE Learning

Discovery Series:
Introduction to Psychology
Rod Plotnik and Haig Kouyoumdjian

Publisher: Jon-David Hague

Executive Editor: Jaime Perkins

Sr. Developmental Editors: Renee Deljon and
Kristin Makarewycz

Assistant Editor: Paige Leeds

Editorial Assistant: Jessica Alderman

Sr. Media Editor: Lauren Keyes

Marketing Comunications Manager:
Laura Localio

Sr. Marketing Manager: Elizabeth Rhoden

Marketing Coordinator: Angeline Low

Sr. Content Project Manager: Pat Waldo

Sr. Art Director: Vernon Boes

Manufacturing Planner: Karen Hunt

Rights Acquisitions Specialist:
Don Schlotman

Production and Composition Service:
Graphic World Inc.

Photo Researcher: Terri Wright

Text Researcher: Pablo D'Stair

Copy Editor: Graphic World Inc.

Illustrators: Tim Jacobus and
Graphic World Inc.

Text Designer: Gary Hespenheide

Cover Designer: Irene Morris

For product information and technology assistance, contact us at
Cengage Learning Customer & Sales Support, 1-800-354-9706.

For permission to use material from this text or product,
submit all requests online at **www.cengage.com/permissions**.
Further permissions questions can be e-mailed to
permissionrequest@cengage.com.

Library of Congress Control Number: 2011946247

ISBN-13: 978-1-111-34702-4

ISBN-10: 1-111-34702-6

Wadsworth
20 Davis Drive
Belmont, CA 94002-3098
USA

Cengage Learning is a leading provider of customized learning solutions with office
locations around the globe, including Singapore, the United Kingdom, Australia,
Mexico, Brazil, and Japan. Locate your local office at **www.cengage.com/global**.

Cengage Learning products are represented in Canada by Nelson Education, Ltd.

To learn more about Wadsworth, visit **www.cengage.com/wadsworth**

Purchase any of our products at your local college store or at our preferred online
store **www.cengagebrain.com**.

Printed in the United States of America
4 5 15

Brief Contents

Contents

3 *Sensation and Perception* 98

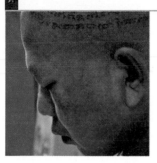

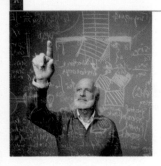

9 *Motivation and Emotion*   404

10 *Social Psychology* 454

12 *Psychological Disorders* 548

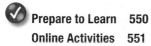

14 Stress, Health, and Coping 638

Introducing Psychology

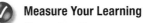

Prepare to Learn

1 **GO** to your **Psychology CourseMate** at **login.cengagebrain.com** and take the **Chapter Pre-Test** to introduce yourself to this chapter's topics and see what you may already know.

2 **READ** the **Learning Objectives (LOs)** (in the left sidebars) and begin the chapter.

3 **COMPLETE** the **Online Activities** (in the right sidebars) *as you read each module*. Activities include **videos**, **animations**, **readings**, and **quizzes**.

4 **CHECK Your Learning** by going online to take the quiz at the end of each module and review material as necessary.

5 **MEASURE Your Learning** after reading the chapter by taking the online **Chapter Post-Test**. Use the chapter review guide at the end of the chapter as needed.

WATCH for these **Online Activities** icons as you read:

Video

Animation

Reading

Assessment

Think Critically

These online activities are important to mastering this chapter. As you read each module, access these materials by going to **login.cengagebrain.com**.

Video Explore studies and firsthand accounts of biological and psychological processes:

- Learn what school is like for a first-grader with autism
- Compare the symptoms of five siblings diagnosed with autism
- Watch how a pigeon is trained to perform new behaviors
- Witness why careful assessment and diagnosis is so important
- Learn more about several prescription treatments for ADHD
- Watch how behavioral therapy helps children with ADHD
- See how teacher beliefs about students' academic abilities affect student performance
- Observe rats helping researchers to understand nicotine addiction

Animation Interact with and visualize important processes and concepts:

- Master the historical and modern approaches to psychology
- Understand the difference between scientific and armchair psychology
- Find out how strength and direction define a correlation

- Use the seven rules to conduct and understand an experiment

Reading Delve deeper into key content:

- Read about how taking notes in class addresses psychology's four goals
- Learn how early American psychologists discriminated against women and minorities
- Learn how the biological approach applies to test anxiety
- Find out how the cognitive approach applies to test anxiety
- Learn how the behavioral approach applies to test anxiety
- Find out how the psychoanalytic approach applies to test anxiety
- Learn how the humanistic approach applies to test anxiety
- Find out how the sociocultural approach applies to test anxiety
- Learn how the evolutionary approach applies to physical attraction
- Find out how to improve study skills based on findings in cognitive and experimental psychology
- Examine the controversies surrounding ADHD diagnosis and treatment
- Learn about problems in using surveys to determine if adolescents accurately recall their sexual histories

- Find out about placebos and some cultural differences affecting their popularity
- Read about how Jane Goodall studied the behavior of chimps
- Learn how informed consent, debriefing, and deception were used in Milgrams's Obedience Study
- Learn how the animal model helps further understanding about schizophrenia

Statistics: The Basics Become familiar with some of the statistics psychologists use in research:

- Learn the basics of descriptive and inferential statistics

Think Critically Challenge your thinking by applying content from this chapter and making connections to related material:

- How Do People with Autism Think?

Assessment Measure your mastery:

- Chapter Pre-Test
- Check Your Learning Quizzes
- Chapter Post-Test

▶ **LO1** Describe autism.

WHEN DONNA WAS about 3 years old, she ate lettuce because she liked rabbits and they ate lettuce. She ate jelly because it looked like colored glass and she liked to look at colored glass. She was told to make friends, but Donna had her own friends. She had a pair of green eyes named Willie, which hid under her bed, and wisps, which were tiny, transparent spots that hung in the air around her.

▼

When people spoke, their words were strange sounds with no meaning, like mumbo jumbo. Although she didn't learn the meanings of words, she loved their sounds when she said them out loud. As a child, she was tested for deafness because she did not use language like other children. She did not learn that words had meaning until she was a teenager.

When people talked to Donna, especially people with loud or excited voices, she heard only "blah, blah, blah." Too much excited talk or overstimulation caused Donna to stare straight ahead and appear to be frozen.

Donna was in and out of many schools because she failed her exams, refused to take part in class activities, walked out of classes she didn't like, and sometimes threw things.

When Donna did make a friend, she tried to avoid getting a friendly hug, which made her feel as if she were burning up inside and going to faint. Eventually she learned to tolerate being hugged but never liked it (D. Williams, 1992). Donna Williams had all the symptoms of autism.

Courtesy of Chris Samuel, by permission of Chris Samuel

Unless otherwise noted, all images are © Cengage Learning

Autism is marked by especially abnormal or impaired development in social interactions, such as hiding to avoid people, not making eye contact, and not wanting to be touched. Autism is marked by difficulties in communicating, such as grave problems in developing spoken language or in initiating conversations.

Individuals with autism are characterized as having very few activities and interests, spending long periods repeating the same behaviors (hand flapping), or following the same rituals. Signs of autism usually appear when a child is 2 or 3 years old (American Psychiatric Association, 2000).

As we describe Donna's experiences, you'll see how psychologists try to answer questions about complex behaviors, such as autism, as well as countless other behaviors discussed throughout this text.

Autism: Christina

Learn what school is like for a first-grade student with autism.

Autism: A Spectrum Disorder

Compare the symptoms of five siblings diagnosed with autism.

Check Your Learning Quiz 1.1

Go to **login.cengagebrain.com** and take the online quiz.

Definition of Psychology

Psychologists study a broad range of behaviors, including Donna's autistic behaviors, as well as hundreds of other behaviors. For this reason, we need a very broad definition of psychology.

Psychology is the systematic, scientific study of behaviors and mental processes.

Behaviors refers to observable actions or responses in both humans and animals. Behaviors might include eating, speaking, laughing, running, reading, and sleeping. *Mental processes,* which are not directly observable, refer to a wide range of complex mental processes, such as thinking, imagining, studying, and dreaming.

Although the definition of psychology is broad, psychologists have four specific goals when they study some behavior or mental process, such as autism.

Goals of Psychology

If you were a psychologist studying Donna's autistic experiences, you would have the following four goals in mind: to describe, explain, predict, and control her behavior.

1 Describe

The first goal of psychology is to describe the different ways that organisms behave.

Donna says that when she was a child, she wondered what people were saying to her because words were just lists of meaningless sounds. When people or things bothered her, she would endlessly tap or twirl her fingers to create movements that completely held her attention and helped her escape from a world that often made no sense.

Courtesy of Chris Samuel, by permission of Chris Samuel

2 Explain

After describing behavior, psychologists try to explain behavior.

The second goal of psychology is to explain the causes of behavior.
Donna's mother believed that autism was caused by evil spirits. Donna thinks her autism may result from metabolic imbalance.

3 Predict

After describing and explaining behavior, psychologists try to predict behavior.

The third goal of psychology is to predict how organisms will behave in certain situations.
Donna says that one of her biggest problems is being so overloaded by visual sensations that she literally freezes in place. She tries to predict when she will freeze up by estimating how many new stimuli she must adjust to.

4 Control

If psychologists can predict behavior, then they can often control behavior.

For some psychologists, the fourth goal of psychology is to control an organism's behavior.
Donna knows one reason she fears meeting people is that social interactions cause a tremendous sensory overload that makes her freeze up. She controls her social fear by making it a rule to meet only one person at a time.

The idea of control has both positive and negative sides. The positive side is that psychologists can help people, such as Donna, learn to control undesirable behaviors by teaching better methods of self-control and ways to deal with situations and relationships (Eikeseth et al., 2007; Hall, 2008). The negative side is the concern that psychologists might control people's behaviors without their knowledge or consent. In Module 1.8, we'll discuss the strict guidelines that psychologists have established to prevent potential abuse of controlling behavior and to protect the rights and privacy of individuals, patients, and participants in experiments.

Now that you've learned the current definition and goals of psychology, we'll go back over 100 years to give you a glimpse of what psychology looked like in its beginning, which will help you appreciate how much psychology has evolved.

Taking Class Notes

Read about how taking notes in class addresses psychology's four goals.

▶ **LO4** List and explain the historical approaches to psychology.

Imagine living in the late 1800s and early 1900s, when the electric light, radio, and airplane were being invented and the average human life span was about 30 years. This was the time when psychology broke away from philosophy and became a separate field of study. As this new area of study developed, early psychologists hotly debated its definition, approach, and goals (Benjamin, 2000). We'll highlight those early psychologists who shaped the field. We'll begin with the person considered to be the father of psychology, Wilhelm Wundt.

Structuralism: Elements of the Mind

Wilhelm Wundt established the first psychology laboratory in 1879, in Leipzig, Germany. Wundt, now considered the father of psychology, asked subjects to drop balls from a platform or listen to a metronome (a device that produces fixed ticks or beats) and report their own sensations. Wundt and his followers analyzed their subjects' sensations; they thought these sensations were the key to analyzing the structure of the mind (Hergenhahn, 2009). For this reason Wundt and his followers were called structuralists, and their approach was called structuralism.

Wilhelm Wundt
1832–1920

Structuralism was the study of the most basic elements, primarily sensations and perceptions, that make up our conscious mental experiences.

Just as you might assemble hundreds of pieces of a jigsaw puzzle into a completed picture, structuralists tried to combine hundreds of sensations into a complete conscious experience. Perhaps Wundt's greatest contribution was his method of introspection.

Introspection was a method of exploring conscious mental processes by asking subjects to look inward and report their sensations and perceptions.

For example, after listening to a beating metronome, the subjects would be asked to report whether their sensations were pleasant, unpleasant, exciting, or relaxing. However, introspection was heavily criticized for being an unscientific method because it was solely dependent on subjects' self-reports, which could be biased, rather than on objective measurements.

It wasn't long before Wundt's approach was criticized for being too narrow and subjective in primarily studying sensations. These criticisms resulted in another new approach, called functionalism.

Functionalism: Functions of the Mind

For 12 years, William James labored over a book called *The Principles of Psychology,* which was published in 1890 and included almost every topic that is now part of psychology textbooks: learning, sensation, memory, reasoning, attention, feelings, consciousness, and a revolutionary theory of emotions.

William James
1842–1910

For example, why do you feel fear when running from a raging wolf? You might answer that an angry wolf is a terrifying creature that causes fear and makes you run—fear makes you run. Not so, according to James, who reasoned that the act of running causes a specific set of physiological responses that your brain interprets as fear—running makes you afraid. According to James, emotions are caused by physiological changes; thus, running produces fear. You'll find out if James's theory of emotions was correct in Chapter 9.

Unlike Wundt, who saw mental activities as composed of basic elements, James viewed mental activities as having developed through ages of evolution because of their adaptive functions, such as helping humans survive. James was interested in the goals, purposes, and functions of the mind, an approach called functionalism.

Functionalism, which was the study of the function rather than the structure of consciousness, was interested in how our minds adapt to our changing environment.

Functionalism did not last as a unique approach, but many of James's ideas grew into current areas of study, such as emotions, attention, and memory (Hergenhahn, 2009). In addition, James suggested ways to apply psychological principles to teaching, which had a great impact on educational psychology. For all these reasons, James is considered the father of modern psychology.

Notice that James disagreed with Wundt's structural approach and pushed psychology toward looking at how the mind functions and adapts to our ever-changing world.

About the same time that James was criticizing Wundt's structuralism, another group also found reasons to disagree with Wundt; this group was the Gestalt psychologists.

▶ **L05** Describe the early discrimination practices among psychologists.

Gestalt Approach: Sensations Versus Perceptions

When you see a road hazard sign like the one in the photo at right, you think the lights forming the arrow are actually moving in one direction. This motion, however, is only an illusion; the lights are stationary and are only flashing on and off.

The illusion that flashing lights appear to move was first studied in 1912 by three psychologists: Max Wertheimer, Wolfgang Köhler, and Kurt Koffka. They reported that they had created the perception of movement by briefly flashing one light and then, a short time later, a second light. Although the positions of the two bulbs were fixed, the light actually appeared to move from one to the other. They called this the *phi phenomenon;* today it is known as *apparent motion.*

Wertheimer and his colleagues believed that the perception of apparent motion could not be explained by the structuralists, who said that the movement resulted from simply adding together the sensations from two fixed lights. Instead, Wertheimer argued that perceptual experiences, such as perceiving moving lights, resulted from analyzing a "whole pattern," or, in German, a *Gestalt.*

The **Gestalt approach** emphasized that perception is more than the sum of its parts and studied how sensations are assembled into meaningful perceptual experiences.

Max Wertheimer
1883–1943

In our example, Gestalt psychologists would explain that your experience of perceiving moving traffic lights is much more than and very different from what is actually happening—fixed lights flashing in sequence. These kinds of perceptual experiences could not be explained by the structuralists and pointed out the limitations of their approach (D. P. Schultz & Schultz, 2008).

After all these years, many principles of the Gestalt approach are still used to explain how we perceive objects. We'll discuss many of the Gestalt principles of perception in Chapter 3.

© Tony Freeman/PhotoEdit

Unless otherwise noted, all images are © Cengage Learning

Behaviorism: Observable Behaviors

"Give me a dozen healthy infants, well-formed, and my own special world to bring them up in and I'll guarantee to take any one at random and train him to become any type of specialist I might select—doctor, lawyer, artist . . ." (Watson, 1924).

John B. Watson
1878–1958

These words come from John B. Watson, who published a landmark paper "Psychology as a Behaviorist Views It," in which he rejected Wundt's structuralism and its study of mental elements and conscious processes. Instead, Watson boldly stated that psychology should be an objective, experimental science, whose goal should be the analysis of observable behaviors and the prediction and control of those behaviors (Harzem, 2004). Watson's ideas illustrate the behavioral approach.

The **behavioral approach** emphasized the objective, scientific analysis of observable behaviors.

From the 1920s to the 1960s, behaviorism was the dominant force in American psychology. However, beginning in the 1970s and continuing into the present, behaviorism's dominance was challenged by the cognitive approach, whose popularity now surpasses behaviorism (Evans, 1999; Glassman & Hadad, 2004).

Survival of Approaches

The survival of each approach depended on its ability to survive its criticisms. Criticisms of Wundt's structural approach gave rise to the functional approach of James and the Gestalt approach of Wertheimer, Köhler, and Koffka. Criticisms of all three approaches—structural, functional, and Gestalt—gave rise to Watson's behavioral approach. These disagreements resulted in many heated debates, but they helped psychology develop into the scientific field it is today.

Although early American psychologists differed in their approaches, they shared one underlying theme that was a sign of their times. They discriminated against women and minorities in both academic and career settings.

At the present time, at least seven approaches can help psychologists understand behavior and mental process. We'll explore these next.

Shaping a Pigeon

Watch how a pigeon is trained to perform new behaviors.

Early Discrimination

Learn how early American psychologists discriminated against women and minorities.

Check Your Learning Quiz 1.2

Go to **login.cengagebrain.com** and take the online quiz.

▶ **LO6** Describe and distinguish the modern approaches to psychology.

In trying to answer questions about autism or any other behaviors, psychologists would use a combination of approaches. The modern approaches to understanding behavior include *biological, cognitive, behavioral, psychoanalytic, humanistic, sociocultural,* and *evolutionary.*

Biological Approach

Because signs of autism usually appear at a very young age, around 2 to 3 years old, many reseachers are interested in exploring the brain development of these individuals. To examine brain development, researchers use the biological approach.

The **biological approach** examines how our genes, hormones, and nervous system interact with our environments to influence learning, personality, memory, motivation, emotions, and other traits and abilities.

Using the biological approach, researchers found that social problems associated with autism are linked to less activity in brain cells responsible for human empathy (mirror neurons). Reduced activity in these cells helps explain why children with autism misunderstand emotional cues and why they have difficulty empathizing (Dapretto et al., 2006; Iacoboni, 2008).

© Visuals Unlimited/Corbis

Cognitive Approach

Individuals with autism usually have difficulty developing language skills. For example, Donna writes, "Autism makes me hear other people's words but be unable to know what the words mean. Autism stops me from finding and using my own words when I want to" (D. Williams, 1994, p. 237). To discover why individuals with autism differ in their language and social skills, psychologists use the cognitive approach.

The **cognitive approach** focuses on how we process, store, and use information and how this information influences what we attend to, perceive, learn, remember, believe, and feel.

Unless otherwise noted, all images are © Cengage Learning

Behavioral Approach

Children with autism also have difficulty in developing social relationships. For instance, they may not want to be touched, they may not make eye contact, and they may hide to avoid people. Parents, doctors, and policy makers all agree that the best method to address these symptoms is to use the behavioral approach.

Good eye contact!

© Eileen Hart/iStockphoto

The **behavioral approach** analyzes how organisms learn new behaviors or modify existing ones, depending on whether events in their environments reward or punish these behaviors.

Treatment programs for autism change or modify behaviors by adhering to a basic behavioral principle: rewards or punishments can modify, change, or control behavior.

Psychoanalytic Approach

When she was about 3 years old, Donna faced a number of personal problems: having an alcoholic mother who hit and verbally abused her, having a father who was often gone, and being sent to a "special needs" school. Apparently in trying to deal with these problems, Donna developed other personalities. One personality was Willie, a child with "hateful glaring eyes, a pinched-up mouth, rigid corpselike stance, and clenched fists," who stamped and spit but also did well in school. The other was Carol, a charming, cooperative little girl who could act normal and make friends (S. Reed & Cook, 1993). The psychoanalytic approach would look carefully at why Donna developed other personalities to deal with difficult childhood experiences (Lanyado & Horne, 1999).

The **psychoanalytic approach** is based on the belief that childhood experiences greatly influence the development of later personality traits and psychological problems. It also stresses the influence of unconscious fears, desires, and motivations on thoughts and behaviors.

Biological Approach to Test Anxiety

Learn how the biological approach applies to test anxiety.

Cognitive Approach to Test Anxiety

Learn how the cognitive approach applies to test anxiety.

Behavioral Approach to Test Anxiety

Learn how the behavioral approach applies to test anxiety.

Psychoanalytic Approach to Test Anxiety

Learn how the psychoanalytic approach applies to test anxiety.

Humanistic Approach

Even though Donna has serious life challenges, she strives toward reaching her potential, and her achievements are impressive. She has published autobiographies and textbooks on autism. Her creative paintings and sculptures can be seen at exhibits. Donna is also a singer-songwriter who has released two incredible albums. And she married a man she refers to as a "diamond of a person" (D. Williams, 2009).

Donna's struggle to free herself from autism, develop close personal relationships, and reach her potential characterizes the humanistic approach.

The **humanistic approach** emphasizes that each individual has great freedom in directing his or her future, a large capacity for achieving personal growth, a considerable amount of intrinsic worth, and enormous potential for self-fulfillment.

The humanistic approach emphasizes the positive side of human nature, its creative tendencies, and its inclination to build caring relationships. This concept of human nature—freedom, potential, creativity—is the most distinctive feature of the humanistic approach and sets it far apart from the behavioral and psychoanalytic approaches (Giorgi, 2005).

Sociocultural Approach

Autism is believed to exist in every culture, but different cultures have very different perceptions of autism. For example, early diagnosis and multidisciplinary treatment is a priority in the United States. In contrast, children with autism living in South Korea are often kept at home hidden from the public. Parents in South Korea may fear that the family will face stigma if people know someone with autism lives there. The unfortunate result is that these children do not get the treatment they need (Grinker, 2007).

The differences in how autism is perceived in the United States and South Korea show the influence of cultural factors and the use of the sociocultural approach in psychology (Matsumoto & Juang, 2008; Shiraev & Levy, 2009).

The **sociocultural approach** studies the influence of social and cultural factors on behaviors and mental processes.

Evolutionary Approach

The most recent modern approach to psychology emerges out of evolutionary theory and is called the evolutionary approach.

The **evolutionary approach** studies how evolutionary ideas, such as adaptation and natural selection, explain behaviors and mental processes.

This approach asserts that today's behaviors and mental processes can be linked to the challenges our human ancestors encountered in adapting to their environments.

Although the evolutionary approach is relatively new, research has already examined how evolution influences a variety of behaviors and mental processes, such as aggression, mate selection, fears, depression, and decision making (Buss, 2004, 2007, 2009).

Despite the many advances of the evolutionary approach in psychology, research findings on the influence of evolutionary factors on autism are still in their infancy. Perhaps sometime in the near future, we'll gain a new, evolutionary explanation for the causes of autism.

Approaches: Historical versus Modern

Master the historical and modern approaches to psychology.

Humanistic Approach to Test Anxiety

Learn how the humanistic approach applies to test anxiety.

Sociocultural Approach to Test Anxiety

Learn how the sociocultural approach applies to test anxiety.

Evolutionary Approach to Physical Attraction

Learn how the evolutionary approach applies to physical attraction.

Check Your Learning Quiz 1.3

Go to **login.cengagebrain.com** and take the online quiz

Eclectic Approach

Rather than strictly focusing on one of the seven approaches, most of today's psychologists use an eclectic approach. **Eclectic approach** means they use different approaches to study the same behavior.

By combining information from the biological, cognitive, behavioral, psychoanalytic, humanistic, sociocultural, and evolutionary approaches, psychologists stand a better chance of reaching their four goals of describing, explaining, predicting, and controlling behavior.

We have discussed the approaches used by modern psychologists, as well as those used by early psychologists. As you compare early and modern approaches, you can appreciate how much psychology has changed in the past 100 years.

Next, we'll discuss the variety of career settings available to psychologists and the different areas of research specialization.

▶ **L07** Differentiate between a psychologist and a psychiatrist.

▶ **L08** Identify the major career settings of psychology.

Psychologist Versus Psychiatrist

Many students think psychologists are primarily counselors and therapists, even though degrees in psychology are awarded in many areas. Obtaining an advanced degree in psychology requires that one finish college and spend 2 to 3 years in postgraduate study to obtain a master's degree or 4 to 5 years in postgraduate study to obtain a PhD. Many students are confused about the differences between a psychologist, a clinical psychologist, and a psychiatrist.

A **psychologist** is usually someone who has completed 4 to 5 years of postgraduate education and has obtained a PhD, PsyD, or EdD in psychology.

A **clinical psychologist** has a PhD, PsyD, or EdD; has specialized in a clinical subarea; and has spent an additional year in a supervised therapy setting to gain experience in diagnosing and treating a wide range of abnormal behaviors.

Until recently, no psychologists in the United States have been able to prescribe drugs. Now, psychologists in New Mexico and Louisiana who complete special medical training can prescribe drugs as psychiatrists do. Several other states may pass similar legislation in the near future, giving psychologists the right to prescribe medication (Munsey, 2008a, 2008b, 2010).

A **psychiatrist** is a medical doctor (MD) who has spent several years in clinical training, which includes diagnosing possible physical and neurological causes of abnormal behaviors and treating these behaviors, often with prescription drugs.

Psychologists can work in the following career settings.

Unless otherwise noted, all images are © Cengage Learning

Many Career Settings

As you can see in the pie chart below, the majority (49%) of psychologists are therapists working in private practice or a therapy setting, while the rest work in other settings. Here's a breakdown of where psychologists in the United States currently work (D. Smith, 2002).

49% The largest percentage (49%) of psychologists work as clinical or counseling psychologists in either a *private practice* or *therapy setting,* such as a psychological or psychiatric clinic; a mental health center; a psychiatric, drug, or rehabilitation ward of a hospital; or a private office. The duties of clinical or counseling psychologists might involve doing therapy; helping patients with problems involving drugs, stress, weight, family, or career; or testing patients for psychological problems that developed from some neurological problem.

28% The second largest percentage (28%) of psychologists work in the *academic settings* of universities and colleges. Academic psychologists often engage in some combination of teaching in a classroom, mentoring or helping students, and doing research.

13% The third largest percentage (13%) of psychologists work in a variety of other kinds of jobs and *career settings.*

6% The fourth largest percentage (6%) of psychologists work in *industrial settings,* such as businesses, corporations, and consulting firms. These psychologists may work at selecting personnel, increasing production, or improving job satisfaction.

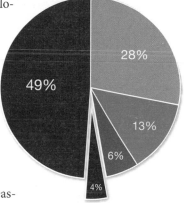

4% The smallest percentage (4%) work in *secondary schools* and *other settings.* For example, school psychologists conduct academic and career testing and provide counseling for a variety of psychological problems.

If you are thinking of entering the field of psychology today, you have a wide and exciting range of career choices. Your career choices are almost limitless! For those who decide to engage in research, we'll next discuss popular research areas to choose from.

▶ **LO9** Describe the areas of research specialization in psychology.

Areas of Research Specialization

As you proceed through your introductory psychology course, you'll find that the world of psychology has been divided into at least eight research areas. Below is a brief description of each of the eight areas.

Clinical and counseling psychology includes the assessment and treatment of people with psychological problems, such as grief, anxiety, or stress.

Social psychology involves the study of social interactions, stereotypes, prejudices, attitudes, conformity, group behaviors, aggression, and attraction.

Developmental psychology examines moral, social, emotional, and cognitive development throughout a person's entire life.

Experimental psychology includes the areas of sensation, perception, learning, human performance, motivation, and emotion.

Unless otherwise noted, all images are © Cengage Learning

Biological psychology involves research on the physical and chemical changes that occur during stress, learning, and emotions, as well as how our genetic makeup, brain, and nervous system interact with our environments and influence our behaviors.

Psychometrics focuses on the measurement of people's abilities, skills, intelligence, personality, and abnormal behaviors.

Cognitive psychology involves how we process, store, and retrieve information and how cognitive processes influence our behaviors.

Industrial/organizational psychology examines the relationships of people and their work environments.

Regardless of which research area a psychologist chooses to pursue, it is essential that the scientific method be used to gain knowledge about behavior and mental processes. Next, we'll discuss the scientific method and why it makes psychology a science.

Study Skills

Find out how to improve study skills based on findings in cognitive and experimental psychology.

Check Your Learning Quiz 1.4

Go to **login.cengagebrain.com** and take the online quiz.

▶ **LO10** Differentiate between scientific and armchair psychology.

▶ **LO11** List and describe the steps to the scientific method.

▶ **LO12** Identify the advantages of the scientific method.

Scientific Method

There are, of course, different ways to answer questions. If we were to answer questions about human behavior and conscious experience through informal observation and speculation, we would be engaging in what's referred to as ***armchair psychology.*** Sometimes, by using armchair psychology we arrive at the correct answer, but sometimes we are wrong in our assumptions about human behavior.

The founders of the science of psychology, such as Wilhelm Wundt and William James, realized that armchair psychology could be improved upon by treating our speculation as hypotheses that could be subjected to scientific scrutiny. Over and over again, psychologists have been surprised to find that what was once thought to be self-evident turned out, on closer examination, to be false. Scientific method allow us a more reliable way to answer questions.

Even though there is an endless array of questions we could ask about people's mental processes and behaviors, psychologists follow the same basic approach to answer each question. This approach is called the *scientific method,* which includes the following six steps:

1. Review the literature: The researcher reads the scientific literature to learn what has already been published on the subject or content he or she is interested in examining.

2. Formulate a hypothesis: The researcher formulates an educated guess about some phenomenon and states it in a very precise way to rule out confusion or error in the meaning of its terms. The variables must have operational definitions, which means they need to be described in a specific, objective manner that allows them to be measured.

The Scientific Method

1. Review the literature

2. Formulate a hypothesis

3. Design the study

4. Collect the data

5. Draw conclusions

6. Report the findings

Unless otherwise noted, all images are © Cengage Learning

3. Design the study: The researcher selects the research method that best answers the hypothesis. In this chapter, you'll learn about several research methods, including the survey, case study, observation, correlation, and experiment.

4. Collect the data: The researcher now begins conducting the study and collecting the data. There are various methods of collecting data. Some examples are questionnaires, observations, interviews, psychological tests, and physiological measurements. The choice a researcher makes primarily depends on the topic being studied. For example, questionnaires are best suited to assess attitudes and beliefs, whereas psychological tests are best suited to assess personality.

5. Draw conclusions: First, the collected data must be analyzed using appropriate statistical techniques, then, the researcher can determine whether or not the data support the hypothesis.

6. Report the findings: The final step in the scientific method is to summarize the research project and its results and submit it to a professional journal. By doing so, researchers contribute to the progression of their specific field of study and science in general. Once their research is published, other researchers can learn from their results, as well as replicate their study, critique it, or pursue research that furthers knowledge of the topic.

Advantages

The scientific method has a few key advantages. First, it is specific and precise. The scientific method precisely states hypotheses and operational definitions, which communicates clearly to others what the researchers are examining. Second, the scientific method is an empirical process that reduces error by making the research findings available to others who can replicate and critique it. This promotes discussion within the scientific inquiry and advances knowledge in the field. Lastly, the scientific method can be used for any of the four goals of psychology. For instance, if a researcher is addressing the goal of predicting behavior, then the hypothesis will state what the researcher expects to find. Then, the researcher will choose a research method, data collection technique, and statistical analysis that best answer the hypothesis.

Now that you've learned the foundation to conducting research in psychology, we'll discuss various research methods, all of which can be used in the scientific method.

Armchair Psychology

Understand the difference between scientific and armchair psychology.

Check Your Learning Quiz 1.5

Go to **login.cengagebrain.com** and take the online quiz.

In the next few modules, we'll be discussing various types of research methods. To help you better understand these research methods, we're going to apply each method to the same specific topic, attention-deficit/hyperactivity disorder (ADHD). We'll begin with the the example of Blake, who has experienced attention and hyperactivity problems since early childhood.

Blake's Problem

When Blake was 3 years old, he crawled into a *T. rex* display at a museum and set off blaring alarms. As a child, he was easily bored, couldn't focus on anything for very long, and never sat still for more than a second. Blake admits that he gets easily bored and is often so desperate to find something interesting to do that he goes "full steam ahead without thinking." One day, to keep himself entertained, he launched rockets (accidentally) into the neighbor's swimming pool! Blake's mother describes him as "exhausting" and "off the wall." "Within minutes, he'd go from concocting baking-soda volcanoes to dumping out all the Lego and K'nex sets, to emptying out the linen closet in order to build a tent city," says his mother (Taylor-Barnes, 2008) (adapted from B.E.S. Taylor, 2007).

At age 5, Blake was diagnosed with a behavioral problem called attention-deficit/hyperactivity disorder, or ADHD (American Psychiatric Association, 2000).

Attention-deficit/hyperactivity disorder, or ADHD, is a behavioral disorder in which a child must have six or more symptoms of inattention, such as making careless mistakes in schoolwork, not following instructions, and being easily distracted, and six or more symptoms of hyperactivity, such as fidgeting, leaving classroom seat, and talking excessively. These symptoms should have been present from an early age, persisted for at least 6 months, and contributed to maladaptive development.

Reprinted with permission by New Harbinger Publications, Inc., "ADHD & Me" by Blake E. S. Taylor

Unless otherwise noted, all images are © Cengage Learning

As you look at the photo of Blake (previous page), you see a mature young adult. However, without medication, Blake has great difficulty focusing: "A way you can think about it is if you're taking a TV remote and somebody else is just changing it uncontrollably and your mind is floating from the History Channel to HBO to the Discovery Channel—it's like you can't really stay concentrated" (B. E. S. Taylor, 2008).

Twenty-five years ago, ADHD was a relatively small problem in the United States, but today it is the most commonly diagnosed behavioral problem in children. The diagnosis of ADHD is not straightforward, because it is based on behavioral symptoms rather than medical tests. There is no objective diagnostic test for ADHD (Hinshaw, 2010). The proposed causes of ADHD are many, including genetic, neurological, cultural, and environmental factors (Barkley, 2006). Finally, the most popular treatment for ADHD is stimulant medication.

The diagnosis, causes, and treatment of ADHD are all topics of controversy. In the middle of these controversies are parents like Blake's mother, who, after dealing with a hyperactive and impulsive child from an early age, have little doubt ADHD exists and stimulant medication decreases hyperactivity and impulsivity. At the same time, critics warn that ADHD may be misdiagnosed or overdiagnosed and that, although stimulant medication may reduce activity, it fails to improve mental functions such as ignoring distractions and recalling information needed to reach a goal (Coghill, 2007).

As researchers work to resolve the controversies surrounding ADHD, they use descriptive, correlational, and experimental research methods—the topics of three modules in this chapter. We'll begin by discussing three types of descriptive research methods: survey, case study, and naturalistic observation.

© Alexander Trinitatov/Shutterstock

ADHD Controversies

Examine the controversies surrounding the diagnosis and treatment of ADHD.

Careful Assessment and Diagnosis

Witness why careful assessment and diagnosis are so important.

Prescriptions to Treat ADHD

Learn more about several prescription treatments for ADHD.

Behavioral Therapy: Kids with ADHD

Watch how behavioral therapy helps children with ADHD.

▶ **LO14** Describe the survey, case study, and observation descriptive research methods.

▶ **LO15** Identify an advantage and a disadvantage of each of the descriptive research methods.

Survey

Suppose you wish to know how many children have ADHD, whether it occurs more in boys or in girls, which treatment is the most popular, and how many children continue to have problems when they become adults. Researchers obtain this information with surveys.

A **survey** is a way to obtain information by asking many individuals—either in person, by telephone, or by mail—to answer a fixed set of questions about particular subjects.

Almost every day the media report some new survey. Although surveys tell us what others believe or how they behave, survey questions can be written to bias the answers; moreover, people may not always answer truthfully (N. Schwartz, 1999). Below are example of questions answered by using surveys:

© Jutta Klee/Getty Images

Do you wash your hands?
Although 92% of the people surveyed by telephone said they always washed their hands after using a public bathroom, direct observation of 6,076 people in four major cities found that only 77% really do and that more women (88%) washed their hands than men (66%) (ASM, 2007).

How many children are diagnosed with ADHD?
Surveys of parents found that 5% of U.S. children between 6 and 17 years old are diagnosed with ADHD. Boys are reported to be diagnosed with ADHD twice as often as girls. ADHD is reported to be more common among adolescents than younger children and more common among white and African American children than Hispanic children (CDC, 2008c).

© Image Source/Getty Images RF

These examples show that surveys can provide a great deal of useful information. However, surveys have potential problems with accuracy (as in the hand-washing survey) and, as you'll see next, with how questions are worded and who asks the questions.

Unless otherwise noted, all images are © Cengage Learning

Disadvantages

How Questions Are Worded

You may be surprised to learn that surveys may get very different results depending on how questions are worded. Here are two examples:

QUESTION: "Would you say that **industry** contributes more or less to air pollution than **traffic**?" **Traffic** contributes more: **24%** **Industry** contributes more: **57%**	**QUESTION:** "Would you say that **traffic** contributes more or less to air pollution than **industry**?" **Traffic** contributes more: **45%** **Industry** contributes more: **32%**

Who Asks the Questions

You may also be surprised to learn that the sex or race of the questioner can also affect how people answer the questions.

QUESTION: "The problems faced by blacks were brought on by blacks themselves."

When the interviewer was **white, 62%** of whites interviewed agreed.

When the interviewer was **black, 46%** of whites interviewed agreed.

We can conclude that surveys can be biased because people may not answer questions truthfully or may feel pressured to answer in certain ways. Also, surveys can be biased by how questions are worded and by interviewing a group of people who do not represent the general population (Gravetter & Forzano, 2009; Jackson, 2009).

Advantages

Surveys can be a useful research tool to efficiently collect information on behaviors, beliefs, experiences, and attitudes from a large sample of people and can compare answers from various ethnic, age, socioeconomic, and cultural groups.

For example, surveys suggest that ADHD interferes with performance in school settings, decreases the chances of graduating from high school, and may lead to conduct disorder problems in adolescence (Root & Resnick, 2003). However, if researchers wish to focus on one individual , they use a case study.

Survey Research: Memory Accuracy

Learn about problems in using surveys to determine if adolescents accurately recall their sexual histories.

Case Study

Sometimes researchers answer questions by studying a single individual in great detail, which is called a case study.

A **case study** is an in-depth analysis of the thoughts, feelings, beliefs, or behaviors of a single person.

We've been discussing the case of Blake Taylor throughout the module. From the age of 3, Blake has had problems paying attention and completing tasks. Throughout his childhood, he felt no one understood the challenges he endured. To help others understand what it's like to live with ADHD, he wrote his autobiography called *ADHD & Me*. In it, he discusses the challenges he faced from early childhood through the present. He talks about how he must take his ADHD medication, keep a daily routine, and make sure to get 9 hours of sleep at night to keep his ADHD symptoms from getting out of control. As a result of his motivation and self-discipline, Blake enjoys a balanced college life spent studying, working out, playing music, socializing, volunteering, and, of course, getting enough sleep (Anwar, 2008; Taylor, 2007). Sometimes case studies help answer questions, but case studies can also result in wrong or biased answers.

Disadvantages

One disadvantage of the case study is that some of the data rely on people's recollections, which can be inaccurate or incomplete. Another problem is that the motives of a researcher may bias the questionning of the person being studied, even though the researcher's intent is to be objective. Also, because case studies rely on individual cases, the results can be misleading if the individual being studied is atypical.

Lastly, results from case studies may be misinterpreted if the observer has preconceived notions of what to look for. For example, beginning in the mid-1970s, parents were told that food with artificial additives, dyes, and preservatives could cause hyperactivity in children (Feingold, 1975). Shortly after, parents reported that, yes indeed, artificial additives caused a sudden increase in restlessness and irritability in their hyperactive children (Feingold, 1975). The parents' reports and beliefs that additives cause hyperactivity are examples of a testimonial.

A **testimonial** is a statement in support of a particular viewpoint based on detailed observations of a person's own personal experience.

However, contrary to the parents' testimonials, researchers have generally found that amounts of artificial additives within a normal range do not affect hyperactivity (Kinsbourne, 1994; Shaywitz et al., 1994).

For all of the above reasons, researchers using the case study cannnot confidently report that their results can be applied to everyone.

Advantages

One of the major advantages of a case study is that psychologists can obtain detailed descriptions and insights into aspects of an individual's life and behaviors that cannot be obtained in other ways. This information may point to potential answers or lead to future studies. Consequently, case studies are useful in psychology to understand the development of a personality or psychological problem or to examine a person's behavior across his or her life span.

You now know that a case study is an in-depth study of a person. The next type of descriptive research method also involves closely studying people, but it involves actually observing their behaviors in a natural setting.

Use of Placebos

Find out about placebos and some cultural differences affecting their popularity.

Naturalistic Observation

In trying to understand the kinds of problems faced by children with ADHD, psychologists study these children in different research settings, which may include observing them in the home, in the classroom, on the playground, at the store, or at their individual work.

Parents and teachers want to know if children with ADHD have different problems at home than in school. Researchers answer this question by conducting naturalistic observations to study children in different settings (home versus school versus grocery store) (Stein, 2004).

A **naturalistic observation** is when researchers gather information by observing individuals' behaviors in a relatively normal environment without attempting to change or control the situation.

For example, naturalistic observations of children with ADHD in school settings indicate that they have difficulty remaining in their seats, don't pay attention to the teacher, can't sit still, interrupt the teacher or students, and get angry when they don't get their way (Junod et al., 2006). Parents report that, at home, ADHD children do not respond when called, throw tantrums when frustrated, and have periods of great activity (Hancock, 1996).

Based on these naturalistic observations, researchers and pediatricians developed a list of primary symptoms of ADHD (AAP, 2000; Stein & Perrin, 2003). Similarly, psychologists study how normal people behave in different naturalistic settings, including schools, workplaces, college dormitories, bars, and sports arenas.

Disadvantages

One problem with naturalistic observations is that the psychologists' own beliefs or values may bias their observations and cause them to misinterpret behaviors. Another problem is that conducting a naturalistic observation can be very time-consuming and requires much training and effort.

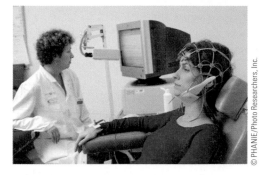

Lastly, because naturalistic settings are uncontrolled and many things happen, researchers find it difficult to identify what causes what. For this reason, researchers may have to answer some questions in a more controlled setting, such as a laboratory or clinic (above right photo).

Advantages

One advantage of naturalistic observations is the opportunity to study behaviors in real-life situations and environments, which cannot or would not be duplicated in the laboratory. Naturalistic observations allow researchers to get a close-up look at everyday life, which means they can be confident that this is really the way people typically behave. Also, because people don't know they are being observed, they won't be motivated to do what they think the observer or researcher wants them to do.

Lastly, an advantage is that the data are collected by first-hand observation and is not based on people's recollections, which at times can be far from accurate.

In conclusion, the purpose of descriptive research methods—survey, case study, and naturalistic observation—is to describe behavior, which as we learned earlier, is the first goal of psychology. These research methods do not predict or explain behavior, the second and third goals of psychology. Next, we'll discuss correlational research, which addresses the predictive goal of psychology.

Naturalistic Observation: Observing Chimps

Read about how Jane Goodall studied the behavior of chimps.

Check Your Learning Quiz 1.6

Go to **login.cengagebrain.com** and take the online quiz.

Correlations

Let's suppose that researchers want to know if ADHD has a genetic basis. One way to identify genetic factors is to study identical twins because they share almost 100% of their genes. Researchers who studied the occurrence of ADHD in identical male twins found that about 75% of the time, if one identical twin had ADHD, so did the second twin (Faraone et al., 2005). This strong relationship suggests a genetic basis for ADHD. Such a relationship is called a correlation.

A **correlation** is an association or relationship in the occurrence of two or more events.

For example, if one twin has ADHD, a correlation will tell us the likelihood of the other twin also having ADHD. The likelihood or strength of a relationship between two events is called a correlation coefficient.

A **correlation coefficient** is a number that indicates the strength of a relationship between two or more events: the closer the number is to –1.00 or +1.00, the greater is the strength of the relationship.

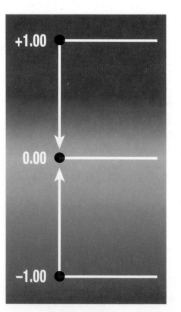

We'll explain correlation coefficients in more detail because they can be confusing.

- A positive correlation coefficient indicates that as one event tends to increase, the second event tends to, but does not always, increase.

  As the coefficient increases from +0.01 to +1.00, it indicates a strengthening of the relationship between the occurrence of two events.
- A zero correlation indicates that there is no relationship between the occurrence of one event and the occurrence of a second event.
- A negative correlation coefficient indicates that as one event tends to increase, the second event tends to, but does not always, decrease.

  As the coefficient increases in absolute magnitude from −0.01 to −1.00, it indicates a strengthening in the relationship of one event increasing and the other decreasing.

Disadvantage

The biggest mistake people make in discussing correlations is assuming that they show cause and effect. For instance, many parents have been told that breast-feeding their infants leads to greater intelligence. There is a positive correlation between duration of breast-feeding and intelligence test scores during adulthood, which means longer duration of breast-feeding is associated with higher intelligence test scores (Mortensen et al., 2002). It's important to remember that although breast-feeding *may* have caused the higher test scores, correlations themselves cannot demonstrate cause and effect between variables.

Let's think carefully about what is actually causing the higher intelligence test scores. Is it something in the breast milk (a hormone or protein) that isn't found in formula or cow's milk? Is it the physical contact between baby and mother during breast-feeding? Or do infants who benefit most from their mother's breast milk have specific genes that process the breast milk (Caspi et al., 2007; Kramer et al., 2008)? The correlation findings leave many questions unanswered.

Advantage

Although correlations cannot indicate cause-and-effect relationships, they do help predict behavior. For example, there is a positive correlation between IQ scores and performance in academic settings (Chamorro-Premuzic & Furnham, 2008; D. M. Higgins et al., 2007). Thus, we would predict that individuals who score high on IQ tests have the skills to do well in college. However, IQ scores are only relatively good predictors for any single individual because doing well in college involves not only academic skills but also other motivational, emotional, and personality factors.

We've discussed the descriptive research methods that describe behavior and correlational research that predicts behavior. Psychologists wishing to explain behavior must use the experimental research method, which we discuss next.

Correlation

Find out how strength and direction define a correlation.

Check Your Learning Quiz 1.7

Go to **cengagebrain.com** and take the online quiz.

▶ LO18 List and describe the seven rules to conducting an experiment.

Remember that information from surveys, case studies, and testimonials has potential for error and bias. Remember, too, that information from correlations can suggest, but not pinpoint, cause-and-effect relationships. One way to reduce error and bias and identify cause-and-effect relationships is to do an experiment.

An **experiment** is a method of identifying cause-and-effect relationships by following a set of rules that minimize the possibility of error, bias, and chance occurrences.

An experiment is the most powerful method for finding what causes what. If we want to find out whether medication improves the behavior of children with ADHD, we would do an experiment. We will divide an experiment into seven rules that are intended to reduce error and bias and identify the cause of an effect.

Conducting an Experiment: Seven Rules

Some researchers and parents claimed that diets without sugar, artificial colors, and additives reduced ADHD symptoms, but most of these claims proved false because the rules to reduce error had not been followed (Kinsbourne, 1994). Here are seven rules that reduce error and bias and that researchers follow when conducting an experiment.

Rule 1: Ask

Every experiment begins with a specific question or questions changed into a specific hypothesis.

A **hypothesis** is an educated guess about some phenomenon and is stated in precise, concrete language to rule out confusion or error in the meaning of its terms.

Researchers develop different hypotheses based on their own observations or previous research findings. Following this first rule, researchers change the general question—Does Ritalin help children with ADHD?—into a very concrete hypothesis.

Hypothesis:
Ritalin will increase positive classroom behaviors of children diagnosed with ADHD.

Rule 2: Identify

After researchers make their hypothesis, they identify a treatment that will be administered to the subjects—the independent variable.

The **independent variable** is a treatment or something the researcher controls or manipulates.

The independent variable may be a single treatment, such as a single drug dose, or various levels of the same treatment, such as different doses of the same drug.

In our experiment, the independent variable is administering three different doses of Ritalin and a placebo.

Independent Variable:
Drug treatment

After researchers choose the treatment, they next identify one or more of the behaviors of the subjects, called the dependent variable, that will be used to measure the effects of the treatment.

The **dependent variable** is one or more of the subjects' behaviors that are used to measure the potential effects of the treatment or independent variable.

In the present experiment, the dependent variable is the teacher's rating of the child's positive classroom behaviors.

Dependent Variable:
Child's positive classroom behaviors

Rule 3: Choose

After researchers identify the independent and dependent variables, they choose participants for the study. Researchers want to choose participants who are representative of the entire group or population, and they do this through a process called random selection.

Random Selection

Random selection means that each participant in a sample population has an equal chance of being selected for the experiment.

An example of random selection is the way lottery numbers are drawn.

The reason researchers randomly select participants is to avoid any potential error or bias that may come from their knowingly or unknowingly wanting to choose the "best" subjects for their experiment.

Rule 4: Assign

After randomly choosing the subjects, researchers then randomly assign participants to different groups, either an experimental group or a control group.

Experimental Group   **Control Group**

The **experimental group** is composed of those who receive the treatment.

The **control group** is composed of participants who undergo all the same procedures as the experimental participants except that the control participants do not receive the treatment.

In this study, some of the children are assigned to the experimental group and receive Ritalin; the other children are assigned to the control group and receive a similar-looking pill that is a placebo.

The reason participants are randomly assigned to either the experimental or control group is to take into account or control for other factors or traits, such as intelligence, social class, age, sex, and genetic differences. Randomly assigning participants reduces the chances that these factors will bias the results.

Rule 5: Manipulate

After assigning participants to experimental and control groups, researchers manipulate the independent variable by administering the treatment to the experimental group. Researchers give the same conditions to the control group but give them a different level of the treatment, no treatment, or a placebo.

In this study, researchers give the experimental group a pill containing Ritalin, whereas the control group receives a placebo. Drugs and placebos are given in a double-blind procedure.

A **double-blind procedure** means neither participants nor researchers know which group is receiving which treatment.

A double-blind procedure is essential in drug research to control for placebo effects and possible influences or biases of the experimenters.

Rule 6: Measure

By manipulating the treatment so that the experimental group receives a different treatment than the control group, researchers are able to measure how the independent variable (treatment) affects those behaviors that have been selected as the dependent variables.

For example, the hypothesis in this study is: Ritalin will increase the positive classroom behaviors of children with ADHD. Researchers observe whether treatment (Ritalin or placebo) changes positive behaviors of ADHD children in the classroom. Positive behaviors include following a variety of classroom rules, such as remaining in seat, not disturbing others, and not swearing or teasing. As the graph below indicates, ADHD children given placebos follow classroom rules 69% of the time, compared with 87% for the children given Ritalin (Pelham et al., 2005). Thus, compared with placebo use, Ritalin use increases positive behaviors in the classroom.

Positive Behaviors in the Classroom	
Ritalin	87%
Placebo	69%

Rule 7: Analyze

Although there appears to be a large increase in positive behaviors, from 69% for the placebo control group to 87% for the Ritalin experimental group, researchers must analyze the size of these differences by using statistical procedures.

Statistical procedures are used to determine whether differences observed in dependent variables (behaviors) are due to independent variables (treatment) or to error or chance occurrence.

Using statistical procedures (see statistics online activity), researchers concluded that, compared with the placebo, Ritalin significantly increased positive behaviors. In this case, significantly means there was a 95% likelihood that it was Ritalin and not some error or chance occurrence that increased positive behaviors (Pelham et al., 2005).

These significant findings support the hypothesis that Ritalin increases positive classroom behaviors of children with ADHD.

Statistics: The Basics

Learn the basics of descriptive and inferential statistics.

Conducting an Experiment

Use the seven rules to conduct and understand an experiment.

Advantages and Disadvantages

By following the seven rules for conducting an experiment, researchers reduce the chances that error or bias will distort their findings. When an experiment is conducted according to its seven rules, it is a much more powerful method for identifying cause-and-effect relationships than are surveys, case studies, observations, or correlations. An experiment can identify cause-and-effect relationships, while other research methods cannot, because it allows researchers to examine the relationship between the independent and dependent variables while controlling for extraneous variables.

Extraneous variables are variables other than the independent variable that may influence the dependent variable in a study.

By randomly assigning participants to the experimental and control groups, researchers reduce the likelihood of extraneous variables influencing the dependent variable. Even so, researchers usually repeat experiments many times before being truly confident that the answers they found were correct. That's why a newly reported finding, no matter how significant, is usually regarded as questionable until other researchers have been able to repeat the experiment and replicate the finding. Still, an advantage of an experiment is that it allows anyone interested to verify its findings by repeating the experiment following the same seven steps.

Another advantage of experiments is they can be used to examine variables precisely as researchers are able to control the variables. For example, in the research example we used to teach you the seven steps of an experiment, researchers were able to use three different doses of Ritalin, rather than simply comparing a single dose of Ritalin to a placebo.

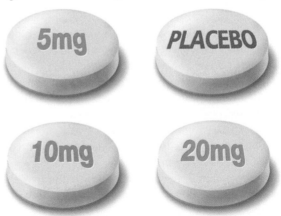

Unless otherwise noted, all images are © Cengage Learning

As wonderful as experiments are, they do have their challenges. One challenge occurs when the participant populations are limited. For instance, many research studies are conducted using college students as their participants. Although college students represent much diversity, there can be some limitations as to how much the results of such a study accurately represent the general population.

Another disadvantage is the possibility of experimenter bias:

Experimenter bias refers to the expectations of the experimenter that participants will behave or respond in a certain way.

Experimenter bias is a problem because it can potentially affect the participants. It's possible, for instance, that experimenters may unconsciously communicate their expectations to participants. They may do so through their facial expression, tone of voice, or choice of words.

To reduce the risk of experimenter bias, the use of a double-blind procedure is advised. Remember, a double-blind procedure means neither participants nor researchers know which group is receiving which treatment.

In addition to the possibility of experimenter expectations presenting problems, participant expectations can also present challenges. It is well known that if we strongly believe something is going to happen, we may unknowingly behave in such a way as to make it happen (R. Rosenthal, 2003). This is called a self-fulfilling prophecy.

A **self-fulfilling prophecy** involves having a strong belief or making a statement (prophecy) about a future behavior and then acting, usually unknowingly, to fulfill or carry out the behavior.

Researchers must try to avoid participant expectations. In the research example we used to teach you the seven steps to an experiment, researchers avoided participant expectations by giving all groups pills that looked and tasted the same. As a result, participants can think they're getting the same drug even though several doses of the drugs are given, as well as a placebo.

Lastly, a major disavantage of an experiment is that it cannot be used to study certain research questions due to ethical concerns. For instance, what if researchers wanted to study the effects of lead exposure on long-term cognitive functioning? They could not use an experiment because randomly assigning participants to a group that forces them to consume lead would be harmful.

As we're about to learn, psychologists conducting research must follow ethical guidlelines to protect participants from physical and psychological harm.

Self-Fulfilling Prophecy

See how teacher beliefs about students' academic abilities affect student performance.

Check Your Learning Quiz 1.8

Go to **login.cengagebrain.com** and take the online quiz.

Unless otherwise noted, all images are © Cengage Learning

▶**LO20** Discuss how psychologists address the concerns of human participants.

Research with Human Participants

If you were asked to volunteer to be a research participant, you would certainly be concerned about whether someone has checked to ensure that the experiment is safe, that there are safeguards to protect you from potential psychological or physical harm, and that you won't be unfairly deceived or made to feel foolish. These are all real concerns, and we'll discuss each one in turn.

The American Psychological Association (APA) has published a code of ethics and conduct for psychologists to follow when doing research, counseling, teaching, and engaging in related activities (APA, 2002). Besides having to follow a code of ethics, psychologists must submit the details of their research programs, especially those with the potential for causing psychological or physical harm, to university and/or federal research committees (institutional review boards). The job of these research committees is to protect the participants (human or animal) by carefully checking the proposed experiments for any harmful procedures (Breckler, 2006).

Before participating in research, individuals must provide informed consent.

Informed consent is an individual's agreement to participate in research after being informed about details of the study, including what their participation will involve and the potential risks.

Are my rights protected?

Even when informed consent is given, participants are still given the right to withdraw from the study at any time and for any reason, and they are informed about treatment alternatives, if applicable. In addition, the researchers must maintain confidentiality.

Confidentiality includes not revealing which data were collected from which participant.

After a participant completes his or her involvement in a research study, the researcher provides a debriefing session.

© Wellaway/Alamy RF

Debriefing includes explaining the purpose and method of the experiment, asking the participants their feelings about being involved in the experiment, and helping the participants deal with possible doubts or guilt that may arise from their behaviors in the experiment.

The purpose of debriefing is to make sure that participants have been treated fairly and have no lingering psychological or physical concerns or worries that come from participating in an experiment (Aronson et al., 2004).

Another ethical concern regarding the treatment of human participants is the use of deception. When recruiting participants for their experiments, psychologists usually give the experiments titles, such as "Study of Eyewitness Testimony" or "Effects of Alcohol on Memory." The reason for using such general titles is that researchers do not want to create specific expectations that may bias how potential participants will behave.

One way that researchers control for participants' expectations is to use bogus procedures or instructions that prevent participants from learning the experiment's true purpose. However, before researchers can use bogus or deceptive methodology, they must satisfy the American Psychological Association's (2002) code of ethics. For example, researchers must justify the deceptive techniques by the scientific, educational, or applied value of the study and can use deception only if no other reasonable way to test the hypothesis is available (APA, 2002).

Another way to avoid bias from participants' expectations is to keep both the researcher and participants in the dark about the experiment's true purpose by using a double-blind procedure, which means that neither participants nor researchers are aware of the experiment's treatment or purpose.

Thus, researchers must be careful not to reveal too many details about their experiments lest they bias how potential subjects may behave.

Next, we'll turn our attention to the ethics of research with animals.

Will they try to trick or deceive me?

© Jack Hollingsworth/Photodisc Green/Getty Images

Milgram's Obedience Study

Learn how informed consent, debriefing, and deception were used in Milgram's obedience study.

▶ **L021** Identify ethical concerns in animal research.

Animal Research

How many animals are used in research?

In the field of psychology, about 7% to 8% of research involves the use of animals. About 90% of the nonhuman animals used by researchers are rats, mice, and birds, while the remaining 10% are other animals such as cats, dogs, and monkeys (C.A.R.E., 2010). We'll examine the justification for using animals in research and how their rights are protected.

Are research animals mistreated?

You may have seen a disturbing photo or heard about a laboratory animal being mistreated (C.A.R.E., 2010). The fact is that, of the millions of animals used in research, only a few cases of animal mistreatment have been confirmed. That is because scientists know that proper care and treatment of their laboratory animals are vital to the success of their research. To abolish the use of all laboratory animals because of one or two isolated cases of mistreatment would be like abolishing all medical practice because of isolated cases of malpractice. Instead, researchers support the Animal Research Act, which balances the rights of animals to be treated with care with the needs for advancing the medical, physiological, and psychological health of humans (Albright et al., 2005).

Courtesy of the Foundation for Biomedical Research

Unless otherwise noted, all images are © Cengage Learning

Is the use of animals justified?

Adrian Morrison, director of the National Institute of Mental Health's Program for Animal Research Issues, offers this view: "Because I do experimental surgery, I go through a soul-searching every couple of months, asking myself whether I really want to continue working on cats. The answer is always yes because I know that there is no other way for medicine to progress but through animal experimentation and that basic research ultimately leads to unforeseen benefits" (Morrison, 1993).

In the field of psychology, animal research has led to a better understanding of how stress affects one's health; the development and treatment of depression, anxiety, and schizophrenia; and critical information about sensory processes of taste, vision, and hearing to mention but a few (C.A.R.E., 2010).

How to strike a balance?

Based on past, present, and potential future benefits of animal research, many experts in the scientific, medical, and mental health communities believe the responsible use of animals in research is justified. This is especially true in light of recent rules that regulate the safe and humane treatment of animals kept in laboratories or used in research (C.A.R.E., 2010; Office of Animal Care and Use, 2010).

It's the animals you don't see that really helped her recover.

Recently, a surgical technique perfected on animals was used to remove a malignant tumor from a little girl's brain. We lost some lab animals. But look what we saved.

Foundation for Biomedical Research

Courtesy of the Foundation for Biomedical Research

Understanding Schizophrenia

Learn how the animal model helps further understanding about schizophrenia.

Understanding Addiction

Observe rats helping researchers to understand nicotine addiction.

Check Your Learning Quiz 1.9

Go to **login.cengagebrain.com** and take the online quiz.

Unless otherwise noted, all images are © Cengage Learning

Think Critically

Challenge Your Thinking

Consider these questions when reading this article:

1. What three childhood symptoms of autism do Donna (introduced in Module 1.1) and Temple share?
2. Which of the four goals of psychology is illustrated by Donna refusing to allow anyone to touch her?
3. Which area of specialization in psychology would be best able to understand how Temple thinks in pictures?
4. Of the seven modern approaches to psychology, which should you use to study someone with autism?
5. What social skill does Temple have (unlike many with autism) that allows her to put herself "inside a cow's head"?
6. How would a humanistic psychologist understand Temple's accomplishments?

How Do People with Autism Think?

As a young child, Temple Grandin had a few peculiarities. She had great difficulty learning to speak and understanding language, but she had an incredible eye for color and great artistic talent. Temple didn't know how to relate with other children and preferred to be alone, often rocking herself back and forth for hours. She was so sensitive to touch that she refused to allow anyone to touch her. Temple was unusually sensitive to sounds. She compared hearing the school bell to a "dentist's drill" (J. P. Shapiro, 1996) sounding in her ear. She

described going through each day feeling anxious as if she were constantly "being mugged on the New York subway" (J. P. Shapiro, 1996).

Temple was diagnosed with autism at the age of 3, and doctors were certain she wouldn't ever be successful. What they didn't know is how much Temple would prove them wrong. Her childhood art projects provided a glimpse into Temple's unique way of thinking. While most of us think in words, Temple, like many others with autism, thinks in pictures. She compares her

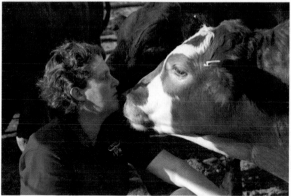

memory to a full-length movie in her head that she can replay over and over again. She can even view the movies from different points of view, which helps her notice small details that otherwise would have been overlooked.

Temple has made remarkable accomplishments by applying her visual way of thinking to her love of animals. For example, she placed herself "inside a cow's head" to see the world through its eyes. By doing so, she realized how frightening it is for cattle to approach the dip vat, a deep swimming pool filled with pesticide that cattle enter to rid them of ticks and other parasites. Cattle would panic while going down a steep and slippery slope and then become even more frightened as they unexpectedly dropped into water. To reduce the fear cattle had of the dip vat, Temple used her visual way of thinking to design equipment with a less steep and slippery walkway, as well as a more comfortable way for cattle to enter the water.

Using her unique way of thinking in pictures, Temple has become the most accomplished and well-known autistic adult in the world. She has taken the lead in designing and advocating for the use of more humane equipment with animals. Her unique understanding of animals led her to publish an insightful book explaining how animals feel. Temple earned a doctorate degree in animal science and is currently a university professor, a prominent author and speaker, and a consultant for the care and handling of livestock. (Adapted from Fenly, 2006; Grandin, 1992, 2002, 2009; J. P. Shapiro, 1996)

Think Critically 1.1

This article and its questions are available in interactive format online.

GO to your Psychology CourseMate at login.cengagebrain.com and take the Chapter Post-Test to see which Learning Objectives you've mastered and which need more review. Use the chapter review guide below and the online activities—including flashcards to review key terms—to measure your learning.

Online Activities

Key Terms	Video	Animation	Reading	Assessment
autism	Autism: Christina, p. 5 Autism: A Spectrum Disorder, p. 5			Check Your Learning Quiz 1.1
psychology, structuralism, introspection, functionalism, gestalt approach, behavioral approach	Shaping a Pigeon, p. 11		Taking Class Notes, p. 7 Early Discrimination, p. 11	Check Your Learning Quiz 1.2
biological approach, cognitive approach, behavioral approach, psychoanalytic approach, humanistic approach, sociocultural approach, evolutionary approach, eclectic approach		Approaches: Historical versus Modern, p. 15	Biological Approach to Test Anxiety, p. 13 Cognitive Approach to Test Anxiety, p. 13 Behavioral Approach to Test Anxiety, p. 13 Psychoanalytic Approach to Test Anxiety, p. 13 Humanistic Approach to Test Anxiety, p. 15 Sociocultural Approaches to Test Anxiety, p. 15 Evolutionary Approach to Physical Attraction, p. 15	Check Your Learning Quiz 1.3
psychologist, psychiatrist, clinical and counseling psychology, developmental psychology, social psychology, experimental psychology, biological psychology, cognitive psychology, psychometrics, industrial/organizational psychology			Study Skills, p. 19	Check Your Learning Quiz 1.4

Online Activities

Key Terms	Video	Animation	Reading	Assessment
armchair psychology, scientific method		Armchair Psychology, p. 21		Check Your Learning Quiz 1.5
attention-deficit/hyperactivity disorder (ADHD), survey, case study, testimonial, naturalistic observation	Careful Assessment and Diagnosis, p. 23 Prescriptions to Treat ADHD, p. 23 Behavioral Therapy: Kids with ADHD, p. 23		ADHD Controversies, p. 23 Survey Research: Memory Accuracy, p. 25 Use of Placebos, p. 27 Naturalistic Observation: Observing Chimps, p. 29	Check Your Learning Quiz 1.6
correlation, correlation coefficient		Correlation, p. 31		Check Your Learning Quiz 1.7
experiment, hypothesis, independent variable, dependent variable, random selection, experimental group, control group, double-blind procedure, statistical procedures, extraneous variable, experimental bias, self-fulfulfilling prophecy	Self-Fulfilling Prophecy, p. 37	Conducting an Experiment, p. 35		Check Your Learning Quiz 1.8
informed consent, confidentiality, debriefing	Understanding Addiction, p. 41		Miligram's Obedience Study, p. 39 Understanding Schizophrenia, p. 41	Check Your Learning Quiz 1.9

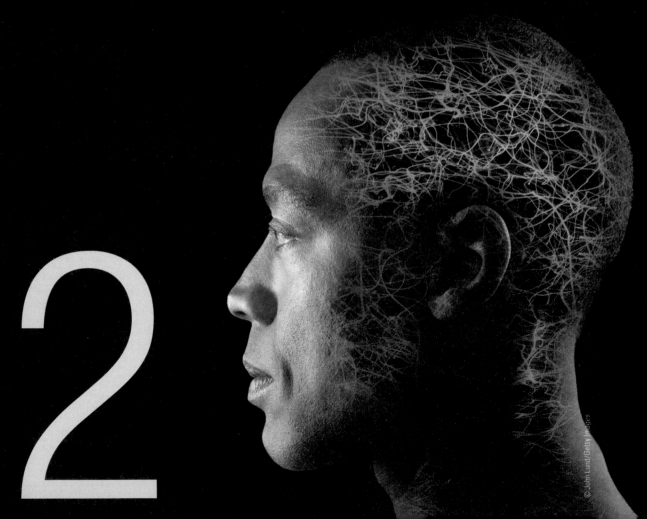

Biological Bases of Behavior

> CHAPTER

2

© John Lund/Getty Images

Chapter Outline and Learning Objectives

Prepare to Learn

1 **GO** to your **Psychology CourseMate** at **login.cengagebrain.com** and take the **Chapter Pre-Test** to introduce yourself to this chapter's topics and see what you may already know.

2 **READ** the **Learning Objectives (LOs)** (in the left sidebars) and begin the chapter.

3 **COMPLETE** the **Online Activities** (in the right sidebars) *as you read each module*. Activities include **videos**, **animations**, **readings**, and **quizzes**.

4 **CHECK Your Learning** by going online to take the quiz at the end of each module and review material as necessary.

5 **MEASURE Your Learning** after reading the chapter by taking the online **Chapter Post-Test**. Use the chapter review guide at the end of the chapter as needed.

WATCH for these **Online Activities** icons as you read:

Video   Animation   Reading   Assessment   Think Critically

These online activities are important to mastering this chapter. As you read each module, access these materials by going to **login.cengagebrain.com**.

Video Explore studies and firsthand accounts of biological and psychological processes:

- See how Alzheimer's disease is diagnosed
- Watch the changes a person with Alzheimer's disease gradually begins to exhibit
- Watch and listen to someone with Alzheimer's disease answer questions about himself
- Discover whether or not the brain can grow and make connections in a person who has been living in a minimally conscious state for 20 years
- Watch how fMRI brain scans are used to evaluate the cognitive functioning of patients
- Watch the exploration of ethical issues associated with stem cell research
- Watch how brain stimulation implants help treat symptoms of Parkinson's disease
- Get a closer look at the hindbrain
- Examine what the exterior cortex of our brain looks like
- Get a closer look at the limbic system
- Learn more about some of the unique aspects of the female brain
- Learn how each hemisphere is specialized for performing certain tasks

Animation Interact with and visualize important processes and concepts:

- Explore how the distribution of genes at fertilization determine individual traits
- Explore the probability of someone developing blue or brown eyes
- Discover how the forces of evolution affect the development of the brain
- Identify the structure of the neuron and understand the action of transmitters
- Identify the overall organization of the bran's several nervous systems
- Get a closer look at how the sympathetic and parasympathetic nervous systems interact
- Explore Broca's and Wernicke's aphasia and how they differ
- Identify the major parts of the brain

Reading Delve deeper into key content:

- Learn more about the ways genetic testing is being used in psychology
- Learn about the effects of alcohol on neurotransmitters
- Learn more about how drugs derived from plants affect neurotransmitters

- Explore how surgeons are able to reattach both of John Thompson's arms and how his arms function post-surgery
- Explore how surgeons are able to transplant a face
- Learn how people can feel sensations and movement from a missing limb
- Learn whether brain size varies among different races and if intelligence is determined by brain size
- Explore how the brains of males and females differ

Assessment Measure your mastery:

- Chapter Pre-Test
- Check Your Learning Quizzes
- Chapter Post-Test

Think Critically Challenge your thinking by applying content from this chapter and making connections to related material:

- Mirrors in Your Brain?

▶ **L01** Describe Alzheimer's disease.

CHARLES SCHNEIDER has had an impressive career—a police officer, fire fighter, and private investigator. He was also quite the craftsman, remodeling houses and building sturdy fences. He has a loving wife, two children, and five grandchildren. In his early fifties, Charles had everything he could ever want in life. But that was before he started to forget things. What could explain why he could no longer remember his lock combination at the firehouse or why he began having to open every compartment in the fire truck to find tools he needed? Why did the names of his coworkers and other people he knew well begin to escape him? Why could he not remember his phone number?

▼

Because Charles had been healthy and his family believed he was too young to have any serious medical problem, he didn't go to the doctor right away. But when he could no longer remember his wife's name, he immediately went for help. When Charles saw a neurologist, he was diagnosed with Alzheimer's *(ALTS-hi-mers)* disease (adapted from Fischman, 2006).

The initial symptoms of **Alzheimer's disease** are problems with memory, such as forgetting and repeating things, getting lost, and being mildly confused. There are also cognitive deficits, such as problems with language, difficulties in recognizing objects, and inability to plan.

In 10% of the cases, Alzheimer's disease begins after age 50, but in 90% of the cases, it begins after age 65. Over a period of 5 to 10 years, these symptoms worsen and result in profound memory loss, lack of recognition of family and

© Jeffrey MacMillan/U.S. News & World Report

Unless otherwise noted, all images are © Cengage Learning

friends, deterioration in personality, and emotional outbursts. There is widespread damage to the brain, especially the hippocampus, which is involved in memory (NIH, 2005; 2008). For Charles, the worst is yet to come. His memory will crumble, he will be bedridden, and he will not know who he is or be able to recognize his family. When he dies—for Alzheimer's has, at present, no cure—Charles will have lost his memory, his wonderful personality, and all signs of humanity.

The reason Alzheimer's disease will eventually destroy Charles's memory, personality, and humanity is that it destroys the brain cells that form the brain's information network. Though the causes of Alzheimer's disease are not certain, scientists are focusing much of their attention on genetics, our next topic.

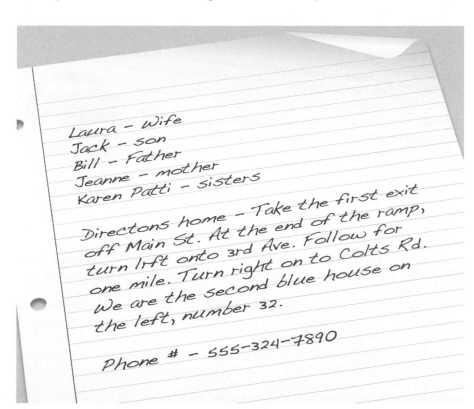

Laura – Wife
Jack – son
Bill – Father
Jeanne – mother
Karen Patti – sisters

Directons home – Take the first exit off Main St. At the end of the ramp, turn lrft onto 3rd Ave. Follow for one mile. Turn right on to Colts Rd. We are the second blue house on the left, number 32.

Phone # – 555-324-7890

Alzheimer's Test

See how Alzheimer's disease is diagnosed.

Alzheimer's Disease

Watch the changes a person with Alzheimer's disease gradually begins to exhibit.

Declining Mental Acuity

Watch and listen to someone with Alzheimer's disease answer questions about himself.

Check Your Learning Quiz 2.1

Go to **login.cengagebrain.com** and take the online quiz.

▶ **L02** Describe the structures and processes involved in genetic transmission.

Genes Overview

1 Fertilization Human life has its beginnings when a father's sperm, which contains 23 chromosomes, penetrates a mother's egg, which contains 23 chromosomes. The result is a fertilized cell called a zygote (shown below).

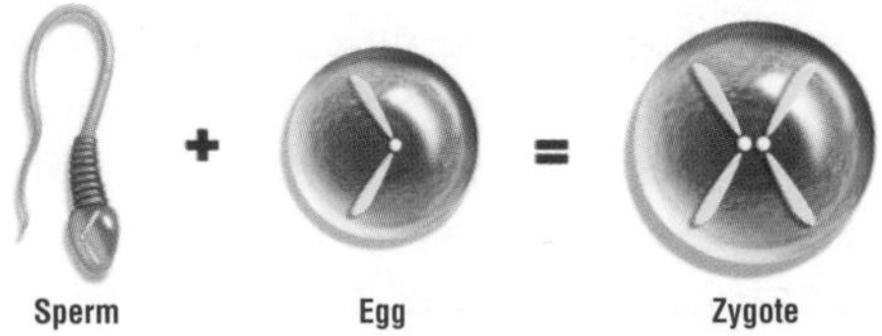

2 Zygote A zygote, about the size of a grain of sand, is the largest human cell.

A **zygote** is a cell that results when an egg is fertilized.

Sperm   Egg   Zygote

A zygote contains 46 chromosomes arranged in 23 pairs. It contains the equivalent of 300,000 pages of type written instructions. For simplicity, the zygote shown at the right has only 1 pair of chromosomes.

3 Chromosomes Inside the very tiny zygote are 23 pairs of chromosomes, which contain chemical instructions for development of the brain and body.

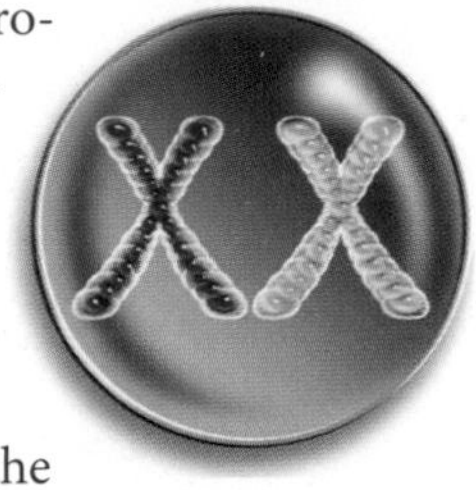

A **chromosome** is a short, rodlike, microscopic structure that contains tightly coiled strands of the chemical DNA, an abbreviation for deoxyribonucleic *(dee-ox-ee-RYE-bow-new-CLEE-ick)* acid.

Each cell of the human body (except for the sperm and egg) contains 46 chromosomes arranged in 23 pairs. For simplicity, the cell shown above has only 2 pairs of chromosomes.

4 Chemical Alphabet Each chromosome contains a long, coiled strand of DNA, which resembles a ladder (left figure) that has been twisted over and over upon itself.

Each rung of the DNA ladder is made up of four chemicals. The order in which the four different chemicals combine to form rungs creates a microscopic chemical alphabet. This chemical alphabet is used to write instructions for the development and assembly of the 100 trillion highly specialized cells that make up the brain and body (R. J. Sternberg, 2001).

Unless otherwise noted, all images are © Cengage Learning

5 Genes and Proteins On each chromosome are specific segments that contain particular instructions. In the chromosome on the right, each segment represents the location of a gene.

A **gene** is a specific segment on the strand of DNA that contains instructions for making proteins.

Proteins are chemical building blocks from which all parts of the brain and body are constructed.

For example, genes determine physical traits (eye color, shape of ear lobes) and contribute to the development of emotional, cognitive, and behavioral traits (Angier, 2003).

6 Polymorphic Genes Although there is only one version of about 99% of our genes, sometimes we have genes that have more than one version.

A **polymorphic gene** is a gene that has more than one version.

Polymorphic genes help explain some of the differences in physical appearance and behaviors in people. For example, there is a polymorphic gene that influences eye color. Depending on which combination of these genes each sibling receives from the parents, two siblings may have different eye colors.

7 Dominant and Recessive Genes Because we can inherit different versions of genes for a particular characteristic (such as eye color) from each parent, conflicts between polymorphic genes can occur. The conflict is resolved by identifying the dominant and recessive genes. In terms of eye color, the gene for brown eyes is dominant and the gene for blue eyes is recessive.

A **dominant gene** is a type of polymorphic gene that determines the development of a specific trait even if it is paired with a recessive gene.

A **recessive gene** is a type of polymorphic gene that determines the development of a specific trait only when it is inherited from both parents.

If you inherit a gene for brown eyes from your father and a gene for blue eyes from your mother, the dominant gene will determine your eye color. The gene for brown eyes is dominant; thus you will develop brown eyes.

Next, we'll learn about how our brains have evolved.

Genes Overview

Explore how the distribution of genes at fertilization determine individual traits.

Inheriting Eye Color

Explore the probability of someone developing blue or brown eye genes.

Genetic Testing

Learn more about the ways genetic testing is being used in psychology.

▶ **L03** Articulate the forces believed to be responsible for the evolution of the human brain and describe the relevance of the theory of evolution in how psychologists conduct research today.

Evolution of the Human Brain

In 1859, Charles Darwin stunned much of the Western world by publishing *Origin of Species,* a revolutionary theory of how species originate, which was the basis for his now-famous theory of evolution.

The **theory of evolution** says that different species arose from a common ancestor and that those species that survived were best adapted to meet the demands of their environments.

Darwin's theory of evolution has received broad scientific support from fossil records and examination of genetic similarities and differences among species (Mayr, 2000; Zimmer, 2009a). The fact that many scientists hold to the theory of evolution clashes with deeply held religious beliefs that place humans on a family tree of their own.

According to evolution theory, present-day humans descended from a creature that split off from apes millions of years ago. Supporting this theory is the finding that humans and chimpanzees share at least 98% of their DNA.

Research suggests that when and how much genes are activated may be what helps set humans apart from chimpanzees (Ehrenberg, 2008). Other research suggests humans are more intelligent than chimpanzees not because of more sophisticated neurons; rather, an enormous number of basic neurons and countless more interactions between neurons are responsible for making humans so brainy (Sapolsky, 2006).

Two forces are thought to be responsible for the evolution of the human brain: **genetic mutations,** which are accidental errors in genetic instructions that lead to a change, and **natural selection,** which means the genes for traits that help an organism survive and reproduce (**adaptive genes**) will be selected and will continue in a species, whereas the genes for traits that prevent survival and reproduction (**maladaptive genes**) will not be selected, consequently being eliminated in a species (Balter, 2002; Toner, 2006).

Unless otherwise noted, all images are © Cengage Learning

The process of natural selection produces **adaptations,** which are common features of a species that provide it with improved function.

Examples of adaptations include a behavior that helps the organism better escape a predator or a physical characteristic providing it with an advantage, such as opposable thumbs for gripping.

A relatively new approach to psychology emerges from the theory of evolution and is called the evolutionary approach.

The **evolutionary approach** studies how evolutionary ideas, such as adaptation and natural selection, explain human behaviors and mental processes.

This approach provides rather persuasive theories in sexual conflict, mating, sexuality, families, social conflict, aggression, morality, depression, and anxiety (Nesse, 2005; Pinker, 2002).

© Stockbyte RF/Getty Images

Research suggests women have a variety of long-standing, adaptive defenses against sexual coercion, a type of sexual conflict, including the formation of female-female coalitions, selection of male friends who serve as "body guards," avoidance of risky activities, and fears of rape (Buss, 2003).

Next we'll discuss the brain's building blocks that form a complex informational network. We'll explain the two groups of brain cells—glial cells and neurons—that make up this network. Also, we'll begin to show you how Alzheimer's disease is changing Charles Schneider's brain.

Evolution of the Human Brain

Discover how the forces of evolution affect the development of the brain.

Check Your Learning Quiz 2.2

Go to **login.cengagebrain.com** and take the online quiz.

▶ **LO4** Identify the main functions of glial cells.

▶ **LO5** Identify the various parts of the neuron and explain how a neuron functions.

Structure of the Brain

We'll begin by explaining the two different kinds of brain cells and which kind is destroyed by Alzheimer's disease.

On the right is a top view of a human brain. It is shaped like a small wrinkled melon, weighs about 1,350 grams (less than 3 pounds), is pinkish-white in color, and has the consistency of firm JELL-O®. Your brain is fueled by sugar (glucose) and has about one trillion cells that can be divided into two groups—glial cells and neurons.

Glial Cells

The most numerous brain cells, about 900 billion, are called glial *(GLEE-all)* cells (shown below).

Glial cells (astrocytes) have at least three functions: (1) providing scaffolding to guide the growth of developing neurons and support mature neurons; (2) wrapping around neurons to form insulation to prevent interference from other electrical signals; and (3) releasing chemicals that influence a neuron's growth and function (Verkhratsky & Butt, 2007).

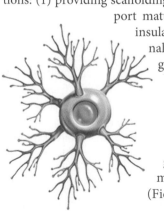

Glial cells grow throughout one's lifetime. If something causes the uncontrolled growth of glial cells, the result is brain cancer. Until recently, glial cells were believed to have only supportive functions (as described above), but research now shows some glial cells may transmit electrical signals, which is the major function of neurons, which we'll discuss next (Fields, 2009; Saey, 2008a).

Neurons

The second group of brain cells, which number about 100 billion, are called neurons (*NER-ons*); one is shown on the right.

A **neuron** is a brain cell with two specialized extensions. One extension is for receiving electrical signals, and a second, longer extension is for transmitting electrical signals.

Depending upon their size, neurons receive and transmit electrical signals at speeds of up to 200 miles per hour over distances from a fraction of an inch to over 3 feet, such as from your toe to your spinal cord.

Neurons form a vast, miniaturized informational network that allows us to receive sensory information, control muscle movement, regulate digestion, secrete hormones, and engage in complex mental processes.

Charles's brain is constructed from two kinds of building blocks—glial cells and neurons. However, Alzheimer's disease gradually destroys the neurons; the result is that Charles's brain is losing its ability to transmit information, causing memory and cognitive difficulties.

Growth and Repair of Neurons

Researchers believe that, with few exceptions, human brains develop almost all their neurons at birth and adult brains do not grow new neurons (Kornack & Rakic, 2001). Human brains are capable only of growing a relatively limited number of new neurons throughout adulthood, and some of these new neurons play an important role in our continuing ability to learn and remember new things (S. Halpern, 2008; Saey, 2008b).

Besides having a limited capacity to grow new neurons throughout adulthood, mature human brains also have a limited capacity to replace, rewire, or repair damaged neurons, such as after a stroke, gunshot wound, or blow to the head (SFN, 2007; J. Silver & Miller, 2004). Recent advances in stem-cell research suggest the human brain may be able to grow more neurons. If this were possible, the brain could repair damage caused by an accident or disease, such as Alzheimer's (Wieloch & Nikolich, 2006).

Next, we'll take a closer look at neurons by examining their structure.

Brain Re-Growth

Discover whether or not the brain can grow and make connections in a person who has been living in a minimally conscious state for 20 years.

Before Charles developed Alzheimer's disease, he was able to engage in a variety of cognitive and physical behaviors. He was able to think, smile, walk, and speak—all because of the activity of microscopic brain cells called neurons.

Structure and Function of Neurons

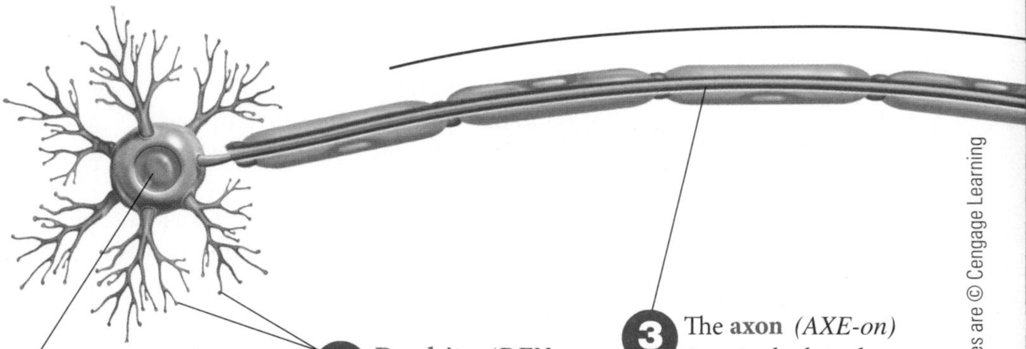

1 The **cell body** (or soma) is a relatively large, egg-shaped structure that provides fuel, manufactures chemicals, and maintains the entire neuron in working order.

In the center of the cell body is a small oval shape representing the nucleus, which contains genetic instructions (in the form of DNA) for both the manufacture of chemicals and the regulation of the neuron.

2 **Dendrites** *(DEN-drites)* are branch-like extensions that arise from the cell body; they receive signals from other neurons, muscles, or sense organs and pass these signals to the cell body.

At the time of birth, a neuron has few dendrites. After birth, dendrites undergo dramatic growth that accounts for much of the increase in brain size. As dendrites grow, they make connections and form communication networks between neurons and other cells or organs.

3 The **axon** *(AXE-on)* is a single thread-like structure that extends from, and carries signals away from, the cell body to neighboring neurons, organs, or muscles.

In the illustration above, the axon is indicated by an orange line inside the tube composed of separate gray segments. Axons vary in length from less than a hair's breadth to as long as 3 feet (from spinal cord to toes). An axon conducts electrical signals to a neighboring organ, a muscle, or another neuron.

Unless otherwise noted, all images are © Cengage Learning

In Alzheimer's disease there is an excessive buildup of gluelike substances, which gradually destroy neurons (Larson, 2008). In Charles's case, these gluelike substances will destroy many of his neurons, causing his brain to actually shrink.

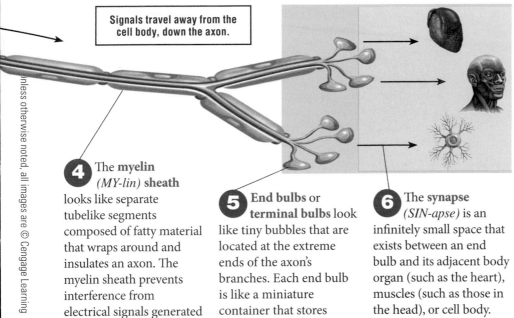

Signals travel away from the cell body, down the axon.

4 The **myelin** *(MY-lin)* **sheath** looks like separate tubelike segments composed of fatty material that wraps around and insulates an axon. The myelin sheath prevents interference from electrical signals generated in adjacent axons.

The axons of most large neurons have myelin sheaths. You may have heard the brain described as consisting of gray and white matter. Gray is the color of cell bodies, while white is the color of myelin sheaths.

5 **End bulbs** or **terminal bulbs** look like tiny bubbles that are located at the extreme ends of the axon's branches. Each end bulb is like a miniature container that stores chemicals called neurotransmitters, which are used to communicate with neighboring cells.

End bulbs reach right up to, but do not physically touch, the surface of a neighboring organ, muscle, or another cell body.

6 The **synapse** *(SIN-apse)* is an infinitely small space that exists between an end bulb and its adjacent body organ (such as the heart), muscles (such as those in the head), or cell body.

When stimulated by electrical signals from the axon, the end bulbs eject neurotransmitters into the synapse. The neurotransmitters cross the synapse and act like switches to turn adjacent cells on or off (Levitan & Kaczmarek, 2002).

▶ **L06** Describe the sequence of the action potential and neural impulse.

Now, that you're familar with the structure and function of neurons, we'll explain the process of how they communicate or send information.

Sequence: Action Potential

1 Feeling a Sharp Object

When you step on a sharp object, you seem to feel the pain almost immediately. To feel the pain involves the following series of electrochemical events:

A. A sharp object produces mechanical pressure on the bottom of your foot.

B. Your skin has sensors that transform the pressure into electrical signals.

C. The electrical signals are sent by the axon to the spinal cord and brain.

D. Finally, your brain interprets these electrical signals as "pain."

We're going to focus on step C and explain how axons send electrical signals by using the analogy of a battery. We'll begin by enlarging the inside of an axon.

2 Axon Membrane: Chemical Gates

Think of an axon as a tube filled and surrounded with fluid. The tube is formed by a thin membrane that keeps the fluid separate and has special gates.

The **axon membrane** has chemical gates (shown in red) that can open to allow electrically charged particles to enter or close to keep out electrically charged particles.

Just as a battery's power comes from its electrically charged chemicals, so does the axon's power to send information.

3 Ions: Charged Particles

The fluid inside and outside the axon contains ions.

Ions are chemical particles that have electrical charges. Ions follow two rules: Opposite charges attract (figure below), and like charges repel.

The axon's function is often explained by discussing sodium and potassium ions. However, it is simpler and easier to focus on just sodium ions, which have positive charges and are abbreviated Na^+, and large protein ions, which have negative charges and are labeled $protein^-$. Because they have opposite charges, Na^+ ions will be attracted to $protein^-$ ions (see figure).

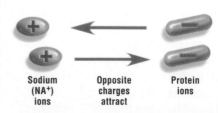

Sodium (NA⁺) ions   Opposite charges attract   Protein ions

4 Resting State: Charged Battery

The axon membrane separates positively charged sodium ions on the outside from negatively charged protein ions on the inside. This separation produces a chemical battery that is not yet discharging and is said to be in its resting state.

The **resting state** means that the axon has a charge, or potential. The charge, or potential, results from the axon membrane separating positive ions on the outside from negative ions on the inside (left figure).

The axon membrane has a charge across it during the resting state because of several factors, the primary one being the sodium pump.

The **sodium pump** is a transport process that picks up any sodium ions that enter the axon's chemical gates and returns them back outside. Thus, the sodium pump is responsible for keeping the axon charged by returning and keeping sodium ions outside the axon membrane.

Sodium
(NA+)
ions

5 Action Potential: Sending Information

If a stimulus, such as a sharp object, is large enough to excite a neuron, two things will happen to its axon. First, the stimulus will eventually open the axon's chemical gates by stopping the sodium pump. Second, when the stoppage of the sodium pump causes the gates to open, thousands of positive sodium ions will rush inside because of their attraction to the negative protein ions. The rush of sodium ions inside the axon is called the action potential.

The **action potential** is a tiny electric current that is generated when the positive sodium ions rush inside the axon.

The enormous increase of sodium ions inside the axon causes the inside of the axon to reverse its charge. The inside becomes positive, while the outside becomes negative. Immediately after the action potential, the sodium pump starts up and returns the axon to the resting state. (Levitan & Kaczmarek, 2002).

Action Potential

Inside = positive

Outside = negative

Sequence: Neural Impulse

6 Sending Information

One mistake students make is to think that the axon has *one* action potential, similar to the bang of a gunshot. However, unlike a gunshot, the axon has numerous individual action potentials that move down the axon, segment by segment; this movement is called the neural impulse.

The **neural impulse** refers to the series of separate action potentials that take place segment by segment as they move down the length of an axon.

Thus, instead of a single bang, a neural impulse goes down the length of the axon very much like a lit fuse. Once lit, a fuse doesn't go off in a single bang but rather burns continuously until it reaches the end. This movement of a neural impulse all the way down to the end of an axon is actually a natural law.

7 All-or-None Law

Why does a neural impulse travel down the axon's entire length? The answer is the all-or-none law.

The **all-or-none law** states that, if an action potential starts at the beginning of an axon, the action potential will continue at the same speed, segment by segment, to the very end of the axon.

You'll see how the all-or-none law works in the figure below.

8 Neural Impulse

Notice in this figure, which continues on the next page, that the neural impulse is made up of a sequence of six action potentials, with the first action potential occurring at the beginning of the axon.

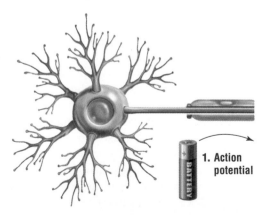

1. Action potential

BATTERY

8a According to the all-or-none law, once a neural impulse begins, it goes to the end of the axon. This means that when action potential 1 occurs, it will be followed in order by potentials 2, 3, 4, 5, and 6. After the occurrence of each action potential, the axon membrane at that point quickly returns to its resting state.

8b Notice that the **myelin sheath** has regular breaks where the axon is bare and uninsulated. It is at these bare points that the axon's gates open and the action potential takes place.

9 End Bulbs and Neurotransmitters

Once the neural impulse reaches the end of the axon, the very last action potential, 6, affects the end bulbs, which are located at the very end of the axon. This last action potential triggers the end bulbs to release their neurotransmitters. Once released, neurotransmitters cross the synapse and, depending upon the kind, they will either excite or inhibit the function of neighboring organs (such as the heart), muscles (such as those in the head), or cell bodies.

As you can now see, neurotransmitters are critical for communicating with neighboring organs, muscles, and other neurons (Levitan & Kaczmarek, 2002). We'll examine transmitters in more detail and show you how they excite or inhibit.

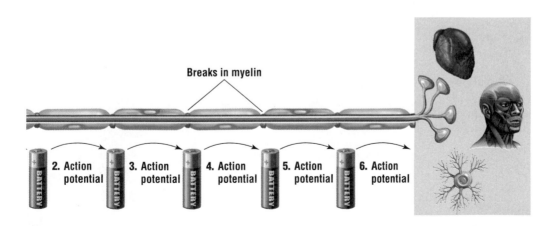

Breaks in myelin

2. Action potential 3. Action potential 4. Action potential 5. Action potential 6. Action potential

▸ **LO7** Describe neurotransmitters and explain how neurons communicate at chemical synapses.

Transmitters

There's no doubt that you have felt your heart pounding when you are afraid, stressed, or angry. One reason for your pounding heart has to do with transmitters.

A **transmitter** is a chemical messenger that carries information between nerves and body organs, such as muscles and heart.

Everything you do, including thinking, deciding, talking, and getting angry, involves transmitters. For example, imagine seeing someone back into your brand new car and then just drive away. You would certainly become angry, and your heart would pound. Let's see why getting angry can increase your heart rate from a normal 60 to 70 beats per minute to over 180.

1 In the figure on the left, you see the end of an axon with three branches. At the end of the bottom branch is a greatly enlarged *end bulb.* Inside the bulb are four colored circles that represent transmitters.

2 When the action potential hits the end bulb, it causes a miniature explosion, and the transmitters are ejected outside. Once ejected, transmitters cross a tiny space, or synapse, and, in this case, reach the nearby heart muscle. Think of transmitters as chemical keys that fit into chemical locks on the surface of the heart muscle. End bulbs usually hold either excitatory or inhibitory transmitters, which have opposite effects.

3 Strong emotions cause the release of *excitatory transmitters,* which open chemical locks in the heart muscle and cause it to beat faster. When you start to calm down, there is a release of *inhibitory transmitters,* which block chemical locks in the heart muscle and decrease its rate (Feldman, 2009). One special class of transmitters that are made in the brain are called neurotransmitters.

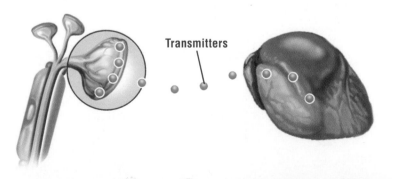

Transmitters

Neurotransmitters

Studying this textbook requires your brain to use millions of neurons that communicate with one another by using chemicals called neurotransmitters.

Neurotransmitters are about a dozen different chemicals that are made by neurons and then used for communication between neurons during the performance of mental or physical activities.

Since billions of neurons are packed tightly together and use different neurotransmitters for eating, sleeping, talking, thinking, and dreaming, why don't neurotransmitters get all mixed up? The answer is that neurotransmitters are similar to chemical keys that fit into only specific chemical locks.

1 The figure on the left again shows the end of an axon with three branches. One *end bulb* is enlarged to show it contains neurotransmitters (four colored circles).

2 The action potential causes the end bulbs to eject their neurotransmitters, which, in turn, cross the synapse and, in this case, land on the surface of nearby dendrites. The surface of one dendrite is enlarged (right figure) to show its *receptors* (notches), which are special areas that function like chemical locks.

3 Each of the many types of neurotransmitters has a unique chemical key that fits and opens only certain chemical locks, or receptors. Thus, billions of neurons use this system of chemical keys that open or close matching locks to communicate and to participate in many different activities (Bohlen und Halbach & Dermietzel, 2006).

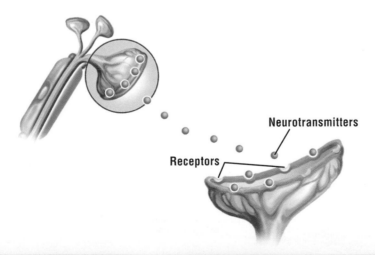

Neurotransmitters

Receptors

Neuron and Transmitters

Identify the structure of the neuron and understand the action of transmitters.

Alcohol

Learn about the effects of alcohol on neurotransmitters.

Plants & Drugs

Learn more about how drugs from plants affect neurotransmitters.

▶ **LO8** Describe the sequence of the reflex response.

Now that you're familiar with neurons and neurotransmitters, we'll explain what enables your hand to instantly move away after touching a very hot object.

Reflex Responses

If you accidentally touched a hot lightbulb, your hand would instantly jerk away, without any conscious thought or effort. This is an example of a reflex.

A **reflex** is an unlearned, involuntary reaction to some stimulus. The network of neural connections underlying a reflex is prewired by genetic instructions.

We are all born with a number of programmed reflexes (such as the knee-jerk reflex), and all reflexes share the same two or three steps, depending upon how they are wired in the nervous system. Here's the sequence for how a reflex occurs:

In some cases, such as when a doctor taps your knee, the knee-jerk reflex is controlled by the spinal cord. In other cases, such as when someone shines a bright light into your eye, the pupillary reflex causes the pupil to constrict. We are all born with a number of programmed reflexes, and all reflexes share the same two or three steps, depending upon how they are wired in the nervous system.

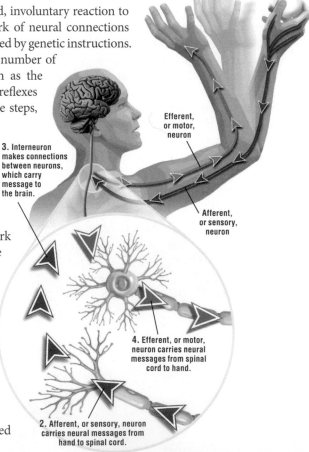

Efferent, or motor, neuron

3. Interneuron makes connections between neurons, which carry message to the brain.

Afferent, or sensory, neuron

4. Efferent, or motor, neuron carries neural messages from spinal cord to hand.

2. Afferent, or sensory, neuron carries neural messages from hand to spinal cord.

One reason reflexes occur so quickly is that they are genetically programmed and involve relatively few neural connections, which saves time. Here's the sequence for how a reflex occurs:

1 Sensors The skin of your fingers has specialized sensors that are sensitive to heat. When you touch a hot lightbulb, these skin sensors trigger neurons that start the withdrawal reflex.

2 Afferent Neurons From the sensors in your skin, long dendrites carry "pain information" in the form of electrical signals to the spinal cord. These dendrites are part of sensory, or afferent, neurons (red arrows).

Afferent *(AFF-er-ent),* or **sensory, neurons** carry information from the sensors to the spinal cord.

Sensory neurons may have dendrites 2 to 3 feet long, to reach from the tips of your fingers to the spinal cord.

3 Interneuron Once the afferent neuron reaches the spinal cord, it transmits the pain information to a second neuron, called an interneuron.

An **interneuron** is a relatively short neuron whose primary task is making connections between other neurons.

In this example, an interneuron transmits the pain information to a third neuron, called the efferent, or motor, neuron.

4 Efferent Neuron Inside the spinal cord, an interneuron transfers information to a third neuron, called an efferent, or motor, neuron (blue arrows).

Efferent *(EFF-er-ent),* or **motor, neurons** carry information away from the spinal cord to produce responses in various muscles and organs throughout the body.

From the spinal cord, an efferent (motor) neuron sends electrical signals on its 2- to 3-foot-long axon to the muscles in the hand. These electrical signals contain "movement information" and cause the hand to withdraw quickly and without any thought on your part.

Functions of Reflex

The primary reason you automatically withdraw your hand when touching a hot object, turn your head in the direction of a loud noise, or vomit after eating tainted food has to do with survival. Reflexes, which have evolved through millions of years, protect body parts from injury and harm and automatically regulate physiological responses, such as heart rate, respiration, and blood pressure (Noback et al., 2005).

Check Your Learning Quiz 2.3

Go to **login.cengagebrain.com** and take the online quiz.

Divisions of the Nervous System

Because you have one brain, you may think that means you have one nervous system. In fact, your brain is much more complex: It has two major nervous systems, one of which has four subdivisions. We'll explain the overall organization of the brain's several nervous systems, beginning with its two major divisions: the central and peripheral nervous systems.

Major Divisions of the Nervous System

Central Nervous System—CNS

You are capable of thinking, speaking, moving, feeling, seeing, and hearing—because of your central nervous system.

The **central nervous system** is made up of the brain and spinal cord. From the bottom of the brain emerges the spinal cord, which is made up of neurons and bundles of axons and dendrites that carry information back and forth between the brain and the body.

People may have numbness or paralysis after damage to their brain or spinal cord because of what neurons cannot easily do. The adult human brain has a limited capacity to grow new neurons and to make new connections. Once damaged, neurons usually die and are not replaced.

Because neurons have a limited capacity for repair and regrowth, people who have an injured or damaged brain or spinal cord experience some loss of sensation and motor movement, depending upon the severity of the damage.

As a result of this damage, messages between the brain and other parts of the body are disrupted, often causing problems in motor coordination, strength, and sensation (Pirko & Noseworthy, 2007).

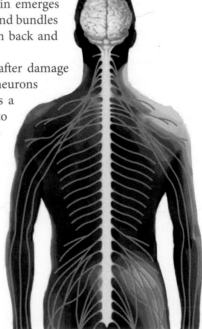

Currently, one of the most exciting areas of research involves techniques that stimulate the regrowth or repair of damaged neurons. The newest approach for treating brain damage is to replace damaged neurons by transplanting stem cells (taken from embyros) into the damaged area (see p. 76). This method has great potential for treating brain and spinal cord diseases, such as Alzheimer's (Karussis & Kassis, 2007; A. M. Wong et al., 2005).

Peripheral Nervous System—PNS

You are able to move your muscles, receive sensations from your body, and perform many other bodily responses because of the peripheral nervous system.

The **peripheral nervous system** includes all the nerves that extend from the spinal cord and carry messages to and from various muscles, glands, and sense organs located throughout the body.

Severed limbs can be reattached and regain movement and sensation because their nerves are part of the peripheral nervous system.

Nerves are stringlike bundles of axons and dendrites that come from the spinal cord and are held together by connective tissue (shown in orange in above figure). Nerves carry information from the senses, skin, muscles, and the body's organs to and from the spinal cord.

Nerves in the peripheral nervous system have the ability to regrow or reattach if severed or damaged. The fact that nerves can regrow means that severed limbs can be reattached and limb transplants are possible. The remarkable ability of nerves to regrow and be reattached distinguishes them from neurons (Kiernan, 2009).

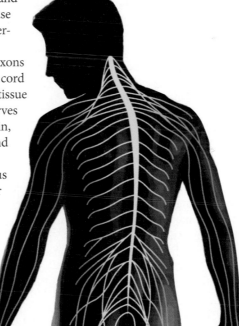

Reattaching Limbs

Explore how surgeons are able to reattach both of John Thompson's arms and how his arms function post-surgery.

Transplanting a Face

Explore how surgeons are able to transplant a face.

Subdivisions of the Peripheral Nervous System

Somatic Nervous System

The **somatic nervous system** consists of a network of nerves that connect either to sensory receptors or to muscles that you can move voluntarily, such as muscles in your limbs, back, neck, and chest.

For example, this gymnast (at right) controls her muscles, knows where her arms and legs are located in space, and maintains her coordination and balance because the somatic nervous system sends electrical signals back and forth to her brain.

ANS—Autonomic Nervous System

The **autonomic nervous system** regulates heart rate, breathing, blood pressure, digestion, hormone secretion, and other functions. The autonomic nervous system usually functions without conscious effort, which means that only a few of its responses, such as breathing, can also be controlled voluntarily.

The autonomic nervous system also has two subdivisions: the sympathetic and parasympathetic divisions.

Subdivisions of the ANS

Sympathetic Division

If you were on a nature hike and suddenly saw a snake, the sympathetic division of the autonomic nervous system would become activiated.

The **sympathetic division,** which is triggered by threatening or challenging physical or psychological stimuli, increases physiological arousal and prepares the body for action.

All of the physiological responses listed in the left-hand column of the table on the next page under *Sympathetic,* such as increased heart rate and dilated pupils, put your body into a state of heightened physiological arousal, which is called the fight-flight response.

The **fight-flight response,** which is a state of increased physiological arousal caused by activation of the sympathetic division, helps the body cope with and survive threatening situations.

Parasympathetic Division

After you have been physiologically aroused by seeing a snake, it usually takes some time before your body returns to a calmer state. The process of decreasing physiological arousal and calming down your body is a result of the activation of the parasympathetic division.

The **parasympathetic division** returns the body to a calmer, relaxed state and is involved in digestion.

As shown in the table, the parasympathetic division, once activated, decreases physiological arousal by decreasing heart rate and constricting pupils. These responses result in the body returning to a more relaxed state.

Sympathetic		Parasympathetic
Pupils dilated, dry; far vision	**Eyes**	Pupils constricted, moist; near vision
Dry	**Mouth**	Salivation
Goose bumps	**Skin**	No goose bumps
Sweaty	**Palms**	Dry
Passages dilated	**Lungs**	Passages constricted
Increased rate	**Heart**	Decreased rate
Supply maximum to muscles	**Blood**	Supply maximum to internal organs
Increased activity	**Adrenal glands**	Decreased activity
Inhibited	**Digestion**	Stimulated
Climax	**Sexual functions**	Arousal

Phantom Limb

Learn how people can feel sensations and movement from a missing limb.

Nervous Systems

Identify the overall organization of the brain's several nervous systems.

Autonomic Nervous System

Get a closer look at how the sympathetic and parasympathetic nervous systems interact.

Check Your Learning Quiz 2.4

Go to **login.cengagebrain.com** and take the online quiz.

▸ **LO12** Describe the different technologies used to investigate the brain.

How can researchers look inside the half-inch-thick skull and study the living brain without causing any damage? There are several brain-scanning techniques that can look through the thick skull and picture the brain with astonishing clarity yet cause no damage to the extremely delicate brain cells.

Brain Scans

A neurologist sees a patient who had recently been hit on the head with a steel rod. The neurologist tells the patient that the front part of her skull has been shattered and the front area of her brain has serious, irreparable damage. The neurologist identified the exact location and extent of the damaged area by using a brain-scanning technique called MRI (right image).

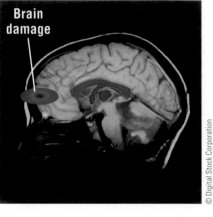

Brain damage

© Digital Stock Corporation

MRI, or **magnetic resonance imaging,** involves passing nonharmful radio frequencies through the brain. A computer measures how these signals interact with brain cells and transforms this interaction into an incredibly detailed image of the brain (or body). MRIs are used to study the structure of the brain.

A newer and different version of the MRI is called the fMRI (left image).

The "f" in **fMRI** (functional magnetic resonance imaging) stands for *functional* and measures the changes in activity of specific neurons that are functioning during cognitive tasks, such as thinking, listening, or reading.

fMRI scans can map activities of neurons that are involved in various cognitive *functions*. In comparison, *MRI* scans show the location of *structures* inside the brain as well as identify sites of brain damage.

Graphic data courtesy of Dr. Ahmad Hariri

Unless otherwise noted, all images are © Cengage Learning

Similar to the fMRI, the PET scan (right image) is also used to identify cognitive functions.

A **PET scan,** or positron emission tomography, involves injecting a slightly radioactive solution into the blood and then measuring the amount of radiation absorbed by brain cells called neurons.

Very active neurons absorb more radioactive solution than less active ones. Different levels of absorption are represented by colors: red and yellow indicate maximum activity of neurons, while blue and green indicate minimal activity.

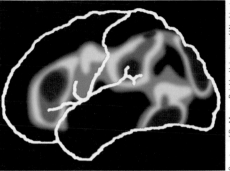

Courtesy of Dr. Marcus Raichle, University of Washington

Both PET and fMRI scans identify and map the living brain's neural activity as a person performs complex behavioral and cognitive tasks, such as seeing, moving, thinking, speaking, and empathizing (McCarthy, 2005). PET scans are now being replaced by the newer fMRI scans because fMRI scans do not require the injection of slightly radioactive solutions (Ropper & Samuels, 2009).

Another technique used to study brain activity is called an EEG.

An **EEG,** or electroencephalograph, involves placing many electrodes on the scalp, which measure changes in electrical voltages at points along the scalp and provide information about brain-wave activity.

© Mike Kepka/San Francisco Chronicle/Corbis

EEGs reveal areas of the brain that are most active, the presence of abnormal brain activation caused by problems with the brain, and changes in mental states, such as sleeping and meditation.

By using these brain-scanning techniques, researchers are mapping a variety of cognitive functions and emotions (Atlas, 2009; Geliebter et al., 2006; Penn, 2006; Purves et al., 2008). Findings have enabled scientists to develop experimental techniques to treat the damaged brain, which we'll discuss next.

Treating Patients with Brain Damage

Watch how fMRI brain scans are used to evaluate the cognitive functioning of patients.

▶ **LO13** Describe experimental procedures to treat the brain.

Experimental Techniques

Stem Cells

About four days after a sperm has fertilized an egg, the resulting embryo, which is about the size of the period at the end of this sentence, has divided and formed embryonic stem cells (shown on right).

Stem cells, not discovered until 1998, have the amazing capacity to change into and become any one of the 220 types of cells that make up a human body, including skin, heart, liver, bones, and neurons.

The discovery of stem cells creates possibilities for treating various diseases. However, the use of human embryonic stem cells is controversial for ethical and political reasons. That's because these embryos, which are fertilized in laboratories and have the potential to develop into humans, are destroyed when the stem cells are removed. Because stem-cell research has such potential, however, it has received wide support and funding from private and state sources.

It's possible for a neurosurgeon to transplant stem cells into a precise location in either animal or human brains by using the stereotaxic procedure.

The **stereotaxic procedure** (see figure below) involves fixing a patient's head in a holder and drilling a small hole through the skull. The holder has a syringe that can be precisely guided to inject cells into a predetermined location in the brain.

In the figure, a large part of the skull has been removed to show the brain, but in actual surgery, only a small, pencil-sized hole is drilled in the skull. A long needle from the syringe is inserted into the designated brain area where the surgeon injects stem cells.

Stem-cell research is still in its infancy, but already some success has been reported in using stem cells to treat people with Parkinson's disease, which is characterized by tremors and shakes in the limb, a slowing of voluntary movements, muscle stiffness, and problems with balance and coordination (Freed, 2008).

Brain Stimulation

About 35,000 people have received **deep brain stimulation (DBS),** a surgical procedure that involves implanting electrodes into a specific area of the brain and placing a battery-powered stimulator under the collarbone. The electrodes are wired to the stimulator, which provides electrical stimulation to the designated brain area. The patient controls the stimulation by using a remote control to turn it on and off. This procedure helps the brain function better and, as a result, reduces or eliminates undesirable symptoms, such as the tremors found in Parkinson's disease (Kluger, 2007b; Kringelbach & Aziz, 2008).

An advantage of DBS is being able to modify the level of stimulation as needed. Also, patients receiving DBS show greater long-term improvement than patients receiving only medication (Deuschl et al., 2006; F. M. Weaver et al., 2009). The limitation of this procedure is that the batteries must be surgically replaced every few years (Pahwa & Lyons, 2003). There is also a minor risk of dangerous bleeding and infection (Kringelbach & Aziz, 2008; F. M. Weaver et al., 2009).

Given its effectiveness and relatively minimal risk, researchers believe DBS will be effective in treating a variety of health problems. DBS is currently being investigated in the treatment of depression, anxiety, phantom limb pain, comas, and Alzheimer's disease, such as that of Charles, described in the beginning of the module (Kluger, 2007b; Kringelbach & Aziz, 2008; G. Miller, 2009; Mullins, 2008; N. D. Schiff et al., 2007).

You've now learned about the brain's building blocks, our incredible nervous system, and how scientists study the living brain. Next, we'll explore the many structures of the human brain and describe their functions.

Stem Cell Research

Watch the exploration of ethical issues associated with stem cell research.

A Brain Pacemaker

Watch how brain stimulation implants help treat symptoms of Parkinson's disease.

Check Your Learning Quiz 2.5

Go to **login.cengagebrain.com** and take the online quiz.

▶ **LO14** Identify and locate the major parts of the brain, and state their functions.

Major Parts of the Brain

A human brain (below figure), which can easily be held in one hand, weighs about 1,350 grams, or 3 pounds, and has the consistency of firm JELL-O. The brain is protected by a thick skull and covered with thin, tough, plasticlike membranes. If shot in the head, a person may or may not die depending on which area was damaged. For example, damage to an area in the forebrain would result in paralysis, damage to an area in the midbrain would result in coma, but damage to an area in the hindbrain would certainly result in death.

In this module we'll explore the various structures in the brain and their functions. First, we'll provide an overview of the major parts of the brain.

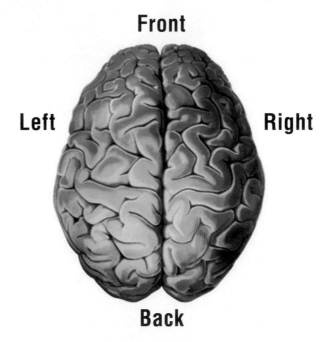

Front

Left

Right

Back

We'll begin our exploration of the brain by looking at its three major parts—forebrain, midbrain, and hindbrain—beginning with the forebrain.

1 Forebrain

The **forebrain,** which is the largest part of the brain, has right and left sides called hemispheres. The hemispheres, connected by a wide band of fibers, are responsible for an incredible number of functions, including learning and memory, speaking and language, having emotional responses, experiencing sensations, initiating voluntary movements, planning, and making decisions.

Forebrain

Side view of the brain's right hemisphere

Midbrain

Pons

Medulla

Cerebellum

2 Midbrain

The **midbrain** has a reward or pleasure center, which is stimulated by food, sex, money, music, attractive faces, and some drugs; it has areas for visual and auditory reflexes and contains the **reticular formation,** which arouses the forebrain so that it is ready to process information from the senses.

3 Hindbrain

The **hindbrain** has three distinct structures: the pons, medulla, and cerebellum.

3a Pons

The **pons** functions as a bridge to transmit messages between the spinal cord and brain. The pons also makes the chemicals involved in sleep.

3b Medulla

The **medulla,** located at the top of the spinal cord, includes cells that control vital reflexes, such as respiration, heart rate, and blood pressure.

3c Cerebellum

The **cerebellum,** which is located at the very back and underneath the brain, is involved in coordinating motor movements but not in initiating voluntary movements.

Of the brain's three parts, the forebrain is the largest, most evolved, and most responsible for a range of personal, social, emotional, and cognitive behaviors. For those reasons, we'll examine the forebrain in more detail.

Brain Size and Myths

Learn whether brain size varies among different races and if intelligence is determined by brain size.

Hindbrain Structures

Get a closer look at the hindbrain.

▶ **LO15** Identify and locate the four lobes in the cerebral cortex, and state their key functions.

Wrinkled Cortex

The picture on the right shows the outside of an adult human brain, which has a very wrinkled surface that is called the cortex (in Latin, *cortex* means "cover").

The **cortex** is a thin layer of cells that essentially covers the entire surface of the forebrain.

The vast majority of our neurons are located in the cortex, which folds over on itself so that it forms a large surface area.

To understand the advantage of having a wrinkled cortex, just imagine having to put a large sheet of paper about 18 inches square into a small match box that is 3 inches square. One solution is to crumple (wrinkle) the sheet of paper until it easily fits into the tiny match box. Similarly, imagine many billions of neurons laid on a sheet of paper about 18 inches square. When this large sheet of neurons is wrinkled, the cortex can fit snugly into our much smaller, rounded skulls.

Early researchers divided the wrinkled cortex into four different areas, or lobes, each of which has different functions.

Four Lobes

As you look at the brain's cortex, you see a wrinkled surface with few distinguishing features. However, the cortex's appearance is deceiving because its hundreds of different functions are organized into four separate areas called lobes.

The cortex is divided into four separate areas, or **lobes,** each with different functions:

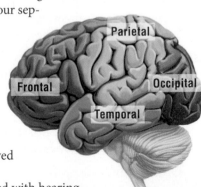

- The **frontal lobe** is involved with personality, emotions, and motor behaviors.
- The **parietal** *(puh-RYE-it-all)* **lobe** is involved with perception and sensory experiences.
- The **occipital** *(ock-SIP-pih-tull)* **lobe** is involved with processing visual information.
- The **temporal** *(TEM-purr-all)* **lobe** is involved with hearing and speaking.

Frontal Lobe: Functions

The frontal lobe is the largest of the brain's lobes and has many important functions.

The **frontal lobe** is involved in many functions: performing voluntary motor movements, interpreting and performing emotional behaviors, behaving normally in social situations, maintaining a healthy personality, paying attention to things in the environment, making decisions, and executing plans.

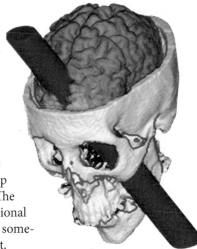

Frontal lobe

Our first clue about the functions of the frontal lobe came from an unusual accident in 1848. Let's meet Phineas Gage, whose accident led to the discovery of one of the frontal lobe's important functions (H. Damasio et al., 1994).

A Terrible Accident

Railroad crewmen were about to blast a rock that blocked their way. Foreman Phineas Gage filled a deep, narrow hole in the rock with powder and rammed in an iron rod to tamp down the charge before covering it with sand. But the tamping iron rubbed against the side of the shaft, and a spark ignited the powder.

The massive rod—3½ feet long, 1¼ inches in diameter, and weighing 13 pounds—shot from the hole under the force of the explosion. It struck Phineas just beneath his left eye and tore through his skull. It shot out the top of his head and landed some 50 yards away. The long-term result caused Phineas to have emotional outbursts and problems in making decisions, something he did not experience before the accident.

Cerebral Cortex

Examine what the cerebral cortex of our brain looks like.

The organization of the frontal lobe is somewhat confusing because it has such a wide range of functions. Now, we'll focus on motor movements, which have a very unusual feature.

The figure on the right shows how the nerves from the left hemisphere (blue) cross over and control the movements of the right side of the body; nerves from the right hemisphere (red) cross over and control the movements of the left side of the body.

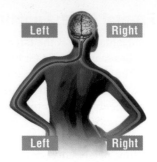

Location of Motor Cortex

The **motor cortex** is a narrow strip of cortex that is located in the frontal lobe. The motor cortex is involved in the initiation of all voluntary movements.

You can move any individual part of your body at will because of how the motor cortex is organized.

Organization and Function of Motor Cortex

The motor cortex is organized in two interesting ways. **First,** a larger body part indicates relatively more area on the motor cortex and thus more ability to perform complex movements. A smaller body part indicates relatively less area on the motor cortex and thus less ability to perform complex movements. **Second,** each body part has its own area on the motor cortex. This means that damage to one part of the motor cortex could result in paralysis of that part yet spare most other parts.

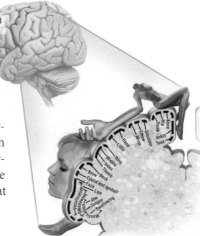

Parietal Lobe: Functions

The parietal lobe is located behind the frontal lobe and processes information from body parts.

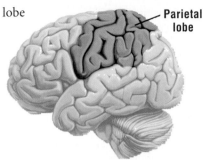

Parietal lobe

The **parietal lobe** functions include processing sensory information from body parts, which includes touching, locating positions of limbs, and feeling temperature and pain, and carrying out several cognitive functions, such as attending to and perceiving objects.

Location of Somatosensory Cortex

The **somatosensory cortex** is a narrow strip of cortex that is located in the parietal lobe. The somatosensory cortex processes sensory information about touch, location of limbs, pain, and temperature.

Your lips are much more sensitive than your elbows because of the way the somatosensory cortex is organized.

Organization of Somatosensory Cortex

The somatosensory cortex is also cleverly organized. First, a larger body part indicates relatively more area on the somatosensory cortex and thus more sensitivity to external stimulation. A smaller body part indicates relatively less area on the somatosensory cortex and thus less sensitivity to external stimulation. Second, notice that each body part has its own area on the somatosensory cortex. This means that damage to one part of the somatosensory cortex could result in loss of feeling to one part of the body yet spare all others.

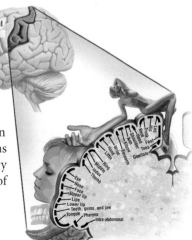

Parietal lobe

Temporal Lobe: Functions

You recognize your name when you hear it spoken; because of the way sound is processed in the temporal lobe, you know it's not just some meaningless noise.

The **temporal lobe** is located directly below the parietal lobe and is involved in hearing, speaking coherently, and understanding verbal and written material.

As you'll see, the process of hearing and recognizing your name involves two steps. The first step in hearing your name occurs when sounds reach specific areas in the temporal lobe called the primary auditory (hearing) cortex.

The **primary auditory cortex** (shown in red), receives electrical signals from receptors in the ears and transforms these signals into meaningless sound sensations, such as vowels and consonants.

The second step in recognizing your name is when the primary auditory cortex sends its electrical signals to the auditory association area.

The **auditory association area** (shown in blue) transforms basic sensory information, such as noises or sounds, into recognizable auditory information, such as words or music.

The temporal lobe has other areas that are critical for speaking and understanding words and sentences. For instance, the temporal lobe is involved in the three-step process required to speak a sentence. The first step is to understand sentences, which involves Wernicke's *(VERN-ick-ees)* area.

Wernicke's area is necessary for speaking in coherent sentences and for understanding speech. Damage to this area results in **Wernicke's aphasia,** which is a difficulty in understanding spoken or written words and in putting words into meaningful sentences.

The second step is putting words together, which involves an area in the frontal lobe called Broca's *(BROKE-ahs)* area.

Broca's area combines sounds into words and arranges words into meaningful sentences. Damage to this area results in **Broca's aphasia** *(ah-fey-zhuh)*, which means a person cannot speak in fluent sentences but can understand written and spoken words.

During the third and final step, Broca's area communicates with the motor cortex (see p. 82), also located in the frontal lobe, to vocalize or pronounce the words.

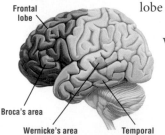

Frontal lobe
Broca's area
Wernicke's area
Temporal lobe

Unless otherwise noted, all images are © Cengage Learning

Occipital Lobe: Functions

Compared to many other animals, humans rely more heavily on visual information, which is processed in the occipital lobe.

The **occipital lobe** is involved in processing visual information, which includes seeing colors and recognizing objects, animals, and people.

Although you see and recognize things with great ease, this is actually a complicated two-step process. For example, the first step in seeing your face when you look into a mirror involves the primary visual cortex.

The **primary visual cortex** (shown in red) receives electrical signals from receptors in the eyes and transforms these signals into meaningless basic visual sensations, such as lights, lines, shadows, colors, and textures.

Since the primary visual cortex produces only meaningless visual sensations, you do not yet see your face. Transforming meaningless visual sensations into a meaningful visual object occurs in the visual association area (Kiernan, 2008).

The **visual association area** (shown in blue) transforms basic sensations, such as lights, lines, and colors into complete, meaningful visual perceptions, such as persons, objects, or animals.

If there are problems in the second step, the person can still see parts of objects but has difficulty combining the parts and recognizing the whole object (see drawing below)(Osborne et al., 2007; Purves et al., 2008). For example, a person with damage to the visual association area may have visual agnosia.

In **visual agnosia,** the individual fails to recognize some object, person, or color, yet has the ability to see and even describe pieces or parts of some visual stimulus.

Broca's and Wernicke's Aphasia

Explore Broca's and Wernicke's aphasia and how they differ.

▶ **LO16** Identify and locate key structures in the limbic system, and state their functions.

▶ **LO17** Identify sex differences in the brain.

Limbic System

Your cortex is involved in numerous cognitive functions, such as thinking, deciding, planning, and speaking, as well as other sensory and motor behaviors. But what triggers your wide range of emotional experiences, such as feeling happy, sad, or angry? The answer lies deeper inside the brain, where you'll find a number of interconnected structures that are involved in emotions and are called the limbic system (J. H. Friedman & Chou, 2007; Ropper & Samuels, 2009).

The **limbic system** refers to a group of about half a dozen interconnected structures that make up the core of the forebrain. The limbic system's structures are involved with regulating many motivational behaviors such as obtaining food, drink, and sex; with organizing emotional behaviors such as fear, anger, and aggression; and with storing memories.

The limbic system is often referred to as our primitive, or animal, brain because its same structures are found in the brains of animals that are evolutionarily very old, such as alligators. The alligator's limbic system, which essentially makes up its entire forebrain, is involved in smelling out prey, defending territory, hunting, fighting, reproducing, eating, and remembering. The human limbic system, which makes up only a small part of our forebrain, is involved in similar behaviors.

We'll discuss some of the major structures and functions of the limbic system. Notice that in the drawing on the next page the limbic structures are surrounded by the forebrain, whose executive functions regulate the limbic system's emotional and motivational behaviors.

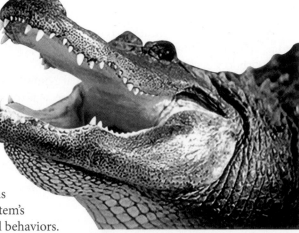

© Ron Dahlquist/Getty Images

Unless otherwise noted, all images are © Cengage Learning

Important Parts of the Limbic System

1 One limbic structure that is a master control for many emotional responses is the hypothalamus *(high-po-THAL-ah-mus)*.

The **hypothalamus** regulates many motivational behaviors, including eating, drinking, and sexual responses; emotional behaviors, such as arousing the body when fighting or fleeing; and the secretion of hormones, such as occurs at puberty.

In addition, the hypothalamus controls the two divisions of the autonomic nervous system discussed earlier.

The next limbic structure, the amygdala *(ah-MIG-duh-la)*, is also involved in emotions but more in forming and remembering them.

2 The **amygdala** plays a major role in evaluating the emotional significance of stimuli and facial expressions, especially those involving fear, distress, or threat.

3 The limbic structure, which is like a miniature computer that gathers and processes information from all of your senses (except smell), is called the thalamus *(THAL-ah-mus)*.

The **thalamus** is involved in receiving sensory information, doing some initial processing, and then relaying the sensory information to areas of the cortex, including the somatosensory cortex, primary auditory cortex, and primary visual cortex.

For example, if the thalamus malfunctions, you might have difficulty processing sensory information (hearing or seeing).

Our last limbic structure, the hippocampus, is involved in saving your memories.

4 The **hippocampus** is involved in saving many kinds of fleeting memories by putting them into permanent storage in various parts of the brain.

The hippocampus functions like the "Save" command on your computer.

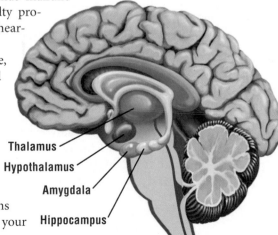

Thalamus
Hypothalamus
Amygdala
Hippocampus

Parts of the Brain

Identify the major parts of the brain.

Limbic System

Get a closer look at the limbic system.

Inside the Female Brain

Learn more about some of the unique aspects of the female brain.

Sex Differences in the Brain?

Explore how the brains of males and females differ.

▶ **LO18** Describe lateralization of brain functions.

Before we complete our journey through the brain, we'll see what happens when the brain is literally cut in two.

Split Brain

Many children, such as 6-year-old Victoria, experience seizures. During the seizures, Victoria would lose consciousness and fall to the floor. As a child, she was given anticonvulsant medicine, which prevented any further seizures until she was 18. When Victoria was 18, for some unknown reason, her seizures returned with greater intensity. And to her dismay, anticonvulsant medication no longer had any effect.

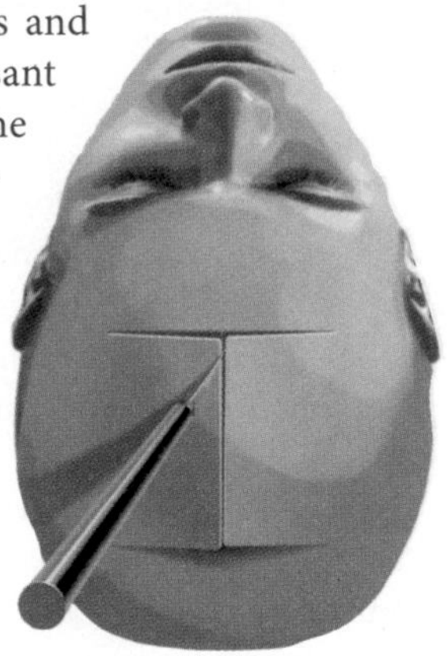

Finally, when she was 27, she decided that her best chance of reducing her frightening, uncontrollable seizures was to have an operation that had a high probability of producing serious side effects (Sidtis et al., 1981). In this operation, a neurosurgeon severed the major connection between her right and left hemispheres, leaving her with what is called a split brain (Gazzaniga, 2008b).

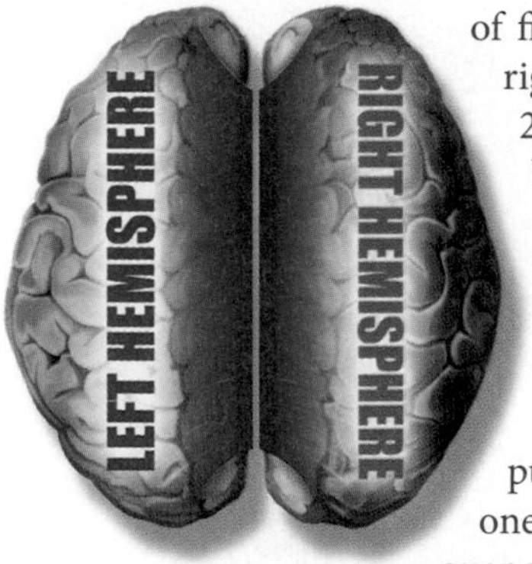

A **split-brain operation** involves cutting the wide band of fibers, called the corpus callosum, that connects the right and left hemispheres. The corpus callosum has 200 million nerve fibers that allow information to pass back and forth between the hemispheres.

A split-brain operation not only disrupts the major pathway between the hemispheres but also, to a large extent, leaves each hemisphere functioning independently.

In many split-brain patients, severing the corpus callosum prevents the spread of seizures from one hemisphere to the other and thus reduces their frequency and occurrence (Gazzaniga, 2008b).

LEFT HEMISPHERE · RIGHT HEMISPHERE

Unless otherwise noted, all images are © Cengage Learning

Lateralization of Functions

After testing split-brain patients, researchers discovered that each hemisphere is specialized for performing certain tasks (Gazzaniga, 2005, 2008a).

Left Hemisphere

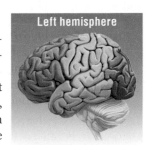

Left hemisphere

- **Verbal** The left hemisphere is very good at all language-related abilities: speaking, understanding language, carrying on a conversation, reading, writing, and spelling.
- **Mathematical** The left hemisphere is very good at mathematical skills: adding, subtracting, multiplying, dividing, and so on. Generally, the right hemisphere can perform simple addition and subtraction but not more complex mathematics (Sperry, 1974).
- **Analytic** The left hemisphere appears to process information by analyzing each separate piece that makes up a whole. For example, the left hemisphere would recognize a face by analyzing piece by piece its many separate parts: nose, eyes, lips, cheeks, and so on (J. Levy & Trevarthen, 1976).

Right Hemisphere

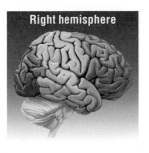

Right hemisphere

- **Nonverbal** Although usually mute, the right hemisphere has a childlike ability to read, write, spell, and understand speech (Gazzaniga, 1998). For example, the right hemisphere can understand simple sentences and read simple words.
- **Spatial** The right hemisphere is very good at solving spatial problems, such as arranging blocks to match a geometric design. Because the hemispheres control opposite sides of the body, the left hand (right hemisphere) is best at completing spatial tasks.
- **Holistic** The right hemisphere appears to process information by combining parts into a meaningful whole. For example, the right hemisphere is better at recognizing and identifying whole faces (J. Levy et al., 1972).

After comparing the functions of the left and right hemispheres, you see that each hemisphere has specialized skills and is better at performing particular tasks. How-ever specialized they may be, it's important to note that both hemispheres work together to successfully complete many tasks (Zimmer, 2009b).

Split-Brain Demonstration

Learn how each hemisphere is specialized for performing certain tasks.

Check Your Learning Quiz 2.6

Go to **login.cengagebrain.com** and take the online quiz.

▶ **LO19** Locate and describe the key elements of the endocrine system.

▶ **LO20** Discuss some ways that hormones regulate behavior.

Defining the Endocrine System

You have two major systems for sending signals to the body's muscles, glands, and organs. We have already discussed the nervous system, which uses neurons, nerves, and neurotransmitters to send information throughout the body. The second major system for sending information is called the endocrine system.

The **endocrine system** is made up of numerous glands that are located throughout the body. These glands secrete various chemicals, called **hormones,** which affect organs, muscles, and other glands in the body (Hinson et al., 2010).

The location of some of the endocrine system's glands are shown in the figure on the next page; their functions are described on the next page.

In many ways, the **hypothalamus,** which is located in the lower middle part of the brain, controls much of the endocrine system by regulating the pituitary gland, which is located directly below and outside the brain. The hypothalamus is often called the control center of the endocrine system.

We'll describe some of the endocrine system's major glands.

The **pituitary gland** hangs directly below the hypothalamus, to which it is connected by a narrow stalk. The pituitary gland is divided into anterior (front) and posterior (back) sections.

Posterior pituitary. The rear portion of the pituitary regulates water and salt balance.

Anterior pituitary. The front part of the pituitary regulates growth through secretion of growth hormones and produces hormones that control the adrenal cortex, pancreas, thyroid, and gonads.

Thyroid. This gland, which is located in the neck, regulates metabolism through the secretion of hormones.

Pancreas. This organ regulates the level of sugar in the bloodstream by secreting insulin.

Adrenal glands. The adrenal glands secrete hormones that regulate sugar and salt balances and help the body resist stress; they are also responsible for growth of pubic hair, a secondary sexual characteristic.

Gonads. In females, the ovaries produce hormones that regulate sexual development, ovulation, and growth of sex organs. In males, the testes produce hormones that regulate sexual development, production of sperm, and growth of sex organs.

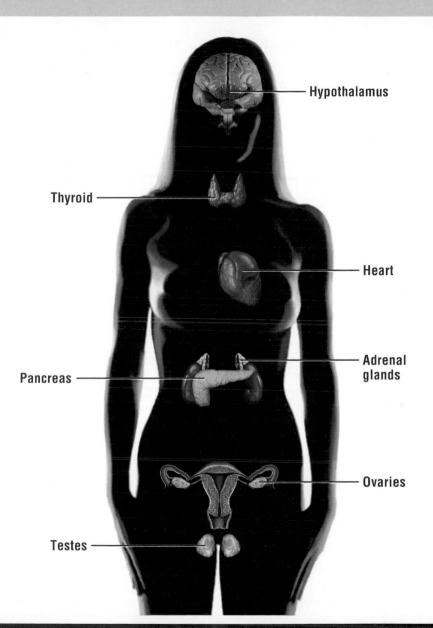

Hypothalamus

Thyroid

Heart

Pancreas

Adrenal glands

Ovaries

Testes

Check Your Learning Quiz 2.7

Go to **login.cengagebrain.com** and take the online quiz.

Think Critically

Challenge Your Thinking

Consider these questions when reading this article:

1. How might mirror neurons explain the social problems of people with autism? (See Modules 1.1, 1.3)
2. In what type of research setting do brain scan studies take place? What are an advantage and disadvantage of this type of research setting? (See Module 1.6)
3. How are mirror neurons different from nerves? (See Module 2.4)
4. What would it be like to have no mirror neurons?
5. How might mirror neurons be involved in the enjoyment of watching pornography?
6. Which modern approaches to psychology are best suited to study mirror neurons? (See Module 1.3)

Mirrors in Your Brain?

When we see someone yawn, we yawn, too. When we watch a spider crawl up someone's leg, we get creepy sensations on our leg. When we see someone in danger, we experience a wave of fear. When we see someone's arm get jabbed with a sharp needle, the muscles in our arms tense up and our breathing intensifies. When we watch our favorite Olympic athlete near the finish line to win first place, our heart races with excitement.

How can simply observing others lead us to experience such intense responses so similar to those experienced by the people we are observing? The answer is found in our brain cells. A type of neuron, called a mirror neuron, helps explain how we effortlessly "read" other people's minds and empathize with them—feel what they do. Mirror neurons automatically put us in somebody else's shoes. Not convinced? Just consider brain-scan research that finds romantic partners who observe loved ones in pain show similar activity in their emotional brain areas as that experienced by the loved ones. It turns out that when we empathize with someone's pain, on some level we actually feel pain!

One fascinating characteristic of mirror neurons is they are the only brain cells that are activated the same way whether

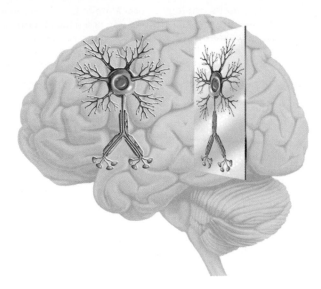

we are "seeing" or "doing." These special neurons mirror what the other person is doing. For instance, when we see someone smiling, our mirror neurons for smiling get activated, which triggers neural activity leading to experiencing feelings associated with smiling, such as happiness. In other words, we get all the benefits of smiling without making even the slightest movement of our lips!

Mirror neurons also help us understand someone's intentions. They get activated when we watch someone do something, which helps us predict what the person's goal is and what he or she may do next. For example, if you see a boy begin to reach for candy on the counter in front of him, you have a copy of what he is doing in your brain, which helps you to understand his goal (getting the candy).

Research on mirror neurons is still in its infancy, and much has yet to be learned. But for now, those of us who are embarrassed by our free-flowing tears during dramatic scenes in television programs, movies, and, yes, sometimes even commercials, should be relieved to know that the emotions we experience may be out of our control; that is, we may not be able to contain our tears after all. (Adapted from Blakeslee, 2006a; Blakeslee & Blakeslee, 2007; Iacoboni, 2008a, 2008b; Iacoboni & Mazziotta, 2007; Ramachandran & Oberman, 2006; T. Singer et al., 2004; Winerman, 2005).

Think Critically 2.1

This article and its questions are available in interactive format online.

GO to your Psychology CourseMate at login.cengagebrain.com and take the Chapter Post-Test to see which Learning Objectives you've mastered and which need more review. Use the chapter review guide below and the online activities—including flashcards to review key terms—to measure your learning.

Measure ^Your Learning

Online Activities

Key Terms	Video	Animation	Reading	Assessment
Alzheimer's disease	Alzheimer's Test, p. 53 Alzheimer's Disease, p. 53 Declining Mental Acuity, p. 53			Check Your Learning 2.1
zygote, chromosome, gene, proteins, polymorphic gene, dominant gene, recessive gene, theory of evolution, genetic mutations, natural selection, adaptive genes, maladaptive genes, adaptations, evolutionary approach		Genes Overview, p. 55 Inheriting Eye Color, p. 55 Evolution of the Human Brain, p. 57	Genetic Testing, p. 55	Check Your Learning 2.2
glial cells, neuron, cell body (soma), dendrites, axon, myelin sheath, end bulbs (terminal buttons), synapse, axon membrane, ions, resting state, sodium pump, action potential, neural impulse, all-or-none law, transmitter, excitatory transmitters, inhibitory transmitters, neurotransmitter, notches, reflex, afferent (or sensory) neuron, efferent (or motor) neuron, interneuron	Brain Re-Growth, p. 59	Neuron and Transmitters, p. 67	Alcohol, p. 67 Plants & Drugs, p. 67	Check Your Learning 2.3

Measure
^Your Learning

Online Activities

Key Terms	Video	Animation	Reading	Assessment
central nervous system, peripheral nervous system, nerves, somatic nervous system, autonomic nervous system, sympathetic nervous system, parasympathetic nervous system, fight-flight response		Nervous Systems, p. 73 Autonomic Nervous System, p. 73	Reattaching Limbs, p. 71 Transplanting a Face, p. 71 Phantom Limb, p. 73	Check Your Learning 2.4
MRI (or magnetic resonance imaging), fMRI (or functional magetic resonance imaging), PET (or positron emission tomography) scan, EEG or electroencephalograph, stem cells, stereotaxic procedure, deep brain stimulation (DBS)	Treating Patients with Brain Damage, p. 75 Stem Cell Research, p. 77 A Brain Pacemaker, p. 77			Check Your Learning 2.5
midbrain, reticular formation, hindbrain, pons, medulla, cerebellum, forebrain, cortex frontal lobe, parietal lobe, occipital lobe, temporal lobe, motor cortex, somatosensory cortex, primary auditory cortex, auditory association area, Broca's area, Broca's aphasia, Wernicke's area, Wernicke's aphasia, primary visual cortex, visual association area, visual agnosia, limbic system, hypothalamus, amygdala, thalamus, hippocampus, split-brain operation	Hindbrain Structure, p. 79 Cerebral Cortex, p. 81 Limbic System, p. 87 Inside the Female Brain, p. 87 Split-brain Demonstration, p. 89	Broca's and Wernicke's Aphasia, p. 85 Parts of the Brain, p. 87	Brain Size and Myths, p. 79 Sex Differences in the Brain?, p. 87	Check Your Learning 2.6
endocrine system, hypothalamus, pituitary gland, posterior pituitary, anterior pituitary, thyroid, pancreas, adrenal glands, gonads				Check Your Learning 2.7

Sensation and Perception

3

Prepare ^ to Learn

1 **GO** to your **Psychology CourseMate** at **login.cengagebrain.com** and take the **Chapter Pre-Test** to introduce yourself to this chapter's topics and see what you may already know.

2 **READ** the **Learning Objectives (LOs)** (in the left sidebars) and begin the chapter.

3 **COMPLETE** the **Online Activities** (in the right sidebars) *as you read each module*. Activities include **videos**, **animations**, **readings**, and **quizzes**.

4 **CHECK Your Learning** by going online to take the quiz at the end of each module and review material as necessary.

5 **MEASURE Your Learning** after reading the chapter by taking the online **Chapter Post-Test**. Use the chapter review guide at the end of the chapter as needed.

WATCH for these **Online Activities** icons as you read:

Video

Animation

Reading

Assessment

Think Critically

These online activities are important to mastering this chapter. As you read each module, access these materials by going to **login.cengagebrain.com**.

Video Explore studies and firsthand accounts of biological and psychological processes:

- See what it's like to have synesthesia
- Get a closer look at how artificial visual systems work
- Learn why a ringtone can be inaudible to adults, yet audible to young people
- Find out how much a child born with a hearing impairment can benefit from receiving a cochlear implant
- Experience the Ames Room

Animation Interact with and visualize important processes and concepts:

- Explore the difference between sensation and perception
- Experience the Gestalt laws of perception
- Explore binocular cues and interact with monocular cues for depth

Reading Delve deeper into key content:

- Explore how the concept of absolute threshold applies to the detection of breast cancer
- Discover how researchers answered the question of whether "unsensored messages" can change behavior
- Explore how implanting artificial photoreceptors into the retina and brain implants help to restore vision in people who are blind
- Learn how color genes affect color vision
- Explore how doctors test for color blindness during a routine eye exam
- Learn more about how cochlear implants are used and how effective they are
- Explore how foods we think are truly disgusting can be delicacies in other parts of the world
- Learn about how it's possible for some smells to encourage us to make purchases

- Explore the role of the vestibular system in motion sickness and how motion sickness can be reduced
- Explore the effectiveness of placebo treatments in reducing pain
- Get a close look at how gate control theory explains an athlete's ability to continue playing in a game after breaking his ankle
- Learn how culture influences perception

Assessment Measure your mastery:

- Chapter Pre-Test
- Check Your Learning Quizzes
- Chapter Post-Test

Think Critically Challenge your thinking by applying content from this chapter and making connections to related material:

- How Do You Train a Killer Whale?

3.1 Introduction

▶ **L01** Describe synthesia.

WHEN CAROL CRANE HEARS the sound of guitars, she feels as if someone is blowing on her ankles. Hearing the piano gives her a tapping sensation on her chest. Hearing jazz music makes her feel as if heavy, sharp raindrops are falling all over her body! When Carol looks at the number *4*, she sees red, and when she looks at the letter *b*, she sees blue. Carol is unique because of the complex way she experiences many sensations. Carol, shown below, has an uncommon condition called synesthesia.

Synesthesia is a condition in which stimulation of one sense results in the automatic and involuntary stimulation of another sense.

Perceiving colors with letters and numbers is a common form of synesthesia. Less common are experiencing sounds with smells and shapes with flavors. Sometimes, the associations are logical, such as the smell of lemons leading people to see yellow. But other times, the associations are surprising, such as the smell of lavender leading people to feel stickiness.

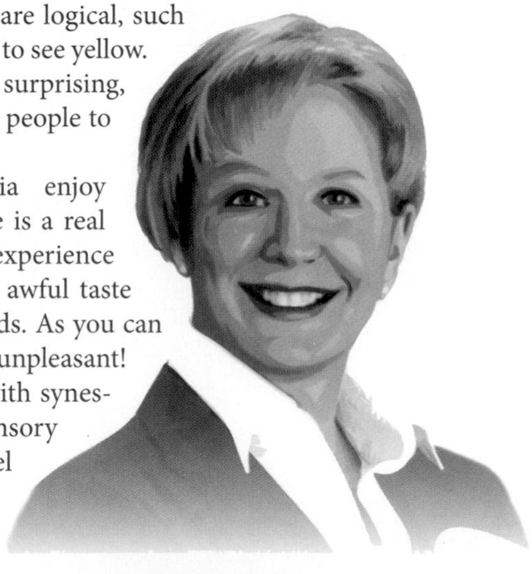

Many people with synesthesia enjoy their special abilities; however, there is a real downside for others. Some people experience unpleasant associations, such as the awful taste of earwax when hearing certain words. As you can imagine, this can make reading very unpleasant!

Research shows that in people with synesthesia, the signals that come from sensory organs, such as the eyes and ears, travel to places in the brain they shouldn't necessarily be going to, which leads to the signals being interpreted as multiple sensations. For example, when people experience color sensations when hearing words, hearing words activates areas of the brain responsible for both hearing and vision. Understanding how sensory experiences are processed in people with synesthesia may ultimately lead to a better understanding of human perception (Cytowic, 1999; Hitti, 2006b; Hubbard & Ramachandran, 2005; Lemley, 1999; Nunn et al., 2002; Rouw & Scholte, 2007; Weir, 2009).

In this chapter, we'll discuss human senses and the process of organizing sensations into meaningful perceptions. We'll begin by identifying and explaining the basic characteristics shared by each of your sense organs.

Synesthesia

See what it's like to have synesthesia.

Check Your Learning Quiz 3.1

Go to **login.cengagebrain.com** and take the online quiz.

Definitions

Your eyes, ears, nose, skin, and tongue are complex, miniaturized, living sense organs that automatically gather information about your environment. We begin with a few definitions that will help you understand sensation.

Transduction

The first thing each sense organ must do is to change or transform some physical energy, such as molecules of skunk spray, into electrical signals, a process called transduction.

Electrical signal

Transduction refers to the process in which a sense organ changes, or transforms, physical energy into electrical signals that become neural impulses, which may be sent to the brain for processing.

For example, transduction occurs when a skunk's molecules enter your nose, which transforms the molecules into electrical signals, or impulses, that are interpreted by your brain as the very unpleasant odor of a skunk.

Adaptation

A short period of time after putting on glasses, jewelry, or clothes, you no longer "feel" them, a process called adaptation.

Adaptation refers to the decreasing response of the sense organs, the more they are exposed to a continuous level of stimulation.

For example, the continuous stimulation of glasses, jewelry, or clothes on your skin results in adaptation so that soon you no longer feel them. Some sense organs adapt very quickly, and some very slowly. However, sense organs do not adapt to intense forms of stimulation, because such stimulation may cause physical damage.

© Royalty-free/Masterfile

Unless otherwise noted, all images are © Cengage Learning

Sensations versus Perceptions

Gathering information about the world involves two steps. In the first step, electrical signals reach the brain and are changed into sensations.

Sensations are relatively meaningless bits of information (top figure) that result when the brain processes electrical signals that come from the sense organs.

In the second step, the brain quickly changes sensations, which you're not aware of, into perceptions.

Perceptions are meaningful sensory experiences (bottom figure) that result after the brain combines hundreds of sensations.

For example, visual sensations would resemble the top figure, showing meaningless lines, colors, and shapes. Visual perceptions would be like the bottom figure, showing a complete "sad-happy" face.

Any one of our sensory organs must be able to detect varying amounts or intensities of electrical signals. When our sensory organs detect enough of an electrical signal, our senses inform us that something is present, and our perceptions tells us what that something is. But not every electrical signal reaching our sense organs necessarily results in our sensing something is present. Some signals are too weak for us to be aware of anything present, so at what point do we become aware of seeing, hearing, smelling, tasting, or feeling some stimulus, object, or event? The answer to this basic question involves thresholds, which we examine next.

▶ **L04** Explain absolute threshold, subliminal stimulus, just noticeable difference (JND), and Weber's law.

Measurement

There are some sounds and objects you may not be aware of because the level of stimulation is too low and does not exceed the threshold of a particular sense.

Threshold refers to a point above which a stimulus is perceived and below which it is not perceived. The threshold determines when we first become aware of a stimulus.

For example, let's suppose you are listening to a recording that contains subliminal messages, which are messages below your absolute threshold for hearing. To understand how the absolute threshold is determined, imagine you are presented with a series of auditory messages that slowly increase in intensity. You're asked to press a button when you first hear a message. You may think that there will be a certain level or absolute value of intensity (loudness) at which you will first report hearing a tone.

The idea that there is an absolute threshold was proposed by Gustav Fechner *(FECK-ner)* (1860), an important historical figure in perceptual research. However, as you'll see, Fechner had difficulty identifying the absolute threshold as he defined it.

At first, Gustav Fechner defined the absolute threshold as the smallest amount of stimulus energy (such as sound or light) that can be observed or experienced. Although Fechner tried various methods to identify absolute thresholds, he found that an individual's threshold was not absolute and, in fact, differed depending on the subject's alertness and the test situation. Because of this variability in measurement, researchers had to redefine absolute threshold.

Absolute threshold is the intensity level of a stimulus such that a person will have a 50% chance of detecting it.

Once we have determined your absolute threshold for hearing messages, we can define a subliminal stimulus.

A **subliminal stimulus** has an intensity that gives a person less than a 50% chance of detecting the stimulus.

Because subliminal messages can occur in a wide range (0–49%), you may or may not report hearing them on the CD. For example, you would never report hearing messages of very low intensity (0% level) but might sometimes report hearing messages of higher intensity (49%).

Next, let's suppose you have no difficulty hearing a stimulus. In fact, this time people are playing music that is too loud and you ask them to turn down the volume. Even after they turn it down, it may still seem just as loud as before. The explanation for this phenomenon can be found in the work of another historical figure in perception, E. H. Weber *(VEY-ber).*

Weber worked on the problem of how we judge whether a stimulus, such as loud music, has increased or decreased in intensity. This problem involves measuring the difference in thresholds between two stimuli, such as very loud music and not-quite-so-loud music. To solve this problem, Weber (1834) developed the concept of a just noticeable difference.

A **just noticeable difference,** or **JND,** refers to the smallest increase or decrease in the intensity of a stimulus that a person is able to detect.

For example, to measure a just noticeable difference in weight, Weber asked people to compare stimuli of varying intensities and indicate when they could detect a difference between them. He discovered that if he presented two stimuli with very low intensities, such as a 2-ounce weight versus a 3-ounce weight, people could easily detect the difference between them. However, if he presented stimuli with high intensities, such as a 40-pound weight versus a 41-pound weight, people could no longer detect the difference. For higher-intensity stimuli, such as heavy weights, a much larger difference in intensity was required for the difference to be noticed (Kantowitz et al., 2009).

Weber's observations on what it takes to detect just noticeable differences formed the basis for what became known as Weber's law.

Weber's law states that the increase in intensity of a stimulus needed to produce a just noticeable difference grows in proportion to the intensity of the initial stimulus.

You've now learned some of the basics of sensation and perception. Later, we'll take a closer look at the relationship between sensations and perceptions, including how sensations are actually turned into perceptions. But first, we'll examine how each of our sensory systems work, beginning with vision.

Detecting Breast Cancer

Explore how the concept of absolute threshold applies to the detection of breast cancer.

Can Subliminal Messages Change Behavior?

Discover how researchers answered the question of whether "unsensed messages" can change behavior.

Check Your Learning Quiz 3.2

Go to **login.cengagebrain.com** and take the online quiz.

▶ **LO5** Discuss the role of light waves and the visual spectrum in vision.

▶ **LO6** Locate the structures of the eyes and describe their functions.

Stimulus: Light Waves

Each sense organ has a different shape and structure; it can receive only a certain kind of stimulus, or physical energy. In the figure below, notice that only a small, specific range of wavelengths from a light source is able to excite receptors in your eyes; this is called the visible spectrum.

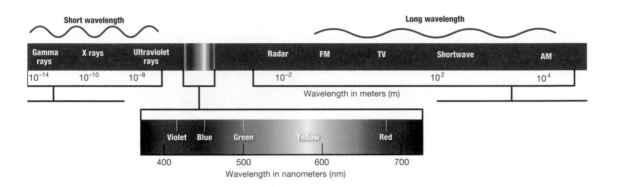

Unless otherwise noted, all images are © Cengage Learning

Invisible—too short

These waves are invisible to the human eye because their lengths are too short to stimulate our receptors. However, some birds (such as hummingbirds) and insects can see ultraviolet rays to help them find food.

Visible—just right

Near the middle of the electromagnetic spectrum is a small range of waves that make up the visible spectrum.

The **visible spectrum** is one particular segment of electromagnetic energy that we can see because these waves are the right length to stimulate receptors in the eye.

Invisible—too long

These waves are invisible to the human eye because their lengths are too long to stimulate the receptors in the eye. Imagine the awful distraction of seeing radio and television waves all day long!

Structure and Function

For you to see a 16-foot-tall giraffe, your eyes perform a series of seven steps.

1 Image Reversed Notice that, at the back of the eye, the giraffe appears upside down. Even though the giraffe is focused upside down in the eye, the brain turns the giraffe right side up so we see the world as it really is.

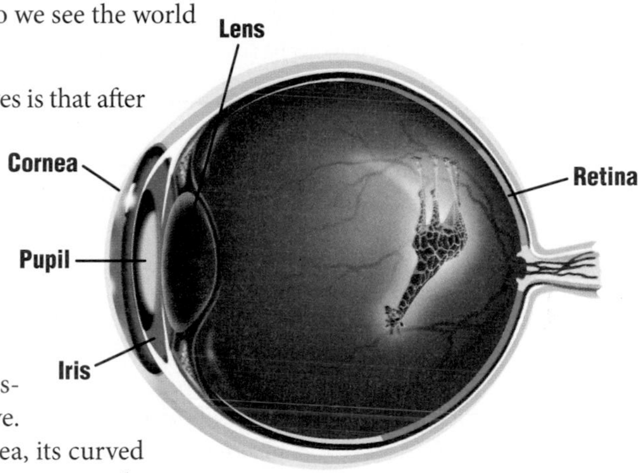

2 Light Waves The problem with light waves is that after they strike an object, such as a giraffe, they are reflected back in a broad beam. You cannot see the giraffe unless your eyes change this broad beam of light waves into a narrow, focused one. The beam of light reflected from the giraffe passes first through the cornea.

3 Cornea The **cornea** is the rounded, transparent covering over the front of your eye. As the light waves pass through the cornea, its curved surface bends, or focuses, the waves into a narrower beam.

4 Pupil The **pupil** is a round opening at the front of your eye that allows light waves to pass into the eye's interior.

5 Iris The **iris** is a circular muscle that surrounds the pupil and controls the amount of light entering the eye. The iris muscle contains the pigment that gives your eye its characteristic color.

6 Lens The **lens** is a transparent, oval structure whose curved surface bends and focuses light waves into an even narrower beam. The lens is attached to muscles that adjust the curve of the lens, which, in turn, adjusts the focusing.

7 Retina The **retina,** located at the very back of the eyeball, is a thin film that contains cells that are extremely sensitive to light. These light-sensitive cells, called photoreceptors, begin the process of transduction by absorbing light waves.

Lens

Cornea

Pupil

Iris

Retina

▶ **LO7** Explain how we adapt to light and dark, see color, and how our brain processes visual information.

Retina

We'll explain the function of the retina's three layers.

1 Each eye has about 120 million rods, most located in the retina's periphery.

Rods are photoreceptors that contain a single chemical, called rhodopsin *(row-DOP-sin),* which is activated by small amounts of light. Because rods are extremely light sensitive, they allow us to see in dim light, but to see only black, white, and shades of gray.

To see color, we need the cones. **Cones** are photoreceptors that contain three chemicals called opsins *(OP-sins),* which are activated in bright light and allow us to see color.

2 The process of *transduction* begins when chemicals in the rods and cones break down after absorbing light waves. This chemical breakdown generates a tiny electrical force that, if large enough, triggers *nerve impulses* in neighboring *ganglion* cells.

3 *Nerve impulses* exit the back of the eye through the *optic nerve,* which carries impulses toward the brain. The point where the optic nerve exits the eye has no receptors and is called the *blind spot.* You don't notice the blind spot because your eyes are continually moving.

What's surprising about the eye is that it does not "see." For you to "see something," impulses must reach visual areas in the brain.

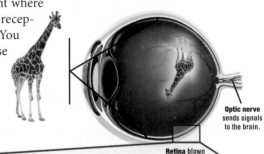

Optic nerve sends signals to the brain.

Retina blown up to show its three layers.

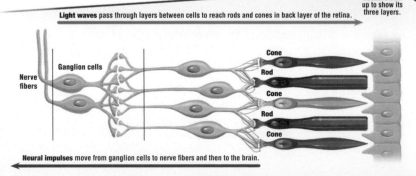

Light waves pass through layers between cells to reach rods and cones in back layer of the retina.

Cone
Rod
Cone
Rod
Cone

Ganglion cells

Nerve fibers

Neural impulses move from ganglion cells to nerve fibers and then to the brain.

Color Vision

The answer to the question "What color is a red apple?" seems obvious. But you are about to discover otherwise. Objects, such as a red apple, do not have colors. Instead, objects reflect light waves whose different wavelengths are transformed by your visual system into the experience of seeing colors. So, what is red? The answer is that the color red is actually produced by a certain kind of wavelength.

How light waves are turned into millions of colors is a wondrous and interesting process, which begins with a ray of sunlight.

Making Colors from Wavelengths

1. A ray of sunlight is called white light because it contains all the light waves in the visible spectrum, which is what humans can see.

2. As white light passes through a prism, it is separated into light waves that vary in length. Nature creates prisms in the form of raindrops, which separate the passing sunlight into waves of different lengths, creating a spectrum of colors that we call a rainbow.

3. Our visual system transforms light waves of various lengths into millions of different colors. For example, in the figure below, notice that the numbers, which vary from about 400 to 700 nanometers, or nm, indicate the length of light waves. We see shorter wavelengths as shades of violet, blue, and green, and longer wavelengths as shades of yellow, orange, and red (Silbernagl & Despopoulous, 2008).

You see an apple as red because the apple reflects longer light waves, which your brain interprets as red.

Actually, how our visual system transforms light waves into color is explained by two different theories—the trichromatic and opponent-process theories—which we'll examine next.

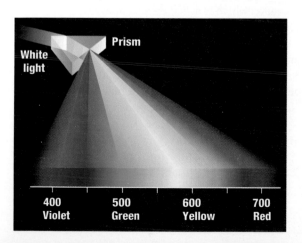

Artificial Visual System

Explore how implanting artifical photoreceptors into the retina and brain implants help to restore vision in people who are blind.

Artificial Visual System

Get a closer look at how artificial visual systems work.

Trichromatic Theory

The explanation of how you see the many colors in the native face (right photo) began over 200 years ago with the early work of a British physicist, Thomas Young. His research laid the basis for a theory of how you see colors, called the trichromatic *(TRI-crow-MAH-tic)* theory of color.

© Digital Stock Corporation

The **trichromatic theory** says that there are three different kinds of cones in the retina, and each cone contains one of three different light-sensitive chemicals called opsins. Each of the three opsins is most responsive to wavelengths that correspond to each of the three primary colors: blue, green, and red. All the other colors can be mixed from these three primary colors.

To understand how color coding occurs in the brain, we need to examine the second theory of color vision, the opponent-process theory.

Opponent-Process Theory

If you stare at a red square for about 20 seconds and then immediately look at a white piece of paper, you'll see a green square, which is called an afterimage.

An **afterimage** is a visual sensation that continues after the original stimulus is removed.

And if you stare at a blue square, you'll see a yellow afterimage. On the basis of his work with afterimages, physiologist Ewald Hering suggested that the visual system codes color by using two complementary pairs: red-green and blue-yellow. Hering's idea became known as the opponent-process theory.

The **opponent-process theory** says that ganglion cells in the retina and cells in the thalamus of the brain respond to two pairs of colors: red-green and blue-yellow. When these cells are excited, they respond to one color of the pair; when inhibited, they respond to the complementary pair.

Unless otherwise noted, all images are © Cengage Learning

Theories Combined

Because we see colors so automatically and naturally, we don't realize it involves both the opponent-process and trichromatic theories.

First, the trichromatic theory says that there are usually three different kinds of cones in the retina. Each cone absorbs light waves of different lengths, which correspond to the three primary colors of blue, green, and red. Second, when electrical signals (color information) reach the ganglion cells in the retina and neurons in the thalamus, they use the opponent-process theory, which involves a pair of colors: Activation results in one color of a pair, and inhibition results in the other color. Third, nerve impulses carry this color information to the visual area of the brain, where other neurons respond and give us the experience of seeing thousands of colors, which can be made by combining the three primary colors of red, green, and blue.

Although most of us have good color vision, some individuals have varying degrees of color blindness.

Color Blindness

The vast majority of us have normal color vision. We see the vibrant colors of the leaves on the top photo: green, red, and yellow. However, some people see these same leaves in shades of blue and yellow (bottom photo) because they have inherited a form of color blindness (HHMI, 2008).

Color blindness is the inability to distinguish two or more shades in the color spectrum.

There are different kinds of color blindness.

Monochromats *(MOHN-oh-crow-mats)* have total color blindness; their worlds look black-and-white. This kind of color blindness is rare and results from individuals having only rods or only one kind of functioning cone (instead of three).

Dichromats *(DIE-crow-mats)* usually have trouble distinguishing red from green because they have just two kinds of cones. This is an inherited genetic defect that results in seeing mostly shades of blue and yellow (bottom photo), which differs in severity (Gerl & Morris, 2008).

© Robert Harding/Masterfile

© Robert Harding/Masterfile

Color Vision and Genes

Learn how color genes affect color vision.

Color Blindness Test

Explore how doctors test for color blindness during a routine eye exam.

Check Your Learning Quiz 3.3

Go to **login.cengagebrain.com** and take the online quiz

▸ **LO8** Discuss the role of sound waves in hearing.

Stimulus: Sound Waves

When a person yells, she produces the yell by letting out air so that it is alternately compressed and expanded into traveling waves called sound waves.

Sound waves, which are the stimuli for hearing, resemble ripples of different sizes.

Similar to ripples on a pond, sound waves travel through space with varying amplitude (height) and frequency (speed).

Amplitude is the distance from the bottom to the top of a sound wave. **Frequency** refers to the number of sound waves that occur within 1 second.

We'll demonstrate the concept of amplitude by comparing sound waves of a cheerleader's yell with a child's whisper.

Amplitude

Yell. As a person yells, she lets out an enormous amount of air that is compressed and expanded into very large traveling waves (shown below). Large sound waves are described as having high amplitude, which the brain interprets as loud sounds.

© Stephen Smith/Getty Images

YELL!

High amplitude means big sound waves and loud sounds.

Whisper. As a child whispers to his friend, he lets out a small amount of air that is compressed and expanded into very small traveling waves. Small sound waves are described as having low amplitude, which the brain interprets as soft sounds.

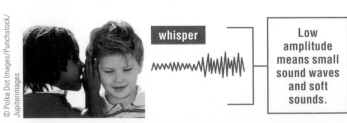

© Polka Dot Images/Punchstock/Jupiterimages

whisper

Low amplitude means small sound waves and soft sounds.

Unless otherwise noted, all images are © Cengage Learning

Frequency and Pitch

Screech or boom. As you listen to someone playing a keyboard, you can tell the difference between high and low notes because your brain is continually discriminating between high and low sounds, or pitch.

High frequency   Low frequency

High note. Striking the top key on a keyboard produces sound waves that travel rapidly and are described as having high frequency. The brain interprets high frequency as high notes or high pitch.

Low note. Striking the bottom key on a keyboard produces sound waves that travel slowly and are described as having low frequency. The brain interprets low frequency as low notes or low pitch.

Relationship: frequency and pitch. When you hear a sound, your auditory system automatically uses frequency to calculate pitch (Barrett et al., 2009).

Pitch is our subjective experience of a sound being high or low, which the brain calculates from specific physical stimuli, in this case the speed or frequency of sound waves. The frequency of sound waves is measured in cycles, which refers to how many sound waves occur within 1 second.

The keyboard's highest key produces sound waves with a high frequency, which results in high sounds or high pitch; the keyboard's lowest key produces sound waves of lower frequency, which results in low sounds or low pitch.

Hearing range. Humans hear sounds within only a certain range of frequencies, and this range decreases with age. For example, infants have the widest range of hearing, from frequencies of 20 to 20,000 cycles per second. For college students, the range is 30 to 18,000 cycles per second. With further aging, the hearing range decreases, so that by age 70, many people can't hear sounds above 6,000 cycles per second.

Next, we'll see how loud a jet plane is compared to a whisper.

Ringtones and the Cochlea

Learn why a ringtone can be inaudible to adults, yet audible to young people.

Measuring Sound Waves

If the sign on the right were posted in the library, you might not know that it refers to loudness, which is measured in decibels (dB).

A **decibel** is a unit to measure loudness. Our threshold for hearing ranges from 0 decibels, which is absolutely no sound, to 140 decibels, which can produce pain and permanent hearing loss.

Please Do Not Talk Above 30 Decibels

The table on the next page contains common sounds with their decibel levels. Notice especially those sound levels that can cause permanent hearing loss.

Decibels and Deafness

It is well established that continuous exposure to sounds with higher decibel levels (over 85 dB) for certain periods of time can produce permanent hearing loss (Barone, 2009; B. Healy, 2007). For example, rock musicians, hunters, operators of heavy machinery, airplane workers, and stereo headphone listeners who take no precautions against higher decibel levels may suffer permanent hearing loss (Lalwani & Snow, 2006). Most young adults are unaware of the risk of going deaf by listening to loud MP3 players for extended periods of time (Godlasky, 2008).

At the end of this module we'll discuss different causes of deafness and treatment. After you review the table on the next page, we'll take you inside the ear and explain how it turns sound waves into wonderful sounds.

Decibel (dB) level	Sounds and their decibel levels		Exposure time and permanent hearing loss
140	Jet engine, gun muzzle blast, firecracker explosion		Any exposure to sounds this loud is painful and dangerous. That's why aircraft ground personnel must wear ear protectors.
120	Rock concert near speakers, thunderclap, record-setting human yell (115 dB)		Exposure for 15 minutes or less can produce hearing loss. Rock musicians and fans who do not use ear plugs risk hearing loss.
100	Chain saw, jackhammer, baby screaming, inside of racing car		Exposure for 2 hours or more can cause hearing loss. Workers using loud power tools who do not use ear protectors risk hearing loss.
80	Heavy city traffic, alarm clock at 2 feet, subway, MP3 player/iPod		Constant exposure for 8 hours can produce hearing loss. Music lovers should know that stereo headphones can produce sounds from 80 to 115 dB.
60	Conversation, air conditioner at 20 feet		Aging decreases hearing sensitivity, and that's why older adults may ask, "What did you say?" indicating that they may not easily hear normal conversations.
30	Whisper, quiet library, gasoline-only car idling in neutral (45 dB)		Today's cars are engineered for quietness. At idle, many cars are almost as quiet as a library; and at 65 mph (70 dB), they are not much louder than a conversation.
0	Threshold of hearing, hybrid car operating on battery only (3–5 dB)		If you were boating in the middle of a calm lake, you might say, "Now, this is really quiet." In comparison, most of us are accustomed to relatively noisy city environments.

▶ **LO9** Locate the structures of the outer, middle, and inner ear, and describe their functions.

Outer, Middle, and Inner Ear

Most of us think we hear with our ears and that's how we tell the difference between, for example, the music of our favorite band and the barking of a dog. But nothing is further from the truth. What really happens is that both music and a dog's barks produce only sound waves, which are just the stimulus for hearing (audition). Your ears receive sound waves, but your brain does the hearing. It's a complicated journey; the first step begins in the outer ear.

1 Outer Ear

The only reason your ear has that peculiar shape and sticks out from the side of your head is to gather in sound waves.

The **outer ear** consists of three structures: external ear, auditory canal, and tympanic membrane.

The **external ear** is an oval-shaped structure that protrudes from the side of the head. The function of the external ear is to pick up sound waves and send them down a long, narrow tunnel called the auditory canal.

The **auditory canal** is a long tube that funnels sound waves down its length so that the waves strike a thin, taut membrane—the eardrum, or tympanic membrane.

In some cases, the auditory canal may become clogged with ear wax, which interferes with sound waves on their way to the eardrum.

The **tympanic** *(tim-PAN-ick)* **membrane** is a taut, thin structure commonly called the eardrum. Sound waves strike the tympanic membrane and cause it to vibrate. The tympanic membrane passes the vibrations on to the first of three small bones to which it is attached.

The tympanic membrane marks the boundary between the outer ear and the middle ear, described next.

2 Middle Ear

The middle ear functions like a radio's amplifier; it picks up and increases vibrations.

The **middle ear** is a bony cavity that is sealed at each end by membranes. The two membranes are connected by three small bones.

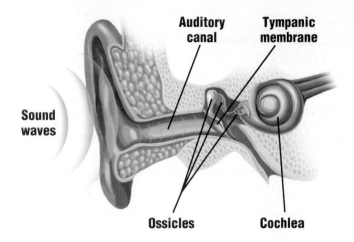

The three tiny bones are collectively called **ossicles** *(AW-sick-culls)* and, because of their shapes, are referred to as the hammer, anvil, and stirrup. The first ossicle—hammer—is attached to the back of the tympanic membrane. When the tympanic membrane vibrates, so does the hammer. In turn, the hammer sends the vibrations to the attached anvil, which further sends the vibrations to the attached stirrup. The stirrup makes the connection with the end membrane, the oval window.

Thus, the function of the middle ear is to pick up vibrations produced by the tympanic membrane, amplify these vibrations, and pass them on to the oval window, which marks the end of the middle ear and beginning of the inner ear.

3 Inner Ear

The **inner ear** contains two main structures: the cochlea, which is involved in hearing, and the vestibular system, which is involved in balance. We'll discuss the vestibular system later in this chapter; now, we'll focus on the cochlea.

The **cochlea** *(KOCK-lee-ah),* located in the inner ear, has a bony coiled exterior that resembles a snail's shell. The cochlea contains the receptors for hearing, and its function is transduction, transforming vibrations into nerve impulses that are sent to the brain for processing into auditory information.

Once nerve impulses reach the brain's auditory areas, you can actually hear.

▶ **LO10** Explain how our brain processes auditory information.

Auditory Cues

The brain calculates not only the direction of a sound but also whether the sound is high or low and loud or soft.

Calculating Direction

The brain determines the **direction of a sound** by calculating the slight difference in time that it takes sound waves to reach the two ears, which are about 6 inches apart.

If you have difficulty telling where a sound is coming from, the sound is probably arriving at both ears simultaneously. To locate the direction, you can turn your head from side to side, causing the sound to reach one ear before the other.

Calculating Pitch

Imagine the low, menacing growl of a lion and then the high screech of fingernails on the chalkboard. Your subjective experience of a sound being high or low is referred to as pitch. Exactly how the cochlea codes pitch and the brain interprets the code is rather complicated. We'll focus on two theories of pitch: the frequency theory and the place theory.

The **frequency theory,** which applies only to low-pitched sounds, says that the rate at which nerve impulses reach the brain determines how low the pitch of a sound is.

For example, the brain interprets a frequency rate of 50 impulses per second as a lower sound than one with a frequency rate of 200 impulses per second. Hearing the low-pitched lion growl involves the frequency theory. Hearing the high-pitched screech of fingernails on the chalkboard involves the place theory.

The **place theory** says that the brain determines medium- to higher-pitched sounds on the basis of the place on the basilar membrane where maximum vibration occurs.

For example, lower-pitched sounds cause maximum vibrations near the beginning of the cochlea's basilar membrane, while higher-pitched sounds cause maximum vibrations near the end of the membrane. The frequency and place theories help explain how our auditory system transforms sound waves into perceptions of low- to high-pitched sounds (Goldstein, 2010).

Calculating Loudness

The brain calculates **loudness** primarily from the frequency or rate of how fast or how slowly nerve impulses arrive from the auditory nerve.

For example, the brain interprets a slower rate of impulses as a softer tone, such as a whisper, and a faster rate as a louder tone, such as a yell (Goldstein, 2010).

Kinds of Deafness

There are two major kinds of deafness: conduction deafness and neural deafness.

Conduction deafness can be caused by wax in the auditory canal, injury to the tympanic membrane, or malfunction of the ossicles. These conditions interfere with the transmission of vibrations from the tympanic membrane to the fluid of the cochlea, resulting in degrees of hearing loss. Conduction deafness can often be treated with a hearing aid, which picks up sound waves, changes them to vibrations, and sends them through the skull to the inner ear (Ruben, 2007).

In contrast, neural deafness is not helped by hearing aids.

Neural deafness can be caused by damage to the auditory receptors (hair cells), which prevents the production of impulses, or by damage to the auditory nerve, which prevents nerve impulses from reaching the brain. Because neither hair cells nor auditory nerve fibers regenerate, neural deafness was generally untreatable until the development of the cochlear implant.

Cochlear Implant

The **cochlear implant** is a miniature electronic device that is surgically implanted into the cochlea. The cochlear implant changes sound waves into electrical signals that are fed into the auditory nerve, which carries them to the brain for processing.

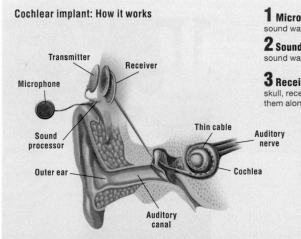

Cochlear implant: How it works

Transmitter
Receiver
Microphone
Sound processor
Outer ear
Thin cable
Auditory nerve
Cochlea
Auditory canal

1 **Microphone** gathers and sends sound waves to a sound processor.

2 **Sound processor** transforms sound waves into electrical signals.

3 **Receiver,** which is implanted in the bony skull, receives the electrical signals and sends them along a thin wire cable to the cochlea.

4 **Thin cable** is threaded through the cochlea to the auditory nerve. The electrical signals trigger impulses in the auditory nerve.

5 **Auditory nerve** carries the "manufactured" impulses to the auditory areas in the brain, which interpret and transform impulses into auditory impulses.

Cochlear Implants

Learn more about how cochlear implants are used and how effective they are.

Child with Cochlear Implant

Find out how much a child born with a hearing impairment can benefit from receiving a cochlear implant.

Check Your Learning Quiz 3.4

Go to **login.cengagebrain.com** and take the online quiz

Unless otherwise noted, all images are © Cengage Learning

▶ **LO11** Explain the processes involved in taste and smell or olfaction.

Taste

As you imagine eating your favorite food, we'll explain how your tongue tastes.

Tongue: Five Basic Tastes

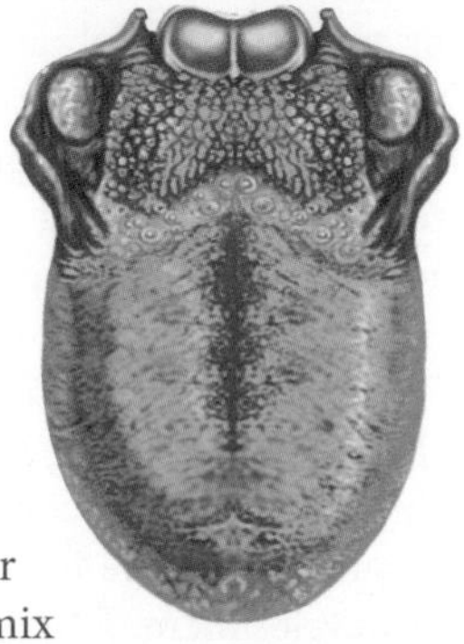

You're probably familiar with four basic tastes: sweet, salty, sour, and bitter. There appears to be a fifth, called *umami,* a meaty-cheesy taste found in cheese, meat, pizza, and MSG (Gilbert, 2008). The right figure shows the areas (shaded in blue) on the tongue that have the most sensors or taste buds.

Surface of the Tongue

As you chew food, its chemicals, which are the **stimuli** for taste, break down into molecules. In turn, these molecules mix with saliva and run down into narrow trenches on the surface of the tongue (bottom right figure).

Taste Buds

Buried in the trenches on the surface of the tongue are many taste buds.

Taste buds, which are shaped like miniature onions, are the receptors for taste. Chemicals dissolved in the saliva activate the taste buds, which produce nerve impulses that eventually reach areas in the brain's parietal lobe. The brain transforms these nerve impulses into sensations of taste.

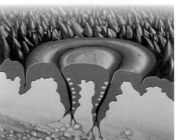

Flavor: Taste and Smell

If taste receptors are sensitive to only five basic tastes, how can you tell the difference between two sweet tastes, such as a brownie and vanilla ice cream? Much of the sensations we attribute to taste are actually contributed by our sense of smell.

We experience **flavor** when we combine the sensations of taste and smell. Because taste is enhanced by the sense of smell, we'll examine smell next.

Smell, or Olfaction

The incredible sense of smell (olfaction) is 10,000 times more sensitive than taste (Lindstrom, 2005). We'll explain the steps for olfaction by having you imagine crossing paths with an angry skunk.

1 Stimulus

An angry skunk protects itself by spraying thousands of molecules, which are carried by the air and drawn into your nose as you breathe. The reason you can smell substances such as skunk spray is that these substances are volatile. A volatile substance is one that can release molecules into the air at room temperature. For example, volatile substances include skunk spray, perfumes, and warm brownies, but not glass or steel. We can smell only volatile substances, but first they must reach the olfactory cells in the nose.

2 Olfactory Cells

Olfactory cells are the receptors for smell and are located in two 1-inch-square patches of tissue in the uppermost part of the nasal passages. The olfactory cells trigger nerve impulses that travel to the brain, which interprets the impulses as different smells.

As you breathe, a small percentage of the air entering your nose reaches the upper surface of your nasal passages, where the olfactory receptors are located. People can lose their sense of smell if a virus or inflammation destroys the olfactory receptors, or if a blow to the head damages the neural network that carries impulses to the brain. But remember, you don't actually smell anything until neural impulses reach your brain.

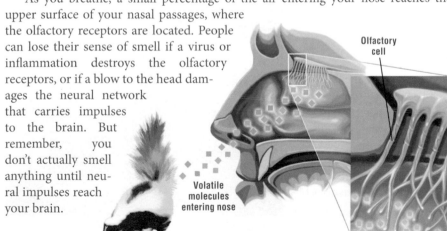

Olfactory cell

Volatile molecules entering nose

Disgust

Explore how foods we think are truly disgusting can be delicacies in other parts of the world.

Can Smells Increase Buying?

Learn about how it's possible for some smells to encourage us to make purchases.

Check Your Learning Quiz 3.5

Go to **login.cengagebrain.com** and take the online quiz

▶ **LO12** Discuss the role of the vestibular system in the positioning and balancing of our bodies.

▶ **LO13** Locate the receptors in the skin and describe their functions.

Position and Balance

We guarantee that one question you never ask is "Where is my head?" Even though your head is in a hundred different positions throughout the day, you rarely forget to duck as you enter a car or forget whether you're standing on your feet or your hands. That's because the position of your head (and usually your body) is automatically tracked by your vestibular sense (Brody, 2008b).

Semicircular canals

The **vestibular sense** provides information about balance and movement.

The vestibular system allows us to walk, bend over to touch our toes, and stand on one leg without falling over.

The **semicircular canals** provide input to the vestibular system. They are located in the inner ear and resemble bony arches, which are set at different angles. Each of the semicircular canals is filled with fluid that moves in response to movements of your head. In the canals are sensors that respond to the movement of the fluid.

A gymnast relies heavily on his or her vestibular sense to keep balance. Any tilt or change in position of the head and body is detected by the sensors in the semicircular canals, which send the information to the brain. The brain interprets these signals to determine the position of the head and body.

© John Lund/Blend Images/Corbis

Unless otherwise noted, all images are © Cengage Learning

Touch

The sense of **touch** includes pressure, temperature, and pain. Beneath the outer layer of skin are a half dozen miniature sensors that are receptors for the sense of touch. The function of the touch sensors is to change mechanical pressure or temperature into nerve impulses that are sent to the brain for processing.

We'll examine several miniature mechanical sensors and explain how they function. However, first we need to exmaine the different layers of the skin.

1 Skin The skin has three layers. The outermost layer is a thin film of dead cells containing no receptors. In the middle and fatty layers of skin are a variety of receptors with different functions. Some of the major sensors in the middle layer are hair receptors.

2 Hair Receptors In the middle layer are free nerve endings that are wrapped around the base of each hair follicle; these are called *hair receptors.* Hair receptors fire with a burst of activity when hairs are first bent. However, if hairs remain bent, the receptors cease firing, an example of *sensory adaptation.*

3 Free Nerve Endings Near the bottom of the outer layer of skin is a group of threadlike extensions; these are called *free nerve endings*. One of their major functions is to transmit information about temperature and pain.

4 Pacinian Corpuscle In the fatty layer of skin is the largest touch sensor, the *Pacinian corpuscle (pa-SIN-ee-in CORE-pus-sole).* This receptor is highly sensitive to touch, responds to vibration, and adapts very quickly.

All these receptors send their electrical signals to the brain.

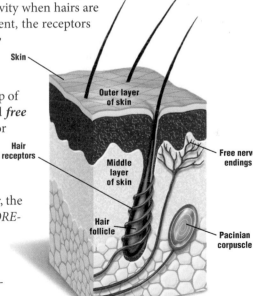

Motion Sickness

Explore the role of the vestibular system in motion sickness and how motion sickness can be reduced.

> ▶ **LO14** Define pain, explain how its definition differs from other senses, and discuss the gate control theory of pain.

Pain

All of us can relate to pain because we have all felt various degrees of it.

Pain is an unpleasant sensory and emotional experience that may result from tissue damage, one's thoughts or beliefs, or environmental stressors.

As much as we don't like to experience it, pain is essential for survival: It warns us to avoid or escape dangerous situations and makes us take time to recover from injury. You'll really appreciate the importance of pain after reading the Think Critically article at the end of the chapter.

The definition of pain differs from the other senses in three ways. First, pain results from many different stimuli (for example, physical injury, psychological and social stressors), whereas the other senses respond primarily to a single stimulus. Second, pain's intensity depends not only on the physical stimulus but also on social and psychological factors. Third, the treatment of pain depends not only on treating any physical injury but also on reducing emotional distress that may have caused or contributed to the painful sensations (Kerns, 2006, 2007).

Researchers recognize pain is a complex process that may or may not include tissue damage and usually involves social, psychological, and emotional factors, which can cause, increase, or decrease painful sensations (Innes, 2005; Nicholson & Martelli, 2004). For instance, researchers found that practicing Catholics perceive electric shocks as less painful when looking at an image of the Virgin Mary (Wiech et al., 2008). Other research finds that people who believe they are receiving an electric shock from another person on purpose, as opposed to accidentally, rate the same shock as more painful (Gray & Wegner, 2008). These studies show that the psychological experiences of pain are different even when the physical sensations are the same!

Research also finds placebo treatments can result in a lower perception of pain. For example, after men had hot metal plates placed on their hands, they were given an injection of either a painkiller or a placebo (they didn't know which). Brain scans showed that the placebo injections activated pain-reducing brain circuits similar to the circuits activated by real painkillers (Petrovic et al., 2002; Ploghaus et al., 2003). This and other studies demonstrate how one's beliefs can activate circuits in the brain that, in turn, result in changes in perception such as decreased pain (Erdmann, 2008; Scott et al., 2007).

Gate Control Theory

Although a headache is painful, the pain may come and go as you shift your attention or become absorbed in some project. This phenomenon is explained by the gate control theory of pain (Melzack & Katz, 2004).

The **gate control theory** of pain says that nonpainful nerve impulses (such as shifting attention) compete with pain impulses (such as a headache) in trying to reach the brain.

This competition creates a bottleneck, or neural gate, that limits the number of impulses that can be transmitted. Thus, shifting one's attention or rubbing an injured area may increase the passage of nonpainful impulses and thereby decrease the passage of painful impulses; as a result, the sensation of pain is

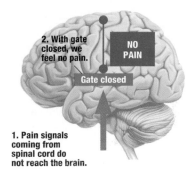

2. With gate open, we feel pain.

PAIN

Gate open

1. Pain signals coming from spinal cord reach the brain.

2. With gate closed, we feel no pain.

NO PAIN

Gate closed

1. Pain signals coming from spinal cord do not reach the brain.

dulled. The neural gate isn't a physical structure but rather refers to the competition between nonpainful and painful impulses as they try to reach the brain.

According to the gate control theory, your perception of pain depends not only on a stressful mental state or physical injury but also on a variety of psychological, emotional, and social factors, which can either decrease or increase your perception of pain (Pincus & Morley, 2001).

Your perception of pain from an injury can also be reduced by your brain's ability to secrete its own pain-reducing chemicals, called endorphins. Someone who has experienced a serious injury will usually report that initially the pain was bearable but with time the pain became much worse. One reason pain seems less intense immediately after injury is the brain produces endorphins.

Endorphins *(en-DOOR-fins)* are chemicals produced by the brain and secreted in response to injury or severe physical or psychological stress.

Overall, there is a strong relationship between an increase in endorphin release and a decrease in pain perception (Zubieta, 2007).

Mind over Body?

Explore the effectiveness of placebo treatments in reducing pain.

Pain from a Sports Injury

Get a close look at how gate control theory explains an athlete's ability to continue playing in a game after breaking his ankle.

Check Your Learning Quiz 3.6

Go to **login.cengagebrain.com** and take the online quiz.

Basic Differences

The first step in responding and adapting to changes in your environment involves gathering millions of meaningless sensations and changing them into useful perceptions. As you are about to discover, sensing and perceiving are as different as night and day. For example, quickly glance at the black-and-white figure below on the left and then look away and describe what you saw.

Sensations

Initially, the top figure appears to be a bunch of meaningless lines, spaces, and blobs, which, for the sake of simplicity, we'll take the liberty of calling visual sensations.

Sensations are relatively meaningless bits of information that result when the brain processes electrical signals that come from the sense organs.

Obviously, it would be impossible to respond, adapt, and survive if you had to rely only on sensations. You can now appreciate the importance of changing sensations into perceptions.

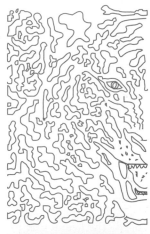

Perceptions

As you look at the bottom figure, your brain is processing many thousands of visual sensations involving lines, curves, textures, shadows, and colors. Then, instantaneously, automatically, and without awareness, your brain combines these thousands of sensations into a perception—an orange tiger's face against a green background.

Perceptions are meaningful sensory experiences that result after the brain combines hundreds of sensations.

However, our perceptions are rarely exact replicas of the original stimuli. Rather, they are usually changed, biased, or distorted by our unique set of experiences. Thus, perceptions are our personal interpretations of the real world.

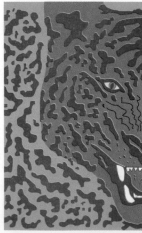

Unless otherwise noted, all images are © Cengage Learning

Changing Sensations into Perceptions

It is most unlikely that you have ever experienced a "pure" sensation because your brain automatically and instantaneously changes sensations into perceptions. To understand how sensations become perceptions, we have divided the perceptual process into a series of discrete steps that, in real life, are much more complex and interactive.

1 Stimulus

Since we normally experience only perceptions, we are not aware of many preceding steps. The first step begins with some stimulus, such as light waves, sound waves, mechanical pressure, or chemicals. The stimulus activates sense receptors in the eyes, ears, skin, nose, or mouth.

2 Transduction

After entering the eyes, light waves are focused on the retina, which contains photoreceptors that are sensitive to light. The light waves are absorbed by photoreceptors, which change physical energy into electrical signals, through a process called transduction. The electrical signals are changed into impulses that travel to the brain. Sense organs do not produce sensations but simply transform energy into electrical signals.

3 Brain: Primary Areas

Impulses from sense organs first go to different primary areas of the brain. For example, impulses from the ear go to the temporal lobe, from touch to the parietal lobe, and from the eye to areas in the occipital lobe. When impulses reach any of the primary areas, they are first changed into sensations. However, you would not report any sensations.

4 Brain: Association Areas

Each sense sends its impulses to a different primary area of the brain where impulses are changed into sensations. The "sensation" impulses are then sent to the appropriate association areas in the brain. The association areas change meaningless bits into meaningful perceptions.

5 Personalized Perceptions

Each of us has a unique set of personal experiences, emotions, and memories that are automatically added to our perceptions by other areas of the brain. As a result, our perceptions are not a mirror but a changed, biased, or even distorted copy of the real world (Goldstein, 2010).

Sensation Versus Perception

Explore the difference between sensation and perception.

Cultural Influences on Perception

Learn how culture influences perception.

Check Your Learning Quiz 3.7

Go to **login.cengagebrain.com** and take the online quiz.

▶ **LO17** Describe top-down and bottom-up perceptual processing and explain the differences between them.

Top-Down versus Bottom-Up Processing

In the previous module, we discussed how sensations are turned into perceptions. Specifically, you learned that our brain's association areas transform meaningless bits of information into meaningful perceptions.

This module focuses on how perceptions are organized. Let's begin by using an example: I (H.K.) am looking at a picture of my dog, Cocoa. How does my brain know I'm seeing Cocoa?

Top-Down Processing

Because I've seen Cocoa countless times and have stored what she looks like in my memory, I would use top-down processing to interpret this stimulus (photo of Cocoa).

Top-down processing is when perception is guided by previous knowledge, experience, beliefs, or expectations to recognize the whole pattern.

It's "top" first because we begin with brain processes. We use our cognitive processes to apply context to the information we are sensing.

Top-down processing also helps us fill in missing gaps. For instance, in the photo of Cocoa, I can't see her tail, but I know that she does have a tail; therefore, I will safely assume her tail is not missing.

But top-down processing cannot occur on its own; it relies on bottom-up processing, which we discuss next.

© Haig Kouyoumdjian

Bottom-Up Processing

Try reading the following sentence: Th- bo-s w-nt -o t-e p-rk -o p-ay -oc-er. Although you may have had to slow down your reading and pay more attention to the sentence, you probably were able to figure out the sentence read "The boys went to the park to play soccer" without too much effort.

You were able to determine what the sentence stated due to your previous reading experiences. Also, you may have had expectations that we wouldn't have you read a very challenging or complex sentence. Thus, you may have correctly thought the sentence would be rather straightforward and simple. This is an example of top-down processing.

However, the task of reading the fragmented sentence demonstrates that top-down and bottom-up processing occur together.

Bottom-up processing is when perception begins with bits and pieces of information that, when combined, lead to the recognition of a whole pattern.

It's "bottom" first because we begin with the raw, sensory information. We use the information we take in and try to bring meaning to it.

Without being able to recognize the bits and pieces of information about the stimuli (in this case the curves and lines that make up the letters, we would not be able to recognize the sentence (Johnston & McClelland, 1974).

Just as in the case of reading, top-down and bottom-up processing work together to help us accurately perceive countless aspects of the world around us. For example, let's consider the perceptual process that occurs as a child looks at a parrot; it involves both bottom-up and top-down processing. First, raw sensory information, which in this case is the image on the child's retina created by light being reflected off of the parrot, provides incoming information (bottom-up processing). Then, the knowledge the child already has about parrots influences her perception (top-down processing).

Perception helps makes sense of our sensations. Top-down and bottom-up processing is only one example of perceptual organization. In the remaining pages of this module, we'll present various other ways our perceptions are organized.

© ARCO/O. Diez/Age fotostock

> ▶ **LO18** List and explain the Gestalt rules for organizing perceptions.

Gestalt Psychology

In the early 1900s, psychologists engaged in a heated debate over how perceptions are formed. Some psychologists, called structuralists, strongly believed that we added together thousands of sensations to form a perception. Others, called Gestalt psychologists, just as strongly believed that sensations were not added but combined according to a set of innate rules to form a perception (Peterson et al., 2007). The Gestalt psychologists won the debate.

Gestalt psychologists believed that our brains follow a set of rules that specify how individual elements are to be organized into a meaningful pattern, or perception.

Organizational Rules

Take a moment to look at the scene below. Would you believe it was painted on a flat wall? One reason you perceive this scene as complex and three-dimensional is that the painter followed many of the Gestalt rules of organization (Han & Humphreys, 1999).

Rules of organization, which were identified by Gestalt psychologists, specify how our brains combine and organize individual pieces or elements into a meaningful perception.

As you look at the scene, your brain automatically organizes many hundreds of visual stimuli, including colors, textures, shadows, bricks, steel, glass, leaves, and branches, according to one or more of the perceptual rules of organization described on the next page. We'll use a relatively simple figure to illustrate each rule.

Painting by Richard Haas, photo © Bill Horsman Photography

Unless otherwise noted, all images are © Cengage Learning

Figure Ground

As you look at the figure on the left, you will automatically see a white object standing out against a red background, which illustrates the figure-ground principle.

The **figure-ground rule** states that, in organizing stimuli, we tend to automatically distinguish between a figure and a ground: The figure, with more detail, stands out against the background.

This particular image is interesting because, as you continue to stare at it, the figure and ground will reverse and you'll see profiles of two faces. However, in the real world, the images and objects we perceive are not reversible because they have more distinct shapes (Humphreys & Muller, 2000).

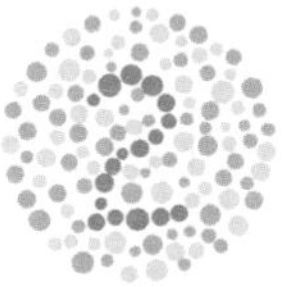

Similarity

As you look at the figure on the left filled with light and dark blue dots, you see a dark blue numeral 2, as opposed to random blue dots. The **similarity rule** states that, in organizing stimuli, we group together elements that appear similar.

Closure

Although the lines are incomplete, you can easily perceive this drawing as a cat or dog. The **closure rule** states that, in organizing stimuli, we tend to fill in any missing parts of a figure and see the figure as complete.

Proximity

Notice that although there are exactly eight circles in each horizontal line, you perceive each line as formed by a different number of groups of circles. The **proximity rule** states that, in organizing stimuli, we group together objects that are physically close to one another.

Continuity

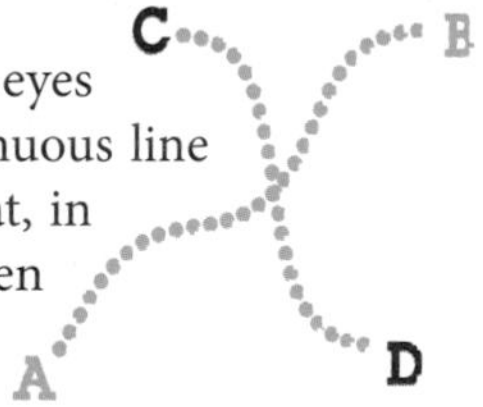

As you scan the figure on the left, keep track of the path your eyes follow. Most people's eyes move from left to right in a continuous line (from A to B or from C to D). The **continuity rule** states that, in organizing stimuli, we tend to favor continuous paths when interpreting a series of points or lines.

Gestalt Laws

Experience the Gestalt laws of perception.

▶ **L019** Define perceptual constancy and describe the four types of perceptual constancy.

Perceptual Constancy

The study of perception is full of interesting puzzles, such as how cars, people, and pets can change their shapes as they move about, yet we perceive them as remaining the same size and shape. For example, a car doesn't grow smaller as it speeds away, even though its shape on your retina grows smaller and smaller. A door doesn't become a trapezoid as you walk through it, even though that's what happens to its shape on your retina. These examples illustrate a phenomenon called perceptual constancy.

Perceptual constancy refers to our tendency to perceive sizes, shapes, brightness, and colors as remaining the same even though their physical characteristics are constantly changing.

We'll discuss four kinds of perceptual constancy: size, shape, brightness, and color.

Size Constancy

Imagine a world in which you perceived that every car, person, or animal became smaller as it moved away. Fortunately, we are spared from coping with so much stimulus change by perceptual constancy, one type of which is size constancy.

Size constancy refers to our tendency to perceive objects as remaining the same size even when their images on the retina continually grow or shrink.

As a car drives away, it projects a smaller and smaller image on your retina (figure above). Although the retinal image grows smaller, you do not perceive the car as shrinking because of size constancy. A similar process happens as a car drives toward you.

As the same car drives closer, it projects a larger image on your retina (right figure). However, because of size constancy, you do not perceive the car as becoming larger.

Shape Constancy

Each time you move a book, its image on your retina changes from a rectangle to a trapezoid. But you see the book's shape as remaining the same because of shape constancy.

Shape constancy refers to your tendency to perceive an object as retaining its same shape even though when you view it from different angles, its shape is continually changing its image on your retina.

The figure on the top right shows that when you look down at a rectangular book, it projects a rectangular shape on your retina.

However, if you move the book farther away, it projects trapezoidal shapes on your retina (bottom right figure), although you still perceive the book as rectangular because of shape constancy.

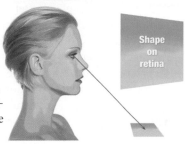

Brightness and Color Constancy

If you look into your dimly lit closet, all the brightly colored clothes will appear dull and grayish. However, because of brightness and color constancy, you still perceive brightness and colors and have no trouble selecting a red shirt.

Brightness constancy refers to the tendency to perceive brightness as remaining the same in changing illumination.

Color constancy refers to the tendency to perceive colors as remaining stable despite differences in lighting.

For example, if you looked at this young girl's sweater in bright sunlight, it would appear to be a bright yellow (left photo).

If you looked at her same yellow sweater in dim light, you would still perceive the color as a shade of yellow, although it appears duller (right photo). Because of color constancy, colors seem about the same even when lighting conditions change.

© Patricia J. Bruno/Positive Images

▶ **LO20** Explain depth perception, including binocular and monocular depth cues.

Depth Perception

Binocular (Two Eyes) Depth Cues

Normally, movies are shown in only two dimensions: height and width. But if you have seen a movie in 3-D (using special glasses to see three dimensions: height, width, and depth), you know the thrill of watching objects leap off the screen so realistically that you duck or turn your head. You may not have realized that your eyes give you a free, no-glasses, 3-D view of the world. And the amazing part of seeing in 3-D is that everything projected on the retina is in only two dimensions, height and width, which means that your brain combines different cues to add a third dimension: depth (Harris & Dean, 2003).

Depth perception refers to the ability of your eye and brain to add a third dimension, depth, to all visual perceptions, even though images projected on the retina are in only two dimensions, height and width.

The above object has been given a three-dimensional look by making it seem to have depth. The cues for depth perception are divided into two major classes: binocular and monocular.

Binocular depth cues depend on the movement of both eyes (bi means "two"; ocular means "eye").

We'll discuss two types of binocular depth cues: convergence and retinal disparity.

Convergence

When you have an eye exam, the doctor usually asks you to follow the end of her finger as she holds it a few feet away and then slowly moves it closer until it touches your nose. This is a test for convergence.

Convergence refers to a binocular cue for depth perception based on signals sent from muscles that turn the eyes. To focus on objects that are near or approaching, these muscles turn the eyes inward, toward the nose. The brain uses the signals sent by these muscles to determine the distance of the object.

The woman in the photo at the right is demonstrating the ultimate in convergence as she looks at the bubble. The more her eyes turn inward or converge, the nearer the object appears in space. The woman in the photo sees the bubble because of convergent clues from her turned-in eyes.

Unless otherwise noted, all images are © Cengage Learning

Retinal Disparity

An advantage of having an eye on each side of your face is that each eye has a slightly different view of the world, which provides another binocular cue for depth perception: retinal disparity.

Retinal disparity refers to a binocular depth cue that depends on the distance between the eyes. Because of their different positions, each eye receives a slightly different image. The difference between those images is the retinal disparity. The brain interprets a large retinal disparity to mean a close object and a small retinal disparity to mean a distant object.

The figure below shows how retinal disparity occurs: The difference between the image seen by the left eye (1) and the one seen by the right eye (2) results in retinal disparity (3).

Another example of retinal disparity occurs when viewers wear special glasses to watch a 3-D movie. Standard 3-D glasses use a red and a green lens, which is a technique to allow the right and left eyes to perceive slightly different views of the same scene. As a result, the brain receives two slightly different images. As the brain automatically combines the slightly different images, we get the feeling of depth (for example, seeing a mad dog jump out of the movie screen into the audience, followed by much screaming).

Individuals who have only one eye still have depth perception because there are a number of one-eyed, or monocular, cues for depth perception, which we'll explain next.

1. Left eye sees a slightly different image of the fly.

3. Brain combines the two slightly different images from left and right eyes and gives us a perception of depth.

2. Right eye sees a slightly different image of the fly.

Monocular (One-Eyed) Depth Cues

An individual with only one seeing eye would lack depth-perception cues associated with retinal disparity, but he would have depth-perception cues associated with having one eye, or being monocular (*mon* means "one").

Monocular depth cues are produced by signals from a single eye. Monocular cues most commonly arise from the way objects are arranged in the environment.

We'll show you seven common monocular cues for perceiving depth.

Linear perspective makes you see the road as going on forever.

Linear perspective is a monocular depth cue that results as parallel lines come together, or converge, in the distance.

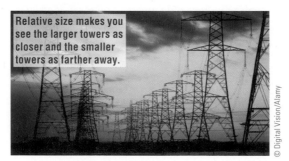

Relative size makes you see the larger towers as closer and the smaller towers as farther away.

Relative size is a monocular cue for depth that results when we expect two objects to be the same size and they are not. In that case, the larger of the two objects will appear closer and the smaller will appear farther away.

Interposition makes you see the fish in front as closer and those in back as farther away.

Interposition is a monocular cue for depth perception that comes into play when objects overlap. The overlapping object appears closer, and the object that is overlapped appears farther away.

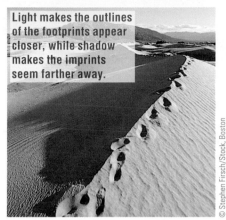

Light makes the outlines of the footprints appear closer, while shadow makes the imprints seem farther away.

Light and shadow make up monocular cues for depth perception: Brightly lit objects appear closer, while objects in shadows appear farther away.

Texture gradient makes you see the sharply detailed, cracked mud as being closer.

Texture gradient is a monocular depth cue in which areas with sharp, detailed texture are interpreted as being closer and those with less sharpness and poorer detail are perceived as more distant.

Atmospheric perspective is a monocular depth cue that is created by the presence of dust, smog, clouds, or water vapor. We perceive clearer objects as being nearer, and we perceive hazy or cloudy objects as being farther away.

Atmospheric perspective makes clear objects seem nearer and hazy objects as being farther away.

Motion parallax makes blurry objects appear closer and clear objects appear farther away.

Motion parallax is a monocular depth cue based on the speed of moving objects. We perceive objects that appear to be moving at high speed as closer to us than those moving more slowly or appearing stationary.

Depth Perception

Explore binocular cues and interact with monocular cues for depth.

Check Your Learning Quiz 3.8

Go to **login.cengagebrain.com** and take the online quiz.

© Stephen Firsch/Stock, Boston

© Photodisc/SuperStock

© HENRYS/Gamma-Rapho via Getty Images

© Robert Holmes/Corbis

▶ **LO21** Describe the common illusions we experience and explain their causes.

Illusions

There are two reasons that much of the time your perceptions of cars, people, food, trees, and animals are reasonably accurate reflections but, because of emotional, motivational, and cultural influences, are never exact copies of reality.

First, we inherit similar sensory systems whose information is processed and interpreted by similar areas of the brain (Franz et al., 2000). The second reason our perceptions are reasonably accurate is because we learn from common experience about the sizes, shapes, and colors of objects. But we've already discussed how perceptions can be biased or distorted by previous emotional and learning experiences. Now we come to another way that perceptions can be distorted: by changing the actual perceptual cues so you perceive something unlikely, which is called an illusion.

An **illusion** is a perceptual experience in which you perceive an image as being so strangely distorted that, in reality, it cannot and does not exist. An illusion is created by manipulating the perceptual cues so that your brain can no longer correctly interpret space, size, and depth cues.

For example, if you look at the illustration below, you'll notice the orange circles are moving right before your eyes! You have to admit this

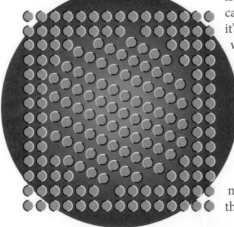

is a fun and impressive illusion. But how can the circles appear to be moving when it's actually a still illustration? In this case, we do not know for sure. The illustration somehow activates motion-detecting neurons in the visual pathway. Patterns in illustrations like this one fool the visual system into seeing motion when it doesn't really exist (Ramachandran & Rogers-Ramachandran, 2007). (If you cannot see the circles move, please don't worry; some people with otherwise normal vision cannot see movement in this illustration.)

Unless otherwise noted, all images are © Cengage Learning

Perception of Motion

In the illusion on the previous page, many of you saw the orange circles move even though it was a still illustration. We can perceive motion that actually exists and motion that is an illusion.

For instance, if you attend a track meet and watch a 100-meter race and then, minutes later, watch a videotaped replay of the same race, you perceive motion produced in two very different ways. One kind of motion is real, while the other is an illusion.

Real motion refers to your perception of any stimulus or object that actually moves in space.

As you watch a live 100-meter race, you are perceiving real motion. However, when you watch a replay of that same race, you are seeing apparent motion.

Apparent motion refers to an illusion that a stimulus or object is moving in space when, in fact, the stimulus or object is stationary. The illusion of apparent motion is created by rapidly showing a series of stationary images, each of which has a slightly different position or posture than the one before.

© Globus Brothers

The principle for creating apparent motion is simple and can be easily noticed by examining the positions of the runner's body in each frame of the time-lapse photo shown above. Beginning on the left side, notice that each frame shows only a slight change in the position of the runner's body. However, if these frames were presented rapidly (for example, at the movie standard of 24 frames per second), you would perceive the illusion of an athlete running down the track.

In a series of ingenious experiments, researchers discovered that several complex mechanisms built into our visual system detect cues that produce the illusion of motion (Ramachandran & Anstis, 1986). One such cue is the closure principle, which means that our brains fill in the motion expected to occur between images that vary only slightly in position and are presented in rapid sequence. Without apparent motion, there would be no movies or television.

Ames Room

In the Ames room (right photo), you perceive the boy on the right to be twice as tall as the woman on the left. In fact, the boy is smaller than the woman but appears larger because of the design of the Ames room.

Adult woman appears smaller than young boy.

© Baron Wolman/Woodfin Camp & Associates

The **Ames room,** named after its designer, shows that our perception of size can be distorted by changing depth cues.

The reason the boy appears to be twice as tall as the woman is that the room has a peculiar shape and you are looking in from a fixed peephole. To see how the Ames room changes your depth cues, look at the diagram of the Ames room in the drawing below. If you view the Ames room from the fixed peephole, the room appears rectangular and matches your previous experience with rooms, which are usually rectangular. However, as the right figure shows, the Ames room is actually shaped in an odd way: The left corner is twice as far away from the peephole as the right corner. This means that the woman is actually twice as far away from you

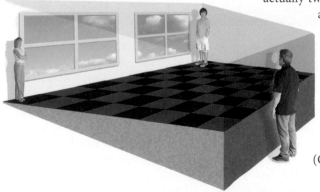

as the boy. However, the Ames room's odd shape makes you think that you are seeing the two people from the same distance, and this illusion makes the farther woman appear to be shorter than the boy (Goldstein, 2010).

Unless otherwise noted, all images are © Cengage Learning

Ponzo Illusion

In the right figure, the top black bar appears to be much longer than the bottom black bar. However, if you measure these two bars, you will discover that they are exactly the same size. This is the *Ponzo illusion.*

You perceive the top bar as being farther away, and you have learned from experience that if two objects appear to be the same size but one is farther away, the more distant object must be larger; thus, the top bar appears longer.

Black bars are the same length.

Müller-Lyer Illusion

The figures below illustrate the *Müller-Lyer illusion.* Notice that the arrow in the left figure appears noticeably shorter than the arrow in the right figure. However, if you measure them, you'll prove that the arrows are of equal length.

One explanation for this illusion is that you are relying on size cues learned from your previous experience with corners of rooms. You have learned that if a corner of a room extends outward, it is closer; this experience distorts your perception so that the left arrow appears to be shorter. In contrast, you have learned that if a corner of a room recedes inward, it is farther away, and this experience makes you perceive the right arrow as longer (Goldstein, 2010).

Left and right arrows are the same length.

Illusions are fun, but what have we learned? Illusions teach us that when proven perceptual cues are changed or manipulated, our reliable perceptual processes can be deceived. Illusions also teach us that perception is a very active process, in which we continually rely on and apply previous experiences with objects when we perceive new situations.

Ames Room

Experience the Ames room.

▶ **L022** Describe ESP and explain how researchers study so-called psychic abilities.

Extrasensory Perception

No one doubts your ability to receive information through one or more of your major senses—seeing, hearing, tasting, smelling, and touching—because this ability has been repeatedly demonstrated and reliably measured. In comparison, most research psychologists do not believe you can receive information outside normal sensory channels, because this phenomenon which is called extrasensory perception has been neither repeatedly demonstrated nor reliably measured (D. J. Bem & Honorton, 1994).

Extrasensory perception (ESP) is a group of psychic experiences that involve perceiving or sending information (images) outside normal sensory processes or channels.

ESP includes four general abilities such as: telepathy, precognition, clairvoyance, and psychokinesis.

Telepathy is the ability to transfer one's thoughts to another or to read the thoughts of others. **Precognition** is the ability to foretell events. **Clairvoyance** is the ability to perceive events or objects that are out of sight. **Psychokinesis** is the ability to move objects without touching them.

Together, these extrasensory perceptions are called psi phenomena.

The term **psi** refers to the processing of information or transfer of energy by methods that have no known physical or biological mechanisms and that seem to stretch the laws of physics.

According to the Gallup polls, 41% of adult Americans believe in ESP, 31% believe in communication between minds without the use of regular senses, 21% believe they can communicate mentally with someone who has died, and as many as 55% believe in psychics (Moore, 2005). In fact, only 7 to 10% of Americans do not believe in any of these extrasensory perceptions (Begley, 2007c, 2008c).

The reason so many Americans but so few research psychologists believe in ESP is that researchers demand hard, scientific evidence rather than evidence from testimonials (p. 30), which are based on personal beliefs or experiences and have a high potential for error and bias. Another reason researchers demand reliable and repeatable evidence to prove the existence of ESP is that some demonstrations of psi phenomena have involved trickery or questionable methodology.

Unless otherwise noted, all images are © Cengage Learning

Trickery and Magic

According to James Randi, known as the Amazing Randi (right photo), and others acquainted with magic, much of what passes for extrasensory perception is actually done through trickery (Randi, 2005, 2009; Ybarra, 1991). For example, many years ago, a television show under the supervision of James Randi offered $100,000 to anyone who could demonstrate psychic powers. Twelve people claimed to have psychic powers, such as identifying through interviews the astrological signs under which people were born, seeing the auras of people standing behind screens, and correctly reading Zener cards (showing five symbols: square, circle, wavy lines, plus sign, and star). Of the 12 people who claimed psychic powers, none scored above chance on any of these tasks (Steiner, 1989).

© Jeffery Allan Salter/Corbis

Although people may claim psychic powers, most cannot demonstrate such powers under controlled conditions, which eliminate trickery, magic, and educated guessing. To eliminate any trickery, claims of psychic abilities must withstand the scrutiny of scientific investigation. Researchers interested in testing psi phenomena use a state-of-the-art method called the Ganzfeld procedure.

The **Ganzfeld procedure** is a controlled method for eliminating trickery, error, and bias while testing telepathic communication between a sender, the person who sends the message, and a receiver, the person who receives the message.

In the Ganzfeld procedure, the receiver is placed in a reclining chair in an acoustically isolated room. Translucent ping-pong ball halves are taped over the eyes, and headphones are placed over the ears. The sender, who is isolated in a separate soundproof room, concentrates for about 30 minutes on a target, which is a randomly selected visual stimulus, such as the Zenar cards described above. At the end of this period, the receiver is shown four different stimuli and asked which one most closely matches what the receiver was imagining. Because there are four stimuli, the receiver will guess the target correctly 25% of the time. Thus, if the receiver correctly identifies the target more than 25% of the time, it is above chance level and indicates something else is occurring, perhaps extrasensory perception (Bem & Honorton, 1994).

Check Your Learning Quiz 3.9

Go to **login.cengagebrain.com** and take the online quiz.

Think Critically

Challenge Your Thinking

Consider these questions when reading this article:

1. What type of research method would you use to learn about the life of a person who cannot feel pain? (See Modules 1.6–1.8)

2. What type of neuron is responsible for people experiencing pain, heat, and cold? (See Module 2.3)

3. Which areas of our brain and body help regulate body temperature and other vital physiological responses, such as respiration, heart rate, and digestion? (See Modules 2.4 & 2.6)

4. How might CIPA affect Ashlyn's ability to learn from her mistakes of injuring herself?

5. How helpful would acupuncture be as a treatment for people with CIPA?

6. Why is it that Ashlyn cannot sense pain or heat, but she can feel her parents tickling and hugging her?

What Would It Be Like Never to Feel Pain?

At the young age of 5, Ashlyn Blocker has already experienced many serious physical injuries. She's had a massive abrasion to the cornea of her eye, terrible burns, and hundreds of bite marks from fire ants. She's also severely damaged her tongue, cheek, and lips, knocked out most of her front teeth, and crushed her fingers in a door frame. Other children would scream in pain from experiencing any of these injuries, but Ashlyn never yelled, nor did she shed a tear. "I can't feel my boo-boos," she says (Tresniowski et al., 2005). Ashlyn is unique because she cannot feel pain.

Ashlyn has a rare and incurable genetic disorder called CIPA (congenital insensitivity to pain with anhidrosis). People with CIPA lack pain and temperature sensation, yet have no other sensory deficits. These individuals cannot feel pain and temperature because they lack nerve fibers responsible for carrying the sensation of pain, heat, and cold to the brain. Anhidrosis, or the inability to sweat, can cause life-threatening problems, such as

© Eric Larson/jensonlarson.com

developing dangerously high fevers because people aren't able to lower their body temperature by sweating.

Living life without feeling pain is not as wonderful as one might think. Pain serves an important function by telling our brain that something is wrong and something needs to be done to correct it. Imagine having appendicitis and not feeling pain. Appendicitis is especially dangerous for people with CIPA because they wouldn't know a problem existed until after their appendix burst. Also, while most people shift their body weight when feeling pain in their joints, CIPA prevents people from sensing this pain and often results in joint problems. Lack of pain sensitivity can lead to other problems, including bone fractures and infections. For example, Ashlyn recently had tonsillitis that went undetected for six months.

Despite the daily challenges Ashlyn faces, she looks like an ordinary girl who enjoys doing the same things others her age do. She likes to swing on the playground and enjoys being tickled and hugged by her parents. Ashlyn is fortunate to have support from her parents and school officials to ensure her safety while allowing her to enjoy her childhood. "There is no reason to think she won't have a normal life," says Dr. Lawrence Shapiro, an internationally recognized child psychologist. Ashlyn's parents describe her as having the "best laugh in the world" and state "she's going to conquer the world" (Tresniowski et al., 2005). (Adapted from Morton, 2004; Tresniowski et al., 2005)

Think Critically 3.1

This article and its questions are available in interactive format online.

GO to your Psychology CourseMate at login.cengagebrain.com and take the Chapter Post-Test to see which Learning Objectives you've mastered and which need more review. Use the chapter review guide below and the online activities—including flashcards to review key terms—to measure your learning.

Measure ^Your Learning

Online Activities

Key Terms	Video	Animation	Reading	Assessment
synesthesia	Synesthesia, p. 103			Check Your Learning Quiz 3.1
transduction, adaptation, sensations, perceptions, threshold, absolute threshold, subliminal stimulus, just noticeable difference (JND), Weber's law			Detecting Breast Cancer, p. 107 Can Subliminal Messages Change Behavior?, p. 107	Check Your Learning Quiz 3.2
visible spectrum, cornea, pupil, iris, lens, retina, rods, cones, trichromatic theory, afterimage, opponent-process theory, color blindness, monochromats, dichromats	Artificial Visual System, p. 111		Artificial Visual System, p. 111 Color Vision and Genes, p. 113 Color Blindness Test, p. 113	Check Your Learning Quiz 3.3
sound waves, amplitude, frequency, pitch, decibel, outer ear, external ear, auditory canal, tympanic membrane, middle ear, ossicles, inner ear, cochlea, direction of a sound, frequency theory, place theory, loudness, conduction deafness, neural deafness, cochlear implant	Ringtones and the Cochlea, p. 115 Child with Cochlear Implant, p. 121		Cochlear Implants, p. 121	Check Your Learning Quiz 3.4
taste buds, flavor, olfactory cells			Disgust, p. 123 Can Smells Increase Buying?, p. 123	Check Your Learning Quiz 3.5

Measure
^Your Learning

Online Activities

Key Terms	Video	Animation	Reading	Assessment
vestibular sense, semicircular canals, skin, hair receptors, sensory adaptation, free nerve endings, Pacinian corpuscle, pain, gate control theory, endorphins			Motion Sickness, p. 125 Mind Over Body?, p. 127 Pain from a Sports Injury, p. 127	Check Your Learning Quiz 3.6
sensations, perceptions		Sensation versus Perception, p. 129	Cultural Influences on Perception, p. 129	Check Your Learning Quiz 3.7
top-down processing, bottom-up processing, Gestalt psychologists, rules of organization, figure-ground rule, similarity rule, closure rule, proximity rule, continuity rule, perceptual constancy, size constancy, shape constancy, brightness constancy, color constancy, depth perception, binocular depth cues, convergence, retinal disparity, monocular depth cues, linear perspective, relative size, interposition, light and shadow, atmospheric persective, texture gradient, motion parallax		Gestalt Laws, p. 133 Depth Perception, p. 139		Check Your Learning Quiz 3.8
illusion, real motion, apparent motion, Ames room, Ponzo illusion, Müller-Lyer illusion, extrasensory perception (ESP), telepathy, precognition, clairvoyance, psychokinesis, psi, Ganzfeld procedure	Ames Room, p. 143			Check Your Learning Quiz 3.9

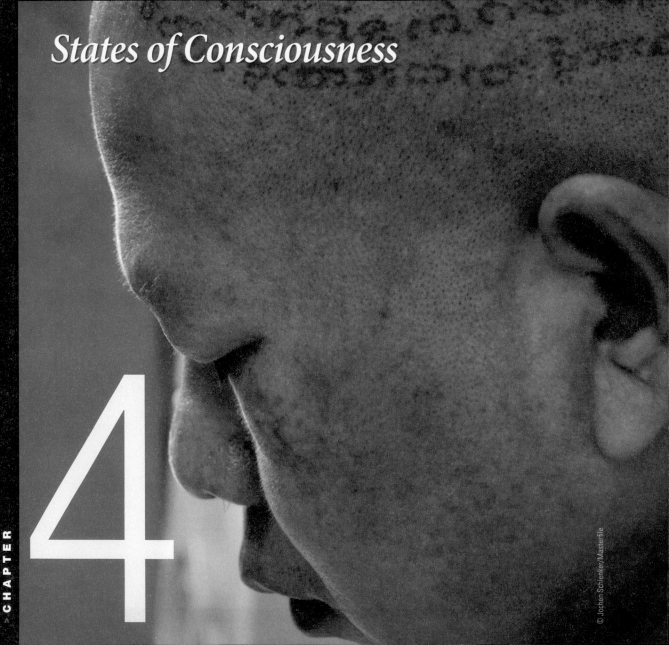

States of Consciousness

4

© Jochen Schlenker/Masterfile

1 **GO** to your **Psychology CourseMate** at **login.cengagebrain.com** and take the **Chapter Pre-Test** to introduce yourself to this chapter's topics and see what you may already know.

2 **READ** the **Learning Objectives (LOs)** (in the left sidebars) and begin the chapter.

3 **COMPLETE** the **Online Activities** (in the right sidebars) *as you read each module.* Activities include **videos**, **animations**, **readings**, and **quizzes**.

4 **CHECK Your Learning** by going online to take the quiz at the end of each module and review material as necessary.

5 **MEASURE Your Learning** after reading the chapter by taking the online **Chapter Post-Test.** Use the chapter review guide at the end of the chapter as needed.

WATCH for these **Online Activities** icons as you read:

Video

Animation

Reading

Assessment

Think Critically

These online activities are important to mastering this chapter. As you read each module, access these materials by going to **login.cengagebrain.com**.

 Video Explore studies and firsthand accounts of biological and psychological processes:

- Explore whether it is possible to unintentionally act in a violent manner during deep sleep.
- Observe how researchers study people's sleep patterns.
- Watch how a non-drug treatment is used to treat insomnia.
- Watch how hypnosis can help reduce pain in people undergoing surgery.
- Watch how hypnosis may be able to help people lose weight.
- Watch how heroin addiction affects the lives of teens.
- Watch what it's like to have a substance use disorder.

 Animation Interact with and visualize important processes and concepts:

- Identify the different states of consciousness.
- Learn how the sleep–wake clock is affected by the 24-hour night–day cycle.

- Observe the physiological and behavioral changes that occur during the stages of sleep.
- See how amphetamine affects neurotransmitters
- See how cocaine affects neurotransmitters

 Reading Delve deeper into key content:

- Explore why some people are early birds while others are night owls
- Learn about seasonal affective disorder
- Learn about the effects of sleep deprivation on the bodies and brains of doctors
- Explore what people typically dream about
- Learn about the non-drug and drug treatments for insomnia
- Explore how studying narcolepsy in dogs leads to improved treatment of this disorder in humans
- Learn how imagery rehearsal helps people escape terrifying nightmares
- Explore why a person would get on stage and imitate Elvis after being hypnotized
- Learn whether caffeine has any effect on intellectual functioning

- Learn how methadone is used in the treatment of heroin addiction
- Explore whether marijuana impairs memory
- Explore the rates and risk factors of alcoholism across cultures
- Learn more about some of the major societal problems that result from alcohol use and abuse

 Assessment Measure your mastery:

- Chapter Pre-Test
- Check Your Learning Quizzes
- Chapter Post-Test

 Think Critically Challenge your thinking by applying content from this chapter and making connections to related material:

- Texting: How Distracting Can it Be?

▶ **LO1** Define persistent vegetative state.

AT AGE 27, TERRI SCHIAVO suffered a heart attack that resulted in her losing consciousness. During the next 15 years, she never regained consciousness and lived in nursing homes under constant care. Terri was fed and hydrated through tubes and had her diapers changed regularly. She could still breathe without a respirator and could even open her eyes. At times, Terri turned toward her mother's voice, made sounds similar to laughter, and had seemingly followed a balloon with her eyes. Despite these abilities and movements, Terri remained completely unaware of her surroundings. Doctors described Terri's condition as a persistent vegetative state.

A **persistent vegetative state** occurs when a person has severe brain damage to the cortex resulting in long-term loss of cognitive function and awareness, but retains basic physiological functions, such as breathing and the sleep-wake cycle.

Doctors stated that Terri's responses were reflexive, not requiring conscious intent, and commonly occur spontaneously with people in a persistent vegetative state. As a result of being in a vegetative state for so long, Terri's brain severely deteriorated. All that remained of her brain was enough to keep certain basic

© Reuters/HO/Landov

life functions working (such as heart rate, breathing, arousal, visual and auditory reflexes). Many doctors concluded Terri would forever remain unconscious and be completely dependent on others.

The question of how long Terri should remain on a feeding tube stirred tremendous debate between her husband and her parents, and even received attention by the courts, the President of the United States, religious leaders, and countless protestors all over the world. After years of controversy, the court ordered the removal of the feeding tube, and Terri died 13 days following its removal. Her autopsy showed she had massive and irreversible brain damage that had shrunk her brain to about half of its expected size, leaving her with no chance of recovery (adapted from Associated Press, 2005a, 2005d; Eisenberg, 2005; Russell, 2005; Schrock, 2007).

Consciousness is a fascinating phenomenon. In this chapter, you'll learn about its many complexities and wonders.

 Check Your Learning Quiz 4.1

Go to **login.cengagebrain.com** and take the online quiz.

▶ **LO2** Define consciousness and the continuum of consciousness.

▶ **LO3** Identify and describe the different states of consciousness.

Different States

How do you know that at this very moment you are conscious?

Consciousness refers to different levels of awareness of one's thoughts and feelings. It may include creating images in one's mind, following one's thought processes, or having unique emotional experiences.

You may think that when awake you are conscious and when asleep you are unconscious, but there is actually a continuum of consciousness.

The **continuum of consciousness** refers to a wide range of experiences, from being acutely aware and alert to being totally unaware and unresponsive.

Below are some experiences that make up the continuum of consciousness.

Controlled Processes

The ability to focus all of our attention on only one thing, such as talking on a cell phone, is an example of controlled processes.

Controlled processes are activities that require full awareness, alertness, and concentration to reach some goal. The focused attention required in carrying out controlled processes usually interferes with the execution of other ongoing activities.

A controlled process such as talking on a cell phone while driving involves focusing most of your attention on talking and little on driving. Consequently, people who use cell phones while driving have four times the risk of having an accident (Kirtland, 2009). The use of a cell phone is the most common distraction while driving (NHTSA, 2008).

Automatic Processes

The attention of the man in the right photo is focused primarily on reading; thus, he is almost automatically eating the apple. This is an example of an automatic process.

Automatic processes are activities that require little awareness, take minimal attention, and do not interfere with other ongoing activities.

Although we seem to concentrate less during automatic processes, at some level we are conscious of what is occurring. For instance, as we drive on automatic pilot, we avoid neighboring cars and can usually take quick evasive action during emergencies.

© PhotosIndia/Getty Images

Unless otherwise noted, all images are © Cengage Learning

Daydreaming

Many of us engage in a pleasurable form of consciousness called daydreaming.

Daydreaming is an activity that requires a low level of awareness, often occurs during automatic processes, and involves fantasizing or dreaming while awake.

We may begin daydreaming in a relatively conscious state and then drift into a state between sleep and wakefulness. Usually we daydream in situations that require little attention or during repetitious or boring activities.

Most daydreams are rather ordinary, such as thinking about getting one's hair cut, planning where to eat, or fantasizing about a date. These kinds of daydreams serve to remind us of important things in our future. Although you might guess otherwise, men's and women's daydreams are remarkably similar in frequency, vividness, and realism (Klinger, 1987).

Altered States

Over 3,000 years ago, Egyptians brewed alcohol to reach altered states of consciousness (Samuel, 1996).

Altered states of consciousness result from using any number of procedures (such as meditation, psychoactive drugs, hypnosis, or sleep deprivation) to produce an awareness that differs from normal consciousness.

For example, the woman in the right photo is using meditation to focus her attention on a single image or thought, free her mind from external restraints, and enter an altered state of consciousness.

Regardless of how altered states are produced, the chief characteristic is that we perceive our internal and external environments or worlds in ways different from normal perception.

Next, we'll briefly discuss sleep, dreams, and unconsciousness to continue the overview of the experiences that make up the continuum of consciousness. Later in this chapter, we'll explore the world of sleep and dreams in more detail.

© Image Source/Jupiterimages

© smikhailov/Shutterstock

Sleep and Dreams

We enter an altered state of consciousness when we go to sleep.

Sleep consists of five different stages that involve different levels of awareness, consciousness, and responsiveness, as well as different levels of physiological arousal.

Because of our decreased awareness, 8 hours of sleep may seem like one continuous state. However, it is actually composed of different states of body arousal and consciousness (Lee-Chiong, 2008). One interesting sleep state involves dreaming.

Dreaming is a unique state of consciousness in which we are asleep but experience a variety of astonishing visual, auditory, and tactile images, often connected in strange ways and often in color.

During the initial stage of sleep, we are often aware of stimuli in our environment. However, as we pass into the deepest stage of sleep, which actually borders on unconsciousness, we may sleeptalk or sleepwalk, and children may experience frightening night terrors but have no awareness or memory of them.

Unconscious

Earlier in this text (Module 1.3) we discussed the psychoanalytic approach, which is based on the ideas of Sigmund Freud. One of his revolutionary ideas was the concept of the unconscious.

According to Freud, when we are faced with very threatening wishes or desires, especially if they are sexual or aggressive, we automatically defend our self-esteem by placing these psychologically threatening thoughts into a mental place called the unconscious.

The **unconscious,** according to Freud, is a mental place that contains unacceptable thoughts, wishes, and feelings that are beyond our conscious awareness.

Freud believed that we can become aware of our unconscious thoughts, wishes, and feelings only through very specialized techniques, which we discuss much later (Module 13.4).

Unless otherwise noted, all images are © Cengage Learning

© Haig Kouyoumdjian

© SGO/VOGIN/Age fotostock

Unconsciousness

If you have ever fainted, gotten general anesthesia, or been knocked out from a blow to the head, you have experienced being unconscious.

Unconsciousness, which can result from disease, trauma, a blow to the head, or general medical anesthesia, results in total lack of sensory awareness and complete loss of responsiveness to one's environment.

For example, a boxer's goal is to knock out the opponent with a quick blow to the head that produces a temporary state of unconsciousness. Being in an accident can damage the brain and cause different levels of unconsciousness and result in different kinds of comas. In some comas, a person appears to be asleep and has absolutely no awareness or responsiveness; this is called a vegetative state (such as the case of Terri Schiavo, who was in a vegetative coma for over a decade). People in vegetative comas are unconscious and in some cases brain-dead, which means they will never again regain consciousness.

Conclusion

Consciousness is so mysterious because it is a continuum of states, which ranges from the tragic unconsciousness of being in a vegetative coma to the keen alertness of controlled processes during a final exam. Although it is difficult to define consciousness, you know what it feels like to be conscious and aware of your thoughts and surroundings.

Neuroscientists find there is no single seat of consciousness; rather it results from interactions among many areas of the brain, depending upon the kinds of thoughts, images, or stimuli to which you are attending (Edelman, 2003).

One obvious sign of consciousness is being awake, which is regulated by a clock in the brain, our next topic.

Continuum of Consciousness

Identify the different states of consciousness.

Check Your Learning Quiz 4.2

Go to **login.cengagebrain.com** and take the online quiz.

THE ADVERTISEMENT READ:
"WE ARE LOOKING FOR A HARDY SUBJECT TO LIVE ALONE IN AN UNDERGROUND CAVE FOR 4 MONTHS. WE'LL PROVIDE BOARD, ROOM, AND A MONTHLY ALLOWANCE. IT WILL BE NECESSARY TO TAKE DAILY PHYSIOLOGICAL MEASUREMENTS, MEASURE BRAIN WAVES, AND COLLECT BLOOD SAMPLES."

Twenty people answered this ad, but researchers selected Stefania because she seemed to have the inner strength, motivation, and stamina to complete the entire 4 months. On the chosen day, Stefania crawled 30 feet underground with her favorite books into a 20-by-12-foot Plexiglas module, which had been sealed off from sunlight, radio, television, and other time cues.

© Murrae Haynes

Without clocks, radio, television, or the sun, Stefania found it difficult to keep track of time, which seemed to have slowed down. When told she could leave her underground cave (above photo) because her 130 days were up, she thought she had been underground only about 60 days (Associated Press, 1989; Toufexis et al., 1989).

Biological Clocks

Stefania was asked to live in a cave, so researchers could study her biological clocks.

Biological clocks are internal timing devices that are genetically set to regulate various physiological responses for different periods of time.

Biological clocks can be set for hours (secretion of urine), for a single day (rise and fall in internal body temperature), or for many days (women's 28-day menstrual cycle). We are interested in a biological clock that is set for a single day and produces what is called a circadian *(sir-KAY-dee-un)* rhythm (*circa* means "about"; *diem* means "day").

A **circadian rhythm** refers to a biological clock that is genetically programmed to regulate physiological responses within a time period of 24 hours (about one day).

You are most familiar with the circadian rhythm that regulates your sleep-wake cycle. In previous studies, when researchers removed all time cues (light, clock, radio, television) from cave dwellers like Stefania, the circadian clock day was believed to lengthen from 24 hours to about 25 hours (Young, 2000). However, in a better-controlled study, researchers reported that the sleep-wake circadian clock is genetically set for a day lasting an average of 24 hours and 18 minutes (Czeisler et al., 1999). The biological circadian sleep-wake clock is located in a group of cells in the brain's suprachiasmatic *(SUE-pra-kye-as-MAT-ick)* nucleus (Lee-Chiong, 2008; Wallisch, 2008).

The **suprachiasmatic nucleus** is a biological clock that uses light entering the eyes to regulate a number of circadian rhythms, including the sleep-wake cycle.

Because your circadian clock is genetically set for about 24 hours, 18 minutes, the regulation process involves it being reset each day to match our agreed-upon 24-hour-long day. The resetting stimulus is morning sunlight, which stimulates light-detecting cells in the eye's retina (see p. 110) (Purves et al., 2008). These *retinal cells,* which are involved in sensing the amount of light and are not involved in seeing, send electrical signals to the brain's circadian clock and reset it by about 18 minutes each day (Purves et al., 2008).

Suprachiasmatic nucleus   **Optic nerve**

If your circadian clock is not properly reset each day, it may result in problems getting to sleep, getting over jet lag, and adjusting to working the night shift (see next page).

Length of Day

24 hr, 18 min Body's circadian clock	24 hr Industrial world's clock

Circadian Preference

Explore why some people are early birds while others are night owls.

▶ **LO5** Discuss circadian problems and treatment.

Circadian Problems and Treatments

For most of the industrial world, a day is agreed to be exactly 24 hours long, but for your genetically set sleep-wake circadian clock, a day is about 24 hours and 18 minutes. The daily resetting of our sleep-wake clocks usually occurs automatically. However, if our circadian clocks are not properly reset, we may experience decreased cognitive performance, work-related and traffic accidents, jet lag, and various sleep disorders (Aamodt & Wang, 2008; Wright, 2002).

Shift Workers

Staying awake when your sleep-wake clock calls for sleep results in decreased performance in cognitive and motor skills (Drummond, 2000). For example, employees who work the graveyard shift (about 1 to 8 A.M.) experience the highest number of accidents, reaching their lowest point, or "dead zone," at about 5 A.M., when it is very difficult to stay alert (Stutts et al., 2002).

The reason shift workers and late-night drivers have more accidents is their sleep-wake clocks have prepared their bodies for sleep, which means they feel sleepy, and are less attentive and alert (Ohayon et al., 2002).

© Philip Rostron/Masterfile

Jet Lag

If you flew from west coast to east coast, you experienced a 3-hour time difference and most likely had jet lag.

Jet lag is the experience of fatigue, lack of concentration, and reduced cognitive skills that occurs when travelers' biological circadian clocks are out of step, or synchrony, with the external clock times at their new locations.

Generally, it takes about one day to reset your circadian clock for each hour of time change. Consider how severe jet lag can be for flight attendants who frequently make long trips.

Next, you'll see how researchers are studying ways to more effectively reset our biological clocks.

Unless otherwise noted, all images are © Cengage Learning

Resetting Clock

Researcher Charles Czeisler (1994) spent 10 years convincing his colleagues that light could reset circadian clocks. After he finally succeeded, other researchers used his and their own research to obtain patents for light therapy (Nowak, 1994).

Light therapy is the use of bright artificial light to reset circadian clocks and to combat the insomnia and drowsiness that plague shift workers and jet-lag sufferers. It also helps people with sleeping disorders in which the body fails to stay in time with the external environment.

For example, researchers report that workers who had been exposed to bright light and then shifted to night work showed improvement in alertness, performance, and job satisfaction (Czeisler et al., 1995). Exposure to bright light at certain times reset the workers' suprachiasmatic nucleus and resulted in a closer match between their internal circadian clocks and their external shifted clock times.

Light therapy has enormous potential for resetting our sleep-wake clocks, and it has also been used to treat depression (Bower, 2005; Tompkins, 2003a, 2003b).

Melatonin

The discovery of a use for melatonin has been a big scientific breakthrough (Kraft, 2007).

Melatonin is a hormone that is secreted by the pineal gland, a group of cells located in the center of the human brain. Melatonin secretion increases with darkness and decreases with light.

The suprachiasmatic nucleus regulates the secretion of melatonin, which plays a role in the regulation of circadian rhythms and in promoting sleep.

Although early testimonials and studies claimed melatonin reduced jet lag, a later double-blind study reported that melatonin was no better than a placebo in reducing jet lag (Spitzer et al., 1999). However, melatonin helped individuals with medical problems resulting from chronically disrupted circadian clocks sleep better and experience less fatigue (Nagtegaal et al., 2000).

Next, we'll examine what happens inside the brain and body during the different stages of sleep.

Pineal gland

Circadian Sleep–Wake Clock

Learn how the sleep–wake clock is affected by the 24-hour night–day cycle.

Seasonal Affective Disorder

Learn about seasonal affective disorder.

Check Your Learning Quiz 4.3

Go to **login.cengagebrain.com** and take the online quiz.

▶ **LO6** Describe the stages of sleep and their sequence during a night of sleep.

The first thing to know about sleep is that your brain never totally sleeps but is active throughout the night. To track your brain's activity during sleep, researchers would attach dozens of tiny wires or electrodes to your scalp and body and record electrical brain activity as you passed through the stages of sleep.

The **stages of sleep** refer to distinctive changes in the electrical activity of the brain and accompanying physiological responses of the body that occur as you pass through different phases of sleep.

As shown in the graph to the right, brain waves are described in terms of frequency (speed) and amplitude (height). They are recorded by a complex machine called an EEG, or electroencephalogram. Each stage of sleep can be recognized by its distinctive pattern of EEGs, which we'll explain here.

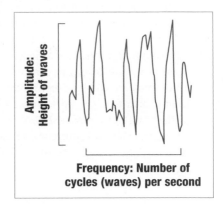

Alpha Stage

Before actually going into the first stage of sleep, you briefly pass through a relaxed and drowsy state, marked by characteristic alpha waves.

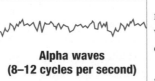

Alpha waves (8–12 cycles per second)

The **alpha stage** is marked by feelings of being relaxed and drowsy, usually with the eyes closed. Alpha waves have low amplitude and high frequency (8 to 12 cycles per second).

After spending a brief time relaxing in the alpha stage, you enter stage 1 of non-REM sleep.

Non-REM Sleep

The second thing to know about sleep is that it is divided into two major categories, called non-REM and REM. (REM stands for rapid eye movement.) We'll discuss non-REM first.

Non-REM sleep is where you spend approximately 80% of your sleep time. Non-REM is divided into sleep stages 1, 2, 3, and 4; each stage is identified by a particular pattern of brain waves and physiological responses.

You begin in sleep stage 1 and gradually enter stages 2, 3, and 4.

Stage 1 sleep is a transition from wakefulness to sleep and lasts from 1 to 7 minutes. In it, you gradually lose responsiveness to stimuli and experience drifting thoughts and images. Stage 1 is marked by the presence of theta waves, which are lower in amplitude and frequency than alpha waves.

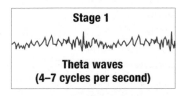

Stage 1

Theta waves
(4–7 cycles per second)

Although stage 1 is usually labeled a sleep stage, some individuals who are aroused from it feel as if they have been awake. Next, you enter stage 2 sleep, which is the first stage of what researchers call real sleep.

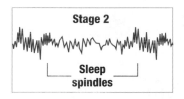

Stage 2

Sleep spindles

Stage 2 sleep marks the beginning of what we know as sleep, since subjects who are awakened in stage 2 report having been asleep. EEG tracings show high-frequency bursts of brain activity called sleep spindles.

As you pass through stage 2, your muscle tension, heart rate, respiration, and body temperature gradually decrease, and it becomes more difficult for you to be awakened. About 30 to 45 minutes after drifting off into sleep, you pass through stage 3 and then enter into stage 4 sleep.

Stage 4 sleep, which is also called slow-wave or delta sleep, is characterized by waves of very high amplitude and very low frequency, called delta waves.

As you pass through stages 3 and 4, your muscle tension, heart rate, respiration, and temperature decrease still further. Stage 4 is often considered to be the deepest stage of sleep because it is the most difficult from which to be awakened.

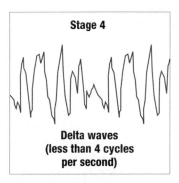

Stage 4

Delta waves
(less than 4 cycles
per second)

REM Sleep

We have discussed one major category of sleep, non-REM; we now move on to the second major category of sleep, which goes by the initials REM.

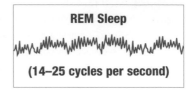

REM Sleep

(14–25 cycles per second)

REM sleep makes up the remaining 20% of your sleep time. It stands for rapid-eye-movement sleep because your eyes move rapidly back and forth behind closed lids. REM brain waves have high frequency and low amplitude. During REM sleep, your body is physiologically very aroused, but all your voluntary muscles are paralyzed. REM sleep is highly associated with dreaming.

You pass into REM sleep about five or six times throughout the night with about 30 to 90 minutes between periods. You remain in each period of REM sleep for 15 to 45 minutes and then pass back into non-REM sleep.

Characteristics of REM Sleep

When REM sleep was first discovered in the early 1950s, researchers found it difficult to believe their unusual findings: Although you are asleep during REM, your body and brain are in a general state of physiological arousal (Aserinsky & Kleitman, 1953). For example, during REM sleep, your heart rate and blood pressure are significantly higher than during non-REM sleep (Rosenthal, 2006).

Because of this strange combination of being asleep yet physiologically aroused, REM sleep is often called *paradoxical sleep*. (A *paradox* is something with contradictory qualities.)

Another unusual feature of REM sleep is that its brain waves are very similar to those recorded when a person is wide awake and alert. By looking at brain-wave recordings alone, researchers cannot tell whether a person is in REM sleep or wide awake. Only the additional recording of rapid eye movements indicates the occurrence of REM sleep.

Although many physiological responses are greatly increased, you completely lose the muscle tension in your neck and limbs so you are essentially paralyzed. However, involuntary muscles that regulate heart, lungs, and other organs continue to function. Researchers think humans evolved muscle paralysis of their limbs during REM sleep so they would not act out violent dreams by running, fighting, or jumping about and injuring themselves (Schenck, 2003). In fact, this actually happens in REM behavior disorder.

In **REM behavior disorder,** which usually occurs in older people, voluntary muscles are not paralyzed, and sleepers can and do act out their dreams, such as fighting off attackers in dreams.

People with this condition have been known to break a hand, punch a wall, or hurt a spouse (Seppa, 2009).

Dreaming

One of the biggest breakthroughs in dream research was the finding that about 80 to 90% of the times when subjects are awakened from a REM period, they report having vivid, complex, and relatively long dreams (Dement, 1999). In contrast, only about 10% of subjects awakened from non-REM sleep report similar kinds of dreams.

One of the first questions asked was what happens when people are deprived of REM sleep and dreaming. Many subjects have been deprived of REM sleep and dreaming without showing any major behavioral or physiological effects (Bonnet, 2005). However, suppressing REM sleep does produce a phenomenon called REM rebound.

REM rebound refers to individuals spending an increased percentage of time in REM sleep if they were deprived of REM sleep on the previous nights.

The occurrence of REM rebound suggests a need for REM sleep, and one such need involves memory. Researchers concluded that REM sleep helps us store or encode information in memory, and they advise students to get a good night's sleep so that what they studied the previous day has a chance to be stored in the brain's memory (Stickgold, 2000, 2005).

Although you now have an overview of the different sleep stages, you may be surprised to discover that how you go through the different stages is somewhat like riding a roller coaster.

Sleep Dangers: Sleep Violence

Explore whether it is possible to unintentionally act in a violent manner during deep sleep.

Sequence of Stages

When you go to sleep at night, you may think that you simply sleep for 8 hours, perhaps toss and turn a little, and even do some dreaming. But sleep is not one unbroken state; rather, it is a series of recurring stages, similar to the ups and downs of a rollercoaster ride. Researchers have studied and plotted changes in brain waves, physiological arousal, and dreaming as subjects progressed through the stages of sleep (Rosenthal, 2006).

We'll describe a typical night's pattern for George, a college sophomore, who goes to bed about 11 P.M. and gets up about 7 A.M. As we take you through the figure below, notice that non-REM sleep is indicated by the wide blue line and REM sleep is indicated by red inserts. The numbers 1 to 4 refer to sleep stages 1, 2, 3, and 4 of non-REM sleep, which we discussed earlier.

As you review the figure below to learn the sequence of sleep stages, read the following page to understand what happens to George as he goes through the different stages of sleep.

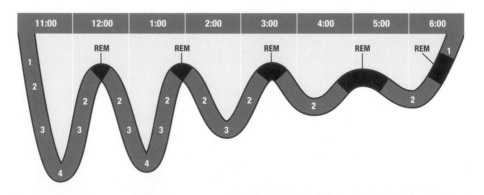

What Happens to George as He Sleeps Throughout the Night?

As George becomes drowsy, he will enter non-REM stage 1, which is the transition between being awake and asleep.

As sleep progresses, he will continue to the next stage, non-REM stage 2, which is the first stage of real sleep. During stage 2, he may experience short, fragmented thoughts, so that if he is awakened, he may think he was dreaming.

He will continue through non-REM stage 3 and finally reach non-REM stage 4. When George enters non-REM stage 4, which is slow-wave, or delta, sleep, he will be very difficult to waken. After staying in stage 4 for some minutes to an hour, he will backtrack to stages 3 and then 2.

After George reaches non-REM stage 2, he does not awaken but rather enters REM sleep. He will remain in REM for 15 to 45 minutes and, if awakened, will likely report dreaming. When in REM, his body is in a high state of physiological arousal, but his voluntary limb muscles are essentially paralyzed. If George experiences night-mares during REM, he will not act them out or injure himself because he cannot move.

After the REM period, he goes back through non-REM stages 2, 3, and 4. It is during stage 4 that George may sleepwalk, sleeptalk, or perform other activities, such as partially awakening to turn off the alarm, pull up the covers, or get up and go to the bathroom. However, George will remember nothing of what happens in non-REM stage 4, such as sleeptalking with his roommate or walking to the kitchen and getting a snack. He will remain in stage 4 for a period of time before again backtracking to non-REM stages 3 and 2, and then to his second REM period of the night.

Like George, we may go in and out of REM sleep five or six times, with REM periods becoming longer toward morning.

Like George, we all go through the sleep stages in about the same sequence.

Awakening

A short time after awakening from sleep, we enter a state of being awake and alert. This state has distinctive brain activity called beta waves (right figure), which are characterized by high frequency and low amplitude and are very similar to those waves observed during REM sleep.

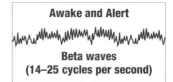

Awake and Alert

Beta waves
(14–25 cycles per second)

Sleep Lab

Observe how researchers study people's sleep patterns.

Sleep Cycles

Observe the physiological and behavioral changes that occur during the stages of sleep.

Check Your Learning Quiz 4.4

Go to **login.cengagebrain.com** and take the online quiz.

▶ **LO7** Discuss how much sleep a typical person needs.

▶ **LO8** Explain theories of why we sleep.

▶ **LO9** Describe what happens when we miss sleep.

Students usually ask three questions about sleep: How much sleep do I need? Why do I sleep? What happens if I go without sleep? We'll discuss each of these questions in turn.

How Much Sleep Do I Need?

Overall, adults in America sleep an average of about 8 hours a night (NSF, 2008). Beginning at birth and continuing through old age, there is a gradual change in the total time we spend sleeping, the percentage of time we spend in REM sleep, and the kinds of sleep problems we have.

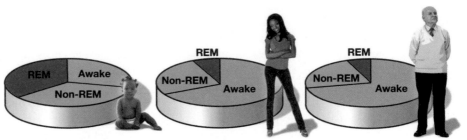

Infancy & Childhood

From infancy to adolescence, the amount of sleep time and the percentage spent in REM decline. For example, a newborn sleeps about 17 hours a day, and 50% of that time is spent in REM; a 4-year-old sleeps about 10 hours a day, and 25% to 30% of that time is spent in REM.

Adolescence & Adulthood

Compared to adults, adolescents need more sleep (about 9 hours) and their circadian clocks favor going to bed later and getting up later (Hathaway, 2006; MFMER, 2005). At about age 20, adolescents adopt the sleep pattern of adults, which is to get approximately 7 to 8 hours of sleep a night, with about 20% or less being REM sleep.

Old Age

Upon reaching our sixties, total sleep time drops to about 6.5 hours a day, but the percentage of REM sleep remains the same (20%) (Ropper & Samuels, 2009). In people over 55, 66% experience symptoms of a sleep problem (such as trouble getting to sleep), and they compensate by taking a daytime nap (NSF, 2003, 2005).

Why Do I Sleep?

Why we sleep remains one of the greatest mysteries of nature (Frank, 2006). We'll describe two currently popular theories—the repair and adaptive theories—of why we spend about one-third of each day asleep.

The **repair theory** suggests that activities during the day deplete key factors in our brain or body that are replenished or repaired by sleep. The repair theory says that sleep is primarily a restorative process.

Repair Theory

The **adaptive theory** suggests that sleep evolved because it prevented early humans and animals from wasting energy and exposing themselves to the dangers of nocturnal predators (Webb, 1992).

The adaptive and repair theories are not really at odds. Both have support but just focus on different reasons for sleep.

Adaptive Theory

What If I Go Without Sleep?

Lack of sleep has various effects on the body and the brain. Here is a brief sample of what happens when people are sleep deprived.

Sleep deprivation may compromise our immune system, which increases an individual's vulnerability to viral infections and may lead to inflammation-related diseases (Dement, 1999; Irwin et al., 2008). Also, sleep deprivation puts the body on alert, increasing production of stress hormones and elevating blood pressure, which are major risk factors for health conditions such as heart disease, stroke, and cancer (Stein, 2005a).

Sleep deprivation can deplete the brain's vital energy stores (glycogen) and interfere with completing tasks that require vigilance and concentration (Geiger, 2002; Ropper & Samuels, 2009). Also, sleep deprivation increases activity of the emotional centers of the brain, leading to irritability, and interferes with the ability to make rational or logical decisions (Yoo et al., 2007).

Sleep-Deprived Doctors

Learn about the effects of sleep deprivation on the bodies and brains of doctors.

Check Your Learning Quiz 4.5

Go to **login.cengagebrain.com** and take the online quiz.

▶ **LO10** Describe and differentiate the major theories of dream interpretation.

Theories of Dream Interpretation

Everyone dreams, but what do dreams mean? It seems the majority of people believe dreams have meaning, but how does one go about interpreting dreams? We'll discuss three currently popular psychological theories of dream interpretation, beginning with the most famous and still controversial theory, Freud's theory of dream interpretation.

Freud's Theory of Dream Interpretation

Before 1900, psychologists believed that dreams were meaningless and bizarre images. However, Sigmund Freud's theory changed all that when he said dreams were a way to reach our unconscious thoughts and desires.

Freud's theory of dreams says that we have a "censor" that protects us from realizing threatening and unconscious desires or wishes, especially those involving sex or aggression. To protect us from having threatening thoughts, the "censor" transforms our secret, guilt-ridden, and anxiety-provoking desires into harmless symbols that appear in our dreams and do not disturb our sleep or conscious thoughts.

Freud made two main points no one had made before: Dreams contain symbols that have meaning, and dreams can be interpreted. For example, Freud (1900) said long objects, such as sticks, umbrellas, and pencils, are male sex symbols; hollow things, such as caves, jars, and keyholes, are female sex symbols. Freud believed the task of a psychoanalyst (that is, a Freudian therapist) was to interpret dream symbols, which were "the royal road" to uncover a client's threatening but unconscious desires, needs, and emotions (Bower, 2001).

As you'll see next, many non-Freudian therapists disagree with Freud's idea that a dream's contents are necessarily symbols or disguised thoughts for threatening, unconscious wishes and desires (Domhoff, 2003).

Extensions of Waking Life

Many therapists believe that dreams are extensions of waking life (Kramer, 2006b; Pesant & Zadra, 2006).

The theory that **dreams are extensions of waking life** says that our dreams reflect the same thoughts, fears, concerns, problems, and emotions that we have when awake.

Therapist and researcher Rosalind Cartwright believes that patients suffering from depression or anxiety, for instance, cope by repeating their fears and concerns in their dreams. She advises that as soon as you awaken from a recurring bad dream, you should figure out why the dream is upsetting and then visualize how you would like the dream to end the next time it occurs. With practice, people can gain control over recurring bad dreams. Cartwright concludes there is little reason to pay attention to dreams unless they keep you from sleeping or cause you to wake up in a panic (Cartwright, 2002). In these cases, therapists find dream interpretation a useful tool in helping clients better understand the personal and emotional problems that are contributing to their bad dreams.

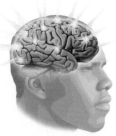

Activation-Synthesis Theory

In the late 1970s, psychiatrist and neurophysiologist J. Allan Hobson published a theory of dreams that disagreed with many existing theories, including Freud's theory of dreams. In 2002, Hobson published a revised version of his theory.

The **activation-synthesis theory** says that dreaming occurs because brain areas that provide reasoned cognitive control during the waking state are shut down. As a result, the sleeping brain is stimulated by random chemical and neural influences that result in hallucinations, high emotions, and bizarre thought patterns that we call dreams.

Unlike Freud, Hobson believes that dream interpretation is questionable, since there is no way to know whether dreams are just bizarre events or contain useful or valid information about a person's problems.

Typical Dreams

Explore what people typically dream about.

Check Your Learning Quiz 4.6

Go to **login.cengagebrain.com** and take the online quiz.

Types of Sleep Problems

In the United States, about 50 to 70 million people experience some kind of sleep problem (Gupta, 2006). For example, some adults have trouble going to or staying asleep (insomnia); some stop breathing in their sleep (sleep apnea); and some go from being wide awake to a very deep sleep quickly and without warning (narcolepsy) (Carskadon, 2006). We'll discuss a number of these sleep problems, as well as possible treatments, beginning with one of the more common problems, insomnia.

Insomnia

In the United States, about 33% of adults report some type of insomnia (Ohayon & Guilleminault, 2006).

Insomnia refers to difficulties in either going to sleep or staying asleep through the night. Insomnia is associated with a number of daytime complaints, including fatigue, impairment of concentration, memory difficulty, and lack of well-being.

Common psychological causes of insomnia include experiencing an overload of stressful events, worrying about personal or job-related difficulties, grieving over a loss or death, and coping with mental health problems. For many middle-aged working people, job stress is a major cause of insomnia and other sleep problems (Kalimo et al., 2000). For students, common causes of insomnia are worry about exams, personal problems, and changes in sleep schedule, such as staying up late Saturday night and sleeping late on Sunday morning. Then, on Sunday night, students are not tired at the usual time and may experience insomnia.

Common physiological causes of insomnia include changing to night-shift work, which upsets circadian rhythms, having medical problems or chronic pain, and abusing alcohol or other substances (such as sedatives).

There are effective treatments for bouts of insomnia, including nondrug (establishing an optimal sleep pattern) and drug treatments (benzodiazepines and nonbenzodiazepines).

Sleep Apnea

In the United States, about 20 million adults have insomnia because they stop breathing, a problem called sleep apnea.

Sleep apnea refers to repeated periods during sleep when a person stops breathing for 10 seconds or longer. The person may repeatedly stop breathing, momentarily wake up, resume breathing, and return to sleep. Repeated awakenings leave the person exhausted during the day but not knowing the cause of the tiredness.

The chances of developing sleep apnea increase if a person is an intense snorer, is overweight, uses alcohol, or takes sedatives (such as benzodiazepines) (Chokroverty, 2000). Some people with sleep apnea may wake up an astonishing 200 to 400 times a night, which also results in insomnia (Czeisler et al., 2006).

The simplest treatment is to sew tennis balls into the back of a pajama top so the person cannot lie on his or her back, which increases the chances of sleep apnea. For more severe cases, the most effective therapy is a device that blows air into a mask worn over the nose, which helps keep air passages open (right photo).

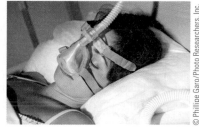

© Philipe Garo/Photo Researchers, Inc.

Narcolepsy

As a child, Rainer would nod off in classes. As an adult, he may fall asleep in the middle of a meeting, during a conversation, or while driving! He has fleeting urges to sleep throughout the day and always feels fatigued (Marschall, 2007). Rainer has narcolepsy.

Narcolepsy *(NAR-ko-lep-see)* is a chronic disorder that is marked by excessive sleepiness, usually in the form of sleep attacks or short periods of sleep throughout the day. The sleep attacks are accompanied by brief periods of REM sleep and loss of muscle control, which may be triggered by big emotional changes.

Narcoleptics describe their sleep attacks as irresistible. They report falling asleep in inappropriate places, such during an important meeting with their boss. In many cases, these sleep attacks make it difficult for narcoleptics to lead normal lives.

Researchers believe that a hypocretin-based medicine could soon be on the market and provide a new and effective way to treat narcolepsy, which affects about 150,000 Americans (Marschall, 2007).

Insomnia Treatment: Nondrug and Drug

Learn about the non-drug and drug treatments for insomnia.

Narcolepsy in Dogs

Explore how studying narcolepsy in dogs leads to improved treatment of this disorder in humans.

Curing Insomnia

Watch how a non-drug treatment is used to treat insomnia.

▸ **L012** Describe other sleep disturbances, including night terrors, nightmares, sleeptalking, and sleepwalking.

Night Terrors

A 4-year-old girl sits up in the night and begins screaming. This is an example of a night terror.

Night terrors, which occur during stage 3 or 4 (delta sleep), are frightening experiences that often start with a piercing scream, followed by sudden waking in a fearful state with rapid breathing and increased heart rate. However, the next morning the child has no memory of the frightening experience. About 3% to 7% of children have night terrors.

A child in the grip of night terrors is difficult to calm and, even if severely shaken, may need several minutes to regain full awareness. Night terrors are most common in children aged 5 to 7 and usually disappear by adolescence (Heussler, 2005). Caregivers should take enough time to comfort and soothe the frightened child, who usually will go back to sleep.

Nightmares

Besides night terrors, about 25% to 70% of children aged 3 to 6 have nightmares, and 47% of college students report having them once a month (Picchioni et al., 2002).

Nightmares, which occur during REM sleep, are very frightening and anxiety-producing images that occur during dreaming. Nightmares usually involve great danger, such as being attacked, injured, or pursued. Upon awakening, the person can usually describe the nightmare in great detail.

Nightmares usually stop when the person wakes, but feelings of anxiety or fear may persist for some time; it may be difficult to go back to sleep. One effective treatment for nightmares involves psychotherapy. A therapist may help clients better understand the personal and emotional problems contributing to their bad dreams or guide clients through imagery rehearsal to help them envision a positive outcome to the recurring bad dream (Cartwright, 2002; Kershaw, 2010).

Sleeptalking

Anyone can experience sleeptalking, but the condition is more common in males and children.

Sleeptalking, which can occur during any stage of sleep, usually occurs in non-REM sleep and involves talking during sleep without being aware of it.

Sleeptalking can range from mumbling gibberish to rather complicated speech. Interestingly, the voices and the type of language people use during sleeptalking may sound very different from their wakeful speech. Sleeptalking may be spontaneous or induced by conversation with the sleeper. We must note that as much as some of us may wish to ask someone who sleeptalks questions while they're asleep, we can't be sure their answers to our questions are really true, as these individuals have no awareness of what they are saying.

Sleeptalking is not physically harmful, but as you can imagine, it can cause embarrassment and can annoy a bed partner or roommate. There isn't really any treatment for sleep talking; those who fear possible embarassment often avoid situations where others may hear them talk during their sleep (NSF, 2010).

Sleepwalking

One of the more unusual sleep disturbances is sleepwalking.

Sleepwalking usually occurs in stage 3 or 4 (delta sleep) and consists of walking while literally sound asleep. Sleepwalkers generally have poor coordination, are clumsy but can avoid objects, can engage in limited conversation, and have no memory of sleepwalking.

Occasional sleepwalking is considered normal in children; frequent sleepwalking in adults may be caused by increased stress, sleep deprivation, or mental problems (Cartwright, 2006). Sleepwalking can be a serious problem because of the potential for injury and harm to oneself and others (imagine sleepwalking out of the house onto the highway). As such, if you see someone sleepwalking, you should gently guide him or her back to bed. You won't cause harm by doing so; in fact, you may be keeping the person away from danger.

© Laurent/Bouhier/Age fotostock

Nightmare Treatment

Learn how imagery rehearsal helps people escape terrifying nightmares.

Check Your Learning Quiz 4.7

Go to **login.cengagebrain.com** and take the online quiz.

▶ **L013** Define hypnosis and explain hypnotic induction.

Background of Hypnosis

In the late 1700s, Anton Mesmer was the hit of Paris, France, as he claimed to cure a variety of symptoms by passing a force into a patient's body; he called this force animal magnetism. So many patients testified to the success of animal magnetism as a treatment that a committee of the French Academy of Science was appointed to investigate. The committee concluded that many of Mesmer's patients were indeed cured of various psychosomatic problems (real physical problems with no physical causes). However, the committee thought it safer to ban the future use of animal magnetism because they could neither identify what it was nor verify Mesmer's claims that such a force existed (Shermer, 2002). Mesmer's name lives on in our vocabulary: We use the term *mesmerized* to describe someone who is acting strangely because he or she has been spellbound or hypnotized.

Today we know that Mesmer was not creating animal magnetism but rather was inducing hypnosis. Here's the definition agreed to by the American Psychological Association's Division of Psychological Hypnosis (1993):

Hypnosis is a procedure in which a researcher, clinician, or hypnotist suggests that a person will experience changes in sensations, perceptions, thoughts, feelings, or behaviors.

We'll begin by answering three questions that are often asked about hypnosis. Then, we'll discuss a heated debate surrounding hypnosis (what happens when a person is hypnotized). We'll also discuss how hypnosis can influence behaviors.

Who Can Be Hypnotized?

Despite what you may have seen on television or at a stage show, not everyone can be easily hypnotized. There is considerable variation in susceptibility to being hypnotized: About 20% of adults have low susceptibility to hypnosis, which means that they cannot be easily hypnotized. About 65% to 70% of adults have medium susceptibility, and the remaining 10% to 15% have high susceptibility to being hypnotized (Song, 2006a; Spiegal, 2005). The one trait that is highly correlated with susceptibility to hypnosis is a remarkable ability to respond to imaginative suggestions (Kirsch & Braffman, 2001).

Who Is Susceptible?

The standard test for susceptibility is to hypnotize a person and then give a fixed set of suggestions (Weitzenhoffer, 2002). For instance, the person in the right picture is carrying out the hypnotic suggestion, "Your right arm is weightless and moving up." Individuals who score high on the standard test are usually easily hypnotized (Nash, 2001).

How Is Someone Hypnotized?

Although different procedures are used, most use some of the following suggestions for hypnotic induction.

Hypnotic induction refers to inducing hypnosis by first asking a person to either stare at an object or close his or her eyes and then suggesting that the person is becoming very relaxed.

For example, here is a commonly used method for hypnotic induction:

1. The hypnotist creates a sense of trust, so that the individual feels comfortable.
2. The hypnotist suggests that the subject concentrate on something, such as the sound of the hypnotist's voice, an object, or an image.
3. The hypnotist suggests what the subject will experience during hypnosis (for example, becoming relaxed, feeling sleepy, or having a floating feeling). The hypnotist may say, "I am going to count from one to ten, and with each count you will drift more and more deeply into hypnosis" (Bates, 1994).

This procedure works on both individuals and groups, provided the individuals are all susceptible to hypnosis.

Theories of Hypnosis

The explanation of hypnosis has changed significantly over the past 40 years. Early on, being hypnotized was believed to put a person into a trancelike state. In the late 1990s, some believed that being hypnotized put individuals into an altered state of consciousness. More recently, researchers believe that some individuals, hypnotized or not, have the amazing ability to respond to imaginative suggestions (Lynn et al., 2007a). We'll discuss these two views of hypnosis.

Altered State Theory of Hypnosis

Perhaps hypnosis puts people into an altered or disconnected state (Naish, 2006).

The **altered state theory of hypnosis** holds that hypnosis puts a person into an altered state of consciousness, during which the person is disconnected from reality and so is able to experience and respond to various suggestions (Nash, 2001).

For example, individuals were hypnotized and given suggestions that their raised hands were getting heavy or that they would feel no pain. When no longer hypnotized, these individuals said, "My hand became heavy and moved down by itself" or "Suddenly I found myself feeling no pain" (Nash, 2001, p. 49). Well-published hypnosis researcher Michael Nash believes hypnosis disconnects an individual from reality, so the individual does things without conscious intent. Nash states that with hypnosis, scientists can temporarily create hallucinations, false memories, and delusions (for example, a bee buzzing around your head).

© Will & Deni McIntyre/
Photo Researchers, Inc.

Sociocognitive Theory of Hypnosis

Perhaps hypnosis is possible because of personal abilities and social pressures, which could be explained by the sociocognitive theory (Lynn, 2007).

The **sociocognitive theory of hypnosis** says that behaviors observed during hypnosis result not from being hypnotized, but rather from having the special ability of responding to imaginative suggestions and social pressures (Kirsch & Braffman, 2001).

Psychologist Irving Kirsch, who has published more than 85 articles on hypnosis, found that all the phenomena produced during hypnosis have also occurred in subjects who were not hypnotized.

Recent research supports that hypnosis occurs mostly as a result of people's expectations about hypnosis, rather than due to an altered hypnotic state.

Unless otherwise noted, all images are © Cengage Learning

Behaviors

Stage hypnotists can get volunteers to perform a variety of unusual behaviors, such as pretending they are chickens or singing like Elvis. We'll discuss some of the unusual behaviors that can be experienced through hypnosis.

Hypnosis has long been known to reduce pain; this is called hypnotic analgesia.

NO PAIN

Hypnotic analgesia *(an-nall-GEEZ-ee-ah)* refers to a reduction in pain reported by clients after they have undergone hypnosis and received suggestions that reduce their anxiety and promote relaxation.

"When you wake up, you will not remember what happened." This suggestion is used to produce posthypnotic amnesia.

DON'T REMEMBER

Posthypnotic amnesia is not remembering what happened during hypnosis if the hypnotist suggested that, upon awakening, the person would forget what took place during hypnosis.

When a hypnotized subject responds to a suggestion such as "Try to swat that fly," he or she is responding to an imagined perception.

An **imagined perception** refers to experiencing sensations, perceiving stimuli, or performing behaviors that come from one's imagination.

Aside from being used in entertainment, serious and legitimate uses of hypnosis can be found in medical, dental, and therapeutic settings. For example, hypnosis has been successful in reducing pain, fear, and anxiety associated with medical and dental procedures (Patterson & Jensen, 2003).

Researchers agree hypnotized subjects are not faking their responses but seem to actually experience such behaviors as hypnotic analgesia, posthypnotic amnesia, and imagined perception. But researchers disagree about why these behaviors occur. Some researchers believe these behaviors occur because hypnosis puts people into an altered state. Others believe that individuals who are highly susceptible to hypnosis have a trait called imaginative suggestibility, which allows them to focus and carry out suggestions, whether or not they are hypnotized.

Next, we'll discuss the use, abuse, and effects of drugs.

Theories of Hypnosis

Explore why a person would get on stage and imitate Elvis after being hypnotized.

Hypnosis and Surgery Pain

Watch how hypnosis can help reduce pain in people undergoing surgery.

Weight Loss Hypnosis

Watch how hypnosis may be able to help people lose weight.

Check Your Learning Quiz 4.8

Go to **login.cengagebrain.com** and take the online quiz.

> ▶ **LO17** Define addiction, tolerance, dependency, and withdrawal symptoms.

Overview of Psychoactive Drugs

For the past 6,000 years, humans have used legal and illegal drugs, and current usage continues to increase as do drug-related problems. For example, Americans spend over $150 billion a year on legal and illegal drugs, and the resulting problems—personal, medical, legal, and job related—cost society a whopping $500 billion a year (Volkow, 2007).

The reasons people use drugs include obtaining pleasure, joy, and euphoria; meeting social expectations; giving in to peer pressure; dealing with or escaping stress, anxiety, and tension; avoiding pain; and achieving altered states of consciousness (Goldberg, 2010).

In the sections that follow, we'll discuss stimulants, opiates, marijuana, hallucinogens, alcohol, and other commonly used psychoactive drugs.

Psychoactive drugs are chemicals that affect our nervous systems and, as a result, may alter consciousness and awareness; influence how we sense and perceive things; and modify our moods, feelings, emotions, and thoughts. Psychoactive drugs are both licit (legal drugs such as coffee, alcohol, and tobacco) and illicit (illegal drugs such as marijuana, heroin, cocaine, and LSD).

We'll begin our overview of psychoactive drugs by defining four important terms related to drug use and abuse: addiction, tolerance, dependency, and withdrawal symptoms. We'll then discuss the various ways drugs affect the nervous system.

Unless otherwise noted, all images are © Cengage Learning

© Craig Cozart//iStockphoto

Definition of Terms

One reason people continue to use drugs, even after their drug use has resulted in serious negative consequences affecting relationships with others or physical health, is they have an addiction.

Addiction refers to a behavioral pattern of drug abuse that is marked by an overwhelming and compulsive desire to obtain and use the drug; even after stopping, the person has a strong tendency to relapse and begin using the drug again.

The reason people may relapse after trying to give up their drug use is because of their addiction. As their drug use continues, people may develop a tolerance.

Tolerance means that after a person uses a drug repeatedly over a period of time, the original dose of the drug no longer produces the desired effect, so that a person must take increasingly larger doses of the drug to achieve the same behavioral effect.

Becoming tolerant is a sign that a person has developed a drug dependency.

Dependency refers to a change in the nervous system so that a person now needs to take the drug to prevent the occurrence of painful withdrawal symptoms.

Addiction and dependency combine to make stopping doubly difficult.

Being dependent on a drug typically results in withdrawal symptoms if the person stops using the drug.

Withdrawal symptoms are painful physical and psychological symptoms that occur after a drug-dependent person stops using the drug.

The types of withdrawal symptoms that individuals may experience depend on the specific drug they stopped using. Examples of withdrawal aysmptoms include depression, anxiety, sweating, hot and cold flashes, nausea, muscle tremors, stomach cramps. headaches, and disturbances in appetite and sleep, to name a few.

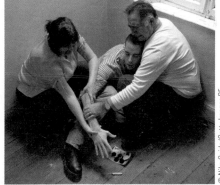

© Niko Guido/Getty Images RF

Next, you'll learn how psychoactive drugs alter one's consciousess, emotions, and thoughts by affecting the brain's communication network.

▶ **LO18** Discuss how drugs affect the nervous system.

▶ **LO19** Discuss the effects that stimulants, opiates, hallucinogens, and alcohol, have on the body and behavior.

Effects on Nervous System

We'll discuss ways that drugs affect the nervous system and activate the brain's reward/pleasure center to cause addiction and dependency.

Drugs Affect Neurotransmitters

As you learned in Chapter 2, your nervous system makes neurotransmitters that act like chemical messengers. After neurons release neurotransmitters, they act like chemical keys that search for and then either open or close chemical locks to either excite or inhibit neighboring neurons, organs, or muscles. For example, morphine's chemical structure closely resembles that of the neurotransmitter

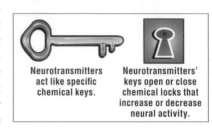

Neurotransmitters act like specific chemical keys.

Neurotransmitters' keys open or close chemical locks that increase or decrease neural activity.

endorphin (see p. 127). As a result of this similarity, morphine acts like, or mimics, endorphin by affecting the same chemical locks, decreasing pain. Thus, some drugs produce their effects by *mimicking* the way neurotransmitters work (Ropper & Samuels, 2009).

After being excited, neurons secrete neurotransmitters, which move across a tiny space (synapse) and affect neighboring neurons' receptors. However, after a brief period, the neurotransmitters are reabsorbed back into the neuron. The action by which neurotransmitters are removed from the synapse through reabsorption is called *reuptake.* If reuptake did not occur, neurotransmitters would remain in the synapse, and neurons would be continuously stimulated. Thus, some drugs block reuptake, which leads to increased neural stimulation that causes increased arousal (Mendelson et al., 2006).

Drugs Affect Brain's Reward/Pleasure Center

Many drugs activate the brain's *reward/pleasure center.* This center includes the nucleus accumbens and ventral tegmental area (right figure) and involves the neurotransmitter dopamine (Saey, 2008a). These drugs produce their effects by directly activating the brain's reward/pleasure center. The reward/pleasure center is also activated when one eats a favorite food, has sex, and does other pleasurable activities (Higgins, 2008).

Next, we'll examine several frequently used drugs.

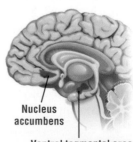

Nucleus accumbens

Ventral tegmental area

Stimulants

Stimulants are psychoactive drugs that increase activity of the central nervous system and result in heightened alertness, arousal, euphoria, and decreased appetite.

The more widely used stimulants include amphetamines, cocaine, caffeine, and nicotine. Dose for dose, amphetamines and cocaine are considered powerful stimulants because they produce a strong effect with a small dose; caffeine and nicotine are considered mild stimulants. We'll discuss each of these stimulants.

Amphetamines

Methamphetamine production is an enormous concern for U.S. law enforcement, who each year raid thousands of illegal crystal methamphetamine laboratories and collect nearly 4,000 lbs of methamphetamine (DEA, 2009). Recent reports estimate that methamphetamine costs U.S. society at least $23 billion a year (Nicosia et al., 2009).

© NY Daily News via Getty Images

Methamphetamine (D-methamphetamine) is close to amphetamine in both its chemical makeup and its physical and psychological effects. Unlike amphetamine, which is taken in pill form, methamphetamine (meth, speed, crank, crystal, ice) can be smoked or snorted and produces an almost instantaneous high.

The primary effect of amphetamines and related drugs (methamphetamine) is to increase the release of the neurotransmitter dopamine and also to block its reuptake, which causes very pleasurable feelings (Bamford et al., 2008). Both amphetamine and methamphetamine cause marked increases in blood pressure and heart rate and produce feelings of enhanced mood, alertness, and energy. However, both have a high risk for addiction and dependency.

The use of amphetamines is dangerous because the initial euphoria is replaced with depression, agitation, insomnia, and true paranoid feelings. Long-term risks include stroke, liver damage, heart disease, memory loss, and extreme weight loss (Dickerson, 2007; Jefferson, 2005). Large doses of methamphetamine can overstimulate the brain, leading to severe convulsions and possibly death (Iversen, 2008).

Another powerful stimulant is cocaine, which we'll discuss next.

Stimulant: Amphetamine

See how amphetamine affects neurotransmitters.

Cocaine

Cocaine is currently a $35-billion-a-year illegal industry with about 1.9 million users (Brodzinsky, 2006; SAMHSA, 2009).

Cocaine, which comes from the leaves of the coca plant, can be sniffed or snorted, since it is absorbed by many of the body's membranes. If cocaine is changed into a highly concentrated form called crack, it can be smoked or injected and produces an instantaneous but short-lived high.

The primary effect of cocaine is to block reuptake of the neurotransmitter dopamine, which means that dopamine stays around longer to excite neighboring neurons (Mendelson et al., 2006). Interestingly though, researchers recently found that the effect of cocaine on our neural system is more complex: cocaine excites dopamine receptors to produce euphoria and glutamate receptors to produce a craving for more of the drug (Uys & LaLumiere, 2008).

In moderate doses, cocaine produces a short-acting high (10 to 30 minutes) that includes bursts of energy, arousal, and alertness. Users tend to believe they are thinking more clearly and performing better, but they overestimate the quality of their work. In large doses, cocaine can result in serious physical and psychological problems, including hallucinations and feelings of bugs crawling under the skin, as well as addiction. An overdose can lead to death (Paulozzi, 2006).

Many physical problems result from cocaine abuse, including lack of appetite, headaches, insomnia, irritability, heart attacks, strokes, seizures, damage to cartilage of the nose (if snorted), and increased risk of HIV (if injected). Also, respiratory failure, which may lead to sudden death, can result from relatively low doses (NIDA, 2006a).

Cocaine users often go through the vicious circle of feeling depressed as the effect wears off, wanting and using more cocaine to relieve the depression, and so on (Ropper & Samuels, 2009). Thus, heavy users often require professional help to break out of their addictive vicious circles (Lamberg, 2004).

Next, we turn to two legal drugs that are the most widely used stimulants: caffeine and nicotine.

Caffeine

Caffeine is the most widely used psychoactive drug in the world (Peng, 2008b). In the United States, 80% to 90% of people routinely consume caffeine, and 170 million are addicted to it (Gupta, 2007; Lemonick, 2007; Price, 2008a).

Caffeine is a mild stimulant and belongs to a group of chemicals called xanthines *(ZAN-thenes),* which have a number of effects. One effect is to block adenosine receptors in the brain, which results in stimulation and arousal (Keisler & Armsey, 2006). Caffeine produces physiological and psychological arousal, including decreased fatigue and drowsiness, feelings of alertness, and improved reaction times.

For 40% to 70% of people who abruptly stop the consumption of caffeine, especially medium to heavy doses, a number of uncomfortable withdrawal symptoms occur, such as headaches, fatigue, jitteriness, nausea, cramps, tremors, and sleeplessness (Gupta, 2007; Lemonick, 2007).

Nicotine

After caffeine, nicotine is the world's most widely used psychoactive drug (Julien, 2005). In the United States, 60 million people are active cigarette smokers, which is equivalent to 24% of the country's population (SAMHSA, 2009).

Nicotine is a stimulant because it triggers the production of dopamine, which is used by the brain's reward/pleasure center to produce good feelings. Nicotine also stops other cells from turning off the pleasure areas, so the overall result is a long-lasting good feeling (Mansvelder et al., 2003).

Nicotine has serious health consequences. Over 400,000 American smokers die each year from lung and heart problems (Price, 2008c). Also, secondhand smoke kills tens of thousands of nonsmokers a year (ALA, 2006; O'Neil, 2006).

Withdrawal symptoms include irritability, attentional deficits, cramps, sleep disturbances, increased appetite, and a strong craving to light up again (NIDA, 2006c).

Stimulant: Cocaine

See how cocaine affects neurotransmitters.

Does Caffeine Make You Smarter?

Learn whether caffeine has any effect on intellectual functioning.

© luchschen/Shutterstock

© K13 ART/Shutterstock

Opiates

In spite of restrictive laws and billions spent on enforcement, opiates are still readily available in most major U.S. cities (Schuckit, 2000). In fact, the production of illegal opiates has reached record levels (*Time,* 2007a).

Opiates are a group of narcotics made from the opium poppy (right photo) that depress the nervous system and provide euphoria, which is often described as a pleasurable state between waking and sleeping, and analgesia (pain reduction).

© Dr. Jeremy Burgess/Photo Researchers, Inc.

Opium, morphine, and heroin are all types of opiates and produce similar effects. But users generally prefer to inject heroin because then it reaches the brain more quickly and produces the biggest euphoric "rush."

Over the past 40 years, researchers have learned much about the effects of opiates on the nervous system. In the 1970s, researchers discovered that the brain has naturally occurring receptors for opiates (Pert et al., 1974). When morphine reaches the brain's receptors, it produces feelings of euphoria and analgesia.

It turns out that the brain not only has its own opiate receptors but also produces its own morphinelike chemicals. These chemicals, which function as neurotransmitters, are called *endorphins* and are found to have the same analgesic properties as morphine (Pleuvry, 2005).

After several weeks of regularly using opiates, a person's brain produces less of its own endorphins and relies more on the outside supply of opiates. As a result, a person becomes addicted to taking opiates and must administer one or more doses daily to prevent withdrawal symptoms.

Withdrawal symptoms, which include hot and cold flashes, sweating, muscle tremors, nausea, and stomach cramps, are not life threatening and last 5 to 8 days. An overdose of opiates depresses the neural control of breathing, and a person dies from respiratory failure (Mendelson et al., 2006).

Interestingly, heroin was once used to treat the addiction of morphine. Now, the most common treatment for heroin addiction is to maintain addicts on methadone, which is an addictive synthetic drug similar to opium. Methadone does not provide the euphoric rush of heroin, but it does prevent withdrawal symptoms that can truly be unbearable (Vocci et al., 2005).

Unless otherwise noted, all images are © Cengage Learning

Hallucinogens

In many parts of the world and in many different cultures, plants and fungi (mushrooms) have long been used to produce visions or hallucinations as part of cultural or religious experiences. However, whites in the United States rarely used hallucinogens until the 1950s and 1960s, when these drugs gained popularity as part of the hippie subculture.

Hallucinogens are psychoactive drugs that can produce strange and unusual perceptual, sensory, and cognitive experiences, which the person sees or hears but knows that they are not occurring in reality. Such nonreality-based experiences are called *hallucinations*.

We'll focus on four of the more commonly used hallucinogens: LSD, marijuana, psilocybin, and MDMA (or ecstasy).

LSD

LSD is a very potent drug because it produces hallucinogenic experiences at very low doses. **LSD** produces strange experiences, which include visual hallucinations, perceptual distortions, increased sensory awareness, and intense psychological feelings. An LSD experience, or "trip," may last 8 to 10 hours.

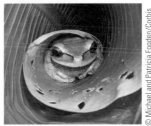

LSD resembles the naturally occurring neurotransmitter serotonin. LSD binds to receptors that normally respond to serotonin, and the net effect is increased stimulation of these neurons (Nelson, 2004). The majority of serotonin receptors are located on neurons in the cerebral cortex, which is involved in receiving sensations, creating perceptions, thinking, and imagining.

LSD's psychological effects partially depend on the setting and the person's state of mind. If a person is tense or anxious or in an unfamiliar setting, he or she may experience a bad trip. If severe, a bad trip may lead to psychotic reactions (especially paranoid feelings) that require hospitalization. Sometime after the hallucinogenic experience, users may experience frightening flashbacks that occur for no apparent reason.

There have been no reports of physical addiction to LSD or death from overdose, but users do quickly develop a tolerance to LSD (Goldberg, 2010).

Teen Drug Use

Watch how heroin addiction affects the lives of teens.

Heroin Addiction Treatment

Learn how methadone is used in the treatment of heroin addiction.

Marijuana

The most widely used illegal drug in the United States is marijuana. In this country, 42% of people have tried marijuana and 14.4 million are current users (SAMHSA, 2008; *Time,* 2008).

Marijuana is a psychoactive drug whose primary active ingredient is THC (tetrahydrocannabinol), which is found in the leaves of the cannabis plant.

THC is rapidly absorbed by the lungs and as such, the use of marijuana can cause many of the same kinds of respiratory problems as tobacco, including bronchitis and asthma attacks. Moreover, marijuana smoke contains 50% more cancer-causing substances and because users hold smoke in their lungs longer, the effects of smoking one joint of marijuana are similar to those of five cigarettes (Time, 2007c).

© Rachel Whenman/Alamy

Unless otherwise noted, all images are © Cengage Learning

A high can be achieved very quickly and last for hours. The type of high is closely related to the dose: Low doses produce mild euphoria; moderate doses produce perceptual and time distortions; and high doses may produce hallucinations, delusions, and distortions of body image (Hanson et al., 2002).

Research shows that marijuana can be effective in treating nausea and vomiting associated with chemotherapy, appetite loss in AIDS patients, eye disease (glaucoma), muscle spasticity, and some forms of pain (Cole, 2005). For these reasons, several states passed laws, and others are considering laws that allow marijuana to be prescribed by doctors and used legally for medical problems (Associated Press, 2006a; Johnson, 2006).

The understanding of the effects of marijuana on the nervous system made leaps and bounds in 1990 when researchers discovered we have THC receptors located throughout areas of the brain involved in motor behavior, memory, emotions, and other higher cognitive functions (Iversen, 2000). Soon after, researchers found that the brain itself makes a chemical or neurotransmitter, called anandamide, that stimulates THC receptors (Piomelli, 1999). Thus, the brain not only has receptors for THC but also makes a THC-like chemical.

Some, but not all, regular heavy users of marijuana develop addiction and dependency. And when heavy users stop, some experience withdrawal symptoms, including irritability, restlessness, and anxiety, as well as strong cravings for more of the drug (Smith, 2002; Wolfing et al., 2008).

Psilocybin

Magic or psychedelic mushrooms are native to Mexico and have earned the "magic" name due to the mystical experiences they cause people to have (Talan, 2006b). However, some people have adverse reactions to magic mushrooms, such as intense fears and paranoia (Griffiths, 2006). The active ingredient in magic mushrooms is psilocybin.

Psilocybin in low doses produces pleasant and relaxed feelings; medium doses produce perceptual distortions in time and space; high doses produce distortions in perceptions and body image and sometimes hallucinations.

Psilocybin is chemically related to LSD and, like LSD, binds to serotonin receptors. The hallucinatory effects produced by psilocybin are comparable to those from LSD but last half as long (Carter et al., 2005).

The primary danger associated with psilocybin is its potential to induce psychotic states that persist long after the experience is expected to end (Espiard et al., 2005). In addition, accidental poisonings are common among those who eat poisonous mushrooms, mistaking them for magic mushrooms.

MDMA or Ecstasy

MDMA was first used in the 1970s with the street name "ecstasy." Today, ecstasy is the most popular hallucinogen and the drug of choice at rave parties (right photo), which feature all-night music and dancing (SAMHSA, 2008).

In recreational doses, MDMA heightens sensations, gives a euphoric rush, raises body temperature, and creates feelings of warmth and empathy. At higher doses, trips include panic, rapid heart beat, high body temperature, paranoia, and psychotic-like symptoms (Baylen & Rosenberg, 2006).

MDMA causes neurons to release large amounts of two neurotransmitters, serotonin and dopamine, which stimulate the brain's reward/pleasure center. Afterward, users may feel depressed and have attention and memory deficits.

Longer-term, heavy use of MDMA can lead to serious cognitive impairments, such as memory loss, weakened immune system, and depression (Falck et al., 2006; Laws & Kokkalis, 2007; Schilt et al., 2007; Ward et al., 2006).

Marijuana and Memory

Explore whether marijuana impairs memory.

▶ **LO20** Discuss the prevention of and treatment for drug abuse.

Alcohol

In 2007, about 127 million Americans age 12 and older drank alcohol. Of these, 23% were binge drinkers (that is, they consumed five drinks in a row at the same occasion), and about 7% were heavy drinkers (they had five drinks in a row on five different days in the past month) (SAMHSA, 2008).

Alcohol (ethyl alcohol) is a psychoactive drug that is classified as a depressant, which means it depresses activity of the central nervous system. Initially, alcohol seems like a stimulant because it reduces inhibitions, but later it depresses many physiological and psychological responses.

The effects of alcohol depend on how much a person drinks. A drink is defined as one cocktail, one 5-ounce glass of wine, or one 12-ounce bottle of beer, and the level of alcohol is measured in percentage in the blood, which is called blood alcohol content, or BAC (Gelles, 2009). After a couple of drinks (0.01–0.05 BAC), alcohol causes friendliness and loss of inhibitions. After four or five drinks (0.06–0.10 BAC), alcohol seriously impairs motor coordination, cognitive abilities, and speech. After many drinks (0.4 BAC and higher), alcohol may cause coma and death.

Alcohol affects many parts of the nervous system. For example, alcohol stimulates the brain's GABA *(GAH-bah)* neural receptors, which leads to feeling less anxious and less inhibited (Schuckit, 2006). Alcohol also impairs the anterior cingulate cortex, which monitors the control of motor actions. When this area is impaired, drinkers will fail to recognize their impaired motor performance (such as driving a car) and continue to drive (Ridderinkhof et al., 2002). In very high doses (0.5 BAC), alcohol depresses vital breathing reflexes in the brain stem (medulla), and this may totally stop breathing and result in death.

The morning after a bout of heavy drinking (3 to 7 drinks), a person usually experiences a ***hangover,*** which may include upset stomach, dizziness, fatigue, headache, and depression. There is presently no cure for hangovers, which are troublesome and painful but not life threatening. Another serious problem is ***blackouts,*** which occur after heavy and repeated drinking. During a blackout, a person seems to behave normally but when sober cannot recall what happened.

Repeated and heavy drinking can also result in liver and brain damage. Withdrawal symptoms may include shaking, nausea, anxiety, diarrhea, hallucinations, and disorientation.

© Craig McClain

Unless otherwise noted, all images are © Cengage Learning

Substance Abuse and Treatment

Now that we've discussed the major psychoactive drugs and their effects, we'll turn our attention to substance abuse and treatment.

Substance abuse refers to a maladaptive behavioral pattern of using a drug so frequently that significant problems develop: failing to meet major obligations and having multiple legal, social, family, health, work, or interpersonal problems. These problems must occur repeatedly during a 12-month period (American Psychiatric Association, 2000).

Substance abuse is one of the most challenging behaviors to change (Ray & Hutchinson, 2007). Most substance abusers need professional treatment to get straightened out. Although there are many approaches to treating substance abuse, most treatment programs in the United States are based on the *Minnesota model,* which recognizes that the drug user has lost control over drugs, may be vulnerable to using other mood-altering substances, cannot solve the drug problem alone, must rebuild his or her life without drugs, and must strive for abstinence (McElrath, 1997; Owen, 2003). The *Minnesota model* involves four steps:

First, the person with a substance-abuse problem must admit that he or she has a problem. Although this step appears obvious, in reality it represents a hurdle that many drug abusers have a difficult time getting over. What happens is that drug users believe that drugs are the solution to their problems, fears, insecurities, and worries.

Second, the person must enter a treatment program, which can be inpatient or outpatient, depending on the severity of the substance-abuse problem.

Third, the person undergoes therapy, which can involve a type of talk therapy; group therapy, such as Alcoholics Anonymous (AA); and/or medications.

Fourth, the person is challenged to remain sober. Typically, the person joins community support groups to help maintain abstinence.

If, after a period of sobriety, a person relapses (uses substances again), there are a variety of options for relapse therapy. However, steadfast determination to remain sober is an essential ingredient to any effective treatment outcome.

Alcoholism Rates

Explore the rates and risk factors of alcoholism across cultures.

Alcohol's Problems on Society

Learn more about some of the major societal problems that result from alcohol use and abuse.

Substance Use Disorder

Watch what it's like to have a substance use disorder.

Check Your Learning Quiz 4.9

Go to **login.cengagebrain.com** and take the online quiz.

Think Critically

Challenge Your Thinking

Consider these questions when reading this article:

1. Which type of brain wave occurs when you are text messaging?
2. How might perception explain why the train driver collided with another train? (See Module 3.7)
3. Why have you forgotten that you're driving while talking or texting?
4. What type of research setting is used to observe people's behaviors in their normal environments? (See Module 1.6)
5. How is walking across the street while talking on your cell phone different from walking while chewing gum?
6. What stage of sleep must people be in if they're unknowingly texting during the night?

Texting: How Distracting Can It Be?

YouTube has videos of young adults texting while driving, and Facebook has a group called *I Text Message People While Driving and I Haven't Crashed Yet!* Many people are routinely texting while on the move, whether it's waiting in line for coffee, walking across the street, or driving.

Is texting a big enough distraction to put people at risk of danger? The American College of Emergency Physicians believes so. They report that many people arrive in the emergency department with serious, sometimes fatal injuries because they weren't paying attention to their surroundings while texting. A large-scale, devastating train crash outside of the Los Angeles area demonstrates the real danger of texting. In this accident, 25 people died and 113 were injured when a commuter train collided head-on with a freight train. An investigation found that text messaging was likely the distraction that led to the tragic accident (the driver of the commuter train had texted just seconds before the crash).

Be honest—how many times have you been talking on your cell phone or texting while driving and looked up only to be surprised you haven't been paying attention to the road and felt thankful to

© Ryan McGinnis/Alamy

be alive? Use of a cell phone in any way while driving increases the risk of an accident, and texting is more dangerous than talking. A driver's risk of getting into an accident is believed to increase sixfold when texting and fourfold when talking on a handheld cell phone.

Such life-threatening distractions are not limited to drivers. Research shows that pedestrians talking on cell phones are less likely to look for traffic before walking into the street and are slower in crossing the road, thereby increasing their risk of getting into an accident with a vehicle. Just imagine how much more serious the distractions would be if they were texting!

Not only is texting distracting during our waking day, but for some, it can be a problem during sleep. Teens and young adults, in particular, go to sleep with their phones plugged in right by their beds. With every beep of a new text message, they awaken, disrupting their sleep and thereby affecting their cognitive and physical performance the next day. There have even been rumors of sleep texting (that is, texting during sleep, only to discover in the morning the texts sent in the middle of night). The dangers of texting seem countless: injuring oneself or others, death, and tremendous embarrassment. (Who knows what you might unknowingly text while asleep!) (adapted from ACEP, 2008; Flagg, 2008; Hatfield & Murphy, 2006; Leming, 2008; Michels, 2008; Novotney, 2009; Villarreal, 2008).

Think Critically 4.1

This article and its questions are available in interactive format online.

GO to your Psychology CourseMate at login.cengagebrain.com and take the Chapter Post-Test to see which Learning Objectives you've mastered and which need more review. Use the chapter review guide below and the online activities—including flashcards to review key terms—to measure your learning.

Measure Your Learning

Module		Learning Objectives
4.1	**Introduction** 156	**LO1** Define persistent vegetative state.
4.2	**Continuum of Consciousness** 158	**LO2** Define consciousness and the continuum of consciousness. **LO3** Identify and describe the different states of consciousness.
4.3	**Rhythms of Sleeping and Waking** 162	**LO4** Describe the circadian clock and identify where it's located in the brain. **LO5** Discuss circadian problems and treatment.
4.4	**Stages of Sleep** 166	**LO6** Describe the stages of sleep and their sequence during a night of sleep.
4.5	**Questions about Sleep** 172	**LO7** Discuss how much sleep a typical person needs. **LO8** Explain theories of why we sleep. **LO9** Describe what happens when we miss sleep.

Online Activities

Key Terms	Video	Animation	Reading	Assessment
persistent vegetative state				Check Your Learning Quiz 4.1
consciousness, continuum of consciousness, controlled processes, automatic processes, daydreaming, altered states of consciousness, sleep, dreaming, unconscious, unconsciousness		Continuum of Consciousness, p. 161		Check Your Learning Quiz 4.2
biological clocks, circadian rhythm, suprachiasmatic nucleus, jet lag, light therapy, melatonin		Circadian Sleep-Wake Clock, p. 165	Circadian Preference, p. 163 Seasonal Affective Disorder, p. 165	Check Your Learning Quiz 4.3
stages of sleep, alpha stage, non-REM sleep, stage 1 sleep, stage 2 sleep, stage 4 sleep, REM sleep, REM behavior disorder, REM rebound	Sleep Dangers: Sleep Violence, p. 169 Sleep Lab, p. 171	Sleep Cycles, p. 171		Check Your Learning Quiz 4.4
repair theory, adaptive theory			Sleep-Deprived Doctors, p. 173	Check Your Learning Quiz 4.5

Measure
^Your Learning

Online Activities

Key Terms	Video	Animation	Reading	Assessment
Freud's theory of dreams, extensions of waking life, activation-synthesis theory			Typical Dreams, p. 175	Check Your Learning Quiz 4.6
insomnia, sleep apnea, narcolepsy, night terrors, nightmares, sleeptalking, sleepwalking	Curing Insomnia, p. 177		Insomnia Treatment: Nondrug and Drug, p. 177 Narcolepsy in Dogs, p. 177 Nightmare Treatment, p. 179	Check Your Learning Quiz 4.7
hypnosis, hypnotic induction, altered state theory of hypnosis, sociocognitive theory of hypnosis, hypnotic analgesia, posthypnotic amnesia, imagined perception	Hypnosis and Surgery Pain, p. 183 Weight Loss Hypnosis, p. 183		Theories of Hypnosis, p. 183	Check Your Learning Quiz 4.8
psychoactive drugs, addiction, tolerance, dependency, withdrawal symptoms, reward/pleasure center, stimulants, reuptake, cocaine, caffeine, nicotine, opiates, hallucinogens, LSD, marijuana, psilocybin, MDMA or ecstasy, alcohol, substance abuse	Teen Drug Use, p. 191 Substance Use Disorder, p. 195	Stimulant: Amphetamine, p. 187 Stimulant: Cocaine, p. 189	Does Caffeine Make You Smarter?, p. 189 Heroin Addiction Treatment, p. 191 Marijuana and Memory, p. 193 Alcoholism Rates, p. 195 Alcohol's Problems on Society, p. 195	Check Your Learning Quiz 4.9

Learning

Prepare to Learn

1 **GO** to your **Psychology CourseMate** at **login.cengagebrain.com** and take the **Chapter Pre-Test** to introduce yourself to this chapter's topics and see what you may already know.

2 **READ** the **Learning Objectives (LOs)** (in the left sidebars) and begin the chapter.

3 **COMPLETE** the **Online Activities** (in the right sidebars) *as you read each module.* Activities include **videos**, **animations**, **readings**, and **quizzes**.

4 **CHECK Your Learning** by going online to take the quiz at the end of each module and review material as necessary.

5 **MEASURE Your Learning** after reading the chapter by taking the online **Chapter Post-Test**. Use the chapter review guide at the end of the chapter as needed.

WATCH for these **Online Activities** icons as you read:

Video

Animation

Reading

Assessment

Think Critically

These online activities are important to mastering this chapter. As you read each module, access these materials by going to **login.cengagebrain.com**.

 Video Explore studies and firsthand accounts of biological and psychological processes:

- Watch what happens in the brain as fear is conditioned in rats
- See how generalization applies to Watson's experiment with Little Albert
- Watch how a rat learns to press the lever in the Skinner box
- Watch how Skinner uses a reward to shape a pigeon's behavior
- Learn how electric shock therapy is used to reduce children's aggressive behaviors
- See a reenactment of Bandura's bobo doll study
- See how a cow demonstrates what seems to be observational learning
- Watch how a crow demonstrates what seems to be insight learning

 Animation Interact with and visualize important processes and concepts:

- Conduct Pavlov's experiment and identify classical conditioning concepts
- Learn more about how to conduct classical conditioning experiments
- Observe and distinguish positive and negative reinforcement and punishment
- Observe and distinguish partial reinforcement schedules

 Reading Delve deeper into key content:

- Learn how cultural factors influence the conditioning of dental fears
- Explore how people develop a fear of needles
- Learn about the adaptive value of a conditioned emotional response

- Learn the pros and cons of punishment
- Learn how social cognitive learning explains fear of snakes
- Explore what the effects are of viewing aggression in the media
- Learn how the Suzuki method is similar to social cognitive learning

 Assessment Measure your mastery:

- Chapter Pre-Test
- Check Your Learning Quizzes
- Chapter Post-Test

 Think Critically Challenge your thinking by applying content from this chapter and making connections to related material:

- How Do You Train a Killer Whale?

Unless otherwise noted, all images are © Cengage Learning

▶ **L01** Define learning.

IT WAS AN UNUSUAL MOVIE for two reasons: First, there was almost no dialogue; human actors spoke only 657 words. Second, the star of the movie was a nonspeaking, nonhuman, 12-year-old, 10-foot-tall, 1,800-pound, enormous brown Kodiak bear named Bart (shown below). Bart is one of the world's largest land-dwelling carnivores and can, with one swipe of his massive 12-inch paw, demolish anything in his path. Yet in the movie, there was big bad Bart, sitting peacefully on his haunches, cradling a small bear cub in his arms. "So what?" you might say, but what you don't know is that, in the wild, a Kodiak bear normally kills and eats any cub it encounters.

▼

Because Bart was found as a cub and raised by a human trainer, Bart grew to act more like an overgrown teddy bear than a natural-born killer. For his role in the movie *The Bear,* Bart learned to perform 45 behaviors on cue, such as sitting, running, standing up, roaring, and, most difficult of all, cradling a teddy bear, which is not what an adult bear does in the wild.

The training procedure seems deceptively simple: Each time Bart performed a behavior on cue, the trainer, Doug Seus, gave Bart an affectionate back scratch, an ear rub, or a juicy apple or pear. For example, when the trainer raised his arms high in the air, it was the signal for Bart to sit and hold the teddy bear. After Bart

© George Frey

correctly performed this behavior, Doug would give him a reward. After Bart learned to perform all these behaviors with a stuffed teddy bear, a live bear cub was substituted, and the scene was filmed for the movie (Cerone, 1989). In all, Bart learned to perform 45 behaviors on cue through specific principles of learning.

Learning is a relatively enduring or permanent change in behavior or knowledge that results from previous experience with certain stimuli and responses. The term behavior includes any observable response (such as fainting, salivating, vomiting).

Because of what Bart learned, he starred in 20 movies and became the highest-paid animal actor, making about $10,000 a day (Brennan, 1997). That's a salary that most of us would be very happy to bear!

In this chapter, you will explore three different kinds of learning: classical conditioning, operant conditioning, and cognitive learning. We'll begin by providing you with an overview of different kinds of learning.

Check Your Learning Quiz 5.1

Go to **login.cengagebrain.com** and take the online quiz.

> ▶ **L02** Define associative and nonassociative learning, and give examples of each.

There are two basic kinds of learning: associative learning and nonassociative learning.

Associative learning involves learning by making a relationship or connection between two events; whereas, nonassociative learning involves learning about a single stimulus.

Below you will learn about two types of associative learning, classical conditioning and operant conditioning, as well as one type of nonassociative learning called cognitive learning. We'll visit three laboratories to see how psychologists identified three principles that underlie three kinds of learning: classical conditioning, operant conditioning, and cognitive learning. Each of the three types of learning will be explored in more detail later in this chapter.

Classical Conditioning

Pretend it is the early 1900s, and you are working as a technician in Russia in the laboratory of Ivan Pavlov. He has already won a Nobel Prize for his studies on the reflexes involved in digestion. He has found that when food is placed in a dog's mouth, the food triggers the reflex of salivation (Evans, 1999).

As a lab technician, your task is to place various kinds of food in a dog's mouth and measure the amount of salivation. But soon you encounter a problem. After you have placed food in a dog's mouth on a number of occasions, the dog begins to salivate merely at the sight of the food.

At first, Pavlov considered this sort of anticipatory salivation to be a bothersome problem. Later, he reasoned that the dog's salivation at the sight of food was also a reflex, but one that the dog had somehow *learned.*

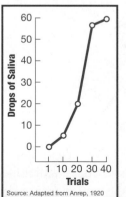
Source: Adapted from Anrep, 1920

In a well-known experiment, Pavlov rang a bell before putting food in the dog's mouth.

As shown in the graph on the left, after a number of trials involving pairing the bell with food, the dog salivated at the sound of the bell alone, a phenomenon that Pavlov called a *conditioned reflex* and today is called classical conditioning. Classical conditioning was an important discovery because it allowed researchers to study learning in an observable, or objective, way (Honey, 2000).

Classical conditioning is a kind of learning in which a neutral stimulus acquires the ability to produce a response that was originally produced by a different stimulus.

Unless otherwise noted, all images are © Cengage Learning

Operant Conditioning

Now let's say it is the late 1800s, and you are working in the laboratory of the American psychologist E. L. Thorndike. Your task is to place a cat in a box with a door that can be opened from the inside by hitting a simple latch. Outside the box is a fish on a dish. You are  to record the length of time it takes the cat to hit the latch, open the door, and get the fish.

On the first trial, the cat sniffs around the box, sticks its paw in various places, accidentally hits the latch, opens the door, and gets the fish. You place the cat back into the box. Again the cat moves around, accidentally strikes the latch, and gets the fish. After many trials, the cat learns to spend its time around the latch and eventually to hit the latch and get the fish in a very short time.

Thorndike's findings have become part of operant conditioning.

Operant conditioning is a kind of learning in which the consequences that follow some behavior increase or decrease the likelihood of that behavior's occurrence in the future.

Cognitive Learning

It is the 1960s, and you are in Albert Bandura's laboratory, where children are watching a film of an adult who is repeatedly hitting and kicking a big plastic doll. Following this film, the children are observed during play.

Bandura found that children who had watched the film of an adult modeling aggressive behavior played more aggressively than children who had not seen the film (Bandura et al., 1963). The children's change in behavior, which was increased aggressive responses, did not seem to be based on associative learning. Instead, the entire learning process appeared to take place in the children's minds, without their performing any observable responses or receiving any noticeable rewards. These mental learning processes are part of a type of nonassociative learning, called cognitive learning (Chance, 2006).

© Craig McClain

Cognitive learning is a kind of learning that involves mental processes, such as attention and memory; may be learned through observation or imitation; and may not involve any external rewards or require the person to perform any observable behaviors.

Check Your Learning Quiz 5.2

Go to **login.cengagebrain.com** and take the online quiz.

▶ **LO3** Describe Pavlov's experiment of classical conditioning.

▶ **LO4** Define the terms in classical conditioning and explain its process.

Pavlov's Experiment

Imagine that you are an assistant in Pavlov's laboratory and your subject is a dog named Sam. You are using a procedure that will result in Sam's salivating when he hears a bell, a response that Pavlov called a *conditioned reflex*. Today, we call Pavlov's procedure *classical conditioning,* which involves the following three steps.

Step 1. Selecting Stimulus and Response

Terms. Before you begin the procedure to establish classical conditioning in Sam, you need to identify three critical terms: *neutral stimulus, unconditioned stimulus,* and *unconditioned response.*

Neutral stimulus. You need to choose a neutral stimulus.

A **neutral stimulus** is some stimulus that causes a sensory response, such as being seen, heard, or smelled, but does not produce the reflex being tested.

Your neutral stimulus will be a tone (bell), which Sam the dog hears but which does not normally produce the reflex of salivation.

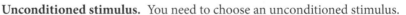

Unconditioned stimulus. You need to choose an unconditioned stimulus.

An **unconditioned stimulus,** or **UCS,** is some stimulus that triggers or elicits a physiological reflex, such as salivation or eye blink.

Your unconditioned stimulus will be food, which when presented to Sam will elicit the salivation reflex (that is, will make Sam salivate).

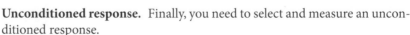

Unconditioned response. Finally, you need to select and measure an unconditioned response.

The **unconditioned response,** or **UCR,** is an unlearned, innate, involuntary physiological reflex that is elicited by the unconditioned stimulus.

For instance, salivation is an unconditioned response that is elicited by food. In this case, the sight of food, which is the unconditioned stimulus, will elicit salivation in Sam, which is the unconditioned response.

Step 2. Establishing Classical Conditioning

Trial. A common procedure to establish classical conditioning is for you first to present the neutral stimulus and then, a short time later, to present the unconditioned stimulus. The presentation of both stimuli is called a *trial.*

Neutral stimulus. In a typical trial, you will pair the neutral stimulus (the tone) with the unconditioned stimulus (the food).

+

Unconditioned stimulus (UCS). Some seconds after the tone begins, you present the unconditioned stimulus, a piece of food, which elicits salivation.

↓

Unconditioned response (UCR). The unconditioned stimulus, food, elicits the unconditioned response, salivation. Food and salivation are said to be unconditioned because the effect on Sam is inborn and not dependent on previous training or learning.

Step 3. Testing for Conditioning

Only CS. After you have given Sam 10 to 100 trials, you will test for classical conditioning. You test by presenting the tone (conditioned stimulus) without showing Sam the food (unconditioned stimulus).

Conditioned stimulus. If Sam salivates when you present the tone alone, it means that the tone has become a conditioned stimulus.

A **conditioned stimulus,** or **CS,** is a formerly neutral stimulus that has acquired the ability to elicit a response that was previously elicited by the unconditioned stimulus.

↓

Conditioned response. When Sam salivates to the tone alone, this response is the conditioned response.

The **conditioned response,** or **CR,** which is elicited by the conditioned stimulus, is similar to, but not identical in size or amount, to the unconditioned response.

This means that Sam's conditioned response will involve less salivation to the tone (conditioned stimulus) than to the food (unconditioned stimulus).

Pavlov's Experiment

Conduct Pavlov's experiment and identify classical conditioning concepts.

▶ **L05** Describe Watson's experiment of classical conditioning.

Conditioned Emotional Responses: Watson's Experiment

One of the first attempts to study the development of emotional responses, such as becoming fearful, occurred in the 1920s. John Watson realized he could use Pavlov's conditioning procedure to study the development of emotional behaviors in an objective way. What follows is a classic experiment on conditioning emotions that John Watson and his student assistant, Rosalie Rayner, published in 1920.

Method: Identify Terms

Watson questioned the role that conditioning played in the develop-ment of emotional responses in children. To answer his question, Watson (right photo) tried to classically condition an emotional response in a child.

© Cengage Learning 2013

Subject: Nine-Month-Old Infant.

The subject, known later as Little Albert, was described as healthy, stolid, and unemotional, since "no one had ever seen him in a state of rage and fear. The infant practically never cried" (Watson & Rayner, 1920, p. 3).

Neutral Stimulus: White Rat.

Watson briefly confronted 9-month-old Albert with a succession of objects, including a white rat, a rabbit, and a dog. "At no time did this infant ever show fear in any situation" (Watson & Rayner, 1920, p. 2).

PhotoDisc, Inc.

Unconditioned Stimulus: Noise.

BANG!

The researchers hit a hammer on a metal bar, which made a loud noise and elicited startle and crying. "This is the first time an emo-tional situation in the laboratory has produced any fear or crying in Albert" (Watson & Rayner, 1920, p. 3).

Unconditioned Response: Startle/Cry.

Startle and crying were observable and measurable emotional responses that indicated the baby was feeling and expressing fear. After Watson identified the three elements of classical conditioning, he and his assistant, Rayner, began the procedure for classical conditioning.

Unless otherwise noted, all images are © Cengage Learning

Procedure: Establish and Test for Classical Conditioning

Establish. At the age of 11 months, Albert was given repeated trials consisting of a neutral stimulus, a white rat, followed by an unconditioned stimulus, a loud noise. During early trials, he startled at the sight of the rat and on later trials he also cried.

Rat (neutral stimulus) plus loud bang (UCS) elicits fear response (UCR).

Test. When first presented with the rat alone (no noise), Albert only startled. Then he was given additional conditioning trials and retested with the rat alone (no noise). "The instant the rat was shown the baby began to cry" (Watson & Rayner, 1920, p. 5). Thus, Watson had succeeded in classically conditioning Albert's emotional response (fear).

Classical conditioning: rat (CS) alone elicits fear response (CR).

Results and Conclusions

Watson and Rayner had shown that Albert developed a conditioned emotional response of startle and crying to the sight of a rat. Watson's conditioning of Albert was more of a demonstration than a rigorously controlled experiment (Field & Nightengale, 2009). For example, Watson and Rayner did not use a standardized procedure for presenting stimuli and sometimes removed Albert's thumb from his mouth, which may have made him cry. Watson was also criticized for not unconditioning Albert's fears before he left the hospital.

Even though there were methodological limitations, Watson's demonstration laid the groundwork for explaining how people can acquire conditioned emotional responses, such as developing dental fears (Field & Nightengale, 2009).

Fear Conditioning

Watch what happens in the brain as fear is conditioned in rats.

▶ **LO6** Identify examples of conditioned emotional responses.

Conditioned Emotional Response: Dental Fear

Classical conditioning occurs not only in experimental settings, but also in our daily lives. For instance, next we'll explore how dental fears can be a result of classical conditioning.

After many trips to her dentist, Carla unknowingly experienced classical conditioning, which explains why she now feels anxious and tense when she smells a certain aftershave lotion. As we review the steps involved in classical conditioning, you will see how they apply to Carla's situation.

Step 1. Selecting Stimulus and Response

Terms. To explain how classical conditioning occurs, it's best to start by identifying three terms: *neutral stimulus, unconditioned stimulus,* and *unconditioned response.*

The ***neutral stimulus*** in Carla's situation was the odor of the dentist's aftershave lotion, which she smelled while experiencing pain in the dentist's chair. The aftershave is a neutral stimulus because although it affected Carla (that is, she smelled it), it did not initially produce feelings of anxiety. In fact, initially Carla liked the smell.

The ***unconditioned stimulus*** for Carla was one or more of several dental procedures, including injections, drillings, and fillings. These dental procedures are unconditioned stimuli (UCS) because they elicited the unconditioned response (UCR), feeling anxious and tense.

The ***unconditioned response*** was Carla's feeling of anxiety, which is a combination of physiological reflexes, such as increased heart rate and blood pressure and rapid breathing, as well as negative emotional reactions. Carla's unconditioned response (anxiety) was elicited by the unconditioned stimulus (painful dental procedure).

Step 2. Establishing Classical Conditioning

Trial. One procedure to establish classical conditioning is for the neutral stimulus to occur first and be followed by the unconditioned stimulus. Each presentation of both stimuli is a *trial.*

In Carla's case, the ***neutral stimulus*** was smelling the dentist's aftershave while she was experiencing a number of painful dental procedures.

Carla's many trips to the dentist resulted in her having repeated trials that involved occurrence of the ***neutral stimulus,*** smelling the dentist's aftershave, and occurrence of the ***unconditioned stimulus,*** having painful dental procedures.

The painful dental procedures elicited the ***unconditioned response*** (anxiety) and other physiological responses (increased heart rate and blood pressure).

Step 3. Testing for Conditioning

Only CS. A test for classical conditioning is to observe whether the neutral stimulus, when presented alone, elicits the conditioned response.

Conditioned stimulus. When Carla smelled her boyfriend's aftershave, which was the same as the dentist's, she felt anxious. The aftershave's smell, formerly a neutral stimulus, had become a ***conditioned stimulus*** because it elicited anxiety, the conditioned response.

Conditioned response. Whenever Carla smelled the aftershave (conditioned stimulus) used by both her dentist and her boyfriend, it elicited the ***conditioned response,*** feeling anxious. However, remember that the conditioned response is similar to, but of lesser intensity than, the unconditioned response. Thus, the anxiety elicited by smelling the aftershave was similar to, but not as great as, the anxiety Carla felt during painful dental procedures.

Conditioning Dental Fears

Learn how cultural factors influence the conditioning of dental fears.

▶ **L04** Define the terms in classical conditioning and explain its process (cont'd).

Other Classical Conditioning Concepts

Carla's experience of being classically conditioned in the dentist's office to feel anxious when she smelled a particular aftershave has some other interesting features. Carla found that similar odors also elicited anxious feelings but that other odors did not; her anxiety when smelling her boyfriend's aftershave gradually decreased, but accidentally meeting the dentist and smelling his aftershave still triggered some anxiety. Pavlov found that these phenomena were associated with classical conditioning, and he named them generalization, discrimination, extinction, and spontaneous recovery.

Generalization

During Carla's conditioning trials, the neutral stimulus, which was the odor of the dentist's aftershave, became the conditioned stimulus that elicited the conditioned response, anxiety. However, Carla may also feel anxiety when smelling other similar odors, such as her own hair shampoo; this is called generalization.

Generalization is the tendency for a stimulus that is similar to the original conditioned stimulus to elicit a response that is similar to the conditioned response. Usually, the more similar the new stimulus is to the original conditioned stimulus, the greater will be the conditioned response.

Discrimination

Carla discovered that smells very different from that of the aftershave did not elicit anxiety; this phenomenon is called discrimination.

Discrimination occurs during classical conditioning when an organism learns to make a particular response to some stimuli but not to others.

For example, Carla had learned that the smell of a particular aftershave predicted the likelihood of a painful dental procedure. In contrast, the smell of her nail polish, which was very different from that of the aftershave, predicted not painful dental procedures but nice-looking fingernails.

Extinction

If Carla's boyfriend did not change his aftershave and she repeatedly smelled it, she would learn that it was never followed by painful dental procedures, and its smell would gradually stop making her feel anxious; this phenomenon is called extinction.

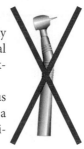

Extinction refers to a procedure in which a conditioned stimulus is repeatedly presented without the unconditioned stimulus and, as a result, the conditioned stimulus tends to no longer elicit the conditioned response.

The procedure for extinguishing a conditioned response is used in therapeutic settings to reduce fears. For example, clients who had a conditioned fear of needles and receiving injections were repeatedly shown needles and given injections by nurses. After exposure to the conditioned stimuli during a 3-hour period, 81% of the clients reported a reduction in fear of needles and receiving injections (Ost et al., 1992).

Spontaneous Recovery

Suppose Carla's conditioned anxiety to the smell of the aftershave had been extinguished by having her repeatedly smell her boyfriend's lotion without experiencing any painful consequences. Some time later, when Carla happened to accidentally meet her dentist in the local supermarket, she might spontaneously show the conditioned response and feel anxiety when smelling his aftershave; this is called spontaneous recovery (Brooks, 2000).

Spontaneous recovery is the tendency for the conditioned response to reappear after being extinguished even though there have been no further conditioning trials.

Spontaneous recovery of the conditioned response will not persist for long and will be of lesser magnitude than the original conditioned response. If the conditioned stimulus (smell of aftershave) is not presented again with the unconditioned stimulus (painful dental procedure), the spontaneously recovered conditioned response will again undergo extinction and cease to occur. Thus, once Carla had been classically conditioned, she would have experienced one or more of these four phenomena.

Now that you are familiar with the procedure and concepts of classical conditioning, we'll explore its widespread occurrence in the real world.

Classical Conditioning

Learn more about how to conduct classical conditioning experiments.

Little Albert

See how generalization applies to Watson's experiment with Little Albert.

▶ **LO7** Explain how classically conditioned responses can be "unconditioned."

"Unconditioning" Conditioned Emotional Responses

Michelle has been receiving chemotherapy treatment for breast cancer. One side effect of the powerful anti-cancer drugs used in chemotherapy is nausea, which may be accompanied by severe vomiting that lasts 6 to 12 hours.

As Michelle received additional chemotherapy injections, she experienced nausea when she smelled the treatment room or smelled her dish soap, which smelled like the treatment room. Michelle's problem is called anticipatory nausea.

Anticipatory nausea refers to feelings of nausea that are elicited by stimuli associated with nausea-inducing chemotherapy treatments.

Patients experience nausea after treatment but also before or in anticipation of their treatment. For example, by their fourth injection, 60% to 70% of patients who receive chemotherapy experience anticipatory nausea when they encounter smells, sounds, sights, or images related to treatment (Montgomery & Bovbjerg, 1997). Once conditioning is established, anticipatory nausea can be very difficult to treat and control with drugs (Brennan, 2004). Even after chemotherapy ends, anticipatory nausea may reappear for a while, which is an example of spontaneous recovery.

However, there is a nonmedical treatment for anticipatory nausea, which is based on classical conditioning and is called systematic desensitization.

Systematic desensitization is a procedure based on classical conditioning, in which a person imagines or visualizes fearful or anxiety-evoking stimuli and then immediately uses deep relaxation to overcome the anxiety.

Essentially, systematic desensitization is a procedure to "uncondition," or overcome, fearful stimuli by pairing anxiety-provoking thoughts or images with feelings of relaxation. Systematic desensitization was developed by Joseph Wolpe in the early 1950s and has become one of the most frequently used nonmedical therapies for relief of anxiety and fears in both children and adults (Williams & Gross, 1994).

In Michelle's case, she will try to "uncondition," or override, the anxiety-producing cues of chemotherapy (smells and sights) with feelings of relaxation. The procedure for systematic desensitization involves following the three steps (Wolpe & Lazarus, 1966).

Systematic Desensitization Procedure: Three Steps

Step 1. Learning to Relax

Michelle is taught to relax by tensing and relaxing sets of muscles, beginning with the muscles in her toes and continuing up to the muscles in her calves, thighs, back, arms, shoulders, neck, and finally face and forehead. She practices doing this intentional relaxation for about 15 to 20 minutes every day for several weeks.

Step 2. Making an Anxiety Hierarchy

Michelle makes up a list of 7 to 12 stressful situations associated with chemotherapy treatment. As shown on the right, she arranges her list of situations in a hierarchy that goes from least to most stressful. For example, the least stressful situations are driving to and entering the clinic, and the most stressful are nausea and vomiting.

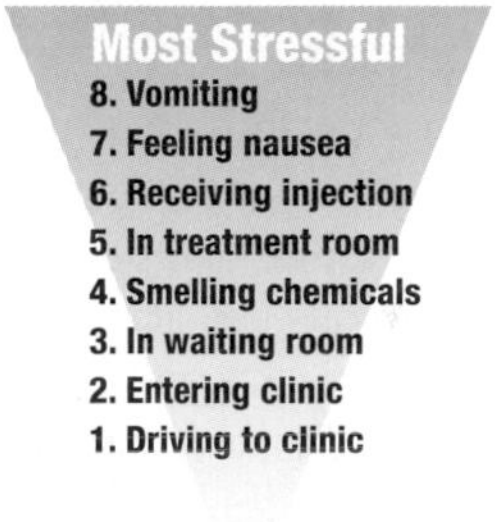

Most Stressful
8. Vomiting
7. Feeling nausea
6. Receiving injection
5. In treatment room
4. Smelling chemicals
3. In waiting room
2. Entering clinic
1. Driving to clinic

Step 3. Imagining and Relaxing

Michelle *first* puts herself into a deeply relaxed state and then vividly imagines the least stressful situation, driving to the clinic. She is told to remain in a relaxed state while imagining this situation. If she becomes anxious or stressed, she is told to stop imagining this situation and return instead to a relaxed state. Once she is sufficiently relaxed, she again imagines driving to the clinic. If she can imagine driving to the clinic while remaining in a relaxed state, she goes to the next stressful situation. She continues up the anxiety hierarchy, imagining in turn each of the eight stressful stimuli while keeping herself in a relaxed state.

As Michelle associates relaxation with each stressful situation in the hierarchy, she overcomes, or counterconditions, each stimulus. In other words, systematic desensitization uses relaxation to get rid of the stressful feelings that have become associated with the stimuli identified in the hierarchy.

You've learned much already about classical conditioning, but there's one side to classical conditioning we have yet to cover, which is its tremendous adaptive value.

Fear of Needles

Explore how people develop a fear of needles.

▶ **LO8** Discuss the adaptive value of classical conditioning.

Adaptive Value

Pavlov believed that animals and people evolved the capacity for classical conditioning because it had an adaptive value (Lieberman, 2004).

Adaptive value refers to the usefulness of certain abilities or traits that have evolved in animals and humans and tend to increase their chances of survival, such as finding food, acquiring mates, and avoiding pain and injury.

We'll discuss several examples, such as learning to avoid certain tastes, salivating at the sight of food, and learning to avoid danger, that support Pavlov's view that classical conditioning is useful because it has an adaptive value. We'll begin by presenting the adaptive value of classical conditioning in animals, followed by humans.

Animals

Rat exterminators have firsthand knowledge of classical conditioning's adaptive value. Exterminators find that while some rats eat enough bait poison to die, others eat only enough to get sick. Once rats get sick on a particular bait poison, they quickly learn to avoid its smell or taste and never again eat that bait poison; this response is called *bait shyness*. This kind of learning is a form of classical conditioning called taste-aversion learning (Bernstein & Koh, 2007).

Taste-aversion learning refers to associating a particular sensory cue (such as smell, taste, sound, or sight) with getting sick and thereafter avoiding that particular sensory cue in the future.

The adaptive value of taste-aversion learning and its adaptive value for rats is obvious: By quickly learning to avoid the smells or taste associated with getting sick, such as eating poison bait, they are more likely to survive.

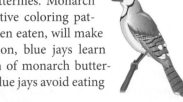

Another example of taste-aversion learning and its adaptive value is seen in blue jays, who feast on butterflies, but learn not to eat monarch butterflies. Monarch butterflies, which have a distinctive coloring pattern, contain a chemical that, when eaten, will make birds sick. Through taste aversion, blue jays learn that the distinctive color pattern of monarch butterflies predicts getting sick, and so blue jays avoid eating monarch butterflies.

Humans

It is likely that in your lifetime, you, too, will experience taste-aversion learning. For example, if you have ever eaten something and gotten sick after taking a thrill ride, you may try to avoid the smell or taste of that particular food. Similarly, people who get sick from drinking too much of a particular alcoholic drink (often a sweet or distinctive-tasting drink) may avoid that drink for a long period of time (Reilly & Schachtman, 2009). Taste-aversion learning may also warn us away from eating poisonous plants that cause illness or even death, such as certain varieties of mushrooms. All these examples of taste-aversion learning show the adaptive value of classical conditioning, which is to keep us away from potentially unpleasant or dangerous situations, such as over-drinking or eating poisonous plants.

I'm starting to get a sick feeling!!!

In contrast, things that taste good can also produce a classically conditioned response in humans that is adaptive. For example, the next time you enter a restaurant, read the menu, think about food (such as the ice cream sundae on the dessert menu), and see people eating, notice that you are salivating, even though you have no food in your own mouth. This is a clear example of how many different kinds of neutral stimuli, such as reading a menu, seeing people eat, or imagining food, can become conditioned stimuli that elicit a conditioned response, such as salivation.

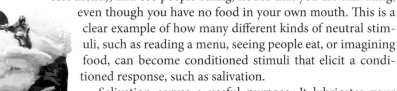

© Michael Stuckey/Comstock

Salivation serves a useful purpose: It lubricates your mouth and throat to make chewing and swallowing food easier. Thus, being classically conditioned to salivate when reading a menu prepares your mouth for the soon-to-arrive food. Conditioned salivation and taste-aversion learning are examples of how classical conditioning has an adaptive value (Aamodt & Wang, 2008; Lieberman, 2004).

We have discussed many sides of classical conditioning. It's evident that classical conditioning has a considerable influence on many of our thoughts, emotions, and behaviors. Next, we'll turn to a different kind of learning called operant conditioning.

Adaptive Value

Learn about the adaptive value of a conditioned emotional response.

Check Your Learning Quiz 5.3

Go to **login.cengagebrain.com** and take the online quiz.

▶ **LO9** Describe Thorndike's experiments that led to the law of effect and Skinner's experiment that led to operant conditioning.

Background: Thorndike and Skinner

At the start of this chapter, we told you how a trainer used principles of learning to teach Bart to perform 45 different behaviors on cue. Bart learned to perform these behaviors through a kind of learning called operant conditioning.

Operant conditioning is a kind of learning in which an animal or human performs some behavior, and the following consequence (that is, the reward or punishment) increases or decreases the chance that the animal or human will again perform that same behavior.

For example, if Bart performed a particular behavior, such as picking up a teddy bear, the consequence that followed—getting a rewarding apple—increased the chance that Bart would again pick up the teddy bear.

Operant conditioning has now been applied to many different settings, such as training animals to perform, training children to use the toilet, and helping autistic children learn social behaviors. However, the discovery of operant behavior involved two different researchers who worked in two different laboratories on two different kinds of problems. We'll visit the laboratories of the two important researchers: E. L. Thorndike and B. F. Skinner.

Thorndike's Law of Effect

It's the late 1800s, and we're in the laboratory of E. L. Thorndike, who is interested in studying the reasoning capacity in animals. Thorndike has devised a simple but clever way to measure reasoning in an objective way. He has built a series of puzzle boxes from which a cat can escape by learning to make a specific response, such as pulling a string or pressing a bar. Outside the puzzle box is a reward for escaping—a piece of fish.

We watch Thorndike place a cat in the puzzle box and record its escape time. After Thorndike records the data, we see a lessening in the time needed to escape. For example, on the first trial the cat needs over 240 seconds to hit the escape latch, but by the last trial, the cat hits the escape latch in less than 60 seconds.

Thorndike explains that, with repeated trials, the cat spends more time around the latch, which increases the chances of hitting it and more quickly escaping to get the fish. To explain why a cat's random trial-and-error behaviors turn into goal-directed behaviors, Thorndike formulated the law of effect.

The **law of effect** states that behaviors followed by positive consequences are strengthened, while behaviors followed by negative consequences are weakened.

Skinner's Operant Conditioning

It's the 1930s, and we're in the laboratory of B. F. Skinner, who is interested in analyzing ongoing behaviors of animals. Skinner explains that Thorndike's law of effect is useful, since it describes how animals are rewarded for making particular responses. However, to analyze ongoing behaviors, you must have an objective way to measure them. Skinner's solution is a unit of behavior he calls an operant response (Skinner, 1938).

An **operant response** is a response that can be modified by its consequences and is a meaningful unit of ongoing behavior that can be easily measured.

For example, suppose that out of curiosity Bart picks up a teddy bear. His picking up the teddy bear is an example of an operant response because Bart is acting or operating on the environment. The consequence of his picking up the teddy bear is that he receives an apple (a desirable effect), which modifies his response by increasing the chances that Bart will repeat the same response.

By measuring operant responses, Skinner can analyze animals' ongoing behaviors during learning. He calls this kind of learning *operant conditioning*, which focuses on how consequences (rewards or punishments) affect behaviors.

A simple example of operant conditioning occurs when a rat in an experimental box accidentally presses a bar. If the bar press is followed by food, this consequence increases the chance that the rat will press the bar again. As the rat presses the bar more times, more food follows, which in turn increases the chances that the rat will continue to press the bar (indicated by the rise of the red line in the figure below).

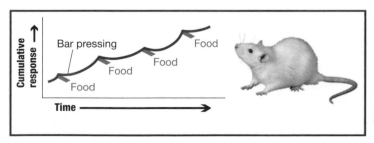

Using his procedure of operant conditioning, B. F. Skinner spent the next 50 years exploring and analyzing learning in rats, pigeons, schoolchildren, and adults.

Now we'll examine Skinner's ingenious procedure for operant conditioning in more detail.

> ▶ **LO10** Describe shaping, superstitious behavior, generalization, discrimination, extinction, and spontaneous recovery.

Principles and Procedures

A rat may initially press a bar out of curiosity; whether it presses the bar again depends on the consequences.

To show how consequences can affect behavior, imagine that you are looking over Skinner's shoulder as he places a rat into a box.

The box is empty except for a bar jutting out from one side and an empty food cup below and to the side of the bar (right figure). This box, called a *Skinner box,* is automated to record the animal's bar presses and deliver food pellets. The Skinner box is an efficient way to study how an animal's ongoing behaviors may be modified by changing the consequences of what happens after a bar press.

As you watch, Skinner explains that the rat is a good subject for operant conditioning because it can use its front paws to manipulate objects, such as a bar, and it has a tendency to explore its environment, which means that it will eventually find the bar, touch it, or even press it.

Skinner goes on to explain the following three factors that are involved in conditioning a rat to press a bar in the Skinner box.

1 The rat has intentionally not been fed for some hours so that it will be active and more likely to eat the food reward. A hungry rat tends to roam restlessly about, sniffing at whatever it finds.

2 The goal is to condition the rat to press the bar. By pressing the bar, the rat operates on its environment; thus, this response is called an ***operant response.***

3 Skinner explains that a naive rat does not usually waltz over and press the bar. In conditioning a rat to press a bar, Skinner will use a procedure called shaping.

Shaping is a procedure in which an experimenter successively reinforces behaviors that lead up to or approximate the desired behavior.

On the next page we'll show you how shaping works if the desired behavior is pressing the bar.

Shaping: Training a Rat in the Skinner Box

Skinner places a white rat into the (Skinner) box, closes the door, and watches the rat through a one-way mirror. At first, the rat wanders around the back of the box, but when it turns and faces the bar, Skinner releases a food pellet into the food cup. The rat hears the pellet drop, approaches the food cup, and then sees, sniffs, and eats the pellet. After eating, the rat moves away to explore the box. But as soon as the rat turns and faces the bar, Skinner releases another pellet. The rat hears the noise, goes to the food cup, sniffs, and eats the pellet.

As shaping continues, Skinner decides to reinforce the rat only when it moves toward the bar. Skinner waits, and when the rat faces and moves toward the bar, Skinner releases another pellet. After eating the pellet, the rat wanders a bit but soon returns to the bar and sniffs it. A fourth pellet immediately drops into the cup, and the rat eats it. When the rat places one paw on the bar, a fifth pellet drops into the cup.

Next Skinner waits until the rat puts its paws on the bar and actually happens to press down; this response releases another pellet. Soon, the rat is pressing the bar over and over to get pellets. Notice how Skinner reinforces the rat's behaviors that lead up to or approximate the desired behavior of bar pressing.

Immediate Reinforcement

Skinner explains that in shaping behavior, the food pellet, or **reinforcer,** should follow *immediately* after the desired behavior. By following immediately, the reinforcer is associated with the desired behavior and not with some other behavior that just happened to occur. If the reinforcer is delayed, the animal may be reinforced for some undesired or superstitious behavior.

Superstitious behavior is a behavior that increases in frequency because its occurrence is accidentally paired with the delivery of a reinforcer.

When I (R. P.) was a graduate student, I conditioned my share of superstitious rat behaviors, such as making them turn in circles or stand up instead of pressing the bar. That's because I accidentally but immediately reinforced a rat after it performed the wrong behavior.

Next, we'll discuss other operant conditioning concepts.

Rat in a Skinner Box

Watch how a rat learns to press the lever in the Skinner box.

B.F. Skinner Shaping a Pigeon

Watch how Skinner uses a reward to shape a pigeon's behavior.

Other Operant Conditioning Concepts

During the time that Bart was being trained (through operant conditioning to a hand signal) to pick up and hold a teddy bear to a hand signal, he simultaneously learned a number of other things, such as to hold a bear cub, not to obey commands from a stranger, and to stop picking up the teddy bear if he was no longer given apples (reinforcers). You may remember these phenomena—generalization, discrimination, extinction, and spontaneous recovery—from our discussion of classical conditioning in Module 5.3. We'll explain how the same terms also apply to operant conditioning.

© George Frey

Generalization

In the movie, Bart was supposed to pick up and hold a bear cub on command. However, in the wild, adult male Kodiak bears don't pick up and hold cubs; instead, they usually kill them.

Although Bart was relatively tame, his trainer took no chances of Bart's wilder nature coming out and killing the bear cub. For this reason, the trainer started by conducting the initial conditioning with a stuffed teddy bear. Only after Bart had learned to pick up and hold the teddy bear on cue did the trainer substitute a live bear cub.

As the trainer had predicted, Bart transferred his holding the teddy bear to holding the live bear cub, a phenomenon called generalization.

© Mateusz Drozd/Shutterstock

In operant conditioning, **generalization** means that an animal or person emits the same response to similar stimuli.

In classical conditioning, **generalization** is the tendency for a stimulus similar to the original conditioned stimulus to elicit a response similar to the conditioned response.

A common and sometimes embarrassing example of generalization occurs when a young child generalizes the word "Daddy" to other males who appear similar to the child's real father. As quickly as possible, embarrassed parents teach their child to discriminate between the real father and other adult males.

Unless otherwise noted, all images are © Cengage Learning

Discrimination

Since Bart had been raised and trained by a particular adult male, he had learned to obey and take cues only from his trainer and not from other males. This is an example of discrimination.

In operant conditioning, **discrimination** means that a response is emitted in the presence of a stimulus that is reinforced and not in the presence of unreinforced stimuli.

In classical conditioning, **discrimination** is the tendency for some stimuli but not others to elicit a conditioned response.

© George Frey

Extinction and Spontaneous Recovery

Even after filming ended, Bart continued to perform his trained behaviors for a while. However, when these behaviors were no longer reinforced, they gradually diminished and ceased. This is an example of extinction.

In operant conditioning, **extinction** refers to the reduction in an operant response when it is no longer followed by the reinforcer.

In classical conditioning, **extinction** refers to the reduction in a response when the conditioned stimulus is no longer followed by the unconditioned stimulus.

After undergoing extinction, Bart may show spontaneous recovery.

In operant conditioning, **spontaneous recovery** refers to a temporary recovery in the rate of responding.

In classical conditioning, **spontaneous recovery** refers to the temporary occurrence of the conditioned response in the presence of the conditioned stimulus.

Extinction: Bart stops behaviors if reinforcers stop.

Spontaneous recovery: After extinction, Bart's behavior returns.

Remember that all four phenomena—generalization, discrimination, extinction, and spontaneous recovery—occur in both operant and classical conditioning.

▶ **L011** Identify and describe the different types of consequences to behavior.

Types of Consequences

In operant conditioning, the performance of some response depends on its consequences (that is, rewards or punishment). We'll discuss the effects of different kinds of consequences next.

Notice where the man is sitting as he saws off a tree limb (figure on right). His behavior illustrates a key principle of operant conditioning, which is that *consequences are contingent on behavior.* In this case, the man will fall on his head (consequence) if he cuts off the tree limb (behavior). Furthermore, this consequence will make the tree trimmer think twice before repeating this stupid behavior. Thus, consequences affect behavior, and in operant conditioning, there are two kinds of consequences: reinforcement and punishment.

Reinforcement is a consequence that occurs after a behavior and *increases* the chance that the behavior will occur again.

For example, one of the main reasons you study hard for exams is to get good grades (reinforcement). The consequence of getting a good grade increases the chances that you'll study hard for future exams.

Punishment is a consequence that occurs after a behavior and *decreases* the chance that the behavior will occur again.

For example, one school used punishment to reduce students' absentee rates. Students who got more than eight unexcused absences lost desirable privileges (for example, no football games, no prom). In this case, punishing consequences decreased the chance of students playing hooky from school from 15% to 4% (Chavez, 1994). However, other research shows that when schools use physical punishment to discourage undesirable behavior, absenteeism rates increase (HRW, 2008).

Next, we'll discuss two kinds of reinforcement.

© Corbis/SuperStock

Unless otherwise noted, all images are © Cengage Learning

Reinforcement

Although getting an apple and getting a grade of "F" seem very different, they are both consequences that can increase the occurrence of certain behaviors. There are two kinds of consequences, or reinforcements—positive and negative—that increase the occurrence of behaviors.

Positive Reinforcement

Immediately after Bart the bear emitted or performed a behavior (for example, holding a teddy bear), the trainer gave him an apple to increase the likelihood of his repeating that behavior. This situation is an example of positive reinforcement.

Positive reinforcement refers to the presentation of a stimulus that increases the probability that a behavior will occur again.

A **positive reinforcer** is a stimulus that increases the likelihood that a response will occur again.

For example, if you ask a friend for money and get it, the money is a positive reinforcer that will increase the chances of your asking again. There's a second kind of reinforcement, called negative reinforcement.

Negative Reinforcement

If you have a headache and take an aspirin to get rid of it, your response of taking an aspirin is an example of negative reinforcement.

Negative reinforcement refers to an aversive (that is, unpleasant) stimulus whose removal increases the likelihood that the preceding response will occur again.

If taking an aspirin removes your headache (aversive or unpleasant stimulus), then your response of taking an aspirin is negatively reinforced because it removes the headache and thus increases the chances of your taking an aspirin in the future. Don't be confused by the fact that both positive and negative reinforcers *increase* the frequency of the responses they follow.

Besides positive and negative reinforcers, there are also primary reinforcers, such as food, and secondary reinforcers, such as money and coupons.

Reinforcers

A student might repeat a behavior, such as study, because the consequence is food (a primary reinforcer), or be quiet on the school bus because the consequence is a coupon (a secondary reinforcer).

Primary Reinforcers

If you made yourself study for 2 hours before rewarding yourself with chocolate, you would be using a primary reinforcer.

© Simon Belcher/Alamy

A **primary reinforcer** is a stimulus, such as food, water, or sex, that is innately satisfying and requires no learning on the part of the subject to become pleasurable.

Primary reinforcers, such as eating, drinking, or having sex, are unlearned and innately pleasurable. In our example, chocolate is a primary reinforcer for studying. However, many behaviors are aided or maintained by secondary reinforcers.

Secondary Reinforcers

A school teacher used a secondary reinforcer when she gave each child a coupon good for fun prizes if he or she ate fruits and vegetables during lunch. A coupon is an example of a secondary reinforcer.

A **secondary reinforcer** is any stimulus that has acquired its reinforcing power through experience; secondary reinforcers are learned, such as by being paired with primary reinforcers or other secondary reinforcers.

Coupons, money, grades, and praise are examples of secondary reinforcers because their value is learned or acquired through experience (Delgado et al., 2006; Klein, 2009). For example, children learned that their teacher's coupons were valuable because they could be redeemed for fun prizes. The coupons became secondary reinforcers that encouraged children to eat fruits and vegetables during lunch at school (Hendy et al., 2005, 2007). Many of our behaviors are increased or maintained by secondary reinforcers.

Unlike primary and secondary reinforcers, which are consequences that increase behaviors, punishment has a very different effect.

©MBI/Alamy

Unless otherwise noted, all images are © Cengage Learning

Punishment

There are two kinds of punishment—positive and negative—that decrease the occurrence of behaviors. Both positive and negative punishment function as "stop signs"; they stop or decrease the occurrence of a behavior.

Positive Punishment

There is a school in Massachusetts that uses a controversial method of punishment to discourage students from engaging in dangerous behaviors. The school requires students to wear backpacks, which contain an electric device that allows staff members to apply a shock to electrodes attached to the student's body whenever the student engages in dangerous or prohibited behaviors (Kaufman, 2007). The goal is to decrease the occurrence of certain behaviors, and the method used is an example of positive punishment.

Positive punishment refers to presenting an aversive (unpleasant) stimulus after a response. The aversive stimulus decreases the chances that the response will recur.

The aversive stimulus in the above example is electric shock, which decreases the chances that dangerous and self-destructive behaviors will occur.

Negative Punishment

One kind of undesirable behavior in young children is the persistent refusal of parental requests, a problem called noncompliance. One method used to decrease children's noncompliance is time-out.

Time-out removes reinforcing stimuli after an undesirable response. This removal decreases the chances that the undesired response will recur.

Time-out is an example of negative punishment.

Negative punishment refers to removing a reinforcing stimulus after a response. This removal decreases the chances that the response will recur.

In time-out, the reinforcing stimulus being removed is the freedom to play, and the undesirable behavior being decreased is noncompliance.

Although somewhat confusing, remember that positive and negative punishment *decrease* the likelihood of a behavior occurring again, while positive and negative reinforcement *increase* the likelihood of a behavior occurring again.

© Design Pics/Ron Nickel/Getty Images

Pain Therapy

Learn how electric shock therapy is used to reduce children's aggressive behaviors.

Types of Consequences

Observe and distinguish positive and negative reinforcement and punishment.

Pros and Cons of Punishment

Learn the pros and cons of punishment.

Unless otherwise noted, all images are © Cengage Learning

▶ **LO12** Identify and describe the different schedules of reinforcement.

Schedules of Reinforcement

As we've learned, Skinner's operant conditioning is a powerful method for analyzing the individual behaviors of animals and humans. Part of Skinner's method was to study how different kinds of consequences or reinforcements affected behavior, and this led to his study of different schedules of reinforcement.

A **schedule of reinforcement** refers to a program or rule that determines how and when the occurrence of a response will be followed by a reinforcer.

Skinner pointed out many examples of how schedules of reinforcement both maintained and controlled behaviors. We'll first look at how two general schedules of reinforcement—continuous and partial reinforcement—can greatly affect ongoing behavior.

When I (H. K.) first began training my dog to "shake hands," I gave her a treat each time she responded to my command and shook my hand. Later on, when she had mostly learned to shake hands, I gave her a treat only some of the time. These situations illustrate continuous reinforcement and partial reinforcement.

Continuous Reinforcement

Giving my dog a treat each time she responded to my command and shook my hand illustrates the schedule of continuous reinforcement.

Continuous reinforcement means that every occurrence of the operant response results in delivery of the reinforcer.

In the real world, relatively few of our behaviors are on a continuous-reinforcement schedule. Continuous reinforcement is often used in the initial stages of operant conditioning because it results in rapid learning of some behavior.

Partial Reinforcement

After my dog had mostly learned to shake hands on command, I gave her a treat about every fifth time, which illustrates the schedule of partial reinforcement.

Partial reinforcement refers to a situation in which responding is reinforced only some of the time.

In the real world, many of our behaviors are on a partial reinforcement schedule, which is very effective in maintaining behavior over the long run. My dog keeps shaking my hand on command because some of the time she gets a treat.

Partial Reinforcement Schedules

There are four different schedules of partial reinforcement, each of which has a different effect on controlling and maintaining animal and human behaviors.

Fixed-Ratio Schedule

If factory workers are paid after packing six boxes, they are on a fixed-ratio schedule.

Fixed-ratio schedule means that a reinforcer occurs only after a fixed number of responses are made by the subject.

A fixed-ratio schedule is often used to pay assembly-line workers because it results in fast rates of work.

© Mike Blank/Getty Images

Fixed-Interval Schedule

If a surfer gets a big wave to ride every 30 seconds, he is on a fixed-interval schedule.

Fixed-interval schedule means that a reinforcer occurs following the first response after a fixed interval of time.

A fixed-interval schedule has slow responding at first, but as the time for the reinforcer nears, responses increase.

© Warren Bolster/Getty Images

Variable-Ratio Schedule

If a slot machine pays off after an average of 25 pulls, the gambler is on a variable-ratio schedule.

Variable-ratio schedule means that a reinforcer is delivered after an average number of correct responses has occurred.

The variable-ratio schedule produces a high rate of responding because the person doesn't know which response will produce the payoff.

© RK Studio/Monashee Frantz/Getty Images

Variable-Interval Schedule

If a bus arrives an average of 7 minutes late but at variable intervals, the bus rider is on a variable-interval schedule. This reinforces arriving just a few minutes late for the bus.

Variable-interval schedule means that a reinforcer occurs following the first correct response after an average amount of time has passed.

A variable-interval schedule results in a more regular rate of responding than does a fixed-interval schedule.

© SuperStock

Schedules of Reinforcement

Observe and distinguish the partial reinforcement schedules.

▶ **LO13** Explain behavior modification and identify some of its applications.

Behavior Modification

In this chapter, we have discussed many examples of how operant conditioning principles are applied to animals and humans. For example, we explained how operant conditioning is used to encourage children to eat fruits and vegetables during lunch, to stop children from engaging in dangerous behaviors, and to train a dog to shake hands. These are all examples of behavior modification (Miltenberger, 2007).

Behavior modification is a treatment or therapy that changes or modifies problems or undesirable behaviors by using principles of learning based on operant conditioning.

Behavior Modification and Autism

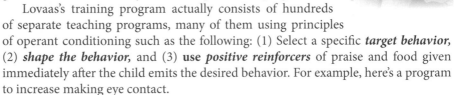

For over 35 years, psychologist and researcher Ivar Lovaas of the University of California at Los Angeles has used behavior modification or, more colloquially, behavior mod to treat autism (we discussed the symptoms of autism in Module 1.1). Lovaas's program at UCLA, which is called the Young Autism Project, treats 2- to 3-year-old autistic children with a 40-hour-per-week program that runs for 2 to 3 years. Here's part of the program:

Lovaas's training program actually consists of hundreds of separate teaching programs, many of them using principles of operant conditioning such as the following: (1) Select a specific *target behavior,* (2) *shape the behavior,* and (3) **use** *positive reinforcers* of praise and food given immediately after the child emits the desired behavior. For example, here's a program to increase making eye contact.

Target behavior is getting the child to make eye contact following the command "Look at me."

Shaping the behavior involves two steps:

Step 1. Have the child sit in a chair facing you. Give the command, "Look at me" every 5 to 10 seconds. When the child makes a correct response of looking at you, say "Good looking" and simultaneously reward the child with food.

Step 2. Continue until the child repeatedly obeys the command, "Look at me." Then gradually increase the duration of the child's eye contact from 1 second to periods of 2 to 3 seconds.

Using this behavior-mod program, therapists and parents have had success in teaching autistic children to make eye contact, to stop constant rocking, to interact with peers, to speak, and to engage in school tasks (Lovaas, 1993).

Biofeedback

Many people develop a variety of psychosomatic problems, which result from stressful or disturbing thoughts that lead to real aches and pains in the body. For example, psychosomatic problems include back pain, muscle tension, high blood pressure, stomach distress, and headaches. One procedure to reduce psychosomatic problems using behavioral modification is based on operant conditioning and is called biofeedback.

Biofeedback is a training procedure through which a person is made aware of his or her physiological responses, such as muscle activity, heart rate, blood pressure, or temperature. After becoming aware of these physiological responses, a person tries to control them to decrease psychosomatic problems.

For example, headaches may be caused or worsened by muscle tension, of which the sufferer may be totally unaware. Through video or audio biofeedback, a person can be made aware of muscle tension and learn how to reduce it.

As shown in the right photo, small sensors attached to the client's head detect

© Will & Deni McIntyre/Photo Researchers, Inc.

activity in the muscles that stretch across the top front part of the head and along the jaw. The man is trying to relax his forehead muscle by imagining relaxing scenes, thinking relaxing thoughts, or actually tensing and relaxing the muscle itself. The target behavior is a decrease in facial muscle tension. To reach this target behavior, the client practices thinking about or imagining relaxing scenes that result in a decrease in muscle tension. A decrease in muscle tension is signaled by a decrease in an audio signal, which acts as a reinforcer. After a number of these sessions, the client learns to decrease muscle tension with the goal of staying relaxed the next time he gets upset.

We'll discuss other methods of reducing stress and associated psychosomatic problems in Chapter 14.

Behavioral Modification and Autism

Learn how behavioral modification is used to treat autism.

▶ **LO14** Distinguish between operant and classical conditioning.

Operant Versus Classical Conditioning

Earlier in this chapter, we discussed how Bart the bear was operantly conditioned to hold a teddy bear and how Sam the dog was classically conditioned to salivate to the sound of a bell. Although both operant and classical conditioning lead to learning, they have very different procedures and principles. Below, we provide a comparison of the principles and procedures of operant and classical conditioning by using the same subject, Bart the bear.

Operant Conditioning

1 **Goal** The goal of operant conditioning is to increase or decrease the rate of some response, which usually involves shaping. In Bart's case, the goal was to increase his rate of holding a teddy bear.

2 **Voluntary Response** Bart's behavior of holding a teddy bear is a voluntary response because he can perform it at will. Bart must perform a voluntary response before getting a reward.

3 **Emitted Response** Bart voluntarily performs or emits some response, which is called the operant response (for example, holding a teddy bear). The term *emit* indicates that the organism acts or operates on the environment.

4 **Contingent on Behavior** Bart's performance of the desired response depends on, or is contingent on, the consequences. For example, each time Bart holds the teddy bear, the consequence is that he receives an apple. The apple, which is a reinforcer, increases the chances that Bart will perform the desired response in the future.

The reinforcer must occur immediately after the desired response. If the reinforcer occurs too late, the result may be the conditioning of unwanted or superstitious responses.

5 **Consequences** An animal or human's performance of some behavior is contingent on its consequences or what happens next. For example, the consequence of Bart's picking up and holding a teddy bear was to get an apple.

Thus, in operant conditioning, an animal or human learns that performing or *emitting* some behavior is followed by a *consequence* (reward or punishment), which, in turn, increases or decreases the chances of performing that behavior again.

Classical Conditioning

1 Goal The goal of classical conditioning is to create a new response to a *neutral stimulus.* In Bart's case, he will make a new response, salivation, to the sound of a horn, which is the neutral stimulus because it does not usually cause Bart to salivate.

2 Involuntary Response Salivation is an example of a *physiological reflex.* Physiological reflexes are triggered or elicited by some stimulus and called involuntary responses.

3 Elicited Response As Bart eats an apple, it will trigger the involuntary reflex of salivation. Eating the apple, which is the *unconditioned stimulus,* triggers or elicits an involuntary reflex response, salivation, which is called the *unconditioned response.*

4 Conditioned Response Bart was given repeated trials during which the neutral stimulus (that is, the horn's sound) was presented and followed by the unconditioned stimulus (apple). After repeated trials, Bart learned a relationship between the two stimuli: The horn's sound is followed by an apple. The horn's sound, or neutral stimulus, becomes the *conditioned stimulus* when its sound alone, before the occurrence of the apple, elicits salivation, which is the *conditioned response.*

5 Expectancy In classical conditioning, an animal or human learns a predictable relationship between, or develops an expectancy about, the neutral and unconditioned stimuli. This means Bart learned to expect that the neutral stimulus (horn's sound) is always followed by the unconditioned stimulus (apple). Thus, in classical conditioning, the animal or human learns a *predictable relationship* between stimuli.

Check Your Learning Quiz 5.4

Go to **login.cengagebrain.com** and take the online quiz.

▶ **LO15** Define cognitive learning.

▶ **LO16** Describe Tolman's cognitive map and Bandura's social cognitive learning.

Introduction to Cognitive Learning

In operant conditioning, the learning process is out in the open: Bart performs an observable behavior (holds a teddy bear), which is followed by an observable consequence (gets an apple). But there is another kind of learning that involves unobservable mental processes and unobservable rewards that you may give yourself. This kind of learning, called cognitive learning, is partly how Tony Hawk learned to skate.

Tony Hawk is recognized as the greatest skateboarder of all time. But Tony did not always have a talent for skating. When Tony was 9 years old, his brother gave him his old skateboard. Tony had seen his brother skate before, and he tried to skate just like him. Tony then visited a skate park, where he was awed by how quickly skaters went up, down, and around walls. Tony wanted to be as talented as the skaters at the park, and he went on to practice every chance he had. When Tony was asked why he enjoyed skating as a child, he replied, "I liked that no one was telling me how to do it" (CBS News, 2004). Instead, Tony learned by observing how his friends and professionals skated at the park: "I would watch them and try to learn from them. I'd imitate them" (Hawk, 2002, p. 30).

The process Tony used to learn skateboarding is very different from the operant conditioning procedure used to teach Bart new behaviors. During operant conditioning, Bart performed observable behaviors that were influenced by observable consequences. In comparison, Tony learned how to skateboard through observation and imitation, which involved unobservable mental processes; this process is called cognitive learning.

Cognitive learning, which involves mental processes, such as attention and memory, says that learning can occur through observation or imitation and such learning may not involve any external rewards or require a person to perform any observable behaviors.

Currently, cognitive learning is extremely useful in explaining both animal and human behavior (Bandura, 2001a). We'll begin by discussing what two famous psychologists had to say about cognitive learning.

Evan Agostini/Getty Images

Unless otherwise noted, all images are © Cengage Learning

Edward Tolman

In the 1930s, Tolman was exploring hidden mental processes. For example, he would place rats individually in a maze, such as the one shown below, and allow each rat time to explore the maze with no food present. Then, with food present in the maze's food box, he would test the rat to see which path it took. The rat learned very quickly to take the shortest path. Next, Tolman blocked the shortest path to the food box. The first time the rat encountered the blocked shortest path, it selected the next shortest path to the food box. According to Tolman (1948), the rat selected the next shortest path because it had developed a cognitive map of the maze.

A **cognitive map** is a mental representation in the brain of the layout of an environment and its features.

Tolman also showed that rats learned the layout of a maze without being reinforced, a position very different from Skinner's. Tolman's study of animals laid the groundwork for the study of cognitive processes in humans, which is best shown by the theory of Albert Bandura (2001a).

Albert Bandura

Bandura began as a behaviorist, which means he focused on observable behaviors and avoided studying mental events. Over the course of his career, he has almost entirely shifted to a cognitive approach. Bandura (1986) has focused on how humans learn through observing things. For example, Bandura says a child can learn to hate spiders simply by observing the behaviors of someone who shows a fear of spiders. This is an example of social cognitive learning.

Social cognitive learning results from watching, imitating, and modeling and does not require the observer to perform any observable behavior or receive any observable reward.

Just as Tolman found that learning occurred while rats were exploring, Bandura found that humans learned while observing and that much, if not most of human learning takes place through observation.

Fear of Snakes

How does social cognitive learning explain the fear of snakes?

Observational Learning

Perhaps a dozen experiments in psychology have become classics because they were the first to demonstrate some very important principles. One such classic experiment demonstrated the conditioning of emotional responses in "Little Albert" (pp. 212–213). Another classic is Albert Bandura (1965) and his colleagues' demonstration that children learned aggressive behaviors by watching an adult's aggressive behaviors. Learning through watching is called *observational learning,* which is a form of cognitive learning.

Bobo Doll Experiment

One reason this Bobo doll study is a classic experiment is that it challenged the idea that learning occurred through classical or operant conditioning. Children learned to perform aggressive responses simply from watching.

Procedure In one part of the room, preschool children were involved in their own art projects. In another part of the room, an adult got up and, for the next 10 minutes, kicked, hit, and yelled, "Hit him! Kick him!" at a large, inflated Bobo doll. Some children watched the model's aggressive behaviors, while other children did not.

Each child was later subjected to a frustrating situation and then placed in a room with toys, including the Bobo doll. Without the child's knowledge, researchers observed the child's behaviors.

Results Children who had observed the model's aggressive attacks on the Bobo doll also kicked, hit, and yelled, "Hit him! Kick him!" at the doll. Through observational learning alone, these children learned the model's aggressive behaviors and were now performing them. In comparison, children who hadn't observed the model's behaviors didn't hit or kick the Bobo doll after becoming mildly frustrated.

Conclusion Bandura's point is that children learned to perform specific aggressive behaviors not by practicing or being reinforced but simply by watching a live model perform behaviors. Observational learning is called *modeling* because it involves watching a model and imitating the behavior.

Based on the Bobo doll study and others, Bandura developed a theory of cognitive learning that we'll examine next.

Bandura's Social Cognitive Theory

The idea that humans gather information about their environments and the behaviors of others through observation is a key part of Bandura's (2001a) social cognitive theory of learning.

Social cognitive theory emphasizes the importance of observation, imitation, and self-reward in the development and learning of social skills, personal interactions, and many other behaviors.

Unlike operant and classical conditioning, this theory says it is not necessary to perform any observable behaviors or receive any external rewards to learn.

Bandura believes that four processes—attention, memory, imitation, and motivation—operate during social cognitive learning. We'll explain how these processes operate in decreasing fear of spiders.

Social Cognitive Learning: Four Processes

1 Attention

The observer must pay attention to what the model says or does. In the photo at right, a nonfrightened person (model) holds a huge spider while a woman (observer) looks on in fear.

2 Memory

The observer must store or remember the information so that it can be retrieved and used later. The observer in the photo will store the image of seeing a nonfrightened person (model) holding a spider.

3 Imitation

The observer must be able to use the remembered information to guide his or her own actions and thus imitate the model's behavior. The observer in the photo will later try to imitate the model's calm behavior when holding a spider.

4 Motivation

The observer must have some reason or incentive to imitate the model's behavior. The observer in the photo is motivated to overcome her fear of spiders because she wants to go on camping trips. If this observer can successfully imitate the model's calm behavior, then she will overcome her fear of spiders.

Bobo Doll Study

See a reenactment of Bandura's bobo doll study.

Clever Cow

See how a cow demonstrates what seems to be observational learning.

Viewing Aggression

Explore what the effects are of viewing aggression in the media.

East Meets West

Learn how the Suzuki method is similar to social cognitive learning.

▶ **LO19** Describe insight learning and explain how Sultan the chimp demonstrated insight.

Insight Learning

Earlier we told you that Thorndike concluded that learning occurred through a process of trial and error as cats gradually formed associations between moving the latch and opening the door in the puzzle box. About the same time that Thorndike in America was studying the trial-and-error learning of cats escaping from a puzzle box, Wolfgang Köhler in Germany was studying how chimpanzees learned to obtain bananas that were out of reach. Köhler challenged Thorndike's conclusion that animals learned only through trial and error. Köhler suggested instead that animals that were observed under the proper circumstances could solve a problem in a sudden flash, known as insight or "ah-ha!" (Cook, 2002).

Insight is a mental process marked by the sudden and unexpected solution to a problem, a phenomenon often called the "ah-ha!" experience.

Here's an example of Köhler's chimp, Sultan, who showed insight in getting a banana that was hanging out of reach.

Insight in Animals

Köhler (1925) hung a banana from the ceiling in a room that had a box placed off to one side. The banana was too high for Sultan the chimp to grab by reaching or jumping. When Sultan first entered the room, he paced restlessly for about 5 minutes. Then he got the box, moved it toward the banana, climbed onto the box, jumped up, and seized the banana. On his second try, Sultan quickly moved the box beneath the banana and jumped up to get it.

What intrigued Köhler about Sultan's problem-solving behavior was that it seemed to differ from the random trial-and-error behavior of Thorndike's cats. Before Sultan arrived at a solution, he might pace about, sit quietly, or vainly grasp at the out-of-reach banana. Then, all of a sudden, he seemed to hit on the solution and immediately executed a complicated set of behaviors, such as standing on a box, to get the banana. Köhler believed that Sultan's sudden solution to a problem was an example of *insight,* a mental process quite different from what Thorndike had observed in the random trial-and-error learning of cats.

Unless otherwise noted, all images are © Cengage Learning

Insight in Humans

Just as Sultan the chimp seemed to suddenly arrive at a solution to a problem, humans also report the experience of suddenly and unexpectedly solving a challenging or difficult problem. You may have an "ah-ha!" experience or flash of insight if you can figure out what critical piece of information is needed to make the following story make sense:

A man walks into a bar and asks for a glass of water. The bartender points a gun at the man. The man says "Thank you" and walks out.

Obviously, something critical happened between the two events: "asks for a glass of water" and "The bartender points a gun at the man." Some subjects solved this problem relatively quickly, while others couldn't solve this problem in the 2-hour time limit.

Neither one of us could solve the problem until we read the hint: The man has hiccups. Think about cures for hiccups and you may have an "ah-ha!" experience (answer at bottom of page). There was a difference between nonsolvers and solvers in the cognitive strategy they used. The nonsolvers focused on the obvious elements, such as man, bartender, gun, and glass of water, and not on new concepts such as hiccups and cure that lead to a solution. In comparison, the solvers spent more time on bringing in new information, and when they finally found the missing piece of information (cure for hiccups), the solution arrived suddenly, like the "ah-ha!" experience Köhler defined as insight (Durso et al., 1994).

We have discussed three examples of cognitive learning: Tolman's idea of cognitive maps, Bandura's theory of social cognitive learning, and Köhler's study of insightful problem solving.

Clever Crow

Watch how a crow demonstates what seems to be insight learning.

Check Your Learning Quiz 5.5

Go to **login.cengagebrain.com** and take the online quiz.

Answer: The man drank the water, but it didn't cure his hiccups. The bartender thought a surprise or fright might do the trick. He points a gun at the man, who is frightened, and so his hiccups stop. The man says "Thank you" and walks out.

Unless otherwise noted, all images are © Cengage Learning

Think Critically

Challenge Your Thinking

Consider these questions when reading this article:

1. How do we know what a reinforcer is for a whale?

2. Why isn't punishment used to train a whale to perform behaviors?

3. Why is it important to reinforce the whale immediately after it performs a desired behavior?

4. In this training example, what is the neutral stimulus? Unconditioned stimulus? Conditioned stimulus?

5. Can whales learn to do tricks by just watching other whales perform?

6. Is the use of animals for entertainment purposes justified? (See Module 1.9)

How Do You Train a Killer Whale?

If you have ever been to a marine park, then you most certainly have been entertained by watching the marvelous marine animal performances. In just one show an enormous killer whale jumps through a ring suspended in air, waves to audience members with its fins, swims backward while standing up on its tail, and gently kisses a brave volunteer. Whales are taught to perform these impressive behaviors with the use of operant and classical conditioning techniques.

Operant conditioning is used to train whales because when the consequences of performing a specific behavior are reinforcing, the whale will likely repeat the behavior. Positive reinforcers for whales may include food, toys, back scratches, being sprayed with a hose, or another favorite activity. Giving the whale positive reinforcers immediately after it performs a specific behavior makes it likely that the behavior will increase in frequency, duration, and intensity in a similar situation.

The use of classical conditioning is also necessary to teach a whale to perform complex behaviors. Because it is not always possible to reinforce the whale immediately after it performs a specific behavior, trainers must use a signal, such as a whistle, to provide the whale with immediate feedback that it has correctly performed the desired behavior. A whale learns the meaning of the whistle by the

© AP Images/Amy Sancetta

trainer whistling before giving the whale food. Over the course of several trials, the whale comes to associate the whistle with receiving food, and the whale performs the behavior to get the reinforcement.

Once the association between the whistle and the reinforcer is established, whales can be taught to perform complex behaviors. First, the whale is taught to follow a target, such as a long stick with a ball at the end. The target guides the whale in a direction, and when the target touches the whale, the trainer blows the whistle and reinforces the whale. After this is done several times, the target is moved farther away and the trainer waits for the whale to touch it before providing reinforcement. The whale learns that

making contact with the target results in being reinforced. Now, when the whale performs a behavior that is close to the desired behavior, the trainer whistles and the whale approaches the trainer to receive a positive reinforce.

Teaching whales to perform behaviors may appear like a relatively easy task while watching the trainers and whales interact on stage, but the truth is training whales to perform is very challenging work. Trainers need to be committed, patient, and friendly to earn the whale's trust, and even then it can take months or even years to teach a whale a complex set of behaviors. (Adapted from Animal training at SeaWorld, 2002; Aqua facts: Training marine mammals, 2006)

Think Critically 5.1

This article and its questions are available in interactive format online.

GO to your Psychology CourseMate at login.cengagebrain.com and take the Chapter Post-Test to see which Learning Objectives you've mastered and which need more review. Use the chapter review guide below and the online activities—including flashcards to review key terms—to measure your learning.

Measure
^Your Learning

Online Activities

Key Terms	Video	Animation	Reading	Assessment
learning				Check Your Learning Quiz 5.1
associative learning, classical conditioning, operant conditioning, cognitive learning				Check Your Learning Quiz 5.2
neutral stimulus (NS), unconditioning stimulus (UCS), unconditioned response (UCR), conditioned stimulus (CS), conditioned response (CR), generalization, discrimination, extinction, spontaneous recovery, anticipatory nausea, systematic desensitization, adaptive value, taste-aversion learning	Fear Conditioning, p. 213 Little Albert, p. 217	Pavlov's Experiment, p. 211 Classical Conditioning, p. 217	Conditioning Dental Fears, p. 215 Fear of Needles, p. 219 Adaptive Value, p. 221	Check Your Learning Quiz 5.3

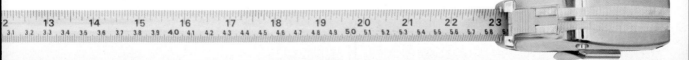

Measure ^Your Learning

Online Activities

Key Terms	Video	Animation	Reading	Assessment
operant conditioning, law of effect, operant response, shaping, superstitious behavior, generalization, discrimination, extinction, spontaneous recovery, reinforcement, punishment, positive reinforcement, positive reinforcer, negative reinforcement, primary reinforcer, secondary reinforcer, positive punishment, time-out, negative punishment, schedule of reinforcement, continuous reinforcement, partial reinforcement, fixed-ratio schedule, variable-ratio schedule, fixed-interval schedule, variable-interval schedule, behavior modification, biofeedback	Rat in a Skinner Box, p. 225 B.F. Skinner Shaping a Pigeon, p. 225 Pain Therapy, p. 231	Types of Consequences, p. 231 Schedules of Reinforcement, p. 233	Pros and Cons of Punishment, p. 231 Behavioral Modification and Autism, p. 235	Check Your Learning Quiz 5.4
cognitive learning, cognitive map, social cognitive learning, social cognitive theory, insight	Bobo Doll Study, p. 241 Clever Cow, p. 241 Clever Crow, p. 243		Fear of Snakes, p. 239 Viewing Aggression, p. 241 East Meets West, p. 241	Check Your Learning Quiz 5.5

Memory

6

Prepare to Learn

1 **GO** to your **Psychology CourseMate** at **login.cengagebrain.com** and take the **Chapter Pre-Test** to introduce yourself to this chapter's topics and see what you may already know.

2 **READ** the **Learning Objectives (LOs)** (in the left sidebars) and begin the chapter.

3 **COMPLETE** the **Online Activities** (in the right sidebars) *as you read each module*. Activities include **videos**, **animations**, **readings**, and **quizzes**.

4 **CHECK Your Learning** by going online to take the quiz at the end of each module and review material as necessary.

5 **MEASURE Your Learning** after reading the chapter by taking the online **Chapter Post-Test**. Use the chapter review guide at the end of the chapter as needed.

WATCH for these **Online Activities** icons as you read:

Video

Animation

Reading

Assessment

Think Critically

These online activities are important to mastering this chapter. As you read each module, access these materials by going to **login.cengagebrain.com**.

 Video Explore studies and firsthand accounts of biological and psychological processes:

- Learn more about Daniel Tammet's amazing memory
- See how short-term memory works
- Explore Clive Wearing's memory problems
- Learn how the brain processes declarative and nondeclarative memory
- Watch how maintenance and elaborative rehearsal work
- Watch how easily false memories can be implanted
- Watch what happens in the brain when we are exposed to an emotionally charged event
- Explore what the implications are of memory abilities for police, the justice system, and eyewitness testimony

 Animation Interact with and visualize important processes and concepts:

- Observe the interaction between the three memory processes
- Test your memory and understand the primacy-recency effect
- Watch how short- and long-term memories are formed in the brain
- See how mnemonic devices help to improve memory

 Reading Delve deeper into key content:

- Learn how culture influences the way information is encoded
- Learn how culture influences the use of retrieval cues
- Find out whether false memories can change your behavior

- Learn whether drugs can block emotional memories
- Explore how accurate your own eyewitness testimony is

 Assessment Measure your mastery:

- Chapter Pre-Test
- Check Your Learning Quizzes
- Chapter Post-Test

 Think Critically Challenge your thinking by applying content from this chapter and making connections to related material:

- Can Bad Memories Be Erased?

DANIEL TAMMET STOOD before the packed house at the Museum of History and Science in Oxford. He recited, from memory, the first 22,514 digits of *pi*, which is often rounded off to two decimal places, or 3.14. He completed this amazing feat in 5 hours and 9 minutes and made no mistakes.

▼

Scientists describe Daniel's memory as nothing less than extraordinary. In fact, Daniel is one of only a half dozen people worldwide with such gargantuan memory powers. Later in the chapter, we'll learn about the memory technique Daniel uses to remember so many digits (Schorn, 2007; Tammet, 2007, 2009). First, we'll learn how Daniel's amazing ability to recall thousands of digits involves three different memory processes.

Memory is the ability to retain information over time through three processes: encoding (forming), storing, and retrieving. Memories are not copies but representations of the world that vary in accuracy and are subject to error and bias.

First, Daniel developed a method or code to form memories for digits, a process called encoding.

Encoding refers to making mental representations of information so that it can be placed into our memories.

For example, Daniel encodes numbers by

© Colin McPherson/Corbis

Unless otherwise noted, all images are © Cengage Learning

visualizing each number as having a different shape, color, and texture. Such a vivid mental representation helps him store numbers in his memory.

Second, Daniel used associations to encode information because associations are also useful for storing information.

Storing is the process of placing encoded information into relatively permanent mental storage for later recall.

New information that is stored by making associations with old or familiar information is much easier to remember, or retrieve.

Third, Daniel was able to recall, or retrieve, 22,514 digits in order.

Retrieving is the process of getting or recalling information that has been placed into short-term or long-term storage.

We'll discuss many fasinating aspects of memory, such as remembering and forgetting, as well as the biology of memory, ways to improve your memory, eyewitness testimony, and unusual memories. We'll start with the three kinds of memory.

3.141592653589793238

Daniel Tammet

Learn more about Daniel Tammet's amazing memory.

Check Your Learning Quiz 6.1

Go to **login.cengagebrain.com** and take the online quiz.

▶ **L03** Describe the characteristics and functions of sensory memory, short-term memory, and long-term memory.

Memory Processes

We often talk about memory as though it were a single process. In fact, a popular model of memory divides it into three different processes: sensory, short-term, and long-term memory (Baddeley, 2006). To illustrate each of these processes, we'll examine what happens as you walk through a big-city mall.

Imagine that as you walk through a busy mall, you are bombarded by hundreds of sights, smells, and sounds, including the music of a lone guitarist playing for spare change. Many of these stimuli reach your sensory memory.

Sensory memory refers to an initial process that receives and holds environmental information in its raw form for a brief period of time, from an instant to several seconds.

For example, after reaching your ears, the guitarist's sounds are held in sensory memory for a second or two. What you do next will determine what happens to the guitarist's sounds that are in your sensory memory.

© PhotoDisc/Getty Images

If you pay no more attention to these sounds in sensory memory, they automatically disappear without a trace. However, if you pay attention to the guitarist's music, the auditory information in sensory memory is automaticiclly transferred into another memory process called short-term memory (Baddeley, 2009c).

Short-term memory, also called **working memory,** refers to another process that can hold only a limited amount of information (an average of seven items) for only a short period of time (2 to 30 seconds).

© Royalty-Free/Masterfile

Once a limited amount of information is transferred into short-term, or working, memory, it will remain there for up to 30 seconds. If during this time you become more involved in the information, such as whistling to the music, the information will remain in short-term memory for a longer period of time, and there is a good chance that this mental activity will transfer the music from short-term into long-term memory (Squire & Kandel, 2009).

Long-term memory refers to the process of storing almost unlimited amounts of information over long periods of time.

For example, you have stored hundreds of songs, terms, and faces in your long-term memory, information that is potentially available for retrieval.

Now that you know what the three memory processes are, we'll explain how they work together.

1 Sensory memory We'll explain how the three types of memory work and how paying or not paying attention to something determines what is remembered and what is forgotten.

Imagine listening to a lecture. All the information that enters your sensory memory remains for seconds or less. If you *do not pay attention* to information in sensory memory, it is forgotten. If you *do pay attention* to particular information, such as the instructor's words, this information is automatically transferred into short-term memory.

2 Short-term memory If you *do not pay attention* to information in short-term memory, it is not encoded and is forgotten. If you *do pay attention* by rehearsing the information, such as taking notes, the information will be encoded for storage in long-term memory. That's why it helps to take lecture notes.

3 Long-term memory Information that is encoded for storage in long-term memory will remain there on a *relatively permanent basis*. Whether or not you can recall the instructor's words from long-term memory depends partly on how they are encoded, which we'll discuss later. This means that poor class notes may result in poor encoding and poor recall on exams. The secret to great encoding and great recall is to associate new information with old, which we'll also discuss later.

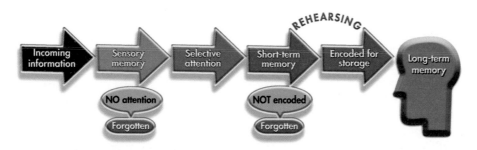

Now that we have given you an overview of memory, we'll discuss each of the three types of memory in more detail.

Memory Processes

Observe the interaction between the three memory processes.

Sensory Memory: Recording

Your brain has a mental video-audio recorder that automatically receives and holds incoming sensory information for only seconds or less. This brief period provides just enough time for you to decide whether some particular incoming sensory information is important or interesting and therefore demands your further attention. We'll examine two different kinds of sensory memory: (1) visual sensory memory, called iconic memory, and (2) auditory sensory memory, called echoic memory.

Iconic Memory

About 14,000 times a waking day, your eyes blink and you are totally blind during the blinks (Casselman, 2006; Garbarini, 2005). However, the world doesn't disappear during the eyeblinks because of a special sensory memory, which is called iconic *(eye-CON-ick)* memory.

Iconic memory is a form of sensory memory that automatically holds visual information for about a quarter of a second or more; as soon as you shift your attention, the information disappears. (The word icon means "image.")

You don't "go blind" when both eyes close completely during a blink (about one-third of a second) because the visual scene is briefly held in iconic memory (O'Regan et al., 2000). When your eyes reopen, you don't realize that your eyes were completely closed during the blink because you "kept seeing" the visual information that was briefly stored in iconic memory. Without iconic memory, your world would disappear into darkness during each eye blink.

Unless otherwise noted, all images are © Cengage Learning

PhotoDisc, Inc.

Echoic Memory

Without realizing, you have already experienced auditory sensory memory, which is called echoic *(eh-KO-ick)* memory.

Echoic memory is a form of sensory memory that holds auditory information for 1 or 2 seconds.

For instance, suppose you are absorbed in reading a novel and a friend asks you a question. You stop reading and ask, "What did you say?" As soon as those words are out of your mouth, you realize that you can recall, or play back, your friend's exact words. You can play back these words because they are still in echoic memory, which may last as long as 2 seconds. In addition to letting you play back things you thought you did not hear, echoic memory lets you hold speech sounds long enough to know that sequences of certain sounds form words (Norman, 1982).

Below is a quick review of the functions of iconic and echoic memories.

Functions of Sensory Memory

Prevents being overwhelmed. Sensory memory keeps you from being overwhelmed by too many incoming stimuli because any sensory information you do not attend to will vanish in seconds.

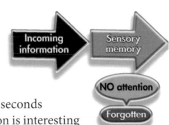

Gives decision time. Sensory memory gives you a few seconds to decide whether some incoming sensory information is interesting or important. Information you pay attention to will automatically be transferred to short-term memory.

Provides stability, playback, and recognition. Iconic memory makes things in your visual world appear smooth and continuous, such as "seeing" even during blinking. Echoic memory lets you play back auditory information, such as holding separate sounds so that you can recognize them as words.

If you attend to information in sensory memory, it goes into short-term memory, the next topic.

Short-Term Memory: Working

You have just looked up a phone number, which you keep repeating as you dial to order a pizza. After giving your order and hanging up, you can't remember the number. This example shows two characteristics of short-term memory.

Short-term memory, more recently called **working memory,** refers to a process that can hold a limited amount of information (an average of seven items) for a limited period of time (2 to 30 seconds).

Short-term memory is also called *working memory* to indicate that it's an active process. For good reason, telephone numbers and postal ZIP codes are seven numbers or fewer because that is about the limit of short-term memory.

Two Features of Short-Term Memory

Limited Duration

The new telephone number you looked up will remain in short-term memory for a brief time, usually 2 to 30 seconds, and then disappear. However, you can keep information longer in short-term memory by using maintenance rehearsal.

Maintenance rehearsal refers to the practice of intentionally repeating or rehearsing information so that it remains longer in short-term memory.

Researchers studied how long information is remembered without practice or rehearsal by asking participants to remember a series of consonants composed of three meaningless letters, such as CHJ. Participants were prevented from rehearsing these consonants by having them count backward immediately after seeing the three letters. As shown in the graph, 80% of the participants recalled the groups of three letters after 3 seconds. However, only 10% of the participants recalled the groups of three letters after 15 seconds (Peterson & Peterson, 1950). Since almost all the participants had forgotten the groups of three letters after 15 seconds (if they were prevented from rehearsing), this study clearly showed that information disappears from your short-term memory within seconds unless you continually repeat or rehearse the information.

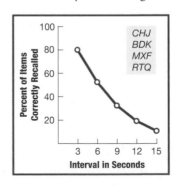

Limited Capacity

In previous chapters, we pointed out several studies that are considered classic because they challenged old concepts or identified significant new information. One such classic study is that of George Miller (1956), who was the first to discover that short-term memory can hold only about seven items or bits, plus or minus two. Although this seems like too small a number, researchers have repeatedly confirmed Miller's original finding (Baddeley, 2004).

It is easy to confirm Miller's finding with a *memory span test,* which measures the total number of digits that we can repeat back in the correct order after a single hearing. For example, students make few errors when they are asked to repeat seven or eight digits, make some errors with a list of eight or nine digits, and make many errors when they repeat a list that is longer than nine digits.

One of the main reasons information disappears from short-term memory is interference (Anderson, 2009a).

Interference results when new information enters short-term memory and overwrites or pushes out information that is already there.

For example, if you are trying to remember a phone number and someone asks you a question, the question interferes with or wipes away the phone number. One way to prevent interference is through rehearsal. However, once we stop rehearsing, the information in short-term memory may disappear.

Although short-term memory has limited capacity and duration, it is possible to increase both. For example, we use a classroom demonstration in which we guarantee that any student can learn to memorize a list of 21 digits, in exact order, in just 25 seconds. This impressive memory demonstration, which always works, is accomplished by knowing how to use something called chunking, our next topic.

Short-Term Memory

See how short-term memory works.

▶ **LO3** Describe the characteristics and functions of sensory memory, short-term memory, and long-term memory. (Cont'd)

Chunking

Although short-term memory briefly holds an average of about seven items, it is possible to increase the length of each item by using a process called chunking (Baddeley, 2009c).

Chunking is combining separate items of information into a larger unit, or chunk, and then remembering chunks of information rather than individual items.

One of the interesting things about Daniel Tammet's prodigious memory for numbers is his ability to chunk. Whereas most of us would see an endless string of random numbers when looking at the digits in *pi*, Daniel is able to chunk the numbers into groups, with each represented by a unique visual image. In his mind, every number up to 10,000 has a unique shape, color, and texture. When he sees a long sequence of numbers, as in *pi*, he effortlessly sees a "landscape of colorful shapes." Daniel describes some numbers as being beautiful (such as 333) and others as quite ugly (such as 289). He has a condition called synesthesia, which we discussed in Module 3.1 (see pp. 102–103). Synesthesia is when people's senses become intertwined. For example, they may hear colors, see music, or taste shapes. Synesthesia has been shown to activate more areas of people's brain, which in turn may improve their memory (Foer, 2006; Schorn, 2007; Tammet, 2007, 2009).

The ability to use chunking is not limited to people with super memories. We all use chunking at times without thinking about it. For example, to remember the 11-digit phone number 16228759211, we break it into four chunks: 1-622-875-9211.

As first suggested by George Miller (1956), chunking is a powerful memory tool that greatly increases the amount of information that you can hold in short-term memory. Daniel's ability to chunk numbers helped him develop an incredible memory, and the use of chunking can improve your memory, too.

Next, we'll review three important functions of short-term memory.

Functions of Short-Term Memory

There are three important points to remember about short-term memory: (1) paying attention transfers information into short-term memory; (2) after a short time, information disappears unless it is rehearsed; and (3) some information is transferred from short-term memory into permanent storage.

Attending

Imagine driving along with your radio on while a friend in the passenger seat is talking about the weekend. A tremendous amount of information is entering your sensory memory, but you avoid stimulus overload because incoming information automatically vanishes in seconds unless you pay attention to it.

The moment you pay attention to information in sensory memory, that information enters short-term memory. For example, while your friend is talking, you don't pay attention to the radio until your favorite song comes on. As you pay attention, you hear the radio, even though it has been playing the whole time. One function of short-term memory is that it allows us to *selectively attend to information that is relevant and disregard everything else.*

Rehearsing

Once information enters short-term memory, it usually remains for only seconds unless you rehearse it. For example, the announcer on the car radio gives a phone number to call for free movie tickets. But unless you rehearse or repeat the number over and over, it will probably disappear from your short-term memory because of interference from newly arriving information. Another function of short-term memory is that it allows you *to hold information for a short period of time until you decide what to do with it.*

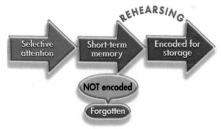

If you rehearse the information in short-term memory, you increase the chances of storing it.

Storing

Rehearsing information not only holds that information in short-term memory but also helps *to store or encode information in long-term memory.*

Next, we'll describe the steps in the memory process and why some things are stored in long-term memory.

▶ **LO3** Describe the characteristics and functions of sensory memory, short-term memory, and long-term memory. (Cont'd)

Long-Term Memory: Storing

Putting Information into Long-Term Memory

Don't think of sensory memory, short-term memory, and long-term memory as *things* or *places* but as ongoing and interacting *processes*. To show how these different memory processes interact, we'll describe what happens as you hear a new song on the car radio or iPod and try to remember the song's title.

1 Sensory Memory As you drive down the highway, let's say you're half listening to the car radio. Among the incoming information, which is held for seconds or less in sensory memory, are the words, "Remember this song, 'Love Is Like Chocolate,' and win two movie tickets."

2 Attention If you do **not** pay attention to information about winning tickets, it will disappear from sensory memory. If the chance to win tickets gets your attention, information about the song title, "Love Is Like Chocolate," is automatically transferred into short-term memory.

3 Short-Term Memory Once the song title is in short-term memory, you have a short time (2 to 30 seconds) for further processing. If you lose interest in the title or are distracted by traffic, the title will most likely disappear and be forgotten. However, if you rehearse the title or, better yet, form a new association, the title will likely be encoded in your long-term memory.

Love Is Like Chocolate

© PhotoDisc/Getty Images

4 Encoding You place information in long-term memory through a process called encoding.

Encoding is the process of transferring information from short-term to long-term memory by paying attention to it, repeating or rehearsing it, or forming new associations.

For example, if you simply repeat the title or don't make any new associations, the title may not be encoded at all or may be poorly encoded and thus difficult to recall from long-term memory. However, if you find the title, "Love Is Like Chocolate," to be catchy or unusual, or you form a new association, such as thinking of a heart-shaped chocolate, you will be successful in encoding this title into long-term memory.

5 **Long-Term Memory** Once the song title is encoded in long-term memory, it has the potential to remain there for your lifetime.

Long-term memory refers to the process of storing almost unlimited amounts of information over long periods of time with the potential of retrieving, or remembering, such information in the future.

For example, later you may try to recall the song title from long-term memory by placing it back into short-term memory. How easily and accurately you can recall or retrieve information depends on many factors (Anderson, 2009c).

6 **Retrieving** When people talk about remembering something, they usually mean retrieving or recalling information from long-term memory.

Retrieving is the process of selecting information from long-term memory and transferring it back into short-term memory.

There are several reasons you can't remember or retrieve the song's title. You might not have effectively encoded the title into long-term memory because you got distracted or neglected to form a new association (for example, a chocolate heart). The key to successfully retrieving information from long-term memory is to effectively encode information, usually by making associations between new and old information, which we'll soon discuss.

Features of Long-Term Memory

Long-term memory has an almost *unlimited capacity* to store information. Anything stored has the potential to last a *lifetime,* provided drugs or disease do not damage the brain's memory circuits (Bahrick, 2000).

Although all information in long-term memory has the potential to be retrieved, how much you can actually retrieve depends on a number of factors, including how it was encoded and any interference from related information.

Researchers found that the *content and accuracy* of long-term memories may undergo change and distortion across time and not always be as accurate as people think. We don't recall all events with the same accuracy, sometimes inflating positive events and eliminating negative ones (Anderson, 2009b; Mather & Carstensen, 2005).

Unless otherwise noted, all images are © Cengage Learning

▶ **L03** Describe the characteristics and functions of sensory memory, short-term memory, and long-term memory. (Cont'd)

Separate Memory Systems

Most researchers agree there are two memory systems (Neath & Surprenant, 2003). One system involves short-term memory, which stores limited information for a brief period of time, and then the information disappears. For example, a stranger tells you his or her name, but a few minutes later you have totally forgotten the name because it disappeared from short-term memory. A second system involves long-term memory, which stores large amounts of information for long periods of time. For example, you can recall in great detail many childhood memories that have been stored in long-term memory. Other evidence for two memory systems comes from research on how you remember items in a relatively long list.

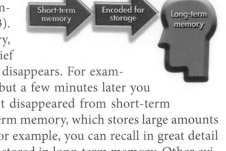

We'll give you a chance to memorize a list of items, which will show that you have two separate memory systems: short- and long-term memory.

Please read the following list only once and try to remember the animals' names:

**bear, giraffe, wolf, fly, deer,
elk, gorilla, elephant, frog, snail,
turtle, shark, ant, owl**

Immediately after reading this list, write down (in any order) as many of the animals' names as you can remember.

If you examine the list of names that you wrote down, you'll discover a definite pattern to the order of the names that you remembered. For example, here's the order in which names in the above list would most likely be remembered.

First Items: Primacy Effect

In studies using similar lists, subjects more easily recalled the *first* four or five items (bear, giraffe, wolf, fly) because subjects had more time to rehearse the first words presented. As a result of rehearsing, these first names were transferred to and stored in long-term memory, from which they were recalled. This phenomenon is called the primacy effect.

The **primacy effect** refers to better recall, or improvement in retention, of information presented at the beginning of a task.

© PhotoDisc, Inc.

6.2

Middle Items

Subjects did not recall many items from the *middle* of the list (for example, gorilla, elephant, frog) because they did not have much time to rehearse them. When they tried to remember items from the middle of the list, their attention and time were split between trying to remember the previous terms and trying to rehearse new ones. Less rehearsal meant that fewer middle items were stored in long-term memory; more interference meant that fewer items remained in short-term memory.

Last Items: Recency Effect

Subjects more easily recalled the *last* four or five items (for example turtle, shark, ant, owl) because they were still available in short-term memory and could be read off a mental list. This phenomenon is called the recency effect.

The **recency effect** refers to better recall, or improvement in retention, of information presented at the end of a task.

Together, these two effects are called the primacy-recency effect.

The **primacy-recency effect** refers to better recall of information presented at the beginning and end of a task.

As we'll explain next, the primacy-recency effect is evidence that short- and long-term memory are two separate processes.

Short-Term versus Long-Term Memory

One reason you probably didn't remember the name "elephant" is that it came from the middle of the list. The middle section of a list is usually least remembered because that information may no longer be retained in short-term memory and may not have been encoded in long-term memory.

For example, subjects showed better recall (70%) for the first items presented, which is the primacy effect. The primacy effect occurs because subjects have more time to rehearse the first items, which increases the chances of transferring these items into long-term memory. In addition, subjects showed better recall (60%) for the last items presented, which is the recency effect. Sometimes subjects say that they can still "hear these words" and usually report these items first. The recency effect occurs because the last items are still in short-term memory, from which they are recalled (Glanzer & Cunitz, 1966).

Primacy-Recency Effect

Test your memory and understand the primary-recency effect.

▶ **LO4** Describe the different types of sensory memory and long-term memory. (Cont'd)

Declarative Versus Procedural or Nondeclarative

Imagine what life would be like without memory. For Clive Wearing, that's a grim reality.

At age 40, Clive Wearing, a musician, got a disease that caused brain damage resulting in severe memory impairment. For instance, despite having written a book on a classical composer, he cannot remember any information about the composer. Clive can no longer enjoy reading books or watching movies because he is unable to follow the plot. Each time Clive sees his wife, he excitedly greets her as if he has not seen her in years, even though she may have left the room for only a moment. He cannot recall his wedding day or the names of his children.

The disease did spare Clive some of his memory. Even though Clive cannot remember being educated in music, he remembers how to play the piano, conduct an orchestra, and sing (Baddeley, 2009d; Sacks, 2008).

When Clive tells others about his life, he says it is "precisely like death. I'd like to be alive" (Goodwin, 2006, p. 125). He does not feel alive because for the past 25 years, his memory problems have robbed him of a past and future. Clive lives in a never-ending present. His wife describes his memory by explaining, "It's as if Clive's every conscious moment is like waking up for the first time" (Goodwin, 2006, p. 126).

Clive retained some memory abilities while losing others because different types of memory are stored differently in the brain. For instance, the ability to play the piano uses one type of long-term memory, and remembering names and personal experiences uses a second type of long-term memory.

The discovery that there are two kinds of long-term memory is a relatively new finding, and like many discoveries in science, it was found quite by accident.

Unless otherwise noted, all images are © Cengage Learning

Researchers were testing a patient, well known in memory circles as H. M. (right photo), who suffered severe memory loss because of an earlier brain operation to reduce his seizures. H. M.'s task seemed simple: draw a star by guiding your hand while looking into a mirror (pictured below). However, this mirror-drawing test is relatively difficult because looking into a mirror reverses all hand movements: up is down and down is up. As H. M. did this task each day, his drawing improved, indicating that he was learning and remembering the necessary motor skills. But here's the strange part. Each and every day, H. M. would insist that he had never seen or done mirror drawing before (Cohen, 1984).

How could H. M. have no memory of mirror drawing, yet show improvement in his performance as he practiced it each day? Based on H. M.'s mirror drawing, as well as data from other patients and many animal studies, researchers discovered there are two kinds of long-term memory, each involving different areas of the brain (Nyberg & Cabeza, 2005; Squire & Kandel, 2009). You'll understand why H. M. could improve at mirror drawing but not remember doing it after you learn about the two kinds of long-term memory, declarative and procedural.

Man Without A Memory

Explore Clive Wearing's memory problems.

▶ **LO4** Describe the different types of sensory memory and long-term memory. (Cont'd)

Declarative Memory

Which bird cannot fly?
What did you eat for breakfast?

You would recall or retrieve answers to these questions from one particular kind of long-term memory called declarative memory.

Declarative memory involves memories for facts or events, such as scenes, stories, words, conversations, faces, or daily events. We are aware of and can recall, or retrieve, these kinds of memories.

There are two kinds of declarative memory: semantic and episodic (Eichenbaum, 2004).

© Digital Stock Corporation

Unless otherwise noted, all images are © Cengage Learning

Semantic Memory "Which bird cannot fly?" asks you to remember a fact, which involves semantic *(sah-MAN-tick)* memory.

Semantic memory is a type of declarative memory and involves knowledge of facts, concepts, words, definitions, and language rules.

Most of what you learn in classes (such as facts, terms, definitions) goes into semantic memory (Eysenck, 2009).

Episodic Memory "What did you eat for breakfast?" asks you to remember an event, which involves episodic *(ep-ih-SAH-dick)* memory.

Episodic memory is a type of declarative memory and involves knowledge of specific events, personal experiences (episodes), or activities, such as naming or describing favorite restaurants, movies, songs, habits, or hobbies.

Most of your college experiences go into episodic memory (Baddeley, 2009a).

Since his brain operation, H. M. cannot remember new facts (semantic memory) or events (episodic memory). Thus, H. M. has lost declarative memory, which explains why he does not remember events, such as doing mirror drawing (Squire et al., 2004).

However, H. M.'s motor skills improved during mirror drawing, which indicates another kind of long-term memory.

Procedural or Nondeclarative Memory

How did you learn to play tennis?
Why are you afraid of spiders?

Even if you can play tennis and are afraid of spiders, you can't explain how you control your muscles to play tennis or why you're so terrified of such a tiny (usually harmless) bug. That's because motor skills and emotional feelings are stored in procedural memory.

Procedural memory, also called **nondeclarative memory,** involves memories for motor skills (such as playing tennis), some cognitive skills (such as learning to read), and emotional behaviors learned through classical conditioning (for example, fear of spiders). We cannot recall or retrieve procedural memories.

Even if you have not played tennis for years, you can pick up a racket and still remember how to serve because that information is stored in procedural memory. But you cannot describe the sequence of movements needed to serve a ball because these skills are stored in procedural memory. Similarly, if you learned to fear spiders through classical conditioning, you cannot explain why you're afraid because the reasons are stored in procedural memory. Although procedural memories greatly influence our behavior, we have neither awareness of nor ability to recall these memories (Baddeley, 2009b).

Now we can explain H. M.'s strange behavior. He was able to improve at mirror drawing because it involved learning a motor skill that was stored in procedural memory. But he could not talk about the skill because no one is aware of or can recall procedural memories. Although H. M. gradually improved at mirror drawing, he could not remember the event of sitting down and drawing because that involves declarative (episodic) memories, which were damaged in his brain surgery (Hilts, 1995). The study of H. M. is a classic study because it first demonstrated the existence of two kinds of long-term memory: declarative memory and procedural memory. We'll discuss the brain systems underlying these types of long-term memory later in Module 6.5.

© PhotoDisc, Inc.

Brain and Memory

Learn how the brain processes declarative and nondeclarative memory.

Check Your Learning Quiz 6.2

Go to **login.cengagebrain.com** and take the online quiz.

▶ **LO6** Describe automatic and effortful encoding.

Two Kinds of Encoding

It's very common for someone to say, "Let me tell you about my day," and then describe in great detail a long list of mostly bad things, including long, word-for-word conversations. You can easily recall these detailed personal experiences, even though you took no notes. That's because many personal experiences are automatically, and with no effort, encoded in your long-term memory.

Encoding refers to acquiring information or storing information in memory by changing this information into neural or memory codes.

Why is it that detailed personal experiences and conversation seem to be encoded effortlessly and automatically and easily recalled? Why is it that much of book learning, such as memorizing terms or definitions, usually requires deliberate effort and considerable time and may still not be easily recalled when taking exams? The answer is there are two different kinds of encoding: automatic and effortful encoding.

Automatic Encoding

Just as most of us can recall all the annoying things that happened today, the person in the figure to the right is recalling a long list of very detailed personal activities that were automatically encoded into his long-term memory. In fact, many personal events (often unpleasant ones), as well as things we're interested in (for example, movies, music, sports) and a wide range of skills (such as riding a bike) and habits, are automatically encoded (Dere et al., 2008).

Automatic encoding is the transfer of information from short-term into long-term memory without any effort and usually without any awareness.

Personal Experiences One reason many of your personal experiences are automatically encoded is they hold your interest and attention and easily fit together with hundreds of previous associations. Because personal experiences, which are examples of *episodic information,* are encoded automatically into long-term memory, you can easily recall lengthy conversations, facts about movies and sports figures, clothes you bought, or food you ate.

I bought this hat at a second-hand store for a quarter, and then I bought these shoes from a guy who said that he makes them from old tires...

Encoded for storage → Long-term memory

Interesting Facts You may know avid sports fans or watchers of popular TV programs who remember an amazing number of facts and details, seemingly without effort. Because these kinds of facts *(semantic information)* are personally interesting and fit with previous associations, they are automatically and easily encoded into declarative long-term memory.

Skills and Habits Learning how to perform various motor skills, such as playing tennis or riding a bike, and developing habits, such as brushing your teeth, are examples of *procedural information,* which is also encoded automatically. For example, H. M. learned and remembered how to mirror-draw because mirror drawing is a motor skill that is automatically encoded into procedural long-term memory.

On the other hand, factual or technical information from textbooks is usually not encoded automatically but requires deliberate, or effortful, encoding, which we'll discuss next.

Effortful Encoding

The person in the figure to the right is pulling his hair because learning unfamiliar or complicated material almost always involves *semantic information,* which is difficult to encode because such information is often uninteresting, complicated, or requires making new or difficult associations. For all these reasons, semantic information, such as terms, can be encoded only with considerable concentration and effort (Squire & Kandel, 2009).

Effortful encoding involves the transfer of information from short-term into long-term memory either by working hard to repeat or rehearse the information or, especially, by making associations between new and old information.

You already know that some information, such as learning a skill, habit, or interesting personal event, is often encoded effortlessly and automatically. In contrast, semantic information, such as learning hundreds of new or difficult terms, facts, concepts, or equations, usually requires effortful encoding because you must form hundreds of new associations. Next, we'll explain two methods of effortful encoding, rehearsing and forming associations.

> I've been studying these terms for hours and I still can't remember their definitions.

Encoding and Cultural Influences

Learn how culture influences the way information is encoded.

▶ **LO7** Describe maintenance and elaborative rehearsal.

▶ **LO8** Explain the levels-of-processing theory.

Rehearsing and Encoding

Think of encoding information in your brain as similar to saving information on a gigantic computer hard drive. Unless you have a very good system for labeling and filing the hundreds of computer files, you will have great difficulty finding or retrieving a particular file from the hard drive. Similarly, how easily you can remember or retrieve a particular memory from your brain depends on how much effort you used to encode the information. There are two kinds of effortful encoding: maintenance rehearsal and elaborative rehearsal (Baddeley, 2009a).

Maintenance Rehearsal

The easiest way to remember information for only a short period of time, such as a new phone number, is to simply repeat or rehearse it. This kind of effortful encoding is called maintenance rehearsal.

Maintenance rehearsal refers to simply repeating or rehearsing the information rather than forming any new associations.

Maintenance rehearsal works best for maintaining or keeping information in *short-term memory*, such as remembering a phone number for a few seconds while dialing it. However, if you want to remember the phone number later, maintenance rehearsal is not a good encoding process because it does not include a system for keeping track of how and where that particular phone number will be stored. If you need to remember a phone number for a long period of time and avoid having to keep looking it up, you'll need to use another form of effortful encoding called elaborative rehearsal.

Elaborative Rehearsal

There are some phone numbers and much information from lectures and textbooks that you want to encode so that you remember the information for long periods of time. To have the greatest chance for remembering something, it's best to encode information using elaborative rehearsal.

Elaborative rehearsal involves using effort to actively make meaningful associations between new information that you wish to remember and old or familiar information that is already stored in long-term memory.

To test the usefulness of elaborative rehearsal, students were asked to remember many groups of three words each, such as *dog, bike,* and *street.* Students who encoded the words with maintenance rehearsal (repeating words) did poorly on recall. In comparison, students who encoded the words using elaborative rehearsal—that is, taking the effort to make associations among the three words (for example, dog rides a bike down the street)—had significantly better recall (McDaniel & Einstein, 1986).

Effectiveness

Elaborative rehearsal is such an effective system of encoding because by making associations between new and old information, you create cues for locating or retrieving the new information from long-term memory. For example, thinking of the association (dog rides a bike down the street) helps you remember the three words (dog, bike, street).

Levels of Processing

The poorest system for encoding information is to simply repeat the information, which is maintenance rehearsal. The best encoding system is to make associations, which is elaborative rehearsal. How much effort and time you put into encoding information is the basis for the levels-of-processing theory (Craik & Lockhart, 1972).

The **levels-of-processing theory** says that remembering depends on how information is encoded. If you encode by paying attention only to basic features (such as length of phone number), information is encoded at a shallow level and results in poor recall. If you encode by making new associations, this information will be encoded at a deeper level, which results in better recall.

Research clearly demonstrates that the system you use to process or encode information has a great effect on how easily you can remember or retrieve the information (Anderson, 2009a). Remember, the ability to recall information depends on how well or deeply the information was processed. As we'll discuss next, a major reason for forgetting is poor encoding (Brown & Craik, 2005).

Rehearsal

Watch how maintenance and elaborative rehearsal work.

Check Your Learning Quiz 6.3

Go to **login.cengagebrain.com** and take the online quiz.

Unless otherwise noted, all images are © Cengage Learning

▶ **LO9** Describe the difference between the types of interference.

If asked to describe what happened today, you can accurately recall many personal events, conversations, and countless irritations. However, in spite of hours of study, there are many things you seem to have forgotten when you take an exam.

Forgetting refers to the inability to retrieve, recall, or recognize information that was stored or is still stored in long-term memory.

We'll summarize a few reasons people forget things.

Interference

Sooner or later, every student faces the problem of having to take exams in several different courses on the same day. This situation can increase the chances of forgetting material because of something called interference.

The theory of **interference** says that we may forget information not because it is no longer in storage or memory but rather because old or newer related information produces confusion and thus blocks retrieval from memory.

Students who take multiple tests on the same day often complain of studying long and hard but forgetting information that they knew they knew. In this case the culprit may be interference. For example, if you are studying for and taking psychology and sociology tests on the same day, you may find that some of the material on social behavior in psychology is similar to but different from material in sociology, and this mix-up will cause interference and forgetting.

Similarly, if you take two or more classes in succession, you may find that information from one class interferes with learning or remembering information from the others. We'll explain the two kinds of interference—proactive and retroactive—and how each can lead to forgetting (Anderson, 2009a). Interference, both proactive and retroactive, is one of the most common reasons for forgetting (Roediger & McDermott, 2005).

Proactive Interference

The prefix *pro* means "forward," so *proactive* interference "acts forward" to interfere with recalling newly learned information.

Proactive interference occurs when old information (learned earlier) blocks or disrupts the remembering of related new information (learned later).

Proactive Interference

1 Psychology information

From 1:00 to 3:00, you study for a test in psychology.

2 Psychology info acts forward

From 3:00 to 5:00, you study for a test in sociology. You may experience difficulty in learning and remembering this new sociology information because the previously learned psychology terms can "act forward" and interfere with remembering terms from sociology.

3 Proactive interference

When you take your sociology exam, you may forget some of the sociology terms you studied because of proactive interference. Previously learned psychology terms "act forward" to interfere with or block the recall of the more recently learned and related sociology terms.

Retroactive Interference

The prefix *retro* means "backward," so *retroactive* interference means "acting backward" to interfere with recalling previously learned information.

Retroactive interference occurs when new information (learned later) blocks or disrupts the retrieval of related old information (learned earlier).

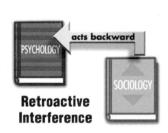

Retroactive Interference

1 Psychology information

From 1:00 to 3:00, you study for a test in psychology. Then from 3:00 to 5:00, you study for a test in sociology.

2 Sociology info acts backward

You may experience difficulty in remembering the psychology terms you learned earlier because the sociology terms recently learned may "act backward" and disrupt earlier learned and related psychology terms.

3 Retroactive interference

When you take the psychology exam, you may forget some of the terms you studied because of retroactive interference. Recently learned sociology terms "act backward" to interfere with or block the recall of earlier learned and related psychology terms.

▶ **LO10** Describe how to form effective retrieval cues.

Retrieval Cues

Have you ever parked your car in a mall and later roamed around the huge lot trying to find it? In that case, the reason for your forgetting probably involved poor retrieval cues (Anderson, 2009c).

Retrieval cues are mental reminders that you create by forming vivid mental images of information or associating new information with information that you already know.

Forgetting parking places (which most of us have done) points to the need for creating good retrieval cues.

Forming Effective Retrieval Cues

One reason we forget things (such as definitions, names, phone numbers) is that we do not take the time to create effective retrieval cues. You can form effective retrieval cues by creating vivid mental images of the information, making associations between new and old information, or making somewhat bizarre but memorable associations.

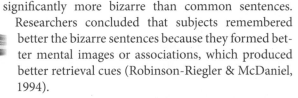

For example, researchers wondered which types of sentences students would remember better: common sentences, such as "The sleek new train passes a field of fresh, juicy strawberries," or bizarre sentences, such as "The sleek new train is derailed by the fresh, juicy strawberries." As a computer randomly presented 12 common and 12 bizarre sentences, students were told to form vivid mental images of the scenes. When retested later, subjects recalled significantly more bizarre than common sentences. Researchers concluded that subjects remembered better the bizarre sentences because they formed better mental images or associations, which produced better retrieval cues (Robinson-Riegler & McDaniel, 1994).

Retrieval Cues and Interference There have been cases in which eyewitnesses identified assailants who were later proven innocent based on DNA evidence (Dowling, 2000). One reason eyewitnesses were mistaken is that the emotional and traumatic events prevented them from forming effective *retrieval cues.* Another reason the eyewitnesses made mistakes is *interference;* that is, the faces of the accused assailants somewhat resembled and interfered with their recognizing the real assailants. These examples show that forgetting can result from poor retrieval cues, no associations, or interference (Brown & Craik, 2005).

Another example of forgetting, which involves retrieval cues and interference, usually begins with someone saying, "It's on the tip of my tongue."

Tip-of-the-Tongue Phenonemon

Most of us have had the frustrating experience of feeling we really do know the name of a movie, person, or song but cannot recall it at this moment. This kind of forgetting is called the tip-of-the-tongue phenomenon.

"It's on the tip of my tongue."

The **tip-of-the-tongue phenomenon** refers to having a strong feeling that a particular word can be recalled, but despite making a great effort, we are temporarily unable to recall this particular information. Later, in a different situation, we may recall the information.

Research shows the tip-of-the-tongue phenomenon is nearly universal, occurs about once a week, and most often involves names of people and objects. Usually the thing is remembered some minutes later (Branan, 2008; B. L. Schwartz, 1999).

An interesting feature of retrieval cues is that such cues can also come from our states of mind.

State-Dependent Learning

When you yell at someone for doing the same annoying thing again, why is it that a long list of related past annoyances quickly comes to mind? One answer involves state-dependent learning.

State-dependent learning means that it is easier to recall information when you are in the same physiological or emotional state or setting as when you originally encoded the information.

For example, getting angry at someone creates an emotional and physiological state that triggers the recall of related past annoyances.

© Ben Welsh Premium/Alamy

Evidence for state-dependent learning comes from an array of research studies that indicate that retrieval cues are created by being in certain physiological or emotional states or in particular settings, and returning to these original states helps recall information that was learned under the same conditions.

Next, we'll look inside the brain to see what happens during remembering and forgetting.

Retrieval and Cultural Influences

Learn how culture influences the use of retrieval cues.

▶ **LO11** Discuss what repressed memories are, how they may be implanted, and their accuracy.

Repressed and Recovered Memories

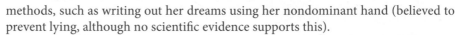

The man in the picture on the right was accused by his daughter, Katrina (left), of molesting her as a child and allegedly being a murderer. Katrina's childhood memories first surfaced during psychiatric treatment many years later, when she was 25. She never made these accusations in a conscious state, but only while under the influence of medication and controversial treatment methods, such as writing out her dreams using her nondominant hand (believed to prevent lying, although no scientific evidence supports this).

It was quickly discovered that the horrors Katrina was describing couldn't possibly be true, and she later withdrew the allegations. Fortunately, Katrina and her father have mended their relationship and are now closer than ever before. Katrina sued the psychiatrist who almost ruined her life by making her believe her so-called repressed memories and won a large settlement (BBC News, 2007; Madeley, 2007).

Katrina's case illustrates one of the more explosive issues in psychology: the problem of repressed and recovered memories.

Repressed Memories

The idea of repressed memories is based on Sigmund Freud's theory of repression, which underlies much of his psychoanalytic theory of personality (discussed in Module 11.2).

Repression is the process by which the mind pushes a memory of some threatening or traumatic event deep into the unconscious. Once in the unconscious, the repressed memory cannot be retrieved at will and may remain there until something releases it and the person remembers it.

Many therapists believe repressed memories of sexual abuse do occur. However, a prominent memory researcher disagrees: "The idea that forgetting in abuse survivors is caused by a special repression mechanism—something more powerful than conscious suppression—is still without a scientific basis" (Schacter, 1996, p. 264). Thus, the controversy over repressed memories continues (Loftus & Davis, 2006).

Implanting False Memories

For many years now, researchers have studied whether false memories could in fact be implanted and later recalled as being "true." Hundreds of studies now report false memories can be implanted in children and adults (Loftus, 2003a, 2005b). However, the fact that false memories can be implanted and later recalled as true does not disprove the occurrence of repressed memories. Rather, these studies simply show that a false suggestion can grow into a vivid, detailed, and believable personal memory (Loftus, 2000, 2005b).

The repeated finding that false memories can be implanted and later remembered as true raises a question about the accuracy of repressed memories that are later recovered and believed to be true.

Accuracy of Recovered Memories

Unfortunately, the accuracy of recovered memories often cannot be established because there is no corroborating evidence of the client's report that the traumatic event really did occur 20 to 30 years earlier (Roediger & McDermott, 2005). Also, there is reason to question the accuracy of recovered memories because people usually do not recall the memories on their own, but often do so with the help of therapists or support groups (Roediger & McDermott, 2005). Additionally, if the memories were obtained under hypnosis or "truth serum" (sodium amytal), they may not be  accurate, since people often become more open to suggestion and may later recall events that were suggested during hypnosis as being true (Lynn et al., 2003).

Another reason to question the accuracy of recovered memories is that hundreds of clients have later retracted charges of childhood sexual abuse based on memories recovered in therapy (Loftus & Davis, 2006). In over a dozen other cases, including the case of Katrina (discussed on the preceding page), clients have successfully sued and won large monetary awards from their therapists for implanting false memories of child abuse (Loftus, 1999; Madeley, 2007).

Although there are valid reasons to question the accuracy of some recovered memories, it's important to note that examples of recovered memories that are accurate do in fact exist (Loftus, 1997a, 2003a).

Suggestibility

Watch how easily false memories can be implanted.

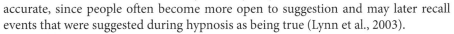

False Memories and Behavior

Find out whether false memories can change your behavior.

Check Your Learning Quiz 6.4

Go to **login.cengagebrain.com** and take the online quiz.

▸ **LO12** Identify the brain structures most important to memory.

Location of Memories in the Brain

If you learned only 500 new things every day, that adds up to storing 180,000 new memories every year and 3,600,000 memories after 20 years. To figure out how the brain stores and files away 3,600,000 memories (a very conservative estimate), researchers have studied the formation of different types of memories. Based on these studies, researchers have identified several areas of the brain involved in processing and storing different kinds of thoughts and memories.

Cortex: Short-Term Memories

When you look up a new phone number, you can hold it in short-term memory long enough to dial the number. Your ability to hold words, facts, and events in short-term memory depends on activity in the *cortex,* which is a thin layer of brain cells that covers the surface of the forebrain (indicated by the thin red line on the outside of the brain).

People may have brain damage that prevents them from storing long-term memories, but if their cortex is intact, they may have short-term memory and be able to carry on relatively normal conversations. However, if they cannot store long-term memories, they would not later remember having those conversations.

Cortex: Long-Term Memories

If you learn the words to a song, these words are stored in long-term memory. Your ability to remember or recall songs, words, facts, and events for days, months, or years depends on areas widely spread throughout the *cortex.*

People may have brain damage that prevents them from learning or remembering any new songs. However, if they have an intact cortex, they may remember the words from songs they learned before their brain damage because such information would have already been safely stored in their cortex.

© PhotoDisc/Getty Images

© Glow Images/SuperStock

Unless otherwise noted, all images are © Cengage Learning

Amygdala: Emotional Memories

Suppose that each time you hear a particular song associated with a special person, you have a romantic feeling. The romantic feeling associated with this emotional memory is provided by the *amygdala* (shown in blue below).

The amygdala plays a critical role in the long-term processing of emotionally intense experiences (Squire & Kandel, 2009). For example, the amygdala helps us recognize emotional facial expressions, especially fearful or threatening ones, and adds a wide range of emotions to our memories (Dolan, 2002; Ohman, 2002). So humans with damage to the amygdala still have memories, but the memories lose their emotional impact, such as no longer finding loud noises unpleasant or no longer recognizing emotional facial expressions (Hamann et al., 2002).

Hippocampus: Transferring & Retrieving Memories

Just as the "Save" command on your computer transfers a file into permanent storage on your hard drive, the *hippocampus* (shown in green below) transfers declarative information (such as words, facts, and personal events) from short-term memory into permanent long-term memory (Zola & Squire, 2005).

Individuals with hippocampal damage cannot save any declarative memories, such as new words, facts, or personal events (Zeineh et al., 2003). However, people with hippocampal damage **can** learn and remember nondeclarative or procedural information, such as acquiring motor skills (tying one's shoes, playing tennis) (Fields, 2005). But, if asked, people with hippocampal damage **cannot** remember performing a motor skill (playing tennis) because performing the skill (I played tennis) is a personal event (declarative memory).

Finally, researchers have long assumed that the hippocampus is also somehow involved in retrieving memories. Only recently have they discovered that the storage and retrieval of memory actually involve activation of the same neurons located in the hippocampus (Gelbard-Sagiv et al., 2008).

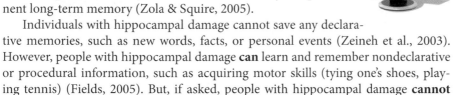

Memories of Emotional Events

Explore whether drugs can block emotional memories

Emotional Memory

Watch what happens in the brain when we are exposed to an emotionally charged event.

▶ **L013** Describe neural assemblies and long-term potentiation.

You just learned that your *cortex* stores both short-term and long-term memories; your *hippocampus* transfers or saves declarative information in long-term memory but does not transfer nondeclarative or procedural information into long-term memory; and your *amygdala* adds emotional content to positive and negative memories (Tulving & Craik, 2005). Now that you know the location of memories in the brain, we can examine how individual memories are formed.

Making a Short-Term Memory

Suppose you just looked up the phone number 555-9013 and repeat it as you dial. Researchers believe that your brain may store that number in short-term memory by using interconnected groups of neurons that are called neural assemblies.

Neural assemblies are groups of interconnected neurons whose activation allows information or stimuli to be recognized and held briefly and temporarily in short-term memory.

This figure shows how a very simplified neural assembly might work. Some information, such as repeating a phone number, activates a neural assembly that holds the phone number in short-term memory. However, if you switch your attention to something else before encoding the number in long-term memory, this neural assembly stops and the phone number is gone and forgotten. Researchers believe that neural assemblies are one mechanism for holding information in short-term memory (Smith, 2000). However, as you'll see next, permanently storing information in long-term memory involves chemical or structural changes in the neurons themselves.

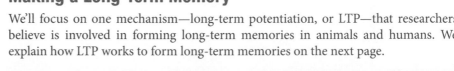

Making a Long-Term Memory

We'll focus on one mechanism—long-term potentiation, or LTP—that researchers believe is involved in forming long-term memories in animals and humans. We explain how LTP works to form long-term memories on the next page.

Long-Term Potentiation (LTP)

1 One way to learn the name of the large orange-beaked bird on the right is to repeat its name, "toucan," several times. After you repeat this name (repeated stimulation), some neurons in your brain actually grow and change to form new connections with other neurons (Goldstein, 2008; Stickgold & Ellenbogen, 2008). This neural change, which is involved in forming long-term memories, is part of a complicated process called long-term potentiation.

Long-term potentiation, or **LTP,** refers to changes in the structure and function of neurons after they have been repeatedly stimulated.

For example, by repeating the name "toucan," you are repeatedly stimulating neurons.

2 We'll use only two neurons (perhaps many hundreds are involved) to make the LTP process easier to understand. In the figure below, repeating the name "toucan" stimulates neuron A, which produces LTP and causes neuron A to grow and form new connections with neuron B.

3 LTP changes the structure and function of neuron A so it becomes associated with the name "toucan." To recall the name of this bird, you activate neuron A, which activates its newly formed connections with neuron B, and this combined neural activation forms basis for your long-term memo the name "toucan."

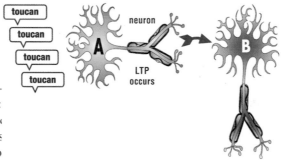

4 When researchers chemically or genetically blocked the occurrence of LTP in sea snails or mice, these animals could not learn a classically conditioned response or a water maze (Mayford & Korzus, 2002; Tonegawa & Wilson, 1997). Blocking the occurrence of LTP blocked the formation of long-term memories. Thus, neuroscientists believe the LTP process, which changes the structure and function of neurons, is the most likely basis for learning and memory in animals and humans (Goldstein, 2008; Tsien, 2000).

Making Memories

Watch how short- and long-term memories are formed in the brain.

Check Your Learning Quiz 6.5

Go to **login.cengagebrain.com** and take the online quiz.

▶ **L014** Describe strategies for improving memory.

Improving Your Memory

At one time or another, almost everyone complains about forgetting something. Many of our students complain about forgetting information that they really knew but couldn't recall during exams. This kind of forgetting has several causes. There may be *interference (proactive and retroactive)* from information studied for related classes; there may be *poor retrieval cues* that result from trying to learn information by using rote memorization; or students may not use *elaborative rehearsal,* which involves making associations between new and old information.

> How can I improve my memory?

If you hear about memory courses that claim to greatly improve your memory, what these courses usually teach are how to use mnemonic methods.

Mnemonic *(ni-MON-ick)* **methods** are ways to improve encoding and create better retrieval cues by forming vivid associations or images, which improve recall.

We'll discuss two common mnemonic methods—method of loci and peg method—that improve memory (Eysenck, 2009b).

Method of Loci

If you need to memorize a list of terms, concepts, or names in a particular order, an efficient way is to use the method of loci.

The **method of loci** *(LOW-sigh)* is an encoding technique that creates visual associations between already memorized places and new items to be memorized.

We'll use the following three steps of the method of loci to memorize names of early psychologists: Wundt, James, and Watson.

Step 1 Memorize a visual sequence of places (*loci* in Latin means "places"), such as places in your apartment where you can store things. Select easily remembered places such as in your kitchen (for example, sink, cabinet, refrigerator, stove, and closet).

Step 2 Create a vivid association for each item to be memorized. For example, picture Wundt hanging from a bridge and saying, "I wundt jump."

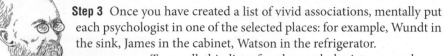

Step 3 Once you have created a list of vivid associations, mentally put each psychologist in one of the selected places: for example, Wundt in the sink, James in the cabinet, Watson in the refrigerator.

To recall this list of early psychologists, you take an imaginary stroll through your kitchen and mentally note the image stored in each of your memorized places.

Peg Method

Another useful mnemonic device for memorizing a long list, especially in the exact order, is the peg method.

The **peg method** is an encoding technique that creates associations between number-word rhymes and items to be memorized.

The rhymes act like pegs on which you hang items to be memorized. Let's use the two steps of the peg method to memorize our three early psychologists: Wundt, James, Watson.

Step 1 Memorize the list of peg words shown on the right, which consists of a number and its rhyming word.

> one is a bun
> two is a shoe
> three is a tree
> four is a door
> five is a hive

Step 2 Next, associate each of the items you wish to memorize with one of the peg words. For instance, imagine Wundt on a bun, James with two left shoes, and Watson stuck in a tree.

To remember this list of early psychologists, you recall each peg along with its image of an early psychologist that you placed there.

Conclusion

As you've now learned, improving one's memory requires making the effort to use good encoding, such as elaborative rehearsal, which means creating good associations that, in turn, produce good retrieval cues and improve memory.

Mnemonic Devices

See how mnemonic devices help to improve memory.

Check Your Learning Quiz 6.6

Go to **login.cengagebrain.com** and take the online quiz.

▶ **LO15** Describe the accuracy of memory and its potential consequences in eyewitness testimony.

How Accurate Is an Eyewitness?

On a hot summer night, Jennifer Thompson, a 22-year-old college student, went to bed in her home only to wake up frightened by a man lying on top of her holding a knife to her throat. While the man proceeded to rape her, she was committed to studying his every physical feature so she could later help police put him behind bars. When police presented Jennifer with a photo and physical lineup of suspects, she picked Ronald Cotton in both instances. When she was asked if her rapist was present in the courtroom, she again confidently pointed to Ronald Cotton.

Eyewitness testimony refers to recalling or recognizing a suspect observed during a potentially very disrupting and distracting emotional situation that may have interfered with accurate remembering.

Jennifer Thompson's eyewitness testimony was the damning evidence that sent the defendant (an alleged rapist) to prison. After Ronald Cotton (right photo) spent 10 years in prison, DNA evidence proved he was not the rapist and implicated another man, Bobby Poole (left photo). The man who had been sent to prison because of eyewitness testimony was set free (Lithwick, 2009; Stahl, 2009). This example points to at least three problems with eyewitness testimony.

The *first* problem is that juries assume eyewitness testimony is the best kind of evidence because it is so accurate and reliable. However, in the United States, more than 230 people have been wrongfully convicted of crimes and later been freed because of DNA evidence. Of the 230 convictions, about 77% (177) were based on (mistaken) eyewitness testimony (Lithwick, 2009).

One of the pitfalls of eyewitness testimony is known as own-race bias. In the rape case discussed here, the eyewitness was a white female and the accused rapist was a black man. This case brings up another source of eyewitness error: problems in identifying individuals of another race. Researchers found that an eyewitness of one race is less accurate when identifying an accused person of another race (Scheck, 2008; Wells, 2009). The finding that people better recognize faces of their own race than faces of other races is called own-race bias (Ferguson et al., 2001). For instance, when white people see the faces of Cotton and Poole (above photos), they report the faces look very similar, but when black people look at the pictures, they say the two men look nothing alike (Wells, 2009).

A *second* problem with eyewitness testimony is that police and juries generally assume the more confident an eyewitness is, the more accurate is the testimony. For example, the witness in this rape case was very confident when she pointed at the accused man and said, "There is no doubt in my mind." However, there is only a moderate association or correlation (+0.37) between how correct the identification of an eyewitness is and how much confidence the eyewitness feels about his or her identification (Wells & Olson, 2003). This means an eyewitness's confidence is not a good indication of accuracy.

A *third* problem is eyewitnesses may make errors if law enforcement officials ask misleading or biased questions or make suggestions about the perpetrator's identification. In these cases, eyewitnesses may unknowingly accept the misinformation as fact and give unreliable testimony (Bower, 2003b). For example, consider the following case of an eyewitness's mistaken identity.

Can an Eyewitness Be Misled?

Some years ago a series of armed robberies occurred in the Wilmington, Delaware, area. The police had few leads in the case until a local citizen said a Roman Catholic priest, Father Bernard Pagano, looked like the sketch of the robber.

At his trial, seven eyewitnesses positively identified Father Pagano (left photo) as the robber. But at the last minute, another man, Ronald Clouser (right photo), confessed to the robberies and Father Pagano was released (Rodgers, 1982).

As you look at these two photos, you will wonder how this case of mistaken identity could possibly have happened. Ronald Clouser is shorter, 14 years younger, and not nearly as bald as Father Pagano; besides, he has different facial features. Why, then, did eyewitnesses say with certainty that Father Pagano was the robber they had seen? One reason involves how the witnesses were questioned. Apparently, before the witnesses were questioned and shown photos of the suspects, the police had suggested the possibility that the robber was a priest. In part because Father Pagano was the only suspect wearing a clerical collar, the witnesses concluded that he must be the robber. This example is but one of many that show how eyewitness testimony may be distorted or biased.

© Bettman/Corbis

© UPI/Corbis Bettman

Eyewitness Experience

Explore how accurate your own eyewitness testimony is.

Can Questions Change the Answers?

Because of concern about the reliability of eyewitness testimony, Elizabeth Loftus (1979, 2003a) studied whether people can be misled and misremember, especially if they are given false information. We'll describe Loftus's experiments, which demonstrate how subjects misremembered what they saw or heard.

Did the Car Pass the Barn?

In one experiment, subjects watched a film of an automobile accident and then were questioned about what they saw. One of the questions contained a false piece of information: "How fast was the red sports car going when it passed the barn while traveling along the country road?" Although there was no barn in the film, 17% of the subjects said they had seen a barn, indicating that people may believe misinformation if it fits the overall scene or pattern (Loftus, 1975).

Was There a Stop Sign?

In another well-known study by Loftus and colleagues, subjects were first shown slides of a traffic accident involving a stop sign and then asked a series of questions about the accident. Some of the questions were not misleading and asked about the presence of a stop sign. Other questions were deliberately misleading and did not mention the stop sign but asked about the presence of a yield sign. Later, when subjects were asked whether they had seen a stop sign or a yield sign, those subjects who had been misled by earlier questions about a yield sign were more likely to report seeing a yield sign than subjects who were not misled (Loftus et al., 1978). These results, which show that subjects can be misled by being given false but related information, have been replicated by many other researchers (Neisser & Libby, 2005).

How Does False Information Alter Memory?

Based on many such studies, Loftus and Hoffman (1989) concluded that if misleading information is introduced during questioning after an event, people may believe this misinformation and report events that they did not see.

Is What You Say, What You Believe?

Sometimes people come to believe that they actually remember seeing things that were merely suggested to them; this phenomenon is called source misattribution.

Source misattribution is a memory error that results when a person has difficulty deciding which of two or more sources a memory came from: Was the source something the person saw or imagined, or was it a suggestion?

For example, suppose you saw a hit-and-run accident involving a dark red car. During questioning, you are asked the color of the car that drove off. As you're thinking that the car was dark red, you remember hearing another bystander say, "The car was dark blue." Source misattribution would occur if you  said that the car was dark blue (suggestion you heard) rather than dark red (something you saw). Researchers have found that false suggestions, misleading questions, and misinformation can result in source misattribution and create false memories (Roediger & McDermott, 2005).

Which Interview Technique Works Best?

Suppose you witnessed a robbery but had trouble picking the suspect out of a police lineup. To help you provide reliable information about the suspect, you might be questioned using a procedure called the cognitive interview (Eysenck, 2009a).

The **cognitive interview** is a technique for questioning people, such as eyewitnesses, by having them imagine and reconstruct the details of an event, report everything they remember without holding anything back, and narrate the event from different viewpoints.

The cognitive interview has proved very useful in police interrogation. Detectives trained in cognitive interview techniques obtained 47% to 60% more information from victims and suspects than detectives using the standard police interrogation method (Gwyer & Clifford, 1997). The cognitive interview is an effective way to increase correct recall and avoid making suggestions that might create false memories and increase errors of source misattribution in children and adults from varying educational backgrounds (Stein & Memon, 2006).

Reconstructive Memory

Explore what the implications are of memory abilities for police, the justice system, and eyewitness testimony.

Check Your Learning Quiz 6.7

Go to **login.cengagebrain.com** and take the online quiz.

Photographic Memory

One kind of unusual memory that many of us wish we had is the ability to remember everything with little or no difficulty. Such an amazing memory is commonly called a photographic memory.

Photographic memory is the ability to form sharp, detailed visual images after examining a picture or page for a short period of time and to recall the entire image at a later date.

There are no reports of someone developing a photographic memory and only one or two reports of adults who had a truly photographic memory (Stromeyer, 1970). Sometimes people with exceptional memories are mislabeled as having photographic memories (Adams, 2006; Higbee, 2001).

At a national memory contest, Tatiana Cooley (photo above) came in first by doing incredible memory feats, such as pairing 70 names and faces after studying a stack of 100 faces for just 20 minutes. As a child, Tatiana's mother would read to her, and when Tatiana was 2½ years old, she read one of the books back to her mother. In college, Tatiana says, "I remember visualizing the notes that I had taken in class and being able to recall them verbatim for tests so I didn't have to study" (Rogers & Morehouse, 1999, p. 90). To keep her memory sharp, she spends 45 minutes each day memorizing the order in which cards appear in a freshly shuffled deck. Wow! Tatiana's ability to visually remember her notes during exams comes close to satisfying the definition for having a photographic memory.

Super Memory for Faces

Most of us cannot remember the faces of people we met a few years ago and only in passing. New research finds that some people (as many as 2%) in fact have this ability and are referred to as *super-recognizers,* meaning they can easily recognize someone they met in passing, even years later.

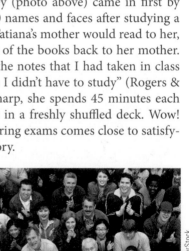

© moodboard/SuperStock

© Doug Levere

Unless otherwise noted, all images are © Cengage Learning

Super-recognizers have an extreme version of memory for faces. They can easily recognize familiar faces, even in very large crowds. They can also recognize people who have changed in appearance, such as aging or changing hair color. Because their memory for faces is so extreme, they often have to pretend to not recognize someone they simply saw in passing to avoid the awkwardness of interacting with them. Imagine how awkward it would be for a stranger to come up and say he saw you 3 years ago at the grocery store while you were buying milk and cookies! People with this incredible memory would be great at providing trustworthy eyewitness testimony (Russell et al., 2009; *Science Daily,* 2009b).

Flashbulb Memory

Although it happened over 20 years ago, I (H. K.) have a detailed memory of my cabin in the Santa Cruz Mountains of California shaking and then seesawing on the edge of a mountain during a frightening earthquake. I can play back this terrible scene in great detail and vivid color as if I were actually experiencing an earthquake. Many individuals have had a similar experience, and this kind of memory event is called a flashbulb memory (Brown & Kulik, 1977).

Flashbulb memories are vivid recollections, usually in great detail, of dramatic or emotionally charged incidents that are of interest to the person. This information is encoded effortlessly and may last for long periods of time.

Do you remember precisely what you were doing when you first learned of the 9/11 attacks? Flashbulb memories usually involve events that are extremely surprising, are emotionally arousing, or have very important meaning for the person. For example, when people were questioned about what they were doing when they heard that President Kennedy or Reagan had been shot, or when the space shuttle *Challenger* exploded, about 80% to 90% could recall vivid details seven months later (Pillemer, 1984).

Examples of Flashbulb Memories

Car accident
High school graduation
Senior prom
18th birthday
First date

Although flashbulb memories are reported with great confidence and in vivid details, researchers report that flashbulb memories do not guarantee any special accuracy (Talarico & Rubin, 2003).

Check Your Learning Quiz 6.8

Go to **login.cengagebrain.com** and take the online quiz.

Think Critically

Challenge Your Thinking

Consider these questions when reading this article:

1. What type of long-term memory includes our recollection of traumatic events we experienced?
2. In this research example, what is the neutral stimulus? Unconditioned stimulus? Conditioned stimulus? (See Module 5.3)
3. Why are scientists primarily focusing on using a drug that targets brain cells in the amygdala and not the hippocampus?
4. Research shows it's more difficult to erase bad memories than to forget good memories. What explains this?
5. Does the phenomenon of source misattribution apply to a person whose memory of the witnessed event gets erased? Why or why not?
6. It's possible to make a memory weaker or even disappear, but is it possible to create false memories and have people believe them to be true?

Can Bad Memories Be Erased?

Imagine a world where no one had any bad memories. New research discoveries suggest that such a world may not be so implausible. For people who are frequently haunted by painful, unpleasant memories, there may be a simple way to alter or even erase the events from their mind.

Scientists believe that after a person experiences a traumatic event, the body releases stress hormones, which act to make the bad memory stronger. To test this theory, scientist Roger Pitman found patients who had just experienced a trau-matic event and gave some of them a drug called propranolol (commonly used to treat blood pressure), which blocks the release of stress hormones; he gave others a placebo. Patients also tape-recorded their recollection of the traumatic experience in detail. Months later, patients listened to the tapes. Over half of the patients who had received placebos exhibited intense physical symptoms of anxiety and fear (such as high heart rate, sweaty palms), whereas none of the patients who received propranolol had such responses.

Other research also supports the use of propranolol to decrease fear associated with bad memories. For instance, Merel Kindt and her colleagues created fearful memories in subjects by administering shocks when they looked at pictures of spiders while instructed to "actively remember" the pictures. One day later, half of the subjects were given propranolol and half a placebo. All were shown pictures of spiders again, and the subjects given medication showed less fearful responses.

The almost magical effects of propranolol occur because the drug affects brain cells in the amygdala, a critical brain structure involved in the processing of emotions in memories and learning fear responses. Using propranolol while actively remembering traumatic events seems to break down unpleasant memories by removing the fear responses associated with them.

Many scientists are excited about using drugs not only to modify memory, but also to permanently erase memory. One such scientist has achieved promising results in his animal research. He found that increasing a particular enzyme to high levels while the subject actively remembers a traumatic experience may actually make the memory vanish.

The future of memory research is full of possibilities. There are, of course, many ethical concerns. For instance, what if murderers and rapists were able to erase from their memory all of the horrific actions they committed? They would thereby eliminate any feelings of guilt or remorse and forfeit the ability to learn from experience. Also, people could interfere with the criminal justice system by erasing the memories of important eyewitnesses. And, there's always the risk of permanently erasing positive, wanted memories in the process.

For now, scientific advances don't help people forget bad memories altogether, but they do help remove the trauma and fear associated with these memories. However, a scientific breakthrough making it possible to completely erase memories in humans may occur sooner than our society prepares itself for the ethical implications of such a discovery. (Adapted from Gutierrez, 2009; Kalb, 2009; Kindt et al., 2009; Lemonick, 2007a; McGowan, 2009)

Think Critically 6.1

This article and its questions are available in interactive format online.

GO to your Psychology CourseMate at login.cengagebrain.com and take the Chapter Post-Test to see which Learning Objectives you've mastered and which need more review. Use the chapter review guide below and the online activities—including flashcards to review key terms—to measure your learning.

Measure ^ Your Learning

Online Activities

Key Terms	Video	Animation	Reading	Assessment
memory, encoding, storing, retrieving	Daniel Tammet, p. 255			Check Your Learning Quiz 6.1
sensory memory, short-term memory, working memory, long-term memory, iconic memory, echoic memory, maintenance rehearsal, interference, chunking, encoding, retrieving, primacy effect, recency effect, primacy-recency effect, declarative memory, semantic memory, episodic memory, procedural memory, nondeclarative memory	Short-Term Memory, p. 261 Man Without a Memory, p. 269 Brain and Memory, p. 271	Memory Processes, p. 257 Primacy-Recency Effect, p. 267		Check Your Learning Quiz 6.2
encoding, automatic encoding, effortful encoding, maintenance rehearsal, elaborative rehearsal, levels-of-processing theory	Rehearsal, p. 275		Encoding and Cultural Influences, p. 273	Check Your Learning Quiz 6.3
forgetting, interference, proactive interference, retroactive interference, retrieval cues, tip-of-the-tongue phenomenon, state-dependent learning, repression	Suggestibility, p. 281		Retrieval and Cultural Influences, p. 279 False Memories and Behavior, p. 281	Check Your Learning Quiz 6.4

Measure
^Your Learning

Module		Learning Objectives	
6.5	Biological Bases of Memory 282	LO12	Identify the brain structures most important to memory.
		LO13	Describe neural assemblies and long-term potentiation.
6.6	Improving Your Memory 286	LO14	Describe strategies for improving memory.
6.7	Eyewitness Testimony 288	LO15	Describe the accuracy of memory and its potential consequences in eye witness testimony.
6.8	Unusual Memories 292	LO16	Describe photographic memory, super-recognizers, and flashbulb memory.
	Think Critically 294		Can Bad Memories Be Erased?

Online Activities

Key Terms	Video	Animation	Reading	Assessment
cortex, amygdala, hippocampus, neural assemblies, long-term potentiation (LTP)	Emotional Memory, p. 283	Making Memories, p. 285	Memories of Emotional Events, p. 283	Check Your Learning Quiz 6.5
mnemonic methods, method of loci, peg method, memory-enhancing drugs		Mnemonic Devices, p. 287		Check Your Learning Quiz 6.6
eyewitness testimony, own-race bias, source misattribution, cognitive interview	Reconstructive Memory, p. 291		Eyewitness Experience, p. 289	Check Your Learning Quiz 6.7
photographic memory, flashbulb memories, super-recognizers				Check Your Learning Quiz 6.8

Intelligence, Thought, and Language

© Ben Hupfer/Corbis

Chapter Outline and Learning Objectives

Prepare to Learn

1 **GO** to your **Psychology CourseMate** at **login.cengagebrain.com** and take the **Chapter Pre-Test** to introduce yourself to this chapter's topics and see what you may already know.

2 **READ** the **Learning Objectives (LOs)** (in the left sidebars) and begin the chapter.

3 **COMPLETE** the **Online Activities** (in the right sidebars) *as you read each module.* Activities include **videos**, **animations**, **readings**, and **quizzes**.

4 **CHECK Your Learning** by going online to take the quiz at the end of each module and review material as necessary.

5 **MEASURE Your Learning** after reading the chapter by taking the online **Chapter Post-Test**. Use the chapter review guide at the end of the chapter as needed.

WATCH for these **Online Activities** icons as you read:

Video

Animation

Reading

Assessment

Think Critically

These online activities are important to mastering this chapter. As you read each module, access these materials by going to **login.cengagebrain.com**.

Video Explore studies and firsthand accounts of biological and psychological processes:

- Learn more about emotional intelligence and why is it important
- Watch an exploration of how important emotions are in making decisions
- Watch how children learn to use morphemes and grammar
- Learn about the sounds infants make
- Learn about how a young child begins to put words together to make sentences
- See how infants and toddlers develop language
- Learn how important it is for parents to talk with young children

Animation Interact with and visualize important processes and concepts:

- Use the exemplar and prototype models to form concepts
- Observe examples of changing one's mental set, using analogies, and forming subgoals

Reading Delve deeper into key content:

- Learn about the practical applications of psychometrics
- Find out about the advantages and disadvantages of the two-factor theory
- Find out about the advantages and disadvantages of the multiple intelligence theory
- Find out about the advantages and disadvantages of the triarchic theory
- Learn about whether or not there are differences in the IQ scores of men and women

- Learn about some of the potential problems of IQ testing
- Learn whether intervention programs can raise IQ scores
- Explore the possible causes of IQ differences between races
- Learn how creative people think and behave
- Explore whether language influences thinking
- Explore whether or not dolphins use language

Assessment Measure your mastery:

- Chapter Pre-Test
- Check Your Learning Quizzes
- Chapter Post-Test

Think Critically Challenge your thinking by applying content from this chapter and making connections to related material:

- Smartest or Strongest Man in America?

▶ **L01** Describe psychometrics.

For the past 200 years, psychologists have debated the question, What is intelligence? Before you learn about how psychologists answer this question, try to answer the question yourself. Then, after reading about the four individuals described below, rank them according to your idea of intelligence.

▼

Based on my idea of intelligence, here's how I have ranked the four individuals: #1___, #2___, #3___, #4___.

A. Halle Berry
She has starred in over 30 Hollywood movies and is the highest-paid African American actress in Hollywood. Not only has she earned an Emmy and a Golden Globe award, but she was also the first African American woman ever to win an Oscar for best actress.

B. Bill Gates
He is the richest man in the United States, worth around $40 billion. As a college sophomore, he dropped out of Harvard and wrote one of the first operating systems to run a computer. In his twenties, he founded Microsoft, whose software operates 90% of the computers in the world.

C. Jay Greenberg
At age 10, Jay enrolled in the world-renowned Juilliard School of Music. Jay has composed more than 100 musical works. He has earned many awards for his compositions and became the youngest composer ever to sign exclusive contracts with major recording labels.

D. Alia Sabur
At only 8 months, Alia began reading. She graduated from college at age 14, becoming the youngest female college graduate in American history. Alia is the youngest person ever to receive awards from the U.S. Department of Defense, U.S. National Science Foundation, and NASA. At the age of 19, she became the world's youngest professor in history.

The problem you faced in trying to rank the intelligence of those four individuals is similar to what psychologists face in measuring intelligence. Measuring intelligence is part of an area of psychology that is called psychometrics.

Psychometrics, which is a subarea of psychology, is concerned with developing psychological tests that assess an individual's abilities, skills, beliefs, and personality traits in a wide range of settings, including school, industry, or clinic.

As you'll discover in this chapter, the measurement of intelligence and the development of intelligence tests are still being debated.

Psychometrics

Learn about some of the practical applications of psychometrics.

Check Your Learning Quiz 7.1

Go to **login.cengagebrain.com** and take the online quiz.

▶ **L02** Explain and distinguish between Spearman's two-factor theory, Gardner's multiple-intelligence theory, Sternberg's triarchic theory, and Goleman's emotional intelligence theory.

Definition of Intelligence

What do you think your IQ score is? When college students were asked to estimate their overall IQs, men's self-reports of IQ were higher than women's self-reports, and both men and women reported higher IQs for their fathers than for their mothers (Petrides et al., 2004). In fact, over the past 20 years, men have consistently overestimated and women have consistently underestimated their IQs, even though researchers find no sex differences in IQ scores (Colom et al., 2000).

People generally believe IQ scores measure intelligence. But it's not so simple. For example, how did you rank the intelligence of the four individuals in the right photos, each of whom shows a different yet extraordinary skill or talent? Do these examples point to the existence of different kinds of intelligence (Gardner, 2006b)?

Many psychologists believe intelligence is best defined by measuring a variety of cognitive abilities, which is what most intelligence tests measure. For example, based on an intelligence test, Alia Sabur received an IQ score so high it was "off the charts." Others argue that a definition of intelligence based entirely on cognitive abilities is much too narrow. Instead, they believe there are many kinds of intelligence, such as involving acting skills (Halle Berry), musical abilities (Jay Greenberg), or problem solving (Bill Gates) (Benson, 2003a; Gardner, 2006b).

More recently, researchers have pointed to the importance of emotional intelligence, which involves how well people perceive, express, and regulate emotions in themselves and others (Salovey et al., 2008). Award-winning actors such as Halle Berry certainly have high emotional intelligence. We'll discuss emotional intelligence later in the module.

Here, we'll examine a few popular definitions of intelligence, beginning with the oldest and perhaps the most widely accepted definition of intelligence, the two-factor theory.

Two-Factor Theory

In 1904, Charles Spearman reported that he had measured intelligence in an objective way. Spearman was one of the first to use the psychometric approach.

The **psychometric approach** measures or quantifies cognitive abilities or factors that are thought to be involved in intellectual performance.

Spearman (1904) reasoned that by measuring related cognitive factors he would have an objective measure of intelligence. This idea led to his two-factor theory of intelligence.

Spearman's two-factor theory says that intelligence has two factors: a general mental ability factor, *g*, which represents what different cognitive tasks have in common, plus many specific factors, *s*, which include specific mental abilities (such as mathematical, mechanical, or verbal skills).

Archives of the History of American Psychology, the Center of the History of Psychology–The University of Akron

Spearman believed that factor *g*, or general mental ability, represented a person's mental energy. Today, factor *g* is defined and measured by a person's performance on various and related cognitive abilities. In other words, modern intelligence tests have essentially changed Spearman's *g* into an objective score, which is commonly known as the IQ score. Today, many psychologists believe that *g*, as represented by IQ scores, is a good measure of a person's general intelligence (Jenson, 2005).

> *On the basis of Spearman's two-factor theory, which of the four individuals on the previous page is most intelligent?*

Many psychologists believe that *g* is the definition of general intelligence, which can be measured by an IQ test and represented by an IQ score. Thus, one way to compare people on intelligence is by using IQ scores. Ranking intelligence by using IQ scores would favor Sabur (with her "off the charts" IQ score), and Gates (whose colleague said he was "the smartest person he ever knew"). However, although Berry (Oscar-winning actress) and Greenberg (composer) might score high on IQ tests, they would get little or no credit for their exceptional acting or music skills.

Some psychologists are critical of *g*'s narrow approach to measuring intelligence and have proposed other definitions and ways to measure intelligence. We'll discuss these definitions next.

Two-Factor Theory

Find out about the advantages and disadvantages of the two-factor theory.

Multiple-Intelligence Theory

Some psychologists reject the idea that intelligence can be reduced to *g* and expressed by a single number, an IQ score. For instance, Howard Gardner (1999, 2006b) argues for broadening the definition of intelligence to include different kinds of abilities, an idea he calls the multiple-intelligence theory.

Gardner's multiple-intelligence theory says that instead of one kind of general intelligence, there are at least nine different kinds, which include verbal intelligence, musical intelligence, logical-mathematical intelligence, spatial intelligence, body-movement intelligence, intelligence to understand oneself, intelligence to understand others, naturalistic intelligence, and existential intelligence.

Gardner states that standard IQ tests measure primarily verbal and logical-mathematical intelligence and neglect other equally important kinds of intelligence, such as the ones listed above. Gardner (1999, 2006b) arrived at his theory of multiple kinds of intelligence after studying which abilities remain following brain damage, how savants and prodigies develop their specialized kinds of intelligence, and how people in different environments develop different abilities to adapt and be successful.

On the basis of Gardner's multiple-intelligence theory, which of the four individuals is most intelligent?

According to Gardner's multiple-intelligence theory, there isn't one kind of general intelligence for ranking all individuals. Rather, Gardner views the special abilities of Berry in acting and Greenberg in music as representing other kinds of intelligence. Gardner argues that none of the four is more intelligent but that each of the four individuals shows a different kind of ability or intelligence that was developed and adapted to his or her environment.

Triarchic Theory

Agreeing with Gardner that Spearman's *g* is too narrow and current IQ tests are limited to measuring only problem-solving skills and cognitive abilities, psychologist Robert Sternberg defined intelligence by *analyzing* three kinds of reasoning processes that people use in solving problems. Sternberg (2003a) calls his approach the triarchic theory of intelligence.

Sternberg's triarchic theory says that intelligence can be divided into three different kinds of reasoning processes (*triarchic* means "three components"). The first is using analytical or logical thinking skills measured by traditional intelligence tests. The second is using problem-solving skills that require creative thinking and the ability to learn from experience. The third is using practical thinking skills that help a person adjust to, and cope with, his or her sociocultural environment.

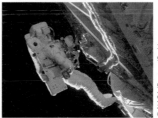

Unlike Spearman's *g*, which measures general intelligence by measuring cognitive abilities, Sternberg's theory breaks intelligence down into three reasoning processes: analytical, problem solving, and practical skills.

On the basis of Sternberg's triarchic theory of intelligence, which of the four individuals (previous page) is most intelligent?

According to Sternberg's triarchic theory, there isn't one kind of general intelligence for evaluating these four individuals but rather three different reasoning processes (analytical, problem solving, practical) that contribute to and predict the success of each of the four individuals.

Multiple-Intelligence Theory

Find out about the advantages and disadvantages of the multiple-intelligence theory.

Triarchic Theory

Explore the advantages and disadvantages of the triarchic theory.

Emotional Intelligence

One of the exciting things about being a researcher is the chance to come up with new ideas. This happened in the early 1990s, when researchers came up with the idea of emotional intelligence, which they suggested made people more effective in social situations (Salovey & Mayer, 1990). By the mid-1990s, popular magazines, such as *Time,* declared that emotional intelligence might redefine what it means to be smart and might be the best predictor of life success (Gibbs, 1995).

Emotional intelligence is the ability to perceive emotions accurately, to take feelings into account when reasoning, to understand emotions, and to regulate or manage emotions in oneself and others (Salovey et al., 2008).

© Carlo Allegri/Getty Images

Unlike the traditional idea of intelligence involving performance on cognitive tests, emotional intelligence involves how well people perceive, express, and regulate emotions in themselves and others. The author of the book *Emotional Intelligence* (Goleman, 1995, 2005) said in an interview, "Oprah Winfrey's ability to read people and identify with them is at the heart of her success" (Brown, 1996, p. 85). In other words, the reason for Oprah's incredible success as a talk-show host is that she rates very high in emotional intelligence.

Here are some common remarks that show how emotions can influence our behaviors:

- "I was so angry, I couldn't think straight."
- "I get worse when people tell me to calm down."
- "When we argue, I get mad and say the wrong thing."
- "Sometimes I act on my feelings, right or wrong."

These kinds of self-reports point to the influence that emotions can have on what we say and do and on our success in life. According to supporters of emotional intelligence, the better our understanding of how emotions work, the more likely we are to find a compromise between our often strong emotional feelings ("I felt like doing that") and our equally strong rational thoughts ("I knew I should not have done that") (Mayer et al., 2000). However, these kinds of self-reports need to be confirmed by more scientific techniques. Researchers are continuing to develop scientifically sound emotional intelligence tests and advance the research on emotional intelligence. Thus, the following findings are considered preliminary.

Preliminary Findings

Here are some findings reported from recent tests to measure emotional intelligence: Youths who scored higher on emotional intelligence tests were less likely to have smoked cigarettes; schoolchildren who scored higher were rated as less aggressive by their peers and more helpful by their teachers; college-age males who scored higher were less likely to use alcohol and other drugs; and higher scores were related to being more empathetic and satisfied with life (Brackett et al., 2004; Lopes et al., 2003; Salovey & Pizarro, 2003).

My life is great!

© Andresr/Shutterstock

Emotional intelligence is also important in romantic relationships. A study with college-age couples found that the unhappiest couples were those in which both individuals had low emotional intelligence test scores, and the happiest couples were those in which both individuals scored high on the same test. Couples in which only one partner scored high on emotional intelligence, on average, fell between the other groups in terms of happiness (Brackett et al., 2005).

Current Status of Intelligence Theories

Western psychologists used the psychometric approach to measure cognitive abilities, which led to the development of intelligence tests and IQ scores and the concept of *g* as the best measure of intelligence (Brody, 2000). Standard intelligence tests remain popular because they have proved useful in predicting performance in academic settings. Critics argue these IQ tests measure only analytical intelligence and ignore other types of intelligence (Nisbett, 2009). Newer approaches, such as Gardner's multiple-intelligence approach and Sternberg's triarchic approach, measure additional abilities and skills and represent different kinds of intelligence. They may replace *g* and its IQ score as the best measure of intelligence (Gardner, 2006b; Sternberg & Pretz, 2005). Many educators have already adopted a multiple-intelligence approach in designing classroom curriculum (Kelly & Tangney, 2006). In terms of emotional intelligence, researchers are only beginning to understand how it is that we can perceive expressions and regulate emotions (Underwood, 2006).

To see how far intelligence testing has come, we'll go back in time and discuss early attempts to define and measure intelligence.

Emotional Intelligence

Learn more about emotional intelligence and why is it important.

Check Your Learning Quiz 7.2

Go to **login.cengagebrain.com** and take the online quiz.

▶ **LO3** Summarize the historical background of measuring intelligence.

Early Attempts to Measure Intelligence

Head Size and Intelligence

Efforts to measure intelligence began in earnest in the late 1800s. That's when Francis Galton noticed that intelligent people often had intelligent relatives and concluded that intelligence was, to a large extent, biological or inherited. In trying to assess intelligence, Galton measured people's heads and recorded the speed of their reactions to various sensory stimuli. However, measures proved to be poorly related to intelligence or academic achievement (Gould, 1996).

Galton later tried to correlate head size with students' grade point average. For example, he reported that the average head size of Cambridge students who received A's was about 3.3% larger than that of students who received C's (Galton, 1888). However, a review of later studies showed a very low correlation of 0.15 between head size and intelligence (IQ scores) (Vernon et al., 2000). Such a low correlation has little practical use in predicting intelligence.

Brain Size and Intelligence

Efforts to measure intelligence continued with the work of Paul Broca, a famous neurologist in the late 1800s. Broca claimed that there was a relationship between brain size and intelligence, with larger brains indicating more intelligence. However, a later reanalysis of Broca's data indicated that measures of brain size proved to be unreliable and poorly correlated with intelligence (Gould, 1996).

More recently, the relative size of living brains was measured with brain scans (pp. 74–75), which permit more precise measurement. A review of brain-scan studies reported medium-sized positive correlations (+0.33) between brain size and intelligence (IQ scores) (McDaniel, 2005). However, such correlations indicate only that a relationship exists; correlations cannot tell us whether bigger brains lead to increased intelligence or whether more cognitive activity leads to bigger brains.

Binet's Breakthrough

As you have seen, the early attempts to use head and brain size to measure intelligence failed. In fact, a paper presented in 1904 to a German psychological society concluded there was little hope of developing psychological tests to objectively measure intelligence (Wolf, 1973).

© Bettmann/Corbis

Alfred Binet (right photo), a gifted French psychologist, strongly believed that intelligence was a collection of mental abilities and that the best way to assess intelligence was to measure a person's ability to perform cognitive tasks, such as understanding the meanings of words or being able to follow directions.

Binet set out to create an intelligence test that would be easy to administer without requiring any special laboratory equipment and would distinguish between normal and abnormal mental abilities (Brody, 1992). In 1905, Binet and psychiatrist Theodore Simon developed the world's first standardized intelligence test, the Binet-Simon Intelligence Scale (Binet & Simon, 1905).

The **Binet-Simon Intelligence Scale** contained items arranged in order of increasing difficulty. The items measured vocabulary, memory, common knowledge, and other cognitive abilities.

The purpose of this first Binet-Simon Intelligence Scale was to distinguish among mentally defective children in the Paris school system. In Binet's time, intellectually deficient children were divided into three groups: idiots (most severely deficient), imbeciles (moderate), and morons (mildest). These terms are no longer used today because they have taken on very negative meanings. The problems with this first test were that it classified children into only the above three categories, and it could not express the results in a single score.

Binet and Simon revised their intelligence scale to solve several problems in their original scale. In this revised test, they arranged the test items in order of increasing difficulty and designed different items to measure different cognitive abilities. For each test item, Binet determined whether an average child of a certain age could answer the question correctly. Because the test items were arranged for each age level (age levels 3 to 13), this new test could identify the average age level at which the child performed. If, for example, a child passed all the items that could be answered by an average 3-year-old but none of the items appropriate for older children, that child would have a mental age of 3. Binet's intelligence test became popular because a single score represented mental age.

Mental age is a method of estimating a child's intellectual progress by comparing the child's score on an intelligence test to the scores of average children of the same age.

At this point, the Binet-Simon scale gave its results in terms of a mental age but not an IQ score, which as you'll learn next, did not occur until years later.

Brain Sizes, Sex Differences & Intelligence

Learn whether or not there are differences in the IQ scores of men and women.

Formula for IQ

The first big change was when Binet and Simon introduced the concept of mental age. The second big change occurred in 1916, when Lewis Terman and his colleagues at Stanford University in California came up with a new and better method to compute the final score. Improving on the concept of expressing the test results in terms of mental age, Terman devised a formula to calculate an intelligence quotient (IQ) score (Terman, 1916).

Intelligence quotient (IQ) is computed by dividing a child's mental age (MA), as measured in an intelligence test, by the child's chronological age (CA) and multiplying the result by 100.

Remember that in Binet's test, mental age was calculated by noting how many items a child answered that were appropriate to a certain age. For example, if a 4-year-old girl passed the test items appropriate for a 5-year-old, she was said to have a mental age of 5. A child's chronological (physical) age is his or her age in months and years. To compute her IQ score, we use Terman's formula, shown below.

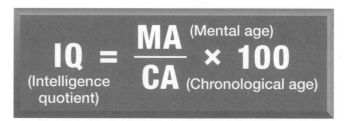

$$\underset{\substack{\text{(Intelligence} \\ \text{quotient)}}}{\text{IQ}} = \frac{\text{MA} \;\text{(Mental age)}}{\text{CA} \;\text{(Chronological age)}} \times 100$$

Thus, for the child in our example, we substitute 5 for MA, 4 for CA, and multiply by 100. We get: $5/4 = 1.25 \times 100 = 125$. So the child's IQ is 125. An IQ score computed in this traditional way is called a *ratio IQ* because the score represents a ratio of mental to chronological age. Today the ratio IQ has been replaced by the *deviation IQ,* whose computation is too complex to explain here. The reason for the switch from ratio IQ to deviation IQ is that deviation IQ scores more accurately reflect test performance as children get older.

Since the original Binet-Simon scale in 1905, IQ tests have become very popular and have grown into a large business. We'll look more closely at one of the most widely used IQ tests.

Examples of IQ Tests

The most widely used IQ tests are the Wechsler Adult Intelligence Scale (WAIS), for ages 16 and older, and the Wechsler Intelligence Scale for Children (WISC), for children of ages 6 to 16.

The **Wechsler Adult Intelligence Scale (WAIS)** and **Wechsler Intelligence Scale for Children (WISC)** have items that are organized into various subtests. Scores from the various subtests are combined to give a single IQ score.

Examples of the subtests for WAIS are shown below. The Verbal Scale (top right) emphasizes language and verbal skills. Because of this emphasis, a person from a deprived environment or for whom English is a second language might have difficulty on this scale because of lack of verbal knowledge rather than lack of cognitive ability.

In an attempt to measure nonverbal skills and rule out other cultural or educational problems, Wechsler added the Performance Scale (lower right). These performance subtests, which measure problem-solving abilities, require concentration and focused effort, which may be difficult for people who are very nervous or are poor test takers.

One reason these IQ tests are widely used is that they have two characteristics of good tests: validity and reliability.

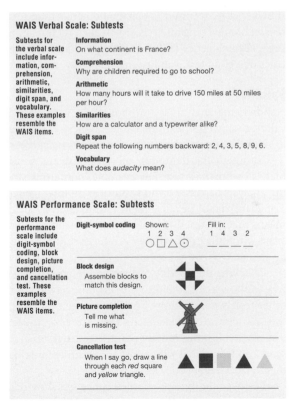

WAIS Verbal Scale: Subtests

Subtests for the verbal scale include information, comprehension, arithmetic, similarities, digit span, and vocabulary. These examples resemble the WAIS items.

Information
On what continent is France?

Comprehension
Why are children required to go to school?

Arithmetic
How many hours will it take to drive 150 miles at 50 miles per hour?

Similarities
How are a calculator and a typewriter alike?

Digit span
Repeat the following numbers backward: 2, 4, 3, 5, 8, 9, 6.

Vocabulary
What does *audacity* mean?

WAIS Performance Scale: Subtests

Subtests for the performance scale include digit-symbol coding, block design, picture completion, and cancellation test. These examples resemble the WAIS items.

Digit-symbol coding   Shown: 1 2 3 4   Fill in: 1 4 3 2

Block design
Assemble blocks to match this design.

Picture completion
Tell me what is missing.

Cancellation test
When I say go, draw a line through each *red* square and *yellow* triangle.

Potential Problems in IQ Testing

Learn about some of the potential problems of IQ testing.

▶ **L06** Discuss the role of validity and reliability in intelligence tests.

Two Characteristics of Tests

How truthful are the claims that intelligence and other personality traits can be identified through analyzing handwriting (Searles, 1998)? For example, which one of the four handwriting samples on the right indicates the highest IQ? (Answer at bottom of next page.)

1. So intelligent
2. so intelligent
3. so intelligent
4. so intelligent

Although handwriting analysis may claim to measure intelligence, research shows that its accuracy is usually no better than a good guess (Tripician, 2000). The reason handwriting analysis or so-called IQ tests in popular magazines are poor measures of intelligence (IQ) is that they lack at least one of the two important characteristics of a good test, validity and reliability.

Validity

Handwriting analysis is fun, but it is a very poor intelligence test because it lacks validity, which is one of the two characteristics of a good test.

Validity means that the test measures what it is supposed to measure.

Although the definition of validity seems simple and short, this characteristic makes or breaks a test. For example, numerous studies have shown that handwriting analysis has little or no validity as an intelligence or personality test (Basil, 1989; Tripician, 2000). Because handwriting analysis lacks the characteristic of validity, it means that this test does not accurately measure what it is supposed to measure. Thus, a test with little or no validity produces results that could be produced by guessing or by chance.

Checking the validity of a test is a long, expensive, and complicated process. One way to show a test's validity is to give the new test to hundreds of subjects along with other tests whose validity has already been established. Then the subjects' scores on the new test are correlated with their scores on the tests with proven validity. Another way to establish the validity of intelligence tests, such as the WAIS, is to show that IQ scores are correlated with another measure of intelligence, such as academic achievement (Deary et al., 2007).

Besides validity, a good intelligence test should also have reliability.

Reliability

If your style of handwriting remained constant over time, such as always boldly crossing your *t*'s, then this trait would be reliable.

Reliability refers to consistency: A person's score on a test at one point in time should be similar to the score obtained by the same person on a similar test at a later point in time.

For example, if boldly crossed *t*'s indicated that a person is intelligent, then this measure of intelligence would be reliable. However, there is no evidence that boldly crossed *t*'s indicate that a person is intelligent. So, in this case, handwriting analysis would be a reliable test of intelligence, but since it lacks validity (doesn't measure intelligence), it is a worthless test of intelligence.

Now, suppose you took the WAIS as a senior in high school and then retook the test as a junior in college. You would find that your IQ scores would be much the same. Because your IQ scores remain similar across time, the Wechsler scales, like other standardized IQ tests, have reliability (Berg, 2000; A. S. Kaufman, 2000).

For example, the graph at right shows the results of verbal IQ scores when seven different age groups of subjects were given the WAIS. Notice that verbal IQ scores are quite stable from ages 20 to 74, indicating that the Wechsler scales score high in reliability (Kaufman et al., 1989).

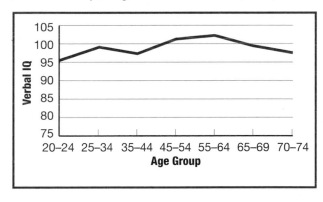

Researchers have shown that current intelligence tests, which measure primarily cognitive abilities, have relatively good validity and reliability (Kaplan & Saccuzzo, 2009). Even though IQ scores can be measured with good reliability and validity, our next question to answer is: What use are IQ scores?

(Handwriting answer: I [R.P.] wrote all four samples so that no matter which one you picked, I would come out a winner!)

Unless otherwise noted, all images are © Cengage Learning

▶ **L07** Discuss the distribution and use of IQ scores.

Normal Distribution of IQ Scores

IQ scores from intelligence tests are said to have a normal distribution.

A **normal distribution** refers to a statistical arrangement of scores so that they resemble the shape of a bell and, thus, is said to be a bell-shaped curve.

A bell-shaped curve means the vast majority of scores fall in the middle range, with fewer scores falling near the two extreme ends of the curve. For example, a normal distribution of IQ scores is shown below. The average IQ score is 100, and 95% of IQ scores fall between 70 and 130. An IQ of 70 and below is one sign of mild retardation. An IQ of 130 or higher is one indication of a gifted individual.

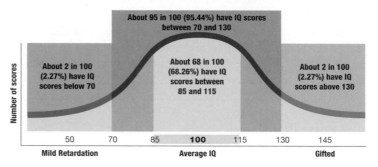

About 95 in 100 (95.44%) have IQ scores between 70 and 130

About 2 in 100 (2.27%) have IQ scores below 70

About 68 in 100 (68.26%) have IQ scores between 85 and 115

About 2 in 100 (2.27%) have IQ scores above 130

Number of scores

50   70   85   **100**   115   130   145

Mild Retardation   Average IQ   Gifted

Mental Retardation: IQ Scores

One use of IQ scores is to help identify individuals with mental retardation.

Mental retardation refers to a substantial limitation in present functioning that is characterized by significantly subaverage intellectual functioning, along with limitations in two of eleven areas, including communication, self-care, home living, social skills, academic skills, leisure, and safety (American Psychiatric Association, 2000).

Three levels of retardation have been identified:

1. *Mild Mental Retardation:* These individuals have IQs that range from 50 to 70. With training, they can learn to read and write, master simple occupational skills, and become self-supporting members of society.

2. *Moderate Mental Retardation:* These individuals have IQs that range from 35 to 55. With training, they can learn to become partially independent in their everyday lives, provided they are in a family or self-help setting.

3. *Severe/Profound Mental Retardation:* These individuals have IQs ranging from 20 to 40. With training, they can acquire limited skills for personal care.

Vast Majority: IQ Scores

Since the vast majority of people, about 95%, have IQ scores that fall between 70 and 130, it is interesting to see what IQ scores can tell us.

For instance, wouldn't you expect IQ scores to predict academic achievement? Because IQ tests measure cognitive abilities similar to those used in academic settings, it is no surprise there is a medium-strength association, or correlation, between IQ scores and grades (0.50) and between IQ scores and total years of education that people complete (0.50) (Brody, 1997). However, based on medium-strength correlations alone, it would be difficult to predict a specific person's academic performance because performance in academic settings also depends on personal characteristics, such as one's interest in school, willingness to study, and belief in one's ability to succeed (Klomegah, 2007; Neisser et al., 1996).

© Sportstock/Shutterstock

Gifted: IQ Scores

Sho Yano (right photo), whose IQ is 200 plus, entered college at age 9, graduated at age 12, plays classical works on the piano, and was the youngest person ever to start a dual MD-PhD program at the University of Chicago. Sho Yano is considered a profoundly gifted child. Although researchers and educators differ in how they define gifted, this definition refers to academically gifted children.

A moderately **gifted** child is usually defined by an IQ score between 130 and 150; a profoundly gifted child has an IQ score about 180 or above.

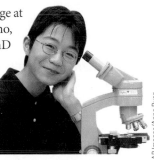

AP Images/Anne Ryan

Like Sho Yano, who excels at the piano and medicine, gifted children usually have some superior talent or skill. When placed in regular classrooms, gifted children may face a number of problems: They may be bored by the lack of stimulation and may develop social problems because they are labeled nerds or geeks. Researchers recommend that gifted children be placed in special academic programs that help them develop their potentials (Goode, 2002; Winner, 2000).

Next, we'll discuss the various influences on intelligence.

Check Your Learning Quiz 7.3

Go to **login.cengagebrain.com** and take the online quiz.

▶ **L08** Discuss the role of nature and nurture in intelligence.

Nature and Nurture

The issue of how much hereditary, or genetic, factors and environmental factors contribute to an individual's intelligence brings us to the nature-nurture question.

The **nature-nurture question** asks how nature (hereditary or genetic factors) interacts with nurture (environmental factors) in the development of a person's intellectual, emotional, personal, and social abilities.

In the early 1900s, intelligence was believed to be primarily inherited, or due to nature (Terman, 1916). In the 1950s, psychology was heavily influenced by behaviorism, which emphasized nurture, or environmental factors, in the development of intelligence (Skinner, 1953). Today, researchers find nature and nurture interact and contribute about equally to the development of intelligence (Davis et al., 2008; Pinker, 2002).

In exploring how nature and nurture contribute to and interact in the development of intelligence, researchers compared IQ scores in non-twin siblings and in fraternal and identical twins.

Fraternal twins, like siblings, develop from separate eggs and have 50% of their genes in common.

Identical twins develop from a single egg and thus have almost identical genes, which means they have nearly 100% of their genes in common.

Nature (Genetic Factors)

The graph on the right shows that the correlation in IQ scores between identical twins (0.85), who share nearly 100% of their genes, is higher than the correlation between fraternal twins (0.60), who share 50% of their genes, or between siblings (0.45), who also share 50% of their genes (Plomin & Petrill, 1997). These findings, which come from over 100 studies, indicate that genetic factors contribute about 50% to the development of intelligence, which has a rather specific definition (Plomin & Spinath, 2004).

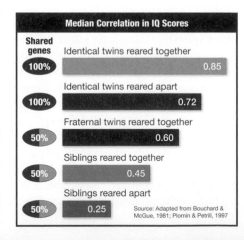

Median Correlation in IQ Scores

Shared genes		
100%	Identical twins reared together	0.85
100%	Identical twins reared apart	0.72
50%	Fraternal twins reared together	0.60
50%	Siblings reared together	0.45
50%	Siblings reared apart	0.25

Source: Adapted from Bouchard & McGue, 1981; Plomin & Petrill, 1997

Nurture (Environmental Factors)

What would happen if children with limited social-educational opportunities and low IQs were adopted by parents who could provide better social-educational opportunities? To determine whether environment can increase IQ scores, one study examined the IQs of African American children from impoverished environments who were adopted into middle-class families, some white and some African American; all of the families provided many social-educational opportunities for the adopted

children. Researchers found that the IQs of the adopted children were as much as 10 points higher than those of African American children raised in disadvantaged homes (Scarr & Weinberg, 1976). In a follow-up study, researchers reported that the adopted children, now adolescents, had higher IQ scores than African American children raised in impoverished communities (Weinberg et al., 1992). Other studies also indicate that as experiences for African Americans improve, so do IQs (Williams, 2009).

These kinds of studies demonstrate that environmental factors clearly contribute to intellectual development (Begley, 2009; Duyme, 1999).

Interaction of Nature and Nurture

An example of how genetic and environmental factors interact in the development of intelligence comes from a study of 3-year-old children who were identified as being either high or low in exploring their environments, which is a personality trait known as stimulation seeking. These children were later given IQ tests at age 11 to determine if being high or low in stimulation seeking affected their IQs. Children who had been rated high in stimulation seeking at age 3 scored significantly higher on IQ tests compared to children who had been rated low in stimulation seeking at age 3. This significant difference in IQ scores (11 points) was not related to the occupation or education of their parents. Researchers concluded that children high in stimulation seeking were more curious and open to learning from their environments, which in turn enhanced the development of their cognitive abilities and resulted in higher scores on IQ tests (Raine et al., 2002).

In conclusion, genetic factors contribute about 50% to the development of one's intelligence (IQ score), while the other 50% comes from the interaction with environmental factors.

Intervention Programs

Learn whether intervention programs can raise IQ scores.

Racial Controversy

Explore the possible causes of IQ differences between races.

Check Your Learning Quiz 7.4

Go to **login.cengagebrain.com** and take the online quiz.

Unless otherwise noted, all images are © Cengage Learning

▶ **LO9** Define thinking and concept.

▶ **LO10** Describe how the exemplar model and prototype theory explain how concepts are formed.

A basic, fundamental process involved in any type of intelligence is the ability to think.

Thinking, which is sometimes referred to as reasoning, involves paying attention to information and engaging in mental processes that are used to form concepts, solve problems, and engage in creative activities.

Let's look at how thinking is involved in learning the difference between a dog, cat, and rabbit. Try to remember back to your childhood. There was probably a time when you named every animal you saw as a "dog." As a child, you gradually learned to tell the difference between a dog, a cat, and a rabbit by forming a different concept for each animal.

A **concept** is a way to group or classify objects, events, animals, or people based on some features, traits, or characteristics that they all share in common.

We'll begin with the exploration of how we learn concepts, as they provide the building blocks for thinking. How you formed the concept of a dog or cat or rabbit has two different explanations: the exemplar model and the prototype theory (Nosofsky & Zaki, 2002; Olsson et al., 2004).

Exemplar Model

You easily recognize the animals below, but the question is: How did you know which animal was which? Is it because your mind contains definitions of hundreds of animals?

The **exemplar model** says that you form a concept of an object, event, animal, or person by defining or making a mental list of the essential characteristics of a particular thing.

According to the exemplar model, you formed a concept of a dog, cat, or rabbit by learning its essential characteristics. The essential characteristics of a dog might include that it barks and has a long nose, two ears, two eyes, four legs, some hair, and usually a tail. Similarly, you made mental lists of the characteristics of other animals. Then, when you looked at the three animals on the previous page, you automatically sorted through hundreds of animal definitions until you found one that included the essential properties of a dog, cat, or rabbit. Once you found the definition, you knew what the animal was. Although the exemplar model seems like a reasonable method of forming concepts, it has two serious problems.

Problems with the Exemplar Model

Too Many Features

In real life, it is very difficult to list all the features that define any object (Rey, 1983). For example, if your list of features to define a dog wasn't complete, the list might also apply to wolves, jackals, coyotes, and skunks. If your list of features to define a dog included every possible feature, such a mental list would be complete but take so long to go through that it would be very slow to use.

> **dog (dog, dag)** *n.; pl.* **dogs, dog.**
> 1. any of a large and varied group of domesticated animals *(Canis familiaris)* that have four legs, a tail, two ears, prominent nose, a hairy coat, and a bark.

And worse, you would need a long list of defining features for each and every animal, person, and object. Such a great number of mental lists would tax the best of memories.

Too Many Exceptions

After making a list of defining features, you would also need to list all the exceptions that do not fit into the dictionary definition of dog. For example, some dogs rarely bark, some are very tiny, some are very large, some are hairless, and some are very fuzzy.

Because of these two problems, you would need to check two mental lists, a long list that contained all the defining features and another that contained all the exceptions, before finding the concept that correctly identified the animal, person, or object.

For these reasons, the exemplar model has generally been replaced by a different theory of how we form concepts: the prototype theory.

▶ **LO11** Describe the functions of concepts.

Prototype Theory

Please look at the three animals on the right, #1, #2, and #3. Despite the great differences in size, color, and facial features of these animals, prototype theory explains why you can easily and quickly recognize each one as a dog.

Prototype theory says that you form a concept by creating a mental image that is based on the average characteristics of an object. This "average" looking object is called a prototype. To identify a new object, you match it to one of your already formed prototypes of objects, people, or animals.

Based on many experiences, you develop prototypes of many different objects, persons, and animals (Rosch, 1978). For example, your prototype of a dog would be a mental image of any particular animal that has average features (such as nose, tail, ears, height, weight). By using your prototype of a dog, you can easily and quickly identify all three animals on the right—the large brown mutt (#1), the tiny Chihuahua (#2), and the spotted Dalmatian (#3)—as being dogs.

Advantages of the Prototype Theory

Average Features

One advantage of the prototype theory over the exemplar model is that you do not have to make a mental list of all the defining features of an object, which is often impossible. Instead, you form a prototype by creating a mental picture or image of the object, animal, or person that has only average features.

Quick Recognition

Another advantage of the prototype theory is that it can result in quick recognition, as happened when you identified these different-looking animals (#1, #2, and #3) as dogs. The more a new object resembles a prototype, the more quickly you can identify it; the less it matches your prototype, the longer it takes.

For example, what is the strange animal on the right (#4)

#1

© PhotoDisc, Inc.

#2

© PhotoDisc, Inc.

#3

© PhotoDisc, Inc.

Unless otherwise noted, all images are © Cengage Learning

and where is its head? Because this animal's features are not close to your dog prototype, it may take you some time to figure out that it has hair like dreadlocks, its head is on the right, and it's an unusual dog (called a Puli).

Prototype theory, which explains that you form concepts by creating and using prototypes, is widely accepted and has generally replaced the exemplar model (Geeraerts, 2006).

Functions of Concepts

If you woke up one day to find that you had lost all your concepts, you would indeed have a very bad day. That's because concepts perform two important functions: They organize information and help us avoid relearning (Humphreys & Forde, 2001).

1 Organize Information Concepts allow you to group things into categories and thus better organize and store information in memory. For example, instead of having to store hundreds of mental images of many different kinds of dogs, you can store a single prototype of the average dog.

2 Avoid Relearning By having concepts that can be used to classify and categorize things, you can easily classify new things without having to relearn what each thing is. For example, once you have a concept for a dog, rabbit, cat, or cookie, you do not have to relearn what that thing is on each new encounter.

Without concepts, our cognitive worlds would consist of unconnected pieces of information. In fact, some forms of brain damage destroy a person's ability to form concepts, so that the person is unable to name or categorize what he or she sees. This is known as visual agnosia (see p. 85). For example, what if you had to always relearn that the picture on the right is of a dog?

There is no doubt that by using concepts, you can identify, categorize, and store information very efficiently. Next, we'll explore the thought processes involved in solving problems.

Concept Formation

Use the exemplar and prototype models to form concepts.

✓

Check Your Learning Quiz 7.5

Go to **login.cengagebrain.com** and take the online quiz.

▶ **L012** Describe problem solving and discuss how algorithms, heuristics, and artificial intelligence are different ways of thinking.

In 1997, world chess champion, Garry Kasparov (photo below), lost a chess match for the first time to a powerful computer (McClain, 2005). He played another computer in 2003 and tied, with three games each (Byrne, 2003). This human-versus-computer chess match was all about thinking and problem solving.

Problem solving involves searching for some rule, plan, or strategy that results in our reaching a certain goal that is currently out of reach.

In previous matches, Kasparov had always beat the computer because he was the better thinker and problem solver. For Kasparov, as well as for most of us, problem solving involves three states: (1) the *initial state,* which is thinking about the unsolved problem; (2) the *operations state,* which involves trying various rules or strategies to solve the problem; and (3) the *goal state,* which is reaching the solution. One plan used by expert problem solvers, such as Kasparov, is to think in broad terms of how to solve the problem, while less successful novices become too focused on specifics (Abernethy et al., 1994). For example, when novice players are in a difficult position, they may spend much time calculating possible moves, often planning many moves ahead, yet never find the best solution. An expert player has more knowledge of chess positions and examines fewer, but better, possibilities in much less time (Ross, 2006). Being a successful problem solver involves using different kinds of thinking, some of which can be programmed into a computer.

> A computer that was unemotional, unconcerned, and uncaring beat me at chess!

© Richard Pohle/Sutcliffe News Features/Sipa

Different Ways of Thinking

In this man-machine chess match, Kasparov's thinking involved a combination of intuition (clever guesses based on years of experience) and creative mental shortcuts, called heuristics. The computer's "thinking" was more fixed because it had been programmed to use a set of rules that lead to specific outcomes, called algorithms. Algorithms or heuristics illustrate two very different ways of thinking or solving problems (Lohman, 2000).

If you wanted to win at a variety of games, such as chess, checkers, or bridge, you would follow a fixed set of rules called algorithms *(AL-go-rhythms).*

Algorithms are a fixed set of rules that, if followed correctly, will eventually lead to a solution.

For example, learning to play chess involves following algorithms that define how pieces move and the results of those moves. The reason relatively few chess players become grand masters like Kasparov is that people vary in their ability to learn and use algorithms.

Initially, the computer was given little chance to beat world chess champion Kasparov because playing chess by using algorithms is a slow process. Instead of using algorithms, chess champion Kasparov was playing with a potentially more powerful set of rules called heuristics.

Kasparov's unique brain, together with his years of experience, allowed him to play chess using heuristics *(hyur-RIS-ticks)*.

Heuristics are rules of thumb, or clever and creative mental shortcuts, that reduce the number of operations and allow one to solve problems easily and quickly.

In the late 1990s, Kasparov's clever and creative shortcuts, or heuristics, had given him the advantage over the fixed and not-so-creative algorithms of computer programs. However, computers now have been programmed with new algorithms that increase their speed of "thinking" from analyzing 100,000 chess moves per second to 2.5 million. As a result of this increased speed, human chess grand masters, whose thinking focuses on using clever heuristics, no longer have a clear advantage over a computer's "thinking" ability (Boyce, 2002).

Besides being used to solve chess problems, heuristics are often used in daily life to make decisions or draw conclusions (Bailenson et al., 2000). A commonly used heuristic is called the availability heuristic.

The **availability heuristic** says we rely on information that is more prominent or easily recalled and overlook other information that is available but less prominent or notable.

For example, the murder rate in the United States actually decreased in the late 1990s. However, during this time, network coverage of homicides increased 473%, which made news of murders more available and, according to the availability heuristic, led people to conclude that murder rates had become epidemic (Comarow, 2001).

Using the availability heuristic to make a decision means taking a mental shortcut. Although heuristics allow us to make quick decisions, they may result in bad decisions, since we make them using shortcuts, which limits the amount of information we use (Bower, 1997).

▶ **LO13** Describe strategies to solve problems.

Three Strategies for Solving Problems

Most of us have had the experience of getting stuck while trying to solve a problem and wondering what to do next. By studying people who are good at problem solving, such as chess players, engineers, and computer programmers, psychologists have identified a number of useful strategies for solving problems. We'll discuss three problem-solving strategies: changing a mental set, using analogies, and forming subgoals.

Changing One's Mental Set

Problem

Connect all nine dots shown on the right by drawing four straight lines without lifting your pencil from the paper or retracing any lines. If, like most people, you have difficulty solving this problem, it may be because of functional fixedness.

Functional fixedness refers to a mental set that is characterized by the inability to see an object as having a function different from its usual one.

For instance, you probably have a mental set that a straight line must begin and end on a dot. To solve the nine-dot problem, you need to break out of functional fixedness, which involves thinking of a line as continuing past a dot (Kershaw & Ohlsson, 2004).

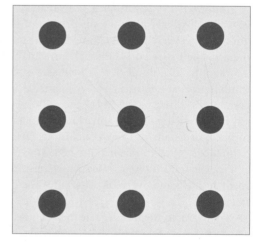

The nine-dot puzzle is a good example of the kind of problem that is often solved in a sudden flash, known as insight, which we discussed earlier (pp. 242–243).

Insight is the sudden grasp of a solution after many incorrect attempts.

You can increase your chances of solving a problem by insight if you consider the problem from many different viewpoints and unusual angles and if you decrease your anxiety and concern, which will in turn help you to overcome functional fixedness.

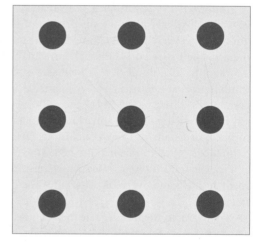

Unless otherwise noted, all images are © Cengage Learning

Using Analogies

Problem

Imagine that you have a box of matches, two candles, a piece of string, and several tacks, as shown in the right photo. How would you mount a candle on the wall so that it could be used as a light?

© Craig McClain

You may solve the candle problem in a flash of insight. However, most of us have to develop a strategy to solve the problem, such as using an analogy.

An **analogy** is a strategy for finding a similarity between the new situation and an old, familiar situation.

If you adopt an analogy to solve the candle problem, here's how your thinking might proceed: "I'm familiar with using a shelf to hold a candle on the wall. Which of the objects—candle, string, or box—could serve as a shelf? If I remove the matches, I can tack the box to the wall."

As you gain more experience and knowledge, you become better at using analogies to solve problems.

Forming Subgoals

Problem

Suppose your assignment is to write a term paper titled "Creativity and Madness." A useful strategy for writing this paper would be to divide the assignment or general problem into a number of subgoals.

Using **subgoals** is a strategy that involves breaking down the overall problem into separate parts that, when completed in order, will result in a solution.

As shown in the right figure, the first subgoal is doing research and finding articles on creativity and madness. The second subgoal is reading the articles and taking notes. The third subgoal is making a detailed outline of the whole paper. A fourth subgoal is using your outline to write the paper. The strategy of working on and completing each specific subgoal makes the overall project more manageable and reduces unproductive worrying that can interfere with starting and completing your paper.

Another problem-solving strategy is to use creative thinking, our next topic.

Problem Solving Strategies

Observe examples of changing one's mental set, using analogies, and forming concepts.

▶ **L014** Explain how creativity is a way of thinking and a problem-solving strategy.

▶ **L015** Describe the different approaches used to measure creativity.

Thinking Creatively

The way one becomes a creative thinker is quite a mystery. Take the case of Shawn Carter, better known as Jay-Z, for example. Carter grew up living in the dangerous projects, dropped out of high school, and began dealing drugs at a young age. Despite overwhelming odds, Carter succeeded in making 10 hit albums, which together have sold nearly 40 million copies. He has received seven Grammy Awards, two MTV Music Awards, an American Music Award, a Billboard Music Award, and countless other honors. Carter is so creative and talented that he completed *The Blueprint,* a critically acclaimed album, in only two days! His creativity helped him succeed outside of the music business as well. Perhaps most notably, Carter's creativity is evident in his urban clothing brand Rocawear, which has become a multimillion-dollar business due to his creative marketing and product development (Ali, 2006; DeCurtis, 2009).

This intriguing story of Shawn Carter raises an interesting question about creativity: How is creativity defined? Although there are more than 60 definitions of creativity, we'll begin with the one most commonly used (Boden, 1994).

How Is Creativity Defined and Measured?

The definition of creative thinking is somewhat different from the definition of a creative individual.

Creative thinking is a combination of flexibility in thinking and reorganization of understanding to produce innovative ideas and new or novel solutions (Sternberg, 2001).

A **creative individual** is someone who regularly solves problems, fashions products, or defines new questions that make an impact on society (Gardner, 1993, 2006a).

People can show evidence of creative thinking in many ways. For example, recognized creative individuals include Albert Einstein, who formulated the theory of relativity; Michelangelo, who painted the Sistine Chapel; Sigmund Freud, who developed psychoanalysis; Dr. Seuss, who wrote rhyming books for children; Ray Kroc, who founded McDonald's; and Shawn Carter (Jay-Z), who is a rapper.

Because there are so many different examples and kinds of creativity, psychologists use three different approaches to measure creativity: the psychometric, case study, and cognitive approaches (Sternberg & O'Hara, 2000).

Psychometric Approach

This approach, which uses objective problem-solving tasks to measure creativity, focuses on the distinction between two kinds of thinking: convergent and divergent (Guilford, 1967; Runco, 2004).

Convergent thinking means beginning with a problem and coming up with a single correct solution.

Examples include answering multiple-choice questions and solving math problems. The opposite of convergent thinking is divergent thinking.

Divergent thinking means beginning with a problem and coming up with many different solutions.

For example, the two problem-solving tasks on page 328 (nine-dot and candle-match puzzles) are used to assess divergent thinking, which is a popular psychometric measure for creativity (Amabile, 1985; Camp, 1994).

Case Study Approach

Because the psychometric approach is limited to using objective tests, it provides little insight into creative minds. In comparison, the case-study approach analyzes creative persons in great depth and thus provides insight into their development, personality, motivation, and problems.

For example, Howard Gardner (1993) used the case-study approach to analyze creative people, including Sigmund Freud. Gardner found that creative people are creative in certain areas but poor in others. For example, Freud was very creative in linguistic and personal areas but very poor in spatial and musical areas. Although case studies provide rich insight into creative minds, their findings are very personal or subjective and not easily applied to others (Freyd, 1994).

Cognitive Approach

The cognitive approach tries to build a bridge between the objective measures of the psychometric approach and the subjective descriptions provided by case studies. The cognitive approach identifies and measures cognitive mechanisms that are used during creative thinking (Freyd, 1994).

For example, many individuals have reported that one cognitive mechanism vital to creative thinking is the use of mental imagery, which involves thinking in images (Finke, 1993). Thus, the cognitive approach involves analyzing the workings of mental imagery and its relationship to creative thinking.

Characteristics of Creative People

Learn about how creative people think and behave.

Check Your Learning Quiz 7.6

Go to **login.cengagebrain.com** and take the online quiz.

▶ **L016** Describe the deductive and inductive reasoning processes.

Reasoning

If you saw a nicely dressed older man standing in the ocean, you would naturally wonder what he was doing.

© Hans Neleman/Getty Images

Unless otherwise noted, all images are © Cengage Learning

To figure out this man's unusual behavior, you could use the personal computer inside your brain, which has a very powerful software program called reasoning (Sloman, 1996).

Reasoning, which often means thinking, is a mental process that involves using and applying knowledge to solve problems, make plans or decisions, and achieve goals.

To figure out why this normal-looking, fully dressed but shoeless man is standing in the ocean, you could use two different kinds of reasoning: deductive or inductive.

Deductive Reasoning

Since you rarely see a nicely dressed older man standing in the ocean, you might assume that he is drunk. The kind of reasoning that begins with a big assumption is called deductive reasoning.

Deductive reasoning begins with making a general assumption that you know or believe to be true and then drawing specific conclusions based on this assumption; in other words, reasoning from a general assumption to particulars.

Your general assumption is that only a drunk person would gleefully walk into the ocean dressed in a suit. This man is doing so. Therefore, he must be drunk. In its simplest form, deductive reasoning follows this formula: If you are given an assumption or statement as true, then there is only one correct conclusion to draw. This formula is often referred to as "If p (given statements), then q (conclusion)." For example:

Given statements ("If p"): Only people who are over 21 years of age drink alcohol. That man is drinking alcohol.

Conclusion ("Then q"): That man must be over 21 years of age.

One mistake people make in deductive reasoning is that they assume but do not always know if the basic statement or assumption (p) is true. If the basic statement is false (that is, drunkenness is not the only explanation for the man's behavior), then so are the conclusions. Another way to figure out why the man is standing in the ocean is to use inductive reasoning.

Inductive Reasoning

Instead of just assuming that this man is standing in the ocean because he's drunk, you walk over and ask some specific questions. After listening to this man's answers, you reach a different explanation for why he's standing in the ocean. The kind of reasoning that starts with specific facts or observations is called inductive reasoning.

Inductive reasoning begins with making particular observations that you then use to draw a broader conclusion; in other words, reasoning from particulars to a general conclusion.

For example, when questioned, the man answers "No" to all the following questions: Did you drink alcohol today? Do you have a job? Are you married? Do you do this often? Have you eaten today? Are you ill? Would you like me to take you home? After considering all these particulars, you reach a general conclusion: Either this man is suffering from Alzheimer's disease or he is lying.

Researchers use inductive reasoning when they use past experiences or observations to form a general hypothesis (Evans, 1993). For instance, researchers observed that when some students take exams, they have rapid heart rate, sweaty palms, muscle tension, and increased blood pressure. Based on these particulars, researchers reached the general conclusion that these students have test anxiety.

One big mistake people make in inductive reasoning is jumping to a conclusion before knowing all the facts (Levy, 1997). Depending on the situation, deductive and inductive reasoning are powerful mental tools provided you're aware of their pitfalls.

Next, you'll learn how it is that we make decisions.

▶ **LO17** Discuss how we make decisions, including the role of emotions.

▶ **LO18** Explain the theory of linguistic relativity.

Decision Making

We make many decisions each day. Some decisions have very important consequences in our lives, such as choosing a college, career, or spouse. Other decisions have much less importance, such as choosing a flavor of ice cream, the color of a shirt, or a movie to watch. We would like to believe that we make decisions, especially important ones, based on thoughtful reasoning. But how do we actually make decisions?

Imagine that you are in the hospital and a doctor tells you about your treatment options. One of the treatments involves surgery, and you must decide whether you want to undergo surgery. Would your decision be influenced differently if a doctor told you that the survival rate of surgery is 80% or that there is a 20% chance of dying from surgery? Even though both statements express the same risk, the 80% chance of survival sounds more appealing than the 20% chance of dying. Thinking about the success of surgery is comforting, but thinking about the failure of surgery makes us uncomfortable (De Martino, 2006a).

Research shows that we often base our decisions on emotion rather than intellect (Koenigs et al., 2007; Lehrer, 2009). As we discuss next, research on gambling shows what happens in our brains as we make decisions.

Gambling Decisions

Benedetto De Martino (2006b) and his team of researchers (2006) at the University College of London took brain scans of men and women while they were being asked to make a decision about whether or not to gamble. At the start of the study, each subject was given about $100. They were then either told they could "keep" 40% of their money or "lose" 60% of their money if they did not gamble. When subjects were told they could "keep" 40% of their money if they chose not to gamble, subjects gambled only 43% of the time. When told they could "lose" 60% of their money if they did not gamble, subjects gambled 62% of the time. Even when the chances of winning and losing were identical, the wording of the instructions made a difference in the subjects' decisions.

Should I have surgery?

The results of brain scans showed that the part of the brain responsible for strong negative emotions (amygdala) was very active while subjects were making their decisions, regardless of the choice they made. Researchers concluded that emotions had a strong influence on how subjects made gambling decisions. Further support for the significant role of emotions in decision making comes from research studies showing that people who lack emotions due to brain trauma or injury often have serious difficulties making even simple decisions (Damasio, 2006).

Thoughts and Words

Because words are so much a part of our reasoning and decision-making processes, we need to know how words can influence or bias our thinking.

Almost everyone has heard the untrue saying that the Inuit (Eskimos) have dozens of words for snow because their survival depends on knowing how to travel and hunt in different kinds of snow. This particular observation was first made by amateur linguist Benjamin Whorf (1956), who noticed that languages differed in their vocabularies depending on how much emphasis they gave to different objects and events in their environment. For example, Whorf reasoned that because the Inuit (Eskimos) have many names for snow, they must be able to perceive many more kinds of snow than Americans, for whom snow conditions are less important. On the basis of these kinds of observations, Whorf formulated the theory of linguistic relativity.

The **theory of linguistic relativity** states that the differences among languages result in similar differences in how people think of and perceive the world.

Therefore, the theory of linguistic relativity states that speakers of different languages think about the world in different ways. Research findings conclude that though there is some support for language determining our thinking, there are many examples of this not being true (Davies & Corbett, 1997, Pinker, 1994).

Next, you'll learn about the basics of language.

Decisions! Decisions!

Watch an exploration of how important emotions are in making decisions.

Thinking in Two Languages

Explore whether language influences thinking.

Check Your Learning Quiz 7.7

Go to **login.cengagebrain.com** and take the online quiz.

© Hans Blohm/Masterfile

▶ **LO19** Describe the four rules of language.

Rules of Language

Now, we turn our attention to an important component of intelligence and thinking, which is language.

Language is a special form of communication that involves learning rules to make and combine symbols (words or gestures) into an endless number of meaningful sentences.

The reason language is such a successful form of communication arises from two amazingly simple principles: words and grammar.

A **word** is an arbitrary pairing between a sound or symbol and a meaning.

For example, consider why it is that we call the object in the right photo a parrot. The word *parrot* does not look like, sound like, or fly like a parrot, but it refers to a bird we call a parrot because all English-speaking people memorized this pairing as children. Adults are estimated to know about 60,000 such pairings or words. (Pinker, 1995). However, these symbols or words are rather useless unless the users follow rules of grammar.

Grammar refers to a set of rules for combining words into phrases and sentences to express an infinite number of thoughts that can be understood by others.

For instance, our mental rules of grammar immediately tell us that the headline "Parrot Bites Man's Nose" means something very different from "Man Bites Parrot's Nose."

As children, each of us learned the four rules of language. Now, as adults, we use these rules without being aware of how or when we use them. To illustrate the four rules of language, we'll use the word *caterpillar*. As a child, you may have watched its strange crawling motion, or perhaps you even picked one up.

1 The first language rule governs phonology.

Phonology *(FOE-nawl-uh-gee)* specifies how we make the meaningful sounds that are used by a particular language.

Any English word can be broken down into phonemes.

Phonemes *(FOE-neems)* are the basic sounds of consonants and vowels.

For example, the various sounds of *c* and *p* represent different phonemes, which are some of the sounds in the word *caterpillar*. We combine phonemes to form words by learning the second rule.

© Corbis/SuperStock

Unless otherwise noted, all images are © Cengage Learning

2 The second language rule governs morphology.

Morphology *(mor-FAWL-uh-gee)* is the system we use to group phonemes into meaningful combinations of sounds and words.

A **morpheme** *(MOR-feem)* is the smallest meaningful combination of sounds in a language.

For example, a morpheme may be

a word, such as **cat**,

a letter, such as the **s** in cat**s**,

a prefix, such as the **un-** in **un**breakable,

or a suffix, such as the -**ed** in walk**ed**.

The word **caterpillar** is actually one morpheme, and the word **caterpillars** is two (**caterpillar-s**). We use the third rule to combine words into meaningful sentences.

3 The third language rule governs syntax, or grammar.

Syntax, or **grammar,** is a set of rules that specifies how we combine words to form meaningful phrases and sentences.

For example, why doesn't the following sentence make sense? **Caterpillars green long and are.**

You instantly realize that this sentence is nonsensical because it doesn't follow the English grammar rules. If you apply the rules of English grammar, you would rearrange the combination of words to read: "Caterpillars are long and green." Although you may not be able to list all the rules of grammar, you automatically follow them when you speak. One way you know whether the word *bear* is a noun or a verb is by using the fourth rule.

4 The fourth language rule governs semantics.

Semantics *(si-MAN-ticks)* specifies the meanings of words or phrases when they appear in various sentences or contexts.

For instance, as you read "Did Pat pat a caterpillar's back?" how do you know what the word **pat** means, since it appears twice in succession. From your knowledge of semantics, you know that the first **Pat** is a noun and the name of a person, while the second **pat** is a verb, which signals some action.

Language Development #1

Watch how children learn to use morphemes and grammar.

Understanding Language

One of the great mysteries of using and understanding language can be demonstrated by the following two simple but very different sentences:

You picked up a caterpillar.

A caterpillar was picked up by you.

Despite a different word order, you know these two sentences mean exactly the same thing. How you know that these different sentences mean exactly the same thing was explained by linguist Noam Chomsky (1957). We'll discuss two of Chomsky's revolutionary principles—mental grammar and innate brain program—that allow us to use and understand spoken language with relative ease.

Mental Grammar

Almost every sentence we speak or understand is formed from a brand-new combination of words. Chomsky pointed out that the brain does not have the capacity to contain a list of all the sentences we will ever use. Instead, Chomsky argued that the brain contains a program or ***mental grammar*** that allows us to combine nouns, verbs, and objects in an endless variety of meaningful sentences. Chomsky's principle of mental grammar answers the question of how we can so easily create so many different sentences. The second question that Chomsky answered was: How do we acquire this mental grammar?

Innate Brain Program

How is it possible that 4-year-old children, with no formal schooling, can speak and understand an endless variety of sentences? For example, the average 4-year-old child can already determine that the sentence "The caterpillar crept slowly across the leaf" is correct but that the sentence "The crept leaf caterpillar slowly the across" is meaningless. Chomsky's answer is that young children can learn these complex and difficult rules of grammar because our brains come with a built-in, or innate, program that makes learning the rules of grammar relatively easy.

But how does an innate grammar program, which could be used by any child in any culture, specify the rules for forming and understanding an endless number of meaningful sentences? Chomsky's answer is perhaps his cleverest contribution.

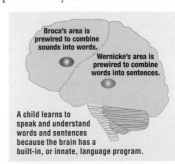

Broca's area is prewired to combine sounds into words.

Wernicke's area is prewired to combine words into sentences.

A child learns to speak and understand words and sentences because the brain has a built-in, or innate, language program.

Different Structure, Same Meaning

One of the most difficult questions Chomsky had to answer was how an idea can be expressed in different ways, with different grammatical structures, yet mean the same thing. He answered this question by making a distinction between two different structures of a sentence: surface structure and deep structure.

Surface structure refers to the actual wording of a sentence, as it is spoken.

Deep structure refers to an underlying meaning that is not spoken but is present in the mind of the listener.

We can illustrate the difference between surface and deep structures with our same two sentences:

You picked up a caterpillar.

A caterpillar was picked up by you.

Notice that these two sentences have different *surface structures,* which means they are worded differently. However, according to Chomsky, you are able to look underneath the different surface structures of the two sentences and recognize that they have the same *deep structure,* which is why you know they have the same meaning.

Chomsky argues that we learn to shift back and forth between surface and deep structure by applying transformational rules.

Transformational rules are procedures by which we convert our ideas from surface structures into deep structures and from deep structures back into surface ones.

For example, when you hear the two sentences about picking up the caterpillar, you transform the words into their deep structure, which you store in memory. Later, when someone asks what the person did, you use transformational rules to convert the deep structure in your memory back into a surface structure, which can be expressed in differently worded sentences. The distinction between surface and deep structures is part of Chomsky's theory of language.

Chomsky's theory of language says that all languages share a common universal grammar and that children inherit a mental program to learn this universal grammar.

Chomsky's theory, which is widely accepted today, was considered a major breakthrough in explaining how we acquire and understand language (Baker, 2002). However, one criticism of Chomsky's theory is that he downplays the importance of different environmental opportunities for hearing and practicing sounds, which have been shown to interact with and influence language development (Schlaggar et al., 2002).

Check Your Learning Quiz 7.8

Go to **login.cengagebrain.com** and take the online quiz.

▶ **LO22** Describe the four stages in acquiring language.

Stages in Acquiring Language

If Chomsky is correct that all children inherit the same innate program for learning grammar, then we would expect children from around the world to go through similar stages in developing language and acquiring the rules for using language. And in fact, all children do go through the same stages (Pinker, 1994).

Language stages refer to the four different periods or stages, that all infants go through—babbling, single words, two-word combinations, and sentences.

All children go through these four stages in the same order, and the occurrence of each stage is associated with further development of the brain. At birth, an infant's brain has almost all of its neurons, but they have not yet made all their connections. For example, a 6-month-old infant's brain (top left figure) has few neural interconnections, which are associated with performing simple behaviors, such as babbling. In comparison, a 24-month-old infant's brain (bottom left figure) has hundreds of neural interconnections, which are associated with more complex behaviors, such as using two-word combinations (Ropper & Samuels, 2009).

Here are the four stages that each of us went through in learning to speak and understand language:

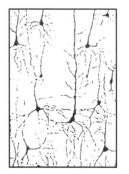

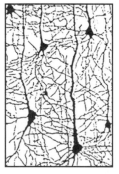

1 Babbling

One of the key features in human development is that infants begin to make sounds long before they can say real words. Infants repeat the same sounds over and over, and these sounds are commonly called babbling.

Babbling, which begins at about 6 months, is the first stage in acquiring language. Babbling refers to making one-syllable sounds, such as "dee-dee-dee" or "ba-ba-ba."

Babbling is an example of an innate "sound" program in the brain involved in making and processing sounds that will eventually be used to form words. Through endless babbling, infants learn to control their vocal apparatus so they can make, change, and imitate the sounds of their parents or caregivers (Hoff, 2009). After babbling, infants begin to say their first words.

2 Single Word

At about 1 year of age, infants begin to say single words.

Single words mark the second stage in acquiring language, which occurs at about 1 year of age. Infants say single words that usually refer to what they can see, hear, or feel.

Unless otherwise noted, all images are © Cengage Learning

The infant's single words, such as "milk" or "go," often stand for longer thoughts, such as "I want milk" or "I want to go out." As the infant learns to say words, parents usually respond by speaking in parentese (motherese).

Parentese (motherese) is a way of speaking to young children in which the adult speaks in a slower and higher-than-normal voice, emphasizes and stretches out each word, uses very simple sentences, and repeats words and phrases.

3 Two-Word Combinations

Starting around age 2, children begin using single words to form two-word combinations.

Two-word combinations, which represent the third stage in acquiring language, occur at about 2 years of age. Two-word combinations are strings of two words that express various actions, such as "Me play" or "See boy," or relationships such as "Hit ball" or "Milk gone."

The relationship between the two words gives hints about what the child is communicating. For example, "See boy" tells us to look at a specific object. At a certain point the child will begin to form sentences.

4 Sentences

Children make a rather large language leap when they progress from relatively simple two-word combinations to using longer and more complex sentences.

Sentences, which represent the fourth stage of acquiring language, occur at about 4 years of age. Sentences range from three to eight words in length and indicate a growing knowledge of the rules of grammar.

However, a child's first sentences differ from adult sentences in that the child may omit the "small words" and speak in a pattern called telegraphic speech.

Telegraphic speech is a distinctive pattern of speaking in which the child omits articles such as *the,* prepositions such as *in* or *out*, and parts of verbs.

For example, an adult may say, "I'm going to the store." A 3- to 4-year-old child may use telegraphic speech and say, "I go store." By age 4 or 5, children learn the rules of grammar, and the structure of their sentences improves. As they learn the rules of grammar, however, they often make errors of overgeneralization.

Overgeneralization means applying a grammatical rule where it should not be used.

For example, after a child learns the rule of forming the past tense of many verbs by adding a *d* sound to the end, he or she may overgeneralize this rule and add a *d* to the past tense of irregular verbs (for example, "I goed to store"). By the time children enter school, they usually have a good grasp of their language rules.

One-Syllable Sound

Learn about the sounds infants make.

Two-Word Combination

Learn about the word combinations toddlers make.

Sentences

Learn about how a young child begins to put words together to make sentences.

Language Development #2

See how infants and toddlers develop language.

Unless otherwise noted, all images are © Cengage Learning

▶ **LO23** Discuss the innate and environmental factors involved in acquiring language.

It is quite amazing how children from different countries around the world, including Bali, China, Nigeria, Sweden, Japan, United States, Mexico, France, Spain, and Thailand, can acquire the sounds, words, and rules of their particular native language. Each child learns his or her own native language as a result of interactions between innate (genetic) and environmental (learning) factors.

What Are Innate Factors?

All children go through the same four language stages because of innate language factors (Albert et al., 2000).

Innate language factors are genetically programmed physiological and neurological features that facilitate our making speech sounds and acquiring language skills.

We'll examine three innate language features that work together so that we can learn to speak and use language.

Innate Physiological Features

We have a specially adapted vocal apparatus (larynx and pharynx) that allows us to make sounds and form words. In comparison, the structures of the vocal apparatus of gorillas and chimpanzees prevent them from making the variety of sounds necessary to form words (Lessmoellmann, 2006; Pinker, 1994).

Innate Neurological Features

When people speak or use sign language, certain brain areas are activated. The PET scan on the right shows a side view of the brain; red and yellow indicate the most neural activity (Petitto, 1997). These findings indicate that the left hemisphere of the brain is prewired to acquire and use language, whether spoken or signed.

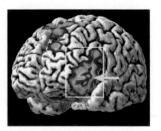

Innate Developmental Factors

Researchers have discovered a critical period when acquiring language is the easiest (Shafer & Garrido-Nag, 2007).

The **critical language period** is the time from infancy to adolescence when language is easiest to learn. Language is usually more difficult to learn anytime after adolescence.

For example, immigrant children do very well learning English as a second language, while immigrant adults, who are past the critical period, have more difficulty and do less well (Jackendoff, 1994). The critical period for learning language also explains why learning your native language was easy as a child but, as an adult, learning a foreign language is many times more difficult.

What Are Environmental Factors?

How each child learns a particular language depends on social interactions, one of the environmental factors.

Environmental language factors refer to interactions children have with parents, peers, teachers, and others who provide feedback that rewards and encourages language development, as well as opportunities for children to observe, imitate, and practice language skills.

What would happen if a child were deprived of almost all social interactions from ages 1 to 13? Such was the case with Genie, whose mentally disturbed father strapped her to a potty chair in a back room, punished her for making any sounds, and forbade the mother or brother to talk to her. When discovered at age 13 by a social worker, Genie could not speak a single word (Curtiss, 1977). Genie's case illustrates that even though children are prewired by heredity to speak a language, they need certain environmental stimuli, such as listening, speaking, and interacting with others, in order to learn to speak and use language. Genie's case also illustrates the importance of social cognitive learning.

Social cognitive learning refers to the acquisition of language skills through social interactions, which give children a chance to observe, imitate, and practice the sounds, words, and sentences they hear from their parents or caregivers.

For example, within 8 months of training, Genie had acquired a vocabulary of about 200 words. However, Genie's long period of social deprivation left its mark, and even after years of continued social interactions, her language ability did not develop beyond that of a 2- or 3-year-old child (Harris, 1995).

Talk to Children

Learn how important it is for parents to talk with young children.

▶ **LO24** Summarize research on the language capabilities of animals.

Do Animals Have Language?

Like most pet owners, I (R.P.) talk to my dog, and he usually behaves as if he understands what I say. For example, my dog Bear (photo at right) behaves as if he understands "get your toy," "go for walk," "time to eat," and "watch television." The obvious question is: Has Bear learned a language? The answer to this question hinges on the difference between communication and language. Like many animals, Bear has the ability to communicate.

Communication is the ability to use sounds, smells, or gestures to exchange information.

But as you've already learned, language is much more than just communication. Although Bear can communicate (that is, understand my commands and act accordingly), he, like most animals, shows no evidence of meeting the four criteria for having real language.

1 Language, which is a special form of communication, involves *learning a set of abstract symbols* (words or signs).

2 Language involves *using abstract symbols* (words or signs) to express thoughts or indicate objects and events that may or may not be present.

3 Language involves *learning complex rules of grammar* for forming words into meaningful phrases and sentences.

4 Language involves using the rules of grammar to *generate an endless number of meaningful sentences.*

Because some animals show an amazing ability to communicate, researchers are debating whether animals can satisfy all four criteria for language. We'll examine how close two animals come to satisfying the four criteria.

Gorilla and Chimpanzee

Shown on the top of the next page is researcher Francine Patterson using sign language to communicate with Koko the gorilla, who has a vocabulary of about 1,000 signs (Boysen, 2009). Similarly, Beatrice and Allen Gardner (1975) taught sign language to a chimpanzee named Washoe, who learned about 250 signs and passed her language skills on to her son (*Time*, 2007b). The finding that gorillas and chimps can learn sign language raised the question of whether they use language in the same way as humans.

Psychologist Herbert Terrace (1981) analyzed videotapes of chimps using sign language with their trainers. He was particularly interested in a chimp named Nim, who learned more than 125 signs. After observing over 20,000 of Nim's signs on videotape, Terrace concluded Nim was using signs more as tools to obtain things than as abstract symbols or words and that Nim never learned to form combinations of more than a few words. Also, Terrace stated Nim had primarily learned to imitate or respond to cues rather than learning and using rules of grammar to produce new sentences.

In the late 1980s, new findings on bonobos (commonly called pygmy chimps) provided the strongest evidence for language in animals. Psychologist Sue Savage-Rumbaugh reported that Kanzi, a bonobo, has remarkable language skills that surpass previous accomplishments of common chimps (Savage-Rumbaugh & Lewin, 1994; Shanker et al., 1999). Instead of using sign language, Kanzi "speaks" by touching one of 256 symbols on a board, each of which stands for a word (Boysen, 2009). For example, Kanzi (right photo) might signal "Want a drink" by touching the symbol for "drink" or signal "Want to play" by touching in sequence two symbols for "hiding" and "play biting." Savage-Rumbaugh suggests that 17-year-old Kanzi has an ability to use abstract symbols (keyboard) and a kind of primitive grammar (word order) for combining symbols that equals the language ability of a 2-year-old child (Savage-Rumbaugh, 1998).

Dolphins

Explore whether or not dolphins use language.

Check Your Learning Quiz 7.9

Go to **login.cengagebrain.com** and take the online quiz.

Think Critically

Challenge Your Thinking

Consider these questions when reading this article:

1. Based on Chris's IQ score, what type(s) of intelligence does he excel at?
2. Based on the normal distribution, where does Chris rank in intelligence?
3. Which intelligence theory takes his weight-lifting and physical strength into consideration?
4. Is Chris's ability to speak and read at an early age mostly attributable to nature or nurture?
5. According to Sternberg's triarchic theory, which type of intelligence stands out most for Chris?
6. Given Chris's high IQ of 195, what size brain must he have?

Smartest or Strongest Man in America?

Smartest, definitely. Though Chris Langan can bench press a whopping 500 pounds, his intellect is far more impressive. Chris's IQ score is off the charts at an estimated 195 (average IQ score is 100). Only one in several billion people has an IQ of 195 or above. Even Einstein didn't compare, as his IQ is estimated to have been 150. Chris is surely a rocket scientist, brain surgeon, or Nobel Prize winner, right? Wrong! Let's take a look at Chris's life to understand why he hasn't achieved the extraordinary career success we might expect from him.

Chris's childhood left much to be desired. His family was so poor he had only one outfit, which consisted of unmatched socks and a shirt, pants, and shoes, all with holes in them. His father left before his birth and his mother had four husbands, three of whom died. Chris's fourth stepfather was physically abusive toward him. For instance, he asked Chris questions and when Chris answered them correctly, he punched Chris in the mouth. Chris took up weight-lifting in his early teens, and one day when his stepfather began beating him, he struck back so hard, his stepfather left and never returned.

Despite harsh living circumstances, Chris's intellect persevered. He began

speaking at 6 months of age, and by age 3 he was reading. He skipped ahead in school, and even then, he felt he knew more than his teachers. All he had to do to ace exams was to quickly skim his textbooks. Chris is one of the few to obtain a perfect score on the SAT, and he even squeezed in a nap during this challenging timed test.

Though doing well in school came easily to Chris, he never finished college. Instead, he has worked labor jobs throughout his life, which include construction worker, lifeguard, farmhand, cowboy, factory worker, firefighter, and, for the past 20 years, a bouncer at a bar. Isn't working as a bouncer one of the last jobs you would expect the smartest man in America, and quite possibly in the world, to have? So, you have to ask yourself, why did Chris end up like this? The answer is because of his disadvantaged environment. There was no one to help him. No one ever encouraged him to pursue greatness. Absolutely nothing in

his background helped him take advantage of his remarkable talents.

Chris is now in his fifties, still lifting weights and working as a bouncer. He's also working on a theory that explains problems scientists and philosophers have been thinking about for thousands of years. He calls his theory Cognitive–Theoretic Model of the Universe (CTMU). He believes CTMU can answer all questions about reality and prove the existence of God. If anyone can answer such questions, surely Chris, with an IQ of 195, is a top contender.

We have to wonder what would have happened to Chris had he been born into a wealthy, well-respected, and well-connected family. Perhaps if he were raised in such an environment he could have become the brain surgeon or Nobel Prize winner we would expect from a man with an unmatched IQ. (Adapted from Brabham, 2001; Gladwell, 2008; Grossman, 2008; Preston, 2008)

Think Critically 7.1

This article and its questions are available in interactive format online.

Measure ^ Your Learning

GO to your Psychology CourseMate at login.cengagebrain.com and take the Chapter Post-Test to see which Learning Objectives you've mastered and which need more review. Use the chapter review guide below and the online activities—including flashcards to review key terms—to measure your learning.

Online Activities

Key Terms	Video	Animation	Reading	Assessment
psychometrics			Psychometrics, p, 305	Check Your Learning Quiz 7.1
psychometric approach, Spearman's two-factor theory, Gardner's multiple-intelligence theory, Sternberg's triarchic theory, emotional intelligence	Emotional Intelligence, p. 311		Two-Factor Theory, p. 307 Multiple-Intelligence Theory, p. 309 Triarchic Theory, p. 309	Check Your Learning Quiz 7.2
Binet-Simon Intelligence Scale, mental age, intelligence quotient (IQ), Wechsler Adult Intelligence Scale (WAIS), Wechsler Intelligence Scale for Children (WISC), validity, reliability, normal distribution, mental retardation, gifted			Brain Sizes, Sex Differences & Intelligence, p. 313 Potential Problems in IQ Testing, p. 315	Check Your Learning Quiz 7.3
nature-nurture questions, fraternal twins, identical twins			Intervention Programs, p. 321 Racial Controversy, p. 321	Check Your Learning Quiz 7.4
thinking, concept, exemplar model, prototype theory		Concept Formation, p. 325		Check Your Learning Quiz 7.5

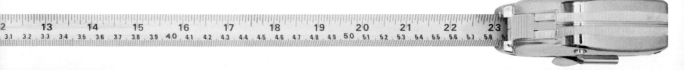

Measure ^Your Learning

Online Activities

Key Terms	Video	Animation	Reading	Assessment
problem solving, algorithms, heuristics, availability heuristic, functional fixedness, insight, analogy, subgoals, creative thinking, creative individual, convergent thinking, divergent thinking		Problem Solving Strategies, p. 329	Characteristics of Creative People, p. 331	Check Your Learning Quiz 7.6
reasoning, deductive reasoning, inductive reasoning, theory of linguistic relativity	Decisions! Decisions!, p. 335		Thinking in Two Languages, p. 335	Check Your Learning Quiz 7.7
language, word, grammar, phonology, phonemes, morphology, morpheme, syntax (or grammar), semantics, surface structure, deep structure, transformational rules, Chomsky's theory of language, language stages, babbling, single words, parentese (motherese), two-word combinations, sentences, telegraphic speech, overgeneralization	Language Development #1, p. 337 One-Syllable Sound, p. 341 Two-Word Combination, p. 341 Sentences, p. 341 Langage Development #2, p. 341			Check Your Learning Quiz 7.8
innate language factors, critical language period, environmental language factors, social cognitive learning, communication	Talk to Children, p. 343		Dolphins, p. 345	Check Your Learning Quiz 7.9

Life Span Development

8

1 **GO** to your **Psychology CourseMate** at **login.cengagebrain.com** and take the **Chapter Pre-Test** to introduce yourself to this chapter's topics and see what you may already know.

2 **READ** the **Learning Objectives (LOs)** (in the left sidebars) and begin the chapter.

3 **COMPLETE** the **Online Activities** (in the right sidebars) *as you read each module*. Activities include **videos**, **animations**, **readings**, and **quizzes**.

4 **CHECK Your Learning** by going online to take the quiz at the end of each module and review material as necessary.

5 **MEASURE Your Learning** after reading the chapter by taking the online **Chapter Post-Test**. Use the chapter review guide at the end of the chapter as needed.

WATCH for these **Online Activities** icons as you read:

Video

Animation

Reading

Assessment

Think Critically

These online activities are important to mastering this chapter. As you read each module, access these materials by going to **login.cengagebrain.com**.

Explore studies and first-hand accounts of biological and psychological processes:

- Learn what it's like to be raised in a Romanian orphanage
- Learn what infants prefer to listen to and look at
- Watch how smell develops in infants
- Learn how taste develops in infants
- Watch how vision develops in infants
- See what motor development is like during infancy
- See what motor development is like during early childhood
- See what motor development is like during middle childhood
- Watch how children develop object permanence
- Learn more about the cognitive abilities of children in the preoperational stage
- Explore the cognitive abilities of children in the concrete operational stage
- Learn more about the characteristics of children with different types of temperaments
- Watch how infants who have a secure attachment respond to unfamiliar people and situations

- Watch young children explain what it means to be a boy or a girl
- Learn more about the cognitive abilities of people in the formal operational stage
- Discover the attitudes teens have about risk-taking behaviors
- Learn more about some of the sexual changes that may occur with aging
- Watch how our cognitive processes change with age

Animation Interact with and visualize important processes and concepts:

- See what happens during each of the three stages of the prenatal period
- See how children perform on the conservation task
- Learn how Freud's and Erikson's theories explain conflicts and problems during a child's social development
- Practice identifying the characteristics of each of Kohlberg's stages of moral development

Reading Delve deeper into key content:

- Find out how children raised by the same parents in the same family can have such different temperaments

- Explore how social role theory explains why children from different countries and cultures develop similar male-female gender roles
- Find out how scientific research answers the question of whether teens should be permitted to drive
- Learn how culture influences one's preference for partners
- Learn the key factors to a successful relationship

Assessment Measure your mastery:

- Chapter Pre-Test
- Check Your Learning Quizzes
- Chapter Post-Test

Think Critically Challenge your thinking by applying content from this chapter and making connections to related material:

- Who Matters More—Parents or Peers?

▶ **L01** Explain the nature-nurture question.

FOR THE FIRST 3 YEARS OF HIS LIFE, Alex was raised in an orphanage in Romania, where the number of infants and children greatly exceeded the number of caregivers. At the orphanage, Alex was given adequate nutrition, allowing him to develop well physically, but the affection, stimulation, and comfort he received were far from adequate. Alex, like other children living in Romanian orphanages, spent most of his days alone in a crib with almost no interaction with others. When he cried, no one came to hold or soothe him. He was never given the opportunity to bond with a caregiver.

▼

When Alex was 3 years old, a family living in the United States adopted him. His adoptive mother described him as being friendly and engaging, but also "self-abusive" and having a "dark side." For instance, Alex would make himself go into a seizure by slamming his head on the floor. He was also aggressive toward others, one time attacking his younger sister, "beating her senseless." When asked if he wanted his adoptive mother to love him, he said to her, "I never want you to love me." When his adoptive mother asked him if he loved her, he replied, "No, I don't love anybody" (Jarriel & Sawyer, 1997).

Children like Alex, whose emotional needs (such as forming an attachment with a caregiver) go unmet during infancy and early childhood, may develop attachment problems. However, this isn't the case with some children. The question of why some children raised in these orphanages later have attachment problems while others don't can be explained by the nature-nurture question.

The **nature-nurture question** asks how much nature (genetic factors) and how much nurture (environmental factors) contributes to a person's biological, emotional, cognitive, personal, and social development.

There are now about 10,000 Romanian children growing up in the United States, and nearly all of them initially had serious developmental problems. One researcher studying the adjustment of Romanian adoptees in the United States found that after the first year, 20% of children reached normal development, 60% showed only mild problems, and the remaining 20% had serious cognitive, behavioral, and emotional problems (Fischer, 1999). The reason some Romanian adoptees have long-term developmental problems while others make significant improvements involves genetic (nature) and environmental (nurture) factors.

Romanian Orphanages

Learn what it's like to be raised in a Romanian orphanage.

Check Your Learning Quiz 8.1

Go to **login.cengagebrain.com** and take the online quiz.

Unless otherwise noted, all images are © Cengage Learning

▶ **L02** Identify and describe the three stages of prenatal development

Prenatal Period

We start the journey across the life span by answering the question: How did you begin? You began as a single cell about the size of a grain of sand. In this tiny cell was the equivalent of about 300,000 pages of instructions for the development of your brain and body. This single cell marks the beginning of the prenatal period.

Prenatal Period: Three Stages

1. Germinal Stage
2. Embryonic Stage
3. Fetal Stage

The **prenatal period** extends from conception to birth and lasts about 266 days (around 9 months). It consists of three successive phases: the germinal, embryonic, and fetal stages. During the prenatal period, a single cell will divide and grow to form 200 billion cells.

As we examine the prenatal period, we'll explore how a human being begins, develops, and is born.

1 Germinal Stage

The germinal stage marks the beginning of our development.

The **germinal stage** is the first stage of prenatal development and refers to the 2-week period following conception.

To understand how conception occurs, we need first explain ovulation.

Ovulation is the release of an ovum or egg cell from a woman's ovaries.

In most cases, only a single ovum is released during ovulation, but sometimes two ova are released. If two separate ova are released and fertilized, the result is fraternal twins, who can be two brothers, two sisters, or a brother and sister. Because fraternal twins come from two separate eggs, they are no more genetically alike than any other two children of the same parents. In contrast, if a single ovum splits into two parts after fertilization, the result is identical twins, whose genes are almost indistinguishable.

How does conception take place? If no sperm are present, there can be no fertilization, and the ovum, together with the lining of the uterus, is sloughed off in the process called menstruation. If, however, sperm have been deposited in the vagina (100 to 500 million sperm may be deposited with each act of intercourse), they make their way to the uterus and into the fallopian tubes in search of an ovum to be fertilized.

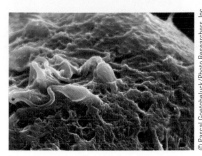

Conception, or **fertilization**, occurs if one of the millions of sperm penetrates the ovum's outer membrane. After the ovum has been penetrated by a single sperm (left photo), its outer membrane changes and becomes impenetrable to the millions of remaining sperm.

Once the ovum has been fertilized, it is called a *zygote*, which is a single cell that is smaller than the dot in the letter *i*. The zygote begins a process of repeated division and, after about a week, consists of about 150 cells. After 2 weeks, it has become a mass of cells and attaches itself to the wall of the uterus. Once the zygote is implanted, or attached to the wall of the uterus, the embryonic stage begins.

2 Embryonic Stage

During this next stage, the organism begins to develop body organs.

The **embryonic stage** is the second stage of the prenatal period and spans the 2 to 8 weeks that follow conception; during this stage, cells divide and begin to differentiate into bone, muscle, and body organs.

At about 21 days after conception, the beginnings of the spinal cord and eyes appear; at about 24 days, cells differentiate to form what will become part of the heart; at about 28 days, tiny buds appear that will develop into arms and legs; and at about 42 days, features of the face take shape.

Toward the end of the embryonic stage, the organism has developed a number of body organs, such as the heart. The embryo is only about 4 cm long but already has the beginnings of major body organs and limbs and begins to look somewhat human (Cunningham et al., 2009).

In the right photo, you can see the head as the large rounded structure at the top, and the black dot on the side of the head is the developing eye. After this second stage of development, which is called the embryonic stage and lasts 2 to 8 weeks, comes the last stage, which is called the fetal stage.

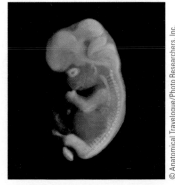

Stages of Prenatal Development

See what happens during each of the three stages of the prenatal period.

▶ **LO3** Explain the interaction of drugs and prenatal development.

3 Fetal Stage

The embryonic stage is followed by the fetal stage.

The **fetal stage,** which is the third stage in prenatal development, begins 2 months after conception and lasts until birth.

At the end of the fetal stage, usually 38 to 42 weeks after conception (or roughly 9 months), birth occurs and the fetus becomes a newborn.

During the fetal stage, the fetus develops vital organs, such as lungs, and physical characteristics that are distinctively human. For example, at about 6 months, a fetus has eyes and eyelids that are completely formed (above photo), a fine coating of hair, relatively well-developed external sex organs, and lungs that are beginning to function.

Infants born very prematurely (under 6 months) will have difficulty surviving because their lungs are not completely formed and they have difficulty breathing. However, a 6-month-old fetus usually has lungs well enough developed to show irregular breathing and, for this reason, can survive if born prematurely.

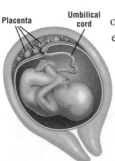

Placenta   Umbilical cord

Because the fetus experiences rapid body growth and development of the nervous system, it is highly vulnerable to the effects of drugs and other harmful agents. However, the blood supply of the fetus is partly protected by the placenta (left figure) (Koren, 2007).

The **placenta** is an organ that connects the blood supply of the mother to that of the fetus. The placenta acts as a filter, allowing oxygen and nutrients to pass through while keeping out some toxic or harmful substances.

However, certain viruses, such as HIV, and drugs, including nicotine, caffeine, and cocaine, pass from the placenta into the fetus's blood vessels and thus can affect development. These potentially dangerous agents are called teratogens.

A **teratogen** *(teh-RAT-oh-gen)* is any agent that can harm a developing fetus, causing deformities or brain damage. It might be a disease (such as genital herpes), a drug (such as alcohol), or another environmental agent (such as chemicals).

We discuss the interactions of drugs and prenatal development next.

© Frans Lanting Studio/Alamy

Unless otherwise noted, all images are © Cengage Learning

Drugs and Prenatal Development

In the womb, the fetus is protected from various teratogens (certain chemicals and drugs) by the filtering system of the placenta. However, we'll discuss several drugs, both legal and illegal, that can pass through the placenta, reach the fetus, and cause potential neurological, physiological, and psychological problems.

Caffeine

Pregnant women who use caffeine, even as little as one cup of coffee a day, are at higher risk of having an underweight baby. Babies born underweight are more likely to have health problems as adults, such as high blood pressure and diabetes (CARE, 2008).

Smoking and Nicotine

Smoking during pregnancy increases the risk of low birth weight, preterm deliveries, and possible physical problems (Cunningham et al., 2009). In addition, infants born to smoking mothers have an increased risk for developing attention-deficit/hyperactivity disorder (p. 22), sudden infant death syndrome (SIDS), oral clefts (birth defect of mouth and lips), and respiratory infections (Braun et al., 2006; Dambro, 2006; Shaw et al., 2009).

Heavy Drinking

Alcohol (ethanol) is a teratogen that crosses the placenta, affects the developing fetus, and can result in fetal alcohol syndrome (Fryer et al., 2007; Riley & McGee, 2005).

Fetal alcohol syndrome, or **FAS,** results from a mother drinking heavily during pregnancy, especially in the first 12 weeks. FAS results in physical changes, such as short stature, flattened nose, and short eye openings (right photo); neurological changes, such as fewer brain connections within the brain structure; and psychological and behavioral problems, such as hyperactivity, impulsive behavior, deficits in information processing and memory, drug use, and poor socialization.

© George Steinmetz

Cocaine Plus Other Drugs

Pregnant women who use crack cocaine along with other drugs, such as alcohol, tobacco, or marijuana, have infants with low birth weights, poor feeding habits, and risks for developing other psychological problems, such as low IQ scores and poor coping skills, which may last into adulthood (Bendersky & Lewis, 1999; Frank et al., 2001).

Check Your Learning Quiz 8.2

Go to **login.cengagebrain.com** and take the online quiz.

▶ **LO4** Describe the sensory and motor development of children.

We have discussed the three stages of prenatal development, which end with the baby's birth. After the baby gets a pat on the backside and lets out a cry, he or she is ready to take on the world. Human infants are born with a surprising number of sensory and motor abilities, such as hearing, grasping, and sucking. How these abilities develop is explained by an inherited genetic program.

Genetic Developmental Program

Conception results in a fertilized egg, which has a genetic program that is equivalent to 300,000 pages of typed instructions for developing the body and brain. The mother and father each contribute 23 chromosomes, so each child receives a unique genetic program.

Brain Growth

After birth, the genetic program regulates how the brain develops, such as making thousands of connections between neurons. A 1-month-old brain has very few neural connections, while a 2-year-old brain has many thousands. This enormous increase in neural connections partly explains why the weight of a baby's brain increases from 25% to 75% of its adult weight between birth and 2 years old (Sigelman & Rider, 2006).

Sensory Development

During the 9 months of development in the womb, a genetic program is guiding the development of sensory functions that are important for the newborn's survival. Here's a summary of a newborn's sensory abilities.

Unless otherwise noted, all images are © Cengage Learning

Faces

Newborns show a preference for their mother's face over strangers' faces in the first few days after birth. Beginning at 4 months of age, an infant can visually distinguish his or her mother's face from a stranger's or an animal's (Wingert & Brant, 2005). By 3 or 4 years of age, an infant's visual abilities are equal to those of an adult.

Hearing

One-month-old infants have very keen hearing and can discriminate small sound variations, such as the difference between *bah* and *pah*. By 6 months, infants have developed the ability to make all the sounds that are necessary to learn the language in which they are raised (Pascalis et al., 2002).

Touch

Newborns have a well-developed sense of touch and will turn their head when touched on the cheek. Touch will also elicit other reflexes, such as grasping and sucking.

Smell and Taste

Six-week-old infants can smell the difference between their mother and a stranger (Macfarlane, 1975). Newborns have an inborn preference for both sweet and salt and an inborn dislike of bitter-tasting things.

Depth Perception

By the age of 6 months, infants have developed depth perception, which was tested by observing whether they would crawl off a visual "cliff" (Gibson & Walk, 1960).

A **visual cliff** is a glass tabletop with a checkerboard pattern over part of its surface; the remaining surface consists of clear glass with a checkerboard pattern several feet below, creating the illusion of a clifflike drop to the floor (see photo).

An infant is placed on the area with the checkerboard pattern and is encouraged to creep off the cliff. Six-month-old infants hesitate when they reach the clear glass "dropoff," indicating that they have developed depth perception.

Although the genetic program is largely responsible for the early appearance of these sensory abilities, *environmental stimulation,* such as parental touch and play, encourages the infant to further develop these sensory abilities (Collins et al., 2000).

Hearing and Faces

Learn what infants prefer to listen to and look at.

Smell

Watch how smell develops in infants.

Taste

Learn how taste develops in infants.

Vision and Depth Perception

Watch how vision develops in infants.

© Mark Richards/PhotoEdit

Motor Development

The development of early motor skills, such as sitting, crawling, and walking, follow two rules: the proximodistal and cephalocaudal principles.

Proximodistal Principle

The **proximodistal principle** states that parts closer to the center of the infant's body (*proximo* in Latin means "near") develop before parts farther away (*distal* in Latin means "far").

For example, activities involving the trunk are mastered before activities involving the arms and legs. For that reason, infants can roll over before they can walk or bring their arms together to grasp a bottle.

Cephalocaudal Principle

The **cephalocaudal principle** states that parts of the body closer to the head (*cephalo* in Greek means "head") develop before parts closer to the feet (*caudal* in Greek means "tail").

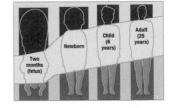

For example, infants can lift their heads before they can control their trunks enough to sit up, and they can sit up before they can control their legs to crawl. In the right figure, notice the head area developing before the feet area.

Maturation

The cephalocaudal and proximodistal principles, which regulate the sequence for developing early motor skills, are part of a process known as maturation.

Maturation refers to developmental changes that are genetically or biologically programmed rather than acquired through learning or life experiences.

In developing motor skills, such as sitting up, crawling, and walking, all infants in all parts of the world go through the same developmental stages at about the same times. However, if children are given more opportunities to practice their stepping reflex earlier in life, they will begin to walk at an earlier age than children who lack such opportunities (Thelen, 1995). Thus, the development of early motor development is heavily influenced by maturation (genetic program), but the timing can be partly slowed or speeded up by experience (nurture).

Developmental Norms

Parents often note the major milestones in their infants' motor development, such as their first time crawling or walking, because they want to know if their children are within the developmental norms.

Developmental norms refer to the average ages at which children perform various kinds of skills or exhibit abilities or behaviors.

The three photos on this page represent stages involved in learning to walk. The development norm for sitting up alone is 5.5 months (range 4.5 to 8.0 months), crawling is 10 months (range 7.0 to 12.0 months), and walking alone is 12.1 months (range 11.5 to 14.5 months). By the age of 2, infants have grown into toddlers who can walk up and down stairs and use their hands to hold glasses of juice, operate toys, and, of course, get into a lot of trouble.

Remember that norms for motor development represent average ages rather than absolute ages. Therefore, parents should not be disturbed if their infant's motor progress does not match the norms.

Neural Connections

The reason infants develop skills and abilities at different times is that neural connections develop at different rates. This means that infants cannot perform complex cognitive, sensory, or motor tasks, such as walking, talking, and reading, until appropriate areas of their brains develop neural connections.

Although we have focused on the role of the genetic developmental program (nature), it's important to remember that nature interacts with the environment (nurture) to encourage or discourage the development of motor, sensory, and cognitive abilities (Hadders-Algra, 2002). For example, infants need appropriate *environmental stimulation.* In other words, for development of their visual systems, they need to see things; for learning to speak, they need to hear parents or caregivers speaking; for emotional development, they must get loving care; for motor development, they must explore objects. These examples show how the genetic program interacts with environmental stimulation for the proper development of a child's sensory, motor, and cognitive abilities.

Motor Development: Infancy

See what motor development is like during infancy.

Motor Development: Early Childhood

See what motor development is like during early childhood.

Motor Development: Middle Childhood

See what motor development is like during middle childhood.

© Vinicius Tupinamba/Shutterstock

© Marina Dyakonova/Shutterstock

Elyse Lewin/Getty Images

▶ **LO5** Describe Piaget's theory of cognitive development as it applies to children.

Cognitive Development

We have explained how a newborn's brain and senses develop relatively quickly so that an infant is soon ready to creep and walk and explore and learn about a wondrous world through a process called cognitive development.

Cognitive development refers to how a person perceives, thinks, and gains an understanding of the world through the interaction and influence of genetic and learned factors.

The person who has had the greatest impact on the study of cognitive development is Jean Piaget, who was a biologist and a psychologist. For much of his life, Piaget studied how children solved problems in their natural settings, such as cribs and playgrounds. Piaget believed that a child acts like a scientist who is actively involved in making guesses about how the world works. He stated that children learn to understand things, such as what to do with blocks, through two processes: assimilation and accommodation.

If you give 5-month-old Sam a block, he will first try to put it into his mouth because at that age, infants "think" that objects are for sucking on. This behavior is an example of assimilation.

© PhotoDisc, Inc.

Assimilation is the process by which a child uses old methods or experiences to deal with new situations.

At 5 months, Sam will first put a new object into his mouth because his knowledge of objects is that they are for eating or sucking. Thus, Sam will assimilate the new object as something too hard to eat but all right for sucking.

Depending on their age and knowledge, children assimilate blocks in different ways: infants assimilate blocks as something to suck; toddlers assimilate blocks as something to stack or throw; and adolescents assimilate blocks as something used to play games. The assimilation of new information leads to accommodation.

If you give 2-year-old Sam the blocks, he will not try to eat them, but he may try to stack them, an example of accommodation.

Accommodation is the process by which a child changes old methods to deal with or adjust to new situations.

© PhotoDisc, Inc.

For example, because of Sam's experience with different kinds of objects, he has learned that square, hard objects are not food but things that can be handled and stacked. Sam's learning to change existing knowledge because of new information is an example of accommodation. Using assimilation and accommodation, children go through a series of cognitive stages.

Unless otherwise noted, all images are © Cengage Learning

Piaget's Cognitive Stages

Piaget is best known for describing the changes or different stages in cognitive development that occur between infancy and adulthood (Bjorklund, 2005).

Piaget's cognitive stages refer to four different stages—sensorimotor, preoperational, concrete operations, and formal operations—each of which is more advanced than the preceding stage because it involves new reasoning and thinking abilities.

We'll explain Piaget's four stages by following Sam's cognitive development.

Stage 1: Sensorimotor Stage

Imagine Sam as a newborn infant. His primary way of interacting with the world is through reflexive responses, such as sucking and grasping. By 5 months, Sam has developed enough voluntary muscle control so that he can reach out, grasp things, and put them into his mouth to discover if the things are good to suck on. Sam is in the sensorimotor stage.

The **sensorimotor stage** (from birth to about age 2) is the first of Piaget's cognitive stages. During this stage, infants interact with and learn about their environments by relating their sensory experiences (such as hearing and seeing) to their motor actions (mouthing and grasping).

Hidden Objects At the beginning of the sensorimotor stage, Sam has one thinking problem: remembering that hidden objects still exist. For example, notice in the right photo that when a screen is placed in front of the toy dog, Sam looks away. He doesn't push the screen away to get at the toy because, at this point, Sam behaves as if things that are out of sight are out of mind and simply no longer exist. Sam has not learned object permanence.

Object Permanence Beginning at around 9 months, if Sam is shown a toy dog that is then covered by a screen, he will try to push the screen away and look for the dog. Sam has learned that a toy dog that is out of sight still exists behind the screen. This new concept is called object permanence.

Object permanence refers to the understanding that objects or events continue to exist even if they can no longer be heard, touched, or seen.

By the end of the sensorimotor period, an infant will search for objects that have disappeared, indicating a fully developed concept of object permanence. At the end of the sensorimotor stage, 2-year-old Sam can think about things that are not present and can form simple plans for solving problems, such as searching for things.

Piaget's Object Permanence

Watch how children develop object permanence.

© Doug Goodman/Photo Researchers, Inc.

Stage 2: Preoperational Stage

As a 4-year-old, Sam is busy pushing a block around the floor and making noises as he pretends the block is a car. The cognitive ability to pretend is a sign that Sam is going through the preoperational stage.

The **preoperational stage** (from about 2 to 7 years old) is the second of Piaget's cognitive stages. During this stage, children learn to use symbols, such as words or mental images, to solve simple problems and to think or talk about things that are not present.

At this stage, Sam is acquiring the cognitive ability to pretend things and to talk about or draw things that are not physically present. However, his thinking has a number of interesting limitations that make his thinking different from an adult's. During the preoperational stage, two of his cognitive limitations involve having problems with conservation and engaging in egocentric thinking.

Conservation As 4-year-old Sam watches you pour milk from a tall, thin glass into a short, wide glass, will he know that the amount of milk remains the same even though its shape changes? To know this, Sam must be able to grasp the concept of conservation.

Conservation refers to the fact that even though the shape of some object or substance is changed, the total amount remains the same.

Here's what happens when 4-year-old Sam faces a conservation problem.

In photo #1, 4-year-old Sam watches as his mother fills two short, wide glasses with equal amounts of milk.

In photo #2, Sam sees his mother pour the milk from one short, wide glass into a tall, thin glass. Mother asks, "Does one glass have more milk?"

In photo #3, Sam points to the tall, thin glass as having more milk because the tall glass looks larger. He makes this mistake even though he just saw his mother pour the milk from a short, wide glass.

Sam, like other children at the preoperational stage, will not be able to solve conservation problems until the next stage.

Egocentric Thinking A second problem that Sam has during the preoperational stage is that he makes mistakes or misbehaves because of egocentric thinking.

Egocentric *(ee-goh-SEN-trick)* **thinking** refers to seeing and thinking of the world only from your own viewpoint and having difficulty appreciating someone else's viewpoint.

Piaget used the term *egocentric thinking* to mean that preoperational children cannot see situations from another person's, such as a parent's, point of view. When they don't get their way, children may get angry or pout because their view of the world is so self-centered.

Stage 3: Concrete Operational Stage

Between the ages of 7 and 11, Sam learns that even if things change their shape, they don't lose any quantity or mass, a new concept that occurs during the concrete operational stage.

The **concrete operational stage** (from about 7 to 11 years) is the third of Piaget's cognitive stages. During this stage, children can perform a number of logical mental operations on concrete objects (ones that are physically present).

Conservation As you may remember, when Sam was 4 years old and in the preoperational stage, he had not mastered the concept of conservation. In the preoperational stage, Sam thought a tall, thin glass held more milk than a short, wide glass. And if 4-year-old Sam watched as a ball of clay (top right picture) was flattened into a long, thin piece (bottom right picture), he would say the long piece was larger.

However, Sam is now 10 years old and has just watched you flatten a ball of clay into a long piece. Sam now says that the long, flattened piece contains the same amount of clay as the ball, even if the shape changed. Similarly, if 10-year-old Sam watched you pour cola from a short glass into a tall glass, he would correctly answer that the amount of cola remained the same. Children gradually master the concept of conservation during the concrete operational stage, and they also get better at classification.

Classification If you gave 4-year old, preoperational Sam some red and blue marbles in different sizes, he would be able to classify the pieces according to a single category, such as size. However, during the concrete operational stage, 10-year-old Sam has acquired the ability to classify the marbles according to two categories, such as color and size, indicating he has learned a new cognitive skill.

New Abilities During the concrete operational stage, children learn to classify or sort objects according to more than one category, and they learn to solve a variety of conservation problems. The reason Piaget called this the *concrete* operational stage is that children can easily classify or figure out relationships between objects, provided the objects are actually physically present, or "concrete."

However, children at the concrete operational stage still have difficulty figuring out relationships among objects that are not present or situations that are imaginary. Thinking about imaginary or hypothetical situations occurs in Piaget's fourth stage, which we'll discuss later in Module 8.4 (p. 382).

Piaget's Conservation

See how children perform on the conservation task.

Piaget's Preoperational Stage

Learn more about the cognitive abilities of children in the preoperational stage.

Piaget's Concrete Operational Stage

Explore the cognitive abilities of children in the concrete operational stage.

▶ **LO6** Discuss the emotional development of children, including different types of temperament and attachment.

Emotional Development

Becki is describing the emotional makeup of her sextuplets (right photo). "Brenna, the oldest by 30 seconds, is the affectionate one. Julian, the second child delivered, is 'Mr. Smiley.' Quinn, the third, is sweet and generous and most adventurous. Claire, fourth oldest, is the boss, as charming as she is tough. Ian,

© 1995 Taro Yamasaki

the fifth, is the smallest and loves music, drawing, and sleep. Adrian, the youngest, is the biggest and most gentle" (Reed & Breu, 1995, p. 127). Each of these 2-year-old sextuplets has a unique emotional development (Bates, 2004).

Emotional development refers to the influence and interaction of genetic factors, brain changes, cognitive factors, coping abilities, and cultural factors in the development of emotional behaviors, expressions, thoughts, and feelings (Goldsmith, 2003).

Temperament

We'll focus on temperament, which is one of the genetic factors invloved in emotional development.

Temperament refers to relatively stable and long-lasting individual differences in mood and emotional behavior, which emerge early in childhood because these differences are largely influenced by genetic factors.

Researchers studied differences in infants' temperaments and divided infants into four categories (Thomas & Chess, 1977).

1 **Easy babies** are happy and cheerful, have regular sleeping and eating habits, and adapt quickly to new situations.

2 **Slow-to-warm-up babies** are more withdrawn, moody, and tend to take longer to adapt to new situations.

3 **Difficult babies** are fussy, fearful of new situations, and more intense in their reactions. During the course of the 7-year study, difficult babies developed more serious emotional problems than the easy or slow-to-warm-up babies.

4 **No-single-category babies** have a variety of traits and cannot be classified into one of the other three categories.

Because an infant's temperament influences emotional development, it also affects the bond or attachment between parent and child, our next topic.

Attachment

For the first 3 years of his life, Alex (right picture) lived in an orphanage where he had no consistent, loving person to take care of him. Living his first few years of life without close bonding to a parent or caregiver led Alex to have problems in attachment.

Attachment is a close, fundamental emotional bond that develops between the infant and his or her parents or caregiver.

Babies form an attachment to their parents through a gradual process that begins shortly after birth and continues through early childhood. As newborns, infants have a powerful social signal, crying, which elicits care and sympathy. As 4- to 6-week-old infants, they will begin smiling at others, which will elicit joy and pleasure in their parents. At about 6 months, infants begin to give their parents a happy greeting (such as holding out their arms) when they reappear after a short absence. By the end of the first year, an infant usually shows a close attachment to her parents, as well as to one or more other family members.

However, depending on the infant's temperament and the mother's attitude, different kinds of attachment occur. Ainsworth (1979) developed a method for studying infants' reactions to being separated from, and then reunited with, their mothers. She used these reactions to describe the infants' attachment. We'll focus on secure (65% of infants) and insecure (20% of infants) attachment.

Secure attachment is characteristic of infants who use their parent or caregiver as a safe home base from which they can wander off and explore their environments.

For example, when infants are placed in an unfamiliar room containing many interesting toys, securely attached infants tend to explore freely as long as their parent looks on. If the parent leaves, most of the infants cry. On the parent's return, securely attached infants happily greet the caregiver and are easily soothed. In contrast, some infants show insecure attachment.

Insecure attachment is characteristic of infants who avoid or show ambivalence or resistance toward their parent or caregiver.

For example, insecurely attached infants may want to be held one minute but push away the next minute, displaying a lack of trust in the parent or caregiver.

The kind of attachment formed in infancy is associated with the success of future relationships. For example, a secure attachment is associated with being more trusting and enjoying relationships more;   an insecure attachment is associated with being dependent and having poor social relationships (Burge et al., 1997; Howard & Medway, 2004). We'll explore social development next.

Temperament

Learn more about the characteristics of children with different types of temperaments.

Attachment

Watch how infants who have a secure attachment respond to unfamiliar people and situations.

Temperament

Find out how children raised by the same parents in the same family can have such different temperaments.

Social Development

At the beginning of this module we described how Alex was raised in an orphanage until age 3, at which time he was adopted. Some psychologists wonder how Alex's early emotional difficulties will affect his future social development.

Social development refers to how a person develops a sense of self, or a self-identity, develops relationships with others, and develops the kinds of social skills important in personal interactions.

After Alex was adopted, we know that even after a few years with his adoptive parents, he never seemed to have made a good adjustment. Some psychologists would not be surprised that Alex never developed close relationships with others or that he never learned social skills important in personal interactions. This is because some psychologists believe the first five years are the most important and that early emotional troubles may lead to later social problems.

Alex's social development is a long and complicated process, which is influenced by many of the emotional and cognitive factors that we have just discussed. We'll describe three different theories of social development.

Freud's Psychosexual Stages

One of the best-known theories is that of Sigmund Freud (1940/1961), who said that each of us goes through five successive psychosexual stages.

The **psychosexual stages** are five different developmental periods—oral, anal, phallic, latency, and genital stages—during which the individual seeks pleasure from different areas of the body that are associated with sexual feelings. Freud emphasized that a child's first 5 years were most important to social and personality development.

© Bettmann/Corbis

According to Freud, Alex will go through five developmental stages, some of which contain potential conflicts between his desires and his parents' wishes. If his desires are over- or undersatisfied, he may become fixated at one of the first three stages. As you'll see, becoming fixated at one of these stages will hinder his normal social development.

Unless otherwise noted, all images are © Cengage Learning

Stage 1: Oral Stage Early infancy (first 18 months of life)
The **oral stage** lasts for the first 18 months of life and is a time when the infant's pleasure seeking is centered on the mouth.
Potential conflict Pleasure-seeking activities include sucking, chewing, and biting. If Alex were locked into or fixated at this stage because his oral wishes were gratified too much or too little, he would continue to seek oral gratification as an adult.

Stage 2: Anal Stage Early infancy (1½ to 3 years)
The **anal stage** lasts from the age of about 1½ to 3 and is a time when the infant's pleasure seeking is centered on the anus and its functions of elimination.
Potential conflict If Alex were locked into or fixated at this stage, he would continue to engage in behavioral activities related to retention or elimination. Retention may take the form of being very neat, stingy, or behaviorally rigid. Elimination may take the form of being generous or messy.

Stage 3: Phallic Stage Early childhood (3 to 6 years)
The **phallic** *(FAL-ick)* **stage** lasts from about age 3 to 6 and is a time when the infant's pleasure seeking is centered on the genitals.
Potential conflict During this stage, Alex will compete with the parent of the same sex (that is, his father) for the affections and pleasures of the parent of the opposite sex (his mother). Problems in resolving this competition may result in Alex going through life trying to prove his toughness.

Stage 4: Latency Stage Middle and late childhood (from age 6 to puberty)
The **latency stage,** which lasts from about age 6 to puberty, is a time when the child represses sexual thoughts and engages in nonsexual activities, such as developing social and intellectual skills.

At puberty, sexuality reappears and marks the beginning of a new stage called the genital stage, which we will discuss in Module 8.4 (p. 387).

▶ **L08** Describe Erikson's psychosocial theory of development as it applies to children.

Erikson's Psychosocial Stages

According to well-known psychologist Erik Erikson, Alex will encounter kinds of problems very different from the psychosexual ones proposed by Freud. Unlike Freud's emphasis on psychosexual issues, Erikson (1963, 1982) focused on psychosocial issues and said that each of us goes through eight psychosocial stages.

The **psychosocial stages** are eight developmental periods during which an individual's primary goal is to satisfy desires associated with social needs. The eight periods are associated, respectively, with issues of trust, autonomy, initiative, industry, identity, intimacy, generativity, and ego integrity.

Erikson hypothesized that from infancy through adulthood we proceed through these stages, each of which is related to a different problem that needs to be resolved. If we successfully deal with the potential problem of each psychosocial stage, we develop positive personality traits and are better able to solve the problem at the next stage. However, if we do not successfully handle the psychosocial problems, we may become anxious or troubled and develop social or personality problems.

Unlike Freud, Erikson believed that psychosocial needs deserve the greatest emphasis and that social development continues throughout one's lifetime. Thus, Erikson would emphasize Alex's psychosocial needs and downplay the importance of sexuality in the first five years.

Stage 1: Trust versus Mistrust Early infancy (birth through first year)

Potential problem Alex comes into the world as a helpless infant who needs much care and attention. If his parents are responsive and sensitive to his needs, Alex will develop what Erikson calls basic trust, which makes it easier for him to trust people later in life. If Alex's parents neglect his needs, he may view his world as uncaring, learn to become mistrustful, and have difficulty dealing with the second stage.

It appears that Alex did not receive the care and attention he needed during his first year of life.

Stage 2: Autonomy versus Shame and Doubt Late
infancy (1 to 3 years)

Potential problem As Alex begins walking, talking,
and exploring, he is bound to get into conflict with the
wishes of his parents. Thus, this second stage is a battle
of wills between his parents' wishes and Alex's desires to
do as he pleases. If his parents encourage Alex to
explore, he will develop a sense of independence, or autonomy. If his parents disap-
prove of or punish Alex's explorations, he may develop a feeling that independence is
bad and feel shame and doubt.

Stage 3: Initiative versus Guilt Early childhood (3 to 5 years)

Potential problem As a preschooler, Alex has developed a number of
cognitive and social skills that he is expected to use to meet the challenges in his small world. Some of these challenges involve assuming
responsibility and making plans. If his parents encourage initiative,
Alex will develop the ability to plan and initiate new things. However, if they discourage initiative, he may feel uncomfortable or
guilty and may develop a feeling of being unable to plan his future.

Stage 4: Industry versus Inferiority Middle and late childhood (5 to
12 years)

Potential problem Alex's grade-school years are an exciting time, filled with participating in school, playing games with other children, and working to complete projects. If

Alex can direct his energy into working at and completing
tasks, he will develop a feeling of industry. If he has difficulty
applying himself and completing homework, he may develop
a feeling of inferiority and incompetence.

According to Erikson, Alex will encounter a particular
psychosocial problem at each stage. If he successfully solves
the problem, he will develop positive social traits that will help
him solve the next problem. If he does not solve the problem,
he will develop negative social traits that will hinder his solv-
ing a new problem at the next stage. We'll explain the remaining four stages in Module
8.4 (p. 387) and Module 8.5 (p. 396)

Next, we'll examine the social cognitive theory of social development.

**Freud's Psychosexual
versus Erikson's
Psychosocial Stages of
Childhood**

Learn how Freud's and Erikson's
theories explain conflicts and
problems during a child's social
development.

Bandura's Social Cognitive Theory

After watching his daddy bowl, this 3-year-old boy (right photo) walked up to his daddy, pointed at the ball, and said, "Me too ball." Neither Freud's nor Erikson's theory explains why this boy wanted to learn to bowl, what motivated him to ask his daddy, or why he clapped his hands just like his daddy when the ball hit the pins. Albert Bandura (below photo) (2001a) says that this little boy, like all of us, develops many of his behaviors and social skills through a variety of social cognitive processes.

The **social cognitive theory** emphasizes the importance of learning through observation, imitation, and self-reward in the development of social skills, interactions, and behaviors. According to this theory, it is not necessary that you perform any observable behaviors or receive any external rewards to learn new social skills because many of your behaviors are self-motivated, or intrinsic.

Social cognitive theory stresses how you learn by modeling and imitating behaviors you observe in social interactions and situations. For example, after watching his daddy, this boy is intrinsically motivated to imitate many of his daddy's social behaviors. Social cognitive theory emphasizes that children develop social behaviors and skills by watching and imitating the social behaviors of their parents, teachers, and peers.

In comparing Bandura's, Freud's, and Erikson's theories, we notice that although the three theories are very different, they are complementary because each emphasizes a different process. Social cognitive theory emphasizes learning through modeling; Freud's theory focuses on parent–child interactions that occur in satisfying innate biological needs; and Erikson's theory points to the importance of dealing with social needs.

We'll use these theories to explain how some children overcame terrible childhood experiences to develop normal social behaviors.

© PhotoDisc, Inc.

© Time& Life Pictures/Getty Images

Unless otherwise noted, all images are © Cengage Learning

Resiliency and Vulnerability

Beginning in his early childhood, Dave Pelzer's extremely disturbed, alcoholic mother did her best to put him through one life-threatening situation after another. She abused him mentally, physically, and emotionally. Some of the ways she tortured him were by denying him food, clothing, and warmth, forcing him to drink ammonia, stabbing him in his stomach, and constantly threatening to kill him. She belittled Dave by referring to him only as "It" rather than his name. The abuse Dave endured was so grave that it has been identified as one of the most serious and disturbing cases of child abuse on record. At age 12, Dave was finally removed from his mother's custody and placed in foster homes. He struggled to adjust to these various caregivers, but he finally developed a trusting, loving relationship with two caregivers he learned to call Mom and Dad.

Courtesy of Dave Pelzer

Dave was exposed to serious life stressors during his childhood. How these stressors affect children depends on each child's vulnerability and resiliency.

Vulnerability refers to psychological or environmental difficulties that make children more at risk for developing later personality, behavioral, or social problems.

Resiliency refers to psychological and environmental factors that compensate for increased life stresses so that expected problems do not develop.

There is no question that Dave was extremely vulnerable. Although other children with such high vulnerability might have later developed serious emotional or behavioral problems, Dave triumphed over seemingly insurmountable odds, displaying tremendous resiliency, and developed into a competent, courageous, and autonomous adult. He served in the armed forces for which he earned personal commendations by three former U.S. presidents. Dave has authored six best-selling inspirational books, two of which were nominated for the Pulitzer Prize. And, given the passion that drives him, Dave's contributions to this world are far from over (Peltzer, 1995, 1997, 1999, 2000, 2003, 2009).

Studies on resilient children show three findings. First, early traumatic events do not necessarily lead to later social-emotional problems, as Freud predicted. Second, a loving, supportive caregiver or teacher can substitute for a disinterested parent. Third, children observe and imitate normal social behaviors modeled by caregivers (Brooks & Goldstein, 2002; Werner & Smith, 2001).

▶ **LO11** Describe gender role development, including different explanations for how children acquire gender roles.

Gender Differences

When you look at the photo of the infant on the right, you can't help asking, Is it a girl or a boy? This question has great importance to social development because it involves gender identity.

By the age of 3, most children learn to label themselves as boys or girls and can classify others as being the same sex or the other sex (Ruble et al., 2006).

Gender identity refers to the individual's subjective experience and feelings of being a female or male.

Once children know their correct sex, they begin to learn and show sex-appropriate behaviors, which are called gender roles.

By ages 2 to 3, American children have learned the preference of each traditional gender role for toys, clothes, games, and tools. By ages 4 to 5, children have developed a clear idea of which occupations are stereotypically for men and for women. And by the relatively early age of 5, children have already learned the thoughts, expectations, and behaviors that accompany their particular gender roles (Eckes & Trautner, 2000).

Gender roles are the traditional or stereotypical behaviors, attitudes, and personality traits that parents, peers, and society expect us to have because we are male or female.

Gender roles become part of who we are and have a relatively powerful effect on how we behave, think, and act. How children acquire gender roles is explained by two somewhat different but related theories: social role theory and cognitive developmental theory (Martin et al., 2002).

Social Role Theory

In many families, the parents expect a son to behave and act differently than a daughter. How parental expectations influence a child's gender identity is explained by the social role theory (Eagly et al., 2000).

The **social role theory** emphasizes the influence of social and cognitive processes on how we interpret, organize, and use information. Applied to gender roles, it says that mothers, fathers, teachers, grandparents, friends, and peers expect, respond to, and reward different behaviors in boys than in girls. Under the influence of this differential treatment, boys learn a gender role that is different from girls'.

©moodboard/Corbis

Unless otherwise noted, all images are © Cengage Learning

For example, the stereotypical gender roles for males include being dominant, controlling, and independent, while gender roles for females include being sensitive, nurturing, and concerned (Eagly & Karau, 2002; Wood et al., 1997). According to social role theory, these gender differences originate, to a large extent, because mothers and fathers respond to and reward different behaviors in girls than in boys.

One criticism of social role theory is that it focuses too much on rewarding and discouraging behaviors and too little on cognitive influences, which are emphasized in the cognitive developmental theory.

Cognitive Developmental Theory

When you were a child, you probably learned that there were rules about what boys and girls could and could not do. This childhood experience supports the cognitive developmental theory (Martin, 2000).

The **cognitive developmental theory** says that, as children develop mental skills and interact with their environments, they learn one set of rules for male behaviors and another set of rules for female behaviors.

In this view, children actively process information that results in their learning gender rules regarding which behaviors are correct for girls and wrong for boys, and vice versa. On the basis of these rules, children form mental images of how they should act; these images are called gender schemas.

Gender schemas are sets of information and rules organized around how either a male or a female should think and behave (Bem, 1985).

For instance, the traditional gender schema for being a boy includes engaging in rough-and-tumble play and sports, initiating conversations, and exploring; the traditional gender schema for being a girl includes playing with dolls, expressing emotions, listening, and being dependent.

Cognitive developmental theory emphasizes that a child is an active participant in learning a male or female set of rules and schemas, which result in different gender roles (Bem, 1981). Therefore, both social role theory and cognitive developmental theory predict that the sexes will develop different gender roles.

Perceiving Gender Roles

Watch young children explain what it means to be a boy or a girl.

Gender Roles

Explore how social role theory explains why children from different countries and cultures develop similar male-female gender roles.

Check Your Learning Quiz 8.3

Go to **login.cengagebrain.com** and take the online quiz.

Unless otherwise noted, all images are © Cengage Learning

▶ **LO12** Describe how puberty changes the bodies of girls and boys.

Following childhood we enter a period of development known as adolescence.

Adolescence is a developmental period from about ages 12 to 18, during which many biological, cognitive, social, and personality traits change from childlike to adultlike.

The great change from child to adult is full of challenge, excitement, and anxiety for the adolescent and the parents. Perhaps the biggest event in changing from a child to an adult is the onset of puberty.

Physical Development: Puberty

Puberty refers to a developmental period, between the ages of 9 and 17, when the individual experiences significant biological changes that result in developing secondary sexual characteristics and reaching sexual maturity.

As puberty triggers dramatic changes in the structure and function of our bodies, we simultaneously experience dramatic changes in our thoughts, personalities, and social behaviors. To understand why puberty changes our minds, we must first learn how puberty changes our bodies.

Girls

Becoming a woman means going through puberty and experiencing three major biological changes that occur between ages 9 and 13. The onset of puberty usually occurs about two years earlier in girls (average of 10.5 years) than in boys (average of 12.5 years).

1 Puberty sets off a surge in physical growth, which is marked by an increase in height that starts on average at 9.6 years. This growth spurt begins about 6 to 12 months before the onset of breast development.

2 Puberty triggers a physiological process that results in a girl's reaching female sexual maturity, which primarily involves the onset of menarche.

Menarche is the first menstrual period; it is a signal that ovulation may have occurred and that the girl may have the potential to conceive and bear a child.

© David Michael Kennedy

The onset of menarche (average of 12.5 years) is triggered by a brain area called the hypothalamus, which releases a hormone called kisspeptin that stimulates the pituitary gland to produce hormones. These hormones stimulate the ovaries to increase production of female hormones (Kotulak, 2006; Messager, 2006).

Estrogen is a major female hormone. At puberty, estrogen levels increase eight-fold, which stimulates the development of both primary and secondary sexual characteristics.

3 Puberty marks a major change in the girl's body as she develops female secondary sexual characteristics.

Female secondary sexual characteristics include growth of pubic hair, development of breasts, and widening of hips.

In girls, the onset of secondary sexual characteristics begins at 10.5 years (the range is from age 9 to age 18) and continues for about 4.5 years.

Boys

Becoming a man means going through puberty and experiencing three major biological changes that occur between ages 10 and 14.

1 Puberty triggers an increase in *physical growth,* especially height, generally at 13 to 14 years of age. The increase in height may be dramatic, and a boy may feel strange as he discovers that he is taller than his mother and as tall as or taller than his father.

2 Puberty starts a physiological process that results in a boy's reaching *male sexual maturity,* which includes growth of the genital organs (testes and penis) and production of sperm. The onset of genital growth begins at around 11.5 years. The production and release of sperm begin at 12 to 14 years of age.

The increase in genital growth and the production of sperm are triggered by the *hypothalamus,* which stimulates the male pituitary gland. The pituitary in turn triggers the testes to increase production of testosterone.

Testosterone, which is the major male hormone, stimulates the growth of genital organs and the development of secondary sexual characteristics.

3 The increased production of testosterone triggers the development of male secondary sexual characteristics.

Male secondary sexual characteristics include the growth of pubic and facial hair, development of muscles, and a deepening in voice.

These changes usually occur between 12 and 16 years of age, but there is a wide range in their development.

Cognitive Development

We have already discussed the physical changes that occur during puberty. Along with these changes, adolescents develop new ways of thinking and reasoning, which represents a major change in their cognitive development.

As you may remember from the prior module, Piaget's theory of cognitive development is that we all go through four cognitive stages (bottom left figure). As we go through each cognitive stage, we acquire a new and distinct kind of reasoning and thinking that is different from and more advanced than the reasoning abilities we possessed at our previous stage. We've already discussed Piaget's first three cognitive stages, which occur during childhood (pp. 367–369). We'll now discuss the formal operational stage, because it begins in adolescence.

Piaget's Cognitive Stage 4: Formal Operational

When adolescents begin to use abstract concepts, such as liberty, justice, animal rights, and God, it is good evidence they are entering the formal operational stage.

The **formal operational stage,** the last of Piaget's four cognitive stages, extends from about age 12 through adulthood. During this stage, adolescents and adults develop the abilities to think about abstract or hypothetical concepts, to consider an issue from another's viewpoint, and to solve cognitive problems in a logical way.

Having the ability to think about and discuss abstract concepts means that adolescents can critically consider their beliefs, attitudes, values, and goals, as well as discuss

a wide range of topics important to their becoming adults. For instance, when adolescents were asked about their major concerns, tops on their lists were getting married, having friends, getting a good job, and doing well in school. Each of these concerns involves the ability to discuss abstract concepts, which is a cognitive skill that they are learning at the formal operational stage.

One of the interesting questions about adolescents is why some seem so slow to develop thinking and reasoning skills that prepare them to deal with typical problems and stressful situations that occur during adolescence. For example, many adolescents report that they are not prepared to have sex (even though they already have) or they do stupid things such as drink and drive. Researchers only recently discovered that the answer involves the developing adolescent's brain.

Brain Development: Reason and Emotion

Parents believe their teens should know better than to act in seemingly irresponsible and impulsive ways, and until recently researchers agreed because they believed teenage brains were fully developed. However, new findings indicate that teenage brains are still developing, especially the areas involved in reasoning (Crews, 2006).

Prefrontal Cortex: Executive Functions

Every company has an executive officer who is responsible for making decisions, planning, organizing, and thinking about the future. Similarly, our brains have an executive area, called the *prefrontal cortex,* which is involved in similar functions and is located near the front of the brain (red area in right figure).

By using brain scans to take pictures of the neural development of teenage brains, researchers found that the adolescent's prefrontal cortex was still developing and thus did not yet have the ability to think, reason, decide, or plan like an adult (Luna, 2006; Shute, 2009). This finding helps explain many of the adolescent's seemingly irresponsible behaviors.

Another reason adolescents have a tendency to engage in risk-taking behaviors involves a different part of their brain that's involved in emotional behaviors.

Limbic System: Emotional Behaviors

Parents often complain about the moodiness and irritability of their teenager. As one parent said, "It's hot and cold, nasty and nice. One minute loving me, one minute hating me." What parents don't realize is that a teenager's prefrontal cortex, which acts like an executive officer, is not fully developed, so an adolescent has less control over his or her emotional and impulsive behaviors. This explains why teens are so easily upset when parents can't understand them (Shute, 2009).

As shown in the above right figure (circled blue area), a circle of structures makes up our limbic system (pp. 86–87). The *limbic system* is involved in a wide range of emotional behaviors, such as being ecstatic over getting a date, feeling depressed when failing a test, and getting angry when insulted. Research has found that sex hormones (testosterone in males and estrogen in females), which are secreted in abundance during puberty, increase the growth of the limbic system. Researchers believe the increased size and function of the limbic system account for a teen's irritability and frequency of talking aggressively with others (Whittle et al., 2008).

Piaget's Formal Operational Stage

Learn more about the cognitive abilities of people in the formal operations stage.

Risk Taking

Discover the attitudes teens have about risk-taking behaviors.

Are Teens Too Young to Drive?

Find out how scientific research answers the question of whether teens should be permitted to drive.

Kohlberg's Theory of Moral Reasoning

An adolescent's lack of a strong executive officer (prefrontal cortex) will affect moral judgment. Suppose your best friend is dying of cancer. You hear of a chemist who has just discovered a wonder drug that could save her life. The chemist is selling the drug for $5,000, many times more than it cost him to make. You try to borrow the full amount but can get only $2,500. You ask the chemist to sell you the drug for $2,500 but he refuses. Later that night, you break into the chemist's laboratory and steal the drug. Should you have done that?

Did you decide that it would be all right to steal the drug to save the life of your dying friend? If you did, how did you justify your moral decision? Lawrence Kohlberg (1984) and associates presented similar dilemmas to individuals who were then asked to explain their moral decisions. On the basis of such studies, Kohlberg explained the development of moral reasoning in terms of three levels.

Level 1: Self-Interest

The **preconventional level,** which represents Kohlberg's lowest level of moral reasoning, has two stages. At stage 1, moral decisions are based primarily on fear of punishment or the need to be obedient; at stage 2, moral reasoning is guided most by satisfying one's self-interest, which may involve making bargains.

For example, individuals at stage 1 might say that you should not steal the drug because you'll be caught and go to jail. Individuals at stage 2 might say that you can steal the drug and save your best friend, but in return you'll have to give up some freedom by going to jail. Most children are at the preconventional level.

Level 2: Social Approval

The **conventional level,** which represents an intermediate level of moral reasoning, also has two stages. At stage 3, moral decisions are guided most by conforming to the standards of others we value; at stage 4, moral reasoning is determined most by conforming to laws of society.

Individuals at stage 3 might say that you should steal the drug since that is what your family would expect you to do. Individuals at stage 4 might say that you should not steal the drug because of what would happen to society if everybody took what they needed. Many adolescents and adults are at the conventional level.

© Deborah Cheramie/iStockphoto

© Shelley Dennis/iStockphoto

Unless otherwise noted, all images are © Cengage Learning

Level 3: Abstract Ideas

The **postconventional level,** which represents the highest level of moral reasoning, has one stage. At stage 5, moral decisions are made after carefully thinking about all the alternatives and striking a balance between human rights and laws of society.

Individuals at stage 5 might say that one should steal the drug because life is more important than money. Some, but not all, adults reach the postconventional level. (Stage 6, which appeared in earlier versions of Kohlberg's theory, has been omitted in later versions because too few people had reached it.)

Moral reasoning and cognitive development are also influenced by the kinds of rules that parents use, which is our next topic.

Baumrind's Parenting Styles

If someone asked how your parents raised you, would you answer that they were strict, supportive, easy, or hard? It turns out that parents' rules, standards, and codes of conduct influence how a teenager develops a sense of independence and achievement (Baumrind, 1991). We'll discuss how parental rules can affect the cognitive and emotional development of teenagers by focusing on three of Baumrind's parenting styles: authoritarian, authoritative, and permissive parents.

Authoritarian parents attempt to shape, control, and evaluate the behavior and attitudes of their children in accordance with a set standard of conduct, usually an absolute standard that comes from religious or respected authorities.

For these parents, obedience is a virtue, and they punish and use harsh discipline to keep the adolescent in line with their rules.

Authoritative parents attempt to direct their children's activities in a rational and intelligent way. They are supportive, loving, and committed, encourage verbal give-and-take, and discuss their rules and policies with their children.

Authoritative parents value being expressive and independent but are also demanding. The children of such parents tend to be competent. In addition, girls are achievement-oriented and boys are friendly and cooperative.

Permissive parents are less controlling and behave with a nonpunishing and accepting attitude toward their children's impulses, desires, and actions; they consult with their children about policy decisions, make few demands, and use reason rather than direct power.

Girls with such parents are less socially assertive, and both boys and girls are less achievement-oriented.

Kohlberg's Theory of Moral Reasoning

Practice identifying the characteristics of each of Kohlberg's stages of moral development.

© Troels Graugaard/iStockphoto

Personality and Social Development

One more change that occurs during adolescence is that adolescents develop a sense of who they are, which involves personality and social development.

Personality and **social development** refer to how a person develops a sense of self or self-identity, develops relationships with others, and develops the skills useful in social interactions.

For example, the teenager in the right photo shows her independence and what she believes is her real identity by having a very noticeable hairstyle and piercings.

Personal identity or **self-identity** refers to how we describe ourselves and includes our values, goals, traits, perceptions, interests, and motivations.

Personal identity grows and changes as adolescents acquire new values, goals, beliefs, and interests (Bandura, 1999). A major influence on the kind of identity teenagers develop is how they feel about themselves, which is called self-esteem.

Self-esteem is how much we like ourselves and how much we value our self-worth, importance, attractiveness, and social competence.

For example, in adolescents, self-esteem is influenced by a number of factors, including how physically attractive and how socially competent they appear to their peers (DuBois et al., 2000). We'll discuss three different patterns of self-esteem development in adolescents (Zimmerman et al., 1997).

High Self-Esteem. A large percentage of adolescents (about 60%) develop and maintain a strong sense of self-esteem through junior high school. These individuals do well in school, develop rewarding friendships, participate in social activities, and are described as cheerful, assertive, emotionally warm, and unwilling to give up if frustrated.

Low Self-Esteem. A small percentage of adolescents (15%) develop and maintain a chronically low sense of self-esteem that continues through junior high school. These adolescents usually have continuing personal and social problems (such as being shy, lonely, and depressed), which have been present for some time and contribute to this low self-esteem.

Reversals. A moderate percentage of adolescents (about 25%) show dramatic reversals in self-esteem, either from high to low or from low to high. For example, some boys change from being stern, unemotional, and lacking social skills into being open and expressive.

© PhotoDisc, Inc.

Unless otherwise noted, all images are © Cengage Learning

Two theories of how individuals progress through their social and personality development are Freud's psychosexual stages and Erikson's psychosocial stages, both of which we began to discuss in Module 8.3.

Freud's Psychosexual Stages

Previously, you learned about the first four psychosexual stages, as they related to childhood (pp. 372–373). Now, we turn our attention to the fifth and final stage.

Stage 5: Genital Stage Puberty through adulthood

The **genital stage** lasts from puberty through adulthood and is a time when the individual has renewed sexual desires that he or she seeks to fulfill through relationships with members of the opposite sex.

If an individual successfully resolved conflicts in the first three stages, he will have the energy to develop loving relationships and a healthy and mature personality.

© Visual Ideas/Camilo M/Age fotostock RF

Erikson's Psychosocial Stages

As you may remember from Module 8.3 (pp. 374–375), Erikson divided life into psychosocial stages, which each contain a unique psychosocial conflict and together span the lifespan. In Module 8.2, we discussed Erikson's stages related to childhood; now, we'll discuss the stage related to adolescence.

Stage 5: Identity versus Role Confusion Adolescence (ages 12 to 20)

Adolescents need to leave behind the carefree, irresponsible, and impulsive behaviors of childhood and develop the more purposeful, planned, and responsible behaviors of adulthood. If adolescents successfully resolve this problem, they will develop a healthy and confident sense of *identity*. If they are unsuccessful in resolving the problem, they will experience *role confusion,* which results in having low self-esteem and becoming unstable or socially withdrawn.

© Tetra Images/Age fotostock RF

Check Your Learning Quiz 8.4

Go to **login.cengagebrain.com** and take the online quiz.

▶ **L020** Describe physical and sexual changes during adulthood.

Physical Development

As you look at the photo on the right, the difference you see between grandmother and granddaughter is an example of normal aging, which is very different from pathological aging.

Normal aging is a gradual and natural slowing of our physical and psychological processes from middle through late adulthood.

Pathological aging may be caused by genetic defects, physiological problems, or diseases, such as Alzheimer's (pp. 52–53), all of which accelerate the aging process.

One goal of the study of aging, which is called *gerontology,* is to separate the causes of normal aging from those of pathological aging. The percentage of people in the United States over 65 is expected to almost double by the year 2040 (right graph). Soon, it is expected that, for the first time in human history, there will be more people over the age of 65 in the world than children under age 5 (USCB, 2008a). Life expectancy in the United States was 45 years in 1945 but is more recently a record 78 years (WHO, 2009). In the 1920s, only 2,300 people in the United States were over 100, but recent data finds more than 96,000 are over that age, and the number is estimated to be 600,000 by 2050 (Wright, 2003; USCB, 2009a)!

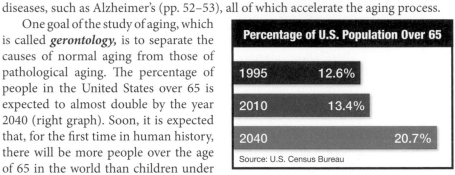

Percentage of U.S. Population Over 65

Year	Percentage
1995	12.6%
2010	13.4%
2040	20.7%

Source: U.S. Census Bureau

So far, the oldest people on record have lived from 113 to 122 years. How long you will live and how fast your body will age depend about 50% on heredity (genes) and 50% on other factors, such as diet, exercise, lifestyle, and diseases (Wright, 2003). In the past decades, the steady increases in life expectancy came primarily from improved public health and new cures for diseases. But advances in controlling diseases are slowing, and researchers believe that even with major improvements in geriatric care, the average life expectancy will not go beyond 85 years (Olshansky, 2003). Instead, researchers believe that large increases in life expectancy must now come from slowing the aging process itself (Miller, 2003).

© David J. Sams/Stock, Boston

Unless otherwise noted; all images are © Cengage Learning

The **aging process** is caused by a combination of certain genes and proteins that interfere with organ functioning and the natural production of toxic molecules (free radicals), which in turn cause random damage to body organs and DNA (the building blocks of life). Such damage eventually exceeds the body's ability to repair itself and results in greater susceptibility to diseases and death (Olshansky et al., 2002).

Researchers recently found that stress, such as that caused by job loss or divorce, results in the aging of DNA (Epel & Blackburn, 2004). Also, studies have identified a half dozen genetic factors in the very old (average age 98) that seemed to have slowed the aging process (Wright, 2003). Although such practices as having a good diet, exercising, reducing stress, and taking vitamins or antioxidants may improve quality of life and help one live into the 100s, none of these things alone has been shown to slow the aging process and allow humans to live to 130 or beyond (Olshansky, 2003).

As our bodies age, they experience many physiological changes.

Physiological Changes

Early Adulthood

In our early to middle 20s, our immune system, senses, physiological responses, and mental skills are at their peak efficiency.

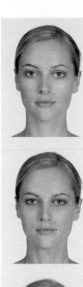

Middle Adulthood

In our 30s and 40s, we usually gain weight, primarily because we are less active. By the late 40s, there is a slight decrease in physiological responses, including heart rate, lung capacity, and muscle strength.

Late Adulthood

In our 50s and 60s, we may experience a gradual decline in height because of loss of bone, a further decrease in output of lungs and kidneys, an increase in skin wrinkles, and a deterioration in joints. Sensory organs become less sensitive, resulting in less acute vision, hearing, and taste. The heart becomes less effective at pumping blood. A decrease occurs in the number and diameter of muscle fibers, which may explain some of the slowing in motor functions that accompanies old age.

Very Late Adulthood

In our 70s and 80s, we undergo further decreases in muscle strength, bone density, nerve conduction, and output of lungs, heart, and kidneys.

As many of the body's physical responses slow down with aging, there are corresponding decreases in related behaviors, such as sexual behaviors.

Sexual Changes with Aging

Surveys of sexual behavior, which usually sample people between ages 17 and 59, generally report that single men have more sex partners, experience orgasm more frequently, and masturbate more frequently than single women and that about one-third of married couples have sex two or three times a week (Crooks & Baur, 2002). People in late adulthood (60 to 80) are often not included in these surveys because of the common ste-

reotype that they no longer have any interest in sexual activity or that it is inappropriate for them to engage in sex. However, a survey of men and women over age 70 found that about 57% of men and 52% of women were sexually active (Beckman et al., 2008). This survey indicates that adults can enjoy sexual activity well into their later years, especially if they know how sexual responses change and learn ways to deal with these changes. We'll discuss some of the normal changes in sexual responses that accompany aging.

Men

As men reach late adulthood (60s, 70s, and 80s), they may experience some physiological changes that decrease sexual responsiveness.

Sexual Responding Because many of the body's physiological responses slow down, older men may require more time and stimulation to have an erection and to reach orgasm. Upon ejaculation, there may be a reduction in the force and amount of fluid. However, healthy men usually have no difficulty in becoming sexually aroused or reaching orgasm. Some men worry that their decreased ability to have an erection or reach orgasm means an end to their sexuality (Masters & Johnson, 1981). Currently, there are a few drugs (such as Viagra) approved for the treatment of impotency, which is the inability to have an erection. These drugs help about 70% of men who have impotency problems (Berenson, 2005).

Psychological Problems The decreased sexual abilities that older men generally experience can make them uncomfortable and threaten their self-esteem. However, having longer periods of stimulation, improving intimate communication, and using more imaginative sexual activity can usually compensate for men's decreased self-confidence (Bartlik & Goldstein, 2001).

Women

The most significant effect on women's sexual behavior in later adulthood is menopause.

Menopause occurs in women at about age 50 (range 35 to 60) and involves a gradual stoppage in secretion of the major female hormone (estrogen), which in turn results in cessation of both ovulation and the menstrual cycle.

Physical Symptoms Most older women experience hot flashes, some sleep disturbance, and dryness of the vagina, which result from a decrease and eventual stoppage in the secretion of the female hormone estrogen. A lack of estrogen results in a reduction of lubrication during arousal. However, there is little or no change in the ability to become sexually aroused or to reach orgasm. Potential problems with lack of lubrication or painful intercourse may be treated with hormone replacement therapy or the use of vaginal creams (Nathan & Judd, 2007; Reed & Sutton, 2006).

Psychological Symptoms Researchers followed 400 healthy women through menopause and observed many psychological changes. They found that women did report psychological symptoms, such as depression, anxiety, and anger. However, these symptoms were related to other stressful issues (such as growing older in a society that glorifies being young), rather than to the physical symptoms of menopause. In addition, women's expectations influenced their psychological outlook during menopause. Women with positive expectations about what they hope to accomplish have few psychological symptoms, compared to women who expect their lives to be over and thus feel depressed during menopause (Dennerstein et al., 1997; Neugarten, 1994).

Sexual Activities Some older women think sexual activity is appropriate only for young people. Others expect sexual activity to be just like it was during their young adulthood, and they may have difficulty accepting the inevitable changes that occur as they age. Overall, half of women age 50 and older are at least as satisfied with their sex life as during their younger years (Potter, 2006). But many women do experience sexual difficulties and often find it difficult to discuss with others. One way to help these women is to have their doctors ask them about their sexual functioning; currently, more than 90% of doctors are reported not to bring up the topic (WSHF, 2008).

Adult Sex Life Changes

Learn more about some of the sexual changes that may occur with aging.

▶ **LO21** Describe changes in cognition during adulthood.

Cognitive Development

As individuals enter their 20s, they face a number of major changes, such as deciding about going to college, leaving home for perhaps the first time, choosing a career or major, entering the job market, and searching for a serious relationship (Arnett, 2000b). The 20s are a time when executive abilities (thinking, planning, deciding, remembering) are sharp, partly because the brain's prefrontal cortex is now more fully developed. Cognitive or executive abilities usually remain sharp through the 30s. But beginning in the 40s and continuing through the 50s and 60s, there is a gradual decline in some cognitive abilities, especially in the ability to remember things. We'll discuss some changes in cognitive abilities as we age.

Changes in Cognitive Speed

From about ages 20 to 40, cognitive skills remain relatively stable. However, between 40 and 80, there is a general slowing of some cognitive processes. Beginning in the late 50s, there is a slowing of three cognitive processes:

Why is my golf game slowing down?

© ImageSource/Age fotostock RF

Unless otherwise noted, all images are © Cengage Learning

1. There is a slowing in **processing speed,** which is the rate at which we encode information into long-term memory or recall or retrieve information from long-term memory.

2. There is a slowing in **perceptual speed,** which is the rate at which we can identify a particular sensory stimulus.

3. There is a slowing in **reaction time,** which is the rate at which we respond (that is, see, hear, move) to some stimulus.

This slowing in processing, perceiving, and reacting partly explains why older people react more slowly when driving a car or playing golf and are slower to make decisions or understand and follow instructions. For example, partly because of the slowdown in these processes, there is a professional golf tour for seniors only (that is, for those over age 50); they can no longer keep up with younger golfers.

Besides a slowing in cognitive speed, older adults experience a problem in remembering things.

Changes in Memory

Researchers concluded that older adults have no trouble remembering the big picture (such as the name of a movie) but do forget many of the small details (such as who played the starring role) (Schacter, 2001). So as people move into their 50s, 60s, and 70s, their complaints are true: They forget details (such as names, places, groceries) that may be bothersome but are usually unimportant.

Memory differences. Young adults in their 20s excel at encoding (storing) and recalling vast amounts of detail but are not as good at making sense of what all the details mean. In comparison, mature adults in their 50s excel at making sense of information but forget many details.

Brain changes. Decreases in memory skills result from the slowing down of memory abilities, reasoning processes, and focusing of attention. Brain scans show these kinds of problems, which occur throughout normal aging, result from the normal loss of brain cells in the prefrontal cortex (Milham et al., 2002).

Now, we'll learn how the brain changes for the better as we age.

Resiliency

Research indicates that as we age, our brains become more flexible and adaptable. Though brain cells may lose processing speed, their connections to other brain cells multiply, and they form more meaningful neural connections as a result of more life experience (Anthes, 2009; McAuliffe, 2008). Also, the brain's left and right hemispheres become better integrated during middle age. This means that brains of older adults can compensate for age-related declines by expanding their neural network to include both brain hemispheres (Cohen, 2006). As brains become more flexible and adaptable, they also manage emotions better.

Emotions

Older adults have a "positivity bias," which means they pay less attention to negative information and more to positive information. Research found that the part of the brain responsible for strong negative emotions (amygdala) becomes less active with age. This focus on the positive explains why older adults have better mental health than younger adults, who mostly focus on negative emotions (Cabeza, 2006, 2008; Carstensen, 2006).

Next, we turn to changes in social and emotional development in adulthood.

Cognitive Models of Aging

Watch how our cognitive processes change with age.

Social and Emotional Development

As we enter adulthood, many of us experience various kinds of love, choose partners for different reasons, and learn some ways to achieve and maintain a successful intimate relationship. In this section, we'll explore kinds of love, choosing a partner, and the characteristics of a long-term commitment.

Kinds of Love

Earlier researchers had thought love too mysterious for scientific study, but current researchers have begun to classify love into various components. As a starting point, researchers distinguish between passionate and companionate love (Rapson & Hatfield, 2005).

Passionate love involves continuously thinking about the loved one and is accompanied by warm sexual feelings and powerful emotional reactions.

Companionate love involves having trusting and tender feelings for someone whose life is closely bound up with one's own.

For example, when people fall madly in love, it's usually passionate love. When mature couples talk about enjoying each other's company, it's usually companionate love, which may or may not involve sexual behaviors. Thus, love is more complex than many think. One of the better known theories of love is Robert Sternberg's (1999) triangular theory of love.

The **triangular theory of love** has three components: passion, intimacy, and commitment. **Passion** is feeling physically aroused and attracted to someone. **Intimacy** is feeling close and connected to someone; it develops through sharing and communicating. **Commitment** is making a pledge to nourish the feelings of love and to actively maintain the relationship.

Love Triangle — Commitment, Intimacy, Passion

Three components of love

What makes you feel in love is the component of passion, which rises quickly, and strongly influences and biases your judgment. What makes you want to share and offer emotional and material support is the component of intimacy. What makes you want to form a serious relationship, such as getting married, and to promise support through difficult times, is the component of commitment. Sternberg believes that the kind of love most of us strive for is complete or consummate love, which is a balanced combination of all three components—passion, intimacy, and commitment.

Choosing a Partner

Researchers suggest that one way we choose a partner for a long-term relationship is by finding someone who matches our ideal-partner schema (Fletcher & Simpson, 2000).

A **schema** is an organized mental or cognitive list that includes characteristics, facts, values, or beliefs about people, events, or objects.

An ideal-partner schema is a mental list of the most desirable characteristics we are seeking. An ideal-partner schema in order of preference for unmarried college students (averaged for men and women) is shown at right (Buss, 1994). Results showed men and women form ideal-partner schemas with two major differences: Men rank physical attractiveness as more important, and women rank earning capacity higher (Buss, 1995, 2003).

IDEAL PARTNER
1. kind/understanding
2. exciting
3. intelligent
4. physically attractive (men rank higher)
5. healthy
6. easygoing
7. creative
8. wants children
9. earning potential (women rank higher)

After Mr. or Ms. Right is chosen, the couple is ready to make a commitment, such as living together or getting married.

Making a Long-Term Commitment

Many couples may choose to make a commitment to each other by living together. In the United States, the number of unmarried, heterosexual couples living together, or cohabiting, increased from 1 million in 1960 to 13.6 million in 2008 (Jayson, 2005; USCB, 2009b). Fewer unmarried people who cohabit are in homosexual relationships. What happens within the first two years of living together really matters, as most couples will either break up or marry by then.

For those who choose to marry, many find long-term happiness and many others get a divorce. Couples who later divorce seem to have commonly shared problems: One or both partners spends too much time criticizing the other; one or both partners become too defensive when one of their faults is criticized; one or both partners show contempt for the other; and one or both partners engage in stonewalling or are unwilling to talk about some problem (Gottman, 2000).

Successful couples learn to confront and deal with stonewalling by settling disagreements in an open, straightforward way; try to be less defensive about negative feedback; criticize their partners less and try to be more supportive; and agree to overlook small problems they are unlikely to change (Gottman, 1999).

Falling in love is grand, but achieving long-term success takes a lot of work (Gottman, 2003).

Preference for Partners

Learn how culture influences one's preference for partners.

Happy Marriages

Learn the key factors to a successful relationship.

Cohabitation

Discover some of the major research findings on cohabiting.

▶ **LO24** Describe Erikson's psychosocial theory of development as it applies to adults.

▶ **LO25** Describe Kübler-Ross's stage theory of the adjustment process in accepting one's death.

Erikson's Psychosocial Stages

As you may remember from Modules 8.3 and 8.4, Erikson divided life into psychosocial stages, which each contain a unique psychosocial conflict and together span the lifespan. In Module 8.3 (pp. 374–375), we discussed Erikson's first four stages that occur during childhood, and in Module 8.4 (p. 387), we discussed the fifth stage, which occurs in adolescence. Now, we'll identify and describe the remaining three stages, which occur during adulthood.

Stage 6: Intimacy versus Isolation Young adulthood (ages 20 to 40)
Young adulthood is a time for finding intimacy by developing loving and meaningful relationships. On the positive side, we can find intimacy in caring relationships. On the negative side, without intimacy we will have a painful feeling of isolation, and our relationships will be impersonal.

Stage 7: Generativity versus Stagnation Middle adulthood (ages 40 to 65)
Middle adulthood is a time for helping the younger generation develop worthwhile lives. On the positive side, we can achieve generativity through raising our own children. If we do not have children of our own, we can achieve generativity through close relationships with children of friends or relatives. Generativity can also be achieved through mentoring at work and helping others. On the negative side, a lack of involvement leads to a feeling of stagnation, of having done nothing for the younger generation.

Stage 8: Integrity versus Despair Late adulthood (ages 65 and older)
Late adulthood is a time for reflecting on and reviewing how we met previous challenges and lived our lives. On the positive side, if we can look back and feel content about how we lived and what we accomplished, we will have a feeling of satisfaction, or integrity. On the negative side, if we reflect and see a series of crises, problems, and bad experiences, we will have a feeling of regret and despair.

Conclusions

Researchers have found evidence that we do go through a sequence of psychosocial stages and that how we handle conflicts at earlier stages affects our personality and social development at later stages (Van Manen & Whitbourne, 1997).

Death and Dying

As we discussed, when individuals enter the last stage of Erikson's psychosocial theory, they confront the crisis of integrity versus despair. By resolving this crisis and achieving integrity, a person meets the end of life with feeling he or she had a meaningful and fullfilling life. On the contrary, if a person has a feeling of regret or despair meeting the end of life, then he or she would feel that life has been meaningless or wasted.

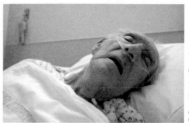

Have you ever wondered about your own death? How will you accept the process of dying? Will you be able to die with integrity or will you be left in despair? These questions are perhaps of most relevance to those who have been told they have a terminal illness. After spending hundreds of hours at the bedsides of people with a terminal illness, Elisabeth Kübler-Ross (1969) developed her stage theory of the psychological process involved in accepting one's death:

1. **Denial**—"This can't be happening to me." " I feel fine, there's nothing wrong with me."
2. **Anger**—"Why me?" "How can this happen to me?" "Why couldn't it have been someone else?"
3. **Bargaining**—"Just let me live long enough to see my daughter's marriage." "Please, I'll do anything, just let me have more time!"
4. **Depression**—"I'm losing everyone I love." "I'm so sad, what's the point of living any longer?"
5. **Acceptance**—"I know I'm going to die soon and I'm ok with it." "There isn't much I can do to postpone death, so why not prepare for it?"

Kübler-Ross (1974) explains that some people may not go through each of these stages, or they may do so in a different sequence. In developing her theory, she was not trying to convey the only way or the best way for people to accept death. Rather she described the typical response to impending death. Still, there has been much discussion during the past few decades regarding the process of death and dying, and much of this is undoubtedly due to Kübler-Ross's pioneering efforts in closely studying the process of dying in people who were terminally ill.

Check Your Learning Quiz 8.5

Go to **login.cengagebrain.com** and take the online quiz.

Think Critically

Challenge Your Thinking

Consider these questions when reading this article:

1. If researchers wanted to observe how children typically behave with parents and with peers, what type of research setting should they use?
2. Which parenting styles would be most likely and least likely to use physical punishment as a method to discipline children?
3. What is the name of the age-old question of which is more important—genetics or environment?
4. How would the evolutionary approach explain Harris's position that peers matter more than parents?
5. What type of learning describes the process of learning by observing peers?
6. What type of parent behavior would likely have a long-term effect on children's development?

Who Matters More—Parents or Peers?

Sigmund Freud argued that parents are to blame for the problems of children. In fact, people all around the world, many psychologists included, believe parents are responsible, at least in some way, for children's problems. But could this notion that seems like indisputable common sense be wrong?

Judith Harris, a researcher, argues that parents have minimal effect on their children's development, while peers have a much more influential role. Skeptical? Let's consider the changes in parenting styles over the years and the influence

they have had on children's behavior. There has been a decrease in the use of physical punishment, yet children are no less aggressive than in previous generations. Parents shower their children with more praise and affection than ever before, yet children's self-confidence, happiness, and overall mental health are no better for it. Could it be that Harris has a valid point?

Harris states that genetics is responsible for half of children's personality and peers are essentially responsible for the other half. Therefore, Harris is not

Unless otherwise noted, all images are © Cengage Learning

saying that environment plays no role in shaping a child's development, but rather that the environment that is important is the one outside of the home. She provides support for this position by presenting research on identical twins (genetically almost indistinguishable) raised together, which shows they are no more alike than identical twins reared apart. Also, how people behave at home with their parents does not predict how they behave with teachers or bosses, and how people behave with siblings does not predict how they interact with peers. Together, these findings suggest the home environment has little effect on behavior and personality development.

Research finds that children learn how to behave appropriately by observing their peers. If they simply imitated their parents' behaviors, their behavior would be considered quite odd. Children are motivated to be similar to their peers and at the same time to be better than them. They compare themselves to their peers to understand their strengths and weaknesses. By comparing their intellectual knowledge and ability with peers, children can judge how smart they really are. After all, children don't have to know more than their parents to be considered smart; they have to know more than their peers.

Harris acknowledges that how parents interact with their child affects the child's behavior at home, as well as how the child will regard the parents when he or she becomes an adult. However, she states that parents do not have a long-term effect on the type of person the child will become. Many researchers disagree with her. They cite studies showing that changes in the behavior of parents affect the behavior of children, even outside of the home. So, which is more important to a child's development—parents or peers? It's difficult to answer with certainty. It seems both may be just as important, but perhaps in different ways. (Adapted from J. R. Harris 1998, 2006, 2007, 2009a, 2009b; Saletan, 2006)

Think Critically 8.1

This article and its questions are available in interactive format online.

GO to your Psychology CourseMate at login.cengagebrain.com and take the Chapter Post-Test to see which Learning Objectives you've mastered and which need more review. Use the chapter review guide below and the online activities—including flashcards to review key terms—to measure your learning.

Measure ^Your Learning

Online Activities

Key Terms	Video	Animation	Reading	Assessment
nature-nurture question	Romanian Orphanages, p. 357			Check Your Learning Quiz 8.1
prenatal period, germinal stage, ovulation, conception (or fertilization), embryonic stage, fetal stage, placenta, teratogen, fetal alcohol syndrome (FAS)		Prenatal Period, p. 359		Check Your Learning Quiz 8.2
visual cliff, proximodistal, cephalocaudal, maturation, developmental norms, cognitive development, assimilation, accommodation, Piaget's cognitive stages, sensorimotor stage, object permanence, preoperational stage, conservation, egocentric thinking, concrete operations stage, emotional development, temperament, attachment, secure attachment, insecure attachment, social development, psychosexual stages, oral stage, anal stage, phallic stage, latency stage, psychosocial stages, social cognitive theory, vulnerability, resiliency, gender identity, gender roles, social role theory, cognitive developmental theory, gender schemas	Hearing and Faces, p. 363 Smell, p. 363 Taste, p. 363 Vision and Depth Perception, p. 363 Motor Development: Infancy, p. 365 Motor Development: Early Childhood, p. 365 Motor Development: Middle Childhood, p. 365 Piaget's Object Permanence, p. 367 Piaget's Preoperational Stage, p. 369 Piaget's Concrete Operational Stage, p. 369 Temperament, p. 371 Attachment, p. 371 Perceiving Gender Roles, p. 379	Piaget's Conservation, p. 369 Freud's Psychosexual versus Eriskon's Psychosocial Stages of Childhood, p. 375	Temperament, p. 371 Gender Roles, p. 379	Check Your Learning Quiz 8.3

Online Activities

Key Terms	Video	Animation	Reading	Assessment
adolescence, puberty, menarche, estrogen, female secondary sexual characteristics, testosterone, male secondary sexual characteristics, formal operations stage, preconventional level, conventional level, postconventional level, authoritarian parents, authoritative parents, permissive parents, personality and social development, personal identity or self-identity, self-esteem, genital stage	Piaget's Formal Operations Stage, p. 383 Risk Taking, p. 383	Kohlberg's Theory of Moral Reasoning, p. 385	Are Teens Too Young to Drive?, p. 383	Check Your Learning Quiz 8.4
normal aging, pathological aging, aging process, menopause, processing speed, perceptual speed, reaction time, passionate love, companionate love, triangular theory of love, passion, intimacy, commitment, schema	Adult Sex Life Changes, p. 381 Cognitive Models of Aging, p. 383 Cohabitation, p. 395		Preference for Partners, p. 395 Happy Marriages, p. 395	Check Your Learning Quiz 8.5

Motivation and Emotion

1 **GO** to your **Psychology CourseMate** at **login.cengagebrain.com** and take the **Chapter Pre-Test** to introduce yourself to this chapter's topics and see what you may already know.

2 **READ** the **Learning Objectives (LOs)** (in the left sidebars) and begin the chapter.

3 **COMPLETE** the **Online Activities** (in the right sidebars) *as you read each module*. Activities include **videos**, **animations**, **readings**, and **quizzes**.

4 **CHECK Your Learning** by going online to take the quiz at the end of each module and review material as necessary.

5 **MEASURE Your Learning** after reading the chapter by taking the online **Chapter Post-Test**. Use the chapter review guide at the end of the chapter as needed.

WATCH for these **Online Activities** icons as you read:

Video

Animation

Reading

Assessment

Think Critically

These online activities are important to mastering this chapter. As you read each module, access these materials by going to **login.cengagebrain.com**.

 Video Explore studies and firsthand accounts of biological and psychological processes:

- Learn how current research is helping to deal with the obesity epidemic
- Watch what it is like to have and overcome anorexia
- Learn more about one type of bulimia nervosa
- Learn about gender identity disorder
- Watch teens describe what it's like to come out as having a homosexual orientation
- Explore a homeless teen's need for achievement
- Watch how facial analysis may be used to improve lie detection
- Watch how emotional expressions vary across cultures

 Animation Interact with and visualize important processes and concepts:

- Distinguish the four components of emotion
- Observe how the James-Lange, facial feedback, and cognitive appraisal theories differ

 Reading Delve deeper into key content:

- Explore how the brain's reward/pleasure center, incentives, and cognitive factors explain why Erik climbs
- Learn the advantages and disadvantages of Maslow's hierarchy of needs
- Read about the role of peripheral and central cues in hunger
- Find out how metabolic rate can be increased
- Learn more about why dieting is so difficult

- Learn how Viagra is used to treat sexual problems
- Learn about the influence of external rewards on intrinsic motivation
- Explore why some people have more fears than others
- Learn how the perception of emotions varies across cultures

 Assessment Measure your mastery:

- Chapter Pre-Test
- Check Your Learning Quizzes
- Chapter Post-Test

 Think Critically Challenge your thinking by applying content from this chapter and making connections to related material:

- Why Do They Have to Learn to Smile?

▶ **LO1** Define motivation.

ONCE A MIDDLE-SCHOOL TEACHER and wrestling coach, Erik Weihenmayer (below) has become one of the most respected and well-known athletes in the world. In 2001, Erik climbed to the top of Mount Everest, the world's highest peak. In 2002, he stood on top of Mount Kosciusko, completing his 7-year journey to climb the Seven Summits, the highest mountain on each of the seven continents. During these adventures, he endured severe winds, –70°F weather, and countless life-threatening situations.

Erik's quests were far from over. In 2003, he joined some of the world's best athletes to compete in the Primal Quest, the toughest multisport adventure race in the world, taking place over 10 days across 457 miles of high elevation in the Sierra Nevadas. It involves intense kayaking, mountain biking, caving, whitewater rafting, and trekking. Averaging only 2 hours of sleep a night, Erik and his team became one of only about half of the teams to cross the finish line.

Erik accomplished these amazing feats while facing another major challenge: blindness. He is the only blind person in history to reach the summit of the world's highest peak, Mount Everest, and one of the youngest to climb the Seven Summits. Erik never allows his blindness to interfere with his pur-

Unless otherwise noted, all images are © Cengage Learning

© Didrik Johnck/Corbis

suit of adventure and life fulfillment. For instance, his blindness is accompanied by increased eye pressure, which is exacerbated in high elevations. Erik described this pressure when he reached 19,000 feet during one of his climbs by saying, "It felt like someone stabbed me in the eye with a fork" (Weihenmayer, 1999). Yet, he continued to the top of the peak (adapted from *Everest News,* 1999; Touchthetop, 2009).

Reporters who question Erik about why he risks his life to climb and pursue dangerous adventures are really asking about his motivation.

Motivation refers to the various physiological and psychological factors that cause us to act in a specific way at a particular time.

We'll discuss various motivating factors, including those involved in hunger, sexual behavior, achievement, and, of course, mountain climbing.

© Melinda Fawver/Shutterstock

Check Your Learning Quiz 9.1

Go to **login.cengagebrain.com** and take the online quiz.

Unless otherwise noted, all images are © Cengage Learning

▸ **LO2** Describe and differentiate the different theories of motivation.

Theories of Motivation

Many people who watch or hear about Erik engaging in his many dangerous climbs or other adventures ask: Why is he doing that? This question is about motivation. We'll discuss four general theories of motivation.

Instinct

In the early 1900s, William McDougall (1908) claimed that humans were motivated by a variety of instincts.

Instincts are innate tendencies or biological forces that determine behavior.

McDougall listed about half a dozen instincts, such as combat, curiosity, sympathy, and self-assertion. He might have explained Erik's motivation to climb as arising from instincts involving curiosity and self-assertion. But attributing mountain climbing to an instinct is more like labeling than explaining the underlying motivation. At one point, psychologists had proposed over 6,000 instincts to explain every kind of human motivation.

Instincts represented an early but failed attempt to explain human motivation. We'll jump from the early 1900s to the early 2000s and examine current research that sheds a new light on human motivation.

Brain: Reward/Pleasure Center

During his climbs up to each of the Seven Summits, Erik was motivated to satisfy various biological needs, such as eating and drinking. The human body is set up genetically to send biological signals to the brain, which is genetically wired to interpret the body's biological signals and thus motivate the person to eat or drink by causing feelings of hunger or thirst (Kalat, 2009).

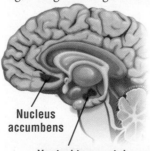

Nucleus accumbens

Ventral tegmental area

One reason you are motivated to eat is that chewing food can be so pleasurable. This "eating" pleasure comes from the brain's reward/pleasure center (Dackis & O'Brien, 2001; Dallman et al., 2005).

The **reward/pleasure center** includes several areas of the brain, such as the nucleus accumbens and the ventral tegmental area, and involves several neurotransmitters, especially dopamine. These components make up a neural circuit that produces rewarding and pleasurable feelings.

Incentives

The issue of motivation becomes personal when we ask you to explain why you worked so hard to get into college. Now that you're in college, what is motivating you to study for exams and write papers? One answer is you are motivated to get a college degree because it is a big incentive (Fiske, 2008; Petri & Govern, 2004).

Incentives are goals that can be either objects or thoughts that we learn to value and that we are motivated to obtain.

Incentives have two common features. First, they can be either thoughts ("I want to get a degree") or objects (such as money or clothes) that we learn to value. For example, when you were 5 years old, you had not yet learned the value of a good education. Second, the value of incentives can change over time. A pizza is not an incentive at 7 A.M., but it may be an incentive at 7 P.M. Many of our behaviors are motivated by a variety of incentives, including grades, praise, money, or clothes. You can think of incentives as pulling us or motivating us to obtain them.

Cognitive Factors

Thousands of people train for months to run grueling 26-mile-long marathons, in which only the top two or three receive any prize money and the rest receive only T-shirts. What motivates people to endure such agony? The answer can be traced back to when psychologists began applying cognitive concepts to explain human motivation (Bandura, 1986; Deci & Ryan, 1985; Fiske, 2008; Weiner, 1991). These cognitive researchers said that one reason people run marathons, usually for no reward other than a T-shirt, has to do with the difference between extrinsic and intrinsic motivation.

Extrinsic motivation involves engaging in certain activities or behaviors that either reduce biological needs or help us obtain incentives or external rewards.

Intrinsic motivation involves engaging in certain activities or behaviors because the behaviors themselves are personally rewarding or because engaging in these activities fulfills our beliefs or expectations.

Intrinsic motivation explains that people volunteer their services, spend hours on hobbies, or run marathons, because these activities are personally rewarding or challenging. Intrinsic motivation emphasizes that we are motivated to engage in many behaviors because of our own personal beliefs, expectations, or goals, rather than external incentives (Linnenbrink-Garcia & Fredricks, 2008).

Erik Weihenmayer's Motivation

Explore how the brain's reward/pleasure center, incentives, and cognitive factors explain why Erik climbs.

▶ **LO3** Describe biological and social needs, as well as Maslow's hierarchy of needs.

Needs

We have a variety of needs we wish to satisfy. We'll discuss some of the more common biological and social needs.

Biological Needs

It's rather obvious that the man in the photo at right is about to satisfy his hunger, a basic biological need.

Biological needs are physiological requirements that are critical to our survival and physical well-being.

Researchers have identified about a dozen biological needs, such as the needs for food, water, sex, oxygen, sleep, and pain avoidance, all of which help to keep our bodies functioning at their best and thus help us survive (Petri & Govern, 2004).

Social Needs

One reason that most adults in the United States get married is that being married satisfies a number of social needs.

Social needs are needs that are acquired through learning and experience.

Depending on your learning and experiences, you may acquire dozens of social needs, such as the needs for achievement, forming social bonds, fun, relaxation, independence, and nurturance (Petri & Govern, 2004). In some cases, the distinction between biological and social needs is blurred. For example, we may engage in sex for reproduction, which is a biological need, or to express love and affection, which is a social need.

Maslow's Hierarchy of Needs

If you were very hungry and very lonely at the same time, which need would you satisfy first, your biological need (hunger) or your social need (affiliation)? One answer to this question can be found in Maslow's (1970) hierarchy of needs,

Maslow's hierarchy of needs is an ascending order, or hierarchy, in which biological needs are placed at the bottom and social needs at the top.

Maslow's hierarchy of needs is represented by a pyramid. Please go to the bottom of the pyramid (below) and begin reading at Level 1. Then continue reading Levels 2, 3, 4, and 5, which takes you up the pyramid.

Level 5 Self-Actualization: Fulfillment of One's Unique Potential
According to Maslow, the highest need is self-actualization, which involves developing and reaching our full potential as unique human beings. However, Maslow cautioned that very few individuals reach the level of self-actualization because it is so difficult and challenging.

Level 4 Esteem Needs: Achievement, Competency, Approval, and Recognition
During early and middle adulthood, people are especially concerned with achieving their goals and establishing their careers. As we develop skills to gain personal achievement and social recognition, we turn our energies to Level 5.

Level 3 Love and Belonging Needs: Affiliation with Others and Acceptance by Others
Adolescents and young adults, who are beginning to form serious relationships, would be especially interested in fulfilling their needs for love and belonging. After we find love and affection, we advance to Level 4.

Level 2 Safety Needs: Protection from Harm
People who live in high-crime or dangerous areas would be very concerned about satisfying their safety needs. After we find a way to live in a safe environment, we advance to Level 3.

Level 1 Physiological Needs: Food, Water, Sex, and Sleep
People who are homeless or jobless would be especially concerned with satisfying their physiological needs above all other needs. We must satisfy these basic needs before we advance to Level 2.

Maslow's Hierarchy of Needs

Learn the advantages and disadvantages of Maslow's hierarchy of needs.

Check Your Learning Quiz 9.2

Go to **login.cengagebrain.com** and take the online quiz.

▸ **LO4** Define optimal weight.

▸ **LO5** Define overweight and obesity, and identify their primary causes and some of their associated medical problems.

▸ **LO6** Discuss the three hunger factors: biological, psychosocial, and genetic.

At first glance, the issue of hunger may seem rather straightforward. When we haven't eaten, we look for food, eat, and feel full and content. However, there are various factors that influence our eating behavior. We'll begin by discussing optimal, or ideal, weight and overweight.

Optimal Weight

The reason you never see fat wolves is that they, like all animals, have an inherited biological system that carefully regulates their eating so that they maintain their optimal, or ideal, weights (Kolata, 2000b).

Optimal or **ideal weight** results from an almost perfect balance between how much food an organism eats and how much it needs to meet its body's energy needs.

In the wild, animals usually eat only to replace fuel used by their bodies, and thus they rarely get fat. In addition, most wild animals use up a tremendous amount of energy in finding food. In comparison, home pets may become fat because their owners give them too much food or food so tasty their pets eat too much. And unlike wild animals, pets may have few opportunities to run around and burn off the extra food. The same factors that make pets overweight also make humans overweight.

Overweight

Like animals, humans have an inherited biological system that regulates hunger to keep us at our ideal weights. However, there is currently a worldwide problem of overweight and obesity.

Overweight means a person is 20% over the ideal body weight.

Obesity means a person is 30% or more above the ideal body weight.

Overweight and obesity are primarily caused by two factors: eating more than is required to fuel the body's energy needs and not getting enough exercise to burn off surplus calories (CDC, 2006c). Being overweight or obese increases their risk for heart disease, stroke, high blood pressure, clogged arteries, and adult-onset diabetes (Healy, 2006; Hsu, 2006; Whitlock et al., 2009). However, solving the problem of being overweight or obese is complicated because eating is influenced by three hunger factors.

9.3

Three Hunger Factors

The way in which you satisfy your hunger drive—when, where, and how much you eat—is influenced by three different factors: biological, psychosocial, and genetic (Hill et al., 2003).

Biological hunger factors come from physiological changes in blood chemistry and signals from digestive organs that provide feedback to the brain, which, in turn, triggers us to eat or stop eating.

If your eating were regulated primarily by biological factors, as in most animals, you would keep your weight at optimal levels. The fact that 67% of U.S. adults are overweight or obese and that some individuals suffer from serious eating problems indicate the influence of both genetic and psychosocial hunger factors.

© Jose Luis Pelaez/Getty Images

Genetic hunger factors come from inherited instructions found in our genes. These instructions determine the number of fat cells or metabolic rates of burning off the body's fuel, which push us toward being normal, overweight, or underweight.

Psychosocial hunger factors come from learned associations between food and other stimuli (such as snacking while watching television); sociocultural influences (such as pressures to be thin); and personality problems (such as low self-esteem).

These three hunger factors interact to influence your weight. For example, because of psychosocial factors, some of us eat when we should not, such as during stress. Because of biological factors, some of us may respond too much or too little to feedback from our digestive organs. Because of genetic factors, some of us can eat more calories and still maintain optimal weight.

Biological Hunger Factors

As discussed above, our eating is partly regulated by biological hunger factors, which come from peripheral and central cues (Woods et al., 2000).

Peripheral cues come from changes in blood chemistry or signals from digestive organs, which secrete various hormones.

Central cues result from activity in different brain areas, which in turn results in increasing or decreasing appetite.

We discuss peripheral and central cues next.

Weight Control

Learn how current research is helping to deal with the obesity epidemic.

Unless otherwise noted, all images are © Cengage Learning

Peripheral Cues

Signals for feeling hungry or full come from a number of body organs that are involved in digestion and regulation of blood sugar (glucose) levels, which is the primary source of fuel for the body and brain.

1 When empty, the **stomach** secretes a hormone, ghrelin, which carries "hunger signals" to the brain's hypothalamus, the master control for hunger regulation (Raloff, 2005). When the stomach is full, stretch receptors in its walls send "full signals" to the brain's hypothalamus, which decreases appetite (Chaudri et al., 2006; Kluger, 2007).

2 The **liver** monitors the level of glucose in the blood. When the level of glucose falls, the liver sends "hunger signals" to the brain's hypothalamus; when the level of glucose rises, the liver sends "full signals" to the hypothalamus (Woods et al., 2000).

3 The **intestines** also secrete ghrelin, which carries "hunger signals" to the hypothalamus, increasing appetite. The intestines also secrete another hormone called PYY, which carries "full signals" to the hypothalamus, decreasing appetite (Raloff, 2005). Finally, the intestines secrete a hormone called CCK (cholecystokinin), which signals the hypothalamus to inhibit eating (Kluger, 2007).

4 **Fat cells** secrete a hormone called leptin, which acts on the brain's hypothalamus. If levels of leptin are falling, the hypothalamus increases appetite; if levels are rising, the hypothalamus decreases appetite. The secretion of leptin helps maintain a constant level of body fat and defend against starving the body to death (Rui, 2005).

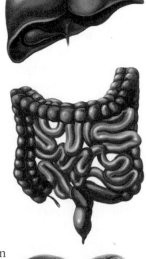

Unless otherwise noted, all images are © Cengage Learning

Central Cues

1 The brain has an area with different groups of cells that are collectively called the **hypothalamus.** Each group of cells is involved in a different kind of motivation, including regulation of thirst, sexual behavior, sleep, intensity of emotional reactions, and hunger. We'll focus on two groups of cells, the lateral and ventromedial hypothalamus, which affect hunger in opposite ways, either increasing or decreasing appetite.

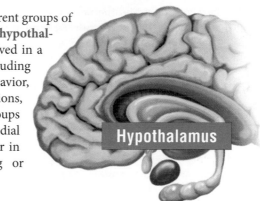

Hypothalamus

2 The **lateral hypothalamus** refers to a group of brain cells that receives "hunger signals" from digestive organs: increase in ghrelin, fall in level of blood glucose, and fall in levels of leptin. The lateral hypothalamus interprets these "hunger signals" and increases the appetite (Kluger, 2007; Woods et al., 2000).

For example, electrical stimulation of the lateral hypothalamus causes rats to start eating, while destruction of the lateral hypothalamus causes rats to stop eating and even starve without special feeding.

3 The **ventromedial hypothalamus** refers to a group of brain cells that receives "full signals" from digestive organs. A full stomach activates stretch receptors, rise in level of blood glucose, rise in levels of leptin, and increase in the hormones PYY and CCK. The ventromedial hypothalamus interprets these "full signals" and decreases appetite (Kluger, 2007).

For example, stimulation of the ventromedial hypothalamus causes rats to stop eating, while destruction of the ventromedial hypothalamus causes rats to overeat.

Next, we'll examine genetic hunger factors.

Biological Hunger Factors

Explore the role of peripheral and central cues in hunger.

Genetic Hunger Factors

Researchers generally find that identical twins (right photo), even when separated soon after birth and reared in adopted families, are much more alike in weight than fraternal twins reared apart (Bouchard et al., 1990). This similarity in weight is due to genetic hunger factors.

Genetic hunger factors come from inherited instructions found in our genes. These instructions determine the number of fat cells or metabolic rates of burning off the body's fuel, which push us toward being normal, overweight, or underweight.

On the basis of twin studies, researchers concluded that inherited factors contribute 70% to 80% to the maintenance of a particular body size and weight, while environmental factors contribute the other 20% to 30% (Bulik et al., 2003). The finding that genetic hunger factors contribute 70% to 80% to having a certain body size and weight explains why identical twins have similar body types. The finding that environmental factors contribute 20% to 30% to body size explains why one twin may weigh a little more or less than the other.

Research shows that people who have a commonly found variation of a gene are at an increased risk of becoming obese. Scientists now believe there may be as many as 100 different fat genes and are working to identify them (Bouchard, 2009; Christman, 2006).

So far, psychologists have identified four genetic hunger factors.

1 We inherit different numbers of fat cells.

Fat cells, whose number is primarily determined by heredity, do not normally multiply except when people become obese. Fat cells shrink if we are giving up fat and losing weight (left) and greatly enlarge if we are storing fat and gaining weight (right) (Fried, 2008; Spalding et al., 2008).

People who inherit a larger number of fat cells have the ability to store more fat and are more likely to be fatter than average.

2 We inherit different rates of metabolism.

Metabolic rate refers to how efficiently our bodies break food down into energy and how quickly our bodies burn off that fuel.

For example, if you had a low metabolic rate, you would burn less fuel, be more likely to store excess fuel as fat, and thus might have a fatter body. In comparison, if you had a high metabolic rate, you would burn off more fuel, be less likely to store fat, and thus might have a thinner body. This means that people can consume the same number of calories but, because of different metabolic rates, either maintain, lose, or gain weight.

3 We inherit a set point to maintain a certain amount of body fat.

The **set point** refers to a certain level of body fat (adipose tissue) that our bodies strive to maintain constant throughout our lives.

For example, a person whose body has a higher set point will try to maintain a higher level of fat stores and thus have a fatter body. In comparison, a person whose body has a lower set point will maintain a lower level of fat stores and thus have a thinner body (Woods et al., 2000).

4 We also inherit weight-regulating genes.

Weight-regulating genes play a role in influencing appetite, body metabolism, and secretion of hormones that regulate fat stores, such as leptin.

For example, in the photo at right, the mouse on the left has a gene that increases a brain chemical (neuropeptide Y) which increases eating, so it weighs three times as much as the normal-weight mouse on the right (Gura, 1997). In total, researchers have found 11 genetic mutations that can disrupt appetite regulation, leading someone to continue to eat without feeling full (Kluger, 2007).

Courtesy of Jeffrey M. Friedman, Rockefeller University

You have seen how genetic hunger factors are involved in the regulation of body fat and weight. But genes alone cannot explain our obesity epidemic (Gillman, 2007). Next, we'll explore several psychological factors involved in the regulation of eating and weight.

Metabolic Rate

Learn how metabolic rate can be increased.

Psychosocial Hunger Factors

Many of us have a weakness for certain foods, and mine (H.K.) is for desserts. Even though my biological and genetic hunger factors may tell my brain when to start and stop eating, I can use my large forebrain to override my innately programmed biological and genetic factors. My forebrain allows me to rationalize that one dessert can do no harm. This kind of rationalizing comes under the heading of psychosocial hunger factors.

Psychosocial hunger factors come from learned associations between food and other stimuli, such as snacking while watching television; sociocultural influences, such as pressures to be thin; and personality problems, such as low self-esteem.

Psychosocial hunger factors can have an enormous effect on our eating habits and weight and contribute to many problems associated with eating, such as becoming overweight, eating when stressed or depressed, and bingeing (Ward et al., 2000). We'll discuss three psychosocial hunger factors: learned associations, social-cultural influences, and personality traits.

Learned Associations

The best examples of how learned associations influence eating are when we eat not because we're hungry but because it's "lunchtime," because foods smell good, because our friends are eating, or because we can't resist on supersizing, even though we don't need it at all.

Americans often rely on external cues to stop eating, such as the end of a TV program or getting to the bottom of a soda, which, combined with a preference for large portions and tasty junk foods high in calories, has led to a rising rate of overweight and obesity in both children and adults (Hellmich, 2005; Rozin et al., 2003; Wansink et al., 2007).

Another learned association that influences eating is that we eat more when we experience stress (Macht, 2007). For instance, 76% of female and 33% of male college students report eating more when they feel stress, and unfortunately for them, college usually involves plenty of stress (Hellmich, 2008)!

Health professionals advise us to unlearn many of our learned food associations. We should eat only when hungry and eat smaller portions and healthier foods (Pi-Sunyer, 2003; Story et al., 2008).

Social-Cultural Influences

Here are examples of how social-cultural influences affect body weight.

Czech Republic In the 1970s, the Czech Republic government subsidized cheap fatty sausage and dairy products. The result was that 45% of Czech women and a smaller percentage of men are obese. The government instituted programs to encourage healthier eating habits, which were effective until fast-food restaurants opened all over the country (Elliott, 1995; Jarrett, 2006).

China In parts of China, fatty fast foods have become very popular along with a more sedentary lifestyle. This has resulted in an increase in obesity rates over the last 15 years: from 12.8% in 1991 to 29% in 2006 (CDC, 2008e). In addition, there has been an alarming increase in obesity among children, who are pampered by a culture that prizes well-nourished children as indicating affluence and well-being (Mydans, 2003).

United States In the United States, there are many cultural pressures on females, in particular, to be thin. For example, the mass media advertise that the ideal female is one with a slender body (think size 0 models). As a result, many American females report being dissatisfied with their weight and see themselves as overweight even when they are not. Some also develop an eating disorder (see pp. 422–423) as a result (Mayo Clinic, 2006a).

Personality & Mood Factors

If a person has certain personality traits, he or she may be at greater risk for overeating, as well as developing serious eating disorders. The particular personality traits that have been associated with eating problems include heightened sensitivity to rejection, excessive concern with approval from others, high personal standards for achievement, and the need to have control (over oneself or one's body) (Polivy & Herman, 2002). Someone with these kinds of personality traits may find it very difficult and sometimes almost impossible to control his or her eating (Brody, 2003).

Mood factors, such as stress, anxiety, and depression, can lead to bursts of overeating or indulgence in sweet and unhealthy foods. Overeating when under emotional strain occurs in otherwise healthy people (Macht, 2007).

Dieting

Learn more about why dieting is so difficult.

© Guang Nu/Reuters Newmedia, Inc./Corbis

▶ **L07** Describe anorexia nervosa and bulimia nervosa and explain their possible causes and treatment options.

Eating Disorders

We'll discuss two serious eating disorders, anorexia nervosa and bulimia nervosa, their causes and treatments.

Anorexia Nervosa

Miss America 2008, Kirsten Haglund (right photo), developed anorexia nervosa at age 15. The lack of nutrition caused her collarbones to stick out, and her energy was so depleted that she felt exhausted after walking up only a few stairs (Haglund, 2008). Kirsten has overcome her eating disorder and helps those struggling with anorexia nervosa *(an-uh-REX-see-ah ner-VOH-sah)* (Haglund, 2008; Wilkins, 2009).

© Steve Marcus/Reuters

Anorexia nervosa is a serious eating disorder characterized by refusing to eat and not maintaining weight at 85% of what is expected, having an intense fear of gaining weight or becoming fat, and missing at least three consecutive menstrual cycles. Anorexics also have a disturbed body image: They see themselves as fat even though they are very thin (APA, 2000).

Risk Factors

One risk factor is having parents who set excessively high standards that cannot possibly be achieved (Eggers & Liebers, 2007). Another risk involves personality factors, such as being very anxious, rigid, and a perfectionist (Gura, 2008a). Lastly, brain areas that normally respond to the pleasurable, rewarding aspects of eating do not work in people with anorexia (Kaye, 2008).

Treatment

Well-established psychological treatments for anorexics have had limited success, and drugs have not been too useful (McIntosh et al., 2005; Walsh et al., 2006). A relatively new treatment program has reported success using a form of family therapy. (Tyre, 2005). Generally, recovery is difficult: About 30% make a full recovery; about 35% regain some weight but maintain a poor body image; about 25% have chronic, recurrent symptoms; and about 5% die from starvation or suicide (Eggers & Liebers, 2007).

Bulimia Nervosa

Carol's life seemed perfect when she was growing up, but all the time something was terribly wrong. "It was like I had to live in this fantasy world where everything was sweet and good and I got straight A's," Carol explains. "I started work when I was really young and everyone thought I was so nice and sweet. And I was just dying inside, literally." Carol, who began binge eating at the age of 15, was not overweight to

begin with. She would eat a huge amount of food in one brief period and then force herself to vomit as a way of avoiding any weight gain (adapted from *The Daily Aztec,* March 22, 1984). Carol's disorder is called bulimia nervosa *(boo-LEE-me-ah ner-VOH-sah).*

Bulimia nervosa is characterized by a minimum of two binge-eating episodes per week for at least three months; fear of not being able to stop eating; regularly engaging in vomiting, use of laxatives, or rigorous dieting and fasting; and excessive concern about body shape and weight (APA, 2000).

Risk Factors

One risk factor involves cultural pressures to develop a slim body, as seen among the Fijian girls discussed earlier. Another risk factor involves personality characteristics, such as being excessively concerned about appearance, being too sensitive, and having low self-esteem and high personal standards for achievement. For some, bouts of depression, anxiety, mood swings, and problems with social relationships may trigger episodes of bulimia nervosa (Stice, 2002).

Treatment

The psychological treatment for bulimia nervosa may involve ways to control weight, as well as one of two kinds of psychotherapy: cognitive-behavioral therapy, which focuses on substituting positive thoughts for negative ones, or interpersonal therapy, which focuses on improving a person's social functioning (Cooper & Shafran, 2008; Hilbert et al., 2007; Wilson et al., 2002). Drug treatment for bulimia nervosa is less effective than psychotherapy (Mitchell et al., 2007). Generally, about 50% of bulimics recover fully (Eggers & Liebers, 2007).

Anorexia

Watch what it is like to have and overcome anorexia.

Exercise Bulimia

Learn more about one type of bulimia nervosa.

Check Your Learning Quiz 9.3

Go to **login.cengagebrain.com** and take the online quiz.

▸ **LO8** Discuss the three sex factors: genetic, biological, and psychological.

Sex Factors

Although we don't look, sound, or behave the same as lions do, we share similar biological and genetic factors that regulate sexual behavior. The sexual behavior of lions and most animals is controlled chiefly by genetic and biological factors, which means that most animals engage in sex primarily for reproduction.

Genetic sex factors include inherited instructions for the development of sexual organs, the secretion of sex hormones, and the wiring of the neural circuits that control sexual reflexes.

Biological sex factors include the action of sex hormones, which are involved in secondary sexual characteristics (such as facial hair, breasts), sexual motivation (more so in animals than in humans), and the development of ova and sperm.

Lions, like most animals, generally avoid sexual interactions unless the female is in heat, which means she is ovulating and can be impregnated. In comparison, humans engage in sexual behavior for many reasons, which points to psychological sex factors.

Psychological sex factors play a role in developing sexual or gender identity, gender role, and sexual orientation. In addition, psychological factors can result in difficulties in the performance or enjoyment of sexual activities.

For example, otherwise healthy men and women may report difficulties in sexual activities arising from stress, anxiety, or guilt, which can interfere with the functioning of genetic and biological sex factors.

As we did for the hunger drive, we'll discuss, in order, the influences of genetic, biological, and psychological factors on sexual behavior.

Genetic Influences on Sexual Behavior

How we develop a particular sex organ, male or female, is determined primarily by a genetic program that is contained in a single human cell about the size of a grain of sand (Faller et al., 2004).

Sex Chromosome

Unlike the other cells of our body, which contain 46 chromosomes (23 pairs), the sperm and egg each contain half that number and are called sex chromosomes.

The **sex chromosome,** which is in the sperm or the egg, contains 23 chromosomes, which in turn have genes that contain instructions for determining the sex of the child.

As we discussed earlier (p. 54), each chromosome is made up of a long strand of DNA (deoxyribonucleic acid). On this long strand of DNA are hundreds of genes, which contain the chemically coded instructions for the development and maintenance of our bodies. Some sperm have an **X** chromosome and some have a **Y;** these contain different genetic instructions and, as you'll see, result in the development of different sex organs (such as penis or vagina).

Egg with X chromosome

1 The human egg contains one of the sex chromosomes, which is always an **X** chromosome. Thus, each human egg has a single **X** chromosome.

2 A human sperm also contains one of the sex chromosomes. However, the sperm's chromosome can be either an **X** chromosome, which has instructions for development of *female sex organs* and body, or a **Y** chromosome, which has instructions for male sex organs and body. Thus, the sperm (**X** or **Y**) determines the sex of the infant.

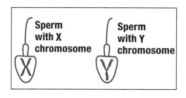

Sperm with X chromosome Sperm with Y chromosome

3 During fertilization, a single sperm penetrates an egg and results in a fertilized egg with 23 pairs of chromosomes. If the last pair has the combination **XY,** it means the egg contains the genetic instructions for developing a male's sex organs (top right figure). If the last pair has the combination **XX,** it means the egg contains the genetic instructions for developing a female's sex organs (below right).

Following fertilization, the human cell, which is called a zygote, will divide over and over many thousands of times during the following weeks and months and eventually develop into a female body with female sex organs or a male body with male sex organs.

Male instructions
XY

Female instructions
XX

▶ **LO9** Describe gender identity and gender roles.

Biological Influences on Sexual Behavior

You have seen how genetic sex factors influence the development of the body's sex organs. The next big event to affect a person's sex organs and sexual motivation occurs at puberty as a result of biological sex factors.

Sex hormones secreted during puberty both directly and indirectly affect our bodies, brains, minds, personalities, self-concepts, and mental health. We'll focus on how sex hormones affect our bodies.

Sex Hormones

Before and shortly after birth, sex hormones are released in our bodies.

Sex hormones, which are chemicals secreted by glands, circulate in the bloodstream to influence the brain, body organs, and behaviors. The major male sex hormones secreted by the testes are **androgens,** such as testosterone; the major female sex hormones secreted by the ovaries are **estrogens.**

Sex hormones remain inactive until puberty, when a recently discovered hormone called kisspeptin stimulates the production of androgens and estrogens to prepare the body for reproduction (Roa et al., 2008).

Male–Female Differences

The presence or absence of testosterone in the womb causes different neural programming so that the male hypothalamus functions differently from the female hypothalamus.

The **male hypothalamus** triggers a continuous release of androgens, such as testosterone, from the testes. The increased level of androgens causes the development of male secondary sexual characteristics, such as facial and pubic hair, muscle growth, and lowered voice.

Testosterone

The **female hypothalamus** triggers a cyclical release of estrogens from the ovaries. The increased level of estrogens causes the development of female secondary sexual characteristics, such as pubic hair, breast development, and widening of the hips. The cyclical release of hormones (such as estrogen and progesterone) also regulates the menstrual cycle.

As genetic and biological factors guide our bodies toward physical sexual maturity, numerous psychological factors prepare our minds for psychological sexual maturity. Next, we'll examine these psychological sex factors.

Estrogen

Psychological Influences on Sexual Behavior

Two major psychological sex factors are gender identity and gender roles.

Gender Identity

Between the ages of 2 and 3, a child can correctly answer the question "Are you a boy or a girl?" The correct answer indicates that the child has already acquired the beginnings of a gender identity (Blakemore, 2003).

Gender identity, which was formerly called sexual identity, refers to the individual's subjective experience and feelings of being either a male or a female.

The doctor's words, "It's a girl" or "It's a boy," set in motion the process for acquiring a gender identity. From that point on, parents, siblings, grandparents, and others behave toward male and female infants differently, so that they learn and acquire their proper gender identity (Martin et al., 2002). For example, the girl in the right photo is checking out a dress in the mirror, a behavior that she has observed her mother doing and that she is now imitating.

Gender Roles

By the age of 5, children have acquired many of the complex thoughts, expectations, and behaviors that accompany their particular gender role of male or female (Best & Thomas, 2004).

Gender roles, which were formerly called sex roles, refer to the traditional or stereotypical behaviors, attitudes, and personality traits that society designates as masculine or feminine. Gender roles greatly influence how we think and behave.

For example, young boys learn stereotypical male behaviors (right photo), such as playing sports, competing in games, engaging in rough-and-tumble play, and acquiring status in his group. In comparison, girls learn stereotypical female behaviors, such as providing and seeking emotional support, emphasizing physical appearance and clothes, and learning to cooperate and share personal experiences (Ruble et al., 2006; Rudman & Glick, 2008).

After acquiring a gender role, the next step is knowing one's sexual orientation.

Gender Identity Disorder

Learn more about gender identity disorder.

▶ **LO10** Define sexual orientation and describe the types of sexual orientation.

▶ **LO11** Discuss research findings on the causes of sexual orientation.

▶ **LO12** Describe the four-stage model of sexual response.

Sexual Orientation

In answering the question "Do you find males or females sexually arousing?" you are expressing your sexual orientation.

Sexual orientation, also called sexual preference, refers to whether a person is sexually aroused primarily by members of his or her own sex, the opposite sex, or both sexes.

Homosexual orientation refers to a pattern of sexual arousal by persons of the same sex.

Heterosexual orientation refers to a pattern of sexual arousal by persons of the opposite sex.

Bisexual orientation refers to a pattern of sexual arousal by persons of both sexes.

A recent national survey of sexual orientation found that the vast majority (90%) of the American population reported having a heterosexual orientation, 2% a homosexual orientation, 2% a bisexual orientation, and the remaining 6% declined to identify their sexual orientation (Mosher et al., 2005).

Of several models that explain how we develop a particular sexual orientation, the interactive model is perhaps the most popular (Money, 1987; Zucker, 1990).

The **interactive model of sexual orientation** says that genetic and biological factors, such as genetic instructions and prenatal hormones, interact with psychological factors, such as the individual's attitudes, personality traits, and behaviors, to influence the development of sexual orientation.

Genetic and Biological Factors

There is debate over how much genetic and biological factors influence sexual orientation. Some researchers prefer the term *sexual preference* because it suggests that we have considerable freedom in choosing a sexual orientation and that genetic and biological factors do not play a major role (Baumrind, 1995; Byne, 1997). Other researchers prefer the term *sexual orientation* because they believe genetic and biological factors play a major role (Diamond & Sigmundson, 1997).

Sexual Response, Problems, and Treatments

Various surveys report that 10% to 52% of men and 25% to 63% of women aged 18 to 59, married and unmarried, experience sexual problems (Heiman, 2002). Some seek help for their problem, while others are ashamed or embarrassed and suffer in silence. When a person seeks help for a sexual problem, the clinician will check whether the causes are organic or psychological.

Organic factors refer to medical conditions or drug or medication problems that lead to sexual difficulties.

For example, certain medical conditions (such as diabetes), medications (such as antidepressants), and drugs (such as alcohol) can interfere with sexual functioning.

Psychological factors refer to performance anxiety, sexual trauma, guilt, and failure to communicate, all of which may lead to sexual problems.

Four-Stage Model of Sexual Response

To understand how psychological factors cause sexual problems, it helps to know Masters and Johnson's (1966) four-stage model of sexual response:

1st Stage: Excitement The body becomes physiologically and sexually aroused, resulting in erection in the male and vaginal lubrication in the female.

2nd Stage: Plateau Sexual and physiological arousal continues in males and females.

3rd Stage: Orgasm Men have rhythmic muscle contractions that cause ejaculation of sperm. Women experience similar rhythmic muscle contractions of the pelvic area. During orgasm, women and men report very pleasurable feelings.

4th Stage: Resolution Physiological responses return to normal.

There were few successful treatments for sexual problems until Masters and Johnson (1970) published their treatment program. First, the therapist provides information about the sexual response and helps the couple communicate their feelings. Then the therapist gives the couple "homework," which is designed to reduce performance anxiety. Homework involves learning to pleasure one's partner without genital touching or making sexual demands. This nongenital pleasuring is called *sensate focus*. After using sensate focus, the couple moves on to genital touching and intercourse.

Gay Teens

Watch teens describe what it's like to come out as having a homosexual orientation.

Viagra

Learn how Viagra is used to treat sexual problems.

Check Your Learning Quiz 9.4

Go to **login.cengagebrain.com** and take the online quiz.

▶ **LO13** Explain the difference between high achievers and underachievers.

Need for Achievement

Victor remembers being in the seventh grade when some of his black buddies called him a "white boy" because they thought he was studying too hard. "You can't be cool if you're smart," says Victor, who was Mission Bay High's student body president, had a 3.7 (A–) grade point average, and planned to attend the University of Southern California in the fall (adapted from the *San Diego Union-Tribune,* June 17, 1994).

It doesn't look cool if you work hard for grades.

Victor didn't allow the negative peer pressure to hold him back. For Victor, academic achievement was one of his many social needs.

Social needs, such as the desire for affiliation or close social bonds; nurturance or need to help and protect others; dominance or need to influence or control others; and achievement or need to excel, are acquired through learning and experience.

If you are working hard to achieve academic success, you are demonstrating your social need for achievement.

The **achievement need** refers to the desire to set challenging goals and to persist in pursuing those goals in the face of obstacles, frustrations, and setbacks.

We'll discuss three questions related to the achievement need: What is high need for achievement? What is fear of failure? What is underachievement?

What Is High Need for Achievement?

There is perhaps no better example of individuals with high need for achievement than Olympic athletes. One example is Michael Phelps, who has won 16 Olympic medals, including 8 gold medals in 2008 (the individual record for the most gold medals at a single Olympics). He trains for at least 5 hours a day, 6 days a week, to be the best swimmer he can be. Michael has all

the traits of someone with a high need for achievement (Atkinson & Raynor, 1974; McClelland, 1985).

High need for achievement is shown by those who persist longer at tasks; perform better on tasks, activities, or exams; set challenging but realistic goals; compete with others to win; and are attracted to careers that require initiative.

Although the vast majority of us will not make the Olympics, most of us will show varying degrees of the need to achieve by doing our best, striving for social recognition, and working to achieve material rewards (Hareli & Weiner, 2002).

What Is Fear of Failure?

Just as some individuals may be motivated by a high need for achievement, others may be motivated by a fear of failure (Atkinson, 1964).

Fear of failure is shown by people who are motivated to avoid failure by choosing easy, nonchallenging tasks where failure is unlikely to occur.

For example, fear of failure may motivate a student to study just enough to avoid failing an exam but not enough to get a good grade. In fact, the greater a student's fear of failure, the poorer his or her grades (Herman, 1990). Atkinson (1964) said that individuals who are motivated primarily by a fear of failure will never do as well, work as hard, or set goals as high as those who are motivated by a need for achievement.

What Is Underachievement?

One of our friends described his 14-year-old son, Rich, as having all the brains in the world but doing nothing with them. Although Rich is a computer wizard, he gets terrible grades in school, never does his homework, and doesn't seem to have any ambition. Rich might be called an underachiever.

Underachievers are individuals who score relatively high on tests of ability or intelligence but perform more poorly than their scores would predict.

The psychological characteristics of underachievers include having a poor self-concept, low self-esteem, and poor peer relationships, as well as being shy or depressed. The cognitive characteristics of underachievers include fear of failure, poor perceptions of their abilities, and lack of persistence. This means that underachievers are less likely to persist in getting their college degrees, holding on to jobs, or maintaining their marriages (McCall, 1994).

$E = mc^2$
$\pi = 3.14$
$y = mx + b$

**Homeless Teen Graduates
High School with a 3.7 GPA**

Explore a homeless teen's need for achievement.

▶ **L014** Discriminate between intrinsic and extrinsic motivation.

Cognitive Influences

One common factor in many successful students is that they like what they are studying. This "enjoyment of work" is an important cognitive factor that greatly influences motivation.

Take for instance the over 1,600 seniors who compete in the Intel Science Talent Search to win the most prestigious high-school science award in the United States. One recent winner was Eric Larson (right photo), a senior from Oregon who has always enjoyed science, especially thinking about questions no one else can answer. Larson's project classified mathematical objects called fusion categories, which no one had labeled before (Bedrosian, 2009; Crepeau, 2009). His work has implications for theoretical physics and computer science (Ehrenberg, 2009). Larson's love of science is a motivating force that comes from various cognitive factors.

Cognitive factors in motivation refer to how people evaluate or perceive a situation and how these evaluations and perceptions influence their willingness to work.

Eric Larson perceives science projects as interesting and enjoyable and works hard to complete them. He describes science and math as "beautiful" (Larson, 2009). Compared to Larson's love of science, others find science projects hard and boring and take science courses only because they are required. The difference between taking science courses because of a love of science and because of course requirements illustrates the difference between two kinds of motivation: intrinsic motivation and extrinsic motivation (Ryan & Deci, 2000).

Intrinsic motivation involves engaging in certain activities or behaviors without receiving any external rewards because the behaviors themselves are personally rewarding or because engaging in these activities fulfills our beliefs or expectations.

Larson's dedication to science is in large part fueled by intrinsic motivation, which is related to feeling competent, curious, and interested, having self-determination, and enjoying the task, whether it's a science project, work you like, a hobby, or volunteer work. In comparison, extrinsic motivation involves different factors.

Courtesy of Intel Corporation

Unless otherwise noted, all images are © Cengage Learning

Extrinsic motivation involves engaging in certain activities or behaviors that either reduce biological needs or help us obtain incentives and external rewards.

If you do a job, task, or assigned work because it is required, your motivation is often extrinsic, which may involve being evaluated or competing, or seeking recognition, money, or other incentives, such as acquiring a car or home. Another major difference between intrinsic and extrinsic motivation is that working because of intrinsic motivation (loving what you're doing) makes you feel powerfully motivated. Without intrinsic motivation, fewer people would volunteer their time, or donate their blood (Deci et al., 1999).

> **EXTRINSIC MOTIVATION**
> Competitive
> Get recognition
> Obtain incentives
> Make money

> **INTRINSIC MOTIVATION**
> Competent
> Determined
> Personally rewarding
> Enjoyable

So, here's an interesting question: What would happen to intrinsic motivation if you got paid for doing something that you love doing? Would receiving money for volunteering to give blood "turn off" or decrease the intrinsic motivation of donors to the point that they might give less blood or none at all?

Researchers generally believed that if people were given external rewards (such as money, awards, or prizes) for doing tasks (such as donating blood) from intrinsic motivation, their performance of and interest in these tasks would decrease (Deci & Moller, 2005). However, recent reviews of this issue indicate that the effects of external rewards on intrinsic motivation are more complex than originally thought.

Recent studies indicate that, unlike previously thought, external rewards that are unexpected or involve positive verbal feedback may increase intrinsic motivation. External rewards that are tied to doing minimal work or completing a specific project may decrease intrinsic motivation. For example, when parents or teachers praise children, the praise is likely to increase intrinsic motivation if the praise is sincere and promotes the child's feelings of being competent and independent. In contrast, insincere praise, praise for very small accomplishments, or praise that is controlling rather than rewarding may decrease intrinsic motivation (Deci & Moller, 2005). All these studies show that external rewards influence cognitive factors, which in turn may increase or decrease intrinsic motivation.

Intrinsic Motivation

Explore the influence of external rewards on intrinsic motivation.

Check Your Learning Quiz 9.5

Go to **login.cengagebrain.com** and take the online quiz.

▶ **LO15** Define emotions.

Components of Emotion

What happened to Bethany Hamilton at 7:30 on a Friday morning was something she would never forget. Bethany paddled her surfboard about a quarter mile off the north shore of Kauai, Hawaii, and as she waited to catch the best waves, she noticed the water was clear and calm, like a swimming pool. The waves turned out to be too small to ride, so she relaxed by holding the surfboard with her right arm and letting her left arm dangle in the warm water. Suddenly she saw a glimmer of gray in the clear blue water. Almost instantly, Bethany felt tremendous pressure and fierce yanking on her left arm. It was then she realized that the razor-sharp teeth of a 15-foot tiger shark were wrapped tightly around her left arm. When she saw the water around her turn bright red with streaks of her blood, her heart pounded like a hammer and her adrenaline flowed like water from a fire hose. The shark eventually let go of her arm and swam away. With great courage and perseverance, Bethany paddled to the beach as quickly as she could with only her right arm. Her left arm had been violently ripped off almost to the armpit, and the shark even took a big chunk out of her surfboard!

© AP Images/Kalahari Photo/Jamie-Andrea Yanak

Unless otherwise noted, all images are © Cengage Learning

As Bethany approached the beach, people helped her off the surfboard and called for help. She was rushed to the hospital for surgery, and about a week after her stitches were removed, Bethany began surfing again. It was difficult learning to surf with only her right arm, but her extraordinary drive helped her win several surfing competitions after the attack. Although Bethany at times experiences dread and fright that something bad is going to happen again, for the most part, she is as comfortable as other surfers are while in the water (adapted from Hamilton, 2004).

Bethany experienced a variety of emotions during and after her shark attack. During the attack, she felt intense anxiety and fear for her life. When she reached the shore, she felt relieved to be alive but worried about her missing arm. Sometime later, she felt fright about surfing again, but she also felt pride and joy after catching her first big wave after the attack. Although Bethany experienced over a half-dozen emotions, they all shared the same four components (Frijda, 2008).

An **emotion** is defined in terms of four components. First, you interpret or appraise some stimulus (event, object, or thought) in terms of your well-being. Second, you experience a subjective feeling, such as fear or happiness. Third, you have physiological responses, such as changes in heart rate or breathing. Fourth, you may show observable behaviors, such as smiling or crying.

Bethany's experience with the shark illustrates the four components of an emotion:

First, she *interpreted* or *appraised* the stimulus, a shark attack, as a very serious threat to her well-being and survival.

Second, she had the *subjective experience* or *feeling* of fear and terror.

Third, she had a variety of *physiological responses,* such as heart pounding and adrenaline pumping, which cause arousal and prepare the body for action, such as swimming away fast.

Fourth, she showed *overt* or *observable behaviors,* such as fearful facial expressions and rapid paddling to the beach. In some cases, such as playing poker, a person may experience a wide range of emotions but try to hide his or her overt behaviors by showing no facial expression, commonly known as a "poker face." In other cases, cultural factors influence overt behaviors, such as allowing American women but not usually American men to cry in public.

Although there is general agreement that emotions have four components, there is much discussion of the order in which these four components occur (Frijda, 2008). For instance, did Bethany have to think about the shark before she felt fear, or did she feel fear immediately and then think about how terrified she was? We'll discuss this question about emotion next.

Components of Emotion

Distinguish the four components of emotion.

▶ **LO16** Describe and differentiate the different theories of emotions.

1. Stimulus (shark) triggers different physiological changes in your body.

2. Your brain interprets different patterns of physiological changes.

Interpret

3. Different physiological changes produce different emotions (fear).

4. You may or may not show observable responses (scream).

Seeing a shark swimming nearby causes instant fear. Explaining how this fear arises depends on the specific approach or theory. We'll begin with the historic James-Lange theory, which says that if you see a bear, you are frightened because you run. Is it true?

James-Lange Theory

This theory, proposed in the late 1800s by two psychologists, William James and Carl Lange, emphasizes physiological patterns as causing emotional feelings.

The **James-Lange theory** says that our brains interpret specific physiological changes as emotions and that there is a different physiological pattern underlying each emotion.

James (1884/1969) illustrated his theory with the example of seeing a bear: If you see a bear, "you are frightened because you run" rather than run because you are frightened. According to the James-Lange theory, the order for the occurrence of the four components of an emotion is shown in the left figure.

Criticisms

There are three major criticisms of the James-Lange theory. First, different emotions are not necessarily associated with different patterns of physiological responses. For instance, anger, fear, and sadness share similar physiological patterns of arousal (Cacioppo et al., 2000). Thus, James's bear example was backward: Instead of the act of running making you feel fear, you feel fear and then run.

Second, people whose spinal cords have been severed at the neck are deprived of most of the feedback from their physiological responses (autonomic nervous system), yet they experience emotions with little or no change in intensity. These data are the opposite of what the James-Lange theory would predict, which is that these people should experience little or no emotion (Chwalisz et al., 1988).

Third, some emotions, such as feeling guilty or jealous, may require a considerable amount of interpretation or appraisal of the situation. The sequence involved in feeling a complex emotion such as guilt or jealousy points to the influence of cognitive factors on emotional feelings (Clore & Ortony, 2008).

Unless otherwise noted, all images are © Cengage Learning

Next, we turn to the facial feedback theory, which says seeing a bear triggers changes in facial muscles & skin that lead to feeling different emotions.

Facial Feedback Theory

The idea that feedback from facial muscles causes emotional feelings originated with Charles Darwin (1872/1965) and evolved into facial feedback theory (Keltner & Ekman, 2000; Matsumoto et al., 2008).

The **facial feedback theory** says that the sensations, or feedback, from the movement of your facial muscles and skin are interpreted by your brain as different emotions.

According to facial feedback theory, the four components of emotions occur in the order shown in the right figure.

Criticisms

While it is true that facial expressions of fear, happiness, sadness, and disgust involve different muscle-skin patterns, little evidence supports that it's the feedback from these different muscle groups that actually causes the emotion. For example, if feedback from facial muscles caused emotions, then individuals whose facial muscles are completely paralyzed should not be able to experience emotions, yet they do report feeling emotions (Heilman, 2000).

Although researchers have not confirmed Darwin's original theory that feedback from facial muscles alone is sufficient to produce emotions, they have found that feedback from facial muscles, such as those involved in smiling or crying, may influence your mood and overall emotional feeling and increase the intensity of your subjective emotional experience (Kolb & Taylor, 2000).

The James-Lange and facial feedback theories of emotions show that physiological changes in the body and feedback from facial muscles contribute to but do not themselves cause different emotions. What can cause an emotion are the thoughts that go on inside your brain (mind), which is our next topic.

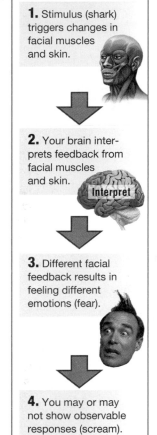

1. Stimulus (shark) triggers changes in facial muscles and skin.

2. Your brain interprets feedback from facial muscles and skin. Interpret

3. Different facial feedback results in feeling different emotions (fear).

4. You may or may not show observable responses (scream).

Theories of Emotion

Observe how the James-Lange, facial feedback, and cognitive appraisal theories differ.

1. Injection of hormone causes physiological arousal (rise in heart rate, etc.).

2. Explain physiological arousal by using situational cues.

3. Depending on situation, feel different emotions (happy or angry).

4. Show observable behaviors that match emotions.

Suppose you won a lottery and felt very happy. Weeks later, the thought of winning still makes you feel very happy. The fact that your thoughts alone can give rise to emotions illustrates the importance of cognitive factors.

Schachter-Singer Experiment

Current cognitive theories of emotions can be traced back to the original research of Stanley Schachter and Jerome Singer (1962), whose classic experiment was the first to show the importance of cognitive interpretation, or appraisal, in contributing to emotional states.

As shown in the figure left, Schachter and Singer first injected their subjects with a hormone, epinephrine (adrenaline), which caused physiological arousal, such as increased heart rate and blood pressure. However, subjects were told that the injections were vitamins and were not told that they would experience physiological arousal. After the injections, subjects were placed in different situations, a happy one or an angry one. Those subjects in the happy situation often reported feeling happy, and their observable behaviors were smiles. However, those in the angry situation often reported feeling angry, and their observable behaviors were angry facial expressions. Schachter and Singer explained that subjects did not know that their physiological arousal was caused by hormone injections, and they looked around for other causes in their environment. Subjects interpreted environmental cues, such as being in a happy or angry situation, as the cause of their arousal and thus reported feeling happy or angry. The Schachter-Singer cognitive theory was the first to show that cognitive factors, such as your interpretation of events, could influence emotional feelings.

The Schachter-Singer finding that cognitive processes, such as thoughts, interpretations, and appraisals of situations, can trigger emotions became the basis for today's cognitive appraisal theory of emotions.

Unless otherwise noted, all images are © Cengage Learning

Cognitive Appraisal Theory

The cognitive appraisal theory began with the experiment of Schachter and Singer and developed into its present form because of many researchers (Ellsworth & Scherer, 2003; Lazarus, 2006).

The **cognitive appraisal theory** says that your interpretation or appraisal or thought or memory of a situation, object, or event can contribute to, or result in, your experiencing different emotional states.

Suppose you're thinking about having won the lottery last week and planning what to do with all that money. According to the cognitive appraisal theory, the sequence for how thinking results in feeling happy is shown in the right figure.

Thought then Emotion

Thinking of your first serious kiss can make you feel happy, while thinking of times you were jealous can make you sad or angry. In these cases, as well as in feeling pride, envy, or compassion, the thinking or appraisal occurs before the emotion (Lazarus, 2006).

Emotion without Conscious Thought

Imagine being on a nature walk, turning a corner, and seeing a huge snake on the path. In this case, the feeling of fear is instant, without conscious thought or appraisal; you don't have to think "that's a dangerous snake and I better be careful." Thus, in some situations, such as those that involve problems at work, fond family memories, or terrible tragedies, thoughts precede and result in emotional feelings. In other situations, such as those involving attack or threat to one's personal survival, emotions can occur instantly, without conscious thought or awareness.

The relatively new finding that certain emotions, especially fear, can occur without conscious thought or awareness brings us to the most recent approach to the study of emotions, called affective neuroscience, which we'll discuss next.

1. The stimulus could be an event, object, or thought: "I won $55 million last week."

2. You appraise or think of what you can do: "I can go on a trip around the world."

Interpret

3. Appraising or thinking about what you can do brings feelings of happiness and joy.

Happy

4. You also have physiological responses and observable behaviors (smiling).

Check Your Learning Quiz 9.6

Go to **login.cengagebrain.com** and take the online quiz.

Unless otherwise noted, all images are © Cengage Learning

▶ **LO17** Describe the affective neuroscience approach and the brain circuits for emotions.

Neuroscientists use brain imaging techniques to identify structures and neural activities in the living brain. These studies contribute to the new affective neuroscience approach to understand emotions (Panksepp, 2008).

The **affective neuroscience approach** studies the underlying neural bases of emotion by focusing on the brain's neural circuits that evaluate stimuli and produce or contribute to experiencing and expressing different emotional states.

The word *affective* suggests affect or emotion. The word *neuroscience* suggests research methods that involve studying patients with neurological disorders and using methods that involve brain imaging to identify activity in the living brain.

Emotional Detector and Memorizer

If you were shown a number of stimuli, would you detect a snake quicker than a flower? Researchers found that compared to detecting unemotional neutral targets such as flowers, we are faster at detecting targets with emotional meaning, such as faces with positive (smiling) or negative (fearful) expressions, and threatening things, such as snakes. However, we are fastest at identifying stimuli that may pose a threat, such as fearful faces or snakes (Williams & Mattingley, 2006).

Amygdala

Your physical survival depends in part on a brain structure about the size and shape of an almond, the amygdala (Whalen & Phelps, 2009).

The **amygdala** *(ah-MIG-duh-la)* receives input from all the senses. Using all this sensory input, the amygdala monitors and evaluates whether stimuli have positive or negative emotional significance for our well-being and survival. It is also involved in storing memories that have emotional content. The amygdala is the reason you can remember that a joke is funny or a face is happy or threatening.

Brain Circuits for Emotions

Researchers have used brain imaging techniques (fMRI—p. 74) to measure neural activity and trace neural pathways or circuits throughout the living brain. We'll focus on the neural activity that occurs when a person is confronted with a fearful stimulus, such as seeing a ferocious wolf. (Quirk, 2007; Siegal, 2005).

A. Slower Circuit

When you see a ferocious wolf, vi information about the wolf's shap size, and color enters the *eyes* (**1**), which send neural information about the "wolf" to the *thalamus* (**2**). In turn, the thalamus relays the neural information to the *visual cortex* (**3**). The visual cortex transforms the neural signals into the image of a ferocious wolf and relays the "wolf" information to the *amygdala* (**4**). The amygdala interprets the neural information and signals the presence of

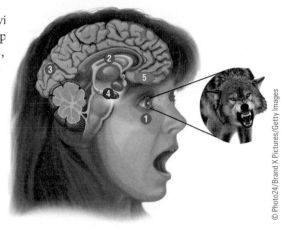

a threat, which results in feelings of fear, an associated fearful facial expression, and probably running to escape from the threat. And this neural activity happens very fast, in about 0.12 second. However, there is an even faster circuit.

B. Faster Circuit

As usual, visual information about the wolf enters the *eyes* (**1**), which send neural information about the "wolf" to the *thalamus* (**2**). The thalamus sends neural information directly to the *amygdala* (**4**), saving time by skipping the *visual cortex* (**3**). This means the amygdala recognizes the threatening wolf and triggers a fearful response almost instantaneously after seeing the wolf. This **faster circuit** provides an amazingly quick warning of a greatly threatening stimulus.

C. Prefrontal Cortex

The part of your brain that is involved in complex cognitive functions, such as making decisions, planning, and reasoning, is called the *prefrontal cortex* (**5**). The prefrontal cortex is involved in remembering and experiencing emotions even when the fear object is not present, such as when you tell a friend about your wolf encounter and again feel fear, or recall a joke and laugh. It is also involved in anticipating and analyzing the potential rewards, punishments, and emotional consequences of performing or not performing certain behaviors (Fuster, 2008).

Fear and the Amygdala

Explore why some people have more fears than others.

© Photo24/Brand X Pictures/Getty Images

▶ **LO18** Explain how the lie detector measures arousal and discuss its validity.

Lie Detection

For 9 years, the Russians paid or promised $4.6 million to Aldrich Ames (right photo), who was a Central Intelligence Agency official. Later, Ames pleaded guilty to espionage, which involved selling secrets to the Russians. Ames is currently serving a life sentence in prison. The Ames case brings up the issue of lie detection because he reportedly passed at least two lie detector (polygraph) tests during the time that he was selling U.S. secrets to Russia (Jackson, 1994). The Ames case raises a couple of questions: What is the theory behind lie detection? How accurate are lie detector tests?

I lied, but I passed two lie detector tests.

© Getty Images

What Is the Theory?

The lie detector test is based on the four components of an emotion (p. 435). The first component is interpreting a stimulus. In this case, Ames will need to interpret questions such as "Have you ever sold secrets to Russia?" The second component is a subjective feeling, such as whether Ames will feel any guilt when he answers "Yes" or "No" to the question "Have you ever sold secrets to Russia?" The third component is the occurrence of physiological responses (right figure). If Mr. Ames feels guilty, then his guilt feeling will be accompanied by physiological arousal, which includes increases in heart rate, blood pressure, breathing, and sweating of the hands. The fourth component is the occurrence of some overt behavior, such as a facial expression. Mr. Ames may be able to control his facial expressions and put on a nonemotional poker face. However, neither the presence nor the absence of expressions is critical to the theory behind lie detector

Chest movement during respiration

Abdominal movement during respiration

Heart rate and blood pressure

Skin conductance

Unless otherwise noted, all images are © Cengage Learning

Lie detector (polygraph) tests are based on the theory that, if a person tells a lie, he or she will feel some emotion, such as guilt or fear. Feeling guilty or fearful will be accompanied by involuntary physiological responses, which are difficult to suppress or control and can be measured with a machine called a polygraph.

A polygraph is about the size of a laptop computer and measures chest and abdominal muscle movement during respiration, heart rate, blood pressure, and skin conductance.

How Accurate Are Lie Detector Tests?

If Floyd was innocent, why did he fail two lie detector exams? The basic problem with lie detector tests is that researchers have been unable to identify a pattern of physiological responses specific to lying. This means a number of different emotions—such as guilt, fear, or worry—can trigger physiological responses that make a person appear to be lying when he or she is telling the truth (Fiedler et al., 2002). Also, the person administering the polygraph test) can have a bias about the subject and not provide objective interpretations of the results (Haseltine, 2008). Because of these serious problems, researchers estimate that lie detector tests are wrong 25% to 75% of the time (Broad, 2002; Saxe, 1994).

Innocent or Faking

Besides high error scores, lie detector tests have two other problems: In one study, about 40% of subjects were judged to be lying or maybe lying when they were telling the truth (Honts, 1994); in another study, about 50% of guilty people who were told to both press their toes to the ground and bite their tongues during questioning passed lie detector tests (Honts et al., 1994).

New Tests

One of the newest tests involves using brain scans (right photo) to detect changes in thinking and associated neural activity that occur when lying. No area of the brain specializes in lying; however, researchers are finding increased activation in regions involved in suppressing information and resolving conflicts when an individual lies (Gamer et al., 2007; Kozel et al., 2005).

Other new tests aimed at improving the accuracy of lie detection include using eye scans to measure blood flow to the eye; observing very brief, involuntary facial expression changes; and analyzing the consistency and amount of detail in someone's testimony (Colwell, 2009; Ekman, 2006; Kluger & Masters, 2006).

Facial Analysis

Watch how facial analysis may be used to improve lie detection.

Check Your Learning Quiz 9.7

Go to **login.cengagebrain.com** and take the online quiz.

▶ **LO19** Define universal emotional expressions and describe the supportive evidence.

As you'll recall, the fourth component of an emotion is showing overt or observable behaviors, such as facial expressions. It turns out that some emotional facial expressions are universal, meaning they are expressed and recognized across cultures.

Universal Facial Expressions

When you were about 4 to 6 weeks old, you began to smile. Smiling is considered one of the universal emotional expressions (Ekman, 2003).

Universal emotional expressions are specific inherited facial patterns or expressions that signal specific feelings or emotional states, such as a smile signaling a happy state.

For example, notice that although the four individuals in the photos come from four different countries, they display similar facial expressions—smiles—which you would interpret as showing happiness.

Researchers generally agree that seven facial expressions for emotions are universal: anger, happiness, fear, surprise, disgust, sadness, and contempt (Ekman, 2003; Ekman & Rosenberg, 2005). Other emotions, such as pride, jealousy, and compassion, do not have particular facial expressions.

We'll review two kinds of evidence—cross-cultural and genetic— that support the idea of universal emotional expressions.

Cross-Cultural Evidence

How do individuals from relatively isolated cultures in New Guinea, Burma, Thailand, and Borneo (photos from top to bottom) know how to smile or what a smile means? One answer is a smile is one of the unlearned, inherited universal emotional expressions. For example, researchers showed photos of different facial expressions to individuals in 20 different Western cultures and 11 different primitive (illiterate and isolated) cultures. As the graph on the next page indicates, individuals in both Western and primitive cultures showed significant agreement on which facial expressions signaled which emotions. Most individuals in Western and primitive cultures agreed that a smile indicated happiness. However, only about one third of individuals in primitive cultures agreed that an open-mouth and raised-eyebrows expression indicated surprise.

Based on the cross-cultural findings shown in the graph at right, researchers concluded that there are innately or biologically determined universal facial expressions for emotions (Ekman, 2003; Ekman & Rosenberg, 2005).

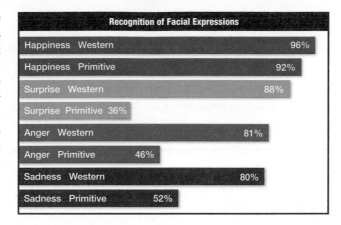

Recognition of Facial Expressions

Happiness Western	96%
Happiness Primitive	92%
Surprise Western	88%
Surprise Primitive	36%
Anger Western	81%
Anger Primitive	46%
Sadness Western	80%
Sadness Primitive	52%

Genetic Evidence

Is it possible that the programming of facial expressions, such as smiling, is in our genetic instructions? One answer to this question comes from observing the development of emotional expressions in infants.

Researchers found that at 4 to 6 weeks of age, infants begin to smile. The question is whether an infant's smiling is biologically programmed or whether the infant has learned to smile by observing and imitating the parents' facial expressions. You might be surprised to learn that even infants born blind, who never observe their parents smiling, begin to smile at 4 to 6 weeks. More recent research found that blind individuals produced the same facial expressions for anger, disgust, surprise, joy, sadness, and contempt as those who are sighted. Together, these results indicate that facial expressions are innate or genetically programmed and not learned through observation (Eibl-Eibesfeldt, 1973; Matsumoto & Willingham, 2009).

Additional evidence for universal emotions comes from reports that infants in all cultures develop facial expressions in a predictable order. For instance, newborns show facial expressions signaling disgust, infants 4 to 6 weeks old begin to smile, infants 3 to 4 months old show angry and sad facial expressions, and infants 5 to 7 months old show fear (Izard, 1993; Kopp & Neufeld, 2003).

Researchers conclude that evidence from cross-cultural studies on facial expressions, the development of emotional expressions in infants, and the shared facial expressions among sighted and blind individuals indicate strong genetic influences on the development of emotional expressions.

Culture and Emotion

Watch how emotional expressions vary across cultures.

Emotions Across Cultures

Learn how the perception of emotions varies across cultures.

Check Your Learning Quiz 9.8

Go to **login.cengagebrain.com** and take the online quiz.

▶ **LO20** Describe positive psychology and explain its influence on emotions.

▶ **LO21** Describe happiness and identify factors that contribute to happiness.

Positive Psychology

Sherrod Ballentine has a stressful job as a court mediator, and although she's not clinically depressed, she wants to learn ways to improve her mood. She takes a class called "Authentic Happiness and How to Obtain It" and learns activities that will train her mind to focus more on the positive. One activity Sherrod learns is to write down three happy events and their causes at the end of each day for a week. After completing the class, she said, "I am happier. Every day, I feel so grateful to wake up this way" (Lemley, 2006). Sherrod's new learned skills are based on positive psychology.

Positive psychology is the scientific study of optimal human functioning, focusing on the strengths and virtues that enable individuals and communities to thrive. It aims to better understand the positive, adaptive, and fulfilling aspects of human life.

Positive psychology has three main concerns. The first is the study of positive emotions, such as happiness, hope, love, and contentment. The second is the study of positive individual traits, such as altruism, courage, compassion, and resilience. The third is the study of positive institutions, or the strengths that promote better communities, such as justice, parenting, tolerance, and teamwork (Seligman, 2003).

Many research examples show that characteristics of positive psychology have a beneficial impact on mood and physical health. For example, research on writing exercises, such as the one Sherrod did, shows impressive results. One study found that after writing about positive experiences for 20 minutes each day for 3 consecutive days, college students reported improved mood and had fewer health-center visits for illness in the months that followed (Burton & King, 2004). Also, happy people report having more friends, more satisfying marriages, higher incomes, healthier lifestyles, and longer lives than their unhappy peers (Hales, 2008).

Next, we turn to a positive emotion, happiness, and the question "Why doesn't happiness last longer?"

Unless otherwise noted, all images are © Cengage Learning

Positive Emotions

Pam was unmarried, 8 months pregnant, and holding down two jobs when she stopped in at Jackson's Food Store for her morning orange juice and one lottery ticket. She remembers praying, "Please, God, let something happen so I can afford a small studio apartment" (Reed & Free, 1995, p. 63). The next day she was ecstatic when she discovered that her single lottery ticket was worth $87 million (right photo).

I won 87 million dollars!

Idaho Statesman/© Tom Shanahan

Happiness, usually indicated by smiling and laughing, can result from momentary pleasures, such as a funny commercial; short-term joys, such as a great date; and long-term satisfaction, such as an enjoyable relationship.

What leads to long-term satisfaction or happiness? When researchers interviewed lottery winners 1 to 24 months after they had won large sums of money, the majority reported positive changes, such as financial security, new possessions, more leisure time, and earlier retirement. However, when asked to rate their happiness 1 year after winning, lottery winners were no happier than before (Diener & Diener, 1996). Why the happy feeling of winning a lottery doesn't last is explained by the adaptation level theory.

The **adaptation level theory** says that we quickly become accustomed to receiving some good fortune (such as money, job, car, or degree); we take the good fortune for granted within a short period of time; and as a result, the initial impact of our good fortune fades and contributes less to our long-term level of happiness.

Researchers find that happiness is not a fixed state and does not primarily result from getting more money, cars, clothes, or promotions because these achievements gradually lose their emotional appeal, as predicted by the adaptation level theory. Rather, being happy is a continuous process associated with making an effort to enjoy simple, daily pleasurable events, people, or situations. It includes a daily diet of little highs, as well as pursuing personal goals, developing a sense of meaningfulness, having intimate relationships, and not judging yourself against what others do but by your own yardstick (Easterlin, 2003; Lykken, 2003; Seligman, 2002).

Check Your Learning Quiz 9.9

Go to **login.cengagebrain.com** and take the online quiz.

Think Critically

Challenge Your Thinking

Consider these questions when reading this article:

1. In the United States, why is smiling in social situations considered an acceptable and even desirable way to behave in public?
2. When having to make money is bucking cultural traditions, what do you think will happen?
3. Even though emotional expressions, such as smiling, are considered universal facial expressions, why don't the Japanese smile more?
4. Why is it so difficult for many highly motivated Japanese to learn to smile?
5. Why do you think that smiley, friendly salespeople are more successful and better at building morale?
6. According to the facial feedback theory, how would not smiling influence emotions?

Why Do They Have to Learn to Smile?

In the United States it's very common to see people smiling in public because it's a friendly way to interact socially. In fact, many businesses insist that their salespeople smile at customers because smiling makes the customers feel more comfortable and more likely to buy something. But in Japan, people are very reluctant to show emotions in public, and that's become a problem.

Japan is currently going through a recession or downturn in business, so there is increased competition to get new customers and keep current customers happy. Said one gas station attendant who is trying to learn to smile more, "In this recession, customers are getting choosy about their gas stations, so you have to think positively. Laughter and a smile are representative of this positive thinking" (Reitman, 1999, p. A1).

But getting salespeople to smile is a radical change in Japan, whose cultural tradition has long emphasized suppressing any public display of emotions, be it happy, sad, or angry. For example, women never smile at their husbands, and members of families rarely touch in public and never hug, even when greeting after a long separation. It's still

© Nobura Hashimoto/Corbis

common for women to place a hand over their mouths when they laugh, and men believe that the correct and proper behavior is to show no emotions in public. Unlike American salespeople, who often smile and make eye contact with their customers, Japanese salespeople are reserved and greet customers with a simple "welcome"; smiling, up until now, was totally frowned upon.

Because getting salespeople to smile is going against a strong tradition, learning how to smile has grown into a big business in Japan. Employees are now being sent to "smile school," which uses various techniques to teach reluctant and bashful students to smile. For example, one technique in learning how to smile is biting on a chopstick (photo above) and then lifting the edges of the mouth higher than the chopstick. Another technique is

to follow "smile" instructions: "Relax the muscle under your nose, loosen up your tongue. Put your hands on your stomach and laugh out loud, feeling the 'poisons' escape" (Reitman, 1999, p. A1).

What is driving all this smiling in Japan is sales and morale. As is well known by American businesses, happy, friendly salespeople are usually the most successful and are great at building company morale. The same is holding true in Japan, where smiley clerks are racking up the most sales and creating a friendly morale.

People in other parts of Asia, such as China, also are not accustomed to smiling in social situations. In fact, volunteers for the 2008 Olympics in Beijing were required to take classes on how to smile to ensure that they portrayed China as hospitable. (Adapted from Mauss, 2005; Reitman, 1999; UPI, 2006)

Think Critically 9.1

This article and its questions are available in interactive format online.

GO to your Psychology CourseMate at login.cengagebrain.com and take the Chapter Post-Test to see which Learning Objectives you've mastered and which need more review. Use the chapter review guide below and the online activities—including flashcards to review key terms—to measure your learning.

Measure ^ Your Learning

Online Activities

Key Terms	Video	Animation	Reading	Assessment
motivation				Check Your Learning Quiz 9.1
insincts, reward/pleasure center, incentives, extrinsic motivation, intrinsic motivation, biological needs, social needs, Maslow's hierarchy of needs			Erik Weihenmayer's Motivation, p. 411 Maslow's Hierarchy of Needs, p. 413	Check Your Learning Quiz 9.2
optimal or ideal weight, overweight, obesity, biological hunger factors, genetic hunger factors, psychosocial hunger factors, peripheral cues, central cues, stomach, liver, intestines, fat cells, hypothalamus, lateral hypothalamus, ventromedial bypothalamus, metabolic rate, set point, weight-regulating genes, anorexia nervosa, bulimia nervosa	Weight Control, p. 415 Anorexia. p. 423 Exercise Bulimia, p. 423		Biological Hunger Factors, p. 417 Metabolic Rate, p. 419 Dieting, p. 421	Check Your Learning Quiz 9.3
genetic sex factors, biological sex factors, psychological sex factors, sex chromosome, sex hormones, androgens, estrogens, gender identity, gender roles, sexual orientation, homosexual orientation, heterosexual orientation, bisexual orientation, interactive model of sexual orientation, organic factors, psychological factors	Gender Identity Disorder, p. 427 Gay Teens, p. 429		Viagra, p. 429	Check Your Learning Quiz 9.4

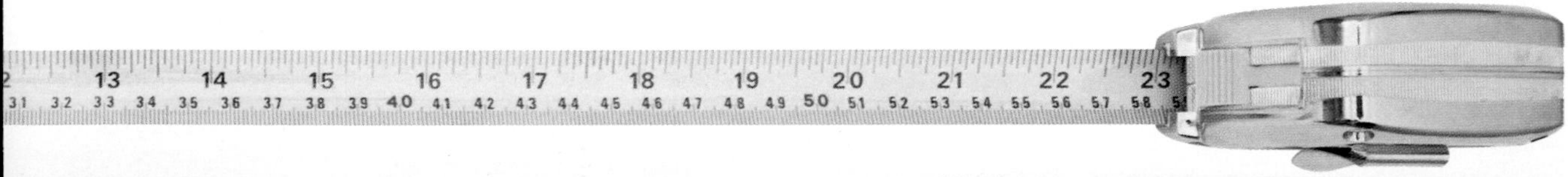

Measure
˅Your Learning

Online Activities

Key Terms	Video	Animation	Reading	Assessment
social needs, achievement need, high need for achievement, fear of failure, underachievers, cognitive factors in motivation, instrinsic motivation, extrinsic motivation	Homeless Teen Graduates High School with 3.7 GPA, p. 431		Instrinsic Motivation, p. 433	Check Your Learning Quiz 9.5
emotion, James-Lange theory, facial feedback theory, cognitive appraisal theory		Components of Emotion, p. 435 Theories of Emotion, p. 437		Check Your Learning Quiz 9.6
affective neuroscience approach, amygdala, lie detector (polygraph) tests	Facial Analysis, p. 443		Fear and the Amygdala, p. 441	Check Your Learning Quiz 9.7
universal emotional expressions	Culture and Emotion, p. 445		Emotions Across Cultures, p. 445	Check Your Learning Quiz 9.8
positive psychology, happiness, adaptation level theory				Check Your Learning Quiz 9.9

Social Psychology

10

Chapter Outline and Learning Objectives

1 **GO** to your **Psychology CourseMate** at **login.cengagebrain.com** and take the **Chapter Pre-Test** to introduce yourself to this chapter's topics and see what you may already know.

2 **READ** the **Learning Objectives (LOs)** (in the left sidebars) and begin the chapter.

3 **COMPLETE** the **Online Activities** (in the right sidebars) *as you read each module*. Activities include **videos**, **animations**, **readings**, and **quizzes**.

4 **CHECK Your Learning** by going online to take the quiz at the end of each module and review material as necessary.

5 **MEASURE Your Learning** after reading the chapter by taking the online **Chapter Post-Test**. Use the chapter review guide at the end of the chapter as needed.

WATCH for these **Online Activities** icons as you read:

Video

Animation

Reading

Assessment

Think Critically

Online Activities

These online activities are important to mastering this chapter. As you read each module, access these materials by going to **login.cengagebrain.com**.

 Video Explore studies and firsthand accounts of biological and psychological processes:

- Watch how physical attractiveness affects a person's perception
- See how stereotypes affect people
- Learn what sexual prejudice is and how prevalent it is in our society
- Watch how we have attitudes that we don't even know we have
- Watch how likely it is that a person will conform to an unusual behavior
- Watch conformity take place in an elevator
- Learn how powerful the pressure to be obedient is and why people obey
- Learn how group polarization shifts people's views
- Learn more about why people help others in distress
- Explore the role mirror neurons play in our social relationships

 Animation Interact with and visualize important processes and concepts:

- Experience the influence of first impressions
- Use internal and external attributions while discovering their errors

 Reading Delve deeper into key content:

- Learn whether changing attributions can change grades
- Explore how culture shapes our attitudes
- Learn more about the difference between cognitive dissonance theory and self-perception theory
- Learn about whether men and women respond differently to the routes for persuasion
- Learn about a modern-day replication of Milgram's experiment and find out how it compares to the original study

- Read about a fascinating example of group membership
- Learn why people did not help a woman who was being violently attacked
- Find out why some abused children become violent adults while others do not

 Assessment Measure your mastery:

- Chapter Pre-Test
- Check Your Learning Quizzes
- Chapter Post-Test

 Think Critically Challenge your thinking by applying content from this chapter and making connections to related material:

- Why the Debate over Teen Vaccination?

▶ **L01** Describe social psychology.

LAWRENCE GRAHAM (below) wanted to get a job at a country club and had phoned numerous clubs to set up personal interviews. Here's what happened when he arrived for one of his interviews:

"We don't have any job openings—and if you don't leave the building, I will have to call security," the receptionist said.

"But I just spoke to Donna, your dining manager, and she said to come by and discuss the waiter job."

"Sorry, but there are no jobs and no one here named Donna" (Graham, 1995, p. 4).

▼

Graham finally got two job offers and decided on the exclusive Greenwich Country Club. This club had been in existence for 100 years and was in the affluent, prestigious, and white town of Greenwich, Connecticut.

Although Graham wanted a job as a waiter, he was hired to be a busboy. Except when a member wanted something and deliberately looked for him, Graham's job made him quite invisible and able to overhear members' conversations.

"Here, busboy. Here, busboy," a woman called out. "Busboy, my coffee is cold. Give me a refill."

"Certainly, I would be happy to," said Graham.

Before he returned to the kitchen, Graham heard the woman say to her companion, "My goodness. Did you hear that? That busboy has diction like an educated white person" (Graham, 1995, p. 12).

© Ted Hardin

In real life, Lawrence Graham was a Harvard Law School graduate and earned $105,000 a year working as an associate in a New York law firm. Although he was ready to move up the social ladder, Graham, who is black, received no invitations to join a country club, as his white associates did. So to find out what goes on in country clubs that do not admit blacks, he got in the only way he could, as a busboy making $7 an hour.

Graham's example brings up several major topics of social psychology.

Social psychology is a broad field whose goals are to understand and explain how our thoughts, feelings, perceptions, and behaviors are influenced by the presence of, or interactions with, others.

Social psychologists study how we form impressions and perceive others, how we form attitudes and stereotypes, how we evaluate social interactions, and why racism exists—all of which are involved in Lawrence Graham's story.

© Cengage Learning 2013

Check Your Learning Quiz 10.1

Go to **login.cengagebrain.com** and take the online quiz.

Person Perception

Compare the photo of Lawrence Graham on the top with that on the bottom. In the top photo, your first impression is that Graham is a busboy or waiter, while in the bottom photo, your first impression is that Graham is a confident businessman or professional. Your first impressions, which were formed in seconds, with little conscious thought, are part of person perception.

Person perception refers to seeing someone and then forming impressions and making judgments about that person's likability and the kind of person he or she is, such as guessing his or her intentions, traits, and behaviors.

As you formed a first impression of Graham from each photo, four factors influenced your judgment (Newman, 2001).

1 **Physical Appearance** Your initial impressions of a person are influenced and biased by a person's physical appearance. For example, Graham makes a very different first impression when he looks like a busboy or a professional.

2 **Need to Explain** You don't just look at a person, but rather you try to explain why he looks, dresses, or behaves in a certain way. You might explain that Graham-as-busboy is working his way through college, while Graham-as-professional is successfully developing his career.

3 **Influence on Behavior** Your first impressions will influence how you would interact with a person. For example, if your first impression of Graham is as a $7-an-hour busboy, you would interact with him very differently than if your impression of him was as a $105,000-a-year professional working for a large corporation.

4 **Effects of Race** Researchers found that we generally perceive faces that are racially different from our own in a biased way because they do not appear as distinct as faces from our own race (Ferguson et al., 2001). Also, the brain area associated with emotional vigilance becomes more activated when white people view photos of unfamiliar black, as compared to unfamiliar white, faces (Fiske, 2006). Clearly, our first impressions of people are subject to our racial biases.

© Ted Hardin

© Ted Hardin

Unless otherwise noted, all images are © Cengage Learning

Physical Attractiveness

One factor that plays a major role in person perception, especially forming first impressions, is physical attractiveness.

Courtesy of Dr. Victor Johnston, from "Why We Feel"

Researchers found that, for better or worse, a person's looks matter, since people who are judged more physically attractive generally make more favorable impressions (Marcus & Miller, 2003). To determine why a face is judged attractive, researchers created faces by combining and averaging physical features taken from different faces. Researchers could make faces more or less attractive by averaging more (32) or fewer (16) faces (Langlois et al., 1994). For example, the face in the right photo, which was rated very attractive, was actually created by averaging thousands of faces (Johnston, 2000). It turns out that averaged faces are more attractive than the originals.

Some researchers believe that physical attraction is completely instinctual and not based on logic. Research suggests that some physical characteristics are considered more universally attractive (Jayson, 2009a). For example, researchers found that both within and across cultures, there is strong agreement (correlation about 0.90) among whites, African Americans, Asians, and Hispanics about which faces of adults and children are and are not attractive (Langlois et al., 2000). According to evolutionary psychologists, judging and valuing attractiveness may have evolved and become a "built-in" ability because attractiveness was a visible sign of a person having good genes, being healthy, and becoming a good mate (Lie, 2009; Quill, 2009).

According to evolutionary psychologists, men are most attracted to youthful women who have an "hourglass figure" (hips larger than waist) (right photo), which signals a childbirth advantage. Women are most attracted to men who have masculine faces, with a larger jaw and greater muscle mass (left photo), which suggests higher testosterone levels (Jayson, 2009a).

© Ismael Lopez/Photolibrary

© Dave Falk/Getty Images

Person Perception

Experience the influence of first impressions.

The Beauty Bonus

Watch how physical attractiveness affects a person's perception.

▶ **LO4** Explain stereotypes and distinguish between prejudice and discrimination.

Stereotypes

On the right are photos of actors who played the roles of patients complaining of chest pains. While describing their symptoms, the actor-patients were videotaped. These videotapes were shown to over 700 physicians, who were asked to recommend treatments. Because the actor-patients all described the same physical symptoms, all the physicians should have generally recommended the same treatments. However, physicians recommended different treatments that depended on the physicians' particular sexual and racial stereotypes (Schulman et al., 1999).

Stereotypes are widely held beliefs that people have certain traits because they belong to a particular group. Stereotypes are often inaccurate and frequently portray the members of less powerful, less controlling groups more negatively than members of more powerful or more controlling groups.

Stereotypes played an important role in the study we just described. Although the actor-patients reported the same symptoms and should have received about the same kinds of treatment, physicians were 40% less likely to recommend sophisticated medical tests for women and blacks compared to white men (Schulman et al., 1999). More recent research also found that blacks were less likely than whites to receive expensive medical procedures (*USA Today*, 2005).

These studies show that racial and sexual stereotypes, which may occur automatically and without awareness, may bias the physicians' perceptions and judgments (Andersen et al., 2007).

As you'll see next, once negative stereotypes are formed, they are difficult to change.

From "The Effect of Race and Sex on Physicians' Recommendations for Cardiac Catheterization" by K.A. Schulman et al., 1999. *The New England Journal of Medicine.* 2/5/99, pp. 621–622. Copyright © 1999, Massachusetts Medical Society.

Unless otherwise noted, all images are © Cengage Learning

Development of Stereotypes

Psychologists believe we develop stereotypes when parents, peers, teachers, and others reward us with social approval for holding certain attitudes and beliefs. There are also cultural pressures to adopt certain values and beliefs about members of different groups. For example, in the weight-conscious culture of the United States, there is an emphasis on being thin, so we might expect a negative stereotype to apply to people who are overweight. In fact, research shows that people have a bias against hiring overweight job applicants, especially overweight women (Pingitore et al., 1994). Other research shows that after taking into account factors such as age, race, and sex, people who are perceived as more attractive make more money (Judge et al., 2009). Another study found that in a trivia competition, a situation in which working with a partner with a high IQ provides a distinct advantage, people are willing to sacrifice 12 IQ points in a partner to have one who is thin (Caruso, 2009).

Why do you think I wasn't hired?

© PhotoDisc, Inc.

These biases identified above are examples of negative stereotypes, which are often accompanied by prejudice and discrimination.

Prejudice refers to an unfair, biased, or intolerant attitude toward another group of people.

An example of prejudice is believing that overweight women are not as intelligent, competent, or capable as women of normal weight.

Discrimination refers to specific unfair behaviors exhibited toward members of a group.

An employer's bias against hiring overweight applicants is an example of discrimination.

The history of the United States provides many examples of racist and sexist cultural stereotypes, such as beliefs that women are not smart enough to vote and that blacks are inferior to whites (Swim et al., 1995). Research shows some stereotypes, including racial prejudice, are so much a part of our society they begin developing as early as 6 years of age (Baron & Banaji, 2006).

Why don't adults like me?

© PhotoDisc, Inc.

Stereotype Threat

See how stereotypes affect people.

Sexual Prejudice

Learn what sexual prejudice is and how prevalent it is in our society.

Check Your Learning Quiz 10.2

Go to **login.cengagebrain.com** and take the online quiz.

▶ **LO5** Define attributions and distinguish between internal and external attributions.

▶ **LO6** Discuss how attributions affect our explanations of behavior.

After 13 seasons and 2,000 games in the minor leagues, this umpire was passed over for promotion to the major leagues and released. An evaluation report by the Office for Umpire Development claimed that this umpire's work had "deteriorated in areas of enthusiasm and execution," even though earlier in the season the rating had been "better than average." What is unusual about this umpire is that she is a woman. Pam Postema (right photo) claims the reason she was passed over for promotion and released was that she was a woman and there are no female umpires in major league baseball (Reed & Stambler, 1992).

Because I'm a woman, I wasn't promoted.

Most sports fans would have an explanation as to why Pam was not promoted to major league baseball. These kinds of explanations are called attributions.

Attributions are things we point to as the causes of events, other people's behaviors, and our own behaviors.

Types of Attributions

If you had to explain why there are no female umpires in major league baseball, you would use either internal or external attributions (Heider, 1958).

Internal attributions are explanations of behavior based on the internal characteristics or dispositions of the person performing the behavior. They are sometimes referred to as **dispositional attributions.**

For example, if you used internal attributions to explain why Pam was not made a major league umpire, you would point to her personal characteristics or dispositions, such as saying that she was not a good judge of balls and strikes.

External attributions are explanations of behavior based on the external circumstances or situations. They are sometimes called **situational attributions.**

If you used external attributions to explain why Postema was not promoted, you would point to external circumstances, such as saying that major league baseball is run by men, and they do not want to have a woman umpire.

Thus, making internal or external attributions has important implications for personal and social behaviors (Derlega et al., 2005).

Attribution Errors

We'll discuss three errors in making attributions.

© Bettman/Corbis

Unless otherwise noted, all images are © Cengage Learning

Fundamental Attribution Error

If you believe women cannot reach high work positions because they lack the skills and intelligence to do so, you may be making the fundamental attribution error (Langdridge & Butt, 2004).

The **fundamental attribution error** refers to our tendency, when we look for causes of a person's behavior, to focus on the person's disposition or personality traits and overlook how the situation influenced the person's behavior.

An example of the fundamental attribution error would be to conclude that women cannot obtain high work positions because of personal or dispositional factors, such as a lack of assertiveness or intelligence. However, the real reason may be the use of subtle discriminatory hiring practices to keep women out.

Actor-Observer Effect

John angrily explains that he got to his car to put more money in the meter just as the police officer was driving away. John adds he's very responsible and the ticket was bad luck because he was only 45 seconds late. John says he got the ticket because the police officer was just being mean. John's explanation is a good example of the actor-observer effect (Malle, 2006).

The **actor-observer effect** refers to the tendency, when you are behaving (or acting), to attribute your own behavior to situational factors. However, when you are observing others, you attribute another's behavior to his or her personality traits or disposition.

In the parking ticket example, John, the *actor*, attributes his getting the ticket to situational factors, just having bad luck, rather than to his own behavior, being late. In addition, John, the *observer*, explains the police officer ticketed him because of a dispositional or personality factor (the officer was mean).

Self-Serving Bias

When we look for the causes of our behaviors, we may make errors because of the self-serving bias (Fiedler, 2007; Mcallister et al., 2002).

The **self-serving bias** refers to explaining our successes by attributing them to our dispositions or personality traits and explaining our failures by attributing them to the situations.

According to the self-serving bias, if you get an A on an exam, you tend to attribute your success to your personality traits or disposition, such as intelligence and perseverance. However, if you get a D on an exam, you tend to attribute your failure to the situation, such as a difficult test or unfair questions.

Types of Attributions

Use internal and external attributions while discovering their errors.

Attributions and Grades

Learn whether changing attributions can change grades.

Check Your Learning Quiz 10.3

Go to **login.cengagebrain.com** and take the online quiz.

▶ **LO7** Define attitude and explain the three components of attitude.

The media regularly report on people's attitudes toward a wide range of hot topics, such as politics, religion, drug use, abortion, and sports. The concept of attitude, which in the 1930s was called the single most indispensable term in social psychology (Allport, 1935), continues to be one of the most studied concepts (Maio et al., 2006).

An **attitude** is any belief or opinion that includes an evaluation of some object, person, or event along a continuum from negative to positive and that predisposes us to act in a certain way toward that object, person, or event.

Attitudes can have a significant impact on behavior, as happened in the tragic death of an 11-year-old boy named Bo. An autopsy showed that Bo had died of complications from diabetes. After suffering painful symptoms for 7 days, he went into a coma and died. At the time, he was 15 to 20 pounds underweight. Bo's parents were members of the Followers of Christ Church in Oregon, and they believed that prayer is a substitute for conventional medical treatment. The leader of the church had preached that God would heal and that anyone seeking worldly (medical) help was weak and lacked faith in God. Because of these attitudes, Bo received no medical treatment for his diabetes, which doctors said was an easily treatable problem. Records showed that as many as 25 children in the congregation had died in the past 20 years because they were treated with prayers instead of conventional medical help.

Bo's case is an example of attitudes that have the power to influence life-and-death decisions. Attitudes influence a wide range of behaviors, which is one reason billions of dollars are spent each year trying to measure and change attitudes and get people to buy certain products or vote for particular candidates. Attitudes, which can have very powerful influences on our lives, have three components.

Components of Attitudes

If we closely examined the attitudes of Bo's parents toward faith healing and conventional medical treatment, we would find that attitudes influence their thoughts (cognitive component), feelings (affective component), and behaviors (behavioral component) (Huskinson & Haddock, 2006; Maio & Haddock, 2007).

Unless otherwise noted, all images are © Cengage Learning

Cognitive Component

Bo's parents did not approve of conventional medical treatment for their son because they believed that only prayers were needed since God does the healing (if that is God's will). The parents' beliefs illustrate the cognitive component of attitudes, which includes both thoughts and beliefs that are involved in evaluating some object, person, or idea.

An attitude's cognitive component can range from a very negative evaluation to a very positive one. For example, Bo's parents have a very positive belief in faith healing and a very negative evaluation of conventional medical treatment.

Affective Component

Bo's parents were fearful of seeking conventional medical treatment because it meant going against God's will. The parents' fearful feelings illustrate the affective component of attitudes, which involves emotional feelings that can be weak or strong, positive or negative. For example, Bo's parents had strong positive feelings about using only prayers to treat their son's medical problem and strong negative feelings about seeking conventional medical treatment.

Behavioral Component

The parents' positive attitude toward using prayer alone and their negative attitude toward seeking conventional medical treatment resulted in their not calling a medical doctor. The parents' refusal to call a medical doctor illustrates the behavioral component of attitudes, which involves performing or not performing some behavior.

In some cases, engaging in some behavior can influence the formation of an attitude (Maio et al., 2006). For example, having a good or bad experience in doing something (for example, snowboarding, sky diving, using drugs, going to concerts) may result in a positive or negative attitude toward that activity.

Implicit Association Test

Watch how we have attitudes that we don't even know we have.

National Attitudes

Explore how culture shapes our attitudes.

▶ **LO8** Describe the different processes that can lead to attitude change.

Attitude Change

At one time, Floyd Cochran (right photo) was an out-and-out hatemonger who was a leader of the neo-Nazi group, Aryan Nation, in Idaho. His goal was to exterminate everyone who wasn't white. He constantly preached hatred, and he recruited many white youths to help him "spread the hate like a disease" (Cochran, 2007). Then, as he was preparing for the annual Hitler Youth Festival, a group of white supremacists told him that his 4-year-old son must be euthanized because he was born with a birth defect. Floyd found himself caught between his own years of preaching hate and members of Aryan Nation hating the son he loved. Floyd resolved his personal dilemma by renouncing his white supremacist values and abandoning the hate organizations. He now speaks out against hate and racism (Charmoli, 2006).

> I was a racist until my values hurt my son.

Courtesy of Floyd Cochran

Why did Floyd radically change his attitudes, from preaching hate and racism to denouncing these beliefs? We'll begin our discussion on attitude change with the theory of cognitive dissonance and self-perception theory.

Cognitive Dissonance

After a group of white supremacists told him his son must be euthanized, Floyd's life became one big conflict. He had spent most of his adult life practicing racism and hate, but now his own personal values were causing him great anguish. Floyd found himself in the middle of a very troubling inconsistency, which Leon Festinger (1957) called cognitive dissonance.

Cognitive dissonance refers to a state of unpleasant psychological tension that motivates us to reduce our cognitive inconsistencies by making our beliefs more consistent with our behavior.

There are two main ways to reduce cognitive dissonance: adding or changing beliefs and counterattidunal behavior. (Andersen et al., 2007).

Adding or Changing Beliefs We can reduce cognitive dissonance by adding new beliefs or changing old beliefs and making them consistent with our behavior. To decrease his cognitive dissonance, Floyd renounced his hateful beliefs so his attitudes became consistent with his behavior, which was loving his son regardless of his birth defect.

Counterattitudinal Behavior Another way we can reduce cognitive dissonance is by engaging in opposite or counterattitudinal behavior (Leippe & Eisenstadt, 1994).

Counterattitudinal behavior involves taking a public position that runs counter to your private attitude.

A classic study by Festinger and Carlsmith (1959) illustrates how counterattitudinal behavior works. In this study, subjects were asked to do an extremely boring task, such as turning pegs in a board. At the end of the task, the experimenter asked the subjects to help out by telling the next group of subjects how interesting the task was. Subjects were asked to lie about the task and say it was interesting, which is engaging in counterattitudinal behavior. For saying the task was interesting, some subjects received $1 and some received $20. Some time later, the original subjects were asked how much they had liked the boring task. A curious finding emerged. Subjects paid just $1 had a more favorable attitude about the boring task than those who were paid $20.

That's because subjects paid $20 felt they were paid well for lying. Subjects paid $1 had no good reason for lying, and so, to resolve the cognitive dissonance between what they'd said (it was interesting) and what they felt (it was boring), they convinced themselves that the task was somewhat interesting. This shows that engaging in opposite or counterattitudinal behaviors can change attitudes. However, there's a different explanation for this experiment's results.

Self-Perception Theory

Perhaps subjects in the previous experiment came to believe their own lies (that the task was interesting) after engaging in counterattitudinal behavior, not to reduce cognitive dissonance but because of changing their own self-perceptions.

Self-perception theory says that we first observe or perceive our own behavior and then, as a result, we change our attitudes.

Daryl Bem (1967), who developed self-perception theory, would explain that subjects paid only $1 for lying would recall their behavior and conclude that they would never have lied for only $1, so the task must have actually been interesting.

We may change our own attitudes in response to cognitive dissonance or self-perception. However, others are continually trying to change our attitudes through various forms of persuasion, our next topic.

Changing Attitudes

Learn more about the difference between cognitive dissonance theory and self-perception theory.

© Mikeledray/Shutterstock

© Patrick McCall/Shutterstock

Persuasion

Political candidates spend much of their time, energy, and money trying to persuade people to vote for them. What politicians have to decide is whether to use an intellectual or emotional appeal, how to appear honest, and what arguments to use. We'll begin with choosing between two different routes: central or peripheral (Maio & Haddock, 2007; Petty & Cacioppo, 1986).

Central Route If the audience is interested in thinking about the real issues, a politician might best use the central route.

The **central route for persuasion** presents information with strong arguments, analyses, facts, and logic.

I think logical arguments and hard facts work best.

A political candidate using the central route for persuasion should present clear, detailed information about his or her views and accomplishments and should appear honest and credible by demonstrating knowledge and commitment to the issues (Priester & Petty, 1995).

The central route for persuasion works with people who think about and analyze the issues. However, not all voters can be persuaded by the central route. For some, a peripheral route is the better persuasion method.

Peripheral Route If the audience is more interested in the candidate's personality or image, a politician might seek votes using the peripheral route.

The **peripheral route for persuasion** emphasizes emotional appeal, focuses on personal traits, and generates positive feelings.

I think emotional and personal appeals work best.

The peripheral route assumes that not all voters will spend the time and energy to digest or discuss the issues. Instead, some audiences are more interested in the candidate's ability to generate excitement by giving an energetic and enthusiastic speech (Priester & Petty, 1995). This route involves bands, banners, parties, and personal appearances, which build an exciting image and create a positive attitude toward the candidate. If audiences like the candidate's image, they will more likely agree with the candidate's views (Carlson, 1990).

Whether the central or peripheral route is used, a number of specific elements are important in persuasion.

© Steve Pope/Landov

Unless otherwise noted, all images are © Cengage Learning

Elements of Persuasion There are a number of important elements in persuasion, including the source, message, and audience.

Source One element in persuading someone to adopt your point of view involves the source of the message. We are more likely to believe sources who have a sense of authority, appear honest and trustworthy, have expertise and credibility, and are attractive and likable (Priester & Petty, 1995). The source element explains why TV newscasters and anchorpersons, exemplified by satirist Jon Stewart on *The Daily Show* (right photo), are usually physically attractive, likable, and believable.

Message Another element of persuasion involves the content of the message. If the persuader is using the *central route,* the messages will contain convincing and understandable facts. If the facts are complicated, a written message is better than a spoken one (Chaiken & Eagly, 1976).

If the persuader is using the *peripheral route,* the messages should be designed to arouse emotion, sentiment, and loyalty. Television infomercials use the peripheral approach by having an attractive and likable demonstrator show how you will look or feel better by buying and using a particular product. However, using fearful messages to persuade people, such as showing blackened lungs to get smokers to quit, may not be effective because arousing fear may interfere with and distract people from hearing and taking precautionary measures to stop unhealthy practices (Ruiter et al., 2001).

Audience Another element of being an effective persuader involves knowing the characteristics of the audience. For example, audiences who are interested in facts are best persuaded using the central route, while audiences interested in personal traits are best persuaded using the peripheral route.

Thus, persuasion is a complicated process that involves the source of the message, the route by which the content is delivered, and the characteristics of the audience. Good persuaders may combine central and peripheral routes to win over the audience to their viewpoints (Cialdini, 2003).

Routes for Persuasion

Learn about whether men and women respond differently to the routes for persuasion

Check Your Learning Quiz 10.4

Go to **login.cengagebrain.com** and take the online quiz.

Conformity

The touch football game had been going on for years and was considered a rite of passage for incoming seniors. During the game, some minor hazing usually took place, such as senior girls dumping various kinds of food (such as ketchup, whipped cream, syrup) on junior girls. About 10 minutes into this particular junior-senior touch football game, something unexpected happened, and the game turned ugly. The senior girls started to act in violent ways that just happened to be videotaped by another student. Later, as CNN played the tape over and over, everyone wondered how these particular senior girls, who came from a well-to-do Chicago suburb and went to a good high school, could have done such disgusting things.

According to the video and police reports, junior girls were beaten, slapped, kicked, splattered in the eyes with Tabasco sauce and vinegar, hit with buckets, covered with animal intestines and urine, and smeared with blood, fish guts, mud, and feces. Five girls ended up in the hospital, some requiring stitches (Black & Flynn, 2003). What kind of group pressure causes normal people to submit to being hazed, and what kind of group pressure turns normal people into violent and ugly hazers?

When students were asked why they agreed to be hazed, many answered they did so because it made them feel part of the group (Hoover & Pollard, 2000). "Going along" with the group is an example of conformity (Levine & Kerr, 2007).

Conformity refers to any behavior you perform because of group pressure, even though that pressure might not involve direct requests.

Some common examples of conforming include wearing clothes that are in style, adopting the "in" slang phrases, and buying the currently popular products. Normally, most people would never conform or agree to be publicly humiliated. Yet reacting to strong group pressures, 48% of high school and college students who participate in group activities conform and agree to be hazed, which means humiliation and possible injury (Lipkins, 2006).

We'll discuss group pressures and why people conform and obey, beginning with a classic experiment in social psychology.

Asch's Experiment

A classic experiment is one that causes us to change the way we think about something—in this case, how social pressures can influence conformity (Blakeslee, 2005; Stasser & Dietz-Uhler, 2003). Solomon Asch's (1958) classic experiment showed very clearly how an individual can be pressured to conform to a group's standards. As we describe Asch's experiment, imagine that you are a subject and guess how you might have behaved.

Procedure

You are seated at a round table with five others and have been told that you are taking part in a visual perception experiment. Your group is shown a straight line and then is instructed to look at three more lines of different lengths and pick out the line equal in length to the original one (right illustration). The three choices are different enough that it is not hard to pick out the correct one. Each person at the round table identifies his or her choice out loud, with you answering next to last. When you are ready to answer, you will have heard four others state their opinions. What you do not know is that these four other people are the experimenter's accomplices. On certain trials, they will answer correctly, making you feel your choice is right. On other trials, they will deliberately answer incorrectly, much to your surprise. In these cases you will have heard four identical incorrect answers before it is your turn to answer. You will almost certainly feel some group pressure to conform to the others' opinion. Will you give in?

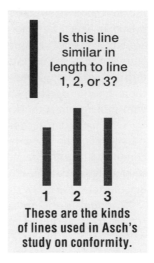

Is this line similar in length to line 1, 2, or 3?

1 2 3

These are the kinds of lines used in Asch's study on conformity.

Results

Out of 50 subjects in Asch's experiment, 75% conformed on some of the trials, but no one conformed on all the trials; 25% never conformed. These data indicate that the desire to have your attitudes and behaviors match those of others in a group can be a powerful force.

Asch's study is considered a classic because it was the first to clearly show that group pressures can influence conformity. However, we may conform publicly but disagree privately, and this is an example of compliance.

Behavior Lab Conformity

Watch how likely it is that a person will conform to an unusual social behavior.

Conformity

Watch conformity take place in an elevator.

▶ **LO11** Summarize Milgram's obedience experiment.

Compliance

One interpretation of Asch's data is that subjects were not really changing their beliefs but rather just pretending to go along with the group. For example, when subjects in Asch's experiment privately recorded their answers, conforming drastically declined. This decline indicated that subjects were conforming but not really changing their beliefs, which is one kind of compliance.

Compliance is a kind of conformity in which we give in to social pressure in our public responses but do not change our private beliefs.

For example, you may conform to your instructor's suggestions on rewriting a paper although you do not agree with the suggestions. In this case, you would be complying with someone in authority.

I disagree, but I'll rewrite it

One particular technique of compliance is used by salespeople, who know that if they get the customer to comply with a small request, the customer is more likely to comply with a later request to buy the product (Cialdini & Goldstein, 2004).

The **foot-in-the-door technique** refers to the technique of starting with a little request to gain eventual compliance with a later request.

A common example of the foot-in-the-door technique is telemarketers who first get you to answer a simple question such as "How are you today?" so that you'll stay on the phone and answer their other questions. The foot-in-the-door technique is one successful way to obtain compliance (Rodafinos et al., 2005).

If you are officially or formally asked to comply with a request, such as "Take a test on Friday," your compliance is called obedience.

Obedience

When it comes to signs, laws, rules, and regulations, such as speed limits, instructors' assignments, and doctors' orders, people differ in what they choose to obey.

Obedience refers to performing some behavior in response to an order given by someone in a position of power or authority.

Most of us obey orders, rules, and regulations that are for the general good. But what if the orders or rules are cruel or immoral?

Milgram's Experiment

Stanley Milgram's (1963) experiment on obedience is a classic experiment in social psychology because it was the first to study whether people would obey commands that were clearly inhumane and immoral (Miller, 2005). As we describe this famous experiment, imagine being the "teacher" and consider whether you would have obeyed the experimenter's commands.

The Setup Imagine that you have volunteered for a study on the effects of punishment on learning. After arriving in the laboratory at Yale University, you are selected to be the "teacher," and another volunteer is to be the "learner." What you don't know is that the learner is actually an accomplice of the experimenter. As the teacher, you watch the learner being strapped into a chair and having electrodes placed on his wrists. The electrodes are attached to a shock generator in the next room. You and the researcher then leave the learner's room, close the door, and go into an adjoining room.

> Whenever you make a mistake, you'll receive an electric shock.

The researcher gives you a list of questions to ask the learner over an intercom, and the learner is to signal his answer on a panel of lights in front of you. For each wrong answer, you, the teacher, are to shock the learner and to increase the intensity of the shock by 15 volts for each succeeding wrong answer. In front of you is the shock machine, with 30 separate switches that indicate increasing intensities. The first switch is marked "15 volts. Slight shock," and the last switch is marked "XXX 450 volts. Danger: Severe shock." You begin to ask the learner questions, and as he misses them, you administer stronger and stronger shocks.

Shock Controller

Slight shock — MAXIMUM XXX 450 volts

Milgram's Experiment: Obedience to Authority

Learn how powerful the pressure to be obedient is and why people obey.

The Conflict As the teacher, you give the learner shocks that increase in intensity up to 300 volts, when the learner pounds on the wall. You continue and after the next miss, you give the learner a 315-volt shock, after which the learner pounds on the wall and stops answering any more questions. Although you plead with the researcher to stop the experiment, the researcher explains that, as the teacher, you are to continue asking questions and shocking the learner for incorrect answers. Even though the learner has pounded on the wall and stopped answering questions after a 315-volt shock, would you continue the procedure until you deliver the XXX 450 volts?

What you, the teacher, don't know is that the learner is part of the experiment and acts like being shocked but never received a single one. The teacher was misled into believing that he or she was really shocking the learner. The question was whether a teacher would continue and deliver the maximum shock.

The Results The scary question was how many "teachers" (that is, subjects) would deliver the maximum intensity shock to the "learner."

0.12% When psychiatrists were asked to predict how many subjects would deliver the full range of shocks, including the last 450 volts, they estimated that only 0.12% of the subjects would do so.

65% To the surprise and dismay of many, including Milgram, 65% of the subjects delivered the full range of shocks, including the final 450 volts. There was no difference between males and females.

When Stanley Milgram conducted these studies on obedience in the early 1960s, they demonstrated that people will obey inhumane orders simply because they are told to do so. This kind of unthinking obedience to immoral commands was something that psychiatrists and Milgram had not predicted. Milgram (1974) repeated variations of this experiment many times and obtained similar results. Additionally, Milgram's experiment was repeated in various parts of the world with similar results (Blass, 2000).

Percentage of Subjects Who Obeyed Experimenter's Commands

Labels on the shock controller

Why Do People Obey? Psychologists have suggested several reasons that 65% of the subjects in Milgram's experiment agreed to deliver the maximum shock to learners. Perhaps the major reason is that people have learned to follow the orders of authority figures, whether they are religious leaders, army commanders, doctors, scientists, or parents. However, people are more likely to obey authority figures when they are present. In one of his follow-up studies, Milgram (1974) found that when subjects received their instructions over the telephone, they were more likely to defy authority than when they received their instructions in person. This also explains why patients don't follow doctors' orders once they leave their offices.

People also obey because they have learned to follow orders in their daily lives, whether in traffic, on the job, or in personal interactions. However, people are more likely to obey if an authority figure (officer, boss, or parent) is present.

Were Milgram's Experiments Ethical? Although the Milgram experiments provided important information about obedience, the study could not be conducted under today's research guidelines. As we discussed (pp. 38–39), all experiments today, especially those with the potential for causing psychological or physical harm, are carefully screened by research committees, a practice that did not exist at the time of Milgram's research. When there is a possibility of an experiment causing psychological harm, the researchers must propose ways to eliminate or counteract the potential harmful effects. This is usually done by debriefing the subjects.

Debriefing occurs after an experimental procedure and involves explaining the purpose and method of the experiment, asking the subjects their feelings about being in the experiment, and helping the subjects deal with possible doubts or guilt arising from their behaviors in the experiment.

Although Milgram's subjects were debriefed, critics doubt that the question of whether any psychological harm had been done to the subjects was resolved. Because the potential for psychological harm to the subjects was so great in Milgram's studies, any related research had to pass very strict ethical standards.

In conclusion, Milgram's experiment demonstrated that ordinary people are capable of hurting others (even when those being hurt beg them to stop), as long as they are ordered by an authority figure to do so. In other words, blind obedience to unreasonable authority or inhumane orders is much more likely than we think.

Next, we'll explore the powerful influence of groups.

Milgram's Experiment Revisited

Learn about a modern-day replication of Millgram's experiment and find out how it compares to the original study.

▶ **LO12** Describe reasons for group membership.

Group Dynamics

When you're with family, friends, or co-workers, you may or may not be aware of the many group influences that can change how you think, feel, and behave.

Groups are collections of two or more people who interact, share some common idea, goal, or purpose, and influence how their members think and behave.

To illustrate the powerful influences of groups, we'll describe the case of Dennis Jay, who almost died in a drunken coma and later heard that his fraternity brothers had lied about the initiation that had almost killed him.

Group Cohesion and Norms

As a pledge at a fraternity initiation party, Dennis Jay and 19 others submitted to hazing: They were forced to drink from a "beer bong," a funnel into which beer was poured; the beer ran down a plastic hose placed in the mouth (right photo). The rule was that once you threw up, you could stop drinking from the beer bong. Because he did not throw up, Jay was given straight shots of whiskey until he fell on his face. By the time his frat brothers got Jay to the hospital, he was in a coma and barely breathing. His blood alcohol content was 0.48, and a level of 0.50 is usually fatal. (Legally drunk in many states is 0.08.)

At first, Jay refused to describe what happened because he wanted to be loyal to his fraternity. Then he heard the fraternity brothers had lied and said he had stumbled drunk into their frat house and they had brought him to the hospital just to help out. The fraternity brothers' lies made Jay angry, and he told the truth (Grogan et al., 1993). As discussed earlier, one reason individuals endure harmful hazing rites is because they wish to become a member of a desired group.

Social psychologists would explain that the fraternity lied about what happened to Jay because of two powerful group influences: group cohesion and group norms.

Group cohesion is group togetherness, which is determined by how much group members perceive that they share common attributes.

One reason many groups have some form of initiation rites and rituals is to have all members share a common experience and thus increase group cohesion.

Group norms are the formal or informal rules about how group members should behave.

Because of powerful group norms to stick together to preserve their group, these fraternity members were willing to lie about what really happened to Jay.

Group Membership

In his hierarchy of human needs (see pp. 412–413), humanistic psychologist Abraham Maslow identified *the need for love and belonging* as fundamental to human happiness (Maslow, 1970). One way to satisfy this social need is by joining a group, which helps individuals feel a sense of belonging, friendship, and support. According to Maslow's theory, the social need to belong points to a **motivational reason** for joining groups. Leon Festinger (1954) offered another reason for joining groups, based on the social comparison theory.

Social comparison theory says that we are driven to compare ourselves to others who are similar to us, so that we can measure the correctness of our attitudes and beliefs. According to Festinger, this drive to compare ourselves motivates us to join groups.

According to Festinger's theory, the drive to compare and judge our attitudes and beliefs against those of others who are similar to us points to a cognitive reason for joining groups. For example, social comparison theory may explain why many young Mormons join missionary groups (right photo).

An additional reason for forming groups is that we can accomplish things in groups that we simply cannot do alone. For example, students form study groups because they want academic help, social support, and motivation. Study groups can take two different forms, each with different goals: task-oriented and socially oriented groups (Burn, 2004).

In a **task-oriented group,** the members have specific duties to complete.

In a **socially oriented group,** the members are primarily concerned about fostering and maintaining social relationships among the members of the group.

For example, a task-oriented group helps members achieve certain academic, business, political, or career goals, while a socially oriented group primarily provides a source of friends, fun activities, and social support.

Group membership can have a powerful influence on many social interactions, such as deciding with whom to socialize, whom to discriminate against and whom to battle, psychologically and physically (Simon & Sturmer, 2003).

Next, we'll discuss how groups and crowds can influence our behaviors.

Teen Pregnancy Pact

Read about a fascinating example of group membership.

Jim LoScalzo/U.S. News & World Report

▶ **LO13** Describe how groups can facilitate or inhibit certain behaviors.

Behavior in Groups

You may not notice, but being in a crowd can cause you to think and behave differently than when you're alone.

A **crowd,** which is a large group of persons who are usually strangers, can facilitate or inhibit certain behaviors.

For example, we'll discuss how being in a crowd can increase or decrease personal performance, encourage individuals to engage in antisocial behaviors, or cause individuals to refuse to help someone in need.

Facilitation and Inhibition

If a runner has a history of successful competition, he may turn in a better performance in front of a large crowd as a result of social facilitation.

Social facilitation is an increase in performance in the presence of a crowd.

In contrast, if a runner has a spotty history in competition, he may turn in a worse performance in front of a large crowd because of social inhibition.

Social inhibition is a decrease in performance in the presence of a crowd.

Whether we show facilitation or inhibition depends partly on our previous experience. Generally, the presence of others will facilitate well-learned, simple, or reflexive responses but will inhibit new, unusual, or complex responses. An example of social facilitation occurs during championship games when a player is awarded the title of "most valuable player." An example of social inhibition also occurs during championship games when a star player, who is expected to do great, instead feels anxiety about performing and plays poorly or "chokes" (Baumeister, 1995).

© Bob Daemmrich/PhotoEdit

Unless otherwise noted, all images are © Cengage Learning

Thus, the presence of a crowd can either facilitate or inhibit behaviors, depending on the situation (Burn, 2004). As you'll learn next, in some instances the presence of a crowd can make it more likely for people to behave in very irrational ways.

Deindividuation in Crowds

During riots, people have been arrested for looting, setting fires, and beating others. Individuals in a crowd are more likely to commit such antisocial acts because being in a crowd conceals the person's identity, a process called deindividuation.

Deindividuation refers to the increased tendency for subjects to behave irrationally or perform antisocial behaviors when there is less chance of being personally identified.

Researchers believe deindividuation occurs because being in a crowd gives individuals anonymity and reduces guilt and self-awareness (Silke, 2003; Zimbardo, 1970).

© WorldFoto/Alamy

The Bystander Effect

As a person lies unconscious on a sidewalk, hundreds of people may walk by without helping. The reasons no one stops to help may include fear of the person's reactions, inexperience with providing help, and the bystander effect.

The **bystander effect** says that an individual may feel inhibited from taking some action because of the presence of others.

© David Grossman/Alamy

Data from over 50 studies indicate that 75% of people offer assistance when alone, but fewer than 53% do so when in a group (Latané & Nida, 1981). One explanation for the bystander effect is the diffusion of responsibility theory.

The **diffusion of responsibility theory** says that, in the presence of others, individuals feel less personal responsibility and are less likely to take action in a situation where help is required (Latané, 1981).

Recent survey results report that 77% of Americans want to help victims of disasters but when it comes to volunteering, many will not because they believe the whole country is already helping (Marchetti & Bunte, 2006).

Kitty Genovese

Learn why people did not help a woman who was being violently attacked.

Unless otherwise noted, all images are © Cengage Learning

▶ **L014** Explain how group polarization and groupthink affect decision making.

Group Decisions

All of us have been in groups, including families, fraternities, sororities, various social or business clubs. What you may not realize is that being in a group creates social pressures that influence how you think and make decisions. We'll discuss two interesting factors in making decisions: group polarization and groupthink.

Group Polarization

Imagine that a young lawyer is trying to decide between two job offers. The first offer is from an established firm that promises security and prestige. However, it has a poor record as an equal opportunity employer of women and has no women partners. The second offer is from a recently established firm that can promise little security or prestige. However, it has an excellent record in promoting women as partners. Which offer should the lawyer accept? Using dilemmas such as this, researchers compared the recommendations from individuals in a group with those made by the group after it engaged in discussion (Gigone & Hastie, 1997; Pruitt, 1971). Group discussions change individuals' judgments, such as when a group urges a more risky decision than do individuals. This phenomenon is known as the *risky shift*.

Researchers later discovered that the direction of a group's risky shift depends on how conservative or liberal the group was to begin with. If a group's members are initially more conservative, group discussion will shift its decision to an even more conservative one. If a group's members are initially more liberal, group discussion will shift its decision to an even more liberal one. The group's shift to a more extreme position is called group polarization (right figure) (Fiedler, 2007).

Group polarization is a phenomenon in which group discussion reinforces the majority's point of view and shifts that view to a more extreme position.

Before group discussion, individual views are generally positive.

After group discussion, individual views shift to more positive views.

Groupthink

In the early 1960s, President John F. Kennedy took the world to the brink of nuclear war when he ordered the invasion of Cuba. This invasion, which occurred at the Bay of Pigs, was a terrible decision and a well-remembered failure. Researchers have analyzed group decision-making processes involved in bad decisions, such as the Bay of Pigs invasion, the escalation of war in Vietnam, the Watergate cover-up, and the *Challenger* disaster, as well as flawed group decisions in business and other organizations. One reason that groups made bad decisions in the above examples is a phenomenon called groupthink (right image) (Janis, 1989; Vallacher & Nowak, 2007).

What's most important is that we stick together.

© PhotoDisc, Inc.

Groupthink refers to a group making bad decisions because the group is more concerned about reaching agreement and sticking together than gathering the relevant information and considering all the alternatives.

According to psychologist Irving Janis (1989), groupthink has a number of clearly defined characteristics: Discussions are limited, few alternatives are presented, and there is increased pressure to conform. In addition, groupthink results in viewing the world in very simple terms: There is the **in-group,** which includes only the immediate members of the group, versus the **out-group,** which includes everyone who is not a part of the group. When a group adopts the in-group–out-group attitude and mentality, the result is that it strengthens groupthink by emphasizing the protection of the group's members over making the best decisions.

Avoiding Groupthink

One authority on groupthink recommends using a method called vigilant decision making, which helps a group avoid falling into groupthink and thus leads to better decisions (Janis, 1989). Major elements of *vigilant decision making* include the following: doing a thorough, open, and unbiased information search; evaluating as many alternative ideas as possible; and having an impartial leader who allows the members to freely and openly express differing opinions without being criticized or being considered a threat to the group. Researchers found that the vigilant decision-making method does result in better and more successful group decisions, although it is criticized for being very time-consuming (Burn, 2004).

Group Polarization

Learn how group polarization shifts people's views.

Check Your Learning Quiz 10.5

Go to **login.cengagebrain.com** and take the online quiz.

▶ **LO15** Discuss how genes and environment may influence aggression.

Influences on Aggression

Drive-by shootings, gang fights and killings, spousal and child abuse, school shootings, hate crimes, revenge shooting by angry workers, bullying, road rage, and extreme forms of hazing are all examples of aggression.

Aggression is any behavior directed toward another that is intended to cause harm.

There is no single reason someone turns into a child bully or an aggressive adult but rather three major components: genetic and environmental influences, social cognitive and personality traits, and situational cues.

© Ben Welsh Premium/Alamy

Genes and Environment

Genes and environment have significant influence on aggressive behavior. We'll begin by focusing on the genetic influence in animals and humans, and then examine the interaction between genes and environment.

Genetic Influences in Animals

You can clearly see that genetic influences can regulate aggression by watching the behavior of animals. Ethologists, who study animal behavior in natural settings, have identified numerous social signals that animals have evolved to regulate aggression. For example, the right photo shows a dominant wolf standing above a submissive wolf. The submissive wolf avoids being attacked by lying down and rolling over to expose its vulnerable belly. Many dominant and submissive gestures observed in animals are largely programmed by genetic factors and help animals avoid potentially damaging aggressive attacks and improve their chances of survival. Compared with animals, reasons for aggressive acts in humans are much more complicated.

© Zigmund Leszcynski/Animals Animals

Unless otherwise noted, all images are © Cengage Learning

Genetic Influences in Humans

We all begin life with a different set of genes (picture below) that contain chemical instructions that regulate the manufacture and assembly of the many thousands of parts that make up our body and brain.

Researchers studied levels of aggression in twins and adopted children to gauge how much genetic factors influence human aggression. If genetic factors influence aggression in humans, then identical twins, who share almost 100% of their genes, should be more alike in committing aggressive behaviors than fraternal twins, who share only 50% of their genes. Also, if genetic factors influence human aggression, then children from aggressive biological parents should be more aggressive, even if adopted by nonaggressive parents. Researchers analyzed over 50 twin and adoption studies and found that genetic factors accounted for about 34% of the total factors that were responsible for developing aggressive and antisocial behaviors (Rhee & Waldman, 2002). These studies show that genetic influences may partly predispose a person to develop aggressive behaviors, but whether this actually occurs depends on the interaction with potentially powerful good or bad environmental influences.

Genes Interact with Good and Bad Environments

The evidence for the interaction of genetic and environmental factors in aggressive behavior is abundant. Researchers found that a specific gene variation influences brain development to make someone more prone to engage in impulsive violence, but only when the gene variation is combined with environmental stress (Mullin & Hinshaw, 2007).

Researchers have also studied the interaction of genetic and environmental factors by following boys who had inherited potentially "bad genes" from their criminally inclined biological parents. Some of these boys were adopted by noncriminal parents and raised in good environments, while others were raised in "bad environments" by criminally inclined adoptive parents. Results showed the combination of "bad genes" interacting with "bad environments" resulted in a large percentage of boys going on to commit criminal acts. However, results also showed that good environments can, to a large extent, compensate for inheriting "bad genes" and can override the development of aggressive or antisocial behaviors (Raine, 2002).

Genes and Child Abuse

Find out why some abused children become violent adults while others do not.

▶ **LO16** Describe how social cognitive theory explains how people learn to be aggressive.

▶ **LO17** Explain the frustration-aggression hypothesis.

Social Cognitive and Personality Factors

We have discussed how genetic factors may predispose a person to be aggressive, but whether this occurs depends upon the interaction with environmental factors, such as one's learning experiences. One theory that explains how people learn to be aggressive is Bandura's (2001a) social cognitive theory.

Social cognitive theory says that much of human behavior, including aggressive behavior, may be learned through watching, imitating, and modeling, and does not require the observer to perform any observable behavior or receive any observable reward.

A classic laboratory study by Bandura (1965) found that children who observed a model's aggressive behaviors performed similar aggressive behaviors (p. 240). Children who were exposed to aggressive models, such as seeing parents use physical punishment, showed increased aggression with their peers, parents, and dating partners (Anderson & Huesmann, 2003).

Children have ample opportunity to see, model, and imitate aggressive adults, since the majority of programs on television contain aggressive actions. Researchers found that adolescents who had watched 2 to 3 hours of daily television (all kinds of programs) were almost 4 times more likely to commit violent and aggressive acts compared to those who had watched less than 1 hour a day. Researchers concluded that frequent TV viewing correlated with committing violent acts later in life (Johnson et al., 2002). However, it's also possible that aggressive-prone adolescents prefer to watch TV rather than engage in other activities.

Model of Aggression

One model of how children develop aggressive behaviors points to an interaction among genetic/environmental factors, which can predispose individuals to develop an irritable or angry temperament and become more or less aggressive depending upon the environment; social cognitive factors, which involve imitating and modeling the observed aggressive behaviors; and personality factors, such as being impulsive, and lacking empathy (Anderson & Bushman, 2002; Tisak et al., 2006).

© Edouard Berne/Getty Images

Unless otherwise noted, all images are © Cengage Learning

Situational Cues

A number of situational cues have been linked to increased aggression, including hot weather, easy access to guns, and exposure to violent TV shows and video games (Anderson & Bushman, 2002). Another situational cue that has made the news is drivers becoming so frustrated and angry by other drivers' annoying driving habits that they respond by aggressively pursuing,

ramming, fighting, and even shooting another driver (Galovski et al., 2006). The press labeled this aggressive action by frustrated drivers *road rage*, which shows how frustration can trigger aggression.

The **frustration-aggression hypothesis** says that when our goals are blocked, we become frustrated and respond with anger and aggression.

However, researchers soon discovered that although frustration may lead to aggression, the link between the two is not absolute. Leonard Berkowitz (1989) examined the frustration-aggression hypothesis and concluded the following:

- Frustration doesn't always lead to aggression.
- Social rules may inhibit aggression.
- Frustration may result in behaviors other than aggression.
- Cognitive factors can override aggression.

Thus, Berkowitz (1993) modified the original hypothesis.

The **modified frustration-aggression hypothesis** says that although frustration may lead to aggression, a number of situational and cognitive factors may override the aggressive response.

Although our daily lives are often filled with frustrations, we usually find ways to control our frustrations. However, a child is more likely to react to frustration with violence if he or she has observed and imitated the aggressive behaviors of adults (Osofsky, 1995). Similarly, adults with a personality trait to be impulsive or a genetic tendency to be aggressive are more likely to react to frustration with aggression (Lindsay & Anderson, 2000).

Remember there is no single reason or cause of aggression. Our discussion points to the importance of biological influences and emphasizes that any explanation of human aggression must consider the interaction among three factors: genes and environment, social cognitive learning and personality traits, and situational cues.

Check Your Learning Quiz 10.6

Go to **login.cengagebrain.com** and take the online quiz.

© Roy Morsch/Age fotostock

▶ **LO18** Describe prosocial behavior and altruism.

▶ **LO19** Explain two models of why people choose to help others.

Helping Behaviors

While Wesley Autrey was waiting for the subway in New York City, he saw a man suffering from a seizure fall onto the tracks. A train was rapidly approaching the station and, knowing the man would be killed in only seconds, Wesley jumped onto the tracks and covered the man with his body. The train passed over their bodies leaving only inches to spare. The train came so close to Wesley's body that it left grease marks on his hat (C. Buckley, 2007; Trump, 2007). Wesley's quick, heroic action is an example of helping, or prosocial behavior.

Prosocial behavior (helping) is any behavior that benefits others or has positive social consequences.

In our society, professionals, such as paramedics, are trained and paid to provide help. However, in Wesley's case, he was the only onlooker who risked his life to save a seizing man who had no possibility of surviving on his own. Wesley's helping may be described as altruistic, since he expected no external reward.

Altruism is one form of helping or doing something, often at a cost or risk, for reasons other than the expectation of a material or social reward.

Altruistic people often do things that touch our hearts. Consider 87-year-old Osceola McCarty (right photo), who handwashed clothes most of her life for grateful clients. When she finally retired at age 86, she donated most of her life savings, an amazing $150,000, to the University of Southern Mississippi to finance scholarships for the area's African American students. "I want them to have an education," said McCarty, who never married and has no children of her own. "I had to work hard all my life. They can have the chance that I didn't have" (Plummer & Ridenhour, 1995, p. 40). As these examples show, some people help in emergencies, and others help by donating time or money. What motivates people to help others?

I donated most of my life savings for student scholarships.

© Alan Weiner

Unless otherwise noted, all images are © Cengage Learning

Why People Help

Researchers suggest at least three different motivations—empathy, personal distress, and norms and values—to explain why people, like McCarty, are altruistic and help others without thought of rewards (Batson, 1998; Schroeder et al., 1995):

- We may help because we feel empathy (that is, we identify with what the victim must be going through).
- We may help because we feel personal distress (that is, we have feelings of fear, alarm, or disgust from seeing a victim in need).
- We may help because of our norms and values (that is, we may feel morally bound or socially responsible to help those in need).

Researchers have combined these three motivations along with several other ideas to construct two different theories of why people come out of a crowd and help perfect strangers. We can use these two theories to explain why Wesley (right photo) was the only onlooker at the subway station who dared to jump on the tracks and risk his life to save that of another man.

© AP Images/Frank Franklin II

Decision-Stage Model

Wesley may have decided to help after going through five stages, which involved making five different decisions.

The **decision-stage model of helping** says that you go through five stages in deciding to help: (1) you notice the situation; (2) you interpret it as one in which help is needed; (3) you assume personal responsibility; (4) you choose a form of assistance; and (5) you carry out that assistance.

According to the decision-stage model, Wesley helped because he went through all five stages. Most onlookers stopped at stage 3 and decided it was not their responsibility, so they did not help. This model explains that people may recognize a situation as an emergency (stages 1 and 2) yet fail to help because they do not take personal responsibility for the situation (Latané & Darley, 1970).

Arousal-Cost-Reward Model

Wesley also may have helped because he thought about the costs and rewards.

The **arousal-cost-reward model of helping** says that we make decisions to help by calculating the costs and rewards of helping.

For example, seeing an accident may cause you to be unpleasantly and emotionally *aroused,* which you wish to reduce. In deciding how to reduce these unpleasant feelings, you calculate the *costs* and *rewards* of helping. For example, those who decided not to help may have felt that the costs of helping, such as getting involved in a potentially dangerous situation, outweighed the rewards (Piliavin et al., 1982).

Why People Help

Learn more about why people help others in distress.

Check Your Learning Quiz 10.7

Go to **login.cengagebrain.com** and take the online quiz.

▶ **LO20** Define social neuroscience.

▶ **LO21** Describe the technology used in social neuroscience.

▶ **LO22** Summarize a major finding in social neuroscience.

As we learned earlier in this chapter (p. 460), the area of the brain associated with emotional vigilance becomes activated when white people view unfamiliar black faces. This research finding is an example of a new interdisciplinary field called social neuroscience.

Social neuroscience refers to an emerging area of research that examines social behavior, such as perceiving others, by combining biological and social approaches. In other words, it focuses on understanding how social behavior influences the brain, as well as on how the brain influences social behavior (Cacioppo & Berntson, 2002).

Research in social neuroscience has grown dramatically in recent years (Cacioppo et al., 2007). We'll discuss the methods researchers use to study social neuroscience and some of the research findings that have emerged from this recent approach to understanding social behavior.

Methods

A variety of techniques are used in social neuroscience to examine the interaction of brain and social processes. As we learned earlier (Module 2.5), there are several techniques for studying the brain. The common techniques used in social neuroscience to examine brain activity include positron emission tomography (PET scan), functional magnetic resonance imaging (fMRI), electroencephalography (EEG), and transcranial magnetic stimulation (TMS).

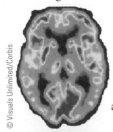

PET scan involves injecting a slightly radioactive solution into the blood and then measuring how much radiation is absorbed by neurons. Different levels of absorption are represented by colors: red and yellow indicate maximum activity of neurons, while blue and green indicate minimal activity.

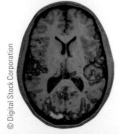

fMRI measures the changes in the activity of specific neurons that are functioning during cognitive tasks, such as thinking about another person.

© Visuals Unlimited/Corbis

© Digital Stock Corporation

Unless otherwise noted, all images are © Cengage Learning

EEG involves placing electrodes at various points across the scalp. The electrodes detect electrical activity (brain-wave activity) throughout the brain's surface.

TMS is a noninvasive technique that sends pulses of magnetic energy into the brain. It works to either activate or suppress brain activity.

Findings

Perhaps the most fascinating research in social neuroscience has been identifying mirror neurons, which are brain cells that are responsible for human empathy. Mirror neurons allow us to put ourselves in other people's shoes and experience how they feel. They are the reason we smile when we see a baby smile or flinch when we see a

person in pain. Mirror neurons also explain why yawning is contagious. When we see another person yawn (left photo), mirror neurons tell our brains to do the same. In fact, I (H. K.) couldn't stop myself from yawning when I looked at this photo! On a more upbeat note, group laughter spreads in much the same way (Dobbs, 2006b). For instance, I always laugh more while watching a comedy in a crowded theater than when I watch one alone at home. Thanks to mirror neurons, I know there is a biological explanation for why these movie-watching experiences are so different.

A major area of social neuroscience research is racial bias. Many people who adamantly report being race-blind may unknowingly hold unconscious racial biases, which can come out in unexpected ways. For instance, when white Americans see photos flashed so quickly they have no conscious awareness of having seen them, the area of the brain that signals "Watch out!" is more active immediately following the appearance of black faces than white faces (Begley, 2008a).

Mirror Neurons

Explore the role mirror neurons play in our social relationships.

Check Your Learning Quiz 10.8

Go to **login.cengagebrain.com** and take the online quiz.

Think Critically

Challenge Your Thinking

Consider these questions when reading this article:

1. What role does brain development play in the likelihood of adolescents having safe sex to reduce the chances of getting infected with HPV? (See Module 8.4)
2. How do the three components of attitude apply to the position of conservatives?
3. Why has preaching abstinence not been more successful in preventing girls from getting HPV?
4. Which group attitudes or norms do conservatives share? How does a group benefit by sharing norms?
5. What type of persuasion are advocates of the vaccine most likely using to pass legislation?
6. If a parent is opposed to vaccinating a teen, what needs to happen to change his or her attitude toward teens getting vaccinated?

Why the Debate over Teen Vaccination?

What if modern medicine could prevent three-quarters of the occurrences of a leading cause of cancer in women and save almost 300,000 lives each year? A major public health breakthrough makes this possible. The first vaccine to protect women against cervical cancer is now available.

Cervical cancer is caused by HPV (human papillomavirus), the most common sexually transmitted infection in the United States. Cervical cancer usually strikes when a woman is young, often before she has had children, and the treatment may cause infertility. Because

cervical cancer is the leading cause of cancer death in women and its treatment has serious risks, prevention is essential.

A vaccine that prevents infection of four types of HPV and comes with minimal side effects is now available. The vaccine is 100% effective in targeting certain causes of cervical cancer that together make up about three-quarters of all cervical cancer cases. Despite its effectiveness and safety, the use of the vaccine has provoked considerable social controversy.

Because many teens contract HPV within only a few years after their first sexual experience, it is recommended that the vaccine be administered to girls during their early teens. Some conservative officials and parents oppose vaccinating teen girls, stating the vaccine undermines their value of abstinence being the best method to avoid getting HPV. These same opponents fear that vaccinating young teens against a sexually transmitted infection, such as HPV, conveys approval to be sexually promiscuous.

Alan Kaye, the executive director of the National Cervical Cancer Coalition, disagrees with opponents who worry the vaccination will result in girls becoming sexually promiscuous. He responds to these moral objections by comparing the vaccine to wearing a seat belt: "Just because you wear a seat belt doesn't mean you're seeking out an accident" (Stein, 2005). Others argue the cervical cancer vaccine is no different from routine vaccines that protect children from diseases such as measles, polio, or chicken pox.

Texas Governor Rick Perry decided the benefits of the vaccine outweighed the moral concerns. Texas became the first state to require girls to be immunized before the sixth grade. Since then about two dozen states considered making similar requirements; however, only Virginia and the District of Columbia have moved toward requiring girls to receive the shot.

Concerns raised about the vaccine that are unrelated to morality include its high cost ($360), uncertainty about

Bob Pardue/Alamy

how long the vaccine will be effective, and possible side effects. Despite these concerns, more than 25% of teenage girls have already received the HPV vaccine. Advocates are optimistic that up to 90% of teenage girls will eventually receive the HPV vaccine.

In addition to the HPV vaccine targeting the major causes of cervical cancer, it protects against the causes of 90% of all genital warts cases and may reduce the risk of oral cancer. Consequently, another social debate is deciding whether boys should be vaccinated as well. (Adapted from Associated Press, 2005e; Bosch et al., 2002; DeNoon, 2008; FDA, 2006; Gostout, 2007; Hitti, 2006a; Kaufman, 2006b; Kotz, 2007c; MSNBC, 2006; Peterson, 2007; Rubin, 2007; Slade et al., 2009; Stein, 2005b; Sternberg, 2009; *Time*, 2007b)

Think Critically 10.1

This article and its questions are available in interactive format online.

GO to your Psychology CourseMate at login.cengagebrain.com and take the Chapter Post-Test to see which Learning Objectives you've mastered and which need more review. Use the chapter review guide below and the online activities—including flashcards to review key terms—to measure your learning.

Measure
^Your Learning

Online Activities

Key Terms	Video	Animation	Reading	Assessment
social psychology				Check Your Learning Quiz 10.1
person perception, stereotypes, prejudice, discrimination	The Beauty Bonus, p. 461 Stereotype Threat, p. 463 Sexual Prejuduce, p. 463	Person Perception, p. 461		Check Your Learning Quiz 10.2
attributions, internal attributions, dispositional attributions, external attributions, situational attributions, fundamental attribution error, actor-observer effect, self-serving bias		Types of Attributions, p. 465	Attributions and Grades, p. 465	Check Your Learning Quiz 10.3
attitude, cognitive dissonance, counterattitudinal behavior, self-perception theory, central route for persuasion, peripheral route for persuasion	Implicit Association Test, p. 467		National Attitudes, p. 467 Changing Attitudes, p. 469 Routes for Persuasion, p. 471	Check Your Learning Quiz 10.4

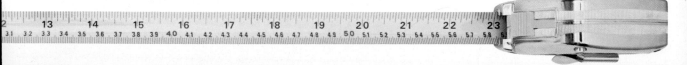

Online Activities

Key Terms	Video	Animation	Reading	Assessment
conformity, compliance, foot-in-the-door technique, obedience, debriefing, groups, group cohesion, group norms, social comparison theory, task-oriented group, socially oriented group, crowd, social facilitation, social inhibition, deindividuation, bystander effect, diffusion of responsibility theory, group polarization, groupthink	Behavior Lab Conformity, p. 473 Conformity, p. 473 Milgram's Experiment: Obedience to Authority, p. 475 Group Polarization, p. 483		Milgram's Experiment Revisited, p. 477 Teen Pregnancy Pact, p. 479 Kitty Genovese, p. 481	Check Your Learning Quiz 10.5
aggression, social cognitive theory, frustration-aggression hypothesis, modified frustration-aggression hypothesis			Genes and Child Abuse, p. 485	Check Your Learning Quiz 10.6
prosocial behavior (helping), altruism, decision-stage model of helping, arousal-cost-reward model of helping	Why People Help, p. 489			Check Your Learning Quiz 10.7
social neuroscience, PET scan (positron emission tomography), fMRI (functional magnetic resonance imaging), EEG (electroencephalography), TMS (transcranial magnetic stimulation)	Mirror Neurons, p. 491			Check Your Learning Quiz 10.8

Personality

11

1 **GO** to your **Psychology CourseMate** at **login.cengagebrain.com** and take the **Chapter Pre-Test** to introduce yourself to this chapter's topics and see what you may already know.

2 **READ** the **Learning Objectives (LOs)** (in the left sidebars) and begin the chapter.

3 **COMPLETE** the **Online Activities** (in the right sidebars) *as you read each module*. Activities include **videos**, **animations**, **readings**, and **quizzes**.

4 **CHECK Your Learning** by going online to take the quiz at the end of each module and review material as necessary.

5 **MEASURE Your Learning** after reading the chapter by taking the online **Chapter Post-Test**. Use the chapter review guide at the end of the chapter as needed.

WATCH for these **Online Activities** icons as you read:

 Video

 Animation

 Reading

 Assessment

 Think Critically

These online activities are important to mastering this chapter. As you read each module, access these materials by going to **login.cengagebrain.com**.

 Video Explore studies and firsthand accounts of biological and psychological processes:

- Learn more about Ted Haggard's inner struggle
- Watch how children express their self-concept
- Learn how twin research helped our understanding of genetic and environmental contributions to psychology
- Find out about the situation model of personality

 Animation Interact with and visualize important processes and concepts:

- Explore the development of the id, ego, and superego and their relationship to anxiety defense
- Identify the personality traits in each of the Big Five categories

 Reading Delve deeper into key content:

- Read about what Freud would say about Haggard's self-confessed "sexual immorality"
- Learn how unconscious forces may have made Ted Haggard act out his sexual desires
- Find out how using defense mechanisms can be helpful and harmful
- Learn about the unique problems the Oedipus complex causes for boys and girls
- Explore the current status of Freud's theory
- Discover what it takes to reach your potential
- Learn how The Freedom Writers were able to shatter stereotypes of at-risk students
- Learn how locus of control explains the difference in stress between the Japanese and British

- Find out how the social cognitive theory of personality development compares with other theories
- Learn how the five-factor theory applies to different cultures
- Learn what your handwriting reveals about your personality
- Learn what your horoscopes reveal about your personality

 Assessment Measure your mastery:

- Chapter Pre-Test
- Check Your Learning Quizzes
- Chapter Post-Test

 Think Critically Challenge your thinking by applying content from this chapter and making connections to related material:

- Personality Tests Help Employers Find Applicants Who Fit

▶ **LO1** Define personality and theory of personality.

TED HAGGARD FOUNDED New Life Church in the basement of his house 25 years ago and became a prominent author and national evangelical Christian leader with a congregation of 14,000 worshippers in the largest church in Colorado. He is married with five children and has boyish dimples and a warm smile.

▼

In 2006, at the peak of his career, a male prostitute accused Haggard of having a three-year sexual affair with him and of using drugs. This accusation was alarming not only because Haggard was a married pastor, but also because he publicly supported a constitutional amendment banning gay marriage.

When the accusations were first broadcast on the news, Haggard confessed to church officials, saying, "Ninety-eight percent of what you know of me was the real me. Two percent of me would rise up, and I couldn't overcome it" (Haggard, 2006a). Then, in a television news interview the next morning, Haggard denied ever having sex with a male prostitute and ever using drugs. Church officials were shocked and appalled when they saw the other side of Ted during the interview as he lied while still smiling at the camera, appearing calm and assured.

As evidence of Haggard having sexual encounters with a male prostitute and using drugs continued to build, he made the following public confession: "The fact is that I am guilty of sexual immorality… I'm a deceiver and a liar. There is part of my life that is so repulsive and dark that I've been warring against it all of my adult life" (Haggard, 2006a). Haggard resigned as pres-

© Dennis Oda

ident of the 30-million-member National Association of Evangelicals and was dismissed as senior pastor of New Life Church.

Figuring someone out involves examining the puzzling, fascinating, and complex components of our innermost selves, our personalities.

Personality refers to a combination of long-lasting and distinctive behaviors, thoughts, motives, and emotions that typify how we react and adapt to other people and situations.

Haggard's moral public persona and dark private self raise a number of questions about personality: How does personality develop? Why do personalities differ? How well do we know ourselves? These kinds of questions can be answered by theories of personality, which we'll be exploring throughout the chapter.

A **theory of personality** is an organized attempt to describe and explain how personalities develop and why personalities differ.

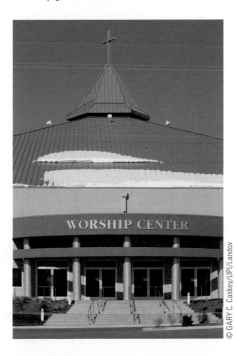

© GARY C. Caskey/UPI/Landov

Ted Haggard

Learn more about Ted Haggard's inner struggle.

Check Your Learning Quiz 11.1

Go to **login.cengagebrain.com** and take the online quiz.

Overview of the Psychoanalytic Approach

Freud's theory of personality begins with a controversial assumption that is an important key to unlocking the secrets of personality. To understand how Freud found this key idea, we'll journey back in time to the late 1800s.

At that time, Freud was wondering why several of his women patients had developed very noticeable physical symptoms, such as losing all sensation in their hands or being unable to control the movements of their legs. What most puzzled Freud, who was a medical doctor, was that despite these physical complaints, he could not identify a physical cause for these symptoms. Somehow, Freud's brilliant mind solved this problem and, in so doing, found an important key to unlocking the secrets of personality. Freud reasoned that since there were no observable physical causes of the women's physical symptoms, the causes must come from unconscious psychological forces (Westen & Gabbard, 1999).

In the 1800s, Freud's belief that human behavior was influenced by unconscious psychological forces was revolutionary, and it led to his equally revolutionary theory of personality.

Freud's psychoanalytic theory of personality emphasizes the importance of early childhood experiences, unconscious or repressed thoughts that we cannot voluntarily access, and the conflicts between conscious and unconscious forces that influence our feelings, thoughts, and behaviors.

Freud believed that unconscious psychological forces had a powerful influence on personality and that these forces originated in early childhood. If Freud were alive today, he would look for reasons behind Ted Haggard's self-confessed "sexual immorality" at age 50 by searching through Ted's childhood and his unconscious thoughts and forces.

Explaining the complex development of someone's personality, such as Ted Haggard's, is such a difficult task that only a dozen or so psychologists have tried. One of the best-known attempts to explain personality is included in Sigmund Freud's (1901/1960, 1924, 1940) overall theory of psychoanalysis, which includes two related theories: a method of psychotherapy, which we'll discuss in Chapter 13, and a theory of personality development, which we'll focus on here.

We'll begin with Freud's controversial and revolutionary assumption that unconscious psychological forces influence behavior.

Conscious Versus Unconscious Forces

Ted Haggard's life was full of inconsistencies. His public behaviors as a pastor and husband were moral and respectable, but his private behaviors of having sexual relations with a male escort were immoral and degrading to his character: "The public person I was wasn't a lie; it was just incomplete...the darkness increased and finally dominated me. As a result, I did things that were contrary to everything I believe" (Haggard, 2006a).

Ted indicated that just as he had preached all along, he believed homosexual acts were immoral and lying about a sexual affair was equivalent to "the stinking garbage of a rotting sin" (Haggard, 2006b). In doing so, he was expressing conscious thoughts.

Conscious thoughts are wishes, desires, or thoughts that we are aware of, or can recall, at any given moment.

However, Freud theorized that our conscious thoughts are only a small part of our total mental activity, much of which involves unconscious thoughts or forces (Westen et al., 2008).

Unconscious forces represent wishes, desires, or thoughts that, because of their disturbing or threatening content, we automatically repress and cannot voluntarily access.

Did Ted have sexual relations with a male escort because of some unconscious forces that he was unaware of and had repressed? According to Freud, although repressed thoughts are unconscious, they may influence our behaviors through unconscious motivation.

Unconscious motivation is a Freudian concept that refers to the influence of repressed thoughts, desires, or impulses on our conscious thoughts and behaviors.

Freud used unconscious forces and motivation to explain why we say or do things that we cannot explain or understand. Once he assumed that there were unconscious forces and motivations, Freud needed to find ways to explore the unconscious.

Ted Haggard and Psychoanalytic Theory

Explore what Freud would say about Haggard's self-confessed "sexual immorality."

© Kevin Moloney/Getty Images

▸ **LO3** Describe techniques used to discover the unconscious.

Techniques to Discover the Unconscious

It was one thing for Freud to propose the existence of powerful unconscious psychological forces and motivations, but it was quite another thing for him to show that such unconscious forces actually existed. For example, were there any signs that unconscious psychological forces were making Ted Haggard act out his sexual desires that were contrary to his conscious beliefs?

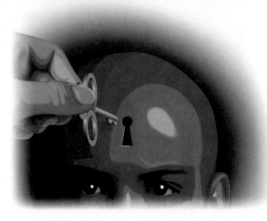

Because neither Ted nor any of us can easily or voluntarily reveal or talk about our unconscious thoughts and desires, Freud needed to find ways for his patients to reveal their unconscious thoughts and desires, some of which might be psychologically threatening or disturbing. From observing his patients during therapy, Freud believed he had found three techniques that uncovered, revealed, or hinted at a person's unconscious wishes and desires.

Freud's three techniques to uncover or unlock the unconscious were free association, dream interpretation, and analysis of slips of the tongue (commonly known as Freudian slips) (Grunbaum, 2006).

Free Association

One of Freud's techniques for revealing the unconscious was to encourage his patients to relax and to sit back or lie down on his now-famous couch and talk freely about anything. He called this process free association.

Free association is a Freudian technique in which clients are encouraged to talk about any thoughts or images that enter their head; the assumption is that this kind of free-flowing, uncensored talking will provide clues to unconscious material.

Free association, which is one of Freud's important discoveries, continues to be used today by some therapists (Lothane, 2006b). However, not all therapists agree that free associations actually reveal a client's unconscious thoughts, desires, and wishes (Grunbaum, 1993).

Dream Interpretation

Freud listened to and interpreted his patients' dreams because he believed that dreams represent a path to the unconscious.

Dream interpretation, a Freudian technique of analyzing dreams, is based on the assumption that dreams contain underlying, hidden meanings and symbols that provide clues to unconscious thoughts and desires. Freud distinguished between the dream's obvious story or plot, called *manifest content,* and the dream's hidden or disguised meanings or symbols, called *latent content.*

For example, Freud interpreted the hidden meaning of dream objects such as sticks and knives as being symbols for male sexual organs and interpreted other objects, such as boxes and ovens, as symbols for female sexual organs. The therapist's task is to look behind the dream's manifest content (including bizarre stories and symbols) and interpret the symbols' hidden or latent content, which provides clues to a person's unconscious wishes or thoughts (Lothane, 2006a).

Freudian Slips

At one time or another, most of us, according to Freud, unintentionally reveal an unconscious thought or desire by making a slip of the tongue (Grunbaum, 2006).

Freudian slips are mistakes that we make in everyday speech; such slips of the tongue, which are often embarrassing, are thought to reflect unconscious thoughts or wishes.

For example, a colleague was lecturing on the importance of regular health care. She said, "It is important to visit a veterinarian for regular checkups." According to Freud, mistakes like substituting *veterinarian* for *physician* are not accidental but rather "intentional" ways of expressing unconscious desires. As it turns out, our colleague, who is in very good health, was having serious doubts about her relationship with a person who happened to be a veterinarian.

Freud assumed that free association, dream interpretation, and slips of the tongue are all mental processes that are the least controlled by our conscious, rational minds. As a result, he believed these techniques allow uncensored clues to slip out and reveal our deeper unconscious wishes and desires.

Ted Haggard and Unconscious Forces

Learn how unconscious forces may have made Ted Haggard act out his sexual desires.

Unless otherwise noted, all images are © Cengage Learning

▶ **LO4** Describe the developmental process and functions of the mind's three divisions.

Divisions of the Mind

According to Freud's theory, a continuing battle goes on in our minds between conscious thoughts and unconscious forces. How our minds fight these battles is perhaps one of Freud's best-known theories, and you'll easily recognize many of the terms, including id, ego, and superego.

To understand how the id, ego, and superego interact, imagine an iceberg floating in the sea. The part of the iceberg that is above water represents conscious forces of which we are aware, while parts below the water indicate unconscious forces of which we are not aware.

Freud divided the mind into three separate processes, each with a different function. Because of their different functions, Freud believed that interactions among the id, ego, and superego would result in conflicts (Westen et al., 2008).

Id: Pleasure Seeker

Freud believed that mental processes must have a source of energy, which he called the id.

The **id,** which is Freud's first division of the mind to develop, contains two biological drives—sex and aggression—that are the source of all psychic or mental energy; the id's goal is to pursue pleasure and satisfy the biological drives.

Freud assumed that the id operated at a totally unconscious level, which is analogous to an iceberg's massive underwater bulk. The id operates according to the pleasure principle.

The **pleasure principle** operates to satisfy drives and avoid pain, without concern for moral restrictions or society's regulations.

You can think of the id as a spoiled child who operates in a totally selfish, pleasure-seeking way without regard for reason, logic, or morality. Simply following the pleasure principle leads to conflict with others (such as parents), and this conflict results in the development of the ego.

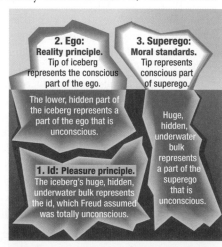

2. Ego: Reality principle. Tip of iceberg represents the conscious part of the ego.

The lower, hidden part of the iceberg represents a part of the ego that is unconscious.

3. Superego: Moral standards. Tip represents conscious part of superego.

Huge, hidden, underwater bulk represents a part of the superego that is unconscious.

1. Id: Pleasure principle. The iceberg's huge, hidden, underwater bulk represents the id, which Freud assumed was totally unconscious.

Ego: Executive Negotiator Between Id and Superego

As infants discover that parents put restrictions on satisfying their wishes, infants learn to control their wishes through the development of an ego.

The **ego,** which is Freud's second division of the mind, develops from the id during infancy; the ego's goal is to find safe and socially acceptable ways of satisfying the id's desires and to negotiate between the id's wants and the superego's prohibitions.

Freud said that a relatively large part of the ego's material is conscious, such as information that we have gathered in adapting to our environments. A smaller part of the ego's material is unconscious, such as threatening wishes that have been repressed. In contrast to the id's pleasure principle, the ego follows the reality principle.

The **reality principle** is a policy of satisfying a wish or desire only if there is a socially acceptable outlet available.

You can think of the ego as an executive negotiator that operates in a reasonable, logical, and socially acceptable way to find outlets for satisfaction. The ego works to resolve conflicts that may arise because of different goals of the id and superego.

Superego: Regulator

As children learn that they must follow rules and regulations in satisfying their wishes, they develop a superego.

The **superego,** which is Freud's third division of the mind, develops from the ego during early childhood; the superego's goal is to apply the moral values and standards of one's parents or caregivers and society in satisfying one's wishes.

Think of the iceberg's visible tip as representing that part of the superego's moral standards of which we are conscious or aware and the huge underwater bulk as representing the part of the superego's moral standards that are unconscious or outside our awareness.

A child develops a superego through interactions with parents or caregivers and by taking on or incorporating their values and rules. The superego's power is in making the person feel guilty if the rules are disobeyed. Because the pleasure-seeking id wants to avoid feeling guilty, it is motivated to listen to the superego. You can think of a superego as a moral guardian or conscience that is trying to control the id's wishes and impulses.

As you'll learn next, conflict often arises between the divisions of mind.

▶ **LO5** List and describe the ego's defense mechanisms.

Defense Mechanisms

Suppose you know that you should study for tomorrow's exam but at the same time you want to go to a friend's party. Freud explained that in this kind of situation, conflict between the desires of the pleasure-seeking id and the goals of the conscience-regulating superego causes anxiety.

Anxiety, in Freudian theory, is an uncomfortable feeling that results from inner conflicts between the primitive desires of the id and the moral goals of the superego.

For example, the study-or-party situation sets up a conflict between the pleasure-seeking goal of the id, which is to go to the party, and the conscience-keeping goal of the superego, which is to stay home and study. Caught in the middle of this id–superego conflict is the ego, which, like any good executive, tries to negotiate an acceptable solution. However, this id–superego conflict, along with the ego's continuing negotiations to resolve this conflict, causes anxious feelings. Freud suggested that the ego tries to reduce the anxious feelings by using a number of mental processes, which he called defense mechanisms (Cramer, 2006).

Defense mechanisms are Freudian processes that operate at unconscious levels and use self-deception or untrue explanations to protect the ego from being overwhelmed by anxiety.

According to Freud, a student's ego has two ways to reduce anxiety over deciding whether to party or study. The student's ego can take realistic steps to reduce anxiety, such as motivating or convincing the student to stay home and study. Or the student's ego can use a number of defense mechanisms, which reduce anxiety by deceiving the student to think it's fine to party and then study tomorrow. In essence, defense mechanisms function like a mental traffic cop to reduce conflict and anxiety.

The following is a brief summary of some of Freud's more well-known defense mechanisms:

Rationalization involves covering up the true reasons for actions, thoughts, or feelings by making up excuses and incorrect explanations.

A student may rationalize that by going to a party tonight, he or she will feel more motivated to study for the exam tomorrow, even if he or she will be very tired and in no mood or condition to study tomorrow.

Denial is refusing to recognize some anxiety-provoking event or piece of information that is clear to others.

Heavy smokers use denial when they disregard the scientific evidence that smoking increases the risk of lung cancer and in addition may be using rationalization if they say they can quit any time they want.

Repression involves blocking and pushing unacceptable or threatening feelings, wishes, or experiences into the unconscious.

Having feelings of jealousy about your best friend's academic success might be threatening to your self-concept, so you may unknowingly block these unwanted feelings by also unknowingly pushing them into your unconscious.

Projection falsely and unconsciously attributes your own unacceptable feelings, traits, or thoughts to individuals or objects.

A student who refuses to accept responsibility for cheating during exams may look at other students and decide that they are cheating.

Reaction formation involves substituting behaviors, thoughts, or feelings that are the direct opposite of unacceptable ones.

A person who feels guilty about engaging in sexual activity may use reaction formation by joining a religious group that bans sex.

Displacement involves transferring feelings about, or response to, an object that causes anxiety to another person or object that is less threatening.

If you were anxious about getting angry at your best friend, you might unknowingly displace your anger by picking an argument with a safer individual, such as a salesclerk, waiter, or stranger.

Sublimation, which is a type of displacement, involves redirecting a threatening or forbidden desire, usually sexual, into a socially acceptable one.

For instance, a person might sublimate strong sexual desires by channeling that energy into physical activities.

We have discussed the three divisions of the mind—id, ego, and superego—and how the ego may use defense mechanisms to reduce anxiety. Now we'll turn to how one's ego and personality develop.

Freud's Divisions of the Mind

Explore the development of the id, ego, and superego and their relationship to anxiety defense.

Use of Defense Mechanisms

Find out how using defense mechanisms can be helpful and harmful.

▶ **LO6** List and describe the five psychosexual stages of development.

1. Oral

2. Anal

3. Phallic

4. Latency

5. Genital

Psychosexual Development

According to Freud (1940), our personality develops as we pass through and deal with potential conflicts at five psychosexual stages.

Psychosexual stages are five developmental periods—oral, anal, phallic, latency, and genital stages—each marked by potential conflict between parent and child. The conflicts arise as a child seeks pleasure from different body areas that are associated with sexual feelings (*erogenous zones*). Freud emphasized that the child's first five years were most important in personality development.

You can think of each psychosexual stage as being a source of potential conflict between the child's id, which seeks immediate gratification, and the parents, who place restrictions on when, where, and how the gratification can take place. For example, the child may want to be fed immediately, while the parent may wish to delay the feeding to a more convenient time. One way a child can deal with or resolve these conflicts (wanting to satisfy all desires but not being allowed to by the parents) is to become fixated at a certain stage.

Fixation, which can occur during any of the first three stages (oral, anal, or phallic) refers to a Freudian process through which an individual may be locked into a particular psychosexual stage because his or her wishes were either overgratified or undergratified.

According to Freud, every child goes through certain situations, such as nursing, bottle feeding, and toilet training, that contain potential conflicts between the child's desire for instant satisfaction and the parents' wishes, which may involve delaying the child's satisfaction. How these conflicts are resolved and whether a child becomes fixated at one stage because of too much or too little satisfaction greatly influence the development of personality.

Next, we discuss each of Freud's five psychosexual stages.

1 Oral Stage

The **oral stage** lasts for the first 18 months of life and is a time when the infant's pleasure seeking is centered on the mouth.

Pleasure-seeking activities include sucking, chewing, and biting. If we were locked into or fixated at this stage because our oral wishes were gratified too much or too little, we would continue to seek oral gratification as adults. Fixation at this stage results in adults who continue to engage in oral activities, such as overeating, gum chewing, or smoking; oral activities can be symbolic as well, such as being overly demanding or "mouthing off."

2 Anal Stage

The **anal stage** lasts from the age of about 1½ to 3 years and is a time when the infant's pleasure seeking is centered on the anus and its functions of elimination.

Fixation at this stage results in adults who continue to engage in activities of retention or elimination. Retention may take the form of being very neat, stingy, or behaviorally rigid (thus the term *anal retentive*). Elimination may take the form of being generous, messy, or carefree (thus the term *anal expulsive*).

3 Phallic Stage

The **phallic** *(FAL-ick)* **stage** lasts from the age of about 3 to 6 and is a time when the infant's pleasure seeking is centered on the genitals.

Freud theorized that the phallic stage is particularly important for personality development because of the occurrence of the Oedipus complex (named for Oedipus, the character in Greek mythology who unknowingly killed his father and married his mother).

The **Oedipus** *(ED-ah-pus)* **complex** is a process in which a child competes with the parent of the same sex for the affections and pleasures of the parent of the opposite sex.

4 Latency Stage

The **latency stage,** which lasts from about age 6 to puberty, is a time when the child represses sexual thoughts and engages in nonsexual activities, such as developing social and intellectual skills.

At puberty, sexuality reappears and marks the beginning of a new stage, called the genital stage.

5 Genital Stage

The **genital stage** lasts from puberty through adulthood and is a time when the individual has renewed sexual desires that he or she seeks to fulfill through relationships with other people.

How a person meets the conflicts of the genital stage depends on how conflicts in the first three stages were resolved. If the individual is fixated at an earlier stage, less energy will be available to resolve conflicts at the genital stage. If the individual successfully resolved conflicts in the first three stages, he or she will have the energy to develop loving relationships and a healthy personality.

Oedipus Complex

Learn about the unique problems the Oedipus complex causes for boys and girls.

▶ **L07** Describe how Jung, Adler, and Horney disagreed with Freud's theory.

▶ **L08** Discuss the current status of Freud's theory.

Evaluation of Psychoanalytic Approach

Because Freud's theory was so creative and revolutionary for its time, it attracted many followers, who formed a famous group called the Vienna Psychoanalytic Society. However, it was not long before members of the society began to disagree over some of Freud's theories and assumptions (Westen et al., 2008). We'll focus on three influential followers who broke with Freud's theory.

Carl Jung

In 1910 Carl Jung became the first president of the Vienna Psychoanalytic Society. Freud said that Jung was to be his "crown prince" and personal successor. However, just four years later, Jung and Freud ended their personal and professional relationship and never again spoke to each other.

The main reason for the split was that Jung disagreed with Freud's emphasis on the sex drive. Jung believed the collective unconscious—and not sex—was the basic force in the development of personality.

National Library of Medicine, Bethesda, MD

The **collective unconscious,** according to Jung, consists of ancient memory traces and symbols that are passed on by birth and are shared by all peoples in all cultures.

Jung's theory of collective unconscious had more influence on the areas of art, literature, philosophy, and counseling than on current areas of psychology.

Alfred Adler

Alfred Adler was another contemporary of Freud's who later became president of the Vienna Psychoanalytic Society. However, after Adler voiced his disagreement with Freud at one of the society's meetings, he was so badly criticized by the other members that he resigned as president.

Courtesy Adler School of Professional Psychology. Reproduced by permission of Kurt Adler.

Unless otherwise noted, all images are © Cengage Learning

Like Jung, Adler disagreed with Freud's theory that humans are governed by biological and sexual urges. Adler believed that the main factors influencing a child's development were sibling influences and child-rearing practices.

In contrast to Freud's biological drives, Adler proposed that humans are motivated by social urges and that each person is a social being with a unique personality.

Karen Horney

Karen Horney was trained as a psychoanalyst; her career reached its peak shortly after Freud's death in 1939. For many years, Horney was dean of the American Institute of Psychoanalysis in New York.

Horney objected to Freud's view that women were dependent, vain, and submissive because of biological forces and childhood sexual experiences. She especially took issue with Freud's idea that penis envy affects girls' development.

In contrast to Freud's psychosexual conflicts, Horney insisted that the major influence on personality development, whether in women or men, can be found in child–parent social interactions. Unlike Freud, who believed that every child must experience child–parent conflicts, Horney theorized that such conflicts are avoidable if the child is raised in a loving, trusting, and secure environment.

Karen Horney is referred to as a neo-Freudian because she changed and renovated Freud's original theory. Neo-Freudians generally agreed with Freud's basic ideas, such as the importance of the unconscious; the division of the mind into the id, ego, and superego; and the use of defense mechanisms to protect the ego. However, they mostly disagreed with Freud's placing so much emphasis on biological forces, sexual drives, and psychosexual stages (Plante, 2005).

Psychoanalytic Approach Today

Current critics of Freud's theory state that his psychoanalytic theory is too comprehensive, too difficult to test or verify, places too much emphasis on the first five years of life, and doesn't take into account genetic factors or brain development in explaining personality.

Despite its criticisms, Freud's theory has had an enormous impact on society, as can be seen in the widespread use of Freudian terms (*ego, id, rationalization*) in literature, art, and our everyday conversations. Freud's theory also has had a great impact on psychology: Many of his concepts have been incorporated into the fields of personality, development, abnormal psychology, and psychotherapy. More recently, neuroscientists began examining many of Freud's questions about the mind and hope to build upon his theory (Solms, 2006).

Freudian Theory Today

Explore the current status of Freud's theory.

Check Your Learning Quiz 11.2

Go to **login.cengagebrain.com** and take the online quiz.

▶ **LO9** Define humanistic theory and describe its three unique characteristics.

Overview of the Humanistic Approach

Charles Dutton (right photo) had been in and out of reform schools since he was 12 years old and was finally sent to prison for manslaughter and illegal possession of a firearm. While in prison, he got into trouble for being a ringleader of a riot and was punished with solitary confinement. To pass his time, he took along a friend's book of plays by black authors. Dutton was so moved by the plays' messages that for the first time he thought about channeling his rage and anger into acting.

At one point he spent more than 60 painful days in the prison hospital after a fellow inmate had plunged an ice pick through his neck. During those long days in the hospital, Dutton decided that it was time to put his life in order and accomplish something worthwhile during his remaining time in prison. He obtained a high-school equivalency certificate and then a 2-year college degree, read dozens of plays, and even started a prison theater. After his parole, he attended college and got his BA in drama. His high point came when he was accepted into Yale drama school.

By the early 1990s, ex-problem boy, ex-con, ex-prisoner Charles Dutton had turned into a very successful actor and starred in his own television series. He has since gone on to star in and direct movies (King, 1991; Schneider, 2007). Dutton's story is an emotionally painful search for identity, culminating in the discovery and development of his acting potential. Developing our potential is at the heart of humanistic theories.

Humanistic theories emphasize our capacity for personal growth, development of our potential, and freedom to choose our destiny.

Humanistic theories reject the biological determinism and the irrational, unconscious forces of Freud's psychodynamic theory. Humanistic theories emphasize freely choosing to go after one's dream and to change one's destiny, as Charles Dutton did.

Three Characteristics of Humanistic Theories

We'll describe each of the three characteristics unique to humanistic theories: a phenomenological perspective, a holistic view, and a goal of self-actualization (Wong, 2006).

Phenomenological Perspective

Humanistic theories stress learning about the world through personal experiences, which illustrates the phenomenological *(feh-nom-in-no-LODGE-uh-cal)* perspective.

The **phenomenological perspective** means that your perception or view of the world, whether or not it is accurate, becomes your reality.

For instance, Charles Dutton's phenomenological perspective of how he perceived his acting abilities may or may not have been accurate. However, because he believed so strongly that he had the abilities, this perception became his reality. Other examples of phenomenological perspectives are long-held beliefs that women could not perform certain jobs, such as police officer, doctor, plumber, truck driver, or lawyer. Since women have demonstrated that they can perform these jobs, this particular perception has been proven false.

Holistic View

Humanistic theories emphasize looking at the whole situation or person, which illustrates the holistic *(hole-LIS-tick)* view.

The **holistic view** means that a person's personality is more than the sum of its individual parts; instead, the individual parts form a unique and total entity that functions as a unit.

For example, the holistic view would explain that Dutton became a very successful actor because of his unique combination of many traits—discipline, ability, motivation, desire—rather than any single trait.

Self-Actualization

Humanistic theories highlight the idea of developing one's true potential, which is called self-actualization.

Self-actualization refers to our inherent tendency to develop and reach our true potentials.

By becoming a professional actor and director, Dutton is a wonderful example of someone who is developing and reaching his true potential and thus is getting closer to achieving a high level of self-actualization. According to humanists, each of us has the capacity for self-actualization.

The beginning of humanistic theories can be traced to two psychologists: Abraham Maslow and Carl Rogers. We'll discuss Abraham Maslow's ideas next.

Carrie Underwood

Discover what it takes to reach your potential.

▶ **LO10** Identify and describe Maslow's hierarchy of needs.

Hierarchy of Needs

We can trace the official beginning of the humanistic movement to the early 1960s and the publication of the *Journal of Humanistic Psychology.* One of the major figures behind establishing this journal was Abraham Maslow. Interestingly enough, Maslow was trained as a behaviorist, but along the way he felt there was too much emphasis on rewards and punishments and observable behaviors and too little emphasis on other important aspects of human nature, such as feelings, emotions, and beliefs. For these reasons, Maslow (1968) broke away from behaviorism and developed his humanistic theory, which emphasized two things: our capacity for growth, or self-actualization, and our desire to satisfy a variety of needs, which he arranged in a hierarchy.

For just a moment, think of all the needs that you try to meet each day: eating, having a safe place to live, talking to your friends, perhaps working at a part-time job, caring for loved ones, and studying for exams. Maslow believed that you satisfy these needs in a certain order. As you may remember from Chapter 9 (pp. 412–413), Maslow arranged all human needs into a hierarchy of five major needs.

Maslow's hierarchy of needs arranges needs in ascending order (figure on left), with biological needs at the bottom and social and personal needs at the top. Only when needs at a lower level are met can we advance to the next level.

Self-Actualization

Esteem Needs

Love and Belonging Needs

Safety Needs

Physiological Needs

Unless otherwise noted, all images are © Cengage Learning

According to Maslow's hierarchy, you must satisfy your biological and safety needs before using energy to fulfill your personal and social needs. Finally, you can devote time and energy to reaching your true potential, which is called self-actualization.

Self-Actualization

Maslow (1971) developed the concept of self-actualization after studying the lives of highly productive and exceptional people, such as Abraham Lincoln, Albert Einstein, and Eleanor Roosevelt. Maslow believed that these individuals had been able to reach the goal of self-actualization because they had developed the personality characteristics listed below.

Characteristics of Self-Actualized Individuals
- They perceive reality accurately.
- They are independent and autonomous.
- They prefer to have a deep, loving relationship with only a few people.
- They focus on accomplishing their goals.
- They report peak experiences, which are moments of great joy and satisfaction.

Maslow believed that, although very few individuals reach the level of self-actualization, everyone has a self-actualizing tendency. This tendency motivates us to become the best kind of person we are capable of being.

There is no doubt that Maslow would also have considered Martin Luther King, Jr., an example of a self-actualized person. Martin Luther King, Jr., devoted his life to achieving civil rights for all people. At right he delivers his famous "I Have a Dream" speech at a civil rights rally in Washington, DC. He was awarded the Nobel Prize for peace at age 35. He was gunned down by an assassin's bullet at age 39. King's achievements exemplify self-actualization.

© Bob Adelman/Magnum Photos

About the same time that Maslow was developing the concept of self-actualization, Carl Rogers was developing a different but related humanistic theory.

▶ **LO11** Describe Rogers' self theory and explain how the self develops.

▶ **LO12** Explain the two types of positive regard.

Self Theory

Carl Rogers was initially trained in the psychoanalytic approach. However, Rogers began to feel that Freud placed too much emphasis on unconscious, irrational forces and on biological urges, and too little emphasis on human potential for psychological growth. As a result, Rogers developed the self theory.

Self theory, also called **self-actualization theory,** is based on two major assumptions: that personality development is guided by each person's unique self-actualization tendency, and that each of us has a personal need for positive regard.

Rogers' first major assumption about self-actualization is similar but slightly different from Maslow's use of the term.

Rogers' **self-actualizing tendency** refers to an inborn tendency for us to develop all of our capacities in ways that best maintain and benefit our lives.

The self-actualizing tendency relates to biological functions, such as meeting our basic needs for food, water, and oxygen, as well as psychological functions, such as expanding our experiences, encouraging personal growth, and becoming self-sufficient. The self-actualizing tendency guides us toward positive or healthful behaviors rather than negative or harmful ones. For example, one of the two boys in the photo below has lost the use of his legs and must use a wheelchair. Part of his self-actualizing process will include learning to deal with his disability, engaging in positive healthful behaviors, and getting to know himself.

Self or **self-concept** refers to how we see or describe ourselves. The self is made up of many self-perceptions, abilities, personality characteristics, and behaviors that are organized and consistent with one another.

Because of very different experiences, the boy in the wheelchair will develop a self-concept different from that of his friend. According to Rogers (1980), self-

© Don Smetzer/Getty Images

concept is a key factor in personality because it influences our behaviors, feelings, and thoughts. For example, if you have a positive self-concept, you will tend to act, feel, and think optimistically and constructively; if you have a negative self-concept, you will tend to act, feel, and think pessimistically and destructively.

Now that you know what the self is, here's how Rogers says that it develops.

Unless otherwise noted, all images are © Cengage Learning

Positive Regard

The second assumption of Carl Rogers' self theory is that we have a need to receive positive regard.

Positive regard includes love, sympathy, warmth, acceptance, and respect, which we crave from family, friends, and people who are important to us.

Rogers believed that positive regard was essential for the healthy development of one's self and for successful interpersonal relationships (Liebert & Spiegler, 1994).

One reason I (H. K.) am one of millions of dog owners is that my dog Cocoa (right photo) shows great happiness at seeing me, no matter how grouchy, distracted, or sad I may feel or act. Unlike friends and family, pets never pass judgment; they provide endless amounts of positive regard no matter how their owners look, feel, dress, or talk. In contrast, friends and family can be judgmental and may give only conditional positive regard.

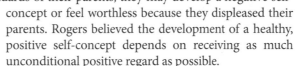

Conditional positive regard refers to the positive regard we receive if we behave in certain acceptable ways, such as living up to or meeting the standards of others.

For instance, one way teenagers display their independence is by choosing different (that is, radical, awful, outrageous) hairstyles and fashions (photo at bottom left). In this case, if the teenagers receive only conditional positive regard based on conforming to the traditional fashion standards of their parents, they may develop a negative self-

concept or feel worthless because they displeased their parents. Rogers believed the development of a healthy, positive self-concept depends on receiving as much unconditional positive regard as possible.

Unconditional positive regard refers to the warmth, acceptance, and love that others show you because you are valued as a human being even though you may disappoint people by behaving in ways that are different from their standards or values or the way they think.

Parents who provide love and respect, even if a teenager does not always abide by their fashion standards, are showing unconditional positive regard, which will foster the development of a healthy self-concept.

Self-Concept

Watch how children express their self-concept.

Applying Humanistic Ideas

Unlike almost every other theory of personality, humanism holds that people are basically good and can achieve their true potentials if the roadblocks placed by society, poverty, drugs, or other evil influences are removed (Megargee, 1997). One of the primary goals of the humanistic approach is to find ways of removing blocking influences so people can grow and self-actualize.

In the United States, there are many mentoring programs, such as Big Brothers/Big Sisters of America, that instill a sense of pride and self-confidence and give children the motivation to achieve success. Children who participated in mentoring programs reported significantly higher self-confidence, grades, and social skills than children without men-

© Najlah Feanny/Corbis

tors (Vredenburgh, 2007). Thus, applying humanistic principles helped improve the self-confidence, grades, and social skills of children who came from problem families or neighborhoods.

Next, we'll review the important humanistic concepts and discuss what critics have to say about humanistic theories.

Evaluation of Humanistic Theories

Perhaps the main reason humanistic theories, such as those of Maslow and Rogers, continue to be popular is that they view people as basically good and believe that people can develop their true potentials (Clay, 2002).

Humanistic theories have had their greatest impact in counseling, clinical settings, and personal growth programs, where ideas like self-concept, self-actualization, and self-fulfillment have proven useful in developing healthy personalities and interpersonal relationships (Rabasca, 2000a; Soyez & Broekaert, 2005). Compared to Freud's idea that we are driven by unconscious irrational forces, humanism says we are driven by positive forces that point us toward realizing our good and true selves. However, these optimistic views of human nature have triggered a number of criticisms.

Criticisms

Humanistic theories have come under considerable criticism because Rogers and Maslow provided little or no scientific evidence that an inherent (biological) tendency to self-actualization really exists. Because the major assumption of self-actualization and other humanistic concepts, such as positive regard and self-worth, are difficult to demonstrate experimentally, critics argue that humanistic theories primarily describe how people behave rather than explain the causes of their behaviors. For these reasons, critics regard humanistic theories more as a wonderfully positive view of human nature or a very hopeful philosophy of life rather than as a scientific explanation of personality development (Burger, 2008). One major problem is that humanistic theories generally ignore research showing that 20% to 60% of the development of intellectual, emotional, social, and personality traits comes from genetic factors (Jang, 2005; McClearn et al., 1997; Parens et al., 2006). This means that genetic factors must be considered when discussing a person's true potential or a person's ability to achieve self-actualization.

Maslow hoped that humanistic theories would become a major force in psychology. Although the humanistic approach has not achieved Maslow's goal, humanism's ideas inspired the human potential movements in the 1960s to 1970s and have been integrated into approaches for counseling, psychotherapy, and education (Clay, 2002). Humanistic theories are becoming more widespread as positive psychology (pp. 672–673), a relatively recent approach, is bringing humanistic ideas into the mainstream (Seligman & Csikszentmihalyi, 2000).

© Andresr/Shutterstock

Positive psychology is the scientific study of optimal human functioning, focusing on the strengths and virtues that enable individuals and communities to thrive. It aims to better understand the positive, adaptive, and fulfilling aspects of human life.

One reason for the growing interest in positive psychology is that it provides a change from the tendency of researchers in psychology to focus more on problems or weaknesses than on strengths or virtues, which is at the core of humanistic psychology.

The Freedom Writers

Learn how The Freedom Writers were able to shatter stereotypes of at-risk students.

Check Your Learning Quiz 11.3

Go to **login.cengagebrain.com** and take the online quiz.

▶ **LO14** Define Bandura's social cognitive theory and explain the three factors that influence personality development.

Overview of the Social Cognitive Approach

Humanistic theories, such as those of Abraham Maslow and Carl Rogers, assume that we are basically good and that our personality is shaped primarily by our inborn tendency for self-actualization or self-fulfillment.

Now we discuss social cognitive theory, which grew out of the research of a number of psychologists, especially Albert Bandura (1986, 2001a).

Social cognitive theory says that personality development is shaped primarily by three forces: cognitive-personal factors, behaviors, and environmental conditions (learning), which all interact to influence how we evaluate, interpret, organize, and apply information.

According to social cognitive theory, we are neither good nor bad but are shaped primarily by three influential factors.

Interaction of Three Factors

For about 30 years, Wangari Maathai (right photo) fought for human rights and conservation of the environment. During this time, she suffered tremendous personal hardships, including being beaten and imprisoned (Maathai, 2006). You can't help wondering what shaped her personality and gave her the strength, determination, and character to sacrifice so much to reach her goals of preserving the environment and empowering women. According to social cognitive theory, Maathai's personality was influenced and shaped by the interactions among three significant forces—namely, cognitive-personal factors, behaviors, and environmental factors.

© Siphwe Sibeko/Reuters/Landov

Unless otherwise noted, all images are © Cengage Learning

Cognitive-Personal Factors

Maathai was born to a family of peasant farmers and grew up during a time when Kenya had an abundance of greenery. Her childhood experiences taught her the beauty of nature's wonders. Being born into a farming family and being taught to value nature are examples of cognitive-personal factors that helped shape Maathai's personality.

Cognitive factors include our beliefs, expectations, values, intentions, and social roles. **Personal factors** include our emotional makeup and our biological and genetic influences.

Cognitive factors guide personality development by influencing the way we view and interpret information. For example, Maathai views the world from the standpoint of someone whose livelihood depended on nature. These kinds of beliefs (cognitions) give Maathai the strength and determination to fight to plant more trees. Thus, cognitive-personal factors influence our personalities by affecting what we think, believe, and feel, which in turn affect how we act and behave.

Behaviors

For the past 30 years, Maathai has spoken forcefully against deforestation, founded the Green Belt Movement, and empowered countless women. These kinds of behaviors also shaped her personality. Behaviors include a variety of personal actions, such as things we do and say.

In Maathai's case, the political and social behaviors that she engaged in to help preserve the environment in turn strengthened her belief that the government's actions to replace greenery with buildings was morally and politically wrong.

Just as behavior influences our beliefs, so does our environment influence both.

Environmental Factors

Maathai lived in Kenya at a time of political oppression, which resulted in harsh beatings, imprisonment, and sometimes death when speaking out against the government's corrupt actions. These environmental factors certainly affected Maathai's personality development.

Environmental factors include our social, political, and cultural influences, as well as our particular learning experiences.

We can assume that living in such an oppressive environment strengthened Maathai's determination to devote her life to restoring trees and empowering women.

According to Bandura (2001a), personality development is influenced by the interactions among these three factors (right figure).

▶ **LO15** Define Rotter's locus of control and differentiate between internal and external locus of control.

▶ **LO16** Define self-efficacy and demonstrate the ability to apply self-efficacy to a real-life example.

To make the relationship between cognitive factors and personality more concrete, we'll focus on two specific beliefs: locus of control and self-efficacy.

Locus of Control

Can you control when you'll graduate? This is the kind of question that intrigued Julian Rotter (1990), who was interested in how social cognitive theory applied to human behavior. Rotter developed a well-known scale to measure a person's expectancies about how much control he or she has over situations, which Rotter called the locus of control.

Locus of control refers to our beliefs about how much control we have over situations or rewards. We are said to have an internal locus of control if we believe that we have control over situations and rewards. We are said to have an external locus of control if we believe that we do not have control over situations and rewards and that events outside ourselves (for example, fate) determine what happens. People fall on a continuum between internal and external locus of control.

For example, if you believe that when you graduate depends primarily on your motivation and determination, then you have more of an internal locus of control. If you believe that when you graduate depends mostly on chance or things outside your control, then you have more of an external locus of control. Having more of an internal locus of control is an advantage because hundreds of studies report a positive relationship between internal locus of control and psychological functioning. For example, people with an internal locus of control are generally higher achievers, cope better with chronic illness, and report less stress, anxiety, and depression than those with an external locus of control. Also, an internal locus of control during childhood seems to protect people against some health problems in adulthood (Burger, 2008; Gale et al., 2008; Livneh et al., 2004; Spector et al., 2001).

Can you control when you will graduate?

© Phil Date/Shutterstock

These findings indicate that a specific belief influences how you perceive your world, which, in turn, affects how you behave. Another cognitive process that affects personality and behavior is how much we believe in our own capabilities.

Unless otherwise noted, all images are © Cengage Learning

Self-Efficacy

Students often ask about how to improve their grades. According to Albert Bandura (2004), one reason students differ in whether they receive high or low grades is related to self-efficacy.

Self-efficacy refers to the confidence in your ability to organize and execute a given course of action to solve a problem or accomplish a task.

For example, saying "I think that I am capable of getting a high grade in this course" is a sign of strong self-efficacy. You judge your self-efficacy by combining four sources of information (Bandura, 1999; Higgins & Scholer, 2008):

1. You use previous experiences of success or failure on similar tasks to estimate how you will do on a new, related task.
2. You compare your capabilities with those of others.
3. You listen to what others say about your capabilities.
4. You use feedback from your body to assess your strength, vulnerability, and capability.

You would rate yourself as having strong self-efficacy for getting good grades if you had previous success with getting high grades, if you believe you are as academically capable as others, if your friends say you are smart, and if you do not become too stressed during exams. Research shows that students' levels of self-efficacy are good predictors of their motivation and learning during college (Chemers et al., 2001; Zimmerman, 2000).

According to Bandura's self-efficacy theory, your motivation to achieve, perform, and do well in tasks and situations is largely influenced by how strongly you believe in your own capabilities. Some people have a strong sense of self-efficacy that applies to many situations (such as academic settings, sports, and social interactions), others have a strong sense that applies to only a few situations (for example, computers but not social interactions), while still others have a weak sense of self-efficacy, which predicts having less success in many of life's tasks (Eccles & Wigfield, 2002).

Why do my friends say that I should be getting better grades?

© PhotoDisc, Inc.

Stress and Coping

Learn how locus of control explains the difference in stress between the Japanese and British.

▶ **LO17** Evaluate the social cognitive approach to personality development.

Evaluation of Social Cognitive Theory

Sometimes a person's experience better illustrates the power and importance of beliefs than all the research in the world. Such an experience is that of Michael J. Fox, a talented actor who has starred in popular TV shows, such as "Spin City," and movies, including the *Back to the Future* trilogy. At age 30, Michael was diagnosed with young-onset Parkinson's disease (p. 76), which led to relentless tremors in his arms and legs. Acting was his livelihood, but the progression of his symptoms made it increasingly difficult for him to act, even with the use of powerful medications to help control his tremors (Dudley, 2006; Fox, 2002).

The worsening of his symptoms forced Michael to make a key life decision: Would he allow his disease to lower his life's ambitions *or* would he believe in his ability to fight harder than ever before to reach his life's goals? Michael was unwilling to allow Parkinson's disease to take over his life. He began fighting against the disease and did so in incredible ways. Michael has continued to act by guest starring in television shows, such as "Boston Legal" and "Rescue Me." Also, by starting his own charitable foundation, which has become a leader in Parkinson's disease research, and speaking in favor of stem-cell research, he has taken an active role in discovering a cure for Parkinson's disease.

I believe I can continue to act.

In his memoir titled *Lucky Man* (Fox, 2002), Michael speaks of the pleasure he has had in increasing public awareness of Parkinson's disease: "The ten years since my diagnosis have been the best ten years of my life, and I consider myself a lucky man." Michael's story illustrates a major assumption of social cognitive theory: Beliefs have a great influence on personality, motivation, and behavior.

We'll evaluate social cognitive theory's approach to personality development.

Unless otherwise noted, all images are © Cengage Learning

© AP Images/Charles Sykes

Comprehensive Approach

Social cognitive theory focuses on the interaction of three primary forces in the development of personality: cognitive-personal factors, which include beliefs, expectations, social roles, and genetic influences; behaviors, which include actions, conversations, and emotional expressions; and environmental influences, such as social, political, and cultural forces.

Experimentally Based

Many of the concepts used in social cognitive theory have been developed from, and based on, objective measurement, laboratory research, and experimental studies. Because the concepts of social cognitive theory, such as locus of control and self-efficacy, are experimentally based, they can be manipulated, controlled, and tested and have reduced susceptibility to error and bias.

Programs for Change

Because many of the concepts of social cognitive theory are experimentally based and objectively defined, these concepts have been used to develop very successful programs for changing behavior and personality. For example, in one study, individuals who had developed an intense fear of snakes showed decreased fear after observing a fearless model touching and handling a snake; in another study, children who had observed an adult's aggressive behaviors imitated and performed similar aggressive behaviors when given an opportunity (Bandura, 1965; Bandura et al.,1969).

Criticisms and Conclusions

Critics say that because social cognitive concepts focus on narrowly defined behaviors, such as self-efficacy and locus of control, social cognitive theory is a somewhat piecemeal explanation of personality development. Also, critics contend that social cognitive theory pays too little attention to the influence of genetic factors, emotional influences, and childhood experiences on personality development (Bouchard & Loehlin, 2001; Loehlin et al., 2003).

Despite these criticisms, social cognitive theory has had a profound impact on personality theory by emphasizing the objective measurement of concepts, the influence of cognitive processes, and its application for behavioral change programs.

Social Cognitive Theory vs. Other Theories

Explore how the social cognitive theory of personality development compares with other theories.

Check Your Learning Quiz 11.4

Go to **login.cengagebrain.com** and take the online quiz.

▶ **LO18** Define trait and trait theory.

Overview of the Trait Approach

At just 5 feet 3 inches, Kiran Bedi (right photo) wouldn't normally attract much attention. Yet, with her petite stature and only a wooden baton, she once turned back a 3,000-member, sword-wielding group of rioters by herself. Her male colleagues felt overwhelmed and ran away.

In 1972, Kiran Bedi became the first female police officer in India. This was no small achievement in a country where women struggle to break free of their second-class status (Bedi, 2006; Turnbull, 2008). But even in the United States, the land of opportunity, throughout the 1970s, 1980s, and 1990s, women had to fight discrimination and harassment from male police officers who believed that women did not have the physical or mental strength to be police officers (Copeland, 1999).

© India Today Group/Getty Images

Kiran Bedi, like the many thousands of female officers around the world, has shown that women make good cops, partly because of their particular personality traits: Women are less authoritarian, more open, better listeners, and less likely to trigger showdowns than are their male counterparts (Lonsway et al., 2003; Munoz, 2003). The reason female police officers act more as peacekeepers and male police officers act more as enforcers may be explained by trait theory.

Trait theory is an approach for analyzing the structure of personality by measuring, identifying, and classifying similarities and differences in personality characteristics or traits.

The basic unit for measuring personality characteristics is the trait.

A **trait** is a relatively stable and enduring tendency to behave in a particular way.

For example, traits of female police officers include being compassionate, sympathetic, and diplomatic, which help them function as peacekeepers, while traits of male police officers include being assertive, aggressive, and direct, which help them function as enforcers.

Identifying Traits

Researchers were determined to find a list of traits whose two characteristics seemed mutually exclusive. The list had to contain very few traits but at the same time be able to describe differences among anyone's and everyone's personality, from farmer to business executive to singer (photos on next page).

Unless otherwise noted, all images are © Cengage Learning

© Alexander Raths/Shutterstock

© Yuri Arcurs/Shutterstock

© Dmitriy Shironosov/Shutterstock

How would you describe their personalities?

How Many Traits Can There Be?

In the 1930s, Gordon Allport and an associate went through the dictionary and selected every term that could distinguish differences among personalities (Allport & Odbert, 1936). They found about 18,000 terms that dealt with all kinds of personality differences; of these, about 4,500 were considered to fit their definition of personality traits. Allport defined traits as stable and consistent tendencies in how an individual adjusts to his or her environment. The advantage of Allport's list was that it was comprehensive enough to describe anyone's and everyone's personality. The disadvantage was that it was incredibly long and thus impractical to use in research. His list of thousands of traits needed to be organized into far fewer basic traits. This task fell to Raymond Cattell.

Aren't Some Traits Related?

In the 1940s, Raymond Cattell (1943) took Allport's list of 4,500 traits and aimed to reduce the list to the most basic traits. Cattell used statistical analysis to search for relationships among hundreds of traits on Allport's list so that the original list could be reduced to 35 basic traits, which Cattell called source traits. He claimed that these 35 basic traits could describe all differences among personalities. Although Cattell's achievement was remarkable, his list of 35 traits—and even his further reduction of the list to 16 traits—still proved too long to be practical for research and only moderately useful in assessing personality differences. Obviously, Cattell's list needed more reducing, but that was to take another 30 years.

▶ **LO19** Describe the five-factor model.

Five-Factor Model

From the 1960s to the early 1990s, about a dozen researchers in several countries were using factor analysis to find relationships among lists of adjectives that describe personality differences. Doing what some thought impossible, researchers reduced the list of 35 traits to only 5, which make up the five-factor model of personality (Burger, 2008; Durrett & Trull, 2005).

The **five-factor model** organizes personality traits and describes differences in personality using five categories: **openness, conscientiousness, extraversion, agreeableness,** and **neuroticism.**

These five factors became known as the Big Five and are easy to remember if you note that their first letters make the acronym OCEAN. Each of the five factors actually represents a continuum of behavior, as briefly described in the at right figure.

You can think of each Big Five factor as a supertrait because each factor's continuum includes dozens of related traits. For example, conscientiousness, on one end of the continuum, includes the traits of being dependable, responsible, deliberate, hardworking, and precise; at the other end are the traits of being impulsive, careless, late, lazy, and aimless.

© Joshua-Ets-Hokin/PhotoDisc, Inc.

© PhotoDisc, Inc.

© PhotoDisc, Inc.

© PhotoDisc, Inc.

© PhotoDisc, Inc.

Openness

Is open to novel experience.	Has narrow interests.

Conscientiousness

Is responsible and dependable.	Is impulsive and careless.

Extraversion

Is outgoing and decisive.	Is retiring and withdrawn.

Agreeableness

Is warm and good-natured.	Is unfriendly and cold.

Neuroticism

Is stable and not a worrier.	Is nervous and emotionally unstable.

Unless otherwise noted, all images are © Cengage Learning

Importance of the Big Five

Unlike earlier attempts to identify traits, there is now convincing evidence that the Big Five, or five-factor model, can indeed describe personality differences among many thousands of individuals by using only five categories or traits.

The five-factor model has been replicated in many different countries, which led researchers to ask if the structure of personality was shaped primarily by different cultural factors (such as child-rearing practices, religious and moral values, language similarities) or primarily by differences in the basic human ways of acting and experiencing that are universal, or similar across all peoples and countries.

Because support for the five-factor model was found in very different countries or cultures, researchers concluded that the basic structure of human personality arises from some universal living experience or biological basis rather than being shaped by individual countries or cultures (Jang et al., 2006; McCrae & Costa, 2003; Yamagata et al., 2006). If basic human personality structure is universal, it means that the personalities of individuals in different countries can be described by using the Big Five traits.

Big Five in the Real World

Questionnaires based on the five-factor model can assess personality more accurately than those based on prior trait models, which is one of the major tasks of therapists and psychologists.

For instance, the Big Five traits can be used to describe differences between male and female police officers. Compared with policemen, policewomen are generally more agreeable (sympathetic, friendly, helpful), more open (insightful, intelligent), and more extraverted (sociable, talkative). These kinds of traits result in policewomen being less authoritarian, more diplomatic, and better at defusing potentially dangerous situations (Spillar & Harrington, 2000).

Researchers generally agree that the five-factor theory is a leap forward in trait theory and is useful in defining personality, predicting behaviors, and identifying personality problems (Burger, 2008; McCrae & Costa, 2003).

Five-Factor Model

Identify the personality traits in each of the Big Five categories.

Big Five and Cultural Differences

Learn how the five-factor model applies to different cultures.

▶ **LO20** Discuss the genetic and environmental influences on traits.

Influences on Traits

Jim Lewis (top photo) and Jim Springer (bottom photo) drove the same model blue Chevrolet, smoked the same brand of cigarettes, owned dogs named Toy, held jobs as deputy sheriff, enjoyed the same woodworking hobby, and had vacationed on the same beach in Florida. When they were given personality tests, they scored almost alike on traits of flexibility, self-control, and sociability. The two Jims are identical twins who were separated four weeks after birth and reared separately. When reunited at age 39, they were flabbergasted at how many things they had in common (Leo, 1987).

Identical twins Jim Lewis and Jim Springer were subjects in the now famous Minnesota twin study. Their scores were similar on personality tests that measured the Big Five traits: openness, conscientiousness, extraversion, agreeableness, and neuroticism. One reason their scores on tests were so similar was their genetic factors were identical.

There are now many studies on thousands of twins, both identical and fraternal, who were reared together and apart and whose data were analyzed by different groups of researchers. Results from earlier studies and two large and recent studies are shown in the graph below (Bouchard & Loehlin, 2001). Researchers estimate the heritability of personality traits ranges from 0.41 to about 0.51, which means that genetic factors contribute about 40% to 50% to the development of an individual's personality traits (Bouchard, 2004).

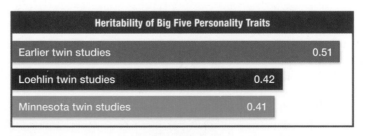

Heritability of Big Five Personality Traits	
Earlier twin studies	0.51
Loehlin twin studies	0.42
Minnesota twin studies	0.41

© Michael Nichols/National Geographic Stock

Unless otherwise noted, all images are © Cengage Learning

Even though genetic factors are responsible for about half of each of the Big Five personality traits we develop, that still leaves about half coming from environmental factors. We'll describe four factors that influence personality development, including two types of environmental factors (shared and nonshared).

Four Factors

The contributions to personality development include four factors.

40% Genetic Factors

The fingerprints of the two Jims were almost identical because they shared nearly 100% of their genes, and genetic factors contribute 97% to the development of ridges on fingertips (Bouchard et al., 1990). In comparison, their scores were similar but not identical on personality traits of self-control, flexibility, and sociability because genetic factors contribute 40% to 50% to personality traits.

27% Nonshared Environmental Factors

Although we know that the two Jims showed remarkable similarities in personality, they also displayed unique differences. For example, Jim Lewis says he is more easy-going and less of a worrier than his identical twin, Jim Springer. One reason the two Jims developed different personality traits is due to nonshared environmental factors. About 27% of the influence on personality development comes from how each individual's genetic factors react and adjust to his or her own environment (Bouchard & Loehlin, 2001; De Fruyt et al., 2006).

26% Error

About 26% of the influence on personality development cannot as yet be identified and is attributed to errors in testing and measurement procedures.

7% Shared Environmental Factors

About 7% of the influence on personality development comes from shared environmental factors that involve how family members interact and share experiences.

Behavioral Genetics

Learn how twin research helped our understanding of genetic and environmental contributions to psychology.

▶ **LO21** Evaluate the trait approach to analyzing the structure of personality.

Evaluation of Trait Theory

It would be very difficult to live without traits because you use them constantly, usually without knowing it. For example, whenever you describe someone or predict how he or she will behave, your descriptions of personality and predictions of behaviors are based almost entirely on knowing the person's traits. Online dating sites are full of personal profiles, which are essentially a list of most-desired traits.

Although traits are very useful as a shorthand to describe a person's personality and predict a person's behaviors, critics raise three major questions about traits: How good is the list? Can traits predict? What influences traits?

© Peter Scholey/Getty Images RF

How Good Is the List?

The Big Five, or five-factor trait model, assumes that all similarities and differences among personalities can be described by an amazingly short but comprehensive list of five traits: openness, conscientiousness, extraversion, agreeableness, and neuroticism (OCEAN). Each of the Big Five traits has two poles or dimensions, which include dozens of related traits. The ability to describe personality using the Big Five has now been verified in many different countries, with different populations and age groups (Allik & McCrae, 2004; Schmitt et al., 2007).

Critics of the five-factor model point out that the data for the model came from questionnaires that may be too structured to give real and complete portraits of personalities. As a result, data from questionnaires may paint too simplistic a picture of human personality and may not reflect its depth and complexity (Block, 1995). Critics also point out that traits primarily describe a person's personality rather than explain or point out its causes (Digman, 1997).

In defense of the five-factor model, researchers have shown that the Big Five traits provide a valid and reliable way to describe personality differences and consistencies in our own lives and in our social interactions with others (McCrae & Costa, 2003).

Unless otherwise noted, all images are © Cengage Learning

Can Traits Predict?

One of the more serious problems faced by early trait theory involved the assumption that, since traits are consistent and stable influences on our behaviors, traits should be very useful in predicting behaviors.

But how does trait theory explain why Rush Limbaugh (right photo) behaved so inconsistently? He preached law and order and right-wing conservative moral standards on his radio talk show, but in his private life he had become a drug addict and was allegedly having his maid buy drugs on the black market.

One explanation is that Limbaugh did behave in a consistent moral way in public situations (such as radio talk shows). However, in other situations, such as his private life, he had become a drug addict. This problem of predicting behavior across situations is known as the person-situation interaction. Researchers found that situations may have as much influence on behavior as traits do, so situational influences must be taken into account when predicting someone's behavior (Funder, 2008). Currently, the Big Five traits are considered useful concepts for describing consistent and stable behavioral tendencies in similar situations, but traits do not necessarily predict behaviors across different situations.

What Influences Traits?

One major surprise from twin studies was the relatively small effect shared environmental experiences have on personality development (p. 535). This finding questioned a major belief of developmental psychologists, who hold that sharing parental or family environment greatly influences personality development among siblings. Instead, twin research suggests that psychologists need to look more closely at each child's reactions to his or her family environment as a major influence on personality development.

According to behavioral geneticists, genetic factors exert a considerable influence on many complex human behaviors, including personality traits (Bouchard, 2004). Yet these same researchers warn that because genetic influences on human behavior generally do not exceed 50%, this means the remaining 50% or more involves environmental influences, especially nonshared environmental influences.

Personality Traits

Find out about the situation model of personality.

Check Your Learning Quiz 11.5

Go to **login.cengagebrain.com** and take the online quiz.

© AP Images/Joseph Kaczmarek

▸ **LO22** Describe projective and objective personality tests, and identify an example of each.

▸ **LO23** Distinguish between projective and objective personality tests, and detail their advantages and disadvantages.

Projective Personality Tests

You'll recall that a core component in Freud's psychoanalytic theory is unconscious thoughts that we cannot voluntarily access. As we've learned, Freud developed three techniques for revealing unconscious forces: free association, dream interpretation, and slips of the tongue. We now add a fourth technique to reveal unconscious forces: projective tests (Butcher, 2009b; Groth-Marnat, 2009).

Projective tests require individuals to look at some meaningless object or ambiguous photo and describe what they see. In describing the ambiguous object, individuals are assumed to project both their conscious and unconscious feelings, needs, and motives.

Examples of Projective Tests

What do you see in this inkblot?
The Rorschach *(ROAR-shock)* inkblot test, which was published in the early 1920s by a Swiss psychiatrist, Hermann Rorschach (1921/1942), contains five inkblots printed in black and white and five that have color. (The inkblot shown on the right is similar to but is not an actual Rorschach inkblot.)

The **Rorschach inkblot test** is used to assess personality by showing a person a series of ten inkblots and then asking the person to describe what he or she thinks each image is.

This test is used primarily in the therapeutic setting to assess personality traits and identify potential problems of clients (Weiner & Meyer, 2009).

What's happening in this picture?
A person would be shown a picture like the one on the right and asked to make up a plot or story about what the young man is thinking, feeling, or doing. (This is an example of, but not a real, Thematic Apperception Test card.)

The **Thematic Apperception Test (TAT)** involves showing a person a series of 20 pictures of people in ambiguous situations and asking the person to make up a story about what the people are doing or thinking in each situation.

The TAT, which was developed by Henry Murray (1943), is used to assess the motivation and personality characteristics of normal individuals, as well as clients with personality problems (Butcher, 2009a; Kaplan & Saccuzzo, 2009).

Projective tests, such as the Rorschach inkblot test, have been used for over 80 years. However, therapists, who report that projective tests are useful in assessing personality traits and problems (Mestel, 2003b; Society for Personality Assessment, 2005), still debate their advantages and disadvantages.

Advantages

Individuals who take projective tests do not know which are the best, correct, or socially desirable answers to give because the stimuli (the inkblot or the TAT picture) are ambiguous and have no right or wrong answers. Thus, one advantage of projective tests such as the Rorschach and the TAT is that they are difficult to fake or bias, since there are no correct or socially desirable answers. When clients respond to Rorschach's meaningless inkblots or make up stories about what is happening in TAT's ambiguous pictures, clinicians assume that clients project their hidden feelings, thoughts, or emotions onto these ambiguous stimuli. Based on this assumption, some clinicians believe that projective tests provide another method for assessing a client's hidden and unconscious thoughts and desires (Groth-Marnat, 2009). Thus, the Rorschach test's advantage is obtaining information about the person in a setting where there are no right or wrong answers.

Disadvantages

One disadvantage of projective tests is the difficulty of interpreting responses to ambiguous stimuli to which there are no right or wrong answers. The current method of scoring the Rorschach is based on analyzing and making judgments about so many different variables (such as content, theme, color, and detail of the cards) that disagreements often arise over interpretations and classifications (Mestel, 2003b). In fact, though the Rorschach is one of the more popular personality assessment tests, some studies point to serious problems in scoring and interpreting responses and making assessments based on the Rorschach test (Society for Personality Assessment, 2005; Wood et al., 2003, 2006). Thus, a clinician's training and experience play a major role in the accuracy of assessing a client's personality though the use of projective tests (Kaplan & Saccuzzo, 2009).

Handwriting Analysis

Learn what your handwriting reveals about your personality.

Objective Personality Tests

If you're applying for a job, you may be asked to fill out a written questionnaire, which is really an honesty or integrity test. These tests aim to predict how likely an applicant is to engage in counterproductive work behaviors (such as stealing, arguing, lying, blaming) (Berry et al., 2007; Spector et al., 2006). Integrity tests are examples of objective personality tests (Mumford et al., 2001).

Objective personality tests, also called **self-report questionnaires,** consist of specific written statements that require individuals to indicate, for example, by checking "true" or "false," whether the statements apply to them.

Because objective personality tests use specific questions and require specific answers, they are considered to be structured, or objective. In comparison, projective tests (pp. 538–539) use ambiguous stimuli, have widely varying responses, and are considered to be unstructured, or projective, personality tests.

Examples of Objective Tests

In business settings, self-report questionnaires are often used in selecting employees for certain traits, such as being honest and trustworthy (Berry et al., 2007; Spector et al., 2006). Other self-report questionnaires, such as the MMPI-2, are used primarily in clinical settings and measure a number of traits and personality problems.

Minnesota Multiphasic Personality Inventory-2

Suppose a parole board needed to decide if a convicted murderer had changed enough in prison to be let out on parole. To help make this decision, they might use a test that identifies the range of normal and abnormal personality traits, such as the well-known Minnesota Multiphasic Personality Inventory-2 (MMPI-2), which has recently been updated to include fewer test items while retaining the effectiveness of the longer version (Ben-Porath, 2010). The revised test is named MMPI-2-RF (Restructured Form), but for simplicity, we will continue to refer to it as MMPI-2.

Could a test show if I'm ready for parole?

Unless otherwise noted, all images are © Cengage Learning

© PhotoDisc, Inc.

The **Minnesota Multiphasic Personality Inventory-2-RF (MMPI-2)** is a true-false self-report questionnaire that consists of 338 statements describing a wide range of normal and abnormal behaviors. The purpose of the MMPI-2 is to measure the personality style and emotional adjustment in individuals with mental illness.

The MMPI-2 asks about and identifies a variety of specific personality traits, including depression, hostility, high energy, and shyness, and plots whether these traits are in the normal or abnormal range. The statements below are similar to actual statements in the MMPI-2:

- I tire quickly.
- I am not worried about sex.
- I believe people are plotting against me.

Advantages

One advantage of the MMPI-2, specifically, is that it has three kinds of scales: (1) validity scales, which assess whether the client was faking good or bad answers; (2) clinical scales, which identify psychological disorders, such as depression or schizophrenia; and (3) content scales, which identify specific areas, such as the anger scale, which includes references to being irritable and to difficulties controlling anger (Kaplan & Saccuzzo, 2009). A second advantage of objective personality tests is that they are easily administered and can be taken individually or in groups. A third advantage is that, since the questions are structured and require either a true-false or yes-no answer, the scoring is straightforward.

Disadvantages

One disadvantage of objective personality tests is that their questions and answers are very structured, and critics point out that such structured tests may not assess deeper or unconscious personality factors. A second disadvantage comes from the straightforward questions, which often allow people to figure out what answers are most socially desirable or acceptable and thus bias the test results. Third, many self-report questionnaires measure specific traits, which we know may predict behavior in the same situations but not across situations. This means a person may behave honestly with his or her family but not necessarily with his or her employer.

Because objective and projective personality tests have different advantages and disadvantages, counselors and clinical psychologists may use a combination of both to assess a client's personality traits and problems.

Horoscopes

Learn what your horoscopes reveal about your personality.

Check Your Learning Quiz 11.6

Go to **login.cengagebrain.com** and take the online quiz.

Think Critically

Challenge Your Thinking

Consider these questions when reading this article:

1. Why do some employers use both interviews and objective personality tests in deciding whom to hire?

2. Why do companies look for certain traits in selecting employees, and why would Freud question the importance of selecting for traits?

3. If you were using the Big Five traits to design a test for salespeople who work as a team, which traits would you look for?

4. What are some objections to or disadvantages of using objective personality tests in the hiring process?

5. An applicant's behavior during an interview is important, but does it generalize to good behavior on the job? Why or why not?

6. Which objective personality test has a scale to detect lying? Can objective personality tests prevent a person from "faking his or her character"?

Unless otherwise noted, all images are © Cengage Learning

Personality Tests Help Employers Find Applicants Who Fit

More and more job applicants are being required to take personality tests. Already, at least one-third of employers, ranging from governments to hospitals, retail stores to restaurants, and airlines to manufacturing plants, use personality tests in their hiring and promotion process.

There are many personality tests, and each measures something different. For instance, the Myers-Briggs measures personality traits necessary for leadership and teamwork and is used by 89 of the Fortune 100 companies. The Minnesota Multipha-

sic Personality Inventory (pp. 540–541) measures an individual's tendency toward substance abuse and psychopathology and is used by 60% of police departments as a way to screen applicants. Personality tests look at a variety of other characteristics, such as thought processes, sociability, motivation, self-awareness, emotional intelligence, stress management, dependability, and work style.

Some experts believe personality tests are overused and overinterpreted, and they caution employers about the

© AJA Productions/Getty Images

potential negative impact of the tests on minority applicants. Others believe personality tests have an important place in the hiring process because the tests can predict how well an applicant "fits" with the job description. For instance, when hiring a salesperson, a company can have a list of the personality traits of successful salespeople and then match an applicant's test results against that standard.

Many companies that have used personality tests showed a decrease in absenteeism and turnover, which means big savings for the company. By using personality tests, one California theme park increased levels of employee retention and customer satisfaction, and reduced levels of absenteeism and theft. Also, a bottling company in Milwaukee reduced the number of sick days in half, and an airline reduced tardiness by one-third.

Personality tests are increasingly being used in the hiring process to supplement interviews and a resumé review. So how should you respond to test questions to be sure you get the job? Although ideal responses vary by job position and company, experts suggest that you not falsify your responses, as many personality tests have a sophisticated way of knowing if you're lying. Luis Valdes, an executive consultant, explains, "For any given character trait, say independence, there's an optimal amount. If a person seems to be really extreme, well, most people aren't that extreme, so it suggests they tried to answer all the questions in a positive but not very realistic way" (Valdes, 2006). In the case of personality tests, it appears that honesty is the best policy. (Adapted from Cha, 2005; Cullen, 2006; Frieswick, 2004; Gladwell, 2004; Gunn, 2006; Smith, 1997; Valdes, 2006; Wessel, 2003)

Think Critically 11.1

This article and its questions are available in interactive format online.

GO to your Psychology CourseMate at login.cengagebrain.com
and take the Chapter Post-Test to see which Learning Objectives
you've mastered and which need more review. Use the chapter
review guide below and the online activities—including
flashcards to review key terms—to measure your learning.

Measure
>Your Learning

Online Activities

Key Terms	Video	Animation	Reading	Assessment
personality, theory of personality	Ted Haggard, p. 503			Check Your Learning Quiz 11.1
Freud's psychoanalytic theory of personality, conscious thoughts, unconscious forces, unconscious motivation, free association, dream interpretation, Freudian slips, id, pleasure priniple, ego, reality principle, superego, anxiety, defense mechanism, rationalization, denial, repression, projection, reaction formation, displacement, sublimation, psychosexual stages, fixation, oral stage, anal stage, phallic, Oedipus complex, latency stage, genital stage, collective unconscious		Freud's Divisions of the Mind, p. 511	Ted Haggard and Psychoanalytic Theory, p. 505 Ted Haggard and Unconscious Forces, p. 507 Use of Defense Mechanisms, p. 511 Oedipus Complex, p. 513 Freudian Theory Today, p. 513	Check Your Learning Quiz 11.2
humanistic theories, phenomenological, holistic view, self-actualization, Maslow's hierarchy of needs, self-actualization, self-theory (self-actualization theory), self-actualizing tendency, self (self-concept), positive regard, conditional positive regard, unconditional positive regard, positive psychology	Self-Concept, p. 521		Carrie Underwood, p. 517 The Freedom Writers, p. 523	Check Your Learning Quiz 11.3

Online Activities

Key Terms	Video	Animation	Reading	Assessment
social cognitive theory, cognitive factors, personal factors, environmental factors, locus of control, self-efficacy			Stress and Coping, p. 527 Social Cognitive Theory vs. Other Theories, p. 529	Check Your Learning Quiz 11.4
trait theory, trait, five-factor model	Behavioral Genetics, p. 535 Personality Traits, p. 537	Five-Factor Model, p. 533	Big Five and Cultural Differences, p. 533	Check Your Learning Quiz 11.5
projective tests, Rorschach inkblot test, Thematic Apperception Test (TAT), objective personality tests (self-report questionnaires), Minnestota Multiphasic Personality Inventory-2-RF (MMPI-2)			Handwriting Analysis, p. 539 Horoscopes, p. 541	Check Your Learning Quiz 11.6

Psychological Disorders

12

Chapter Outline and Learning Objectives

1 GO to your **Psychology CourseMate** at **login.cengagebrain.com** and take the **Chapter Pre-Test** to introduce yourself to this chapter's topics and see what you may already know.

2 READ the **Learning Objectives (LOs)** (in the left sidebars) and begin the chapter.

3 COMPLETE the **Online Activities** (in the right sidebars) *as you read each module.* Activities include **videos**, **animations**, **readings**, and **quizzes**.

4 CHECK Your Learning by going online to take the quiz at the end of each module and review material as necessary.

5 MEASURE Your Learning after reading the chapter by taking the online **Chapter Post-Test**. Use the chapter review guide at the end of the chapter as needed.

WATCH for these **Online Activities** icons as you read:

Video

Animation

Reading

Assessment

Think Critically

These online activities are important to mastering this chapter. As you read each module, access these materials by going to **login.cengagebrain.com**.

Video Explore studies and firsthand accounts of biological and psychological processes:

- Learn more about Dennis Rader
- Watch panic disorder being diagnosed
- Learn what it's like to live with panic disorder
- Watch PTSD being diagnosed
- Learn what it's like to live with PTSD
- Learn what it's like to live with OCD
- Learn what it's like for children to have OCD
- Learn what it's like to live with major depressive disorder
- Learn what it's like to live with bipolar disorder
- Explore what it's like to have a schizophrenic disorder
- See what it's like to have a disorder of thought
- Explore what it's like to have dissociative identity disorder
- Explore what it's like to successfully cope with having dissociative identity disorder

- Learn what it's like to have body dysmorphic disorder
- Explore what it's like to have borderline personality disorder
- Learn what it's like to have anti-social personality disorder

Animation Interact with and visualize important processes and concepts:

- Learn the three ways to define abnormal behaviors
- Use three methods to assess mental disorders and determine their causes

Reading Delve deeper into key content:

- Learn what a clinical assessment can tell us about a person
- Learn how revisions have improved the DSM
- Explore examples of culture-specific mental disorders
- Learn which DSM labels are applied to people most frequently

- Learn about taijin kyofusho
- Learn what seasonal affective disorder is and how it develops
- Explore how thoughts can influence our behaviors and emotions
- Learn about the major breakthroughs in identifying genetic markers for schizophrenia
- Explore how someone with dissociative fugue can adapt to a loss of identity

Assessment Measure your mastery:

- Chapter Pre-Test
- Check Your Learning Quizzes
- Chapter Post-Test

Think Critically Challenge your thinking by applying content from this chapter and making connections to related material:

- What Is a Psychopath?

▶ **L01** Define insanity and mental disorder.

HE WAS A LOVING HUSBAND, devoted father, respected church elder, and straitlaced county official. He also worked for a home security company, where he would help individuals protect themselves from dangerous people. Until the day he was caught, he blended into the Wichita community as an average next-door neighbor. But over a period of 17 years, Dennis Rader planned and carried out the cruel murders of 10 people. He became known as the "BTK killer," which stands for Bind, Torture, and Kill, describing the methods he used with his victims.

▼

In a very real sense, Rader led two different lives. In public, Rader seemed like a quiet, law-abiding guy who helped to protect the safety of others. However, in private, Rader would break into people's homes, hide, and then sneak up on his victims. He would proceed to tie them up, callously strangle them, and eventually murder them.

When Rader's trial began, his defense attorneys had to decide whether they wanted to claim he was legally insane when he committed the murders. You are probably thinking that a person who coldheartedly plans and carries out 10 violent murders must be insane, but let's consider what it means to be insane.

Insanity, according to its legal definition, means not knowing the difference between right and wrong.

As inhumane as Rader's behaviors may seem, his defense did not claim he was insane. Based on Rader's testimony, it was clear he knew all along that his actions were wrong and conducted for his own selfish interests. In 2005, Rader was charged with 10 counts of first-degree murder for which he must serve 10 life sentences (Davey, 2005; O'Driscoll, 2005; Wilgoren, 2005).

When mental health professionals examine Rader's behaviors, they are trying to identify his particular mental disorder.

A **mental disorder** is generally defined as a prolonged or recurring problem that seriously interferes with an individual's ability to live a satisfying personal life and function adequately in society.

We'll begin this chapter with the different factors that are involved in defining, explaining, and treating mental disorders, such as that of Dennis Rader.

BTK KILLER GUILTY OF 10 COUNTS OF FIRST-DEGREE MURDER

Dennis Rader

Learn more about Dennis Rader.

Check Your Learning Quiz 12.1

Go to **login.cengagebrain.com** and take the online quiz.

▶ **LO2** Explain three ways to define abnormal behavior.

Definitions of Abnormal Behavior

In some cases, such as Dennis Rader's murder and mutilation of 10 individuals, we have no doubt that he demonstrated abnormal behaviors. In other cases, such as that of 54-year-old Richard Thompson (right photo), it is less clear what is abnormal behavior.

The City of San Diego evicted Thompson and all his belongings from his home. His belongings included shirts, pants, dozens of shoes, several Bibles, a cooler, a tool chest, lawn chairs, a barbecue grill, tin plates, bird cages, two pet rats, and his self-fashioned bed. For the previous 9 months, Thompson had lived happily and without any problems in a downtown storm drain (sewer). Because the city does not allow people to live in storm drains, however, Thompson was evicted from his underground storm-drain home and forbidden to return. Although Thompson later lived in several care centers and mental hospitals, he much preferred the privacy and comfort of the sewer (Grimaldi, 1986).

There are three different ways to decide whether Richard Thompson's behavior—living in the sewer—was abnormal.

Statistical Frequency

Although Thompson caused no problems to others, his preferred living style could be considered abnormal according to statistical frequency.

The **statistical frequency approach** says that a behavior may be considered abnormal if it occurs rarely or infrequently in relation to the behaviors of the general population.

By this definition, Thompson's living in a storm drain would be considered very abnormal since, out of over 300 million people in the United States, only a very few prefer his kind of home. By this criterion, getting a PhD, being president, living in a monastery, and selling a million records are abnormal. However, we would not consider individuals who do those things to necessarily have mental disorders.

As all these examples demonstrate, the statistical frequency definition of abnormality has very limited usefulness.

Deviation from Social Norms

Thompson's behavior (preferring to live in a sewer) could also be considered abnormal based on social norms.

The **social norms approach** says that a behavior is considered abnormal if it deviates greatly from accepted social standards, values, or norms.

Thompson's decision to live by himself in a storm drain greatly deviates from society's norms about where people should live. However, a definition of abnormality based solely on deviations from social norms runs into problems when social norms change with time. For example, 25 years ago, very few males wore earrings, whereas today many males consider earrings very fashionable.

Thus, defining abnormality on the basis of social norms can be risky, as social norms may, and do, change over time.

Maladaptive Behavior

The major problem with the first two definitions of abnormal behavior (statistical frequency and deviation from social norms) is that they don't say whether a particular behavior is psychologically damaging or maladaptive.

The **maladaptive behavior approach** defines a behavior as psychologically damaging or abnormal if it interferes with the individual's ability to function in his or her personal life or in society.

For example, being terrified of flying, being so depressed one feels completely hopeless about the future, feeling compelled to wash one's hands for hours on end, starving oneself to the point of death (anorexia nervosa), and committing serial murders would all be considered maladaptive and, in that sense, abnormal.

However, Thompson's seemingly successful adaptation to living in a sewer may not be maladaptive for him and has no adverse consequences to society.

Mental health professionals find that the most useful definition of abnormal behaviors is the maladaptive definition (that is, whether a behavior interferes with a person's ability to function normally in society) (Sue et al., 2010).

Definitions of Abnormal Behavior

Learn the three ways to define abnormal behaviors.

© Leftleg/Shutterstock

© Kelly Redinger/Design Pics/Corbis

▶ **L03** Discuss the causes of abnormal behavior.

Causes of Abnormal Behavior

Explanations for the causes of mental disorders have changed through the centuries. In the Middle Ages, mental disorders were thought to be the result of demons or devils, who inhabited individuals and made them do horrible things. In the 1600s, mental disorders were thought to involve witches, who were believed to speak to the devil. In the 1960s, one major cause of mental disorders was thought to be environmental factors, such as stressful events. In the 1990s came advances in studying genetic factors and living brains. As a result, researchers and clinicians now believe mental disorders result from a number of factors, which include biological, cognitive-emotional-behavioral, and environmental influences (Hersen & Thomas, 2006).

Biological Factors

Biological influences include genetic or inherited factors and various neurological factors that influence how the brain functions.

Genetic factors that contribute to the development of mental disorders are inherited tendencies that influence how a person thinks, behaves, and feels.

Genetic factors operate by affecting the developing brain and/or the neurotransmitters the brain uses for communication. Researchers estimate that genetic factors contribute 30% to 60% to the development of mental disorders, such as depression, schizophrenia, and anxiety disorders (Rutter & Silberg, 2002).

Another reason people develop mental disorders is due to neurological factors. For example, people may develop an anxiety disorder if their brain's emotional detector, called the amygdala (see left illustration) is overactive and too often identifies stimuli as threatening when they are only new or novel. In fact, individuals who have social phobias (such as an anxiety disorder), show far more amygdala activity when looking at angry, fearful, or disgusted faces than do individuals without social phobias (Luan et al., 2006).

Amygdala-emotions

Although research studies show that biological factors—genetic and neurological—can contribute to the development of mental disorders, not everyone with an overactive amygdala develops a mental disorder. This means that other factors are also involved in the development of mental disorders.

Unless otherwise noted, all images are © Cengage Learning

Cognitive-Emotional-Behavioral and Environmental Factors

Because biological factors themselves do not always explain why people develop mental disorders, psychologists point to various cognitive-emotional-behavioral factors that interact with and contribute to developing mental disorders.

Cognitive-emotional-behavioral and **environmental factors** that contribute to the development of mental disorders include deficits in cognitive processes, such as having unusual thoughts and beliefs; deficits in processing emotional stimuli, such as under- or overreacting to emotional situations; behavioral problems, such as lacking social skills; and environmental challenges, such as dealing with stressful situations.

For example, Dennis Rader (right photo) was a shy and polite child who preferred to spend time alone. As a boy, he recalls watching his grandparents strangle chickens at their farm, and by the time he reached high school, he was strangling cats and dogs. Rader's hobby during childhood was looking at pictures of women in bondage. By his teens, he fantasized about tying up, controlling, and torturing women. He was becoming increasingly bothered by murderous impulses but did not know how to tell anyone about it (Ortiz, 2005; Singular, 2006). Rader's many maladaptive thoughts, emotions, and behaviors interacted with his biological factors and resulted in his serious mental disorder.

In some cases, traumatic events, such as being in a war, having a serious car accident, watching some horrible event (such as a dog attacking and killing a child), or being brutally mugged, assaulted, or raped, can result in a long-lasting emotional disorder called posttraumatic stress disorder, or PTSD. As we will discuss later in this chapter (p. 567), a person with PTSD may relive the terrible event through memories and nightmares and have serious emotional problems that often require professional help (Resick et al., 2008). Experiencing PTSD is an example of how traumatic environmental factors can contribute to developing a serious mental disorder.

Conclusion

The answer to why Dennis Rader became a serial killer, or why a family member or friend developed a mental disorder involves a number of factors: genetic, neurological, cognitive-emotional-behavioral, and environmental. As several or more of these factors interact, the result in some cases can be the development of one of the mental disorders that we'll discuss in this chapter.

Check Your Learning Quiz 12.2

Go to **login.cengagebrain.com** and take the online quiz.

© Jeff Tuttle/AFP/Getty Images

▶ **L04** Describe three methods of assessing mental disorders.

Assessing Mental Disorders

In some cases, it's relatively easy to identify what's wrong with a person. For example, it's clear that Dennis Rader was a serial killer. But in other cases, it's more difficult to identify exactly what the person's motivation and mental problem are. Take the tragic case of Susan Smith.

Susan Smith appeared on the *Today* show, crying for the return of her two little boys (right photo), Michael, 3 years old, and Alex, 14 months old, who, she said, had been kidnapped. She begged the kidnapper to feed them, care for them, and return them. And then, 9 days later, after an investigation turned up doubts about the kidnapping story, the police questioned Susan again. Not only did she change her story, but she made the teary confession that she had killed her two children. She said she had parked her car by the edge of the lake, strapped her two children into their car seats, shut the windows and doors, got out of the car, and pushed the car into the lake. The two little boys drowned to death.

© Time & Life Pictures/Getty Images

Susan's confession stunned the nation as everyone asked, "How could she have killed her own children?" "What's wrong with Susan?" To answer these questions, mental health professionals did a clinical assessment (Wood et al., 2002).

A **clinical assessment** involves a systematic evaluation of an individual's various psychological, biological, and social factors, as well as identification of past and present problems, stressors, and other cognitive or behavioral symptoms.

Mental health professionals use one or more of three major techniques—neurological exams, clinical interviews, and psychological tests—to do clinical assessments.

Neurological Tests

We can assume Susan was given neurological tests to check for possible brain damage or malfunction. These tests might include evaluating reflexes, brain structures, and brain functions.

Neurological exams are part of a clinical assessment because a variety of abnormal psychological symptoms may be caused by tumors, diseases, or infections of the brain. Neurological tests are used to distinguish physical or organic causes (such as tumors) from psychological ones (such as strange beliefs) (Zillmer et al., 2008). Susan was reported to have no neurological problems.

Unless otherwise noted, all images are © Cengage Learning

Clinical Interviews

As part of her clinical assessment, psychiatrists spent many hours interviewing Susan. This method is called a clinical interview (Hersen & Thomas, 2007).

The **clinical interview** is one method of gathering information about a person's past and current behaviors, beliefs, attitudes, emotions, and problems. Some clinical interviews are unstructured, which means they have no set questions; others are structured, which means they follow a standard format of asking a similar set of questions.

During the clinical interview, Susan would have been asked about the history of her current problems, such as when they started and what other events accompanied them. Based on 15 hours of interviews, Dr. Seymour Halleck testified that Susan was scarred by her father's suicide and her stepfather sexually abusing her, which led to periods of depression, her current problem (Towle, 1995).

Psychological Tests

As part of her assessment, psychologists may have given Susan a number of personality tests (Module 11.6).

Personality tests include two different kinds of tests: objective tests (self-report questionnaires), such as the MMPI, which consist of specific statements or questions to which the person responds with specific answers, and projective tests, such as the Rorschach inkblot test (right image), which have no set answers but consist of ambiguous stimuli that a person interprets or makes up a story about.

Personality tests help clinicians evaluate a person's traits, attitudes, emotions, and beliefs.

Purpose

A major goal of doing a clinical assessment is to decide which mental health disorder best accounts for a client's symptoms. For example, based on her symptoms, Susan was described as having a mood disorder, which you'll learn in Module 12.5 is one of many possible mental health problems.

Clinical Assessment

Use the three methods to assess mental disorders and determine their causes.

Real-Life Assessment of Susan Smith

Learn what a clinical assessment can tell us about a person.

▶ **L05** Describe the DSM model for diagnosing mental disorders.

Diagnosing Mental Disorders

Those who knew Susan tried to diagnose the problem that led to her tragic crime.

"Maybe Susan was just plain crazy." "Maybe she was too depressed to know what she was doing." "Maybe she had bad genes." "Maybe something bad happened to her as a child."

Using a more rigorous method, mental health professionals conduct clinical assessments to identify symptoms, which are then used to make a clinical diagnosis.

A **clinical diagnosis** is a process of matching an individual's specific symptoms to those that define a particular mental disorder.

Making a clinical diagnosis was very difficult prior to the 1950s because there was no uniform code or diagnostic system. However, since 1952, the American Psychiatric Association (APA) has been developing a uniform diagnostic system, whose most recent version is known as the *Diagnostic and Statistical Manual of Mental Disorders*-IV-Text Revision, abbreviated as DSM-IV-TR (APA, 2000).

The **Diagnostic and Statistical Manual of Mental Disorders**-IV-Text Revision (DSM-IV-TR) describes a uniform system for assessing specific symptoms and matching them to almost 300 different mental disorders.

With each revision of the DSM, there have been improvements in diagnosing mental disorders. For instance, the DSM-II gave only general descriptions of mental problems, which resulted in disagreements in diagnosing problems. The DSM-III listed more specific symptoms and criteria for mental disorders; however, the criteria were based primarily on clinical opinion, not on research, so the disagreements continued. A major improvement in the current DSM-IV-TR is that it establishes criteria and symptoms for mental disorders based more on research findings than on clinical opinions (Clark et al., 1995). When the next DSM is published, likely in 2012, mental health experts predict that it will use new findings from genetics and neuroscience to better identify the underlying causes of mental disorders (First, 2007; Miller, 2007).

We'll use the cases of Dennis Rader (serial killer) and Susan Smith (murderer), to show how mental health professionals use the DSM-IV-TR to make a diagnosis. The DSM-IV-TR has five major dimensions, called axes, which serve as guidelines for making decisions about symptoms. We'll first describe Axis I and show how it can be used to diagnose the problems of Susan Smith.

Nine Major Problems: Axis I

Axis I: Nine Major Clinical Syndromes

Axis I contains lists of symptoms and criteria about the onset, severity, and duration of these symptoms. These lists of symptoms are used to make a clinical diagnosis of the following nine major clinical syndromes.

1 Disorders Usually First Diagnosed in Infancy, Childhood, or Adolescence

This category includes disorders that arise before adolescence, such as attention-deficit disorders, autism, mental retardation, and stuttering.

2 Organic Mental Disorders

These disorders are temporary or permanent dysfunctions of brain tissue caused by diseases or chemicals, such as delirium, dementia (such as Alzheiner's disease), and amnesia.

3 Substance-Related Disorders

This category refers to the maladaptive use of drugs and alcohol. Mere consumption and recreational use of such substances are not disorders. This category requires an abnormal pattern of use (such as alcohol abuse, cocaine dependence).

4 Schizophrenia and Other Psychotic Disorders

The schizophrenias are characterized by psychotic symptoms (for example, grossly disorganized behavior, delusions, and hallucinations) and by over six months of behavioral deterioration. This category, which also includes delusional disorder, will be discussed in Module 12.6.

Revisions of the DSM

How have revisions improved the DSM?

Culture-Specific Mental Disorders

Explore examples of culture-specific mental disorders.

5 Mood Disorders

The cardinal feature is emotional disturbance. Patients may or may not have psychotic symptoms. These disorders, including major depression, bipolar disorder, and dysthymic disorder, which will be discussed in Module 12.5. Next, we will discuss how Susan Smith is an example of a person with a mood disorder.

Susan Smith: Diagnosis—Mood Disorder

From childhood on, Susan showed symptoms of being depressed, attempting suicide, seeking sexual alliances to escape loneliness, and having low self-esteem and hopelessness, all of which match the DSM-IV-TR's list of symptoms for a mood disorder. In Susan's case, the specific mood disorder most closely matches major depressive disorder but without serious thought disorders and delusions.

© AP Images/Lou Krasky

6 Anxiety Disorders

These disorders are characterized by physiological signs of anxiety (such as palpitations) and subjective feelings of tension, apprehension, or fear. Anxiety may be acute and focused (as in phobias) or continual and diffuse (as in generalized anxiety disorder).

7 Somatoform Disorders

These disorders are dominated by somatic symptoms that resemble physical illnesses. These symptoms cannot be accounted for by organic damage. There must also be strong evidence that these symptoms are produced by psychological factors or conflicts. This category, which includes somatization disorder, conversion disorder, and hypochondriasis, will be discussed in Module 12.8.

8 Dissociative Disorders

These disorders all feature a sudden, temporary alteration or dysfunction of memory, consciousness, identity, and behavior, as in dissociative amnesia and multiple personality disorder, which will be discussed in Module 12.7.

9 Sexual and Gender-Identity Disorders

There are three types of disorders in this category: gender-identity disorders (discomfort with identity as male or female), paraphilias (preference for unusual acts to achieve sexual arousal), and sexual dysfunctions (impairments in sexual functioning).

Next, we'll describe how the other four axes are used in diagnosing problems.

Other Problems and Disorders: Axes II, III, IV, V

Axis II: Personality Disorders

This axis refers to disorders that involve patterns of personality traits that are long-standing, maladaptive, and inflexible and involve impaired functioning or subjective distress. Personality disorders will be discussed in Module 12.9. An example of a personality disorder is that of Rader.

Dennis Rader: Diagnosis—Antisocial Personality Disorder

Dennis Rader's symptoms include torturing and killing 10 individuals, feeling no guilt or remorse, and exhibiting this behavior over a considerable period of time. According to the DSM-IV-TR, the essential features of an antisocial personality disorder are strange inner experiences that differ greatly from the expectations of one's culture, that lead to significant impairment in personal, occupational, or social functioning, and that form a pattern of disregard for, and violation of, the rights of others. This list of symptoms from the DSM-IV-TR matches those of Rader.

Axis III: General Medical Conditions

This axis refers to physical disorders or conditions, such as diabetes, arthritis, and hemophilia, that have an influence on someone's mental disorder.

Axis IV: Psychosocial and Environmental Problems

This axis refers to psychosocial and environmental problems that may affect the diagnosis, treatment, and prognosis of mental disorders in Axes I and II. A psychosocial or environmental problem may be a negative life event (such as a traumatic event), an environmental difficulty, a familial or other interpersonal stress, or an inadequacy of social support or personal resources.

Axis V: Global Assessment of Functioning Scale

This axis is used to rate the overall psychological, social, and occupational functioning of the individual on a scale from 1 (severe danger of hurting self) to 100 (superior functioning in all activities).

© Jeff Tuttle/AFP/Getty Images

▶ **L06** Identify the advantages and disadvantages of the DSM model for diagnosing mental disorders.

Usefulness of DSM-IV-TR

The figure at right shows the steps in making a clinical diagnosis. Mental health professionals begin by using three different methods to identify a client's symptoms, a process called clinical assessment. Next, the client's symptoms are matched to the five axes in the DSM-IV-TR to arrive at a diagnosis of the client's particular mental disorder.

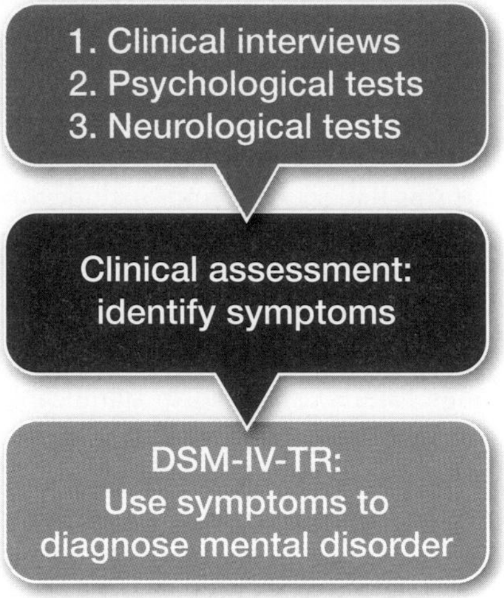

For mental health professionals, there are three advantages of using the DSM-IV-TR's uniform system to diagnose and classify mental disorders (Widiger & Clark, 2000).

First, mental health professionals use the classification system to communicate with one another and discuss their clients' problems.

Second, researchers use the classification system to study and explain mental disorders.

Third, therapists use the classification system to design their treatment program so as to best fit a particular client's problem.

Although using the DSM-IV-TR system to diagnose mental problems has advantages, it also has a number of potential problems. For example, mental health professionals do not always agree on whether a client fits a particular diagnosis. In addition, there may be social, political, and labeling problems, which we'll discuss next.

1. Clinical interviews
2. Psychological tests
3. Neurological tests

Clinical assessment:
identify symptoms

DSM-IV-TR:
Use symptoms to
diagnose mental disorder

Unless otherwise noted, all images are © Cengage Learning

Potential Problems with Using the DSM-IV-TR

It's not uncommon to hear people use labels, such as "Jim's really anxious," "Mary Ann is compulsive," or "Vicki is schizophrenic." Although the goal of the DSM-IV-TR is to give mental disorders particular diagnostic labels, once a person is labeled, the label itself may generate a negative stereotype. In turn, the negative stereotype results in negative social and political effects, such as biasing how others perceive and respond to the labeled person (Greatley, 2004).

Labeling Mental Disorders

Mental health professionals make a clinical diagnosis that results in giving a label to an individual's problem.

Labeling refers to identifying and naming differences among individuals. The label, which places individuals into specific categories, may have either positive or negative associations.

The advantage of diagnostic labels is their ability to summarize and communicate a whole lot of information in a single word or phrase. But, the disadvantage is that if the label has negative associations (for example, mentally ill, retarded, schizo), the very label may elicit negative or undesirable responses. For this reason, mental health professionals advise that we not respond to people with mental disorders by their labels and instead respond to the person behind the label (Albee & Joffe, 2004).

© Jerome Scholler/Shutterstock © Junichi Kusaka/Getty Images

Would you perceive these individuals differently if they were labeled with a mental disorder?

Social and Political Implications

Diagnostic labels can change how a person is perceived and thus have political and social implications. For instance, in the 1970s, gays protested that homosexuality should not be included in the DSM-I and II as a mental disorder. When studies found homosexuals were no more or less mentally healthy than heterosexuals, homosexuality as a mental disorder was eliminated from the DSM-III.

In the 1980s, women protested the DSM label of self-defeating personality disorder because the label applied primarily to women who were said to make destructive life choices, such as staying in abusive relationships (Japenga, 1994). This label was dropped from the DSM-IV because it suggested that women were choosing bad relationships, which wasn't true (Caplan, 1994).

Despite these advances, labeling continues to be a serious problem. For instance, 68% of Americans don't want someone with a mental illness marrying into their family and 58% don't want people with mental illness at their workplace (Martin et al., 2000). Also, even though mental illness does not increase the chance of someone being violent, many Americans still believe that people with mental illness tend to behave in violent ways (Elbogen & Johnson, 2009).

Frequency of Mental Disorders

Learn which DSM labels are applied to people most frequently.

Check Your Learning Quiz 12.3

Go to **login.cengagebrain.com** and take the online quiz.

▶ **LO7** Describe and distinguish between the five anxiety disorders.

The most common mental disorder reported by adults in the United States is any kind of anxiety disorder (Kessler et al., 2005). Here we'll discuss generalized anxiety disorder, panic disorder, post-traumatic stress disorder, three kinds of phobias, and obsessive-compulsive disorder.

Generalized Anxiety Disorder

During his initial therapy interview, Fred (right photo) was sweating, fidgeting in his chair, and repeatedly asking for water to quench a never-ending thirst. From all indications, Fred was visibly distressed and extremely nervous. At first, Fred spoke only of his dizziness and problems with sleeping. He later admitted to a long history of difficulties in interacting with others. He constantly worried about all kinds of possible disasters that might happen to him (Davison & Neale, 1990). Fred's symptoms showed that he was suffering from generalized anxiety disorder.

© Photo_Concepts/iStockphoto

Unless otherwise noted, all images are © Cengage Learning

Generalized anxiety disorder (GAD) is characterized by excessive or unrealistic worry about almost everything or feeling that something bad is about to happen. These anxious feelings occur on a majority of days for a period of at least six months (APA, 2000).

Generalized anxiety disorder includes both psychological and physical symptoms. Psychological symptoms include being irritable, having difficulty concentrating, and being unable to control one's worry, which is out of proportion to the actual event. Constant worrying causes significant distress or impaired functioning in social, occupational, and other areas. Physical symptoms include restlessness, fatigue, sweating, flushing, pounding heart, insomnia, headaches, and muscle tension or aches (APA, 2000).

Panic Disorder

One afternoon, Luisa (next page), a 23-year-old college student, was walking on campus and she suddenly felt her heart rate rapidly accelerate, her throat tighten up, and her arms and legs tremble. She became so nauseous she almost vomited. Then, weeks later, while at the movies, she had another episode during which she experienced dizziness, chest pain, shortness of breath, and weakness in her legs and feet. She feared she was having a heart attack and might die, but after a series of tests, her doctors found no medical problem. Luisa's symptoms indicate she had panic disorder.

Panic disorder is characterized by recurrent and unexpected panic attacks (described below). The person becomes so worried about having another panic attack that this intense worrying interferes with normal psychological functioning (APA, 2000).

A **panic attack** is a period of intense fear or discomfort in which four or more of the following symptoms are present: pounding heart, sweating, trembling, shortness of breath, feelings of choking, chest pain, nausea, feeling dizzy, and fear of losing control or dying (American Psychiatric Association, 2000).

Posttraumatic Stress Disorder

Mark was driving home from work when a huge truck unexpectedly lost control and rammed his car from behind. He was lucky to walk away alive. However, since the accident Mark has become so fearful of driving that he works from home now. He still experiences troublesome, recurring memories of the event and frequently has terrifying nightmares about being in a car accident. Mark's symptoms would be diagnosed as posttraumatic stress disorder.

Posttraumatic stress disorder, or PTSD, is a disabling condition that results from personally experiencing an event that involves actual or threatened death or serious injury or from witnessing or hearing of such an event happening to a family member or friend. People suffering from PTSD experience a number of psychological symptoms, including recurring and disturbing memories, terrible nightmares, and intense anxiety (APA, 2000).

These horrible memories and feelings of fear keep stress levels high and result in a range of psychosomatic symptoms, including sleep problems, pounding heart, and stomach problems (Marshall et al., 2006; Schnurr et al., 2002).

Panic Disorder I

Watch panic disorder being diagnosed.

Panic Disorder 2

Learn what it's like to live with panic disorder.

PTSD I

Watch PTSD being diagnosed.

PTSD 2

Learn what it's like to live with PTSD.

© Chip Simons/Science Faction/Corbis

Phobias

When common fears of seeing blood, spiders, or mice, having injections, meeting new people, speaking in public, flying, or being in small places turn into very intense fears, they are called phobias (over 500 phobias are listed on www.phobialist.com).

A **phobia** *(FOE-bee-ah)* is an anxiety disorder characterized by an intense and irrational fear that is out of all proportion to the possible danger of the object or situation. Because of this intense fear, which is accompanied by increased physiological arousal, a person goes to great lengths to avoid the feared event. If the feared event cannot be avoided, the person feels intense anxiety.

Here we'll discuss three common phobias: social phobias, specific phobias, and agoraphobia (graph at right) (Durand & Barlow, 2006).

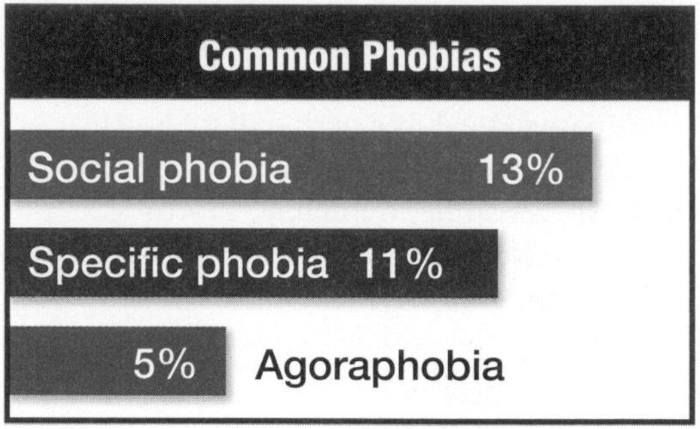

Common Phobias

Social phobia   13%

Specific phobia   11%

5%   Agoraphobia

Social Phobias

In junior high school, Billy (pictured right) never, never spoke up in class or answered any questions. The school counselor said that Billy would be sick to his stomach the whole day if he knew that he was going to be called on. Billy began to hide out in the restrooms to avoid going to class. Billy's fear of speaking up in class is an example of a social phobia (Durand & Barlow, 2010).

Social phobias are characterized by irrational, marked, and continuous fear of performing in social situations. The individuals fear that they will humiliate or embarrass themselves (APA, 2000).

As a fearful social situation approaches, anxiety builds up and may result in considerable bodily distress, such as nausea, sweating, and other signs of heightened physiological arousal. Although a person with a social phobia realizes that the fear is excessive or irrational, he or she may not know how to deal with it, other than by avoiding the situation.

Specific Phobias

Mary's (right picture) fear of flying began in her childhood, when she experienced a turbulent flight that left her scared and anxious. Later, as a young adult, her fear of flying was greatly worsened by memories of the infamous September 11, 2001, terrorist attacks on the World Trade Center, which killed thousands of innocent people. After that incident, her phobia of flying kept her from visiting friends and family. She would try to fly and even make reservations but always cancelled them at the last minute. Mary's traumatic experiences with flying turned into a phobia of flying, which is called a specific phobia.

Specific phobias are characterized by marked and persistent fears that are unreasonable and triggered by anticipation of, or exposure to, a specific object or situation (such as flying, heights, spiders, seeing blood) (APA, 2000).

Among the more common specific phobias seen in clinical practice are fear of animals (zoophobia), fear of heights (acrophobia), fear of confinement (claustrophobia), fear of injury or blood, and fear of flying (Durand & Barlow, 2006).

Agoraphobia

Fear trapped Jane (right picture) in her house for years. If she thought about going outside to do her shopping, pain raced through her arms and chest. She grew hot and perspired. Her heart beat rapidly and her legs felt like rubber. The thought of leaving the house to enter a crowd of people created a sense of real terror. Jane's intense fear of being in public places is called agoraphobia.

Agoraphobia is characterized by anxiety about being in places or situations from which escape might be difficult or embarrassing if a panic attack or panic-like symptoms (sudden dizziness or onset of diarrhea) were to occur (APA, 2000).

Agoraphobia arises out of an underlying fear of either having a full-blown panic attack or having a sudden and unexpected onset of panic-like symptoms.

Social Phobia in Asia

Learn about taijin kyofusho.

▶ **L08** Summarize the possible causes of anxiety disorders.

Obsessive-Compulsive Disorder

Shirley (right picture) was an outgoing, popular high school student with average grades. Her one problem was she was late for school almost every day. Before she could leave the house in the morning, she had to be sure she was clean, so she needed to take a shower that lasted a full 2 hours. After her shower, she spent a long time dressing because, for each thing she did, such as putting on her stockings, underclothes, skirt, and blouse, she had to repeat the act precisely 17 times. When asked about her washing and counting, she said she knew it was crazy but she just had to do it and couldn't explain why (Rapoport, 1988). Shirley's symptoms would be diagnosed as indicative of obsessive-compulsive disorder.

© mediablitzimages (uk) Limited/Alamy

An **obsessive-compulsive disorder** consists of obsessions, which are persistent, recurring irrational thoughts, impulses, or images that a person is unable to control and that interfere with normal functioning, and compulsions, which are irresistible impulses to perform over and over some senseless behavior or ritual (such as hand washing, checking things, counting, putting things in order) (APA, 2000).

Shirley's symptoms included both obsession (her need to be clean and careful about dressing) and compulsions (her need to take 2-hour showers and to perform each act of dressing 17 times). These kinds of obsessive-compulsive behaviors interfere with normal functioning and make holding a job or engaging in social interactions difficult.

Causes of Anxiety Disorders

We'll review some of the factors researchers have identified as having a role in the development of anxiety disorders.

Biological Factors

Using recently developed techniques for studying the living brain and information from mapping the genetic code, researchers have been actively studying biological factors involved in anxiety disorders.

Biological factors underlying anxiety are genetic, neurological, chemical, and physiological components that may predispose or put someone at risk for an anxiety disorder.

Genetic Factors

Studies involving twins and adoptees show that genetic factors are involved in the development of anxiety disorders (Leckman & Kim, 2006; Mosing et al., 2009; Smoller et al., 2008). For instance, there is a higher concordance rate for anxiety disorders among identical twins than among fraternal twins, and adoptee studies show that the biological parent places the child at risk for anxiety disorders. Although no specific genes have yet been identified, some progress has been made in identifying genetic regions that may be involved in anxiety disorders (Hettema et al., 2005; Politi et al., 2006).

Neurological Factors

Several neurotransmitters, including serotonin, norepinephrine, and GABA, seem to be involved in anxiety disorders (Goddard et al., 2010). Also, brain-scan research has found differences in the structure and functioning of specific brain regions to be linked to different anxiety disorders. For example, the amygdala (see pp. 440–441), which plays a key role in negative emotions (such as fear), has been found to be more active in people with PTSD (Rogers et al., 2009)

Psychosocial Factors

Psychosocial factors may also place an individual at risk for anxiety disorders.

Psychosocial factors, such as personality traits, cognitive styles, social supports, and the ability to deal with stressors, interact with predisposing biological factors to put one at risk for developing an anxiety disorder.

Negative Cognitive Style

If people perceive their environment as being uncontrollable, unpredictable, and threatening, they are at risk for anxiety disorders. People with anxiety disorders tend to anticipate something bad will occur, misinterpret their bodily sensations, and dwell on negative information. For example, they may minimize their successes and overgeneralize their failures. Or they may interpret an experience in an exaggerated manner, such as convincing themselves that their momentary increase in heart rate is evidence of a serious heart attack (Armfield, 2006; Beck, 1976, 1991; Barlow, 2000).

Maladaptive Learning

Some anxiety disorders may be learned through classical conditioning (see Module 5.3), as in the case of Little Albert (see pp. 212–213). Other anxiety disorders may be a result of observational learning (see p. 240); simply observing an individual's negative experiences may result in the development of an anxiety disorder.

Obsessive-Compulsive Disorder

Learn what it's like to live with OCD.

Children with Obsessive-Compulsive Disorder

Learn what it's like for children to have OCD.

Check Your Learning Quiz 12.4

Go to **login.cengagebrain.com** and take the online quiz.

Depression is not choosy; it happens to about 6 million Americans a year. Major depression is one example of a mood disorder.

A **mood disorder** is a prolonged and disturbed emotional state that affects almost all of a person's thoughts, feelings, and behaviors.

Most of us have experienced a continuum of moods, with depression on one end and elation on the other. However, think of the depression or blues that most of us feel as having a paper cut on our finger. Then major depression is more like having to undergo open-heart surgery. It's some of the worst news you can get.

We'll focus on the symptoms of three common forms of mood disorders: major depressive disorder, bipolar I disorder, and dysthymic disorder.

Major Depressive Disorder

Popular singer-songwriter Sheryl Crow (right photo) says that she has battled major depression most of her life.

Major depressive disorder is marked by at least two weeks of continually being in a bad mood, having no interest in anything, and getting no pleasure from activities. In addition, a person must have at least four of the following symptoms: problems with eating, sleeping, thinking, concentrating, or making decisions, lacking energy, thinking about suicide, and feeling worthless or guilty (APA, 2000).

Sheryl Crow says that she had been on a world tour with Michael Jackson, singing in front of 70,000 screaming fans. When the tour ended, she was back in her lonely apartment with the anxiety of having to get a record contract. All this stress triggered her first bout of depression, which resulted in her lying in bed, hardly able to move, going unshowered, stringy-haired, and ordering take-out for seven straight months (Hirshey, 2003).

To help understand mood disorders, look at the graph at right. The top bar shows a manic episode or period of incredible energy and euphoria that we'll discuss on the next page. The middle bar shows a normal period when a person's moods and emotions do not interfere with normal psychological functioning. However, some event may cause a person to go from a normal period to a period of depression (bottom bar).

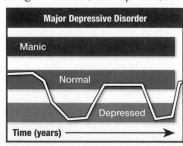

Bipolar I Disorder

Chuck Elliot (right photo) was checking out the exhibits at an electronics convention in Las Vegas when suddenly his mind seemed to go wild and spin at twice its regular speed. His words could not keep up with his thoughts, and he was talking in what sounded like some strange code, almost like rapid fire "dot, dot, dot." Then he stripped off all his clothes and ran stark naked through the gambling casino of the Hilton Hotel. The police were called, and Chuck was taken to a mental hospital (Brooks, 1994). After his symptoms were reviewed, Chuck was diagnosed with what is now called Bipolar I disorder.

Bipolar I disorder is marked by fluctuations between episodes of depression and mania. A manic episode goes on for at least a week, during which a person is unusually euphoric, cheerful, and high and has at least three of the following symptoms: has

great self-esteem, has little need for sleep, speaks rapidly and frequently, has racing thoughts, is easily distracted, and pursues pleasurable activities (APA, 2000).

Chuck Elliot has the typical pattern of bipolar I disorder. As shown in the graph at right, Elliot may have periods of being normal, which may turn into extreme manic episodes followed by periods of extreme depression.

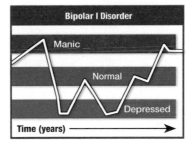

Dysthymic Disorder

Another mood disorder that is less serious than major depression is called dysthymic *(dis-THY-mick)* disorder.

Dysthymic disorder is characterized by being chronically but not continuously depressed for a period of two years. While depressed, a person experiences at least two of the following symptoms: poor appetite, insomnia, fatigue, low self-esteem, poor concentration, and feelings of hopelessness (APA, 2000).

Individuals with dysthymic disorder are often described as "down in the dumps." Some of these individuals become accustomed to such feelings and describe themselves as "always being this way."

Major Depressive Disorder

Learn what it's like to live with major depressive disorder.

Bipolar Disorder

Learn what it's like to live with bipolar disorder.

▶ **LO10** Summarize the possible causes of mood disorders.

Causes of Mood Disorders

Sheryl Crow thought her depression was due to some chemical imbalance in her brain and that depression ran in families (partly inherited or genetic) because her father suffered from similar mood problems (Hirshey, 2003). Let's see if she's right.

Biological Factors

Using recently developed techniques for studying the living brain and information from mapping the genetic code, researchers have been actively studying biological factors involved in mood disorders.

Biological factors underlying depression are genetic, neurological, chemical, and physiological components that may predispose or put someone at risk for developing a mood disorder.

Genetic Factors

Sheryl Crow was right about depression having a genetic component. Research studies comparing depression rates of identical twins with those of fraternal twins, who share only 50% of their genes, find that 40% to 60% of each individual's susceptibility to depression is explained by genetics (Canli, 2008). Researchers believe there is no single gene but rather a combination of genes that produces a risk, or predisposition, for developing a mood disorder (Bower, 2009b; Levinson, 2009).

Neurological Factors

Sheryl Crow was also right about depression involving a chemical imbalance in her brain. Abnormal levels of a group of neurotransmitters (orange circles in right figure), called the monoamines (serotonin, norepinephrine, and dopamine), can interfere with the 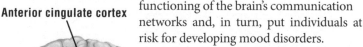 functioning of the brain's communication networks and, in turn, put individuals at risk for developing mood disorders.

Anterior cingulate cortex

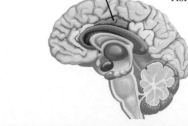

Researchers took computerized photos of the structure and function of living brains and compared brains of depressed patients with those of individuals with normal moods. Researchers reported that a brain area called the anterior cingulate cortex (left figure) was overactive in very depressed patients.

When the anterior cingulate cortex is overactive, it

When the anterior cingulate cortex is overactive, it allows negative emotions to overwhelm thinking and mood. This and other research suggest that faulty brain structure or function contributes to the onset and/or maintenance of mood disorders (Thase, 2009).

Psychosocial Factors

In addition to biological factors, an individual may be at risk for depression because of psychosocial factors.

Psychosocial factors, such as personality traits, cognitive styles, social supports, and the ability to deal with stressors, interact with predisposing biological factors to put one at risk for developing a mood disorder.

We'll discuss a few key psychosocial factors.

Stressful Life Events

Sheryl Crow says that her period of depression was triggered by the overwhelming stress of seeing a fantastic world tour end with her living in a lonely apartment, having to wait on tables while struggling to get a record contract. Researchers found that stressful life events are strongly related to the onset of mood disorders, such as depression (Kendler et al., 2004).

Negative Cognitive Style

Considerable research supports Aaron Beck's (1991) idea that depression may result from one's perceiving the world in a negative way, which in turn leads to feeling depressed. Having a negative cognitive style or negative way of thinking and perceiving can put one at risk for developing a mood disorder.

Personality Factors

Individuals who are especially sensitive to and overreact to negative events (such as rejections, criticisms) with feelings of fear, anxiety, guilt, sadness, and anger are at risk for developing a mood disorder (Klein et al., 2002). Also, individuals who make their self-worth primarily dependent on what others say or think are at risk for becoming depressed when facing the end of a close personal relationship. Some individuals have a need for control, which puts them at risk for depression when they encounter uncontrollable stress (Mazure et al., 2000).

The above psychosocial factors interact with underlying biological factors to increase one's risk of developing a mood disorder (Thase, 2006).

Seasonal Affective Disorder

Learn what seasonal affective disorder is and how it develops.

Beck's Theory of Depression

Explore how thoughts can influence our behaviors and emotions.

Check Your Learning Quiz 12.5

Go to **login.cengagebrain.com** and take the online quiz.

▶ **LO11** Describe three types of schizophrenia and discuss the recovery process for people with schizophrenia.

Michael McCabe (right photo) said that his mind began to weaken when he was 18 years old. "I totally hit this point in my life where I was so high on life, it was amazing. I had this sense of independence. I was 18 and turning into an adult. Next thing I knew I got this feeling that people were trying to take things from me. Not my soul, but physical things from me. I couldn't sleep because they [his mother and sister] were planning to do something to me. I think there was a higher power inside the 7-Eleven that was helping me out the whole time, just bringing me back to a strong mental state" (Brooks, 1994, p. 9). Michael was diagnosed as having schizophrenia *(skit-suh-FREE-nee-ah).*

© Robert Gauthier

Schizophrenia is a serious mental disorder that lasts for at least six months and includes at least two of the following symptoms: delusions, hallucinations, disorganized speech, disorganized behavior, and decreased emotional expression. These symptoms interfere with personal or social functioning (APA, 2000).

Michael has a number of these symptoms, including delusions (higher power inside the 7-Eleven), hallucinations (hearing voices), and disorganized behavior. Schizophrenia affects about 0.2% to 2% of the adult population, or about 4.5 million people (equal numbers of men and women) in the United States (APA, 2000).

Types of Schizophrenia

The DSM-IV-TR describes five subcategories of schizophrenia, each of which is characterized by different symptoms. We'll briefly describe three of the more common schizophrenia subcategories.

Paranoid schizophrenia is characterized by auditory hallucinations or delusions, such as thoughts of being persecuted by others or thoughts of grandeur.

Disorganized schizophrenia is marked by bizarre ideas, often about one's body (such as bones melting), confused speech, childish behavior (such as giggling for no apparent reason or making faces at people), great emotional swings (such as fits of laughing or crying), and often extreme neglect of personal appearance and hygiene.

Catatonic schizophrenia is marked by periods of wild excitement or periods of rigid, prolonged immobility; sometimes the person assumes a frozen posture for hours on end.

Differentiating between types of schizophrenia can be difficult because some symptoms, such as disordered thought processes, are shared by all types.

Symptoms

Schizophrenia is a serious mental disorder that lasts for at least six months and includes at least two of the following symptoms:

Disorders of Thought

These are characterized by incoherent thought patterns, formation of made-up words, inability to stick to one topic, and irrational beliefs or delusions. For example, Michael believed his family was plotting against him.

Disorders of Attention

These include difficulties in concentration and in focusing on a single chain of events. For instance, one patient said he could not concentrate on television because he couldn't watch and listen at the same time.

Disorders of Perception

These include strange bodily sensations and hallucinations, which are sensory experiences without any stimulation from the environment. For example, about 70% of people with schizophrenia report hearing voices that sound real and talk either to them or about them (Thraenhardt, 2006).

Motor Disorders

These include making strange facial expressions, being extremely active, or (the opposite) remaining immobile for long periods of time.

Emotional (Affective) Disorders

These may include having little or no emotional responsiveness or having emotional responses that are inappropriate to the situation (for example, laughing when told of the death of a close friend).

Chances of Recovery

Chances of recovery are dependent upon a number of factors, which have been classified into positive and negative symptoms of schizophrenia (Crow, 1985).

Positive symptoms include hallucinations and delusions, which are a distortion of normal functions. In addition, individuals with positive symptoms have no intellectual impairment, good reaction to medication, and thus a good chance of recovery.

Negative symptoms include dulled emotions and little inclination to speak, which are a loss of normal functions. In addition, individuals with negative symptoms have intellectual impairment, poor reaction to medication, and thus a poor chance of recovery (Dyck et al., 2000).

Schizophrenic Disorder

Explore what it's like to have a schizophrenic disorder.

Disorders of Thought

See what it's like to have a disorder of thought.

▶ **LO12** Summarize the possible causes of schizophrenic disorders.

Causes of Schizophrenia

There are three major factors—biological, neurological, and environmental—that interact in the development of schizophrenia.

Biological Factors

Genetic Predisposition

In 1930, the birth of four identical baby girls (quadruplets) was a rare occurrence (1 in 16 million) and received great publicity. By young adulthood, all four of the Genain quadruplets (right photo), who share nearly 100% of their genes, were diagnosed with schizophrenia (Mirsky & Quinn, 1988). This finding indicates that  increased genetic similarity is associated with increased risk for developing schizophrenia and suggests that a person inherits a predisposition for developing the disorder.

Genetic Markers

Because researchers knew that schizophrenia might have a genetic factor, they compared rates of schizophrenia in identical twins, who share nearly 100% of their genes, with rates in fraternal twins and siblings, who share only 50% of their genes. If one identical twin has schizophrenia, there is a 48% to 83% chance the other twin will also develop the disorder. In comparison, if one brother or sister (sibling or fraternal twin) has schizophrenia, there is only a 10% to 17% chance the other will develop the disorder (Gottesman, 2001). Researchers believe schizophrenia depends on a combination of genes and no one gene by itself has a strong genetic influence (ISC, 2009; Walsh et al., 2008).

Infections

Infections may play a role in the development of schizophrenia. For instance, pregnant women who get the flu are more likely to give birth to children who will develop schizophrenia. Also, some childhood infections, such as the mumps virus, are associated with an increased risk of later developing schizophrenia symptoms. Researchers believe that some infections directly affect the brain, whereas others trigger immune reactions that interfere with normal brain development (Dalman et al., 2008; Wenner, 2008a).

Courtesy of Edna Morlok

Unless otherwise noted, all images are © Cengage Learning

Neurological Factors

Ventricle Size

Most of us don't realize our brains have four fluid-filled cavities called ventricles (right figures). The fluid in these cavities helps to cushion the brain against blows and serves as a reservoir of nutrients and hormones for the brain. In up to 80% of the brains of people with schizophrenia, the ventricles are larger than normal (Niznikiewicz et al., 2003). Researchers conclude that some people with schizophrenia have abnormally large ventricles, which results in a decrease in brain size and may contribute to the development of schizophrenia (Wright et al., 2000). However, not all brains of people with schizophrenia have larger ventricles or an overall decrease in brain size.

Frontal Lobe: Prefrontal Cortex

A brain structure involved in many executive functions, such as reasoning, planning, and paying attention is the prefrontal cortex (see p. 383). In pairs of identical twins in which one twin has schizophrenia and the other does not, the brain of the twin with schizophrenia is characterized by less activation of the prefrontal cortex (Torrey et al., 1994). This decreased prefrontal lobe activity is consistent with the deficits in executive functions observed in people with schizophrenia, such as disorganized thinking, irrational beliefs, and poor concentration (Niznikiewicz et al., 2003).

Environmental Factors

Because biological and neurological factors alone cannot explain the development of schizophrenia, researchers look at the influence of environmental factors, such as the incidence of stressful events. Stressful events, such as hostile parents, the death of a loved one, and career problems, can contribute to the development and onset of schizophrenia. This relationship between stress and the onset of schizophrenia is called the diathesis stress theory.

The **diathesis stress theory** *(die-ATH-uh-sis)* of schizophrenia says that some people have a genetic predisposition (a diathesis) that interacts with life stressors to result in the onset and development of schizophrenia. (Jones & Fernyhough, 2007).

The diathesis stress theory assumes that biological or neurological factors have initially produced a predisposition for schizophrenia. If a person already has a predisposition for schizophrenia, then being faced with stressful environmental factors can increase the risk for developing schizophrenia, as well as trigger the onset of schizophrenia symptoms (Jones & Fernyhough, 2007).

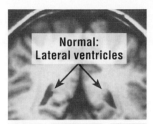

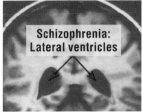

Courtesy of Drs. E. Fuller Torrey & Daniel R. Weinberger, NIMH, Neuroscience Center, Washington D.C.

Genetic Breakthroughs

Learn about the major breakthroughs in identifying genetic markers for schizophrenia.

Check Your Learning Quiz 12.6

Go to **login.cengagebrain.com** and take the online quiz.

▶ **LO13** Describe and distinguish between the three dissociative disorders.

▶ **LO14** Summarize the possible causes of dissociative disorders.

You have probably had the experience of being so absorbed in a fantasy, thought, or memory that, for a short period of time, you cut yourself off from the real world. This is an example of a normal "break from reality," or dissociative experience (Berlin & Koch, 2009; Kihlstrom et al., 1994). Now imagine a dissociative experience so extreme that your own self splits, breaks down, or disappears.

A **dissociative disorder** is characterized by a person having a disruption, split, or breakdown in his or her normal integrated self, consciousness, memory, or sense of identity. This disorder is relatively rare and unusual (APA, 2000).

We'll discuss three of the more common dissociative disorders: dissociative amnesia, dissociative fugue, and dissociative identity disorder.

Dissociative Amnesia

Mark (right picture) is brought into the hospital emergency room. He looks exhausted and is badly sunburned. When questioned, he gives the wrong date, answering September 27 instead of October 1. He has trouble answering specific questions about what happened to him. With much probing, he gradually remembers going sailing with friends on about September 25 and hitting bad weather. He cannot recall anything else; he doesn't know what happened to his friends or the sailboat, how he got to shore, where he has been, or where he is now. Each time he is told that it is really October 1 he looks very surprised (Spitzer et al., 1994). Mark is suffering from dissociative amnesia.

I can't remember anything about the past month.

Dissociative amnesia is characterized by the inability to recall important personal information or events and is usually associated with stressful or traumatic events. The importance or extent of the information forgotten is too great to be explained by normal forgetfulness (APA, 2000).

Causes

In Mark's case, you might think his forgetfulness was due to a blow to the head suffered on the sailboat. However, doctors found no evidence of head injury or neural problems. To recall the events between September 25 and October 1, Mark was given a drug (sodium amytal) that helps people relax and recall events that may be blocked a drug (sodium amytal) that helps people relax and recall events that may be blocked by stressful experiences. While under the effect of the drug, Mark recalled a big storm that washed his companions overboard but spared him because he had tied himself to the boat. Thus, Mark did suffer from dissociative amnesia, which was triggered by the stressful event of seeing his friends washed overboard (Spitzer et al., 1994). In dissociative amnesia, the length of memory loss varies from days to weeks to years and is often associated with a series of stressful events (Eich et al., 1997).

Dissociative Fugue

A 40-year-old man wanders the streets of Denver with $8 in his pocket. He asks people to help him figure out who he is and where he lives. He feels lost, alone, anxious, and desperate to learn his identity. He appears on news shows pleading for help: "If anybody recognizes me, knows who I am, please let somebody know" (Ingram, 2006). After his parents and fiancée see him on television, they contact the police, informing them that the man's name is Jeffrey Ingram (right photo) and that he lives in Seattle. Upon reuniting with his fiancée and family, Jeffrey fails to recognize their faces. He also cannot recall anything about his past (Woodward, 2006). Jeffrey Ingram had experienced dissociative fugue.

Who am I? What's my name?

© AP Images/The Denver Post/Karl Gehring

Dissociative fugue is a disturbance marked by suddenly and unexpectedly traveling away from one's home or place of work and being unable to recall one's past. The person may not remember his or her identity or may be confused about his or her new assumed identity (APA, 2000).

Causes

Before clinicians diagnosed Jeffrey as suffering from dissociative fugue, they ruled out drugs, medications, and head injuries. His fiancée explained that Jeffrey had been on his way to Canada to visit his friend's wife, who was dying of cancer. She believes the stress of seeing his friend's wife dying led him to an amnesia state.

As Jeffrey's case illustrates, the onset of dissociative fugue is related to stressful life events. Usually, fugue states end quite suddenly, and the individual recalls most or all of his or her identity and past.

Dissociative Fugue

Explore how someone with dissociative fugue can adapt to a loss of identity.

Dissociative Identity Disorder

The idea that one individual could possess two or more "different persons" who may or may not know one another and who may appear at different times to say and do different things describes one of the more remarkable and controversial mental disorders (Eich et al., 1997). Previously this disorder was called multiple personality disorder, but now it's called dissociative identity disorder. We'll begin our coverage of this fascinating disorder by discussing a real case.

Herschel Walker (right photo) is recognized for being an NFL legend, Heisman Trophy winner, track star, Olympic competitor, and successful businessman. You would think Herschel would feel as though he were on top of the world. On the contrary, Herschel felt that his life was out of his control. He had difficulty managing his anger, he struggled to feel connected to people, and he experienced unexplained periods of memory loss.

Herschel's wife of 16 years (now divorced) described him as having many different sides, such as the side with an interest in the Marines, the side interested in ballet, the side interested in the FBI, and the side interested in sports. She even noticed that he would occasionally speak in different voices and show uniquely different physical mannerisms.

After Herschel got the courage to seek professional help to understand what had been happening to him, his therapist diagnosed him as suffering from a very rare and complex disorder called dissociative identity disorder.

Dissociative identity disorder (formerly called multiple personality disorder) is the presence of two or more distinct identities or personality states, each with its own pattern of perceiving, thinking about, and relating to the world. Different personality states may take control of the individual's thoughts and behaviors at different times (APA, 2000).

© Kabik/Retna Ltd./Corbis

© Ron Nickel/Photolibrary

Unless otherwise noted, all images are © Cengage Learning

The worldwide occurrence of dissociative identity disorder was very rare before 1970, with only 36 cases reported. However, an "epidemic" occurred in the 1970s and 1980s, with estimates ranging from 300 to 2,000 cases (Spanos, 1994). Reasons for the upsurge include incorrect diagnosis, renewed professional interest, the trendiness of the disorder, and therapists' (unknowing) encouragement of patients to play the roles. The patients most often diagnosed with dissociative identity disorder (DID) are females, who outnumber males by 8 to 1. In addition, patients with DID usually have a history of other mental disorders.

Causes

There are two opposing explanations for DID. One is that DID results from the severe trauma of childhood abuse, which causes a mental splitting or dissociation of identities as one way to defend against or cope with the terrible trauma. A second explanation is that DID has become commonplace because of cultural factors, such as DID becoming a legitimate way for people to express their frustrations or to manipulate or gain personal rewards (Lilienfeld et al., 1999). These opposing explanations reflect the current controversy about why so many patients have been diagnosed with DID.

In Herschel's case, it seems plausible that his early childhood trauma may be the primary cause of his condition. As a young boy, he was severely teased and bullied for being an overweight child who had a severe stutter. His therapist explains that Herschel developed his alter personalities to help him overcome the abuse by his peers, as well as other major challenges he faced later in life.

Herschel identifies about a dozen alter personalities, including "The Hero," who came out in public appearances, and "The Warrior," who was in charge of playing football and coping with the physical pain that came with it. Herschel's therapist describes meeting the alter personalities in therapy by saying, "They will come out and say, I am so-and-so. I'm here to tell you Herschel is not doing too good. . . . When he finishes, it would just disappear back in him, and Herschel comes out" (Mungadze, 2008).

As in Herschel's case, the personalities are usually quite different and complex, and the original personality is seldom aware of the others. After nearly 10 years of psychotherapy, Herschel managed to obtain great insight about his condition and says he is doing much better now. In his book, *Breaking Free*, he discusses his life experiences with dissociative identity disorder and how he has managed to successfully cope with the challenging condition (Walker, 2008; Woodruff et al., 2008).

Dissociative Identity Disorder I

Explore what it's like to have dissociative identity disorder.

Dissociative Identity Disorder 2

Explore what it's like to successfully cope with having dissociative identity disorder.

Check Your Learning Quiz 12.7

Go to **login.cengagebrain.com** and take the online quiz.

▶ **LO15** Describe and distinguish between the three somatoform disorders.

▶ **LO16** Summarize the possible causes of somatoform disorders.

Imagine someone whose whole life centers around physical symptoms, some that are imagined and others that appear real, such as developing paralysis in one's legs. This intense focus on imagined, painful, or uncomfortable physical symptoms is characteristic of individuals with somatoform *(so-MA-tuh-form)* disorders.

Somatoform disorders are marked by a pattern of recurring, multiple, and significant bodily (somatic) symptoms that extend over several years. The bodily symptoms (such as pain, vomiting, paralysis, blindness) are not under voluntary control, have no known physical causes, and are believed to be caused by psychological factors (APA, 2000).

Although not easily diagnosed, somatoform disorders are among the most common health problems seen in general medical practice (Wise & Birket-Smith, 2002). The DSM-IV-TR lists seven kinds of somatoform disorders. We'll discuss three forms: somatization, conversion, and body dysmorphic disorders.

Somatization Disorder

One kind of somatoform disorder, which was historically called hysteria, is now called somatization disorder.

Somatization disorder begins before age 30, lasts several years, and is characterized by multiple symptoms, including pain, gastrointestinal, sexual, and neurological symptoms, which have no physical causes but are triggered by psychological problems or distress (APA, 2000).

All tests are negative.

I have a lot of symptoms.

This disorder is especially common among women (Fink et al., 2004). Those who have somatization disorder use health services frequently and have twice the annual medical care costs of people without somatization disorder (Barsky et al., 2005).

Causes

Many people with somatization disorder are raised in emotionally cold and unsupportive family environments and are often victims of emotional or physical abuse (Brown et al., 2005). Somatization disorders may be a means of coping with a stressful situation or obtaining attention (Durand & Barlow, 2010).

Unless otherwise noted, all images are © Cengage Learning

© Monkey Business Images/Shutterstock

Conversion Disorder

Some people report serious physical problems, such as blindness, that have no physical causes and are examples of conversion disorder, a type of somatoform disorder.

A **conversion disorder** refers to changing anxiety or emotional distress into real physical, motor, sensory, or neurological symptoms (such as headaches, nausea, dizziness, loss of sensation, paralysis), for which no physical or organic cause can be identified (APA, 2000).

©Yuri Arcurs/Shutterstock

Causes

Usually the symptoms of a conversion disorder are associated with psychological factors, such as depression, concerns about health, or the occurrence of a stressful situation. The development of real physical symptoms gets the person attention, removes the person from anxiety-producing situations, and thus reinforces the occurrence and maintenance of the symptoms involved in the conversion disorder (Durand & Barlow, 2010).

Body Dysmorphic Disorder

Some people become preoccupied and obsessed with an imagined defect in their appearence, which in turn results in them going to great lengths to conceal or hide this imagined flaw. Individuals who have an abnormal and extreme concern about their appearence, and who perceive physical defects that are not real, have what is called body dysmorphic disorder.

© OSTILL/iStockphoto

Body dysmorphic disorder involves having an overwhelming preoccupation with an imagined or exaggerated physical defect in one's appearance (APA, 2000).

Causes

The age of onset tends to be in adolescence, when people generally become preoccupied with their appearance. People who develop body dysmorphic disorder may have a strong drive to be perfectionistic, as well as a strong need for approval from others.

Body Dysmorphic Disorder

Learn what it's like to have body dysmorphic disorder.

Check Your Learning Quiz 12.8

Go to **login.cengagebrain.com** and take the online quiz.

▶ **LO17** Define personality disorder and identify which axis it belongs to on the DSM.

▶ **LO18** Describe the symptoms and causes of borderline personality disorder.

Defining Personality Disorder

We have all heard the expression "Don't judge a book by its cover." That advice proved absolutely true when we heard what their friends and neighbors said about the following individuals.

His boss said David Berkowitz was "quiet and reserved and kept pretty much to himself. That's the way he was here, nice—a quiet, shy fellow." Berkowitz, known as "Son of Sam," was convicted of killing six people.

A neighbor said John Esposito "was such a quiet, caring person. He was a very nice person." Esposito was charged with kidnapping a young girl and keeping her in an underground bunker for 16 days.

A friend said Jeffrey Dahmer "didn't have much to say, was quiet, like the average Joe." Dahmer confessed to killing and dismembering 15 people (*Time,* July 12, 1993, p. 18).

While these individuals appeared very ordinary in public appearance and behavior, each was hiding a deep-seated, serious, and dangerous personality disorder.

Throughout this chapter we've been discussing psychological disorders that belong on Axis I of the DSM-IV-TR. We'll wrap up our discussion of psychological disorders by focusing on personality disorders, which belong on Axis II.

A **personality disorder** consists of inflexible, long-standing, maladaptive traits that cause significantly impaired functioning or great distress in one's personal and social life (APA, 2000).

Causes

Individuals with personality disorders often have the following characteristics: troubled childhoods, childhood problems that continue into adulthood, and maladaptive or poor personal relationships. Their difficulties arise from a combination of genetic, psychological, social, and environmental factors (Vargha-Khadem, 2000).

We'll focus on two particular personality disorders, the borderline personality and antisocial personality, because they are mentioned most often by the media.

Borderline Personality Disorder

People who have borderline personality disorder have intense, unpredictable emotional outbursts and lack impulse control, which causes them to express inappropriate anger and engage in very dangerous behaviors.

Borderline personality disorder is a pattern of instability in personal relationships, self-image, and emotions, as well as impulsive behavior (APA, 2000).

About 75% of patients with borderline personality disorder hurt themselves through cutting, burning, or other forms of self-mutilation, and another 10% eventually commit suicide. Patients with borderline personality are so emotionally erratic that they are capable of expressing profound love and intense rage almost simultaneously. Such emotional volatility makes it difficult for them to maintain stable interpersonal relationships. They are terrified of losing the people most close to them, yet they attack these same people in rage, only to later show sweetness and affection toward them (APA, 2000; Cloud, 2009).

© Angela Hampton Picture Library/Alamy

Causes

Borderline personality disorder appears to have both environmental and genetic causes. Experiencing trauma during childhood, such as being abused or prohibited from expressing negative emotions, places individuals at risk for this condition. Brain-scan studies have shown that the amygdala (emotional center of the brain) in these patients is overactive, while the brain areas responsible for controlling emotional responses are underactive. This helps explain why these patients lack emotional regulation. Although no specific genes have been identified, we know that the major symptoms of this condition, such as impulsivity and aggression, are highly heritable (Brody, 2009; Cloud, 2009; Meyer-Lindenberg, 2009).

Borderline Personality Disorder

Explore what it's like to have borderline personality disorder.

▶ **LO19** Describe the symptoms and causes of antisocial personality disorder.

Antisocial Personality Disorder

The "nice," "quiet" killers we described at the start of this module would probably be diagnosed as having antisocial personality disorder or some combination of personality disorders. Between 50% and 80% of prisoners meet the criteria for a diagnosis of antisocial personality disorder (Ogloff, 2006).

Antisocial personality disorder refers to a pattern of disregarding or violating the rights of others without feeling guilt or remorse (3% of population, predominantly males) (APA, 2000).

But not all people diagnosed with antisocial personality disorder are alike, and the diagnostic symptoms vary along a continuum. At one end of the continuum are the chronic delinquents, bullies, and lawbreakers; at the other end are the serial killers.

An example of someone on the delinquent end of the continuum is Tom, who always seemed to be in trouble. As a child, he would steal items (such as silverware) from home and sell or swap them for things he wanted. As a teenager, he skipped classes in school, set deserted buildings on fire, forged his father's name on checks, stole cars, and was finally sent to a federal institution. After Tom served his time, he continued to break the law, and by the age of 21, he had been arrested and imprisoned 50 to 60 times (Spitzer et al., 1994).

At the other end of the psychopathic continuum are serial killers, such as Dennis Rader (right photo) and Jeffrey Dahmer (bottom photo). We discussed Dennis Rader at the start of this chapter. Over a period of 17 years, he planned and carried out the cruel murders of 10 people. He became known as the "BTK killer," which stands for Bind, Torture, and Kill, describing the brutal methods he used with his victims.

© Jeff Tuttle/AFP/Getty Images

Jeffrey Dahmer would pick up gay men, bring them home, drug them, strangle them, have sex with their corpses, and then, in some cases, eat their flesh. As Dahmer said in an interview, "I could completely control a person—a person that I found physically attractive, and keep them with me as long as possible, even if it meant just keep a part of them" (Gleick et al., 1994, p. 129).

© Alan Fredrickson/Reuters/Corbis

Unless otherwise noted, all images are © Cengage Learning

Causes

Antisocial personality disorder involves complex psychosocial and biological factors.

Psychosocial Factors

Researchers have found that aggressive and antisocial children whom parents find almost impossible to control are at risk for developing an antisocial personality (Morey, 1997). Also, children who experience physical or sexual abuse are at an increased risk of developing antisocial personality disorder (Black, 2006). However, since many abused children do not develop an antisocial personality, it is difficult to determine how much childhood abuse contributes to its development.

Biological Factors

Researchers suggest that the early appearance of serious behavioral problems, such as having temper tantrums, bullying other children, torturing animals, and habitually lying, indicates that underlying biological factors, both genetic and neurological, may predispose or place a child at risk for developing antisocial personality disorder (Pinker, 2008). Evidence for genetic factors comes from twin and adoption studies that show that genetic factors contribute 30% to 50% to the development of antisocial personality disorder (Thapar & McGuffin, 1993). Evidence for neurological factors comes from individuals with brain damage and from brain-scan studies of individuals with antisocial personality disorder. For example, researchers found that early brain damage to the prefrontal cortex (left image) resulted in two children who did not learn normal social and moral behaviors and showed no empathy, remorse, or guilt as adults. In addition, brain scans indicated that individuals with antisocial personality disorder had 11% fewer brain cells in their prefrontal cortex (Raine et al., 2000). Since the prefrontal cortex is known to be involved in important executive functions, such as making decisions and planning, researchers suggest that damage to or maldevelopment of the prefrontal cortex predisposes or increases the risk of an individual developing antisocial personality disorder.

Prefrontal cortex

Researchers believe that biological factors can predispose individuals to act in certain ways, but the interaction between biological and psychosocial factors results in the development and onset of personality disorders (Morgan & Lilienfeld, 2000).

Antisocial Personality Disorder

Learn what it's like to have antisocial personality disorder.

Check Your Learning Quiz 12.9

Go to **login.cengagebrain.com** and take the online quiz.

Think Critically

Challenge Your Thinking

Consider these questions when reading this article:

1. According to the three definitions of abnormal behavior, are Dahmer and Rader abnormal?

2. What objective test can be used to best assess for these psychopathic personality traits? (See Module 11.6)

3. Which theory can explain how an individual can display such drastically inconsistent behaviors? (See Module 11.5)

4. What part of the limbic system explains how psychopaths can be so cold and fearless? (See Module 2.6)

5. How would a psychopath do on a lie detector test? (See Module 9.7)

6. What is it called when someone has inherited a gene for psychopathic behaviors but develops those behaviors only if he or she has a stressful childhood?

What Is a Psychopath?

Jeffrey Dahmer would pick up young gay men, bring them home, drug them, strangle them, have sex with their corpses, and then, in some cases, eat their flesh.

Dennis Rader would break into people's homes, tie them up, strangle them, and eventually murder them. His murder method earned him the name "BTK killer," which stands for Bind, Torture, and Kill.

Dahmer and Rader share much in common. They are superficially charming, unemotional, impulsive, and self-

centered. They are pathological liars who constantly manipulate others. Also, both men completely lack remorse, guilt, and empathy. Finally, they have low self-esteem, a strong desire to be in control, and a lifelong sense of loneliness. Dahmer, for example, felt so lonely that he admitted to killing people for company. Together, the above characteristics define a psychopath.

What may seem surprising is that psychopaths can love their parents, spouses, and children but have great difficulty loving the rest of the world. Rader, for instance,

was a loving husband and father. Yet, he seemed completely devoid of humanity as he plainly recounted the details of how he murdered his many victims.

Some of the fascinating characteristics and behaviors of psychopaths may be explained by biological and neurological factors. For example, some psychopaths have abnormalities in their limbic system, which is responsible for motivational behaviors, such as eating and sex, as well as emotional behaviors, such as fear, anger, and aggression. Also, some psychopaths have a disruption in the communication between the hippocampus and the prefrontal cortex, which is believed to contribute to their lack of control, inability to regulate aggression, and insensitivity to cues that predict they will get caught and punished. Interestingly, psychopaths also have lower autonomic arousal and consequently experience less distress when exposed to threats.

The life histories of psychopaths often include a chaotic upbringing, lack of parental attention, parental substance abuse, and child abuse. These life experiences may interact with biological or neurological factors linked to psychopathic behaviors. For instance, children may have genes for psychopathic behaviors that get activated only under stress; if they are raised in a nurturing environment, they may very well develop into well-behaved, moral adults. In other words, at least for some children, the consequences of having a stressful childhood can be deadly. (Adapted from Bower, 2006b, 2008e; Crenson, 2005; Goldberg, 2003; Hickey, 2006; Larsson et al., 2006; Lilienfeld & Arkowitz, 2007; Martens, 2002; Raine et al., 2004; Wilgoren, 2005; Yang et al., 2005b)

Think Critically 12.1

This article and its questions are available in interactive format online.

GO to your Psychology CourseMate at login.cengagebrain.com and take the Chapter Post-Test to see which Learning Objectives you've mastered and which need more review. Use the chapter review guide below and the online activities—including flashcards to review key terms—to measure your learning.

Measure ∧**Your Learning**

Online Activities

Key Terms	Video	Animation	Reading	Assessment
insanity, mental disorder	Dennis Rader, p. 553			Check Your Learning Quiz 12.1
statistical frequency approach, social norms approach, maladaptive behavior approach, genetic factors, cognitive-emotional-behavioral factors, environmental factors		Definitions of Abnormal Behavior, p. 555		Check Your Learning Quiz 12.2
clinical assessment, clinical interview, personality tests, clinical diagnosis, Diagnostic and Statistical Manual of Mental Disorders-IV-Text Revision (DSM-IV-TR), labeling		Clinical Assessment, p. 559	Real-Life Assesssment of Susan Smith, p. 559 Revisions of the DSM, p. 561 Culture-Specific Mental Disorders, p. 561 Frequency of Mental Disorders, p. 565	Check Your Learning Quiz 12.3
generalized anxiety disorder, panic disorder, panic attack, post-traumatic stress disorder, phobia, social phobias, specific phobias, agoraphobia, obsessive-compulsive disorder, biological factors underlying anxiety, psychosocial factors	Panic Disorder 1, p. 567 Panic Disorder 2, p. 567 PTSD 1, p. 567 PTSD 2, p. 567 Obsessive-Compulsive Disorder, p. 571 Children with Obsessive-Compulsive Disorder, p. 571		Social Phobia in Asia, p. 569	Check Your Learning Quiz 12.4

Measure
^Your Learning

Online Activities

Key Terms	Video	Animation	Reading	Assessment
mood disorder, major depressive disorder, bipolar I disorder, dysthymic disorder, biological factors underlying depression, psychosocial factors	Major Depressive Disorder, p. 573 Bipolar Disorder, p. 573		Seasonal Affective Disorder, p. 575 Beck's Theory of Depression, p. 575	Check Your Learning Quiz 12.5
schizophrenia, paranoid schizophrenia, disorganized schizophrenia, catatonic schizophrenia, positive symptoms, negative symptoms, diathesis stress theory	Schizophenic Disorder, p. 577 Disorders of Thought, p. 577		Genetic Breakthroughs, p. 579	Check Your Learning Quiz 12.6
dissociative disorder, dissociative amnesia, dissociative fugue, dissociative identity disorder	Dissociative Identity Disorder 1, p. 583 Dissociative Identity Disorder 2, p. 583		Dissociative Fugue, p. 581	Check Your Learning Quiz 12.7
somatoform disorders, somatization disorder, conversion disorder, body dysmorphic disorder	Body Dysmorphic Disorder, p. 585			Check Your Learning Quiz 12.8
personality disorder, borderline personality disorder, antisocial personality disorder	Borderline Personality Disorder, p. 587 Antisocial Personality Disorder, p. 589			Check Your Learning Quiz 12.9

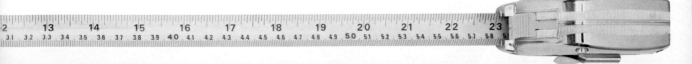

Therapies

13

Prepare to Learn

1 **GO** to your **Psychology CourseMate** at **login.cengagebrain.com** and take the **Chapter Pre-Test** to introduce yourself to this chapter's topics and see what you may already know.

2 **READ** the **Learning Objectives (LOs)** (in the left sidebars) and begin the chapter.

3 **COMPLETE** the **Online Activities** (in the right sidebars) *as you read each module*. Activities include **videos**, **animations**, **readings**, and **quizzes**.

4 **CHECK Your Learning** by going online to take the quiz at the end of each module and review material as necessary.

5 **MEASURE Your Learning** after reading the chapter by taking the online **Chapter Post-Test**. Use the chapter review guide at the end of the chapter as needed.

WATCH for these **Online Activities** icons as you read:

Video

Animation

Reading

Assessment

Think Critically

These online activities are important to mastering this chapter. As you read each module, access these materials by going to **login.cengagebrain.com**.

 Video Explore studies and firsthand accounts of biological and psychological processes:

- Learn more about how psychoanalysis treats psychological problems
- Learn more about how client-centered therapy treats psychological problems
- Learn more about how cognitive therapy treats psychological problems
- Learn more about how behavior therapy treats psychological problems
- Learn more about how antidepressants are used to treat depression
- Learn more about how transcranial magnetic stimulation works
- Learn more about how electroconvulsive therapy works

 Animation Interact with and visualize important processes and concepts:

- Treat a phobia using the three steps of systemic desensitization
- Compare psychoanalytic, humanistic, cognitive, behavior, and biomedical therapies

 Reading Delve deeper into key content:

- Find out how someone can learn to fear blood
- Learn more about psychoanalysis
- Find out how deinstitutionalization led to an increase in homelessness
- Learn about the fascinating case of Anna O.
- Read about why psychoanalysis has lost much of its popularity

- Explore how systematic desensitization is used to uncondition fears
- Learn more about how cognitive-behavioral therapy can be used to treat phobias
- Learn more about how EMDR works

 Assessment Measure your mastery:

- Chapter Pre-Test
- Check Your Learning Quizzes
- Chapter Post-Test

 Think Critically Challenge your thinking by applying content from this chapter and making connections to related material:

- Can Virtual Reality Be More Than Fun and Games?

> ▶ **LO1** Identify the three basic characteristics of psychotherapy.

THE DOCTOR EXPLAINS THAT, as part of my physical exam, the nurse will take a couple of samples of my blood. The nurse enters the room, smiles, and says, "This will only take a minute." I slowly roll up my sleeve and look at my bare arm as if it were about to be cut off.

▼

After the nurse tightens a rubber tourniquet around my upper arm, she says in a gentle voice, "Please make a fist and hold it." As the nurse brings the needle to my vein, she says, "You'll feel a tiny prick but it won't hurt." With a swift movement, she sticks the thin needle into my vein.

She pulls the plunger back and I see my blood, which is a deep red color, flow rapidly into the syringe.

She removes the first syringe and starts to fill a second.

By now my heart is beating crazily and I have broken out in a fine, cold sweat. I try to distract myself by looking away and thinking about my wonderful fuzzy dog, but it's not helping. Now I am floating in space, and all is white and so peaceful. In the distance I hear someone calling my name, "Rod, Rod," but I'm frozen in a deep dream and cannot move a single muscle.

As I come to with the odor of smelling salts, the nurse tells me that I fainted and should just lie still for several minutes. The nurse looks down and asks, "What's the big deal about giving a little blood?"

The big deal is that I have developed a phobia of seeing blood and this overwhelming fear causes me to faint.

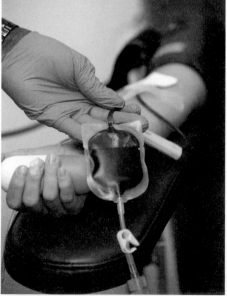

© Sean Locke/iStockphoto

Unless otherwise noted, all images are © Cengage Learning

It turns out that 5% to 15% of the population has developed the same intense fear of blood (Vogele et al., 2003).

The good news for people with phobias or any of the other mental disorders we discussed in Chapter 12 is that there are many different types of therapy that can be used to treat their problems. In fact, there are about a dozen tested psychotherapies that may differ in assumptions and methods but generally share three characteristics.

Psychotherapy has three basic characteristics: verbal interaction between therapist and client(s); the development of a supportive relationship in which a client can bring up and discuss traumatic or bothersome experiences that may have led to current problems; and analysis of the client's experiences and/or suggested ways for the client to deal with or overcome his or her problems.

Before we explore the various types of current psychotherapies, we'll begin with a historical overview of how mental disorders were once treated.

© lightkey/iStockphoto

Conditioned Fear

Find out how someone can learn to fear blood.

Check Your Learning Quiz 13.1

Go to **login.cengagebrain.com** and take the online quiz.

▶ **LO2** Summarize the historical background in treating mental illness.

We'll discuss the major changes in treating mental disorders, including early inhumane treatments, the reform movement, the breakthrough in the use of drugs, and community mental health centers.

Early Treatments

From 1400 to 1700, people who today would be diagnosed as schizophrenics were considered insane and called lunatics. They were primarily confined to asylums or hospitals for the mentally ill, where the treatment was often inhumane and cruel. For example, patients were treated by being placed in a hood and straitjacket, chained to a cell wall, swung back and forth until they were quieted, strapped into a chair (right drawing), locked in handcuffs, hosed down with water until they were exhausted, or twirled until they passed out.

National Library of Medicine, #A-13392

In the late 1700s, Dr. Benjamin Rush, who is considered the father of American psychiatry, developed the "tranquilizing chair" (bottom drawing). A patient was strapped into this chair and remained until he or she seemed calmed down. Dr. Rush believed that mental disorders were caused by too much blood in the brain. To cure this problem, he attempted to treat patients by withdrawing huge amounts of blood, as much as 6 quarts over a period of months. Dr. Rush also tried to cure patients with fright, such as putting them into coffins and convincing them they were about to die. Despite these strange and inhumane treatments, Dr. Rush encouraged his staff to treat patients with kindness and understanding (Davison & Neale, 1994).

In the 1700s, some hospitals even sold tickets to the general public. People came to see the locked-up "wild beasts" and to laugh at the tragic and pathetic behaviors of individuals with severe mental disorders. However, in the late 1700s and early 1800s, a few doctors began to make reforms by removing the patients' chains, forbidding physical punishment, and using a more psychological approach to treat mental disorders (Harris, 2003).

National Library of Medicine, #A-13394

Unless otherwise noted, all images are © Cengage Learning

Reform Movement

In the 1800s, a Boston schoolteacher named Dorothea Dix (right photo) began to visit the jails and poorhouses where most of the mental patients in the United States were kept. Dix publicized the terrible living conditions and the lack of reasonable treatment of mental patients. Her work was part of the reform movement that emphasized moral therapy.

Moral therapy, which was popular in the early 1800s, was the belief that mental patients could be helped to function better by providing humane treatment in a relaxed and decent environment.

During the reform movement, pleasant mental hospitals were built in rural settings so that moral therapy could be used to treat patients. However, these mental hospitals soon became overcrowded, the public lost interest, funds became tight, and treatment became scarce.

By the late 1800s, the belief that moral therapy would cure mental disorders was abandoned. Mental hospitals began to resemble human snake pits, in which hundreds of mental patients, in various states of dress or undress, milled about in a large room while acting out their symptoms with little or no supervision. Treatment went backward, and once again patients were put into straitjackets, handcuffs, and various restraining devices (Routh, 1994).

By the early 1900s, Sigmund Freud (left photo) had developed psychoanalysis, the first psychotherapy. Psychoanalysis eventually spread from Europe to the United States and reached its peak of popularity in the 1950s. However, psychoanalysis was more effective in treating less serious mental disorders (neuroses) than in treating the serious mental disorders (psychoses) that kept people in mental hospitals.

Thus, the wretched conditions and inhumane treatment of patients with serious mental disorders persisted until the early 1950s. By then, more than half a million patients were locked away. But in the mid-1950s, two events dramatically changed the treatment of mental patients: one was the discovery of antipsychotic drugs, and the other was the development of community mental health centers.

Psychoanalysis

Learn more about psychoanalysis.

Photo by Ken Smith of Painting in Harrisburg State Hospital/LLR Collection

© Hulton-Deutsch Collection/CORBIS

Phenothiazines and Deinstitutionalization

The discovery of drugs for treating mental disorders often occurs by chance. Such was the case in the 1950s as a French surgeon, Henri Laborit, searched for a drug that would calm down patients before surgery without causing unconsciousness. He happened to try a new drug on a woman about to have surgery and who also had schizophrenia. To the doctor's great surprise, the drug not only calmed the woman down but also decreased her schizophrenic symptoms. Chlorpromazine *(klor-PRO-ma-zeen)* belongs to a group of drugs called phenothiazines *(fee-no-THIGH-ah-zeens).*

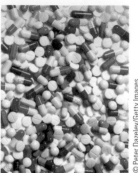

Phenothiazines, which were discovered in the early 1950s, block or reduce the effects of the neurotransmitter dopamine and reduce schizophrenic symptoms, such as delusions and hallucinations.

After 200 years of inhumane treatments for mental disorders, chlorpromazine was the first drug shown to be effective in reducing severe mental symptoms, such as delusions and hallucinations. For this reason, the discovery of chlorpromazine is considered the first revolution in the drug treatment of mental disorders.

In 1954, one of the phenothiazines, chlorpromazine (trade name: Thorazine), reached the United States and had two huge effects. First, it stimulated research on neurotransmitters and on the development of new drugs to treat mental disorders. Second, chlorpromazine reduced severe mental symptoms, such as delusions and hallucinations, to the point that patients could function well enough to be released from mental hospitals, a policy called deinstitutionalization.

Deinstitutionalization refers to the release of mental patients from mental hospitals and their return to the community to develop more independent and fulfilling lives.

In 1950, before the discovery of phenothiazines, there were 550,000 patients in mental hospitals in the United States. After the use of phenothiazines and deinstitutionalization, the number of patients in mental hospitals had dropped to about 150,000 in 1970 and to about 80,000 in 2000.

The goal of deinstitutionalization has been only partly realized. Some former mental patients do live in well-run halfway houses (Lipton et al., 2000). However, many deinstitutionalized patients end up living on the streets. To provide mental health treatment for the homeless, as well as those released from hospitals or too poor to pay for services, community mental health centers offer a place to receive treatment.

Community Mental Health Centers

There is a need for treatment of mental disorders in the homeless, county prisoners, those released from mental hospitals, as well as about 26% of Americans who experience a mental disorder in the course of a year (NIMH, 2008b). Some of these individuals may have less serious mental disorders that require professional help but not hospitalization. One way to provide professional help to individuals with less serious mental disorders is through community mental health centers.

Community mental health centers offer low-cost or free mental health care to members of the surrounding community, especially the underprivileged. The services may include psychotherapy, support groups, and telephone crisis counseling.

Just as the 1950s saw the introduction of a new drug treatment for mental disorders (phenothiazines), the 1960s saw the growing availability of new treatment facilities (community mental health centers). The goal of these centers, as well as other outpatient centers, is to provide treatment for the poor and those who have no other forms of treatment for their mental health problems. These kinds of mental health centers provide briefer forms of therapy that are needed in emergencies and focus on the early detection and prevention of psychological problems. To meet these ambitious goals required an enormous increase in the number of mental health personnel (Burns, 2004; Rosenberg, 2006).

In the 1960s, psychiatrists provided the majority of psychological services, which mainly served individuals in the middle and upper social classes who were not very seriously disturbed. Because of the limited number of psychiatrists, community mental health centers turned to clinical psychologists and social workers to provide the new mental health services. This demand increased the number of clinical and counseling psychologists and social workers and stimulated the development of new therapy approaches (Garfield & Bergin, 1994).

Before discussing specific psychotherapies, we'll answer three general questions about psychotherapy.

Deinstitutionalization and Homelessness

Find out how deinstitutionalization led to an increase in homelessness.

Check Your Learning Quiz 13.2

Go to **login.cengagebrain.com** and take the online quiz.

Unless otherwise noted, all images are © Cengage Learning

© Mira/Alamy

▶ **LO3** Describe when a person should seek psychotherapy, the types of therapists, and the effectiveness of psychotherapy.

If you or a family member, friend, or relative has a mental health problem, you might ask at least three questions about seeking professional help or psychotherapy: Do I need professional help? Are there different kinds of therapists? How effective is psychotherapy? We'll answer each question in turn.

Do I Need Professional Help?

Each year, more than 30 million Americans need help in dealing with a variety of mental disorders (NIMH, 2009a). For example, a person may feel overwhelmed by a sense of sadness, depression, or helplessness so that he or she cannot form a meaningful relationship. A person may worry or expect such terrible things to happen that he or she cannot concentrate or carry out everyday activities. A person may become so dependent on drugs that he or she has difficulty functioning in personal, social, or professional situations. If these problems begin to interfere with daily functioning in social, personal, business, academic, or professional interactions and activities, then a person may need help from a mental health professional (APA, 2009a).

Are There Different Kinds of Therapists?

We'll discuss three of the more common kinds of therapists: psychiatrists, clinical psychologists, and counseling psychologists, each of whom receives a different kind of training in psychotherapy techniques. Together, they provide psychotherapy to 3% of the U.S. population each year (Weissman et al., 2006).

Psychiatrists go to medical school, receive an MD degree, and then take a psychiatric residency, which involves additional training in pharmacology, neurology, psychopathology, and psychotherapeutic techniques.

Psychiatrists usually prescribe drugs to treat mental health disorders. Since the 1990s, psychiatrists have been providing less psychotherapy and instead focusing primarily on biological factors. Currently, less than 30% of psychiatrist office visits involve psychotherapy (Westly, 2008).

Clinical psychologists go to graduate school in clinical psychology and earn a doctorate degree (PhD, PsyD, or EdD). This training, which includes one year of work in an applied clinical setting, usually requires five to six years of work after obtaining a college degree.

Unless otherwise noted, all images are © Cengage Learning

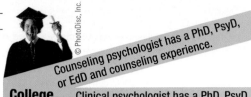

Clinical psychologists focus on psychosocial and environmental factors and use psychotherapy to treat mental health disorders.

Counseling psychologists go to graduate school in psychology or education and earn a doctorate degree (PhD, PsyD, or EdD). This training, which includes work in a counseling setting, usually requires about 4 to 6 years after obtaining a bachelor's degree.

College degree

Counseling psychologist has a PhD, PsyD, or EdD and counseling experience.

Clinical psychologist has a PhD, PsyD, or EdD and clinical experience.

Psychiatrist has an MD and psychiatric residency.

Counseling psychologists, who function in settings such as schools, industry, and private practice, generally deal more with problems of living than with the mental disorders that are treated by clinical psychologists.

In addition, other mental health professionals, such as clinical social workers and psychiatric nurses, provide mental health services.

How Effective Is Psychotherapy?

Researchers have analyzed the results of over 1,500 studies that examined the effects of psychotherapy on a variety of problems, such as depression, anxiety disorders, family problems, and headaches (Butler et al., 2006; L. Luborsky et al., 2002; Nathan et al., 2000). We'll discuss three of the major findings:

- Psychotherapy was effective in relieving a wide variety of psychological and behavioral symptoms in comparison with control groups who were on a waiting list to receive therapy or who received no systematic treatment.
- There was little or no significant difference in effectiveness among the approaches used by different therapies. In other words, the same psychological or behavioral symptoms were treated effectively with different approaches.
- The vast majority of patients (75%) showed measurable improvement by the end of 6 months of once-a-week psychotherapy sessions (24 sessions).

Based on data from thousands of patients, psychotherapy is effective in treating many mental and behavioral problems, and the greatest improvement occurs in a relatively brief time (13 to 18 sessions) (Lambert et al., 2004). However, the amount of improvement varies across patients (Brown et al., 2005; Sotsky et al., 2006).

We'll begin our presentation of the major therapeutic approaches with one of the oldest and best-known approaches, Freud's system of psychoanalysis.

Check Your Learning Quiz 13.3

Go to **login.cengagebrain.com** and take the online quiz.

▶ **LO4** Describe psychoananalysis, including its therapeutic techniques and problems encountered during therapy.

Psychoanalysis

Freud constructed one of the first amazingly complete and interesting descriptions of mental disorder and treatment, which he called psychoanalysis.

Psychoanalysis focuses on the idea that each of us has an unconscious part that contains ideas, memories, desires, or thoughts that have been hidden or repressed because they are psychologically dangerous or threatening to our self-concept. To protect our self-concept from these threatening thoughts and desires, we automatically build a mental barrier that we cannot voluntarily remove. However, the presence of these threatening thoughts and desires gives rise to unconscious conflicts, which, in turn, can result in psychological and physical symptoms and mental disorders.

Freud began developing psychoanalytic theory in the late 1800s. Psychoanalysis makes three major assumptions (Corey, 2009; E. B. Luborsky et al., 2008):

1 Unconscious Conflicts

Freud believed that unconscious conflicts were the chief reason for the development of psychological problems (such as paranoia) and physical symptoms (such as loss of feeling in a hand). To overcome psychological and physical problems, patients needed to become aware of, and gain insight into, their unconscious conflicts and repressed thoughts.

2 Techniques

Freud developed techniques, such as free association and dream interpretation, which he believed provide clues to unconscious conflicts and repressed thoughts.

3 Transfer

Freud found that at some point during therapy the patient would react to the therapist as a substitute parent, lover, sibling, or friend and, in the process, project or **transfer** strong emotions onto the therapist.

Next, we'll take you inside a therapy session to show you how psychoanalysis works.

Unless otherwise noted, all images are © Cengage Learning

Therapy Session

To give you an appreciation of what happens during psychoanalysis, we'll begin with an excerpt from a therapy session.

Henry is in his mid-forties and is well advanced in treatment. As he arrives, he casually mentions his somewhat late arrival at the analyst's office, which might otherwise have gone unnoticed.

"You will think it is a resistance," Henry remarked sarcastically, "but it was nothing of the kind. I had hailed a taxi that would have gotten me to the office on time. However, the traffic light changed just before the cab reached me, and someone else got in instead. I was so annoyed that I yelled 'F___ you!' after the cab driver."

A brief pause ensued, followed by laughter as Henry repeated "F___ you!"—this time clearly directed to the analyst.

The analyst interpreted this interaction to mean that the cabbie had represented the analyst in the first place. Henry's anger at the analyst was relieved by the opportunity to curse out the analyst (cabbie).

After another brief pause, it was the analyst who broke the silence and injected his first and only interpretation of the 50-minute session. He asserted that Henry seemed to be angry about a previously canceled therapy session.

Henry was furious over the interpretation. "Who are you that I should care about missing that session?" he stormed.

Henry paused again, and then tranquilly reflected, "My father, I suppose."

"My father was distant, like you," he began. "We never really had a conversation" (adapted from Lipton, 1983).

Role of the Analyst

This brief excerpt from a psychoanalytic session illustrates some of the basic assumptions of psychoanalysis.

- **Free association.** Notice that the patient is encouraged to free-associate or say anything that comes into his mind, while the analyst makes few comments.
- **Interpretation.** When the analyst does comment, he or she interprets or analyzes something the patient says, such as the meaning of the anger at the cab driver.
- **Unconscious conflicts.** By analyzing the client's free associations, the analyst hopes to reveal the client's unconscious and threatening desires, which are causing unconscious conflicts that, in turn, cause psychological problems.

We'll examine two of Freud's therapy techniques in more detail.

Beginning of Psychoanalysis

Learn about the fascinating case of Anna O.

Techniques to Reveal the Unconscious

One of Freud's major challenges was to find ways to uncover unconscious conflicts, which, he believed, led to psychological problems that he labeled neuroses.

Neuroses, according to Freud, are maladaptive thoughts and actions that arise from some unconscious thought or conflict and indicate feelings of anxiety.

In order to treat neuroses or neurotic symptoms, such as phobias, anxieties, and obsessions, Freud wanted to discover what was in the patient's unconscious. To do this, he developed two major techniques: free association and dream interpretation. To show how these techniques work, we'll describe two of Freud's most famous cases, Rat Man and Wolf-Man.

Rat Man: Free Association

Freud encouraged patients to relax, sit back, or lie down on his now-famous couch and engage in something called free association.

Free association is a technique that encourages clients to talk about any thoughts or images that enter their heads; the assumption is that this kind of free-flowing, uncensored talking will provide clues to unconscious material.

For example, here is how Freud described a session with one of his most famous patients, a 29-year-old lawyer later named the Rat Man because of his obsession that rats would destroy his father and lover.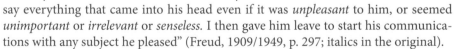

Freud writes, "The next day I made him [Rat Man] pledge himself to submit to the one and only condition of the treatment—namely, to say everything that came into his head even if it was *unpleasant* to him, or seemed *unimportant* or *irrelevant* or *senseless*. I then gave him leave to start his communications with any subject he pleased" (Freud, 1909/1949, p. 297; italics in the original).

Freud is actually telling Rat Man to free-associate. By this means, Freud uncovered a number of Rat Man's repressed memories, such as how Rat Man, as a child, would get into rages and bite people, just like a rat.

Free association was one of Freud's important methodological discoveries. Psychoanalysts still use this technique today to probe a client's unconscious thoughts, desires, and conflicts (Corey, 2009).

Unless otherwise noted, all images are © Cengage Learning

Wolf-Man: Dream Interpretation

Freud listened to and interpreted his patients' dreams because he believed that dreams represent the purest form of free association.

Dream interpretation is a psychoanalytic technique based on the assumption that dreams contain underlying, hidden meanings and symbols that provide clues to unconscious thoughts and desires.

For example, here is one of the best-known dreams in psychoanalytic literature. This dream was told to Freud by a 23-year-old patient who was later named Wolf-Man because he had a phobia of wolves and other animals (Buckley, 1989).

"I dreamt that it was night and that I was lying in my bed. Suddenly the window opened of its own accord, and I was terrified to see that some white wolves were sitting on the big walnut tree in front of the window. . . The wolves were quite white, and looked more like foxes or sheep-dogs, for they had big tails like foxes and they had their ears pricked like dogs when they are attending to something. In great terror, evidently of being eaten up by the wolves, I screamed and woke up. . . I was 3, 4, or at most 5 years old at the time. From then until my 11th or 12th year I was always afraid of seeing something terrible in my dreams" (Freud, 1909/1949, p. 498).

Freud's interpretation of this dream was that, as a young boy, Wolf-Man was "transformed" into a wolf and had witnessed his parents' sexual intercourse (looking through the bedroom window). Later, sexual fears created unconscious conflicts and resulted in a phobia of wolves and other animals.

As Freud demonstrates, the psychoanalyst's task is to look behind the dream's often bizarre disguises and symbols and decipher clues to unconscious, repressed memories, thoughts, feelings, and conflicts (Greenberg & Perlman, 1999).

Case studies, such as those of Rat Man and Wolf-Man, were very important because from these Freud developed the major concepts of psychoanalysis. Freud's case studies read like mystery stories, with Freud being the master detective who searches for psychological clues that will reveal the person's repressed feelings and unconscious conflicts. At the time, Freud's assumptions and theories, such as repressed feelings and unconscious motivation, were revolutionary. However, as we'll discuss later, Freud's theories and assumptions have been very difficult to verify or prove with experimental methods.

Psychoanalysis

Learn more about how psychoanalysis treats psychological problems.

▶ **LO5** Distinguish between traditional psychoanalysis and short-term psychodynamic therapy.

▶ **LO6** Evaluate the current status of psychoanalysis.

Problems During Therapy

Freud was the first to notice that, during therapy, his clients became somewhat hostile toward him, a problem he called transference. He also found that patients became very resistant about dealing with their feelings. Freud believed that how these two problems, called transference and resistance, were handled determined how successful therapy would be. We'll explain these two concepts by using the cases of Rat Man and Wolf-Man, both of which we have already discussed.

Rat Man: Transference

Freud describes Rat Man as expressing hostile feelings toward him. For example, Rat Man refused to shake hands with Freud, accused Freud of picking his nose, called Freud a "filthy swine," and said that Freud needed to be taught manners (Freud, 1909/1949). According to Freud, Rat Man was projecting negative traits of his own controlling mother onto Freud, who became a "substitute mother." This process of transferring feelings to the therapist is called transference.

Transference is the process by which a client expresses strong emotions toward the therapist because the therapist substitutes for someone important in the client's life.

Freud said that if the feelings involved in transference were not worked out, therapy would stall and treatment would not occur. For this reason, Freud believed that one of the major roles of the analyst was to help the client deal with, work through, and resolve the transferred feelings.

Wolf-Man: Resistance

For most patients, the process of working out transference and achieving insight into their problems is long and difficult. One reason for the difficulty is that the client has so many defenses against admitting repressed thoughts and feelings into consciousness. These defenses lead to resistance.

Resistance is characterized by the client's reluctance to work through or deal with feelings or to recognize unconscious conflicts and repressed thoughts.

Resistance may show up in many ways: Clients may cancel sessions or come late, argue continually, criticize the analyst, or develop physical problems. For example, Wolf-Man constantly complained of severe constipation. Freud said that Wolf-Man used constipation as an obvious sign he was resisting having to deal with his feelings (Freud, 1909/1949). A necessary role of the analyst is to overcome the client's resistance so the therapy can proceed and stay on course.

Short-Term Psychodynamic Psychotherapy

Resolving the problems of transference and resistance may take 200 to 600 sessions across several years of traditional psychoanalysis. However, therapists have developed a briefer version of psychoanalysis, which is called short-term psychodynamic psychotherapy.

Short-term dynamic psychothe
emphasizes a limited time for treatment an
focuses on limited goals, such as solving a
relatively well-defined problem. Therapists
take a more active and directive role by
identifying and discussing the client's problems, resolving issues of transference, interpreting the patient's behaviors, and offering
an opportunity for the patient to foster
changes in behavior and thinking that
will result in more active coping and
an improved self-image (Prochaska &
Norcross, 2010).

How long will it take me to get over my fears?

Short-term dynamic psychotherapy, which incorporates techniques of traditional psychoanalysis, has proven effective for treating a number of problems, including generalized anxiety, panic, depression, and several personality disorders (Lewis et al., 2008; Milrod et al., 2007).

Psychoanalysis: Evaluation

During the past 25 years or so, psychoanalytic societies and their members have made a major effort to encourage research on the methods, concepts, and outcomes of psychoanalytic therapy. For example, when researchers compared psychoanalysis with different kinds of long-term psychotherapies, they found that psychoanalysis was just as successful in improving patients' mental status (Blomberg et al., 2001). Supporters add that other Freudian concepts, such as the influence of unconscious forces, long-term effects of early childhood patterns, and the existence of defense mechanisms, resistance, and transference, have been experimentally tested and supported (Fotopoulou, 2006; Luborsky & Barrett, 2006; Ramachandran, 2006; Westen, 2007). It is clear that Freud's influence is very much alive in today's culture.

Decline in Popularity of Psychoanalysis

Read about why psychoanalysis has lost much of its popularity.

Check Your Learning Quiz 13.4

Go to **login.cengagebrain.com** and take the online quiz.

▶ **LO7** Describe humanistic therapy approach and Rogers' client-centered therapy.

The **humanistic therapy approach** argues that people naturally strive to reach their potential. In contrast to psychoanalytic therapy's emphasis on the past and the unconscious, humanistic therapy focuses on the present and the conscious.

Client-Centered Therapy

As a therapist, Carl Rogers used the most popular therapy of his time, which was Freud's psychoanalytic approach. However, before long Rogers became dissatisfied with Freud's view that human nature was dependent on biological urges and instincts—sex and aggression—and that psychological problems arose from unconscious thoughts and desires that threatened one's self-concept. Rogers also disagreed with Freud's belief that the analyst—and not the client—was responsible for the client's progress. Using these ideas, Rogers developed client-centered therapy, which is a form of humanistic therapy (Rogers, 1951, 1986).

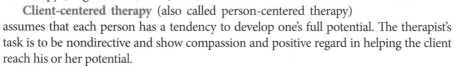

Client-centered therapy (also called person-centered therapy) assumes that each person has a tendency to develop one's full potential. The therapist's task is to be nondirective and show compassion and positive regard in helping the client reach his or her potential.

Therapy Session

Here is a brief excerpt from a client-centered therapy session in which a mother is talking about her problems with letting her daughter be more independent (adapted from Rogers, 1989).

Client: I'm having a lot of problems dealing with my daughter. She's 20 years old; she's in college; I'm having a lot of trouble letting her go . . . And I have a lot of guilt feelings about her; I have a real need to hang on to her. And it's very hard with a lot of empty places now that she's not with me.

Rogers: The old vacuum, sort of, when she's not there.

Client: Yes, yes. I also would like to be the kind of mother that could be strong and say, you know, "go and have a good life."

Rogers: It's hard to give up something that's been so precious in your life, but also something that I guess has caused you pain when you mentioned guilt.

Client: Yeah, and I'm aware that I have some anger toward her that I don't always get what I want. I have needs that are not met. And, uh, I don't feel I have a right to

Unless otherwise noted, all images are © Cengage Learning

those needs. You know . . . she's a daughter; she's not my mother though sometimes I feel as if I'd like her to mother me.

Rogers: So it may be unreasonable, but still, when she doesn't meet your needs, it makes you mad.

Client: Yeah. I get very angry, very angry with her. *(pause)*

Rogers: You're also feeling a little tension at this point, I guess.

Client: Yeah, yeah. A lot of conflict . . .

Rogers: A lot of pain.

Client: A lot of pain.

Rogers: A lot of pain. Can you say anything more what that's about?

There are a few hallmarks of client-centered therapy. First, Rogers avoids giving any suggestions, advice, or disapproval and primarily shows the client he understands what the client is feeling. Second, one technique Rogers uses for showing understanding is *reflecting* or restating the client's concerns. In addition, humanistic therapists believe that clients have the capacity to discover and reach their true potential; it is the therapist's role to help and remove any roadblocks in their paths (Prochaska & Norcross, 2010).

Therapist's Traits

Rogers believed that personal characteristics of the therapist (empathy, positive regard, genuineness) would bring about the client's change. Empathy is the ability to understand what the client is saying and feeling. Positive regard is the ability to communicate caring, respect, and regard for the client. Genuineness is the ability to be real and nondefensive in interactions with the client. Rogers and his followers assumed that a therapist with these three characteristics would be able to help a client change and grow (Raskin et al., 2008).

Effectiveness

Client-centered therapy has been effective in producing significant changes in clients in comparison with no-treatment control groups, but no more or less effective than other forms of therapy (Hill & Nakayama, 2000). Although few therapists currently identify themselves as primarily client-centered in their approach, the principles of client-centered therapy have contributed to making therapists aware of the importance of and the need to develop a positive working relationship with their clients (Kirschenbaum & Jourdan, 2005).

The therapist takes a much more directive role in other types of therapy, such as in cognitive therapy, which we will discuss next.

Client-Centered Therapy

Learn more about how client-centered therapy treats psychological problems.

Check Your Learning Quiz 13.5

Go to **login.cengagebrain.com** and take the online quiz.

▶ **LO8** Describe Beck's cognitive therapy.

Cognitive Therapy

Similar to Carl Rogers' experience, Aaron Beck was also trained in psychoanalytic techniques and used them to treat patients, many of whom were depressed. When he asked them to free-associate, he noticed that depressed patients often expressed negative or distorted thoughts about themselves—"I'm a failure, no one likes me, nothing turns out right." What really caught his attention was how patients would express a string of negative thoughts almost automatically, without paying much attention. Beck reasoned that these automatically occurring negative thoughts had a great impact on the patients' lives, such as by lowering their self-esteem and encouraging self-blame. Beck developed his form of cognitive therapy to stop these thoughts (Beck, 1976, 1991).

Why do I keep thinking all those negative thoughts?

Cognitive therapy, as developed by Aaron Beck, assumes that we have automatic negative thoughts that we typically say to ourselves without much notice. By continually repeating these automatic negative thoughts, we color and distort how we perceive and interpret our world and influence how we behave and feel. Cognitive therapy aims to make a person aware of, and stop, negative self-statements.

Therapy Session

To give you an idea of how negative thoughts occur, here is a brief excerpt from one of Dr. Beck's sessions.

The client is a 26-year-old graduate student who has bouts of depression.

Client: I get depressed when things go wrong. Like when I fail a test.

Therapist: How can failing a test make you depressed?

Client: Well, if I fail, I'll never get into law school.

Therapist: Do you agree that the way you interpret the results of the test will affect you? You might feel depressed, you might have trouble sleeping, not feel like eating, and you might even wonder if you should drop out of the course.

Client: I have been thinking that I wasn't going to make it. Yes, I agree.

Therapist: Now what did failing mean?

Client: *(tearful)* That I couldn't get into law school.

Therapist: And what does that mean to you?

Client: That I'm just not smart enough.

Therapist: Anything else?

Client: That I can never be happy.

Therapist: And how do these thoughts make you feel?

Client: Very unhappy.

Therapist: So it is the meaning of failing a test that makes you very unhappy. In fact, believing that you can never be happy is a powerful factor in producing unhappiness. So, you get yourself into a trap—by definition, failure to get into law school equals "I can never be happy" (Beck et al., 1979, pp. 145–146).

Notice the client's negative self-statements, such as "I'm just not smart enough" and "I can never be happy." Beck believes that these kinds of negative self-statements will influence this client's thoughts and feelings and contribute to her major symptom, depression.

Important Factors

Beck identified specific maladaptive thoughts that contribute to various symptoms, such as anxiety and depression. Thus, thinking "I'm a failure" after doing poorly on one test is an example of overgeneralization, which is making blanket judgments

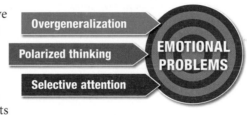

about yourself on the basis of a single incident. Thinking "Most people don't like me" is an example of polarized thinking, which is sorting information into one of two categories, good or bad. Thinking "People always criticize me" is an example of selective attention, which is focusing on one detail so much that you do not notice other events, such as being complimented. Beck believes maladaptive thought patterns cause a distorted view of oneself and one's world, which in turn lead to emotional problems. Thus, cognitive therapy aims to identify and change maladaptive thoughts.

Effectiveness

Cognitive therapy has proved effective in treating a variety of symptoms. For example, it is as effective as various drugs in treating depression, bipolar disorder, general anxiety, social phobia, agoraphobia, panic attacks, smoking, anger, and eating disorders. In some cases, the benefits of cognitive therapy last longer than those of other forms of therapy (Ball et al., 2006; Clark et al., 2006; DeRubeis et al., 2005; Dobson & Khatri, 2000; Rupke et al., 2006).

Cognitive Therapy

Learn more about how cognitive therapy treats psychological problems.

Check Your Learning Quiz 13.6

Go to **login.cengagebrain.com** and take the online quiz.

Unless otherwise noted, all images are © Cengage Learning

▶ **LO9** Describe behavior therapy approach.

Behavior Therapy

In Module 5.3, we told you about Little Albert (right picture), who initially wanted to play with a white rat but, after being conditioned, came to fear it (Watson & Rayner, 1920). This demonstration, which occurred in the 1920s, showed that emotional responses could be conditioned. But it was not until the 1950s that a clinician developed a procedure to unlearn emotional responses. Wolpe's procedure was the first experimental demonstration of reducing fear through conditioning and jump-started the field of behavior therapy (Wolpe, 1958, 1990; Persons, 1997).

Behavior therapy uses the principles of classical and operant conditioning to change disruptive behaviors and improve human functioning. It focuses on changing particular behaviors rather than the underlying mental events or possible unconscious factors.

We'll begin by giving an example of a behavior therapy session.

Therapy Session

In this session, the therapist is talking to a woman who feels bad because she has great difficulty being assertive.

Client: The basic problem is that I have the tendency to let people step all over me. I don't know why, but I just have difficulty in speaking my mind.

Therapist: So you find yourself in situations where you don't respond the way you would like to and you would like to learn how to behave differently.

Client: Yes. But you know, I have tried to handle certain situations differently, but I just don't seem to be able to do so.

Therapist: Well, maybe you tried to do too much or didn't quite know the right technique. For example, imagine yourself at the bottom of a staircase, wanting to get to the top. It's too much to ask to get there in one gigantic leap. Perhaps a better way to go about changing your reaction in these situations is to take it one step at a time.

Client: That makes sense, but I'm not sure if I see how it could be done.

Therapist: Well, there are probably certain situations in which it would be less difficult for you to assert yourself, such as telling your boss that he forgot to pay you for the past four weeks.

Client: *(laughing)* I guess in that situation, I would say something. Although I must admit, I would feel uneasy about it.

Therapist: But not as uneasy as if you went in and asked him for a raise.

Client: No. Certainly not.

Therapist: So, the first situation would be low on the staircase, whereas the second would be higher up. If you can learn to handle easier situations, then the more difficult ones would present less of a problem. And the only way you can really learn to change your reactions is through practice.

Why do I let people walk all over me?

Client: In other words, I really have to go out and actually force myself to speak up more, but taking it a little bit at a time?

Therapist: Exactly. And it's easier and safer to run through some of these situations here because you can't really get into trouble if you make a mistake. Once you learn different ways to speak your mind, you can try them out in the real world (adapted from Goldfried & Davison, 1976).

Notice that the behavior therapist does not encourage the client to free-associate, which is a technique of psychoanalysis. The behavior therapist does not repeat or reflect what the client says, which is a technique of client-centered therapy. The behavior therapist does not discuss the client's tendency to automatically think negative thoughts, which is a technique of cognitive therapy. Instead, the behavior therapist identifies the specific problem, which is the woman's tendency to be unassertive. Next, the behavior therapist discusses a program for behavioral change that will teach this woman to be assertive.

Two Goals

Behavior therapy has two goals. The first is to modify undesirable behaviors and teach the client how to perform new behaviors, which for this woman involves learning ways to be more assertive. The second goal is to help the client meet specific behavioral goals through constant practice and reward (Spiegler & Guevremont, 2009). For example, this woman would be asked to practice initiating conversations and stating her opinions, perhaps beginning in the safety of the therapist's office and gradually practicing these new assertive behaviors in the more threatening situations of the real world.

Next, we discuss the step-by-step exposure process used in behavior therapy.

Behavior Therapy

Learn more about how behavior therapy treats psychological problems.

▶ **LO10** Identify the three steps involved in systematic densensitization.

Systematic Desensitization

Similar to my own phobia of blood, which I shared with you earlier, Jack had developed a phobia of blood that interfered with his plans. He was a high-school senior who wanted to be an ambulance driver. But the problem was that he passed out at the sight or discussion of blood. He had been afraid of blood for years and had fainted about 20 times in science and biology classes. He even felt queasy when bloody accidents or operating-room scenes were shown on television. If his supervisor found out about his phobia, Jack might lose his chance to be an ambulance driver. Except for his phobia, Jack was happy at school, rarely became depressed, and was generally easygoing (Yule & Fernando, 1980).

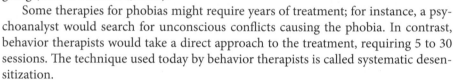

Some therapies for phobias might require years of treatment; for instance, a psychoanalyst would search for unconscious conflicts causing the phobia. In contrast, behavior therapists would take a direct approach to the treatment, requiring 5 to 30 sessions. The technique used today by behavior therapists is called systematic desensitization.

Systematic desensitization is a technique of behavior therapy in which the client is gradually exposed to the feared object while simultaneously practicing relaxation. Desensitization involves three steps: learning to relax, constructing a hierarchy with the least feared situation on the bottom and the most feared situation at the top, and being progressively exposed to the feared situation.

Behavior therapists assume that since Jack's phobia was acquired through a conditioning process, his phobia can be unconditioned by gradually exposing him to the feared object through the process of systematic desensitization.

1 Relaxation

Jack, whose phobia was a fear of blood, underwent systematic desensitization, a very effective treatment for phobias (Cormier & Nurius, 2003). In the first step, Jack learned to relax by practicing progressive relaxation. This method involves tensing and relaxing various muscle groups, beginning with the toes and working up to the head. With this procedure, Jack learned how to put himself into a relaxed state. For most individuals, learning progressive relaxation requires several weeks with at least one 15-minute session every day.

Unless otherwise noted, all images are © Cengage Learning

2 Stimulus Hierarchy

The second step was for Jack to make a stimulus hierarchy, which is a list of feared stimuli, arranged in order from least to most feared. With the help of his therapist, Jack made the stimulus hierarchy shown on the right, which lists various situations associated with blood. A rating of 1 indicates little fear if confronted by this stimulus, while a rating of 7 indicates that Jack would probably pass out from this stimulus.

MOST STRESSFUL

7 Needle drawing blood

6 Finger dripping blood

5 Seeing someone cut

4 Needle entering arm

3 Watching blood on TV

2 Cutting own finger

1 Seeing word "blood"

3 Exposure

Systematic desensitization training means that, after successfully completing steps 1 and 2, Jack was ready for step 3, which was to systematically desensitize himself by exposing himself to the fear stimuli. Desensitization occurs through relaxing while simultaneously imagining the feared stimuli.

Jack put himself into a relaxed state and then imagined the first or least feared item in his hierarchy, seeing the word *blood*. He tried to remain in a relaxed state while vividly imagining the word *blood*. He repeated this procedure until he felt no tension or anxiety in this situation. At this point, he went on to the next item in his hierarchy. Jack repeated the procedure of pairing relaxation with images of each feared item until he reached the last and most feared item.

Through the desensitization program described here, Jack's blood phobia was treated in five 1-hour sessions. A follow-up 5 years later indicated that Jack was still free of his blood phobia, had not developed any substitute symptoms, and was training to be an ambulance driver (Yule & Fernando, 1980).

Exposure: Imagined or In Vivo

Systematic desensitization appears to be most effective if, instead of just imagining the items on the list, which is called imagined exposure, clients gradually expose themselves to the actual situation, which is called in vivo exposure (the phrase *in vivo* is Latin for "in real life") (Moscovitch et al., 2008; Wilson, 2005).

Next, we'll discuss cognitive-behavior, which is actually a combination of behavior and cognitive therapies.

Systematic Desensitization

Treat a phobia using the three steps of systemic desensitization.

Systematic Desensitization and Unconditioning

Explore how systematic desensitization is used to uncondition fears.

▶ **LO11** Describe cognitive-behavioral therapy approach.

Cognitive-Behavioral Therapy

As psychoanalysis reached its peak of popularity in the 1950s, a number of clinicians and researchers were becoming dissatisfied with its procedures, which were time-consuming, costly, and useful for treating only a limited number of clients with relatively minor problems (Franks, 1994).

At this same time, there was a great increase in the popularity of learning principles that came from Pavlov's work on classical conditioning and Skinner's work on operant conditioning. Researchers and clinicians began to apply these learning principles to change human behavior with methods based on a strong experimental foundation rather than Freud's unverified beliefs about unconscious conflicts. Both behavior and cognitive therapies developed out of dissatisfaction with psychoanalysis and the belief that learning principles would provide more effective methods of changing human behavior than would the concepts of psychoanalysis.

One of the interesting developments in therapy has been occurring since the late 1970s, as both behavior and cognitive therapies have become increasingly popular. The major difference between the two therapies is that *behavior therapy* focuses on identifying and changing specific behaviors, while *cognitive therapy* focuses on identifying and changing specific maladaptive thought patterns. Beginning in the early 1990s, researchers and clinicians began combining the methods of behavior and cognitive therapies into what is now called cognitive-behavioral therapy (Grant et al., 2005).

I need to stop thinking all those negative thoughts.

Cognitive-behavioral therapy combines the cognitive therapy technique of changing negative, unhealthy, or distorted thought patterns with the behavior therapy technique of changing maladaptive or disruptive behaviors by learning and practicing new skills to improve functioning.

Techniques

Cognitive-behavioral therapists combine a number of techniques that are designed to change both thoughts and behaviors and thus improve a person's psychological functioning. These techniques include monitoring one's own thoughts and behaviors; identifying thoughts and behaviors that need to be changed; setting specific goals that increase in difficulty; learning to reinforce oneself for reaching a goal; imitating or modeling new behaviors; substituting positive for negative thoughts; and doing homework, which involves practicing new behaviors in a safe setting before performing them in the real world (Beck & Weishaar, 2008). These cognitive-behavioral techniques are the basis for almost all self-help programs, which may be completed without the assistance of a therapist. For more serious problems or additional support, the aid and help of a therapist may be needed.

I need to learn assertive behaviors.

Effectiveness

Cognitive-behavioral therapy is currently being used to treat a wide variety of problems, including eating disorders, marital problems, anxiety and phobias, depression, and sexual dysfunction. Programs based on cognitive-behavioral therapy are widely used to help people stop smoking, become more assertive, improve communication and interpersonal skills, manage stress, and control anger. Researchers report that cognitive-behavioral therapy was significantly more effective in treating this wide variety of problems than were control procedures (Butler et al., 2006; Dobson, 2009). And in some cases, cognitive-behavioral therapy was as effective as drugs in treating some forms of anxiety, phobia, depression, and compulsive behavior (Butler et al., 2006; Spiegler & Guevremont, 2009).

Now that we have discussed the major types of psychotherapy, we will turn our attention to other therapy approaches, such as the fascinating field of biomedical therapies.

Cognitive-Behavioral Treatment of Phobias

Learn more about how cognitive-behavioral therapy can be used to treat phobias.

Check Your Learning Quiz 13.7

Go to **login.cengagebrain.com** and take the online quiz.

▶ **LO12** Describe the common factors among the different psychotherapy approaches.

▶ **LO13** Describe the characteristics of cybertherapy, and identify its advantages and disadvantages.

▶ **LO14** Explain eye movement densensitization and reprocessing.

Common Factors

If you need professional help today, you can choose from a number of different therapies, which are available at a variety of mental health facilities. However, because the current therapy approaches begin with different assumptions and use different methods, you might wonder if one therapy is more effective than another. In answer to this question, researchers have consistently found that there is very little, if any, difference in effectiveness among various therapies (Drisko, 2004; Luborsky et al., 2002). However, for a small number of specific disorders, including panic attacks, phobias, obsessive-compulsions, insomnia, and depression, cognitive-behavioral therapies have generally been shown to be more effective than traditional talk therapies, such as the psychoanalytic approach (Butler et al., 2006; Dobson & Khatri, 2000). One reason different therapies using different techniques achieve the same results is they all share common factors (Luborsky et al., 2002).

Common factors are a basic set of procedures and experiences that different therapies share and that explain why different approaches are equally effective. Common factors include the growth of a supportive and trusting relationship between therapist and client and the development of an accepting atmosphere, in which the client feels willing to admit problems and is motivated to work on changing.

Related to the common factors of various therapeutic approaches is the basic assumption that therapy takes places face to face, with therapist and client in the same room. In this regard, you may find the recent growth in cybertherapy, discussed next, a bit surprising.

Cybertherapy

Cybertherapy challenges the assumption that therapy must take place face-to-face.

Cybertherapy is therapy delivered over the Internet.

Cybertherapy can range from clients e-mailing questions or concerns to a therapist, who in turn responds by e-mail, to clients sitting in front of a camera mounted on their computer and having a live online session with a therapist (right photo).

Unless otherwise noted, all images are © Cengage Learning

© Ingram Publishing/Alamy

The advantages of cybertherapy are that it reduces costs and improves access to therapeutic services in areas with limited availability of mental health services. The disadvantages are that cybertherapists may not have the same credentials or be as well trained as traditional therapists. Also, cybertherapists cannot clearly see body gestures or facial expressions and cannot clearly hear the emotional tone in a client's voice. Initial research on cybertherapy suggests it has promise; however, more controlled experimental research is needed to better assess its effectiveness (Barak et al., 2008; Derrig-Palumbo & Zeine, 2005; Rochlen et al., 2004; Zack et al., 2004).

Cybertherapy may seem strange to some. The next treatment, which is conducted in a traditional therapy environment, may also seem rather odd.

Eye Movement Desensitization and Reprocessing

In the early 1990s, a new kind of psychotherapy appeared that was unlike any we have discussed. This therapy was called Eye Movement Desensitization and Reprocessing (Shapiro, 2002).

Eye Movement Desensitization and Reprocessing (EMDR) involves having the client talk about or imagine a traumatic memory while visually focusing on and following the back-and-forth movement of a therapist's hand. This process usually continues for several 90-minute sessions, after which the traumatic memories are greatly reduced or eliminated.

For about 20 years, researchers have studied EMDR therapy and generally concluded it is not simply a placebo effect but is effective in reducing traumatic memories, such as occur in posttraumatic stress disorder (p. 567).

What is known is that, during EMDR, clients are recalling and confronting their most feared feelings, images, or situations. Thus, many researchers suggest that EMDR may be another form of traditional exposure therapy (pp. 620–621) (Lilienfeld & Arkowitz, 2006). However, others suggest the treatment process of EMDR is unique because the eye movements allow patients to emotionally distance themselves from the trauma experiences (Lee et al., 2006).

Research Findings on EMDR

Learn more about how EMDR works.

▶ **LO15** Identify the different types of drug biomedical therapies and describe their effects.

Biomedical Therapies

The variety of psychotherapy approaches we dicussed in the previous module apply psychological principles to understanding and treating psychological disorders. People with psychological disorders may also be treated with biomedical therapies, either solely or in combination with psychotherapy. Biomedical therapies apply biological principles to understanding and treating psychological disorders. We will begin our discussion of the types of biomedical therapies with the most common form, drug therapies.

Drug Therapies

Since the 1950s, in an effort to treat abnormal psychological and behavioral symptoms, drug companies have developed a diverse array of medications that alter the chemicals in our brains. Various categories of drugs are used to treat symptoms of mental disorders. We'll discuss antidepressant drugs, mood-stabilizer drugs, antianxiety drugs, and antipsychotic drugs.

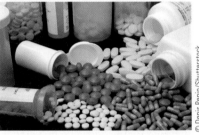

© Denis Pepin/Shutterstock

Antidepressant Drugs

Antidepressants have recently become the most commonly prescribed medication in the United States, used by 10% of the population (Olfson & Marcus, 2009).

Antidepressant drugs act by increasing the levels of a specific group of neurotransmitters (monoamines, such as serotonin, norepinephrine, and dopamine) that are involved in the regulation of emotions and moods.

About 80% of prescribed antidepressant drugs, such as Prozac and Zoloft, belong to a group of drugs called SSRIs (selective serotonin reuptake inhibitors) (Noonan & Cowley, 2002). The SSRIs work primarily by raising the level of the neurotransmitter serotonin. Common side effects include nausea, insomnia, sedation, and sexual problems (such as decreased libido, erectile dysfunction) (Gitlin, 2009; Khawam et al., 2006).

When patients with depression use an antidepressant, which may take up to 8 weeks to work, symptoms for only one-third of the patients will go away (comparable to the recovery rate for a placebo) (Berenson, 2006). The challenge for physicians prescribing antidepressants is that for any given individual, some antidepressants work better than others, but no one antidepressant has been found to be more effective for everyone. Often, patients must try a second or third antidepressant until they find one that works well and has minimal side effects (Arkowitz & Lilienfeld, 2007b).

Mood-Stabilizer Drugs

When a person experiences the highs and lows of mood (mania and depression), they will likely benefit most by taking a mood-stabilizer drug.

Mood-stabilizer drugs act by effecting the levels of neurotransmitters (such as norepinephrine and serotonin) to even out the highs and lows of mood disorders, such as bipolar disorder.

One example of a mood-stablizer drug is lithium, which is used to keep people from becoming too elated (manic) or too depressed. In terms of effectiveness, 50% of bipolar patients are greatly helped with a combined drug program (lithium plus other drugs), 30% are partially helped, and 20% get little or no help (Goodwin, 2003). Also, lithium has been found to be effective in treating individuals with mania (that is, the manic episodes without the depression) (Goodwin, 2003).

However, lithium is a potentially dangerous drug that can in rare cases cause death if its concentration in the blood becomes too high. Therefore, people who use lithium must take regular blood tests.

Antianxiety Drugs

Most antianxiety drugs belong to a class of chemicals known as benzodiazepines *(ben-zo-die-AS-ah-peens)*.

Benzodiazepines (Valium, Xanax, Restoril) reduce anxiety, worry, and stress by lowering physiological arousal, which results in a state of tranquility.

Benzodiazepines provide a sense of tranquility by decreasing the activity of the sympathetic division of the central nervous system, which results in reduced heart rate, respiration, and muscle tension.

Because many people will experience bouts of severe anxiety, worry, and stress at some time in their lives, antianxiety drugs are commonly prescribed. In addition to being used to treat anxiety, benzodiazapines are prescribed for the treatment of sleeping problems, such as insomnia.

However, prolonged use of benzodiazepines, especially at higher doses, may lead to dependence on the drug and serious side effects, such as memory loss and excessive sleepiness.

Treating Depression

Learn more about how antidepressants are used to treat depression.

▶ **LO16** Identify the different types of non-drug biomedical therapies and describe their effects.

Antipsychotic Drugs

Most individuals diagnosed with schizophrenia are prescribed an antipsychotic or neuroleptic (meaning "taking hold of the nerves") drug.

Neuroleptic drugs, also called **antipsychotic drugs,** are used to treat serious mental disorders, such as schizophrenia, by changing the levels of neurotransmitters in the brain.

There are two kinds of neuroleptic drugs: typical and atypical.

Typical neuroleptics were discovered in the 1950s and were the first effective medical treatment for schizophrenia.

Typical neuroleptics: decrease dopamine

Typical neuroleptic drugs primarily reduce levels of the neurotransmitter dopamine.

One group of typical neuroleptics, called the phenothiazines *(pheen-no-THIGH-ah-zeens),* is widely prescribed to treat schizophrenia. Continued use of phenothiazines can produce unwanted motor movements, which is a side effect called tardive dyskinesia *(TAR-div dis-cah-KNEE-zee-ah)* (Dolder, 2008).

Tardive dyskinesia involves the appearance of slow, involuntary, and uncontrollable rhythmic movements and rapid twitching of the mouth and lips, as well as unusual movements of the limbs.

Using typical neuroleptic drugs to treat schizophrenia is being challenged by newer drugs, called atypical neuroleptic drugs.

Atypical neuroleptics: decrease dopamine & serotonin

Atypical neuroleptic drugs (clozapine, risperidone) lower levels of dopamine and other neurotransmitters, especially serotonin.

The first atypical neuroleptic, clozapine, was approved for use in schizophrenia in 1990. Since then, atypical neuroleptics have proven effective in decreasing symptoms of schizophrenia, especially in patients who were not helped by typical neuroleptics (Carpenter, 2003).

One advantage of atypical neuroleptics is they cause tardive dyskinesia in only about 5% of patients, compared to up to 29% of patients given typical neuroleptics (Caroff et al., 2002). However, atypical neuroleptics can cause side effects, the most serious being increased levels of cholesterol and glucose or blood sugar, weight gain, and onset or worsening of diabetes (Burton, 2006; Dolder, 2008). Thus, typical and atypical neuroleptics may produce serious side effects.

Next, we'll focus on biomedical therapies that do not involve the use of drugs.

Unless otherwise noted, all images are © Cengage Learning

Non-Drug Therapies

Brain Stimulation

As you learned in Module 2.5, **deep brain stimulation (DBS)** is a recently implemented surgical procedure that involves implanting electrodes into a specific area of the brain and placing a battery-powered stimulator under the collarbone. The electrodes are wired to the stimulator, which provides electrical stimulation to the designated brain area. The patient controls the stimulation by using a remote control to turn it on and off.

Research supports that DBS is effective and carries relatively minimal risk for treating a variety of health problems. DBS has been most commonly used in the treatment of Parkinson's disease, and is currently being investigated in the treatment of depression, anxiety, phantom limb pain, comas, and Alzheimer's disease (Kluger, 2007b; Kringelbach & Aziz, 2008; G. Miller, 2009; Mullins, 2008; Schiff et al., 2007).

An advantage of DBS is being able to modify the level of stimulation as needed. Also, patients receiving DBS show greater long-term improvement than patients receiving only medication (Deuschl et al., 2006; Weaver et al., 2009). The limitation of this procedure is that the batteries must be surgically replaced every few years (Pahwa & Lyons, 2003). There is also a risk of dangerous bleeding and getting an infection (Kringelbach & Aziz, 2008; Weaver et al., 2009).

Transcranial Magnetic Stimulation

For patients with treatment-resistant depression, a new biomedical treatment option is transcranial magnetic stimulation (right photo).

Transcranial magnetic stimulation (TMS) is a noninvasive technique that activates neurons by sending pulses of magnetic energy into the brain.

Research shows that depressed patients who did not benefit from various medications experienced significant improvement in symptoms after 40 minutes of TMS daily for 4 weeks (O'Reardon et al., 2007). Although side effects, such as headache, light-headedness, and scalp discomfort, may occur, TMS is unlikely to cause seizures and does not require anesthesia, which are both serious concerns of electroconvulsive therapy, our next topic (Baldauf, 2009; George, 2009).

© Canadian Press/Phototake

Magnetic Stimulation to the Brain

Learn more about how transcranial magnetic stimulation works.

Electroconvulsive Therapy

Because the use of shock as therapy has often been portrayed incorrectly in the media, it helps to see the treatment from the eyes of an actual patient.

"... As far as manic-depressive tales go, my stories are typical. My illness went undiagnosed for a decade, a period of euphoric highs and desperate lows highlighted by $25,000 shopping sprees, impetuous trips to Tokyo, Paris, and Milan, drug and alcohol binges.... After seeing eight psychiatrists, I finally received a diagnosis of bipolar disorder on my 32nd birthday. Over the next year and a half, I was treated unsuccessfully with more than 30 medications. My suburban New Jersey upbringing, my achievements as a film major at Wesleyan, and a thriving career in public relations couldn't help me.... As a last resort, I'm admitted to the hospital for ECT, electroconvulsive therapy, more commonly known as electroshock.... The doctor presses a button. Electric current shoots through my brain for an instant, causing a grand-mal seizure for 20 seconds.... I wake up 30 minutes later and think I'm in a hotel room in Acapulco. My head feels as if I've just downed a frozen margarita too quickly.... After four treatments, there is marked improvement. No more egregious highs or lows. But there are huge gaps in my memory. I avoid friends and neighbors because I don't know their names anymore. I can't remember the books I've read or the movies I've seen. I have trouble recalling simple vocabulary. I forget phone numbers.... But I continue treatment because I'm getting better.... On the one-year anniversary of my first electroshock treatment, I'm clearheaded and even-keeled. I call my doctor to announce my 'new and improved' status.... Two and a half years later, I still miss ECT. But medication keeps my illness in check, and I'm more sane than I've ever been" (Behrman, 1999, p. 67).

This patient received electroconvulsive therapy (ECT).

Electroconvulsive therapy (ECT) involves placing electrodes on the skull and administering a mild electric current that passes through the brain and causes a seizure. Usual treatment consists of a series of 10 to 12 ECT sessions, at the rate of about three per week.

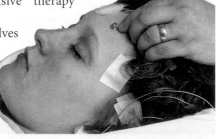

© Photo Researchers, Inc.

Unless otherwise noted, all images are © Cengage Learning

Because antidepressants fail to decrease depression in up to 40% of patients, many of these patients choose to undergo ECT, a last resort option to treat their severe depression. In the United States, ECT is currently used for 100,000 patients per year (Gitlin, 2009; *Newsweek,* 2006; Westly, 2008).

Because antidepressants had not worked, the patient we just described (previous page) agreed to ECT. The reason ECT is the last resort for treating depression is that ECT produces major brain seizures and may cause varying degrees of memory loss (ranging from a loss of memory for events experienced during the weeks of treatment to events both before and after treatment). Following ECT treatment, there is a gradual improvement in memory functions, and for most patients, memory returns to normal levels. However, some patients complain of long-term memory problems (Gitlin, 2009; Sackeim & Stern, 1997).

Even as a last resort treatment option for severe depression, ECT is effective in reducing depressive symptoms in about 70% to 90% of patients (Husain et al., 2004). For example, the right graph shows the results for eight out of nine seriously depressed patients who had received no help from antidepressants. After a series of ECT treatments, they showed a dramatic reduction in depressive symptoms and remained symptom-free after one year (Paul et al., 1981). However, the average relapse rate after ECT treatment exceeds 50%, which means patients may need antidepressant therapy following ECT treatment or additional ECT treatments for depression (Nemeroff, 2007). Researchers are not sure how ECT works but suggest it changes brain chemistry and restores a normal balance to neurotransmitters (Salzman, 2008).

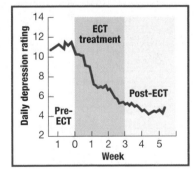

Unlike patients who received ECT in the book *One Flew Over the Cuckoo's Nest,* there is no evidence that modern ECT procedures cause brain damage or turn people into "vegetables" (Ende et al., 2000). Modifications to modern ECT, including the proper placement of electrodes on the scalp and reduced levels of electric current, have lessened the risk for complications (Nemeroff, 2007; Sackeim et al., 2000).

Mental health experts cautiously endorse ECT as a treatment of last resort for severe depression (Glass, 2001; Rasmussen, 2003).

Types of Therapy

Compare psychoanalytic, humanistic, cognitive, behavior, and biomedical therapies.

Electroconvulsive Therapy

Learn more about how electroconvulsive therapy works.

Check Your Learning Quiz 13.8

Go to **login.cengagebrain.com** and take the online quiz.

Think Critically

Challenge Your Thinking

Consider these questions when reading this article:

1. Can virtual-reality therapy be used to treat drug addiction, even though it isn't a fear resulting from a traumatic experience? Explain.
2. What type of DSM-IV-TR disorder is fear of spiders and fear of heights? (See Module 12.4)
3. What are some advantages of virtual-reality therapy over traditional therapy methods?
4. What are some of the physical symptoms you would expect these veterans to exhibit during the reenactment that seems so real? (see Module 12.4)
5. Which type of therapeutic approach and technique is virtual-reality therapy most like?
6. What type of mental health professional(s) would most likely administer virtual-reality therapy?

Can Virtual Reality Be More Than Fun and Games?

Most people experience a traumatic event at some point in their life, but for some, the trauma has lasting effects that interfere with their daily functioning. People who are plagued by nightmares, flashbacks, and constant stress as a result of a traumatic experience, such as abuse, rape, burglary, or watching a person die, are often in desperate need of treatment. For many years, therapists have been working with such clients by helping them confront their fears in a systematic, step-by-step approach.

As you may expect, many clients who have intense fears are reluctant to undergo therapy requiring them to confront the very fear they so badly want to avoid. A relatively new treatment option for these clients is virtual-reality therapy, where they can vividly experience the feared object or situation in a safe and controlled manner. That's right, virtual reality is no longer only about experiencing fun adventures or fantasies. It's a powerful treatment technique. For instance, virtual-reality therapy can help a socially anxious client speak to intimidating crowds of people, or help a client with a phobia of spiders to approach and hold a hideous-looking spider, or even help a client with an intense fear of heights stand on a 30-story building and look straight down.

One of the major advantages of virtual-reality therapy is it can be used when a client's fear is not something a therapist can easily expose him or her to. For this reason, virtual-reality therapy is being used to treat Iraq war veterans diagnosed with PTSD as a result of traumatic combat experiences. These

© AP Images/Ted S. Warren

veterans describe the scene that haunts them, and the therapist uses a computer program to create a virtual environment that consists of the key elements of the reported traumatic experience. The hand-held joystick is used to navigate through the three-dimensional scene, and special goggles help make the scene more real, so real in fact that users feel as though they are back in Iraq. The reenactment takes place on a vibrating platform so the veteran can feel the humming of the tank's motor or the rumbling of explosives being set off. Sounds and smells (such as voices, gunshots, and odors) can be incorporated to add to the realness of the situation. This process is gradual, beginning with only a few elements of the traumatic experience and adding more elements until the scenes become gruesomely realistic,

with images of people getting blown up and terrifying sounds of screaming. The goal is that eventually the veteran can go through an intense re-creation without being overcome with fear.

Because research data on the effectiveness of virtual-reality therapy have been so positive, qualified mental health professionals can now lease software so they can administer treatments in their own offices. The current technology is not nearly as sophisticated as the world portrayed in *The Matrix* trilogy of films, but nevertheless, based on clients' intense reactions, the virtual scenes are realistic enough. (Adapted from Anderson et al., 2005; APA, 2008b; Jardin, 2005; Osborne, 2002; Rizzo et al., 2009; Rizzo, 2008; Rosenthal, 2007; Rothbaum, 2009; Saladin et al., 2006; Williams, 2009)

Think Critically 13.1

This article and its questions are available in interactive format online.

GO to your Psychology CourseMate at login.cengagebrain.com and take the Chapter Post-Test to see which Learning Objectives you've mastered and which need more review. Use the chapter review guide below and the online activities—including flashcards to review key terms—to measure your learning.

Measure
^ Your Learning

Online Activities

Key Terms	Video	Animation	Reading	Assessment
psychotherapy			Conditioned Fear, p. 601	Check Your Learning Quiz 13.1
moral therapy, phenothiazines, deinstitutionalization, community mental health centers			Psychoanalysis, p. 603 Deinstitutionalization and Homelessness, p. 605	Check Your Learning Quiz 13.2
psychiatrists, clinical psychologists, counseling psychologists				Check Your Learning Quiz 13.3
psychoanalysis, neuroses, free association, dream interpretation, transference, resistance, short-term dynamic psychotherapy	Psychoanalysis, p. 611		Beginning of Psychoanalysis, p. 609 Decline in Popularity of Psychoanalysis, p. 613	Check Your Learning Quiz 13.4
humanistic therapy approach; client-centered therapy	Client-Centered Therapy, p. 615			Check Your Learning Quiz 13.5
cognitive therapy	Cognitive Therapy, p. 617			Check Your Learning Quiz 13.6
behavior therapy, systematic desensitization, cognitive-behavior therapy	Behavior Therapy, p. 619	Systemic Desensitization, p. 621	Systematic Desensitization and Unconditioning, p. 621 Cognitive-Behavioral Treatment of Phobias, p. 623	Check Your Learning Quiz 13.7

Measure
^ Your Learning

Online Activities

Key Terms	Video	Animation	Reading	Assessment
common factors, cybertherapy, eye movement desensitization and reprocessing (EMDR), antidepressant drugs, mood-stabilizer drugs, benzodiazepines, neuroleptic drugs, typical neuroleptic drugs, tardive dyskinesia, atypical neuroleptic drugs, deep brain stimulation (DBS), transcranial magnetic stimulation (TMS), electroconvulsive therapy (ECT)	Treating Depression, p. 627 Magnetic Stimulation to the Brain, p. 629 Electroconvulsive Therapy, p. 631	Types of Therapy, p. 631	Research Findings on EMDR, p. 625	Check Your Learning Quiz 13.8

Stress, Health, and Coping

14

Prepare to Learn

1 **GO** to your **Psychology CourseMate** at **login.cengagebrain.com** and take the **Chapter Pre-Test** to introduce yourself to this chapter's topics and see what you may already know.

2 **READ** the **Learning Objectives (LOs)** (in the left sidebars) and begin the chapter.

3 **COMPLETE** the **Online Activities** (in the right sidebars) *as you read each module.* Activities include **videos**, **animations**, **readings**, and **quizzes**.

4 **CHECK Your Learning** by going online to take the quiz at the end of each module and review material as necessary.

5 **MEASURE Your Learning** after reading the chapter by taking the online **Chapter Post-Test**. Use the chapter review guide at the end of the chapter as needed.

WATCH for these **Online Activities** icons as you read:

Video

Animation

Reading

Assessment

Think Critically

These online activities are important to mastering this chapter. As you read each module, access these materials by going to **login.cengagebrain.com**.

Video Explore studies and firsthand accounts of biological and psychological processes:

- See how an individual can overcome the symptoms of PTSD
- Learn what the effects of long-term stress are on a woman's body
- Watch how psychological interventions reduce stress and pain at the doctor's office
- Learn more about the relationship between physical health and psychological stress

Animation Interact with and visualize important processes and concepts:

- Identify the three types of conflict
- Identify the three types of primary appraisals and the two types of coping

Reading Delve deeper into key content:

- Find out how an uplift is the opposite of a hassle
- Learn how people who experience the same situation can make different appraisals
- Explore the physiological and hormonal responses that make up the fight-flight response
- Learn about the use of mind-body therapy
- Explore how Tibetan monks are able to achieve mind-over-body control
- Read about the relationship between locus of control and psychological functioning
- Learn about the differences in use of coping strategy between the sexes across cultures
- Read about how a stress management program helps to reduce levels of stress
- Learn about the role of social support in coping with stress
- Read about the role genes have in a person's long-term happiness

Assessment Measure your mastery:

- Chapter Pre-Test
- Check Your Learning Quizzes
- Chapter Post-Test

Think Critically Challenge your thinking by applying content from this chapter and making connections to related material:

- Coping with Cancer

▸ **LO1** Define stress.

AS YOU APPROACH Brenda Combs's third- and fourth-grade classroom, you hear her enthusiastically lead her students in joyful singing. Brenda has become an extraordinary educator of at-risk children, making a tremendous impact on the lives of her students. But the work is demanding, the hours are long, and the pay is so low she has to also work part-time jobs to make ends meet. She does this all while being a responsible and loving single mother to her son, Mycole, who suffered a massive stroke at birth and requires special care, and being a graduate school student.

▼

Brenda's story is especially impressive because about 10 years ago, she was a homeless crack addict and a petty criminal, who had been shot, beaten, and raped during her years living on the streets. She was fortunate to have escaped many life-threatening moments. Most people would have expected Brenda's life to continue to spiral downward, but Brenda received a wake-up call serious enough to motivate her to drastically improve her life.

The turning point for Brenda was the morning she woke up to find that her shoes had been stolen from her feet as she slept in an alleyway. The day was so scorching hot she couldn't walk anywhere barefoot. But more than shoes were stolen from Brenda that morning—her last shred of dignity was taken, too. At this point, Brenda took complete charge of her life. She is now clean of drugs, lives in a home with her son, and is an inspirational role model to people everywhere (adapted from APB, 2009; Celizic, 2007; Miller, 2007).

Unless otherwise noted, all images are © Cengage Learning

Courtesy of Brenda Combs

For Brenda, her adult life has presented a series of nonstop threatening experiences, which she found to be very stressful.

Stress is the anxious or threatening feeling that comes when we interpret or appraise a situation as being more than our psychological resources can adequately handle (Lazarus, 1999).

To keep her stress from growing out of control, Brenda uses a variety of coping techniques. Spirituality and taking one day at a time are a couple ways she copes. As you can imagine, she must continually guard against being overwhelmed by school, by work, by being a single mother, and by all the other responsibilities of life.

One of the interesting topics we'll discuss in this chapter is the different ways to cope with stress. But first, we'll discuss the types of stressful experiences and responses to stress, as well as personality and health factors associated with stress.

© Cengage Learning 2013

Check Your Learning Quiz 14.1

Go to **login.cengagebrain.com** and take the online quiz.

▶ **LO2** Explain how daily hassles and major life events are stressful experiences that influence mood and psychosomatic problems.

Stressful Experiences

We began this chapter with a description of Brenda's busy day as a single mother, graduate school student, and school teacher. There are countless daily hassles Brenda encounters: managing to be on time to her job and classes, completing her homework and studying, cooking, cleaning, getting her son through the many steps of his day, and managing the behavior of the children in her classroom, to list just a few. Hassles are small stressors, which can add up to make what she would probably call a "bad day."

Courtesy of Brenda Combs

Besides dealing with daily hassles, Brenda has also gone through a number of major life changes: She quit using drugs, became a single mother, and went back to college. Unlike hassles, which seem relatively small, major life events have had a significant impact on Brenda's life and can be very big stressors.

Both hassles and major life events have the potential to become stressful experiences that influence mood and the development of psychosomatic problems.

Hassles

When someone asks, "And how was your day?" people usually reply with a list of hassles.

Hassles are those small, irritating, frustrating events that we face daily and that we usually appraise or interpret as stressful experiences.

For example, a nationwide survey of adults (ages 25 to 74) found the most frequently reported daily hassles involved interpersonal tensions, followed by work-related stressors. The most frequently reported appraisals involved danger (36%), loss (30%), or frustration (27%), and only 2% were appraised as representing opportunity or challenge (Almeida et al., 2002).

Major Life Events

Not only do hassles increase stress levels and predict daily mood and health, but so do major life events.

Major life events are potentially disturbing, troubling, or disruptive situations, both positive and negative, that we appraise as having a significant impact on our lives.

Researchers measure life events using the Social Readjustment Rating Scale (right) (Miller & Rahe, 1997). The number after each event rates the impact that the event would have on one's life; death of one's spouse has the highest rating (119). To obtain your score, add the numbers associated with each event you have experienced in the last year. The total reflects how much life change you have experienced. Researchers predicted that experiencing an increased number of life changes would increase levels of stress and, in turn, increase the chances of developing physical symptoms (such as headaches, stomach problems, muscle pains).

One problem with the Social Readjustment Rating Scale is that it makes no distinction between appraisals of positive events (such as getting married) and negative events (such as

Social Readjustment Rating Scale	
Life event	Mean value
Death of spouse	119
Divorce	98
Death of close family member	92
Fired at work	79
Personal injury or illness	77
Death of a close friend	70
Pregnancy	66
Change in financial state	56
Change in work conditions	51
Marriage	50
Sex difficulties	45
Change in living conditions	42
Change in residence	41
Beginning or ending school	38
Great personal achievement	37
Change in school	35
Trouble with boss	29
Revision of personal habits	27
Change in sleeping habits	26
Vacation	25
Minor violations of the law	22

getting divorced). More recent scales found that the appraisal of negative life events was more important in predicting illnesses or depression than were positive events (Dixon & Reid, 2000; Shimizu & Pelham, 2004).

As we just learned, major life events, such as getting married, moving, beginning college, and losing a job, can cause stress. Most of the time, people adjust to these changes within a few weeks or months. However, in some cases, these life changes may cause people to feel anxious or depressed for many months, which means they have adjustment disorder.

Adjustment disorder is a condition in which a person is unable to cope with or adjust to a major life change. The condition includes emotional symptoms (such as feeling depressed, overwhelmed) and behavioral symptoms (such as avoiding social interaction, performing poorly at school or work, making reckless decisions).

Individuals with adjustment disorder experience an excessive reaction to a life stressor, and their symptoms cause trouble in their daily functioning.

Next, we'll discuss what may happen when a person experiences a major life event that is very traumatic.

Uplifts

Find out how an uplift is the opposite of a hassle.

Traumatic Life Event

Most people experience at least one traumatic situation during their life. About 30% to 50% of children experience at least one traumatic event before they reach 18 (Kazdin, 2008). For some people the experience is so stressful it results in posttraumatic stress disorder (E. J. Ozer et al., 2003).

© David Turnley/Corbis

Posttraumatic stress disorder (PTSD) is a disabling condition that results from personally experiencing an event that involves actual or threatened death or serious injury or from witnessing or hearing of such an event happening to a family member or close friend. People suffering from PTSD experience a number of psychological symptoms, including recurring and disturbing memories, terrible nightmares, and intense fear and anxiety (APA, 2000).

For example, about 32% of women report having PTSD after being raped; about 15% of soldiers report having PTSD after serving in war; and about 20% of people report having PTSD after being in a serious car accident (Elias, 2008a; Hidalgo & Davidson, 2000). These horrible memories and feelings of fear keep stress levels high and result in a range of psychosomatic symptoms, including sleep problems, pounding heart, high blood pressure, and stomach problems (Marshall et al., 2006; Schnurr et al., 2002).

The treatment of posttraumatic stress disorder may involve drugs (such as SSRIs, discussed on p. 626), but some form of cognitive-behavioral therapy (pp. 622–623) has proved more effective in the long term (Bolton et al., 2004). Cognitive-behavioral therapy provides emotional support so victims can begin the healing process, helps to slowly eliminate the horrible memories by bringing out the details of the experience, and gradually replaces the feeling of fear with a sense of courage to go on with life (Harvey et al., 2003; Resick et al., 2008).

In addition to major life events, other situations have the potential to be highly stressful. We'll now turn our attention to frustration, burnout, and conflict.

Frustration

Several years ago, Mariah Carey (next page), a Grammy-winning singer who has sold tens of millions of albums, cancelled all of her public appearances and checked herself

Unless otherwise noted, all images are © Cengage Learning

into a hospital, complaining of "extreme exhaustion." She felt tremendous stress resulting from completing two movies while writing, recording, and producing an album ("Mariah in hospital," 2001). Mariah Carey's example illustrates the difficulties of having a job in which success is judged by how many albums you sell or the number of Grammy awards you win. Having low album sales or not winning an award can be very frustrating.

> Being a pop music star is exhausting.

Frustration is the awful feeling that results when your attempts to reach some goal are blocked.

One reason frustrating situations are especially stressful is that they seem to be beyond your control and they usually elicit strong negative emotions, such as anger or rage (Goldberger & Breznitz, 1993).

If frustration lasts for a long period of time, the result can be burnout.

Burnout

About 5% to 20% of nurses, lawyers, police officers, social workers, managers, counselors, teachers, medical residents, and others whose jobs demand intense involvement with people suffer from burnout (Farber, 2000a, 2000b).

> I'm burnt out after working 10 years in social services.

Burnout refers to being physically overwhelmed and exhausted, finding the job unrewarding, becoming cynical or detached, and developing a strong sense of ineffectiveness and lack of accomplishment in this particular job (Maslach, 2003).

Burnout is accompanied by intense feelings and negative emotions that trigger the fight-flight response, keep the body in a continual state of heightened physiological arousal, and cause many physical symptoms, such as sleep problems, stomach disorders, headaches, and muscle pain (Melamed et al., 2006).

One way to reduce the likelihood of burnout is to take a vacation. Research finds time spent on vacation enhances people's well-being by decreasing their complaints about health problems and exhaustion (Fritz & Sonnentag, 2006).

Next, we'll learn how having to make difficult decisions can be very stressful.

Posttraumatic Stress Disorder

See how an individual can overcome the symptoms of PTSD.

Unless otherwise noted, all images are © Cengage Learning

▶ **LO5** Identify three types of conflict that can cause stress.

▶ **LO6** Explain how stress can be positive.

Conflict

Sometimes situations can be stressful because they involve making difficult decisions. What decisions would you make in the following situations?

- You can go to a party or see a friend who is visiting town for just one day.
- You can study for a psychology exam or write a paper for a history class.
- You can ask a new acquaintance to have lunch, but you risk being rejected.

In making these kinds of decisions, you are most likely to feel stressed because each involves facing a different kind of conflict.

Conflict is the feeling you experience when you must choose between two or more incompatible possibilities or options.

The reason the situations put you in conflict is that, no matter which option you choose, you must give up something you really want to get or you must do something you really want to avoid. We'll describe three common kinds of conflicts: approach-approach, avoidance-avoidance, and approach-avoidance.

Approach-Approach

Deciding between going to a party or seeing a friend involves choosing between two pleasurable options.

Approach-approach conflict involves choosing between two situations that both have pleasurable consequences.

© Laurent Renault/Shutterstock

At first it seems that approach-approach conflicts are the least stressful of the three kinds because, whichever option you choose, you will experience a pleasurable consequence. But, approach-approach conflicts can be the most stressful because you must give up a pleasurable option.

Avoidance-Avoidance

Deciding between studying for a psychology exam or writing a paper for a history class involves choosing between two undesirable options.

Avoidance-avoidance conflict involves choosing between two situations that both have disagreeable consequences.

© Laurent Renault/Shutterstock

In an avoidance-avoidance conflict, you may change your mind many times and wait until the last possible minute before making the final decision. You delay choosing as long as possible in trying to avoid the disagreeable or unpleasant outcome.

Approach-Avoidance

Deciding about asking a new acquaintance to lunch and being afraid of being rejected involves a single situation that has both desirable and undesirable possibilities.

Approach-avoidance conflict involves a single situation that has both pleasurable and disagreeable aspects.

In this example, asking the person to lunch would make you feel good, but at the same time, being rejected is something you want to avoid because it makes you feel bad. Our lives are full of approach-avoidance conflicts, and trying to decide what to do about them can be very stressful.

Situations involving conflict can be very stressful because you must often make undesireable choices. Next, we'll learn about how stress can actually be positive.

Positive Stress

When most people think of stress, negative thoughts immediately come to mind. But did you know that there is a type of stress that is actually healthy and desirable? It's called eustress.

Eustress is a pleasant and desirable type of stress that is healthful and keeps us engaged in situations.

You've likely experienced eustress when purchasing a new car, applying to college, getting a promotion at work, winning first place in a competition, getting married, or having a child.

As a student, you can probably acknowledge that a little bit of stress in school helps motivate you to study. Just imagine if your instructor removed all of the potential stress from the course, such as not requiring you to take exams or not assigning grades! Be honest—how much would you study then?

Eustress arouses and motivates us to achieve and overcome challenges. It is one type of stress we don't want to live without.

Next, we'll learn about how we respond to stress, beginning with our initial evaluation of a situation.

> **I feel great! It was worth the stress!**

Conflict

Identify the three types of conflict.

Check Your Learning Quiz 14.2

Go to **login.cengagebrain.com** and take the online quiz.

▸ **LO7** Discuss the role of primary appraisal in the stress response.

Primary Appraisal

The initial interpretation of a potentially stressful situation is called a primary appraisal (Lazarus, 1999, 2000).

Primary appraisal refers to our initial, subjective evaluation of a situation, in which we balance the demands of a potentially stressful situation against our ability to meet these demands.

For example, think about the following three different primary appraisals when experiencing a racing heart rate. If a doctor gives you medication to treat a headache and says you will initially feel your heart racing, your primary appraisal of your racing heart is that it is irrelevant (your real concern is your headache) and therefore mostly nonstressful. If you're running a marathon and feel your heart beating quickly, your primary appraisal is positive and mostly nonstressful because it makes you feel good. If you're trying to sleep and your heart rate accelerates, your primary appraisal is stressful. Your primary appraisal that a situation is stressful involves three different interpretations: harm/loss, threat, or challenge.

Three Interpretations of Potential Stressors

Harm/Loss

If you broke your arm in a bike accident, you would know that you had suffered harm or loss.

A **harm/loss appraisal** of a situation means that you have already sustained some damage or injury.

Because the harm/loss appraisal elicits negative emotions, such as fear and anxiety, you will feel stressed; the more intense your negative emotions are, the more stressful the situation will seem.

Threat

If you have a terrible fear of giving blood and are asked to do so, you would interpret giving blood as a threat to your well-being.

A **threat appraisal** of a situation means that the harm/loss has not yet taken place but you know it will happen in the near future.

Because a threat appraisal also elicits negative emotions, such as fear, anxiety, and anger, the situation or event may seem especially stressful. In fact, just imagining or anticipating a threatening situation, such as giving blood, can be as stressful as the actual event itself.

Challenge

If you are working hard in college but find you have to take two more classes, you might interpret taking these classes as a way to achieve a goal, an example of a challenge appraisal.

A **challenge appraisal** means you have the potential for gain or personal growth but you also need to mobilize your physical energy and psychological resources to meet the challenging situation.

Because a challenge appraisal elicits positive emotions, such as eagerness, it is usually less stressful than a harm/loss or a threat appraisal.

Situations and Primary Appraisals

Your first reaction to a potentially stressful situation—such as waiting in line, giving blood, making a public speech, dealing with a rude salesperson, taking an exam, or being in a car accident—is to appraise the situation in terms of whether it harms, threatens, or challenges your physical or psychological well-being.

Making primary appraisals about complex situations, such as whether to take a job or get married, may require considerable time as you think over the different ways a situation will affect you. In comparison, making primary appraisals about very emotional situations, such as taking a surprise quiz or getting into a car accident, may occur quickly, even automatically (Lazarus, 2000). However, not all appraisals neatly divide into harm/loss, threat, or challenge. Some primary appraisals are a combination of threat and challenge. For instance, if you are about to ask someone for a first date, you may feel threatened by the possibility of being rejected yet challenged by the chance to prove yourself.

Sequence: Appraisal to Arousal

The first step in feeling stress depends on your primary appraisal. Harm/loss and threat appraisals elicit negative emotions, which, in turn, increase levels of stress. In comparison, challenge appraisals elicit positive emotions, which, in turn, decrease levels of stress. Thus, when you that say a situation is causing you stress, you are forgetting that part of the stress is coming from whether you make a harm/loss or threat appraisal versus a challenge appraisal (Lazarus, 2000). The moment after you make an appraisal, especially a harm/loss or threat appraisal, your body changes from a generally calm state into a state of heightened physiological arousal as it prepares to deal with the stressor.

We'll look inside the body and see what happens when you are stressed.

Same Situation, Different Appraisals

Learn how people who experience the same situation can make different appraisals.

Unless otherwise noted, all images are © Cengage Learning

▶ **LO8** Describe the physiological responses to stress and how these responses influence health.

Fight-Flight Response

Imagine giving a talk in class. As you look at everyone staring at you, you feel your heart pounding, mouth becoming dry, hands sweating, stomach knotting, and muscles tensing; you take in short, rapid breaths. Your body is fully aroused before you have spoken a single word (Tanouye, 1997).

Since speaking in public is no threat to your physical survival and you can neither fight nor flee, why is your body in this state of heightened physiological arousal? The answer is that once you make a primary appraisal that something is a threat—whether it's giving a speech or facing a mugger—these threatening and fearful thoughts automatically trigger one of the body's oldest physiological response systems, the fight-flight response (White & Porth, 2000).

The **fight-flight response** (a) directs great resources of energy to the muscles and the brain; (b) can be triggered by either physical stimuli that threaten our survival or psychological situations that are novel, threatening, or challenging; and (c) involves numerous physiological responses that arouse and prepare the body for action (fight or flight).

We know that the fight-flight response is evolutionarily very old because it can be found in animals such as the alligator, which has been around for millions of years. We presume that our early ancestors evolved a similar fight-flight response to help them survive attacks by wild animals and enemies.

Physical Stimuli

Today you have almost no need to fight wild animals or flee attacking enemies, so you rarely activate your fight-flight response for the reasons important to our early ancestors. However, you would activate the fight-flight response when faced with a potentially dangerous physical stimulus, such as a mugger, accident, police siren, snake, tornado, or other situation that threatened your physical survival.

Psychological Stimuli

Today the most common reason you activate the fight-flight response is exposure to potentially bothersome or stressful psychological stimuli, such as worrying about exams, being impatient in traffic, having to wait in lines, getting angry over a put-down, or arguing with someone (Lazarus, 2000). We'll trace the sequence of how psychological or physical stimuli can trigger the fight-flight response and transform your body into a state of heightened physiological arousal (White & Porth, 2000).

Sequence for Activation of the Fight-Flight Response

1 Appraisal

A number of potentially dangerous physical stimuli, such as seeing a snake or being in an accident, can automatically trigger the fight-flight response. But much more common triggers of the fight-flight response are hundreds of psychological stimuli that you appraise as threatening, such as making a public speech or taking an exam. Thus, either physically or psychologically threatening stimuli can trigger the fight-flight response.

2 Hypothalamus

If you appraise making a public speech as psychologically threatening, these thoughts activate the brain area called the hypothalamus. In turn, the hypothalamus simultaneously activates two stress-related responses: It triggers the pituitary gland to release a stress-fighting hormone called ACTH (adreno-corticotropic hormone), and it activates the sympathetic division of the autonomic nervous system.

3 Sympathetic Division

The autonomic nervous system has two divisions. The sympathetic division, which is activated by the hypothalamus, triggers a number of physiological responses that make up the fight-flight response. In contrast, the parasympathetic division, also activated by the hypothalamus, returns the body to a more calm, relaxed state.

4 Fight-Flight Response

The sympathetic division triggers a very primitive fight-flight response (present in crocodiles), which causes great physiological arousal by increasing heart rate, blood pressure, respiration, and many other responses that prepare the body to deal with an impending threat.

Next, we'll describe what might happen to the body if the fight-flight response is triggered for days, weeks, or months.

Physiological and Hormonal Responses

Explore the physiological and hormonal responses that make up the fight-flight response.

Psychosomatic Symptoms

As a college freshman, Joan was stressed out from having too many classes, spending 28 hours a week on homework, working another 10 hours a week at a part-time job, and not getting enough sleep. Joan is one of the 30% of college students in the United States who reported feeling "frequently overwhelmed" by all they have to do (Sax, 2002). If stress persists for weeks and months, there is a good possibility that you will develop one of a variety of unwanted psychosomatic *(SIGH-ko-so-MAH-tick)* (also called psychophysiological) symptoms (Kemeny, 2003; Selye, 1993).

Psychosomatic symptoms are real and sometimes painful physical symptoms, such as headaches, muscle pains, stomach problems, and increased susceptibility to colds and flu, that are caused by increased physiological arousal that results from psychological factors, such as worry, stress, and anxiety. (The word *psychosomatic* is derived from *psyche* meaning "mind" and *soma* meaning "body.")

"The fact is that we're now living in a world where our bodies aren't allowed a chance to rest . . . they're being driven by inadequate sleep, lack of exercise, by smoking, by isolation or frenzied competition" (McEwen, 2002). Although our bodies are cleverly designed to use the fight-flight response to deal with relatively infrequent stressors, our bodies do need time for rest and relaxation. However, for many, the busy and competitive world is filled with so many stressful situations that they are constantly appraising situations as threatening to their psychological survival and thus giving their bodies little chance to relax (Sapolsky, 2002). The result, as shown in the right figure, is that the constant use of threat appraisals continually triggers the fight-flight response. In turn, the fight-flight response produces a heightened state of physiological arousal that goes on and on and thus increases the risk of developing one or more psychosomatic symptoms (Kemeny, 2003).

We'll discuss different kinds of psychosomatic symptoms, as well as why you may develop one symptom but not others.

1.
Stressful situations

2.
Threat appraisal

3.
Trigger fight-flight

4.
Develop psychosomatic symptoms

Development of Psychosomatic Symptoms

Doctors estimate that 60% to 90% of patients seen in general medical practice have stress-related, psychosomatic symptoms (Benson, 2008). Some of the more common stress-related or psychosomatic symptoms are listed in the figure at right.

Researchers find that whether one develops a psychosomatic symptom, as well as the kind of symptom, depends upon several different factors.

Common Psychosomatic Symptoms
■ **Stomach symptoms:** feelings of discomfort, pain, pressure, or acidity
■ **Muscle pain and tension:** occurring in neck, shoulders, and back
■ **Fatigue:** feeling tired or exhausted without doing physical activity
■ **Headaches:** having either tension or migraine headaches
■ **Intestinal difficulties:** having either constipation or diarrhea
■ **Skin disorders:** exaggerated skin blemishes, pimples, oiliness
■ **Eating problems:** feeling compelled to eat or having no appetite
■ **Insomnia:** being unable to get to sleep or stay asleep
■ **Asthmatic or allergic problems:** worsening of problems
■ **High blood pressure or heart pounding**
■ **Weak immune system and increased chances of getting a cold or flu**

Genetic Predisposition

Because of genetic predispositions, most of us inherit a tendency that targets a particular organ or bodily system for weakening, such as the heart, blood vessels, or immune system. That's why different individuals who are in similar stressful situations experience different kinds of psychosomatic symptoms. For example, some individuals inherit genes that protect their bodies from potentially harmful hormonal effects produced by frequent activation of the fight-flight response. As a result, these individuals may experience fewer psychosomatic symptoms (van Rossum et al., 2002).

Lifestyle

Some lifestyles—such as smoking, being overweight, not exercising, or taking little time for relaxing—promote poor health practices. Such lifestyles give the body little chance to relax and recover from the heightened state of physiological arousal that is produced when the fight-flight response is triggered.

Threat Appraisals

Some of us are more likely to appraise situations as threatening, thus eliciting negative emotions, which automatically trigger the fight-flight response (Kiecolt-Glaser et al., 2002). One solution is to practice changing threat appraisals, which involve negative emotions, into challenge appraisals, which involve positive emotions (Skinner & Brewer, 2002).

Next, we'll examine in more detail how prolonged stressful experiences can affect and break down the body organs.

Women and Stress

Learn what the effects of long-term stress are on a woman's body.

General Adaptation Syndrome

One thing continued stress does is activate the fight-flight response. The continual activation of fight-flight responses results in what Hans Selye (1993) has described as the general adaptation syndrome.

The **general adaptation syndrome** (GAS) refers to the body's reaction to stressful situations during which it goes through a series of three stages—alarm, resistance, and exhaustion—that increase the chances of developing psychosomatic symptoms.

Selye's general adaptation syndrome explains how student Joan, who felt continually overwhelmed, developed a psychosomatic symptom, stomach pain.

1 Alarm Stage

As sleep-deprived Joan worries about having too little time for all she has to do, she appraises that situation as a terrible threat to her well-being, which causes her body to be in the alarm stage.

The **alarm stage** is the initial reaction to stress and is marked by activation of the fight-flight response; in turn, the fight-flight response causes physiological arousal.

Alarm: Initial reaction

Your body may go into and out of the alarm stage (fight-flight response) many times during the day as stressful experiences come and go. Normally, you do not develop psychosomatic problems during the alarm stage because the fight-flight responses come and go. However, if stress continues for a longer period of time, your body goes into the resistance stage.

2 Resistance Stage

As the semester comes to an end, Joan's continual feelings of being overwhelmed cause almost continual fight-flight responses, which in turn cause her body to go into the resistance stage.

The **resistance stage** is the body's reaction to continued stress, during which most of the physiological responses return to normal levels but the body uses up great stores of energy.

Resistance: Fighting back

During the resistance stage, Joan's body will use up vital reserves of hormones, minerals, and glucose (blood sugar) because her body is almost continually in the fight-flight state. Joan doesn't realize that the resistance stage is taking a toll on her stomach by interfering with digestion and causing stomach pain. If her stress continues, her body will go into the exhaustion stage, and her psychosomatic symptom will worsen.

3 Exhaustion Stage

As Joan's feeling of being overwhelmed continues over many weeks, her body may enter the exhaustion stage.

The **exhaustion stage** is the body's reaction to long-term, continuous stress and is marked by actual breakdown in internal organs or weakening of the infection-fighting immune system.

During the exhaustion stage, Joan's stomach problems may become more serious. Extended periods of stress, such as during final exams, may cause your body to go into the stage of resistance or exhaustion. During this time, you may develop a variety of psychosomatic symptoms, such as a cold, flu, cold sore, sore throat, allergy attack, aching muscles, or stomach problems. For example, researchers found that individuals who had prolonged and high levels of anxiety, signaling stages of resistance and exhaustion, were more likely to develop physical health problems than those with normal levels (Hoge et al., 2007).

As you'll see, psychosomatic symptoms develop because of a mind-body interaction.

Exhaustion: Breakdown in organs

Mind-Body Connection

Earlier in this module, you learned that after a prolonged period of fearful or anxious thoughts that continually trigger the fight-flight response, a breakdown in body organs and development of psychosomatic symptoms may occur (Hoge et al., 2007). This is a perfect example of the mind-body connection.

The **mind-body connection** refers to how your thoughts, beliefs, and emotions can produce physiological changes that may be either beneficial or detrimental to your health and well-being.

The mind-body connection is involved in the prevention as well as the development and maintenance of psychosomatic symptoms. More unexpectedly, the mind-body connection is involved in the strengthening or weakening of our immune system, which is the next topic.

Mind-Body Therapy

Learn about the use of mind-body therapy.

Tibetan Monks

Explore how Tibetan monks are able to achieve mind-over-body control.

Reducing Pain at the Doctor's Office

Watch how psychological interventions reduce stress and pain at the doctor's office.

▶ **LO11** Summarize the major findings in the scientific field of psychoneuroimmunology.

Immune System

How often have you gotten a cold, strep throat, or some other bacterial or viral infection when final exams were over? This rather common experience of "coming down with something" when exams are over indicates how prolonged stressful experiences can decrease the effectiveness of your immune system.

The **immune system** is the body's defense and surveillance network of cells and chemicals that fight off bacteria, viruses, and other foreign or toxic substances.

For many years, researchers believed that the immune system was a totally independent bodily system with no input from the brain. However, in the mid-1970s, a psychologist and an immunologist found the first good evidence of a mind-body connection—that psychological factors, such as one's thoughts, influenced the immune system (Ader & Cohen, 1975). Their research led to the development of a new area of medical science that is called psychoneuroimmunology *(SIGH-ko-NOOR-oh-im-you-NAH-luh-gee)*.

Psychoneuroimmunology

Researchers Ader and Cohen (1975) were trying to figure out why some of their rats were dying so young when they chanced upon one of the important scientific discoveries of the 1970s. Previously, immunologists believed the immune system operated independently of psychological influences. Then, to the surprise of all and the disbelief of many, Ader and Cohen reported that psychological factors influenced the immune system's functioning. Today, no one doubts their findings, which launched the field of psychoneuroimmunology (Ader, 2007).

Psychoneuroimmunology is the study of the relationship among three factors: the central nervous system (brain and spinal cord), the endocrine system (network of glands that secrete hormones), and psychosocial factors (stressful thoughts, personality traits, and social influences).

For example, coming down with an illness (such as a cold or flu) after a stressful time results from the interactions among three factors: central nervous system, endocrine system, and psychosocial factors. These three factors can suppress or strengthen the immune system and in turn make the body more or less susceptible to disease and infection (Kiecolt-Glaser et al., 2002).

© Digital Stock Corporation

Unless otherwise noted, all images are © Cengage Learning

The immune system has several ways to kill foreign invaders. In the right photo, an immune system cell sends out a footlike extension to engulf and destroy the small bacterial cell (inside the white oval).

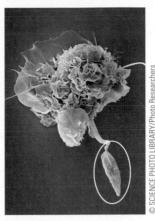

As the scientific field of psychoneuroimmunology progressed, researchers were faced with a difficult question: Why doesn't everyone who is exposed to a disease virus or bacteria actually get the disease? They tackled this question by giving the same amount of cold virus to 394 subjects, all of whom were quarantined for a week. During this period, the researchers checked for symptoms of colds and related the percentage of colds to the levels of stress that subjects had reported before they received the virus. As shown in the graph below, individuals who reported high levels of psychological stress were more likely to develop colds than were those who reported low stress levels. Researchers concluded that, with every increase in psychological stress, there is an increased likelihood of developing a cold, provided we are exposed to the cold virus (Cohen, 2003; Cohen et al., 1997).

Subjects with Colds (%)	
Subjects reporting HIGH psychological stress	48%
Subjects reporting LOW psychological stress	38%

While short-term stress (such as exam stress or traffic) can weaken the immune system, chronic stress (such as relationship conflict or unemployment) has even more severe effects on our health (Segerstrom & Miller, 2004). People who experience chronic stress are more prone to illness because they are continually activating their fight-flight response. When the fight-flight response is activated, your body produces stress hormones, which suppress the immune system and make the body more susceptible to diseases, viruses, and other infections (Ebrecht et al., 2004; Kiecolt-Glaser, 2008).

Health and Stress

Learn more about the relationship between physical health and psychological stress.

Check Your Learning Quiz 14.3

Go to **login.cengagebrain.com** and take the online quiz.

▶ **L012** Describe how hardiness contributes to health.

▶ **L013** Distinguish between external and internal locus of control, and describe their influence on health.

Now, we turn our focus to examining how different kinds of personality variables can help or hinder our experience of stress and ultimately, our health.

Hardiness

Shaun White, nicknamed the "Flying Tomato" for his long, curly red hair, has never been an ordinary athlete. At the age of 6, he began skateboarding on a ramp in his backyard, and he practiced snowboarding during family trips to the mountains. By the time Shaun was 13 years old, he became a pro skateboarder and snowboarder. At age 19, he became the first athlete to compete in both the summer and winter X Games. Shaun always strives to do his very best, even under the most stressful situations. He does not allow the pressure of heated competition or the setback of an awkward landing to compromise his determination to win. Shaun's ability to handle extreme stress became most evident when he won an Olympic gold medal in 2006 (Ruibal, 2006; "Shaun White," 2006).

© JoeKlamar/AFP/Getty Images

Shaun White stays healthy in spite of stressful life situations because he ranks high in hardiness.

Hardiness is a combination of three personality traits—control, commitment, and challenge—that protect or buffer us from the potentially harmful effects of stressful situations and reduce our chances of developing psychosomatic illnesses.

Shaun White is a great example of a hardy person who has the three Cs: control, commitment, and challenge. His disciplined practicing shows he has commitment to his goal of being a snowboarding legend; his participation in the Olympics shows he likes a challenge; and his determination to come back more focused after even the slightest error indicates his desire to be in control (Maddi, 2008).

Hardiness is a personality factor that increases protection against stress and decreases the chances of developing psychosomatic symptoms. Being hardy motivates people like Shaun White to see stressors as opportunities for growth, which gives them a real edge in dealing with potentially stressful situations (Bonanno, 2004; Maddi, 2008).

Next, we'll discuss what researchers have learned by studying control, one of the three traits in hardiness.

Unless otherwise noted, all images are © Cengage Learning

Locus of Control

A daily hassle that most of us hate is having to wait for something or somebody. One reason waiting can be so stressful is that we have little or no control in this situation. How much control you feel you have over a situation is a personal belief that is called locus of control.

Locus of control represents a continuum: At one end is the belief that you are basically in control of life's events and that what you do influences the situation; this belief is called an internal locus of control. At the other end is the belief that chance and luck mostly determine what happens and that you do not have much influence; this belief is called an external locus of control.

Most of us lie somewhere along this continuum, rather than being at one end or the other (Carducci, 2006). For example, when students discuss how much their studying affects their grades, they are in part talking about their locus of control, which in turn affects their stress level.

External Locus of Control

"No matter how much I study, it never seems to help," says the student with an external locus of control. This student will likely appraise exams and papers as less of a challenge and more of a threat, which in turn will generate negative emotions (such as fear, anxiety, or anger) and increase stress levels.

What's the use of studying when I do poorly on exams?

© PhotoDisc, Inc.

Internal Locus of Control

"If I study hard and apply myself, I can get good grades," says the student with an internal locus of control. This student will likely appraise exams and papers less as threats and more as challenges, which in turn will generate positive emotions (such as excitement and enthusiasm) and decrease stress levels. This means that students with internal locus of control have lower levels of stress and, as a result, report fewer psychosomatic symptoms than those with external locus of control (Ruiz-Bueno, 2000).

Another personality trait that can influence stress levels is how pessimistic or optimistic we generally are.

Studying 15 hours a week will lead to better grades.

© Erik Isakson/Age fotostock

Locus of Control and Psychological Functioning

Read about the relationship between locus of control and psychological functioning.

▶ **LO14** Distinguish between optimism and pessimism, and describe their influence on health.

▶ **LO15** Define self-efficacy and desribe its influence on health.

Optimism Versus Pessimism

If you want to experience more positive than negative emotions and reduce your levels of stress, try being more optimistic.

Optimism is a relatively stable personality trait that leads to believing and expecting that good things will happen.

Pessimism is a relatively stable personality trait that leads to believing and expecting that bad things will happen.

I'm an optimist and believe that good things will happen.

© Vorpal Images/Shutterstock

Optimists

One way optimists reduce stress is by focusing on the good things, a process called *positive reappraisal*. Forms of positive reappraisal include discovering new opportunities for personal growth, noticing actual personal growth, and seeing how your actions can benefit others. By using positive reappraisal, you can change the meaning of situations to seem more positive and thus feel positive emotions (Folkman & Moskowitz, 2000). In fact, individuals who perceive themselves as in control (that is, those who have an internal locus of control) are more likely to have an optimistic attitude in dealing with stressors (Klein & Helweg-Larsen, 2002). Generally, optimists cope more effectively with stress and experience more positive emotions and fewer psychosomatic symptoms than pessimists (Nes & Segerstrom, 2006; Taylor et al., 2000).

Pessimists

I'm a pessimist and believe that bad things will happen.

Because pessimists expect bad things to happen, they are likely to change the meaning or appraisal of situations to seem more negative and thus experience more negative emotions, such as anger, rage, fear, or anxiety. For example, researchers found that men with high levels of negative emotions were four times more likely to suffer sudden heart death. In comparison, optimistic patients who received heart transplants reported more positive emotions and dealt better with setbacks than patients with more pessimistic outlooks (Leedham et al., 1995). Numerous studies associate pessimism and negative emotions with increasing stress levels, decreasing functioning of the immune system, and a wide range of psychosomatic symptoms such as high blood pressure, heart problems, and headaches (Vahtera et al., 2000).

© PhotoDisc, Inc.

Another characteristic that affects our experience of stress is how much we believe in our own capabilities.

Unless otherwise noted, all images are © Cengage Learning

Self-Efficacy

Students often share with us how stressed they are when it comes to getting good grades, and ask about how to improve their grades. According to Albert Bandura (2004), one reason students differ in whether they receive high or low grades is self-efficacy.

Why do my friends say that I should be getting better grades?

Self-efficacy refers to the confidence in your ability to organize and execute a given course of action to solve a problem or accomplish a task.

You judge your self-efficacy by combining four sources of information (Bandura, 1999; Higgins & Scholer, 2008):

1. You use previous experiences of success or failure on similar tasks to estimate how you will do on a new, related task.
2. You compare your capabilities with those of others.
3. You listen to what others say about your capabilities.
4. You use feedback from your body to assess your strength, vulnerability, and capability.

You would rate yourself as having strong self-efficacy for getting good grades if you had previous success with getting high grades, if you believe you are as academically capable as others, if your friends say you are smart, and if you do not become too stressed during exams.

Higher levels of self-efficacy are associated with the ability to effectively manage stress (Maciejewski et al., 2000). Also, according to Bandura's self-efficacy theory, your motivation to achieve, perform, and do well in a variety of tasks and situations is largely influenced by how strongly you believe in your own capabilities. People with higher self-efficacy have been shown to have greater success at stopping smoking, losing weight, overcoming a phobia, recovering from a heart attack, performing well in school, adjusting to new situations, coping with job stress, and tolerating pain (Caprara et al., 2004; Joseph et al., 2003; Luszczynska & Sutton, 2006). These findings indicate that having either high or low self-efficacy influences stress levels, and can increase or decrease your performance and success in various tasks and personal behaviors.

Next, we'll discuss two particular combinations of personality traits, which are associated with increasing stress and increasing chances of having a heart attack.

▶ **LO16** Distinguish between Type A and Type D personalities, and describe their influence on health.

Type A Behavior

In the mid-1970s, a new expression—"You're a Type A person"—was coined when two doctors published the book *Type A Behavior and Your Heart* (Friedman & Rosenman, 1974). This book startled the medical world by describing a combination of personality traits that made up a psychological risk factor, which was called Type A behavior.

1970s: Type A Behavior—Impatient, Hostile, Workaholic

We'll begin with the original 1970s definition of Type A behavior (Friedman & Rosenman, 1974).

Type A behavior referred to a combination of personality traits that included an overly competitive and aggressive drive to achieve, a hostile attitude when frustrated, a habitual sense of time urgency, a rapid and explosive pattern of speaking, and being a workaholic.

The reason Type A behavior made such a big scientific splash was because it was associated with an increase in risk of having heart attacks. By 1978, Type A behavior was officially recognized as an independent risk factor for heart disease. However, at about the same time that Type A behavior was declared a risk factor, researchers began having trouble replicating earlier findings and began to seriously question the definition of Type A behavior.

1980s–1990s: Type A Behavior—Depressed, Angry

In the 1980s, research did not support the association between coronary disease and being impatient or a workaholic; those traits were then dropped from the new definition of Type A behavior.

Type A behavior was defined in the 1980s as being depressed, easily frustrated, anxious, and angry, or some combination of these traits.

Despite using this new and improved definition, a review of many studies between 1983 and 1992 led one researcher to conclude that the relationship between Type A behavior and cardiac disease is so weak as to have no practical meaning (Myrtek, 1995). Because of the continuing failure to replicate the original relationship, researchers again redefined Type A behavior.

The 1990s definition of **Type A behavior** specifies an individual who feels angry and hostile much of the time but may or may not express these emotions publicly.

This definition made prolonged hostility or anger (felt or expressed) the major component of Type A behavior (Leventhal & Patrick-Miller, 2000). Research indicates that angry/hostile individuals are three times more likely to have heart attacks, and individuals who are quick to anger under stress are five times more likely to develop a premature heart disease (Smith, 2003). Researchers concluded that individuals who either always show their anger/hostility or always suppress it have large increases in physiological arousal, which can have damaging effects on one's heart and one's health (Finney, 2003).

Type D Behavior

In his work with cardiac patients, Johan Denollet, a psychologist, noticed that some heart-attack survivors remained happy and optimistic, while others became discouraged and pessimistic. He went on to describe a set of behaviors, called Type D Behavior, which he believed predicted health risk (Miller, 2005).

2000s: Type D Behavior—Chronic Distress: Negative Affectivity, Social Inhibition

Type D behavior is defined as chronic distress in terms of two emotional states: negative affectivity (such as worry, irritability or gloom) and social inhibition (such as being shy and reserved, or lacking self-assurance).

People with Type D behavior tend to experience negative emotions and inhibit self-expression in social interactions. Their chronic distress and lack of strong social support help explain why they are at an increased risk for various health problems (Pelle et al., 2009; Williams et al., 2008). For instance, Type D behavior is associated with greater cortisol reactivity to stress and consequently increased risk for coronary artery disease (Sher, 2004). Research on patients who had recently received stents to open their coronary arteries showed Type D patients were four times as likely as others to have a heart attack or die within 6 to 9 months of the procedure (Miller, 2005).

Even though research supports the link between Type D behavior and health problems, Type D behavior is a relatively new concept and needs more research to better determine its impact on health conditions (Miller, 2005).

The next module discusses how to successfully cope with stress.

Check Your Learning Quiz 14.4

Go to **login.cengagebrain.com** and take the online quiz.

▶ **LO17** Discuss the role of secondary appraisal in the stress response.

▶ **LO18** Compare and contrast problem-focused and emotion-focused coping.

Secondary Appraisal

Sooner or later, every couple gets into an argument. In this case, Susan complained that Bill always got home late, but Bill had had a bad day and said that he didn't want to talk about it. Bill's reply angered Susan, who complained more, which made Bill quieter and madder. One reason Bill and Susan's argument quickly became very stressful was that each one made a primary appraisal of being threatened, which elicited negative emotions and triggered the

fight-flight response, which in turn increased physiological arousal and further intensified their negative feelings. How Bill and Susan deal with their stressful situation depends on what kind of secondary appraisal they make next (Lazarus, 2000).

Secondary appraisal involves deciding to deal with a potentially stressful situation by using one or both of two different coping patterns: Problem-focused coping means doing something about the particular problem, while emotion-focused coping means dealing with one's negative feelings.

Kinds of Coping

Which coping strategy Bill and Susan use to deal with their stressful situation—that is, whether they use problem-focused or emotion-focused coping—will affect how their argument gets resolved and what happens to their levels of stress.

If Bill or Susan tried to decrease the stress by stopping the argument and making up, he or she would be using problem-focused coping.

Problem-focused coping means we try to decrease stress by solving the problem through seeking information, changing our own behavior, or taking whatever action is needed to resolve the difficulty.

For example, if Bill agreed to talk about ways of not being late, he would be using problem-focused coping. If Susan agreed to interpret Bill's being late as something he cannot always control and something not to get angry about, she would be using problem-focused coping. The goal of problem-focused coping is to reduce stress by solving the problem.

Another coping strategy that Bill and Susan might use to decrease stressful feelings is called emotion-focused coping.

Emotion-focused coping means that we do things primarily to deal with our emotional distress, such as seeking support and sympathy or avoiding or denying the situation.

For example, Bill may use emotion-focused coping to get over his anger by going to a bar to drink and watch television with the "boys." Susan may use emotion-focused coping to deal with her hurt feelings by calling her friends to talk about what happened and get advice and support.

In the short term, emotion-focused coping may help Bill and Susan deal with their negative emotions, but it doesn't usually solve the basic stressful problem, which means the problem will likely reoccur and cause more stress (Lazarus, 2000). In contrast, a big advantage of using problem-focused coping is that it's a long-term coping strategy, which can help identify and solve the underlying problem that is causing the stressful and negative emotional feelings. In addition, compared to using emotion-focused coping, using problem-focused coping is positively correlated with having and maintaining good physical and mental health (Largo-Wight et al., 2005; Penley et al., 2002).

Choosing a Coping Strategy

Which coping strategy you choose depends partly on the situation and on your personality. For example, one personality factor that influences whether you use primarily problem-focused or emotion-focused coping is how much control you believe you have over the situation. If you appraise a situation (for example, being late) as something under your control, you can use primarily problem-focused coping to solve this problem. On the other hand, if you appraise a situation (for example, dealing with your partner's complaints) as being out of your control, you may first use emotion-focused coping to get over your negative emotions (anger). Once you calm down, you can use problem-focused coping to take some direct action to solve the basic problem (being late), which may involve changing some undesirable behavior (being disorganized). The more frustrating a situation is, the more likely you will need to use both emotion-focused coping and problem-focused coping (Lazarus, 2000).

Next, we'll discuss how changing your way of thinking can be a very effective way to reduce stress.

Primary and Secondary Appraisals

Identify the three types of primary appraisals and the two types of coping.

Sex Differences in Use of Coping Strategy

Learn about the differences in use of coping strategy between the sexes across cultures.

► **LO19** Describe ways to change thinking to more effectively manage stress.

Healthy Thinking

Many daily hassles (such as dealing with long lines, slow traffic, rude people, loud neighbors, and sloppy roommates) can be made more or less stressful depending on how you appraise these situations. Since your appraisal of a situation as threatening or challenging is related to increasing or decreasing your stress levels, it follows that an effective way to decrease stressful experiences is to work at changing how you initially appraise a situation (Lazarus, 2000). We'll explain two effective strategies for changing your appraisals: thinking of potentially stressful situations as challenging rather than threatening and changing negative self-statements into positive ones.

Use Challenge Appraisals

The reason you want to think of or appraise potentially stressful situations as challenging rather than threatening is that threat appraisals elicit negative emotions (such as fear, anxiety, depression), which in turn raise stress levels, while challenge appraisals elicit positive emotions, which lower stress levels. For example, students who emphasize threat appraisals of exams, such as thinking they will not have time to study or expecting to do poorly, are more likely to experience negative emotions, such as anxiety and fear (Shannon, 1994). In turn, anxiety and fear trigger the fight-flight response, which raises the level of stress and often leads to emotion-focused coping, such as complaining, seeking sympathy, or avoiding studying. However, emotion-focused coping does not usually motivate actions, such as studying, that are needed to prepare students for exams.

In comparison, students who emphasize challenge appraisals of exams, such as wanting to do their best or to prove themselves, are more likely to experience positive emotions, such as excitement or eagerness, which decrease levels of stress. In turn, challenge appraisals are more likely to result in problem-focused coping, which means taking direct action to deal with the situation itself, such as developing a study program.

Thus, a good way to deal with potentially stressful situations is to focus on challenging rather than threatening appraisals (Skinner & Brewer, 2002).

Unless otherwise noted, all images are © Cengage Learning

© PhotoDisc, Inc.

I see life as one big challenge!

Substitute Positive Self-Statements

Another way to prevent a situation, such as taking an exam, from becoming more stressful is to work at removing negative self-statements by substituting positive ones. Specifically, on one side of a sheet of paper write your negative self-statements; then next to them on the other side write the positive ones that you can substitute. The example below shows negative self-statements changed into positive ones.

Negative self-statements	Positive self-statements
"I know I'll do badly."	*"I know I can do OK."*
"I always get so anxious."	*"I'm going to stay calm."*
"I'm not smart enough."	*"I've got plenty of ability."*
"I'm never going to learn it."	*"I can learn the material."*

The reason you want to avoid making negative self-statements is that they elicit negative emotions (such as fear, anger, or anxiety), which increase stress levels. By substituting positive self-statements, which elicit positive emotions, you can decrease stress levels. For example, each time you begin to think of a negative self-statement, stop yourself and substitute a positive one. For regularly occurring stressors, such as taking exams, waiting in lines, fighting with traffic, and dealing with rude people, it is best to have prepared a different list of self-statements to go with each different situation. Researchers found that a program of substituting positive self-statements proved very effective in helping people change their thought patterns and reduce their stress levels (Spiegler & Guevremont, 2009).

We can also reduce stress by changing our behaviors and learning to relax.

I believe I can.
I believe I can.
I believe I can.

Stress Management Program

Read about how a stress management program helps to reduce levels of stress.

Changing Behaviors

Students generally get ready for exams in one of two different ways. Some students prepare for an exam by complaining about how much work there is, making excuses about not studying, or blaming the instructor for too much material. These behaviors involve emotion-focused coping, which in the short term reduces stress by decreasing negative emotional feelings. However, in the long run, students may need to change these behaviors and engage in problem-focused coping, which means developing a study plan (Skinner & Brewer, 2002).

If a student is using primarily emotion-focused coping (such as making excuses, procrastinating, or blaming others), he or she will likely do poorly on exams. Instead, a student needs to start a program of problem-focused coping (such as making a study program or rewriting class notes) by using some of the self-reward and behavior modification techniques that we discussed in Chapter 5 (Spiegler & Guevremont, 2009). Thus, one way to reduce stress is to change your behaviors (that is, to emphasize problem-focused over emotion-focused activities).

Learning to Relax

Learning to relax allows your body to turn off the fight-flight response and decrease your heightened physiological arousal. We'll describe three techniques that have proved almost equally effective at getting people to relax, and each involves using one's mind to control one's body's responses (Shapiro et al., 2000).

Biofeedback

You could learn a relaxing response, such as decreasing muscle tension, by having small sensors placed on your forehead. The sensors are attached to a machine that records, amplifies, and displays changes in muscle tension. Each time you think thoughts or images that increase tension, you hear a high tone; if you decrease tension, you hear a low tone. This procedure is called biofeedback.

Biofeedback refers to voluntarily learning to control physiological responses, such as muscle activity, blood pressure, or temperature, by recording and displaying these responses (Spiegler & Guevremont, 2003).

After 12 to 30 biofeedback training sessions (about 20 minutes per session), most individuals have some success in turning on relaxing responses.

Progressive Relaxation

Progressive relaxation involves practicing tensing and relaxing the major muscle groups of the body until you are able to relax any groups of muscles at will.

With progressive relaxation, you usually begin by first tensing and relaxing your toes and then continuing up the body, tensing and relaxing the muscles of your calves, thighs, pelvis, stomach, shoulders, arms, hands, neck, face, and forehead.

After several weeks of daily practice, about 20 minutes per session, you would be able to use this exercise to relax your body at will, especially immediately after being stressed.

Meditation

We'll discuss one popular type of mediation.

Transcendental meditation (TM) involves assuming a comfortable position, closing your eyes, and repeating a sound or concentrating on your breathing so that you clear your head of all thoughts, worrisome and otherwise.

Because meditation involves removing all worrisome or stressful thoughts and replacing them with peaceful ones, it can be an effective method for relaxing and reducing stress. Research on the benefits of meditation for stress management is so conclusive that many hospitals and medical clinics are teaching meditation to their patients. Meditation also provides some relief from anxiety and depression, and improved alertness, focus, and memory (Andrews, 2005; Lazar et al., 2005; Peng, 2008a).

Learning to use meditation to relax at will usually requires practicing about 20 minutes a day for many weeks (Stein, 2003).

Our last topic in this chapter is about the exciting and relatively new area of scientific study focused on optimal human functioning called positive psychology.

© Photosindia/Getty Images

Social Support

Learn about the role of social support in coping with stress.

▶ **LO22** Describe positive psychology and discuss some of its major research findings.

Positive Psychology

Sherrod Ballentine has a stressful job as a court mediator, and although she's not clinically depressed, she wants to learn ways to improve her mood. She takes a class called "Authentic Happiness and How to Obtain It" and learns activities that will train her mind to focus more on the positive. One activity Sherrod learns is to write down three happy events and their causes at the end of each day for a week. After completing the class, she said, "I am happier. Every day, I feel so grateful to wake up this way" (Lemley, 2006). Sherrod's new learned skills are based on positive psychology.

Positive psychology is the scientific study of optimal human functioning, focusing on the strengths and virtues that enable individuals and communities to thrive. It aims to better understand the positive, adaptive, and fulfilling aspects of human life.

Positive psychology has three main concerns. The first is the study of positive emotions, such as happiness, hope, love, and contentment. The second is the study of positive individual traits, such as altruism, courage, compassion, and resilience. The third is the study of positive institutions, or the strengths that promote better communities, such as justice, parenting, tolerance, and teamwork (Seligman, 2003).

One theoretical model states that positive emotions and positive traits enhance health by pushing away negative ones. For instance, it is difficult to be angry or bitter when one is showing compassion and love for others (Anderson, 2003).

Many research examples show that characteristics of positive psychology have a beneficial impact on mood and physical health. For example, research data on altruism and its relationship to mental and physical health found that volunteering and other supportive behaviors (such as providing emotional support to others) are associated with higher life satisfaction, as well as better physical and mental health (Post, 2005). Also, research on writing exercises, such as the one Sherrod did, shows impressive results. One study found that after writing about positive experiences for 20 minutes each day for 3 consecutive days, college students reported improved mood and had fewer health center visits for illness in the following months (Burton & King, 2004).

Unless otherwise noted, all images are © Cengage Learning

Positive psychology has shown us that the benefits of improved mood are endless. Let's consider what factors contribute to happiness and the many benefits of being a happy person. Researchers find that happiness is not a fixed state and does not primarily result from getting more money, cars, clothes, or promotions, because these achievements gradually lose their emotional appeal, as predicted by the adaptation level theory. Rather, being happy is a continuous process associated with making an effort to enjoy simple, daily pleasurable events, people, or situations. It includes a daily diet of little highs, as well as pursuing personal goals, developing a sense of meaningfulness, having intimate relationships, and not judging yourself against what others do but by your own yardstick (Lykken, 2003; Seligman, 2002).

The benefits of being happy are evident as researchers find that happy people report having more friends, more satisfying marriages, higher incomes, healthier lifestyles, and longer lives than their unhappy peers (Frey, 2011; Hales, 2008).

Happiness is an example of only one small area of research within the growing field of positive psychology. One reason there is an increasing interest in positive psychology is that it provides a refreshing and much needed change from the tendency of researchers in psychology to focus more on problems or weaknesses than on strengths or virtues.

© PEOPLESTOCK RF/Alamy

Long-Term Happiness

Read about the role genes have in a person's long-term happiness.

Check Your Learning Quiz 14.5

Go to **login.cengagebrain.com** and take the online quiz.

Think Critically

Challenge Your Thinking

Consider these questions when reading this article:

1. After Lance noticed his right testicle was swollen, which Freudian defense mechanism did he use to deal with this potentially damaging news, and what was his primary appraisal of the situation? (See Module 11.2)
2. Which kinds of personality traits help Lance cope with the stress of knowing that he has cancer?
3. Why was it good news that his family and friends kept calling and visiting?
4. Which type of coping is Lance using by educating himself about cancer?
5. Which Freudian defense mechanism(s) was Lance using during treatment? (See Module 11.2)
6. How did Lance cope with cancer near the end of his treatment and also now that he has survived cancer?

Coping with Cancer

At age 25, world-renowned cyclist Lance Armstrong was training rigorously and cycling better than ever. His training schedule resulted in his legs, feet, back, neck, and just about every other body part being in pain. So he didn't pay much attention when he noticed his right testicle was slightly swollen. Soon, he began to feel much more tired than usual. Then he began having vision trouble, and one morning he coughed up blood. He could no longer pretend something wasn't wrong.

Doctors diagnosed Lance with testicular cancer that had spread to his abdomen, lungs, and brain. When he first heard his doctor say, "You have cancer," his fear became very real. Lance had third-degree testicular cancer (the most serious kind), and he was given less than a 40% chance of surviving. He would have surgery to remove his right testicle and brain lesions, followed by months of chemotherapy.

After leaving the doctor's office, Lance shared his diagnosis with family and friends. He received an overwhelming amount of support as his friends and family routinely called and visited.

Lance also began learning as much as he could about cancer, what it is and how it is treated. He even began seeking second, third, and fourth medical opinions. Learning more about cancer provided him with some reassurance and comfort.

Lance felt so anxious about his diagnosis and treatment that he blocked out memory of what he thought and felt the morning of his risky brain surgery. In the midst of chemotherapy, he kept cycling, wanting to believe that if he could continue to cycle, then somehow he wouldn't be sick. Eventually, Lance became so weak from chemotherapy he could barely walk. Then, instead of feeling hopeless, he chose to believe in his doctors and in his treatment. He began to envision himself overcoming cancer.

Today, Lance Armstrong is a cancer survivor. He now seizes each day as an opportunity to enjoy his life. Since his recovery, he won the Tour de France—the 2,290-mile road race that's considered the single most grueling sporting event in the world—a record seven consecutive times! When asked about his trying experience with cancer, he said, "The truth is that cancer was the best thing that ever happened to me. I don't know why I got the illness, but it did wonders for me, and I wouldn't want to walk away from it. Why would I want to change,

© Robert Laberge/Getty Images

even for a day, the most important and shaping event in my life?" (Armstrong, 2001, p. 4).

Lance is now trying to make a change in the lives of others. He accomplishes this by being a role model to people all over the world and by being a passionate advocate for better cancer research and treatment to improve the experiences of people who have cancer. Lance is definitely a fighter while on his bicycle, and he's no different when it comes to doing everything he can to help find the cure for cancer. (Adapted from Armstrong, 2001, 2007; Hutchinson, 2009)

Think Critically 14.1

This article and its questions are available in interactive format online.

Measure ^ Your Learning

GO to your Psychology CourseMate at login.cengagebrain.com and take the Chapter Post-Test to see which Learning Objectives you've mastered and which need more review. Use the chapter review guide below and the online activities—including flashcards to review key terms—to measure your learning.

Online Activities

Key Terms	Video	Animation	Reading	Assessment
stress				Check Your Learning Quiz 14.1
hassles, major life events, adjustment disorder, post-traumatic stress disorder, frustration, burnout, conflict, approach-approach conflict, avoidance-avoidance conflict, approach-avoidance conflict, eustress	Posttraumatic Stress Disorder, p. 647	Conflict, p. 649	Uplifts, p. 645	Check Your Learning Quiz 14.2
primary appraisal, harm/loss appraisal, threat appraisal, challenge appraisal, fight-flight response, psychosomatic symptoms, general adaptation syndrome, alarm stage, resistance stage, exhaustion stage, mind-body connection, immune system, psychoneuroimmunology	Women and Stress, p. 655 Reducing Pain at the Doctor's Office, p. 657 Health and Stress, p. 659		Same Situation, Different Appraisals, p. 651 Physiological and Hormonal Responses, p. 653 Mind-Body Therapy, p. 657 Tibetan Monks, p. 657	Check Your Learning Quiz 14.3
hardiness, locus of control, optimism, pessimism, self-efficacy, Type A behavior, Type D behavior			Locus of Control and Psychological Functioning, p. 661	Check Your Learning Quiz 14.4

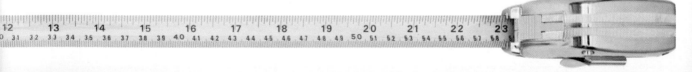

Measure
^Your Learning

Online Activities

Key Terms	Video	Animation	Reading	Assessment
secondary appraisal, problem-focused coping, emotion-focused coping, biofeedback, progressive relaxation, transcendental meditation, positive psychology		Primary and Secondary Appraisals, p. 667	Sex Differences in Use of Coping Strategy, p. 667 Stress Management Program, p. 669 Social Support, p. 671 Long-Term Happiness, p. 673	Check Your Learning Quiz 14.5

absolute threshold Intensity level of a stimulus such that a person will have a 50% chance of detecting it.

accommodation Process by which a child changes old methods to deal with or adjust to new situations.

achievement need Desire to set challenging goals and to persist in pursuing those goals in the face of obstacles, frustrations, and setbacks.

action potential Tiny electric current that is generated when the positive sodium ions rush inside the axon.

activation-synthesis theory States that dreaming occurs because brain areas that provide reasoned cognitive control during the waking state are shut down.

actor-observer effect Tendency to attribute one's own behavior to situational factors.

adaptation Decreasing response of the sense organs the more they are exposed to a continuous level of stimulation.

adaptation level theory Quickly becoming accustomed to receiving some good fortune (such as money, job, car, or degree); taking the good fortune for granted within a short period of time. As a result, the initial impact of good fortune fades and contributes less to long-term levels of happiness.

adaptations Common features of a species that provide it with improved function.

adaptive genes Genes for traits that help an organism survive and reproduce.

adaptive theory States that sleep evolved because it prevented early humans and animals from wasting energy and exposing themselves to the dangers of nocturnal predators.

adaptive value Usefulness of certain abilities or traits that have evolved in animals and humans and tend to increase their chances of survival, such as finding food, acquiring mates, and avoiding pain and injury.

addiction Behavioral pattern of drug abuse that is marked by an overwhelming and compulsive desire to obtain and use the drug; even after stopping, there is a strong tendency to relapse and begin using the drug again.

adjustment disorder Condition in which a person is unable to cope with or adjust to a major life change.

adolescence Developmental period from about ages 12 to 18, during which many biological, cognitive, social, and personality traits change from childlike to adultlike.

adrenal glands Part of the endocrine system; secrete hormones that regulate sugar and salt balances and help the body resist stress; also responsible for secondary sexual characteristics.

affective neuroscience approach Studies underlying neural bases of emotion by focusing on the brain's neural circuits that evaluate stimuli and produce or contribute to experiencing and expressing different emotional states.

afferent neurons (sensory neurons) Carry information from the sensors to the spinal cord.

afterimage Visual sensation that continues after the original stimulus is removed.

aggression Any behavior directed toward another that is intended to cause harm.

aging process Caused by a combination of certain genes and proteins that interfere with organ functioning and the natural production of toxic molecules (free radicals), which in turn cause random damage to body organs and DNA (the building blocks of life).

agoraphobia Characterized by anxiety about being in places or situations from which escape might be difficult or embarrassing if a panic attack or panic-like symptoms (sudden dizziness or onset of diarrhea) were to occur.

agreeableness One of the five categories for describing personality through the five-factor model.

alarm stage Initial reaction to stress; marked by activation of the fight-flight response.

alcohol Psychoactive drug classified as a depressant, meaning it depresses activity of the central nervous system.

algorithms Fixed set of rules that, if followed correctly, will eventually lead to a solution.

all-or-none law States that if an action potential starts at the beginning of an axon, the action potential will continue at the same speed, segment by segment, to the very end of the axon.

alpha stage Stage of sleep marked by feelings of being relaxed and drowsy, usually with the eyes closed.

altered state theory of hypnosis States that hypnosis puts a person into an altered state of consciousness, during which the person is disconnected from reality and so is able to experience and respond to various suggestions.

altered states of consciousness An awareness that differs from normal consciousness; such awareness may be produced by using any number of procedures, such as meditation, psychoactive drugs, hypnosis, or sleep deprivation.

altruism One form of helping or doing something, often at a cost or risk, for reasons other than the expectation of a material or social reward.

Alzheimer's disease Disease associated with memory problems, such as forgetting and repeating things, getting lost, and being mildly confused; also includes associated cognitive deficits, such as problems with language, difficulties in recognizing objects, and inability to plan.

amplitude Distance from the bottom to the top of a sound wave.

amygdala Part of the limbic system; evaluates the emotional significance of stimuli and facial expressions, especially those involving fear, distress, or threat.

anal stage Lasts from the age of about 1½ to 3; a time when the infant's pleasure seeking is centered on the anus and its functions of elimination.

analogy Strategy for finding a similarity between the new situation and an old, familiar situation.

androgens Major male sex hormones secreted by the testes, such as testosterone.

anorexia nervosa Serious eating disorder characterized by refusing to eat and not maintaining weight at 85% of what is expected, having an intense fear of gaining weight or becoming fat, and missing at least three consecutive menstrual cycles.

anterior pituitary Part of the endocrine system; regulates growth through secretion of growth hormones and produces hormones that control the adrenal cortex, pancreas, thyroid, and gonads.

anticipatory nausea Feelings of nausea that are elicited by stimuli associated with nausea-inducing chemotherapy treatments.

antidepressant drugs Act by increasing the levels of a specific group of neurotransmitters (monoamines, such as serotonin, norepinephrine, and dopamine) that are involved in the regulation of emotions and moods.

antipsychotic drugs Used to treat serious mental disorders, such as schizophrenia, by changing the levels of neurotransmitters in the brain.

antisocial personality disorder Pattern of disregarding or violating the rights of others without feeling guilt or remorse.

anxiety In Freudian theory, an uncomfortable feeling that results from inner conflicts between the primitive desires of the id and the moral goals of the superego.

apparent motion Illusion that a stimulus or object is moving in space when, in fact, the stimulus or object is stationary.

approach-approach conflict Choosing between two situations that both have pleasurable consequences.

approach-avoidance conflict A single situation that has both pleasurable and disagreeable aspects.

arousal-cost-reward model of helping Decisions to help are made by calculating the costs and rewards of helping.

assimilation Process by which a child uses old methods or experiences to deal with new situations.

associative learning Learning by making a relationship or connection between two events.

atmospheric perspective Monocular depth cue that is created by the presence of dust, smog, clouds, or water vapor.

attachment A close, fundamental emotional bond that develops between the infant and his or her parents or caregiver.

attention-deficit/hyperactivity disorder ADHD; a behavioral disorder in which a child must have six or more symptoms of inattention, such as making careless mistakes in schoolwork, not following instructions, and being easily distracted, and six or more symptoms of hyperactivity, such as fidgeting, leaving classroom seat, and talking excessively.

attitude Any belief or opinion that includes an evaluation of some object, person, or event along a continuum from negative to positive and that predisposes a person to act in a certain way toward that object, person, or event.

attributions Things one points to as the causes of events, other people's behaviors, and one's own behaviors.

atypical neuroleptic drugs Clozapine or risperidone; lower levels of dopamine and other neurotransmitters, especially serotonin.

auditory association area Part of the temporal lobe; transforms basic sensory information, such as noises or sounds, into recognizable auditory information, such as words or music.

auditory canal A long tube that funnels sound waves down its length so that the waves strike the tympanic membrane.

authoritarian parents Parents who attempt to shape, control, and evaluate the behavior and attitudes of their children in accordance with a set standard of conduct, usually an absolute standard that comes from religious or respected authorities.

authoritative parents Parents who attempt to direct their children's activities in a rational and intelligent way. They are supportive, loving, and committed, encourage verbal give-and-take, and discuss their rules and policies with their children.

autism Abnormal or impaired development in social interactions, such as hiding to avoid people, not making eye contact, or not wanting to be touched; may also be marked by difficulties in communicating, such as grave problems in developing spoken language or in initiating conversations.

automatic encoding Transfer of information from short-term into long-term memory without any effort and usually without any awareness.

automatic processes Activities that require little awareness, take minimal attention, and do not interfere with other ongoing activities.

autonomic nervous system Regulates heart rate, breathing, blood pressure, digestion, hormone secretion, and other functions.

availability heuristic States that people rely on information that is more prominent or easily recalled and overlook other information that is available but less prominent or notable.

avoidance-avoidance conflict Choosing between two situations that both have disagreeable consequences.

axon Single threadlike structure that extends from, and carries signals away from, the cell body to neighboring neurons, organs, or muscles.

axon membrane Has chemical gates that can open to allow electrically charged particles to enter or close to keep out electrically charged particles.

babbling Begins at about 6 months; the first stage in acquiring language.

behavior modification Treatment or therapy that changes or modifies problems or undesirable behaviors by using principles of learning based on operant conditioning.

behavior therapy Uses the principles of classical and operant conditioning to change disruptive behaviors and improve human functioning.

behavioral approach The objective, scientific analysis of observable behaviors.

benzodiazepines Valium, Xanax, Restoril; reduce anxiety, worry, and stress by lowering physiological arousal, which results in a state of tranquility.

Binet-Simon intelligence scale Contained items arranged in order of increasing difficulty; measured vocabulary, memory, common knowledge, and other cognitive abilities; purpose was to distinguish among mentally defective children in the Paris school system.

binocular depth cues Depend on the movement of both eyes.

biofeedback A training procedure through which a person is made aware of his or her physiological responses, such as muscle activity, heart rate, blood pressure, or temperature.

biological approach Studies how human genes, hormones, and nervous system interact with their environments to influence learning, personality, memory, motivation, emotions, and other traits and abilities.

biological clocks Internal timing devices that are genetically set to regulate various physiological responses for different periods of time.

biological factors underlying anxiety Genetic, neurological, chemical, and physiological components that may predispose or put someone at risk for developing an anxiety disorder.

biological factors underlying depression Genetic, neurological, chemical, and physiological components that may predispose or put someone at risk for developing a mood disorder.

biological hunger factors Physiological changes in blood chemistry and signals from digestive organs that provide feedback to the brain, which, in turn, triggers people to eat or to stop eating.

biological needs Physiological requirements that are critical to humans' survival and physical well-being.

biological psychology Research on the physical and chemical changes that occur during stress, learning, and emotions, as well as how humans' genetic makeup, brain, and nervous system interact with environments and influence behaviors.

biological sex factors Action of sex hormones that are involved in secondary sexual characteristics (such as facial hair, breasts), sexual motivation (more so in animals than in humans), and the development of ova and sperm.

bipolar I disorder Marked by fluctuations between episodes of depression and mania.

bisexual orientation Pattern of sexual arousal by persons of both sexes.

body dysmorphic disorder Having an overwhelming preoccupation with an imagined or exaggerated physical defect in one's appearance.

borderline personality disorder Pattern of instability in personal relationships, self-image, and emotions, as well as impulsive behavior.

bottom-up processing Perception begins with bits and pieces of information that, when combined, lead to the recognition of a whole pattern.

brightness constancy Tendency to perceive brightness as remaining the same in changing illumination.

Broca's aphasia Person cannot speak in fluent sentences but can understand written and spoken words.

Broca's area Part of the temporal lobe; combines sounds into words and arranges words into meaningful sentences.

bulimia nervosa Eating disorder characterized by a minimum of two binge-eating episodes per week for at least 3 months; fear of not being able to stop eating; regularly engaging in vomiting, use of laxatives, or rigorous dieting and fasting; and excessive concern about body shape and weight.

burnout Being physically overwhelmed and exhausted, finding a job unrewarding, becoming cynical or detached, and developing a strong sense of ineffectiveness and lack of accomplishment in this particular job.

bystander effect Feeling inhibited from taking some action because of the presence of others.

caffeine Mild stimulant that belongs to a group of chemicals called xanthines.

case study In-depth analysis of the thoughts, feelings, beliefs, or behaviors of a single person.

catatonic schizophrenia Marked by periods of wild excitement or periods of rigid, prolonged immobility; sometimes the person assumes a frozen posture for hours on end.

cell body (soma) Relatively large, egg-shaped structure that provides fuel, manufactures chemicals, and maintains the entire neuron in working order.

central cues Activity in different brain areas, which in turn result in increasing or decreasing appetite.

central nervous system Brain and spinal cord.

central route for persuasion Presents information with strong arguments, analyses, facts, and logic.

cephalocaudal principle States that parts of the body closer to the head develop before parts closer to the feet.

cerebellum Part of the hindbrain; involved in coordinating motor movements but not in initiating voluntary movements.

challenge appraisal Has the potential for gain or personal growth but will also require mobilization of physical energy and psychological resources to meet the challenging situation.

Chomsky's theory of language States that all languages share a common universal grammar and that children inherit a mental program to learn this universal grammar.

chromosome Short, rodlike, microscopic structure that contains tightly coiled strands of the chemical DNA.

chunking Combining separate items of information into a larger unit, or chunk, and then remembering chunks of information rather than individual items.

circadian rhythm Biological clock that is genetically programmed to regulate physiological responses within a time period of 24 hours (about 1 day).

clairvoyance Ability to perceive events or objects that are out of sight.

classical conditioning Learning in which a neutral stimulus acquires the ability to produce a response that was originally produced by a different stimulus.

client-centered therapy Assumes that each person has a tendency to develop one's full potential.

clinical and counseling psychology Assessment and treatment of people with psychological problems, such as grief, anxiety, or stress.

clinical assessment Systematic evaluation of an individual's various psychological, biological, and social factors, as well as identification of past and present problems, stressors, and other cognitive or behavioral symptoms.

clinical diagnosis Process of matching an individual's specific symptoms to those that define a particular mental disorder.

clinical interview One method of gathering information about a person's past and current behaviors, beliefs, attitudes, emotions, and problems.

clinical psychologist Has a PhD, PsyD, or EdD; has specialized in a clinical subarea; and has spent an additional year in a supervised therapy setting to gain experience in diagnosing and treating a wide range of abnormal behaviors.

closure rule States that, in organizing stimuli, people tend to fill in any missing parts of a figure and see the figure as complete.

cochlea Contains the receptors for hearing; its function is transduction, transforming vibrations into nerve impulses that are sent to the brain for processing into auditory information.

cochlear implant The cochlear implant is a miniature electronic device that is surgically implanted into the cochlea. The cochlear implant changes sound waves into electrical signals that are fed into the auditory nerve, which carries them to the brain for processing.

cognitive appraisal theory Interpretation or appraisal or thought or memory of a situation, object, or event can contribute to, or result in, experiencing different emotional states.

cognitive approach Studies how people process, store, and use information and how this information influences what they attend to, perceive, learn, remember, believe, and feel.

cognitive development How a person perceives, thinks, and gains an understanding of the world through the interaction and influence of genetic and learned factors.

cognitive developmental theory States that, as children develop mental skills and interact with their environments, they learn one set of rules for male behaviors and another set of rules for female behaviors.

cognitive dissonance State of unpleasant psychological tension that motivates people to reduce their cognitive inconsistencies by making their beliefs more consistent with their behavior.

cognitive factors Beliefs, expectations, values, intentions, and social roles.

cognitive factors in motivation How people evaluate or perceive a situation and how these evaluations and perceptions influence their willingness to work.

cognitive interview A technique for questioning people, such as eyewitnesses, by having them imagine and reconstruct the details of an event, report everything they remember without holding anything back, and narrate the event from different viewpoints.

cognitive learning Mental processes, such as attention and memory; learning can occur through observation or imitation and may not involve any external rewards or require a person to perform any observable behaviors.

cognitive map Mental representation in the brain of the layout of an environment and its features.

cognitive psychology How people process, store, and retrieve information and how cognitive processes influence behaviors.

cognitive therapy Developed by Beck; people have automatic negative thoughts that they typically say to themselves without much notice.

cognitive-behavioral therapy Combines the cognitive therapy technique of changing negative, unhealthy, or distorted thought patterns with the behavior therapy technique of changing maladaptive or disruptive behaviors by learning and practicing new skills to improve functioning.

cognitive-emotional-behavioral and environmental factors Contribute to the development of mental disorders and include deficits in cognitive processes, such as having unusual thoughts and beliefs; deficits in processing emotional stimuli, such as under- or overreacting to emotional situations; behavioral problems, such as lacking social skills; and environmental challenges, such as dealing with stressful situations.

collective unconscious According to Jung, consists of ancient memory traces and symbols that are passed on by birth and are shared by all peoples in all cultures.

color blindness Inability to distinguish two or more shades in the color spectrum.

color constancy Tendency to perceive colors as remaining stable despite differences in lighting.

commitment Making a pledge to nourish the feelings of love and to actively maintain the relationship.

common factors Basic set of procedures and experiences that different therapies share and that explain why different approaches are equally effective.

communication Ability to use sounds, smells, or gestures to exchange information.

community mental health centers Low-cost or free mental health care to members of the surrounding community, especially the underprivileged.

companionate love Having trusting and tender feelings for someone whose life is closely bound up with one's own.

compliance Kind of conformity in which people give in to social pressure in their public responses but do not change their private beliefs.

concept Way to group or classify objects, events, animals, or people based on some features, traits, or characteristics they all share in common.

conception Occurs when one of the millions of sperm penetrates the ovum's outer membrane.

concrete operational stage Third of Piaget's cognitive stages; from about 7 to 11 years, during which children can perform a number of logical mental operations on concrete objects (ones that are physically present).

conditional positive regard Positive regard people receive if they behave in certain acceptable ways, such as living up to or meeting the standards of others.

conditioned response (CR) Elicited by the conditioned stimulus; is similar to, but not identical in size or amount, to the unconditioned response.

conditioned stimulus (CS) Formerly neutral stimulus that has acquired the ability to elicit a response that was previously elicited by the unconditioned stimulus.

conduction deafness Less severe kind of deafness caused by problems in the middle ear, whether by wax in the auditory canal, injury to the tympanic membrane, or malfunction of the ossicles.

cones Photoreceptors that contain three chemicals called opsins, which are activated in bright light and allow humans to see color.

confidentiality Not revealing which data were collected from which participant.

conflict Feeling experienced when one must choose between two or more incompatible possibilities or options.

conformity Any behavior performed because of group pressure, even though that pressure might not involve direct requests.

conscientiousness One of the five categories for describing personality through the five-factor model.

conscious thoughts Wishes, desires, or thoughts that people are aware of, or can recall, at any given moment.

consciousness Different levels of awareness of one's thoughts and feelings; may include creating images in one's mind, following one's thought processes, or having unique emotional experiences.

conservation Even though the shape of some object or substance is changed, the total amount remains the same.

continuity rule States that, in organizing stimuli, people tend to favor continuous paths when interpreting a series of points or lines.

continuous reinforcement Every occurrence of the operant response results in delivery of the reinforcer.

continuum of consciousness A wide range of experiences, from being acutely aware and alert to being totally unaware and unresponsive.

control group Group composed of participants who undergo all of the same procedures as the experimental participants except that the control participants do not receive the treatment.

controlled processes Activities that require full awareness, alertness, and concentration to reach some goal.

conventional level Represents an intermediate level of moral reasoning; has two stages, stage 3 and stage 4.

convergence Binocular cue for depth perception based on signals sent from muscles that turn the eyes.

convergent thinking Beginning with a problem and coming up with a single correct solution.

conversion disorder Changing anxiety or emotional distress into real physical, motor, sensory, or neurological symptoms (such as headaches, nausea, dizziness, loss of sensation, paralysis), for which no physical or organic cause can be identified.

cornea Rounded, transparent covering over the front of the eye.

correlation An association or relationship in the occurrence of two or more events.

correlation coefficient Number that indicates the strength of a relationship between two or more events: the closer the number is to −1.00 or +1.00, the greater the strength of the relationship.

cortex Thin layer of cells that essentially covers the entire surface of the forebrain.

counter attitudinal behavior Taking a public position that runs counter to one's private attitude.

creative individual Someone who regularly solves problems, fashions products, or defines new questions that make an impact on society.

creative thinking Combination of flexibility in thinking and reorganization of understanding to produce innovative ideas and new or novel solutions.

critical language period Time from infancy to adolescence when language is easiest to learn.

crowd Large group of people who are usually strangers; can facilitate or inhibit certain behaviors.

cybertherapy Therapy delivered over the Internet.

daydreaming Activity that requires a low level of awareness, often occurs during automatic processes, and involves fantasizing or dreaming while awake.

debriefing Explaining the purpose and method of the experiment, asking the participants their feelings about being involved in the experiment, and helping the participants deal with possible doubts or guilt that may arise from their behaviors in the experiment.

decibel Unit to measure loudness.

decision-stage model of helping States that a person goes through five stages in deciding to help: (1) notice the situation, (2) interpret it as one in which help is needed, (3) assume personal responsibility, (4) choose a form of assistance, and (5) carry out that assistance.

declarative memory Memories for facts or events, such as scenes, stories, words, conversations, faces, or daily events.

deductive reasoning Making a general assumption that one knows or believes to be true and then drawing specific conclusions based on this assumption.

deep brain stimulation (DBS) Surgical procedure that involves implanting electrodes into a specific area of the brain and placing a battery-powered stimulator under the collarbone. This procedure helps the brain function better and, as a result, reduces or eliminates undesirable symptoms, such as the tremors found in Parkinson's disease.

deep structure Underlying meaning that is not spoken but is present in the mind of the listener.

defense mechanisms Freudian processes that operate at unconscious levels and use self-deception or untrue explanations to protect the ego from being overwhelmed by anxiety.

deindividuation Increased tendency for subjects to behave irrationally or perform antisocial behaviors when there is less chance of being personally identified.

deinstitutionalization Release of mental patients from mental hospitals and their return to the community to develop more independent and fulfilling lives.

dendrites Branchlike extensions that arise from the cell body; receive signals from other neurons, muscles, or sense organs and pass these signals to the cell body.

denial Refusing to recognize some anxiety-provoking event or piece of information that is clear to others.

dependency Change in the nervous system so that a person now needs to take a drug to prevent the occurrence of painful withdrawal symptoms.

dependent variable One or more of the subjects' behaviors that are used to measure the potential effects of the treatment or independent variable.

depth perception Ability of the eye and brain to add a third dimension, depth, to all visual perceptions, even though images projected on the retina are in only two dimensions, height and width.

developmental norms Average ages at which children perform various kinds of skills or exhibit abilities or behaviors.

developmental psychology Examines moral, social, emotional, and cognitive development throughout a person's entire life.

Diagnostic and Statistical Manual of Mental Disorders A uniform system for assessing specific symptoms and matching them to almost 300 different mental disorders.

diathesis stress theory States that some people have a genetic predisposition (a diathesis) that interacts with life stressors to result in the onset and development of schizophrenia.

dichromats Usually have trouble distinguishing red from green because they have just two kinds of cones.

diffusion of responsibility theory States that in the presence of others, individuals feel less personal responsibility and are less likely to take action in a situation where help is required.

direction of a sound Calculated by the slight difference in time that it takes sound waves to reach the two ears, which are about 6 inches apart.

discrimination Specific unfair behaviors exhibited toward members of a group. In classical conditioning, the tendency for some stimuli but not others to elicit a conditioned response. In operant conditioning, a response is emitted in the presence of a stimulus that is reinforced and not in the presence of unreinforced stimuli.

disorganized schizophrenia Marked by bizarre ideas, often about one's body (such as bones melting), confused speech, childish behavior (such as giggling for no apparent reason or making faces at people), great emotional swings (such as fits of laughing or crying), and often extreme neglect of personal appearance and hygiene.

displacement Transferring feelings about, or response to, an object that causes anxiety to another person or object that is less threatening.

dispositional attributions Explanations of behavior based on the internal characteristics or dispositions of the person performing the behavior.

dissociative amnesia Characterized by the inability to recall important personal information or events and is usually associated with stressful or traumatic events.

dissociative disorder Characterized by a person having a disruption, split, or breakdown in his or her normal integrated self, consciousness, memory, or sense of identity.

dissociative fugue Disturbance marked by suddenly and unexpectedly traveling away from one's home or place of work and being unable to recall one's past.

dissociative identity disorder Presence of two or more distinct identities or personality states, each with its own pattern of perceiving, thinking about, and relating to the world.

divergent thinking Beginning with a problem and coming up with many different solutions.

dominant gene Type of polymorphic gene that determines the development of a specific trait even if it is paired with a recessive gene.

double-blind procedure Procedure in which neither participants nor researchers know which group is receiving which treatment.

dream interpretation Freudian technique of analyzing dreams; based on the assumption that dreams contain underlying, hidden meanings and symbols that provide clues to unconscious thoughts and desires.

dreaming Unique state of consciousness in which people are asleep but experience a variety of astonishing visual, auditory, and tactile images, often connected in strange ways and often in color.

dreams are extensions of waking life States that people's dreams reflect the same thoughts, fears, concerns, problems, and emotions that they have when awake.

dysthymic disorder Characterized by being chronically but not continuously depressed for a period of 2 years.

echoic memory Form of sensory memory that holds auditory information for 1 or 2 seconds.

eclectic approach Using different approaches to study the same behavior.

efferent neurons (motor neurons) Carry information away from the spinal cord to produce responses in various muscles and organs throughout the body.

effortful encoding Transfer of information from short-term into long-term memory either by working hard to repeat or rehearse the information or, especially, by making associations between new and old information.

ego Freud's second division of the mind; develops from the id during infancy; the ego's goal is to find safe and socially acceptable ways of satisfying the id's desires and to negotiate between the id's wants and the superego's prohibitions.

egocentric thinking Seeing and thinking of the world only from one's own viewpoint and having difficulty appreciating someone else's viewpoint.

elaborative rehearsal Using effort to actively make meaningful associations between new information that one wishes to remember and old or familiar information that is already stored in long-term memory.

electroconvulsive therapy (ECT) Places electrodes on the skull and administering a mild electric current that passes through the brain and causes a seizure.

electroencephalograph (EEG) Uses electrodes on the scalp to measure changes in electrical voltages at points along the scalp and provide information about brain-wave activity.

embryonic stage Second stage of the prenatal period and spans the 2 to 8 weeks that follow conception.

emotion Defined in terms of four components: interpret or appraise some stimulus (event, object, or thought) in terms of well-being; experience a subjective feeling, such as fear or happiness; have physiological responses, such as changes in heart rate or breathing; show observable behaviors, such as smiling or crying.

emotional development Influence and interaction of genetic factors, brain changes, cognitive factors, coping abilities, and cultural factors in the development of emotional behaviors, expressions, thoughts, and feelings.

emotional intelligence Ability to perceive emotions accurately, to take feelings into account when reasoning, to understand emotions, and to regulate or manage emotions in oneself and others.

emotion-focused coping Dealing with emotional distress by seeking support and sympathy or avoiding or denying the situation.

encoding Process of transferring information from short-term to long-term memory by paying attention to it, repeating or rehearsing it, or forming new associations.

end bulbs (terminal bulbs) Located at the extreme ends of the axon's branches. Each end bulb is like a miniature container that stores chemicals called neurotransmitters, which are used to communicate with neighboring cells.

endocrine system Numerous glands located throughout the body that secrete hormones.

endorphins Chemicals produced by the brain and secreted in response to injury or severe physical or psychological stress.

environmental factors Social, political, and cultural influences, as well as particular learning experiences.

environmental language factors Interactions children have with parents, peers, teachers, and others who provide feedback that rewards and encourages language development, as well as opportunities for children to observe, imitate, and practice language skills.

episodic memory Type of declarative memory; involves knowledge of specific events, personal experiences (episodes), or activities, such as naming or describing favorite restaurants, movies, songs, habits, or hobbies.

estrogen Major female hormone. At puberty, estrogen levels increase eightfold, which stimulates the development of both primary and secondary sexual characteristics.

estrogens Major female sex hormones secreted by the ovaries.

eustress Pleasant and desirable type of stress that is healthful and keeps people engaged in situations.

evolutionary approach Studies how evolutionary ideas, such as adaptation and natural selection, explain behaviors and mental processes.

exemplar model States that one forms a concept of an object, event, animal, or person by defining or making a mental list of the essential characteristics of a particular thing.

exhaustion stage Body's reaction to long-term, continuous stress; is marked by actual breakdown in internal organs or weakening of the infection-fighting immune system.

experiment Method of identifying cause-and-effect relationships by following a set of rules that minimize the possibility of error, bias, and chance occurrences.

experimental group Group composed of those who receive the treatment.

experimental psychology Areas of sensation, perception, learning, human performance, motivation, and emotion.

experimenter bias Expectations of the experimenter that participants will behave or respond in a certain way.

external attributions Explanations of behavior based on the external circumstances or situations.

external ear Oval-shaped structure that protrudes from the side of the head; its function is to pick up sound waves and send them down a long, narrow tunnel called the auditory canal.

extinction Procedure in which a conditioned stimulus is repeatedly presented without the unconditioned stimulus, and as a result, the conditioned stimulus tends to no longer elicit the conditioned response. In classical conditioning, the reduction in a response when the conditioned stimulus is no longer followed by the unconditioned stimulus. In operant conditioning, the reduction in an operant response when it is no longer followed by the reinforcer.

extraneous variables Variables other than the independent variable that may influence the dependent variable in a study.

extrasensory perception (ESP) Group of psychic experiences that involve perceiving or sending information (images) outside normal sensory processes or channels.

extraversion One of the five categories for describing personality through the five-factor model.

extrinsic motivation Engaging in certain activities or behaviors that either reduce biological needs or help obtain incentives or external rewards.

eye movement desensitization and reprocessing (EMDR) Having the client talk about or imagine a traumatic memory while visually focusing on and following the back-and-forth movement of a therapist's hand.

eyewitness testimony Recalling or recognizing a suspect observed during a potentially very disrupting and distracting emotional situation that may have interfered with accurate remembering.

facial feedback theory Sensations, or feedback, from the movement of facial muscles and skin are interpreted by the brain as different emotions.

fat cells Secrete a hormone called leptin, which acts on the brain's hypothalamus.

fear of failure Choosing easy, nonchallenging tasks where failure is unlikely to occur.

female hypothalamus Triggers a cyclical release of estrogens from the ovaries.

female secondary sexual characteristics Growth of pubic hair, development of breasts, and widening of hips.

fetal alcohol syndrome (FAS) Physical changes, such as short stature, flattened nose, and short eye openings; neurological changes, such as fewer brain connections within the brain structure; and psychological and behavioral problems, such as hyperactivity, impulsive behavior, deficits in information processing and memory, drug use, and poor socialization, that results from a mother drinking heavily during pregnancy, especially in the first 12 weeks.

fetal stage Third stage in prenatal development; begins 2 months after conception and lasts until birth.

fight-flight response State of increased physiological arousal caused by activation of the sympathetic division; helps the body cope with and survive threatening situations.

figure-ground rule States that, in organizing stimuli, one tends to automatically distinguish between a figure and a ground.

five-factor model Organization of personality traits; describes differences in personality using five categories: openness, conscientiousness, extraversion, agreeableness, and neuroticism.

fixed-interval schedule Reinforcer occurs following the first response after a fixed interval of time.

fixed-ratio schedule Reinforcer occurs only after a fixed number of responses are made by the subject.

flashbulb memories Vivid recollections, usually in great detail, of dramatic or emotionally charged incidents that are of interest to the person.

flavor Sensations of taste and smell combined.

foot-in-the-door technique Technique of starting with a little request to gain eventual compliance with a later request.

forebrain Largest part of the brain; has right and left sides called hemispheres.

forgetting Inability to retrieve, recall, or recognize information that was stored or is still stored in long-term memory.

formal operational stage Last of Piaget's four cognitive stages; extends from about age 12 through adulthood.

fraternal twins Twins that develop from separate eggs and have 50% of their genes in common.

free association Freudian technique in which clients are encouraged to talk about any thoughts or images that enter their heads; the assumption is that this kind of free-flowing, uncensored talking will provide clues to unconscious material.

frequency Number of sound waves that occur within 1 second.

frequency theory Applies only to low-pitched sounds; states that the rate at which nerve impulses reach the brain determines how low the pitch of a sound is.

Freud's psychoanalytic theory of personality Emphasizes the importance of early childhood experiences, unconscious or repressed thoughts that one cannot voluntarily access, and the conflicts between conscious and unconscious forces that influence one's feelings, thoughts, and behaviors.

Freud's theory of dreams States that people have a "censor" that protects them from realizing threatening and unconscious desires or wishes, especially those involving sex or aggression.

Freudian slips Mistakes that people make in everyday speech; such slips of the tongue, which are often embarrassing, are thought to reflect unconscious thoughts or wishes.

frontal lobe Part of the cortex; involved with personality, emotions, and motor behaviors.

frustration Awful feeling that results when attempts to reach some goal are blocked.

frustration-aggression hypothesis States that when goals are blocked, people become frustrated and respond with anger and aggression.

functional fixedness A mental set that is characterized by the inability to see an object as having a function different from its usual one.

functional magnetic resonance imaging (fMRI) Measures the changes in activity of specific neurons that are functioning during cognitive tasks, such as thinking, listening, or reading.

functionalism Study of the function rather than the structure of consciousness; interested in how minds adapt to changing environments.

fundamental attribution error Tendency, when looking for causes of a person's behavior, to focus on the person's disposition or personality traits and overlook how the situation influenced the person's behavior.

Ganzfeld procedure Controlled method for eliminating trickery, error, and bias while testing telepathic communication between a sender, the person who sends the message, and a receiver, the person who receives the message.

Gardner's multiple-intelligence theory States that instead of one kind of general intelligence, there are at least nine different kinds.

gate control theory States that nonpainful nerve impulses (such as shifting attention) compete with pain impulses (such as a headache) in trying to reach the brain.

gender identity An individual's subjective experience and feelings of being either a male or a female.

gender roles Traditional or stereotypical behaviors, attitudes, and personality traits that society designates as masculine or feminine.

gender schemas Sets of information and rules organized around how either a male or a female should think and behave.

gene Specific segment on the strand of DNA that contains instructions for making proteins.

general adaptation syndrome (GAS) Body's reaction to stressful situations during which it goes through a series of three stages—alarm, resistance, and exhaustion—that increase the chances of developing psychosomatic symptoms.

generalization Tendency for a stimulus that is similar to the original conditioned stimulus to elicit a response that is similar to the conditioned response. In classical conditioning, the tendency for a stimulus similar to the original conditioned stimulus to elicit a response similar to the conditioned response. In operant conditioning, an animal or person emits the same response to similar stimuli.

generalized anxiety disorder Characterized by excessive or unrealistic worry about almost everything or feeling that something bad is about to happen.

genetic factors Inherited tendencies that influence how a person thinks, behaves, and feels.

genetic hunger factors Inherited instructions found in humans' genes that determine the number of fat cells or metabolic rates of burning off the body's fuel, which push them toward being normal, overweight, or underweight.

genetic mutations Accidental errors in genetic instructions that lead to a change.

genetic sex factors Inherited instructions for the development of sexual organs, the secretion of sex hormones, and the wiring of the neural circuits that control sexual reflexes.

genital stage Lasts from puberty through adulthood; a time when the individual has renewed sexual desires that he or she seeks to fulfill through relationships with members of the opposite sex.

germinal stage First stage of prenatal development and refers to the 2-week period following conception.

gestalt approach Perception is more than the sum of its parts; sensations are assembled into meaningful perceptual experiences.

gestalt psychologists Believed that humans' brains follow a set of rules that specify how individual elements are to be organized into a meaningful pattern, or perception.

gifted Person usually defined by an IQ score between 130 and 150.

glial cells (astrocytes) Cells that provide scaffolding to guide the growth of developing neurons and support mature neurons; wrap around neurons to form insulation to prevent interference from other electrical signals; and release chemicals that influence a neuron's growth and function.

gonads (ovaries in females and testes in males) The ovaries produce hormones that regulate sexual development, ovulation, and growth of sex organs. The testes produce hormones that regulate sexual development, production of sperm, and growth of sex organs.

grammar Set of rules for combining words into phrases and sentences to express an infinite number of thoughts that can be understood by others.

group cohesion Group togetherness; determined by how much group members perceive that they share common attributes.

group norms Formal or informal rules about how group members should behave.

group polarization Phenomenon in which group discussion reinforces the majority's point of view and shifts that view to a more extreme position.

groups Collections of two or more people who interact, share some common idea, goal, or purpose, and influence how their members think and behave.

groupthink A group making bad decisions because the group is more concerned about reaching agreement and sticking together than gathering the relevant information and considering all the alternatives.

hallucinogens Psychoactive drugs that can produce strange and unusual perceptual, sensory, and cognitive experiences that the person sees or hears but knows that they are not occurring in reality.

happiness Indicated by smiling and laughing; can result from momentary pleasures.

hardiness Combination of three personality traits—control, commitment, and challenge—that protect or buffer people from the potentially harmful effects of stressful situations and reduce their chances of developing psychosomatic illnesses.

harm/loss appraisal Situation in which one has already sustained some damage or injury.

hassles Small, irritating, frustrating events that people face daily and that they usually appraise or interpret as stressful experiences.

heterosexual orientation Pattern of sexual arousal by persons of the opposite sex.

heuristics Rules of thumb, or clever and creative mental shortcuts, that reduce the number of operations and allow one to solve problems easily and quickly.

high need for achievement Doing one's best, striving for social recognition, and working to achieve material rewards; shown by those who persist longer at tasks; perform better on tasks, activities, or exams; set challenging but realistic goals; compete with others to win; and are attracted to careers that require initiative.

hindbrain Section of the brain with three distinct structures: the pons, medulla, and cerebellum.

hippocampus Part of the limbic system; involved in saving many kinds of fleeting memories by putting them into permanent storage in various parts of the brain.

holistic view States that a person's personality is more than the sum of its individual parts; instead, the individual parts form a unique and total entity that functions as a unit.

homosexual orientation Pattern of sexual arousal by persons of the same sex.

hormones Various chemicals secreted by numerous glands located throughout the body that affect organs, muscles, and other glands in the body.

humanistic approach States that each individual has great freedom in directing his or her future, a large capacity for achieving personal growth, a considerable amount of intrinsic worth, and enormous potential for self-fulfillment.

humanistic theories Emphasizes capacity for personal growth, development of potential, and freedom to choose one's destiny.

humanistic therapy approach States that people naturally strive to reach their potential.

hypnosis Procedure in which a researcher, clinician, or hypnotist suggests that a person will experience changes in sensations, perceptions, thoughts, feelings, or behaviors.

hypnotic analgesia Reduction in pain reported by clients after they have undergone hypnosis and received suggestions that reduce their anxiety and promote relaxation.

hypnotic induction Inducing hypnosis by first asking a person to either stare at an object or close his or her eyes and then suggesting that the person is becoming very relaxed.

hypothalamus Part of the limbic system; regulates many motivational behaviors, including eating, drinking, and sexual responses; emotional behaviors, such as arousing the body when fighting or fleeing; and the secretion of hormones; sometimes referred to as the control center of the endocrine system because it regulates the pituitary gland.

hypothesis Educated guess about some phenomenon; is stated in precise, concrete language to rule out confusion or error in the meaning of its terms.

iconic memory Form of sensory memory that automatically holds visual information for about a quarter of a second or more.

id Freud's first division of the mind to develop; contains two biological drives—sex and aggression—that are the sources of all psychic or mental energy; the id's goal is to pursue pleasure and satisfy the biological drives.

ideal weight Results from an almost perfect balance between how much food an organism eats and how much it needs to meet its body's energy needs.

identical twins Twins that develop from a single egg and thus have almost identical genes, which means they have nearly 100% of their genes in common.

illusion Perceptual experience in which one perceives an image as being so strangely distorted that, in reality, it cannot and does not exist.

imagined perception Experiencing sensations, perceiving stimuli, or performing behaviors that come from one's imagination.

immune system Body's defense and surveillance network of cells and chemicals that fight off bacteria, viruses, and other foreign or toxic substances.

incentives Goals that can be either objects or thoughts that one learns to value and that one is motivated to obtain.

independent variable Treatment or something the researcher controls or manipulates.

inductive reasoning Making particular observations that are then used to draw a broader conclusion; in other words, reasoning from particulars to a general conclusion.

industrial/organizational psychology Examines the relationships of people and their work environments.

informed consent Individual's agreement to participate in research after being informed about details of the study, including what participation will involve and the potential risks.

innate language factors Genetically programmed physiological and neurological features that facilitate making speech sounds and acquiring language skills.

inner ear Two main structures that are sealed in bony cavities: the cochlea, which is involved in hearing, and the vestibular system, which is involved in balance.

insanity According to its legal definition, not knowing the difference between right and wrong.

insecure attachment Characteristic of infants who avoid or show ambivalence or resistance toward their parent or caregiver.

insight Mental process marked by the sudden and unexpected solution to a problem; a phenomenon often called the "ah-ha!" experience.

insomnia Difficulties in either going to sleep or staying asleep through the night.

instincts Innate tendencies or biological forces that determine behavior.

intelligence quotient (IQ) Computed by dividing a child's mental age (MA), as measured in an intelligence test, by the child's chronological age (CA) and multiplying the result by 100.

interactive model of sexual orientation Genetic and biological factors, such as genetic instructions and prenatal hormones, interact with psychological factors, such as the individual's attitudes, personality traits, and behaviors, to influence the development of sexual orientation.

interference Results when new information enters short-term memory and overwrites or pushes out information that is already there.

internal attributions Explanations of behavior based on the internal characteristics or dispositions of the person performing the behavior.

interneuron Relatively short neuron whose primary task is making connections between other neurons.

interposition Monocular cue for depth perception that comes into play when objects overlap.

intestines Secrete ghrelin, which carries "hunger signals" to the hypothalamus, increasing appetite, and another hormone called PYY, which carries "full signals" to the hypothalamus, decreasing appetite.

intimacy Feeling close and connected to someone; develops through sharing and communicating.

intrinsic motivation Engaging in certain activities or behaviors because the behaviors themselves are personally rewarding or because engaging in these activities fulfills one's beliefs or expectations.

introspection A method of exploring conscious mental processes by asking subjects to look inward and report their sensations and perceptions.

ions Chemical particles that have electrical charges. Ions follow two rules: Opposite charges attract, and like charges repel.

iris Circular muscle that surrounds the pupil and controls the amount of light entering the eye; contains the pigment that gives the eye its characteristic color.

James-Lange theory States that brains interpret specific physiological changes as emotions and that there is a different physiological pattern underlying each emotion.

jet lag Experience of fatigue, lack of concentration, and reduced cognitive skills that occurs when travelers' biological circadian clocks are out of step, or synchrony, with the external clock times at their new locations.

just noticeable difference (JND) The smallest increase or decrease in the intensity of a stimulus that a person is able to detect.

labeling Identifying and naming differences among individuals; places individuals into specific categories and may have either positive or negative associations.

language Special form of communication that involves learning rules to make and combine symbols (words or gestures) into an endless number of meaningful sentences.

language stages Refer to the four different periods or stages that all infants go through—babbling, single words, two-word combinations, and sentences.

latency stage Lasts from about age 6 to puberty; a time when the child represses sexual thoughts and engages in nonsexual activities, such as developing social and intellectual skills.

lateral hypothalamus Group of brain cells that receive "hunger signals" from digestive organs: increase in ghrelin, fall in level of blood glucose, and fall in levels of leptin; also interprets these "hunger signals" and increases the appetite.

law of effect Behaviors followed by positive consequences are strengthened, whereas behaviors followed by negative consequences are weakened.

learning Relatively enduring or permanent change in behavior or knowledge that results from previous experience with certain stimuli and responses.

lens Transparent, oval structure whose curved surface bends and focuses light waves into an even narrower beam, which allows the lens to focus.

levels-of-processing theory States that remembering depends on how information is encoded.

lie detector (polygraph) tests Tests based on the theory that, if a person tells a lie, he or she will feel some emotion, such as guilt or fear. Feeling guilty or fearful will usually be accompanied by involuntary physiological responses, which are difficult to suppress or control and can be measured with a machine called a polygraph.

light and shadow Monocular cues for depth perception: Brightly lit objects appear closer, whereas objects in shadows appear farther away.

light therapy Using bright artificial light to reset circadian clocks and to combat the insomnia and drowsiness that plague shift workers and jet-lag sufferers.

limbic system Group of about half a dozen interconnected structures that make up the core of the forebrain involved with regulating many motivational behaviors such as obtaining food, drink, and sex; organizing emotional behaviors such as fear, anger, and aggression; and storing memories.

linear perspective Monocular depth cue that results as parallel lines come together, or converge, in the distance.

liver Monitors the level of glucose in the blood. When the level of glucose falls, the liver sends "hunger signals" to the brain's hypothalamus; when the level of glucose rises, the liver sends "full signals" to the hypothalamus.

lobes Areas of the cortex.

locus of control Beliefs about how much control one has over situations or rewards.

long-term memory Process of storing almost unlimited amounts of information over long periods of time with the potential of retrieving, or remembering, such information in the future.

long-term potentiation (LTP) Changes in the structure and function of neurons after they have been repeatedly stimulated.

loudness Calculated primarily from the frequency or rate of how fast or how slowly nerve impulses arrive from the auditory nerve.

LSD Hallucinogenic drug that produces strange experiences which include visual hallucinations, perceptual distortions, increased sensory awareness, and intense psychological feelings.

magnetic resonance imaging (MRI) Measures how nonharmful radio frequencies interact with brain cells and transforms the interaction into a detailed image of the brain (or body); used to study the structure of the brain.

maintenance rehearsal Practice of intentionally repeating or rehearsing information so that it remains longer in short-term memory.

major depressive disorder Marked by at least 2 weeks of continually being in a bad mood, having no interest in anything, and getting no pleasure from activities.

major life events Potentially disturbing, troubling, or disruptive situations, both positive and negative, that people appraise as having a significant impact on their lives.

maladaptive behavior approach States that a behavior is psychologically damaging or abnormal if it interferes with the individual's ability to function in his or her personal life or in society.

maladaptive genes Genes for traits that prevent survival and reproduction.

male hypothalamus Triggers a continuous release of androgens, such as testosterone, from the testes.

male secondary sexual characteristics Growth of pubic and facial hair, development of muscles, and a deepening voice.

Maslow's hierarchy of needs Ascending order, or hierarchy, in which biological needs are placed at the bottom and social needs at the top.

maturation Developmental changes that are genetically or biologically programmed rather than acquired through learning or life experiences.

medulla Part of the hindbrain; includes cells that control vital reflexes, such as respiration, heart rate, and blood pressure.

melatonin Hormone that is secreted by the pineal gland, a group of cells located in the center of the human brain.

memory The ability to retain information over time through three processes: encoding (forming), storing, and retrieving.

menarche The first menstrual period; a signal that ovulation may have occurred and that the girl may have the potential to conceive and bear a child.

menopause Occurs in women at about age 50 (range 35 to 60) and involves a gradual stoppage in secretion of the major female hormone (estrogen), which in turn results in cessation of both ovulation and the menstrual cycle.

mental age Method of estimating a child's intellectual progress by comparing the child's score on an intelligence test to the scores of average children of the same age.

mental disorder Prolonged or recurring problem that seriously interferes with an individual's ability to live a satisfying personal life and function adequately in society.

mental retardation Substantial limitation in present functioning that is characterized by significantly subaverage intellectual functioning, along with limitations in two of 11 areas, including communication, self-care, home living, social skills, academic skills, leisure, and safety.

metabolic rate How efficiently the body breaks food down into energy and how quickly the body burns off that fuel.

methamphetamine Similar to amphetamine in both its chemical makeup and its physical and psychological effects; can be smoked or snorted and produces an almost instantaneous high.

method of loci Encoding technique that creates visual associations between already memorized places and new items to be memorized.

midbrain Reward or pleasure center in the brain, which is stimulated by food, sex, money, music, attractive faces, and some drugs.

middle ear Bony cavity that is sealed at each end by membranes.

mind-body connection How thoughts, beliefs, and emotions can produce physiological changes that may be either beneficial or detrimental to one's health and well-being.

Minnesota Multiphasic Personality Inventory-2-RF (MMPI-2) A true-false self-report questionnaire that consists of 338 statements describing a wide range of normal and abnormal behaviors.

mnemonic methods Ways to improve encoding and create better retrieval cues by forming vivid associations or images, which improve recall.

modified frustration-aggression hypothesis Although frustration may lead to aggression, a number of situational and cognitive factors may override the aggressive response.

monochromats Total color blindness; their worlds look black-and-white; results from individuals having only rods or only one kind of functioning cone (instead of three).

monocular depth cues Produced by signals from a single eye.

mood disorder A prolonged and disturbed emotional state that affects almost all of a person's thoughts, feelings, and behaviors.

mood-stabilizer drugs Drugs that act by effecting the levels of neurotransmitters (such as norepinephrine and serotonin) to even out the highs and lows of mood disorders, such as bipolar disorder.

moral therapy Popular in the early 1800s; the belief that mental patients could be helped to function better by providing humane treatment in a relaxed and decent environment.

morpheme Smallest meaningful combination of sounds in a language.

morphology System humans use to group phonemes into meaningful combinations of sounds and words.

motion parallax Monocular depth cue based on the speed of moving objects.

motivation Various physiological and psychological factors that cause people to act in a specific way at a particular time.

motor cortex Narrow strip of cortex that is located in the frontal lobe involved in the initiation of all voluntary movements.

myelin sheath Composed of fatty material that wraps around and insulates an axon. The myelin sheath prevents interference from electrical signals generated in adjacent axons.

narcolepsy Chronic disorder marked by excessive sleepiness, usually in the form of sleep attacks or short periods of sleep throughout the day.

natural selection States that the genes for traits that help an organism survive and reproduce will be selected and will continue in a species, whereas the genes for traits that prevent survival and reproduction will not be selected, consequently being eliminated in a species.

naturalistic observation Researchers gather information by observing individuals' behaviors in a relatively normal environment without attempting to change or control the situation.

nature-nurture question Asks how nature (hereditary or genetic factors) interacts with nurture (environmental factors) in the development of a person's intellectual, emotional, personal, and social abilities.

negative punishment Removing a reinforcing stimulus after a response. This removal decreases the chances that the response will recur.

negative reinforcement Aversive stimulus whose removal increases the likelihood that the preceding response will occur again.

negative symptoms Dulled emotions and little inclination to speak, which are a loss of normal functions. In addition, individuals with negative symptoms have intellectual impairment, poor reaction to medication, and thus a poor chance of recovery.

nerves Stringlike bundles of axons and dendrites that come from the spinal cord and are held together by connective tissue.

neural assemblies Groups of interconnected neurons whose activation allows information or stimuli to be recognized and held briefly and temporarily in short-term memory.

neural deafness Most severe kind of deafness caused by damage to the inner ear, whether to the auditory receptors, which prevent the production of impulses, or to the auditory nerve, which prevents nerve impulses from reaching the brain.

neural impulse Series of separate action potentials that take place segment by segment as they move down the length of an axon.

neuroleptic drugs Used to treat serious mental disorders, such as schizophrenia, by changing the levels of neurotransmitters in the brain.

neuron Brain cell with two specialized extensions, one extension for receiving electrical signals and a second, the longer extension for transmitting electrical signals.

neuroses According to Freud, maladaptive thoughts and actions that arise from some unconscious thought or conflict and indicate feelings of anxiety.

neuroticism One of the five categories for describing personality through the five-factor model.

neurotransmitters About a dozen different chemicals that are made by neurons and then used for communication between neurons during the performance of mental or physical activities.

neutral stimulus Some stimulus that causes a sensory response, such as being seen, heard, or smelled, but that does not produce the reflex being tested.

nicotine Stimulant that triggers the production of dopamine, which is used by the brain's reward/pleasure center to produce good feelings.

night terrors Occur during stage 3 or 4 (delta sleep); characterized by frightening experiences that often start with a piercing scream, followed by sudden waking in a fearful state with rapid breathing and increased heart rate.

nightmares Occur during REM sleep; frightening and anxiety-producing images that occur during dreaming.

non-REM sleep Accounts for approximately 80% of sleep time. Non-REM is divided into sleep stages 1, 2, 3, and 4.

normal aging Gradual and natural slowing of physical and psychological processes from middle through late adulthood.

normal distribution Statistical arrangement of scores so that they resemble the shape of a bell and, thus, is said to be a bell-shaped curve.

obedience Performing some behavior in response to an order given by someone in a position of power or authority.

obesity Person 30% or more above the ideal body weight.

object permanence Understanding that objects or events continue to exist even if they can no longer be heard, touched, or seen.

objective personality tests Specific written statements that require individuals to indicate, for example, by checking "true" or "false," whether the statements apply to them.

obsessive-compulsive disorder Consists of obsessions, which are persistent, recurring irrational thoughts, impulses, or images that a person is unable to control and that interfere with normal functioning; and compulsions, which are irresistible impulses to perform over and over some senseless behavior or ritual (such as hand washing, checking things, counting, putting things in order).

occipital lobe Part of the cortex; involved with processing visual information.

Oedipus complex Process in which a child competes with the parent of the same sex for the affections and pleasures of the parent of the opposite sex.

olfactory cells Receptors for smell.

openness One of the five categories for describing personality through the five-factor model.

operant conditioning Kind of learning in which the consequences that follow some behavior increase or decrease the likelihood of that behavior's occurrence in the future.

operant response Response that can be modified by its consequences and is a meaningful unit of ongoing behavior that can be easily measured.

opiates Group of narcotics made from the opium poppy that depresses the nervous system and provides euphoria, which is often described as a pleasurable state between waking and sleeping, and analgesia (pain reduction).

opponent-process theory States that ganglion cells in the retina and cells in the thalamus of the brain respond to two pairs of colors: red-green and blue-yellow. When these cells are excited, they respond to one color of the pair; when inhibited, they respond to the complementary pair.

optimal weight Results from an almost perfect balance between how much food an organism eats and how much it needs to meet its body's energy needs.

optimism A relatively stable personality trait that leads to believing and expecting that good things will happen.

oral stage Lasts for the first 18 months of life; a time when the infant's pleasure seeking is centered on the mouth.

organic factors Medical conditions or drug or medication problems that lead to sexual difficulties.

ossicles Collectively, three tiny bones called the hammer, anvil, and stirrup; located in the middle ear.

outer ear Consists of three structures: external ear, auditory canal, and tympanic membrane.

overgeneralization Applying a grammatical rule where it should not be used.

overweight Person 20% over the ideal body weight.

ovulation Release of an ovum or egg cell from a woman's ovaries.

pain Unpleasant sensory and emotional experience that may result from tissue damage, one's thoughts or beliefs, or environmental stressors.

pancreas Part of the endocrine system; regulates the level of sugar in the bloodstream by secreting insulin.

panic attack Period of intense fear or discomfort in which four or more of the following symptoms are present: pounding heart, sweating, trembling, shortness of breath, feelings of choking, chest pain, nausea, feeling dizzy, and fear of losing control or dying.

panic disorder Characterized by recurrent and unexpected panic attacks.

paranoid schizophrenia Characterized by auditory hallucinations or delusions, such as thoughts of being persecuted by others or thoughts of grandeur.

parasympathetic division Returns the body to a calmer, relaxed state and is involved in digestion.

parentese (motherese) Way of speaking to young children in which the adult speaks in a slower and higher than normal voice, emphasizes and stretches out each word, uses very simple sentences, and repeats words and phrases.

parietal lobe Part of the cortex; involved with perception and sensory experiences.

partial reinforcement Situation in which responding is reinforced only some of the time.

passion Feeling physically aroused and attracted to someone.

passionate love Continuously thinking about the loved one; accompanied by warm sexual feelings and powerful emotional reactions.

pathological aging May be caused by genetic defects, physiological problems, or diseases, such as Alzheimer's, all of which accelerate the aging process.

peg method Encoding technique that creates associations between number-word rhymes and items to be memorized.

perceptions Meaningful sensory experiences that result after the brain combines hundreds of sensations.

perceptual constancy Tendency to perceive sizes, shapes, brightness, and colors as remaining the same even though their physical characteristics are constantly changing.

perceptual speed Rate at which people can identify a particular sensory stimulus.

peripheral cues Changes in blood chemistry or signals from digestive organs, which secrete various hormones.

peripheral nervous system All the nerves that extend from the spinal cord and carry messages to and from various muscles, glands, and sense organs located throughout the body.

peripheral route for persuasion Emphasizes emotional appeal, focuses on personal traits, and generates positive feelings.

permissive parents Parents who are less controlling and behave with a nonpunishing and accepting attitude toward their children's impulses, desires, and actions; they consult with their children about policy decisions, make few demands, and use reason rather than direct power.

persistent vegetative state When a person has severe brain damage to the cortex resulting in long-term loss of cognitive function and awareness but retains basic physiological functions, such as breathing and the sleep-wake cycle.

person perception Seeing someone and then forming impressions and making judgments about that person's likability and the kind of person he or she is.

personal factors Emotional makeup and humans' biological and genetic influences.

personal identity How people describe themselves and includes values, goals, traits, perceptions, interests, and motivations.

personality A combination of long-lasting and distinctive behaviors, thoughts, motives, and emotions that typify how people react and adapt to other people and situations.

personality disorder Inflexible, long-standing, maladaptive traits that cause significantly impaired functioning or great distress in one's personal and social life.

personality tests Help clinicians evaluate a person's traits, attitudes, emotions, and beliefs.

pessimism Relatively stable personality trait that leads to believing and expecting that bad things will happen.

phallic stage Lasts from about age 3 to 6; a time when the infant's pleasure seeking is centered on the genitals.

phenomenological perspective One's perception or view of the world, whether it is accurate, becomes one's reality.

phenothiazines Discovered in the early 1950s; block or reduce the effects of the neurotransmitter dopamine and reduce schizophrenic symptoms, such as delusions and hallucinations.

phobia Anxiety disorder characterized by an intense and irrational fear that is out of all proportion to the possible danger of the object or situation.

phonemes Basic sounds of consonants and vowels.

phonology Specifies how humans make the meaningful sounds that are used by a particular language.

photographic memory Ability to form sharp, detailed visual images after examining a picture or page for a short period of time and to recall the entire image at a later date.

Piaget's cognitive stages Four different stages—sensorimotor, preoperational, concrete operations, and formal operations—each of which is more advanced than the preceding stage because it involves new reasoning and thinking abilities.

pitch Subjective experience of a sound being high or low, which the brain calculates from specific physical stimuli, in this case the speed or frequency of sound waves.

pituitary gland Part of the endocrine system; hangs directly below and is regulated by the hypothalamus; divided into anterior (front) and posterior (back) sections.

place theory States that the brain determines medium- to higher-pitched sounds on the basis of the place on the basilar membrane where maximum vibration occurs.

placenta Organ that connects the blood supply of the mother to that of the fetus.

pleasure principle Operates to satisfy drives and avoid pain without concern for moral restrictions or society's regulations.

polymorphic gene Gene that has more than one version.

pons Part of the hindbrain; functions as a bridge to transmit messages between the spinal cord and brain. The pons also makes the chemicals involved in sleep.

positive psychology Scientific study of optimal human functioning, focusing on the strengths and virtues that enable individuals and communities to thrive.

positive punishment Presenting an aversive stimulus after a response. The aversive stimulus decreases the chances that the response will recur.

positive regard Includes love, sympathy, warmth, acceptance, and respect, which people crave from family, friends, and people who are important to them.

positive reinforcer Stimulus that increases the likelihood that a response will occur again.

positive reinforcement Presentation of a stimulus that increases the probability that a behavior will occur again.

positive symptoms Hallucinations and delusions, which are a distortion of normal functions. In addition, individuals with positive symptoms have no intellectual impairment, good reaction to medication, and thus a good chance of recovery.

positron emission tomography (PET scan) Injecting a slightly radioactive solution into the blood and then measuring the amount of radiation absorbed by brain cells called neurons.

posttraumatic stress disorder (PTSD) Disabling condition that results from personally experiencing an event that involves actual or threatened death or serious injury or from witnessing or hearing of such an event happening to a family member or friend.

postconventional level Represents the highest level of moral reasoning; has one stage, stage 5.

posterior pituitary Part of the endocrine system; regulates water and salt balance.

posthypnotic amnesia Not remembering what happened during hypnosis if the hypnotist suggested that, upon awakening, the person would forget what took place during hypnosis.

precognition Ability to foretell events.

preconventional level Represents Kohlberg's lowest level of moral reasoning; has two stages, stage 1 and stage 2.

prejudice Unfair, biased, or intolerant attitude toward another group of people.

prenatal period Extends from conception to birth and lasts about 266 days (around 9 months).

preoperational stage Second of Piaget's cognitive stages; from about 2 to 7 years old.

primacy effect Better recall, or improvement in retention, of information presented at the beginning of a task.

primacy-recency effect Better recall of information presented at the beginning and end of a task.

primary appraisal Initial, subjective evaluation of a situation, in which one balances the demands of a potentially stressful situation against the ability to meet these demands.

primary auditory cortex Part of the temporal lobe; receives electrical signals from receptors in the ears and transforms these signals into meaningless sound sensations, such as vowels and consonants.

primary reinforcer Stimulus, such as food, water, or sex, that is innately satisfying and requires no learning on the part of the subject to become pleasurable.

primary visual cortex Part of the occipital lobe; receives electrical signals from receptors in the eyes and transforms these signals into meaningless basic visual sensations, such as lights, lines, shadows, colors, and textures.

proactive interference Occurs when old information blocks or disrupts the remembering of related new information.

problem solving Searching for some rule, plan, or strategy that results in reaching a certain goal that is currently out of reach.

problem-focused coping Decrease stress by solving the problem through seeking information, changing one's own behavior, or taking whatever action is needed to resolve the difficulty.

procedural memory Also called nondeclarative memory; involves memories for motor skills, some cognitive skills, and emotional behaviors learned through classical conditioning.

processing speed Rate at which one encodes information into long-term memory or recall or retrieves information from long-term memory.

progressive relaxation Tensing and relaxing the major muscle groups of the body until one is able to relax any groups of muscles at will.

projection Falsely and unconsciously attributing one's own unacceptable feelings, traits, or thoughts to individuals or objects.

projective tests Individuals look at some meaningless object or ambiguous photo and describe what they see.

prosocial behavior (helping) Any behavior that benefits others or has positive social consequences.

proteins Chemical building blocks from which all parts of the brain and body are constructed.

prototype theory States that one forms a concept by creating a mental image that is based on the average characteristics of an object.

proximity rule States that, in organizing stimuli, people group together objects that are physically close to one another.

proximodistal principle States that parts closer to the center of the infant's body develop before parts farther away.

psi Processing of information or transfer of energy by methods that have no known physical or biological mechanisms and that seem to stretch the laws of physics.

psychiatrist Medical doctor (MD) who has spent several years in clinical training, which includes diagnosing possible physical and neurological causes of abnormal behaviors and treating these behaviors, often with prescription drugs.

psychoactive drugs Chemicals that affect the nervous systems and, as a result, may alter consciousness and awareness; influence how people sense and perceive things; and modify moods, feelings, emotions, and thoughts.

psychoanalysis Idea that each person has an unconscious part that contains ideas, memories, desires, or thoughts that have been hidden or repressed because they are psychologically dangerous or threatening to one's self-concept.

psychoanalytic approach States that childhood experiences greatly influence the development of later personality traits and psychological problems.

psychokinesis Ability to move objects without touching them.

psychological factors Performance anxiety, sexual trauma, guilt, and failure to communicate, all of which may lead to sexual problems.

psychological sex factors Factors that play a role in developing sexual or gender identity, gender role, and sexual orientation.

psychologist Usually someone who has completed 4 to 5 years of postgraduate education and has obtained a PhD, PsyD, or EdD in psychology.

psychology Systematic, scientific study of behaviors and mental processes.

psychometric approach Measures or quantifies cognitive abilities or factors that are thought to be involved in intellectual performance.

psychometrics Subarea of psychology; concerned with developing psychological tests that assess an individual's abilities, skills, beliefs, and personality traits in a wide range of settings, including school, industry, or clinic.

psychoneuroimmunology Study of the relationship among three factors: the central nervous system (brain and spinal cord), the endocrine system (network of glands that secrete hormones), and psychosocial factors (stressful thoughts, personality traits, and social influences).

psychosexual stages Freud's five different developmental periods—oral, anal, phallic, latency, and genital stages— during which the individual seeks pleasure from different areas of the body that are associated with sexual feelings.

psychosocial factors Personality traits, cognitive styles, social supports, and the ability to deal with stressors.

psychosocial hunger factors Learned associations between food and other stimuli (such as snacking while watching television);

sociocultural influences (such as pressures to be thin); and personality problems (such as low self-esteem).

psychosocial stages Eight developmental periods during which an individual's primary goal is to satisfy desires associated with social needs.

psychosomatic symptoms Real and sometimes painful physical symptoms, such as headaches, muscle pains, stomach problems, and increased susceptibility to colds and flu, that are caused by increased physiological arousal that results from psychological factors, such as worry, stress, and anxiety.

psychotherapy Three basic characteristics: verbal interaction between therapist and client(s); the development of a supportive relationship in which a client can bring up and discuss traumatic or bothersome experiences that may have led to current problems; and analysis of the client's experiences and/or suggested ways for the client to deal with or overcome his or her problems.

puberty Developmental period, between the ages of 9 and 17, when the individual experiences significant biological changes that result in developing secondary sexual characteristics and reaching sexual maturity.

punishment Consequence that occurs after a behavior and decreases the chance that the behavior will occur again.

pupil Round opening at the front of the eye that allows light waves to pass into the eye's interior.

random selection Each participant in a sample population has an equal chance of being selected for the experiment.

rationalization Covering up the true reasons for actions, thoughts, or feelings by making up excuses and incorrect explanations.

reaction formation Substituting behaviors, thoughts, or feelings that are the direct opposite of unacceptable ones.

reaction time Rate at which one responds (i.e., see, hear, move) to some stimulus.

real motion Perception of any stimulus or object that actually moves in space.

reality principle Policy of satisfying a wish or desire only if there is a socially acceptable outlet available.

reasoning Mental process that involves using and applying knowledge to solve problems, make plans or decisions, and achieve goals.

recency effect Better recall, or improvement in retention, of information presented at the end of a task.

recessive gene Type of polymorphic gene that determines the development of a specific trait only when it is inherited from both parents.

reflex Unlearned, involuntary reaction to some stimulus.

reinforcement Consequence that occurs after a behavior and increases the chance that the behavior will occur again.

relative size Monocular cue for depth that results when one expects two objects to be the same size, but they are not.

reliability Person's score on a test at one point in time should be consistent with the score obtained by the same person on a similar test at a later point in time.

REM behavior disorder Usually occurs in older people; voluntary muscles are not paralyzed, and sleepers can and do act out their dreams, such as fighting off attackers in dreams.

REM rebound Spending an increased percentage of time in REM sleep if deprived of REM sleep on the previous nights.

REM sleep Stands for rapid-eye-movement sleep; accounts for the remaining 20% of sleep time.

repair theory Suggests that activities during the day deplete key factors in the brain or body that are replenished or repaired by sleep.

repression Blocking and pushing unacceptable or threatening feelings, wishes, or experiences into the unconscious.

resiliency Psychological and environmental factors that compensate for increased life stresses so that expected problems do not develop.

resistance stage Body's reaction to continued stress, during which most of the physiological responses return to normal levels but the body uses up great stores of energy.

resistance Characterized by the client's reluctance to work through or deal with feelings or to recognize unconscious conflicts and repressed thoughts.

resting state When the axon has a charge, or potential, that results from the axon membrane separating positive ions on the outside from negative ions on the inside.

reticular formation Arouses the forebrain so that it is ready to process information from the senses.

retina Thin film located at the very back of the eyeball that contains cells that are extremely sensitive to light.

retinal disparity Binocular depth cue that depends on the distance between the eyes.

retrieval cues Mental reminders that one creates by forming vivid mental images of information or associating new information with information that is already known.

retrieving Process of getting or recalling information that has been placed into short-term or long-term storage.

retroactive interference Occurs when new information blocks or disrupts the retrieval of related old information.

reward/pleasure center Several areas of the brain, such as the nucleus accumbens and the ventral tegmental area; involves several neurotransmitters, especially dopamine.

rods Photoreceptors that contain rhodopsin, which is activated by small amounts of light; they allow people to see in dim light, but only black, white, and shades of gray.

Rorschach inkblot test Used to assess personality by showing a person a series of ten inkblots and then asking the person to describe what he or she thinks each image is.

rules of organization Identified by gestalt psychologists; specify how the brain combines and organizes individual pieces or elements into a meaningful perception.

schedule of reinforcement Program or rule that determines how and when the occurrence of a response will be followed by a reinforcer.

schema Organized mental or cognitive list that includes characteristics, facts, values, or beliefs about people, events, or objects.

schizophrenia Serious mental disorder that lasts for at least 6 months and includes at least two of the following symptoms: delusions, hallucinations, disorganized speech, disorganized behavior, and decreased emotional expression.

secondary appraisal Deciding to deal with a potentially stressful situation by using one or both of two different coping patterns: Problem-focused coping means doing something about the particular problem, whereas emotion-focused coping means dealing with one's negative feelings.

secondary reinforcer Any stimulus that has acquired its reinforcing power through experience; secondary reinforcers are learned, such as by being paired with primary reinforcers or other secondary reinforcers.

secure attachment Characteristic of infants who use their parents or caregivers as a safe home base from which they can wander off and explore their environments.

self How one sees or describes oneself, also called self-concept.

self-actualization Inherent tendency to develop and reach one's true potential.

self-actualizing tendency An inborn tendency to develop all of one's capacities in ways that best maintain and benefit one's life.

self-concept How one sees or describes oneself.

self-efficacy Confidence in one's ability to organize and execute a given course of action to solve a problem or accomplish a task.

self-esteem How much one likes oneself and how much one values one's self-worth, importance, attractiveness, and social competence.

self-fulfilling prophecy Having a strong belief or making a statement (prophecy) about a future behavior and then acting, usually unknowingly, to fulfill or carry out the behavior.

self-identity How one describes oneself, including one's values, goals, traits, perceptions, interests, and motivations.

self-perception theory People first observe or perceive their own behavior and then, as a result, they change their attitudes.

self-report questionnaires Specific written statements that require individuals to indicate, for example, by checking "true" or "false," whether the statements apply to them.

self-serving bias Explaining one's successes by attributing them to one's disposition or personality traits and explaining one's failures by attributing them to the situation.

semantic memory Type of declarative memory; involves knowledge of facts, concepts, words, definitions, and language rules.

semantics Meanings of words or phrases when they appear in various sentences or contexts.

semicircular canals Provide input to the vestibular system.

sensations Relatively meaningless bits of information that result when the brain processes electrical signals that come from the sense organs.

sensorimotor stage First of Piaget's cognitive stages; from birth to about age 2.

sensory memory Initial process that receives and holds environmental information in its raw form for a brief period of time, from an instant to several seconds.

sentences Represents the fourth stage of acquiring language; occurs at about 4 years of age.

set point Certain level of body fat (adipose tissue) that one's body strives to maintain constant throughout one's life.

sex chromosome In the sperm or the egg; contains 23 chromosomes, which in turn have genes that contain instructions for determining the sex of the child.

sex hormones Chemicals secreted by glands; circulate in the bloodstream to influence the brain, body organs, and behaviors.

sexual orientation Whether a person is sexually aroused primarily by members of his or her own sex, the opposite sex, or both sexes.

shape constancy Tendency to perceive an object as retaining its same shape even though its shape is continually changing its image on the retina when viewed from different angles.

shaping Procedure in which an experimenter successively reinforces behaviors that lead up to or approximate the desired behavior.

short-term dynamic psychotherapy Emphasizes a limited time for treatment and focuses on limited goals, such as solving a relatively well-defined problem.

short-term memory Also called working memory; refers to a process that can hold only a limited amount of information (an average of seven items) for only a short period of time (2 to 30 seconds).

similarity rule States that, in organizing stimuli, one groups together elements that appear similar.

single words Second stage in acquiring language; occurs at about 1 year of age.

situational attributions Explanations of behavior based on the external circumstances or situations.

size constancy Tendency to perceive objects as remaining the same size even when their images on the retina continually grow or shrink.

sleep Five different stages that involve different levels of awareness, consciousness, and responsiveness, as well as different levels of physiological arousal.

sleep apnea Repeated periods during sleep when a person stops breathing for 10 seconds or longer.

sleeptalking Can occur during any stage of sleep; usually occurs in NREM sleep and involves talking during sleep without being aware of it.

sleepwalking Usually occurs in stage 3 or 4 (delta sleep) and consists of walking while literally sound asleep.

social cognitive learning Acquisition of language skills through social interactions, which give children a chance to observe, imitate, and practice the sounds, words, and sentences they hear from their parents or caregivers.

social cognitive theory Emphasizes the importance of observation, imitation, and self-reward in the development and learning of social skills, personal interactions, and many other behaviors.

social comparison theory States that people are driven to compare themselves to others who are similar so that they can measure the correctness of their own attitudes and beliefs.

social development How a person develops a sense of self, or a self-identity, develops relationships with others, and develops the kinds of social skills important in personal interactions.

social facilitation Increase in performance in the presence of a crowd.

social inhibition Decrease in performance in the presence of a crowd.

social needs Affiliation or close social bonds; nurturance or need to help and protect others; dominance or need to influence or control others; and achievement or need to excel; acquired through learning and experience.

social neuroscience Emerging area of research that examines social behavior, such as perceiving others, by combining biological and social approaches.

social norms approach States that a behavior is considered abnormal if it deviates greatly from accepted social standards, values, or norms.

social phobias Characterized by irrational, marked, and continuous fear of performing in social situations.

social psychology Study of social interactions, stereotypes, prejudices, attitudes, conformity, group behaviors, aggression, and attraction.

social role theory Emphasizes the influence of social and cognitive processes on how people interpret, organize, and use information.

socially oriented group Members are primarily concerned about fostering and maintaining social relationships among the members of the group.

sociocognitive theory of hypnosis States that behaviors observed during hypnosis result not from being hypnotized but rather from having the special ability of responding to imaginative suggestions and social pressures.

sociocultural approach Studies the influence of social and cultural factors on behaviors and mental processes.

sodium pump Transport process that picks up any sodium ions that enter the axon's chemical gates and returns them back outside.

somatic nervous system Network of nerves that connect either to sensory receptors or to muscles that a person can move voluntarily, such as muscles in the limbs, back, neck, and chest.

somatization disorder Begins before age 30; lasts several years; characterized by multiple symptoms, including pain, gastrointestinal, sexual, and neurological symptoms, which have no physical causes but are triggered by psychological problems or distress.

somatoform disorders Marked by a pattern of recurring, multiple, and significant bodily (somatic) symptoms that extend over several years.

somatosensory cortex Narrow strip of cortex that is located in the parietal lobe that processes sensory information about touch, location of limbs, pain, and temperature.

sound waves Stimuli for hearing; resemble ripples of different sizes.

source misattribution Memory error that results when a person has difficulty deciding which of two or more sources a memory came from.

Spearman's two-factor theory States that intelligence has two factors: a general mental ability factor, g, which represents what different cognitive tasks have in common, plus many specific factors, s, which include specific mental abilities (such as mathematical, mechanical, or verbal skills).

specific phobias Characterized by marked and persistent fears that are unreasonable and triggered by anticipation of, or exposure to, a specific object or situation (such as flying, heights, spiders, seeing blood).

split-brain operation Involves cutting the corpus callosum, which connects the right and left hemispheres.

spontaneous recovery Tendency for the conditioned response to reappear after being extinguished even though there have been no further conditioning trials. In operant conditioning, a temporary recovery in the rate of responding. In classical conditioning, the temporary occurrence of the conditioned response in the presence of the conditioned stimulus.

stage 1 sleep A transition from wakefulness to sleep; lasts from 1 to 7 minutes.

stage 2 sleep The beginning of what humans know as sleep.

stage 4 sleep Also called slow-wave or delta sleep; characterized by waves of very high amplitude and very low frequency, called delta waves.

stages of sleep Distinctive changes in the electrical activity of the brain and accompanying physiological responses of the body that occur as one passes through different phases of sleep.

state-dependent learning It is easier to recall information when in the same physiological or emotional state or setting as when the information was originally encoded.

statistical frequency approach States that a behavior may be considered abnormal if it occurs rarely or infrequently in relation to the behaviors of the general population.

statistical procedures Used to determine whether differences observed in dependent variables (behaviors) are due to independent variables (treatment) or to error or chance occurrence.

stem cells Cells that have the capacity to change into and become any one of the 220 types of cells that make up a human body, including skin, heart, liver, bones, and neurons.

stereotaxic procedure Involves fixing a patient's head in a holder and drilling a small hole through the skull. The holder has a syringe that can be precisely guided to inject cells into a predetermined location in the brain.

stereotypes Widely held beliefs that people have certain traits because they belong to a particular group.

Sternberg's triarchic theory States that intelligence can be divided into three different kinds of reasoning processes.

stimulants Psychoactive drugs that increase activity of the central nervous system and result in heightened alertness, arousal, euphoria, and decreased appetite.

stomach Secretes a hormone, ghrelin, which carries "hunger signals" to the brain's hypothalamus, the master control for hunger regulation.

storing Process of placing encoded information into relatively permanent mental storage for later recall.

stress Anxious or threatening feeling that comes when one interprets or appraises a situation as being more than his or her psychological resources can adequately handle.

structuralism Study of the most basic elements, primarily sensations and perceptions, that make up conscious mental experiences.

subgoals Strategy that involves breaking down the overall problem into separate parts that, when completed in order, will result in a solution.

sublimation Type of displacement; involves redirecting a threatening or forbidden desire, usually sexual, into a socially acceptable one.

subliminal stimulus Intensity that gives a person less than a 50% chance of detecting the stimulus.

substance abuse Maladaptive behavioral pattern of using a drug so frequently that significant problems develop, such as failing to meet major obligations and having multiple legal, social, family, health, work, or interpersonal problems.

superego Freud's third division of the mind; develops from the ego during early childhood; the superego's goal is to apply the moral values and standards of one's parents or caregivers and society in satisfying one's wishes.

superstitious behavior Behavior that increases in frequency because its occurrence is accidentally paired with the delivery of a reinforcer.

suprachiasmatic nucleus Biological clock that uses light entering the eyes to regulate a number of circadian rhythms, including the sleep-wake cycle.

surface structure Actual wording of a sentence, as it is spoken.

survey Way to obtain information by asking many individuals— either in person, by telephone, or by mail—to answer a fixed set of questions about particular subjects.

sympathetic division Triggered by threatening or challenging physical or psychological stimuli; increases physiological arousal and prepares the body for action.

synapse Infinitely small space that exists between an end bulb and its adjacent body organ (such as the heart), muscles (such as those in the head), or cell body.

synesthesia Condition in which stimulation of one sense results in the automatic and involuntary stimulation of another sense.

syntax Set of rules that specifies how humans combine words to form meaningful phrases and sentences.

systematic desensitization Procedure based on classical conditioning in which a person imagines or visualizes fearful or anxiety-evoking stimuli and then immediately uses deep relaxation to overcome the anxiety.

tardive dyskinesia Appearance of slow, involuntary, and uncontrollable rhythmic movements and rapid twitching of the mouth and lips, as well as unusual movements of the limbs.

task-oriented group Members have specific duties to complete.

taste buds Receptors for taste.

taste-aversion learning Associating a particular sensory cue (such as smell, taste, sound, or sight) with getting sick and thereafter avoiding that particular sensory cue in the future.

telegraphic speech Distinctive pattern of speaking in which the child omits articles such as *the,* prepositions such as *in* or *out*, and parts of verbs.

telepathy Ability to transfer one's thoughts to another or to read the thoughts of others.

temperament Relatively stable and long-lasting individual differences in mood and emotional behavior, which emerge early in childhood because these differences are largely influenced by genetic factors.

temporal lobe Part of the cortex; involved with hearing and speaking.

teratogen Any agent that can harm a developing fetus, causing deformities or brain damage.

testimonial Statement in support of a particular viewpoint based on detailed observations of a person's own personal experience.

testosterone Major male hormone; stimulates the growth of genital organs and the development of secondary sexual characteristics.

texture gradient Monocular depth cue in which areas with sharp, detailed texture are interpreted as being closer and those with less sharpness and poorer detail are perceived as more distant.

thalamus Part of the limbic system; involved in receiving sensory information, doing some initial processing, and then relaying the sensory information to areas of the cortex, including the somatosensory cortex, primary auditory cortex, and primary visual cortex.

Thematic Apperception Test (TAT) Showing a person a series of 20 pictures of people in ambiguous situations and asking the person to make up a story about what the people are doing or thinking in each situation.

theory of evolution States that different species arose from a common ancestor and that those species that survived were best adapted to meet the demands of their environments.

theory of linguistic relativity States that the differences among languages result in similar differences in how people think of and perceive the world.

theory of personality Organized attempt to describe and explain how personalities develop and why personalities differ.

thinking Paying attention to information and engaging in mental processes that are used to form concepts, solve problems, and engage in creative activities.

threat appraisal Situation in which the harm/loss has not yet taken place but will happen in the near future.

threshold Point above which a stimulus is perceived and below which it is not perceived.

thyroid Part of the endocrine system; regulates metabolism through the secretion of hormones.

time-out Reinforcing stimuli after an undesirable response. This removal decreases the chances that the undesired response will recur.

tip-of-the-tongue phenomenon Having a strong feeling that a particular word can be recalled but despite making a great effort, being temporarily unable to recall this particular information.

tolerance After a person uses a drug repeatedly over a period of time, the original dose of the drug no longer produces the desired effect so that a person must take increasingly larger doses of the drug to achieve the same behavioral effect.

top-down processing When perception is guided by previous knowledge, experience, beliefs, or expectations to recognize the whole pattern.

touch Includes sensations of pressure, temperature, and pain.

trait Relatively stable and enduring tendency to behave in a particular way.

trait theory Approach for analyzing the structure of personality by measuring, identifying, and classifying similarities and differences in personality characteristics or traits.

transcendental meditation (TM) Assuming a comfortable position, closing the eyes, and repeating a sound or concentrating on breathing so that one's head is cleared of all thoughts, worrisome and otherwise.

transcranial magnetic stimulation (TMS) Noninvasive technique that sends pulses of magnetic energy into the brain; works to either activate or suppress brain activity.

transduction Process in which a sense organ changes, or transforms, physical energy into electrical signals that become neural impulses, which may be sent to the brain for processing.

transference Process by which a client expresses strong emotions toward the therapist because the therapist substitutes for someone important in the client's life.

transformational rules Procedures by which one converts ideas from surface structures into deep structures and from deep structures back into surface ones.

transmitter Chemical messenger that carries information between nerves and body organs, such as muscles and heart.

triangular theory of love Consists of three components: passion, intimacy, and commitment.

trichromatic theory States that there are three different kinds of cones in the retina and each cone contains one of three different light-sensitive chemicals called opsins.

two-word combinations Represents the third stage in acquiring language; occurs at about 2 years of age.

tympanic membrane Taut, thin structure commonly called the eardrum.

type A behavior Combination of personality traits that included an overly competitive and aggressive drive to achieve, a hostile attitude when frustrated, a habitual sense of time urgency, a rapid and explosive pattern of speaking, and being a workaholic; defined in the 1980s as being depressed, easily frustrated, anxious, and angry, or some combination of these traits; defined in the 1990s as an individual who feels angry and hostile much of the time but may or may not express these emotions publicly.

type D behavior Chronic distress in terms of two emotional states: negative affectivity (such as worry, irritability or gloom) and social inhibition (such as being shy and reserved, or lacking self-assurance).

typical neuroleptic drugs Drugs that reduce levels of the neurotransmitter dopamine.

unconditional positive regard Warmth, acceptance, and love that others show because a person is valued as a human being even though he or she may disappoint people by behaving in ways that are different from their standards or values or the way they think.

unconditioned response (UCR) Unlearned, innate, involuntary physiological reflex that is elicited by the unconditioned stimulus.

unconditioned stimulus (UCS) Some stimulus that triggers or elicits a physiological reflex, such as salivation or eye blink.

unconscious According to Freud, a mental place that contains unacceptable thoughts, wishes, and feelings that are beyond one's conscious awareness.

unconscious forces Wishes, desires, or thoughts that, because of their disturbing or threatening content, one automatically represses and cannot voluntarily access.

unconscious motivation Freudian concept that refers to the influence of repressed thoughts, desires, or impulses on one's conscious thoughts and behaviors.

unconsciousness Can result from disease, trauma, a blow to the head, or general medical anesthesia; results in total lack of sensory awareness and complete loss of responsiveness to one's environment.

underachievers Individuals who score relatively high on tests of ability or intelligence but perform more poorly than their scores would predict.

universal emotional expressions Specific inherited facial patterns or expressions that signal specific feelings or emotional states, such as a smile signaling a happy state.

validity A test measures what it is supposed to measure.

variable-interval schedule When a reinforcer occurs following the first correct response after an average amount of time has passed.

variable-ratio schedule When a reinforcer is delivered after an average number of correct responses has occurred.

ventromedial hypothalamus Group of brain cells that receive "full signals" from digestive organs. A full stomach activates stretch receptors, rise in level of blood glucose, rise in levels of leptin, and increase in the hormones PYY and CCK.

vestibular sense Provides information about balance and movement.

visible spectrum One particular segment of electromagnetic energy that humans can see because these waves are the right length to stimulate receptors in the eye.

visual agnosia Individual fails to recognize some object, person, or color yet has the ability to see and even describe pieces or parts of some visual stimulus.

visual association area Part of the occipital lobe; transforms basic sensations, such as lights, lines, and colors into complete, meaningful visual perceptions, such as persons, objects, or animals.

visual cliff Glass tabletop with a checkerboard pattern over part of its surface; the remaining surface consists of clear glass with a checker board pattern several feet below, creating the illusion of a clifflike drop to the floor.

vulnerability Psychological or environmental difficulties that make children more at risk for developing later personality, behavioral, or social problems.

Weber's law States that the increase in intensity of a stimulus needed to produce a just noticeable difference grows in proportion to the intensity of the initial stimulus.

Wechsler Adult Intelligence Scale (WAIS) Most widely used IQ test for ages 16 and older.

Wechsler Intelligence Scale for Children (WISC) Most widely used IQ test for children of ages 6 to 16.

weight-regulating genes Play a role in influencing appetite, body metabolism, and secretion of hormones that regulate fat stores, such as leptin.

Wernicke's aphasia Difficulty in understanding spoken or written words and in putting words into meaningful sentences.

Wernicke's area Part of the temporal lobe; necessary for speaking in coherent sentences and for understanding speech.

withdrawal symptoms Painful physical and psychological symptoms that occur after a drug-dependent person stops using the drug.

word Arbitrary pairing between a sound or symbol and a meaning.

zygote Cell that results when an egg is fertilized.

Aamodt, S., & Wang, S. (2008). *Welcome to your brain: Why you lose your car keys but never forget how to drive and other puzzles of everyday life.* London: Bloomsbury.

Abernethy, B., Neal, R. J., & Koning, P. (1994). Visual-perceptual and cognitive differences between expert, intermediate, and novice snooker players. Applied Cognitive Psychology, 8, 185–211.

Adams, W. L. (2006, March/April). The truth about photographic memory. *Psychology Today.*

Ader, R. (Ed.). (2007). *Psychoneuroimmunology* (4th ed.). Burlington, MA: Elsevier.

Ader, R., & Cohen, N. (1975). Behaviorally conditioned immunosuppression. *Psychosomatic Medicine, 37,* 333–340.

Ainsworth, M. D. S. (1979). Infant-mother attachment. *American Psychologist, 34,* 932–937.

Albee, G. W., & Joffe, J. M. (2004). Mental illness is not "an illness like any other." *The Journal of Primary Prevention, 24,* 419–436.

Albert, M. L., Connor, L. T., & Obler, L. K. (2000). Brain, language, and environment. *Brain and Language, 71,* 4–6.

Albright, T. D., Dixon, J. E., Gage, F. H., & Macagno, E. R. (2005, May 26). A promise for future of medicine. *The San Diego Union-Tribune,* B11.

Alexander, M. (2007, September). Remember me. *Reader's Digest,* 178–185.

Ali, L. (2006, December 4). The coolest mogul. *Newsweek,* 62–66.

Allen, A., & Hollander, E. (2004). Similarities and differences between body dysmorphic disorder and other disorders. *Psychiatric Annals, 34,* 927-33.

Allik, J., & McCrae, R. R. (2004). Toward a geography of personality traits. *Journal of Cross-Cultural Psychology, 35,* 13–28.

Allport, G. W. (1935). Attitudes. In C. Murchison (Ed.), *Handbook of social psychology* (Vol. 2). Worcester, MA: Clark University Press.

Allport, G. W., & Odbert, H. S. (1936). Trait-names: A psycho-lexical study. *Psychological Monographs, 47* (Whole No. 211).

Almeida, D. M., Wethingon, E., & Kessler, R. C. (2002). The daily inventory of stressful events. *Assessment, 9,* 41–55.

Amabile, T. M. (1985). Motivation and creativity: Effects of motivational orientation on creative writers. *Journal of Personality and Social Psychology, 48,* 393–399.

American Academy of Pediatrics. (2000). Clinical practice guideline: Diagnosis and evaluation of the child with attention-deficit/hyperactivity disorder. *Pediatrics, 105,* 1158–1170.

American College of Emergency Physicians. (2008, August 21). Cited in HealthDay News, Text-messaging injuries blamed on distraction. *U.S. News & World Report.*

American Lung Association. (2006). *Smokeless tobacco fact sheet.* Retrieved from http://www.lungusa.org/site/c.dvLUK9O0E/b.1694879/k.CFC8/Smokeless_Tobacco_Fact_Sheet.htm

American Program Bureau. (2009). *Brenda Combs.* Retrieved from http://www.apbspeakers.com/speaker/brenda-combs

American Psychiatric Association. (2000). *Diagnostic and statistical manual of mental disorders* (4th ed., text revision). Washington, DC: Author.

American Psychological Association. (2002). *Ethical principles of psychologists and code of conduct.* Washington, DC: Author.

American Psychological Association. (2008b, May 8). Cited in J. Gever, Virtual reality PTSD therapy shows promise in Iraq veterans. *MedPage Today.*

American Psychological Association. (2009a). Finding help: How to choose a psychotherapist. *American Psychological Association Help Center.* Retrieved from http://www.apahelpcenter.org/articles/article.php?id=51

American Psychological Association, Division of Psychological Hypnosis. (1993). *Hypnosis.* Psychological Hypnosis, 2(3).

American Society for Microbiology. (2007, September 18). Hygiene habits stall: Public handwashing down. *ScienceDaily.* Retrieved from http://www.sciencedailyt.com/releases/2007/09/070917112526.htm

Andersen, S. M., Moskowitz, G. B., Blair, I. V., & Nosek, B. A. (2007). Automatic thought. In A. W. Kruglanski & E. T. Huggins (Eds.), *Social psychology: Handbook of basic principles* (2nd ed., pp. 138–175). New York: Guilford.

Anderson, C. A., & Bushman, B. J. (2002). Human aggression. *Annual Review of Psychology, 53,* 27–51.

Anderson, C. A., & Huesmann, L. R. (2003). Human aggression: A social-cognitive view. In M.A. Hogg & J. Cooper (Eds.), *The Sage handbook of social psychology* (pp. 296–323). Thousand Oaks, CA: Sage.

Anderson, M. C. (2009a). Incidental forgetting. In A. Baddeley, M. W. Eysenck, & M. C. Anderson (Eds.), *Memory* (pp. 192–216). New York: Psychology Press.

Anderson, M. C. (2009b). Motivated forgetting. In A. Baddeley, M. W. Eysenck, & M. C. Anderson (Eds.), *Memory* (pp. 217–244). New York: Psychology Press.

Anderson, M. C. (2009c). Retrieval. In A. Baddeley, M. W. Eysenck, & M. C. Anderson (Eds.), *Memory* (pp. 163–189). New York: Psychology Press.

Anderson, N. B. (2003). *Emotional longevity: What really determines how long you live.* New York: Viking.

Anderson, P. L., Zimand, E., Hodges, L. F., & Rothbaum, B. O. (2005). Cognitive behavioral therapy for public-speaking anxiety using virtual reality for exposure. *Depression and Anxiety, 22,* 156–158.

Andrews, M. (2005, December 26/2006, January 2). Why you shouldn't forget to meditate. *U.S. News & World Report,* 68–69.

Angier, N. (2003, February 25). Not just genes: Moving beyond nature vs. nurture. *The New York Times,* p. D1.

Animal training at SeaWorld. (2002). Busch Entertainment Corporation. Retrieved October 19, 2006, from http://www.seaworld.org/infobooks/Training/home.html

Anthes, E. (2009, February/March). Six ways to boost brainpower. *Scientific American Mind,* 56–63.

Anwar, Y. (2008, January 24). Youngest student to publish ADHD memoir. *UC Berkeley Press Release.*

Aqua facts: Training marine mammals. (2006, October 19). Vancouver Aquarium. Retrieved October 19, 2006, from http:// www.vanaqua.org/education/trainingmarinemammals.html

Arkowitz, H., & Lilienfeld, S. O. (2007b, October/November). The best medicine? *Scientific American Mind,* 80–83.

Armfield, J. M. (2006). Cognitive vulnerability: A model of the etiology of fear. *Clinical Psychology review, 26,* 746–68.

Armstrong, L. (2001). *It's not about the bike.* New York: Berkley Publishing.

Armstrong, L. (2007, April 9). "We have to be ruthless." *Newsweek,* 37.

Arnett, J. J. (2000b). Emerging adulthood. *American Psychologist, 55,* 469–480.

Aronson, E., Wilson, T. D., & Akert, R. M. (2004). *Social psychology* (5th ed.). Upper Saddle River, NJ: Prentice Hall.

Asch, S. E. (1958). Effects of group pressure upon modification and distortion of judgments. In E. E. Maccoby, T. M. Newcomb, & E. L. Hartley (Eds.), *Readings in social psychology* (3rd ed.). New York: Holt, Rinehart and Winston.

Aserinsky, E., & Kleitman, N. (1953). Regularly occurring periods of eye motility, and concomitant phenomena, during sleep. *Science, 118,* 273–274.

Associated Press. (1989, May 24). After 130 days of cave life, a return to glare of the sun. *The New York Times.*

Associated Press. (2005a, March 28). *Docs: Schiavo videos misleading.* Retrieved from http://www.foxnews.com/story/0,2933,151662m00.html

Associated Press. (2005b, June 15). *Schiavo autopsy shows irreversible brain damage.* Retrieved from http://www.msnbc.msn.com/id/8225637/

Associated Press. (2005c, October 7). More evidence supports cervical cancer vaccine. *MSNBC.* Retrieved from http://www.msnbc.com/id/9609603/

Associated Press. (2006a, January 4). R.I. legalizes medical marijuana. *The San Diego Union-Tribune,* A6.

Atkinson, J. W. (1964). *An introduction to motivation.* Princeton, NJ: Van Nostrand Reinhold.

Atkinson, J. W., & Raynor, J. O. (Eds.). (1974). *Motivation and achievement.* Washington, DC: V. H. Winston.

Atlas, S. W. (Ed.). (2009). *Magnetic resonance imaging of the brain and spine.* Baltimore: Lippincott, Williams, & Wilkins.

Baddeley, A. (2004). *Your memory: A user's guide.* Buffalo, NY: Firefly.

Baddeley, A. (2006). Working memory: An overview. In S. J. Pickering (Ed.), *Working memory and education.* Burlington, MA: Elsevier.

Baddeley, A. (2009a). Episodic memory: Organizing and remembering. In A. Baddeley, M. W. Eysenck, & M. C. Anderson (Eds.), *Memory* (pp. 93–112). New York: Psychology Press.

Baddeley, A. (2009b). Learning. In A. Baddeley, M. W. Eysenck, & M. C. Anderson (Eds.), *Memory* (pp. 69–91). New York: Psychology Press.

Baddeley, A. (2009c). Short-term memory. In A. Baddeley, M. W. Eysenck, & M. C. Anderson (Eds.), *Memory* (pp. 19–40). New York: Psychology Press.

Baddeley, A. (2009d). What is memory? In A. Baddeley, M. W. Eysenck, & M. C. Anderson (Eds.), *Memory* (pp. 1–17). New York: Psychology Press.

Baer, J. S., Sampson, P. D., Barr, H. M., Connor, P. D., & Streissguth, A. P. (2003). A 21-year longitudinal analysis of the effects of prenatal alcohol exposure on young adult drinking. *Archives of General Psychiatry, 60,* 377–385.

Bahrick, H. P. (2000). Long-term maintenance of knowledge. In E. Tulving & F. M. Craik (Eds.), *The Oxford handbook of memory.* New York: Oxford University Press.

Bailenson, J. N., Shum, M. S., & Uttal, D. H. (2000). The initial segment strategy: A heuristic for route selection. *Memory & Cognition, 28,* 306–318.

Baker, M. C. (2002, January 15). Cited in B. Fowler, Expert says he discerns "hard-wired" grammar rules. *The New York Times,* p. D5.

Baldauf, S. (2009, July 15). Brain stimulation: Transcranial magetic stimulation. *U.S. News & World Report.*

Ball, J. R., Mitchell, P. B., Corry, J. C., Skillecorn, A., Smith, M., & Malhi, G. S. (2006). A randomized controlled trial of cognitive therapy for bipolar disorder: Focus on long-term change. *Journal of Clinical Psychiatry, 67,* 277–286.

Balter, M. (2002). What made humans modern? *Science, 295,* 1219–1225.

Bamford, N. S., Zhang, H., Joyce, J. A., Scarlis, C. A., Hanan, W., Wu, N., ... Sulzer, D. (2008). Repeated exposure to methamphetamine causes long-lasting presynaptic corticostriatal depression that is renormalized with drug readministration. *Neuron, 58,* 89–103.

Bandura, A. (1965). Influence of models' reinforcement contingencies on the acquisition of imitative responses. *Journal of Personality and Social Psychology, 1,* 589–596.

Bandura, A. (1986). *Social foundations of thought and action: A social cognitive theory.* Englewood Cliffs, NJ: Prentice Hall.

Bandura, A. (1999). Social cognitive theory of personality. In L. A. Pervin & O. P. John (Eds.), *Handbook of personality: Theory and research* (2nd ed.). New York: Guilford.

Bandura, A. (2001a). Social cognitive theory: An agentic perspective. *Annual Review of Psychology, 52,* 1–26.

Bandura, A. (2004). Health promotion by social cognitive means. *Health Education & Behavior, 31,* 143–164.

Bandura, A., Blanchard, E. B., & Ritter, B. (1969). Relative efficacy of desensitization and modeling approaches for inducing behavioral, affective and attitudinal changes. *Journal of Personality and Social Psychology, 13,* 173–179.

Bandura, A., Ross, D., & Ross, S. A. (1963). Imitation of film-mediated aggressive models. *Journal of Abnormal and Social Psychology, 66,* 3–11.

Barak, A., Hen, L., Boniel-Nissim, M., & Shapira, N. (2008). A comprehensive review and a meta-analysis of the effectiveness of internet-based psychotherapeutic interventions. *Journal of Technology in Human Services, 26,* 109–160.

Barkley, R. A. (2006). *Attention-deficit hyperactivity disorder: A handbook for diagnosis and treatment* (3rd ed.). New York: Guilford.

Barlow, D. H. (2000). Unraveling the mysteries of anxiety and its disorders from the perspective of emotion theory. *American Psychologist, 55,* 1247-63.

Baron, A. S., & Banaji, M. R. (2006). The development of implicit attitudes: Evidence of race evaluations from ages 6 and 10 and adulthood. *Psychological Science, 17,* 53–58.

Baron, R. A., & Richardson, D. R. (2004). *Human aggression* (2nd ed.). New York: Springer.

Barone, J. (2009, July/August). Sounds of science. *Discover,* 52-56.

Guilford.Barrett, K. E., Brooks, H., Boitano, S., & Barman, S. M. (2009). *Ganong's review of medical physiology* (23rd ed.). New York: McGraw-Hill.

Barsky, A. J., Orav, E. J., & Bates, D. W. (2005). Somatization increases medical utilization and costs independent of psychiatric and medical comorbidity. *Archives of General Psychiatry, 62,* 903–910.

Bartlik, B., & Goldstein, M. Z. (2001). Men's sexual health after midlife. *Psychiatric Services, 52,* 291–306.

Basil, R. (1989). Graphology and personality: Let the buyer beware. *Skeptical Inquirer, 13,* 241–248.

Bates, B. L. (1994). Individual differences in response to hypnosis. In J. W. Rhue, S. J. Lynn, & I. Kirsch (Eds.), *Handbook of clinical hypnosis.* Washington, DC: American Psychological Association.

Bates, J. (2004). Temperament as an emotion construct: Theoretical and practical issues. In M. Lewis & J. M. Haviland-Jones (Eds.), *Handbook of emotions* (2nd ed.). New York: Guilford.

Batson, C. D. (1998). Who cares? When? Where? Why? How? *Contemporary Psychology, 43,* 108–109.

Baumeister, R. F. (1995). Disputing the effects of championship pressures and home audiences. *Journal of Personality and Social Psychology, 68,* 644–648.

Baumrind, D. (1991). Effective parenting during the early adolescent transition. In P. A. Cowan & E. M. Hetherington (Eds.), *Advances in family research.* Hillsdale, NJ: Erlbaum.

Baumrind, D. (1995). Commentary on sexual orientation: Research and social policy implications. *Developmental Psychology, 31,* 130–136.

Baylen, C. A., & Rosenberg, H. (2006). A review of the acute subjective effects of MDMA/ecstasy. *Addiction, 101,* 933.

BBC News. (2007, October 20). Settlement for bogus abuse woman. Retrieved from http://news.bbc.co.uk/1/hi/scotland/tayside_and_central/7054249.stm

Beck, A. T. (1976). *Cognitive therapy and the emotional disorders.* New York: International Universities Press.

Beck, A. T. (1991). Cognitive therapy: A 30-year retrospective. *American Psychologist, 46,* 368–375.

Beck, A. T., Rush, A. J., Shaw, B. F., & Emery, G. (1979). *Cognitive therapy of depression.* New York: Guilford.

Beck, A. T., & Weishaar, M. E. (2008). Cognitive therapy. In R. J. Corsini & D. Wedding (Eds.), *Current psychotherapies* (8th ed., pp. 263–294). Belmont, CA: Thomson Brooks/Cole.

Becker, A., Burwell, R. A., Gilman, S. E., Herzog, D. B., & Hamburg, P. (2002). Eating behaviours and attitudes following prolonged exposure to television among ethnic Fijian adolescent girls. *British Journal of Psychiatry, 10,* 509–514.

Beckman, N., Waern, M., Gustafson, D., & Skoog, I. (2008). Secular trends in self reported sexual activity and satisfaction in Swedish 70 year olds: Cross sectional survey of four populations, 1971–2001. *British Medical Journal, 337,* a279.

Bedi, K. (2006). *It's always possible: One woman's transformation of India's prison system.* Honesdale: PA: Himalayan Institute Press.

Bedrosian, J. D. (2009, March 12). Intel Science Talent Search crowns 10 promising young scientists. *USA Today,* p. 7D.

Begley, S. (1998a, January 19). Aping language. *Newsweek.*

Begley, S. (2007c, November 5). The ghosts we think we see. *Newsweek, 56.*

Begley, S. (2008a, March 3). How your brain looks at race. *Newsweek, 26–27.*

Begley, S. (2008c, November 3). Why we believe. *Newsweek, 56–60.*

Begley, S. (2009, April 20). Sex, race, and IQ: Off limits? *Newsweek, 53.*

Behrman, A. (1999, January 27). Electroboy. *The New York Times Magazine,* p. 67.

Bem, D. (1967). Self-perception: An alternative interpretation of cognitive dissonance phenomena. *Psychological Review, 74,* 183–200.

Bem, D. J., & Honorton, C. (1994). Does psi exist? Replicable evidence for an anomalous process of information transfer. *Psychological Bulletin, 115,* 4–18.

Bem, S. L. (1981). Gender schema theory: A cognitive account of sex-typing. *Psychological Review, 88,* 354–364.

Bem, S. L. (1985). Androgyny and gender schema theory: Conceptual and empirical integration. In T. B. Sonderegger (Ed.), *Nebraska symposium on motivation.* Lincoln, NE: University of Nebraska Press.

Bendersky, M., & Lewis, M. (1999). Prenatal cocaine exposure and neonatal condition. *Infant Behavior & Development, 22,* 353–366.

Benjamin, L. T., Jr. (2000). The psychology laboratory at the turn of the 20th century. *American Psychologist, 55,* 318–321.

Ben-Porath, Y. S. (2010). *Interpreting the MMPI-2-RF.* Minneapolis: University of Minnesota Press.

Benson, E. (2003a, February). Intelligent intelligence testing. *Monitor on Psychology,* 48–51.

Benson, H. (2008, October). Cited in S. Martin, The power of the relaxation response. *Monitor on Psychology,* 32–33.

Berenson, A. (2005, December 4). Sales of impotence drugs fall, defying expectations. *The New York Times.*

Berenson, A. (2006, January 1). Antidepressants seem to cut suicide risk in teenagers and adults, study says. *The New York Times,* p. 14.

Berg, C. A. (2000). Intellectual development in adulthood. In R. J. Sternberg (Ed.), *Handbook of intelligence.* New York: Cambridge University Press.

Berkowitz, L. (1989). Frustration-aggression hypothesis: Examination and reformulation. *Psychological Bulletin, 106,* 59–73.

Berkowitz, L. (1993). *Aggression: Its causes, consequences, and control.* New York: McGraw-Hill.

Berlin, H. A., & Koch, C. (2009, April/May). Neuroscience meets psychoanalysis. *Scientific American Mind,* 16–17.

Bernstein, I. L., & Koh, M. T. (2007). Molecular signaling during taste aversion learning. *Chemical Senses, 32,* 99–103.

Berry, C. M., Sackett, P. R., & Wiemann, S. (2007). A review of recent developments in integrity test research. *Personnel Psychology, 60,* 271–301.

Best, D. L., & Thomas, J. J. (2004). Cultural diversity and cross-cultural perspectives. In A. H. Eagly, A. E. Beall, & R. J. Sternberg (Eds.), *The psychology of gender* (2nd ed., pp. 296–327). New York: Guilford.

Binet, A., & Simon, T. (1905). Methodes nouvelles pour le diagnostic du niveau intellectual des anormaux. *L'Annee Psychologique, 11,* 191–244.

Bjorklund, D. F. (2005). *Children's thinking: Cognitive development and individual differences.* Belmont, CA: Wadsworth/Thomson.

Black, D. (2006, December 12). What causes antisocial personality disorder? *PsychCentral.* Retrieved from http://psychcentral.com/lib/2006/12/what-causes-antisocial-personality-disorder/

Black, L., & Flynn, C. (2003, May 7). Glenbrook North, cops investigate brawl at hazing; 5 girls are hurt during "initiation." *Chicago Tribune,* p. 1.

Blakemore, J. E. O. (2003). Children's beliefs about violating gender norms: Boys shouldn't look like girls, and girls shouldn't act like boys. *Sex Roles, 48,* 411–419.

Blakeslee, S. (2005, June 28). What other people say may change what you see. *The New York Times,* p. D3.

Blakeslee, S. (2006, January 10). Cells that read minds. *The New York Times.*

Blakeslee, S., & Blakeslee, M. (2007). *The body has a mind of its own.* New York: Random House.

Blass, T. (Ed.). (2000). *Obedience to authority.* Mahwah, NJ: Lawrence Erlbaum.

Block, J. (1995). Going beyond the five factors given: Rejoinder to Costa & McCrae (1995) and Goldberg & Saucier (1995). *Psychological Bulletin, 117,* 226–229.

Blomberg, J., Lazar, A., & Sandell, R. (2001). Long-term outcome of long-term psychoanalytically oriented therapies: First findings of the Stockholm outcome of psychotherapy and psychoanalysis study. *Psychotherapy Research, 11,* 361–382.

Boden, M. A. (1994). Précis of the creative mind: Myths and mechanisms. *Behavioral and Brain Sciences, 17,* 519–570.

Bohlen und Halbach, O. V., & Dermietzel, R. (2006). *Neurotransmitters and neuromodulators: Handbook of receptors and biological effects.* Weinheim, Germany: Wiley-VCH.

Bolton, E. E., Lambert, J. F., Wolf, E. J., Raja, S., Varra, A. A., & Fisher, L. M. (2004). Evaluating a cognitive-behavioral group treatment program for veterans with posttraumatic stress disorder. *Psychological Services, 1,* 140–146.

Bonanno, G. A. (2004). Loss, trauma, and human resilience. *American Psychologist, 59,* 20–28.

Bonneau, R. H., Padgett, D. A., & Sheridan, J. F. (2007). Twenty years of psychoneurimmunology and viral infections in *Brain, Behavior, and Immunity. Brain Behavior, and Immunity, 21,* 273–280.

Bonnet, M. H. (2005). Acute sleep deprivation. In M. H. Kryger, T. Roth, & W. C. Dement (Eds.), *Principles and practice of sleep medicine* (4th ed., pp. 51–66). Philadelphia: Elsevier Saunders.

Booth-Kewley, S., & Friedman, H. S. (1987). Psychological predictions of heart disease: A quantitative review. *Psychological Bulletin, 101,* 343–362.

Bosch, F. X., Lorincz, A., Munoz, N., Meijer, C. J. L. M., & Shah, K. V. (2002). The causal relation between human papillomavirus and cervical cancer. *Journal of Clinical Pathology, 55,* 244–265.

Bouchard, C. (2009, January). Cited in J. Chen, 13 things you never knew about your weight, *Reader's Digest,* 86–95.

Bouchard, T. J., Jr. (2004). Genetic influence on human psychological traits. *Current Directions in Psychological Science, 13,* 148–151.

Bouchard, T. J., Jr., & Loehlin, J. C. (2001). Genes, evolution, and personality. *Behavior Genetics, 31,* 243–273.

Bouchard, T. J., Jr., Lykken, D. T., McGue, M., Segal, N. L., & Tellegen, A. (1990). Sources of human psychological differences: The Minnesota study of twins reared apart. *Science, 250,* 223–228.

Bower, B. (2001). Brains in dreamland. *Science News, 160,* 90–92.

Bower, B. (2003). Words get in the way. *Science News, 163,* 250–251.

Bower, B. (2005, April 23). Mood brighteners: Light therapy gets nod as depression buster. *Science News, 167,* 261–262.

Bower, B. (2006a, May 27). Violent developments. Disruptive kids grow into their behavior. *Science News, 169,* 328–329.

Bower, B. (2006b, July 8). Feminine side of ADHD. *Science News, 170,* 21–22.

Bower, B. (2008, December 6). Morality askew in psychopaths. *Science News,* 16.

Bower, B. (2009b, July 18). Gene's reported role in depression questioned by subsequent studies. *Science News,* 10.

Bower, F. (1997). The power of limited thinking. *Science News, 152,* 334–335.

Boyce, N. (2002, October 7). Chips vs. the chess masters. *U.S. News & World Report,* 70–71.

Boysen, S. (2009). *The smartest animals on the planet.* Buffalo, NY: Firefly Books.

Brabham, D. (2001, July 23). The smart guy. *Newsday.* Retrieved from http://www.megafoundation.org/CTMU/Press/TheSmartGuy.pdf

Brackett, M. A., Cox, A., Gaines, S. O., & Salovey, P. (2005). *Emotional intelligence and relationship quality among heterosexual couples.* Manuscript submitted for publication.

Brackett, M. A., Mayer, J. D., & Warner, R. M. (2004). Emotional intelligence and the prediction of behavior. *Personality and Individual Differences, 36,* 1387–1402.

Branan, N. (2008, April/May). Wait, don't tell me.... *Scientific American Mind,* 13.

Braun, J., Kahn, R. S., Froehlich, T., Auinger, P., & Lanphear, B. P. (2006, October 7). Cited in B. Harder, Cigarettes and lead linked to attention disorder. *Science News,* 170.

Breckler, S. J. (2006, February). The IRB problem. *Monitor on Psychology, 37,* 21.

Brennan, J. (1997, September 28). This 1,800-pound bear is no 800-pound gorilla. *Los Angeles Times/Calendar.*

Brennan, J. (2004). *Cancer in context: A practical guide to supportive care.* New York: Oxford University Press.

Broad, W. J. (2002, October 9). Lie-detector tests found too flawed to discover spies. *The New York Times,* p. A.

Brody, J. E. (2000a, April 25). Memories of things that never were. *The New York Times,* p. D8.

Brody, J. E. (2003, August 18). Skipping a college course: Weight gain 101. *The New York Times,* p. D7.

Brody, J. E. (2008b, January 15). A stable life, despite persistent dizziness. *The New York Times.*

Brody, J. E. (2009, June 16). An emotional hair trigger, often misread. The New York Times, D7.

Brody, N. (1992). *Intelligence.* New York: Academic Press.

Brody, N. (1997). Intelligence, schooling, and society. *American Psychologist, 52,* 1046–1050.

Brody, N. (2000). Theories and measurements of intelligence. In R. J. Sternberg (Ed.), *Handbook of intelligence.* New York: Cambridge University Press.

Brodzinsky, S. (2006, July 25). *Columbia cracks down on drug cash.* Retrieved from http://www.usatoday.com/news/world/2006-07-25-columbia-smuggling_x.htm

Brooks, C. (1994, February 27). Breakdown into the shadows of mental illness. Special report. *San Diego Union-Tribune.*

Brooks, D. C. (2000). Recent and remote extinction cues reduce spontaneous recovery. *Quarterly Journal of Experimental Psychology, 53B,* 25–58.

Brooks, R., & Goldstein, S. (2002). *Raising resilient children.* New York: McGraw-Hill/Contemporary Books.

Brown, G. S., Lambert, M. J., Jones, E. R., & Minami, T. (2005, August). Identifying highly effective psychotherapists in a managed care environment. *The American Journal of Managed Care, 11,* 513–520.

Brown, R. J., Schrag, A., & Trimble, M. R. (2005). Dissociation, childhood interpersonal trauma, and family functioning in patients with somatization disorder. *American Journal of Psychiatry, 162,* 899–905.

Brown, R., & Kulik, J. (1977). Flashbulb memories. *Cognition, 5,* 73–99.

Brown, S. A. (1996, May 13). Talent for living. *People,* 85–86.

Brown, S. C., & Craik, F. I. M. (2005). Encoding and retrieval of information. In E. Tulving & F. M. Craik (Eds.), *The Oxford handbook of memory.* New York: Oxford University Press.

Buckley, C. (2007, January 3). Man is rescued by stranger on subway tracks. *The New York Times.*

Buckley, P. (1989). Fifty years after Freud: Dora, the Rat Man, and the Wolf-Man. *American Journal of Psychiatry, 146,* 1394–1403.

Bulik, C. M., Sullivan, P. F., & Kendler, K. S. (2003). Genetic and environmental contributions to obesity and eating. *International Journal of Eating Disorders, 33,* 293–298.

Burge, D., Hammen, C., Davila, J., Daley, S. E., Paley, B., Herzberg, D., & Lindberg, N. (1997). Attachment cognitions and college and work functioning two years later in late adolescent women. *Journal of Youth and Adolescence, 26,* 285–301.

Burger, J. M. (2008). *Personality* (7th ed.). Belmont, CA: Wadsworth Cengage.

Burn, S. M. (2004). *Groups: Theory and practice.* Belmont, CA: Wadsworth/Thomson.

Burns, T. (2004). *Community mental health teams.* New York: Oxford University Press.

Burton, C. M., & King, L. A. (2004). The health benefits of writing about intensely positive experiences. *Journal of Research in Personality, 38,* 150–163.

Burton, S. (2006). Symptom domains of schizophrenia: The role of atypical antipsychotic agents. *Journal of Psychopharmacology, 20,* 6–20.

Buss, D. M. (1994). Mate preferences in 37 cultures. In W. J. Lonner & R. Malpass (Eds.), *Psychology and culture.* Boston: Allyn & Bacon.

Buss, D. M. (1995). Psychological sex differences. *American Psychologist, 50,* 164–168.

Buss, D. M. (2003). *The evolution of desire: Strategies of human mating* (2nd ed.) New York: Basic Books.

Buss, D. M. (2004). *Evolutionary psychology: The new science of the mind* (2nd ed.). Boston: Allyn & Bacon.

Buss, D. M. (2007). The evolution of human mating. *Acta Psychologica Sinica, 39,* 502–512.

Buss, D. M. (2009). The great struggles of life: Darwin and the emergence of evolutionary psychology. *American Psychologist, 64,* 140–148.

Butcher, J. N. (2009a). Clinical personality assessment: History, evolution, contemporary models & practical applications. Cited in J. N. Butcher (Ed.), *Oxford handbook of personality assessment* (pp. 5–24). New York: Oxford University Press.

Butcher, J. N. (Ed.). (2009b). *Oxford handbook of personality assessment.* New York: Oxford University Press.

Butler, A. C., Chapman, J. E., Forman, E. M., & Beck, A. T. (2006). The empirical status of cognitive-behavioral therapy: A review of meta-analyses. *Clinical Psychology Review, 26,* 17–31.

Byne, W. (1997). Why we cannot conclude that sexual orientation is primarily a biological phenomenon. *Journal of Homosexuality, 34,* 73–80.

Byrne, R. (2003, March 2). When man pulled ahead of machine, albeit briefly. *The New York Times,* p. 12.

Cabeza, R. (2006, January 16). Cited in G. Cohen, The myth of the midlife crisis. *Newsweek,* 82–87.

Cabeza, R. (2008, December 16). Cited in M. Elias, Older brains act as filters. *USA Today,* p. 7D.

Cacioppo, J. T., Amaral, D. G., Blanchard, J. J., Cameron, J. L., Carter, C. S., Crews, D, ... Quinn, K. J. (2007). Social neuroscience: Progress and implications for mental health. *Perspectives on Psychological Science, 2,* 99–123.

Cacioppo, J. T., & Berntson, G. G. (2002). Social neuroscience. In J. T. Cacioppo, G. G. Berntson, R. Adolphs, C. S. Carter, R. J. Davidson, M. K. McClintock, ... S. E. Taylor (Eds.), *Foundations of social neuroscience* (pp. 1–9). Cambridge, MA: MIT Press.

Cacioppo, J. T., Berntson, G. G., Larsen, J. R., Poehlmann, K. M., & Ito, T. A. (2000). The psychophysiology of emotion. In M. Lewis & J. M. Haviland-Jones (Eds.), Handbook of emotions (2nd ed., pp. 173–191). New York: Guilford.

Camp, G. C. (1994). A longitudinal study of correlates of creativity. *Creativity Research Journal, 7,* 125–144.

Canli, T. (2008, February/March). The character code. *Scientific American Mind,* 52–57.

Caplan, P. (1994, June 5). Cited in A. Japenga, DMS. *Los Angeles Times Magazine.*

Caprara, G. V., Barbaranelli, C., Pastorelli, C., & Cervone, D. (2004). The contribution of self-efficacy beliefs to psychosocial outcomes in adolescence: Predicting beyond global dispositional tendencies. *Personality and Individual Differences, 37,* 751–763.

Carducci, B. J. (2006). *Psychology of personality.* Boston: Blackwell Publishing.

CARE. (2008). Maternal caffeine intake during pregnancy and risk of fetal growth restriction: A large prospective observational study. *Behavioral Medicine Journal, 337,* a2332.

Carlson, J. M. (1990). Subjective ideological similarity between candidates and supporters: A study of party elites. *Political Psychology, 11,* 485–492.

Caroff, S. N., Mann, S. C., Campbell, E. C., & Sullivan, K. A. (2002). Movement disorders associated with atypical antipsychotic drugs. *Journal of Clinical Psychiatry, 63*(Suppl. 4), 12–19.

Carpenter, W. (2003, May 20). Cited in E. Goode, Leading drugs for psychosis come under new scrutiny. *The New York Times,* p. A1.

Carskadon, M. A. (2006). *The sleep of America's children* [On-line]. Available: http://www.sleep foundation.org/ hottopics/index. php?secid=11&id=82. Accessed October 5, 2006.

Carstensen, L. (2006, January 31). Cited in T. Valeo, The aging brain puts accent on the positive. *St. Petersburg Times.*

Carter, O. L., Pettigrew, J. D., Hasler, F., Wallis, G. M., Liu, G. B., Hell, D., & Vollenweider, F. X. (2005). Modulating the rate and rhythmicity of perceptual rivalry alterations with the mixed 5-HT2A and 5-HT1A agonist psilocybin. *Neuropsychopharmacology, 30,* 1154–1162.

Cartwright, R. (2002, July 15). Cited in M. H. Gossard, Taking control. *Newsweek,* 47.

Cartwright, R. D. (2006). Sleepwalking. In T. L. Lee-Chiong (Ed.), *Sleep: A comprehensive handbook* (pp. 429–433). Hoboken, NJ: John Wiley & Sons.

Caruso, E. (2009, February/March). Cited in S. Carpenter, Bias doesn't pay. *Scientific American Mind,* 9.

Caspi, A., Williams, B., Kim-Cohen, J., Craig, I. W., Milne, B. J., Poulton, R....Moffitt, T. E. (2007). Moderation of breastfeeding effects on the IQ by genetic variation in fatty acid metabolism. *Proceedings of the National Academy of Sciences, 104,* 18860–18865.

Casselman, A. (2006, January). Blinking flips an off switch in brain. *Discover,* 42.

Cattell, R. B. (1943). The description of personality: Basic traits resolved into clusters. *Journal of Abnormal and Social Psychology, 38,* 476–506.

CBS News. (2004, June 16). *Tony Hawk takes off.* Retrieved from http://www.cbsnews.com/ stories/ 2002/12/ 10/60II/main532509.shtml

CDC. (2006). *Overweight and obesity: An overview.* Retrieved from http://cdc.gov/nccdphp/dnpa/ obesity/contributing_factors.htm

CDC. (2008a, July 23). About 5% of kids have ADHD. Cited in M. Hitti, *WebMD.* Retrieved from http://www.webmd.com/add-adhd/ news/20080723/ cdc-about-5-percent-of-kids-have-adhd

CDC. (2008b, December 19). Cited in C. Macleod, China wrestles with growing obesity. *USA Today,* p. 16A.

Celizic, M. (2007, November 2). Former addict lifts herself up, becomes a teacher. *Today Show.* Retrieved from http://today.msnbc.com/ id/21595900/

Cerone, D. (1989). How to train an 1,800-pound star. *Los Angeles Times*/Calendar.

Cha, A. E. (2005, March 27). Employers replying on personality tests to screen applicants. *Washington Post,* p. A1.

Chaiken, S., & Eagly, A. H. (1976). Communication modality as a determinant of message persuasiveness and message comprehensibility. *Jour-*

nal of Personality and Social Psychology, 34, 605–614.

Chamorro-Premuzic, T., & Furnham, A. (2008). Personality, intelligence and approaches to learning as predictors of academic performance. Personality and Individual Differences, 44, 1596–1603.

Chance, P. (2006). Learning & behavior (5th ed.). Belmont, CA: Thomson Wadsworth.

Charmoli, R. (2006, May 13). Former Spokesman for Aryan Nations speaks about hate groups. Cadillac News.

Chaudri, O., Small, C., & Bloom, S. (2006). Gastrointestinal hormones regulating appetite. Philosophical Transactions of the Royal Society of London. Series B, Biological Sciences, 29, 1187–1209.

Chavez, S. (1994, January 3). Tough stand on attendance pays off at South Gate High. Los Angeles Times.

Chemers, M. M., Hu, L., & Garcia, B. F. (2001). Academic self-efficacy and first-year college student performance and adjustment. Journal of Educational Psychology, 93, 55–64.

Chokroverty, S. (2000). Sleep disorders medicine (2nd ed.). Boston: Butterworth-Heinemann.

Chomsky, N. (1957). Syntactic structures. The Hague, The Netherlands: Mouton.

Christakis, D. A., Gilkerson, J., Richards, J. A., Zimmerman, F. J., Garrison, M. M., Xu, D., ... Yapanel, U. (2009). Audible television and decreased adult words, infant vocalizations, and conversational turns. Archives of Pediatrics & Adolescent Medicine, 163, 554–558.

Christman, M. F. (2006, April 18). Common genetic link to obesity is discovered. The New York Times, p. O4.

Chwalisz, K., Diener, E., & Gallagher, D. (1988). Autonomic arousal feedback and emotional experience: Evidence from the spinal cord injury. Journal of Personality and Social Psychology, 54, 820–828.

Cialdini, R. B. (2003, February). The science of persuasion. Scientific American, 76–81.

Cialdini, R. B., & Goldstein, N. J. (2004). Social influence: Compliance and conformity. Annual Review of Psychology, 55, 591–621.

Clark, D. M., Ehlers, A., Hackman, A., McManus, F., Fennell, M., Grey, N., ... Wild, J. (2006). Cognitive therapy versus exposure and applied relaxation in social phobia: A randomized controlled trial. Journal of Consulting and Clinical Psychology, 74, 568–578.

Clark, L. A., Watson, D., & Reynolds, S. (1995). Diagnosis and classification of psychopathology: Challenges to the current system and fu-

ture directions. Annual Review of Psychology, 46, 121–153.

Clay, R. A. (2002, September). A renaissance for humanistic psychology. Monitor on Psychology, 42–43.

Clore, G. L., & Ortony, A. (2008). Appraisal theories: How cognition shapes affect into emotion. Cited in M. Lewis, J. M. Haviland-Jones, & L. F. Barrett (Eds.), Handbook of emotions (3rd ed., pp. 628–664). New York: Guilford.

Cloud, J. (2009, January 19). Minds on the edge. Time, 42–46.

Cochran, F. (2007, February 16). About Floyd Cochran. Retrieved from http://www.geocities.com/onemansmind/hg/Cochran.html

Coghill, D. R. (2007, November 3). Cited in B. Bower, Stimulant inaction. Science News, 172.

Cohen, G. (2006, January 16). The myth of the midlife crisis. Newsweek, 82–87.

Cohen, N. J. (1984). Preserved learning capacity in amnesia: Evidence for multiple memory systems. In L. R. Squire & N. Butters (Eds.), Neuropsychology of memory. New York: Guilford.

Cohen, S. (2003). Social stress, social support, and the susceptibility to the common cold. American Psychological Society, 16, 13.

Cohen, S., Tyrrell, D. A. J., & Smith, A. P. (1997). Psychological stress in humans and susceptibility to the common cold. In T. W. Miller (Ed.), Clinical disorders and stressful life events. Madison, CT: International Universities Press.

Cole, S. O. (2005). An update on the effects of marijuana & its potential medical use: Forensic focus. The Forensic Examiner, 14.3, 14.

Collins, W. A., Maccoby, E. E., Steinberg, L., Hetherington, E. M., & Bornstein, M. H. (2000). Contemporary research on parenting. American Psychologist, 55, 218–232.

Colom, R., Juan-Espinosa, M., Abad, F., & Garcia, L. F. (2000). Negligible sex differences in general intelligence. Intelligence, 28, 57–68.

Colwell, K. (2009, May 12). Cited in B. Carey, Judging honesty by words, not fidgets. The New York Times, pp. D1, D4.

Comarow, A. (2001, April 23). Scary news, soothing numbers. U.S. News & World Report, 74.

Committee on Animal Research and Ethics. (2010). Retrieved from http://apa.org/science/anguide.html

Cook, G. (2002, January 2). Aha! Eureka moments start with confusion and end with discovery. San Diego Union Tribune, p. F1.

Cooper, Z., & Shafran, R. (2008). Cognitive behaviour therapy for eating disorders. Behavioural and Cognitive Psychotherapy, 36, 713–722.

Copeland, L. (1999, December 16). Meet South's new sheriffs. USA Today, p. A1.

Corey, G. (2009). Theory and practice of counseling and psychotherapy (8th ed.). Belmont, CA: Thomson Brooks/Cole.

Cormier, S., & Nurius, P. S. (2003). Interviewing and change strategies for helpers: Fundamental skills and cognitive behavioral interventions (5th ed.). Pacific Grove, CA: Brooks/Cole.

Craik, F. I. M., & Lockhart, R. S. (1972). Levels of processing: A framework for memory research. Journal of Verbal Learning and Verbal Behavior, 11, 671–684.

Cramer, P. (2003). Defense mechanisms and physiological reactivity to stress. Journal of Personality, 71, 221–244.

Cramer, P. (2006). Protecting the self: Defense mechanisms in action. New York: Guilford.

Crenson, M. (2005, September 11). What makes a sexual predator? North County Times.

Crepeau, M. (2009, March 10). Eugene high school student wins $100,000, a laptop and a bright future. The Oregonian.

Crews, F. (2006, July 9). Cited in K. Butler, Alcohol harder on teen brains than thought. The San Francisco Chronicle, p. B1.

Crooks, R., & Baur, K. (2002). Our sexuality (8th ed.). Pacific Grove, CA: Wadsworth.

Crow, T. J. (1985). The two syndrome concept: Origins and current status. Schizophrenia Bulletin, 11, 471–486.

Cullen, L. T. (2006, April 3). SATS for J-O-B-s. Time, 89.

Cunningham, F. G., Leveno, K. J., Bloom, S. L., Hauth, J. C., Rouse, D., & Spong, C. (Eds.). (2009). Williams obstetrics (23rd ed.). New York: McGraw-Hill.

Curtiss, S. (1977). Genie: A psycholinguistic study of a modern-day "wild child." New York: Academic Press.

Cytowic, R. E. (1999). The man who tasted shapes. Cambridge, MA: MIT Press.

Czeisler, C. A. (1994). Cited in R. Nowak, Chronobiologists out of sync over light therapy patents. Science, 263, 1217–1218.

Czeisler, C. A., Duffy, J. F., Shanahan, T. L., Brown, E. N., Mitchell, J. F., Rimmer, D. W., ... Kronauer, R. E. (1999). Stability, precision, and near-24-hour period of the human circadian pacemaker. Science, 284, 2177–2181.

Czeisler, C. A., Shanahan, T. L., Klerman, E. B., Martens, H., Brotman, D. J., Emens, J. S., ... Rizzo, J. F. (1995). Suppression of melatonin secretion in some blind patients by exposure to bright light. *New England Journal of Medicine, 332,* 6–11.

Czeisler, C. A., Winkelman, J. R., & Richardson, G. S. (2006). Sleep disorders. In S. L. Hauser (Ed.), *Harrison's neurology in clinical medicine* (pp. 169–183). New York: McGraw-Hill.

Dackis, C. A., & O'Brien, C. P. (2001). Cocaine dependence: A disease of the brain's reward center. *Journal of Substance Abuse Treatment, 21,* 111.

The Daily Aztec. (1984, March 22). San Diego State University.

Dallman, M. F., Pecoraro, N. C., & la Fleur, S. E. (2005). Chronic stress and comfort foods: Self-medication and abdominal obesity. *Brain, Behavior, and Immunity, 19,* 275–280.

Dalman, C., Allebeck, P., Gunnell, D., Harrison, G., Kristensson, K., Lewis, G., ... Karlsson, H. (2008). Infections in the CNS during childhood and the risk of subsequent psychotic illness: A cohort study of more than one million Swedish subjects. *The American Journal of Psychiatry, 165,* 59–65.

Damasio, A. (2006, August 7). Cited in D. Vergano, Study: Ask with care. *USA Today,* p. 5D.

Damasio, H., Brabowski, T., Frank, R., Galaburda, A. M., & Damasio, A. R. (1994). The return of Phineas Gage: Clues about the brain from the skull of a famous patient. *Science, 264,* 1102–1105.

Dambro, M. R. (Ed.). (2006). *Griffith's 5-minute clinical consult* (14th ed.). Philadelphia: Lippincott Williams & Wilkins.

Dapretto, M., Davies, M. S., Pfeifer, J. H., Scott, A. A., Sigman, M., Bookheimer, S. Y.... Iacoboni, M. (2006). Understanding emotions in others: Mirror neuron dysfunction in children with autism spectrum disorders. *Nature Neuroscience, 9,* 28–30.

Darwin, C. (1872; reprinted 1965). *The expression of the emotions in man and animals.* Chicago: University of Chicago Press.

Davey, M. (2005, March 6). Suspect in 10 Kansas murders lived an intensely ordinary life. *The New York Times,* p. 1.

Davies, I. R. L., & Corbett, G. G. (1997). A cross-cultural study of colour grouping: Evidence for weak linguistic relativity. *British Journal of Psychology, 88,* 493–517.

Davis, O. S. P., Arden, R., & Plomin, R. (2008). *g* in middle childhood: Moderate genetic and shared environmental influence using diverse measures of general cognitive ability at 7, 9 and 10 years in a large population sample of twins. *Intelligence, 36,* 68–80.

Davison, G. C., & Neale, J. M. (1990). *Abnormal psychology* (3rd ed.). New York: Wiley.

Davison, G. C., & Neale, J. M. (1994). *Abnormal psychology* (6th ed.). New York: Wiley.

De Martino, B. (2006a, August 3). Cited in University College London Media Relations, *Irrational decisions driven by emotions.* Retrieved from http://ucl.ac.uk/media/library/decisionbrain

De Martino, B. (2006b, August 7). Cited in D. Vergano, Study: Ask with care. *USA Today,* p. 6D.

De Martino, B., Kumaran, D., Seymour, B., & Dolan, R. J. (2006, August). Frames, biases, and rational decision-making in the human brain. *Science, 313,* 684–687.

Deary, I. J., Strand, S., Smith, P., & Fernandes, C. (2007). Intelligence and educational achievement. *Intelligence, 35,* 13–21.

deCharms, R. C., Maeda, F., Glover, G. H., Ludlow, D., Pauly, J. M., Soneji, D., ... Mackey, S. C. (2005). Control over brain activation and pain learned by using real-time functional MRI. *Proceedings of the National Academy of Sciences, 102,* 18626–18631.

Deci, E. L., Koestner, R., & Ryan, R. M. (1999). A meta-analytic review of experiments examining the effects of extrinsic rewards on intrinsic motivation. *Psychological Bulletin, 125,* 627–668.

Deci, E. L., & Moller, A. C. (2005). The concept of competence. In A. J. Elliot & C. S. Dweck (Eds.), *Handbook of competence and motivation* (pp. 579–597). New York: Guilford.

Deci, E. L., & Ryan, R. M. (1985). *Intrinsic motivation and self-determination in human behavior.* New York: Plenum Press.

DeCurtis, A. (2009, March 9). Not a businessman—a business, man. *Best Life.* Retrieved from http://www.bestlifeonline.com/cms/publish/wealth/Jay-Z-Personal-Success_printer.php

Delgado, M. R., LaBouliere, C. D., & Phelps, E. A. (2006). Fear of losing money? Aversive conditioning with secondary reinforcers. *Social Cognitive and Affective Neuroscience, 1,* 250–259.

Dement, W. C. (1999). *The promise of sleep.* New York: Random House.

Dennerstein, L., Dudley, E., & Burger, H. (1997). Well-being and the menopausal transition. *Journal of Psychosomatic Obstetrics and Gynecology, 18,* 95–101.

DeNoon, D. J. (2008, October 9). Children's vaccines health center. 25% of teen girls got HPV vaccine. *WebMD.* Retrieved from http://children.webmd.com/vaccines/news/20081009/25-percent-of-teen-girls-got-hpv-vaccine

Dere, E., Easton, A., Nadel, L., & Huston, J. P. (2008). *Handbook of episodic memory* (Vol. 18). Oxford, England: Elsevier.

Derlega, V. J., Winstead, B. A., & Jones, W. H. (2005). *Personality: Contemporary theory and research* (3rd ed.). Belmont, CA: Thomson Wadsworth.

Derrig-Palumbo, K., & Zeine, F. (2005). *Online therapy: A therapist's guide to expanding your practice.* New York: W. W. Norton & Co.

DeRubeis, R. J., Hollon, S. D., Amsterdam, J. D., Shelton, R. C., Young, P. R., Salomon, R. M., ... Gallop, R. (2005). Cognitive therapy vs. medications in the treatment of moderate to severe depression. *Archives of General Psychiatry, 62,* 409–416.

Deuschl, G., Schade-Brittinger, C., Krack, P., Volkmann, J., Schafer, H., Dillman, U., ... Voges, J. (2006). A randomized trial of deep-brain stimulation for Parkinson's disease. *The New England Journal of Medicine, 355,* 896–908.

Diamond, M., & Sigmundson, H. K. (1997). Sex reassignment at birth. *Archives of Pediatric & Adolescent Medicine, 151,* 298–304.

Dickerson, T. J. (2007, June 30). Cited in N. Seppa, Immune abuse. *Science News, 171,* 405–406.

Diener, E., & Diener, C. (1996). Most people are happy. *Psychological Science, 7,* 181–185.

Digman, J. M. (1997). Higher-order factors of the Big Five. *Journal of Personality and Social Psychology, 73,* 1246–1256.

Dixon, W. A., & Reid, J. K. (2000). Positive life events as a moderator of stress-related depressive symptoms. *Journal of Counseling & Development, 78,* 343–347.

Dobbs, D. (2006b, April/May). A revealing reflection. *Scientific American Mind,* 22–27.

Dobson, K. S. (2009). *Handbook of cognitive-behavioral therapies* (3rd ed.). New York: Guilford.

Dobson, K. S., & Khatri, N. (2000). Cognitive therapy: Looking backward, looking forward. *Journal of Clinical Psychology, 56,* 907–923.

Dolan, R. J. (2002). Emotion, cognition, and behavior. *Science, 298,* 1191–1194.

Dolder, C. R. (2008). Side effects of antipsychotics. In K. T. Mueser & D. V. Jeste (Eds.), *Clinical handbook of schizophrenia* (pp. 168–177). New York: Guilford.

Domhoff, G. W. (2003). *The scientific study of dreams.* Washington, DC: American Psychological Association.

Dowling, C. G. (2000, August, 14). Mistaken identity. *People,* 50–55.

Drisko, J. W. (2004). Common factors in psycho-therapy outcome: Meta-analytic findings and their implications for practice and research. *Families in Society, 85,* 81–90.

Drummond, S. P. A. (2000). Cited in B. Bower, Sleepy-heads' brains veer from restful path. *Science News, 157,* 103.

DuBois, D. L., Tevendale, H. D., Burk-Braxton, C., Swenson, L. P., & Hardesty, J. L. (2000). Self-system influences during early adolescence: Investigation of an integrative model. *Journal of Early Adolescence, 20,* 12–43.

Dudley, D. (2006, January/February). Impact awards 2006 honorees. *AARP: The Magazine.*

Durand, V. M., & Barlow, D. H. (2006). *Essentials of abnormal psychology* (4th ed.). Belmont, CA: Thomson Wadsworth.

Durand, V. M., & Barlow, D. H. (2010). *Essentials of abnormal psychology* (5th ed.). Belmont, CA: Thomson Wadsworth.

Durrett, C., & Trull, T. J. (2005). An evaluation of evaluative personality terms: A comparison of the big seven and five-factor model in predicting psychopathology. *Psychological Assessment, 17,* 359–368.

Durso, F. T., Rea, C. B., & Dayton, T. (1994). Graph-theoretic confirmation of restructuring during insight. *Psychological Science, 5,* 94–98.

Duyme, M. (1999). Cited in B. Bower, Kids adopted late reap IQ increases. *Science News, 156,* 54–55.

Dyck, D. G., Short, R. A., Hendryx, M. S., Norell, D., Myers, M., Patterson, T., ... McFarlane, W. R. (2000). Management of negative symptoms among patients with schizophrenia attending multiple-family groups. *Psychiatric Services, 51,* 513–519.

Eagly, A. H., & Karau, S. J. (2002). Role congruity theory of prejudice toward female leaders. *Psychological Review, 109,* 573–598.

Eagly, A. H., Wood, W., & Diekman, A. B. (2000). Social role theory of sex differences and similarities: A current appraisal. In T. Eckes & H. M. Trautner (Eds.), *The developmental social psychology of gender.* Mahwah, NJ: Lawrence Erlbaum.

Easterlin, R. A. (2003). Explaining happiness. *Proceedings of the National Academy of Sciences, 100,* 11176–11183.

Ebrecht, M., Hextall, J., Kirtley, L. G., Taylor, A., Dyson, M., & Weinman, J. (2004). Perceived stress and cortisol levels predict speed of wound healing in healthy male adults. *Psychoneuroimmunology, 29,* 798–809.

Eccles, J. S., & Wigfield, A. (2002). Motivational beliefs, values and goals. *Annual Review of Psychology, 53,* 109–132.

Eckes, T., & Trautner, H. M. (2000). *The developmental social psychology of gender.* Mahwah, NJ: Lawrence Erlbaum.

Edelman, G. M. (2003). Naturalizing consciousness: A theoretical framework. *Proceedings of the National Academy of Sciences, 100,* 5520–5524.

Eggers, C., & Liebers, V. (2007, April/May). Through a glass, darkly. *Scientific American Mind,* 30–35.

Ehrenberg, R. (2008, September 27). Gene activity makes the difference in development of human qualities. *Science News,* 13.

Ehrenberg, R. (2009, June 6). Intel science fair recognizes top young scientists. *Science News,* 9.

Eibl-Eibesfeldt, I. (1973). The expressive behavior of the deaf-and-blind-born. In M. von Cranach & I. Vine (Eds.), *Social communication and movement.* San Diego, CA: Academic Press.

Eich, E., Macaulay, D., Loewenstein, R. J., & Dihle, P. H. (1997). Memory, amnesia, and dissociative identity disorder. *Psychological Science, 8,* 417–422.

Eichenbaum, H. (2004). An information processing framework for memory representation by the hippocampus. In M. S. Gazzaniga (Ed.), *The cognitive neurosciences III.* Cambridge, MA: MIT Press.

Eikeseth, S., Smith, T., Jahr, E., & Eldevik, S. (2007). Outcome for children with autism who began intensive behavioral treatment between ages 4 and 7. *Behavior Modification, 31,* 264–278.

Eisenberg, D. (2005, April 4). Lessons of the Schiavo battle: What the bitter fight over a woman's right to live or die tells us about politics, religion, the courts and life itself. *Time,* 22–30.

Ekman, P. (2003). *Emotions revealed: Recognizing faces and feelings to improve communication and emotional life.* New York: Times Books.

Ekman, P. (2006, October/November). Cited in S. Schubert, A look tells all. *Scientific American Mind,* 26–31.

Ekman, P., & Rosenberg, E. L. (Eds.). (2005). *What the face reveals: Basic and applied studies of spontaneous expression using the facial action coding system (FACS).* New York: Oxford University Press.

Elbogen, E. B., & Johnson, S. C. (2009). The intricate link between violence and mental disorder. *Archives of General Psychiatry, 66,* 152–161.

Elias, M. (2008a, October 27). Post-traumatic stress is a war within the body. *USA Today,* p. 7D.

Elliott, D. (1995, March 20). The fat of the land. *Newsweek.*

Ellsworth, P. C., & Scherer, K. R. (2003). Appraisal processes in emotion. In R. J. Davidson, K. R. Scherer & H. H. Goldsmith (Eds.), *Handbook of affective sciences.* New York: Oxford University Press.

Ende, G., Braus, D. F., Walter, S., Weber-Fahr, W., & Henn, R. A. (2000). The hippocampus in patients treated with electroconvulsive therapy. *Archives of General Psychiatry, 57,* 937–943.

Epel, E., & Blackburn, E. (2004, November 30). Cited in B. Carey, Stress and distress may give your genes gray hair. *The New York Times,* p. D5.

Erdmann, J. (2008, December 20). Imagination medicine. *Science News,* 26–30.

Erikson, E. H. (1963). *Childhood and society.* New York: Norton.

Erikson, E. H. (1982). *The life cycle completed: Review.* New York: Norton.

Espiard, M., Lecardeur, L., Abadie, P., Halbecq, I., & Dollfus, S. (2005). Hallucinogen persisting perception disorder after psilocybin consumption: A case study. *European Psychiatry, 20,* 458–460.

Evans, J. (1993). The cognitive psychology of reasoning: An introduction. *Quarterly Journal of Experimental Psychology, 46A,* 561–567.

Evans, R. B. (1999, December). A century of psychology. *Monitor on Psychology.*

Everest News. (1999). Erik Weihenmayer. Retrieved from http://www.k2news.com/erik/htm

Eysenck, M. W. (2009). Semantic memory and stored knowledge. In A. Baddeley, M. W. Eysenck & M. C. Anderson (Eds.), *Memory* (pp. 113–135). New York: Psychology Press.

Eysenck, M. W. (2009a). Eyewitness testimony. In A. Baddeley, M. W. Eysenck, & M. C. Anderson (Eds.), *Memory* (pp. 317–342). New York: Psychology Press.

Eysenck, M. W. (2009b). Improving your memory. In A. Baddeley, M. W. Eysenck, & M. C. Anderson (Eds.), *Memory* (pp. 357–380). New York: Psychology Press.

Fabrigar, L. R., MacDonald, T. K., & Wegener, D. T. (2005). The structure of attitudes. In D. Albarracin, B. T. Johnson, & M. P. Zanna (Eds.), *The handbook of attitudes.* Mahwah, NJ: Lawrence Erlbaum.

Falck, R. S., Wang, J., Carlson, R. G., & Siegal, H. A. (2006). Prevalence and correlates of current depressive symptomatology among a community sample of MDMA users in Ohio. *Addictive Behaviors, 31,* 90–101.

Faller, A., Schunke, M., & Shunke, G. (2004). *The human body: An introduction to structure and function*. New York: Thieme Medical.

Faraone, S. V., Perlis, R. H., Doyle, A. E., Smoller, J. W., Goralnick, J. J., Holmgren, M. A .... Sklar, P. (2005). Molecular genetics of attention-deficit/hyperactivity disorder. *Biological Psychiatry, 57*, 1313–1323.

Farber, B. A. (2000a). Introduction: Understanding and treating burnout in a changing culture. *Journal of Clinical Psychology/In Session, 56*, 589–594.

Farber, B. A. (2000b). Treatment strategies for different types of teacher burnout. *Journal of Clinical Psychology/In Session, 56*, 675–689.

Feingold, B. R. (1975). Hyperkinesis and learning disabilities linked to artificial food flavors and colors. *American Journal of Nursing, 75*, 797–803.

Feldman, D. (2009). Synaptic mechanisms for plasticity in neocortex. *Annual Review of Neuroscience* (vol. 32). Palo Alto, CA: Annual Reviews.

Fenly, L. (2006, January 18). Autistic expert feels bond with animals. *The San Diego Union–Tribune*, F1.

Ferguson, D. P., Rhodes, G., Lee, K., & Sriram, N. (2001). "They all look alike to me"; Prejudice and cross-race face recognition. *British Journal of Psychology, 92*, 567–577.

Festinger, L. (1954). A theory of social comparison processes. *Human Relations, 7*, 117–140.

Festinger, L. (1957). *A theory of cognitive dissonance*. Palo Alto, CA: Stanford University Press.

Festinger, L., & Carlsmith, J. M. (1959). Cognitive consequences of forced compliance. *Journal of Abnormal and Social Psychology, 58*, 203–210.

Fiedler, K. (2007). Information ecology and the explanation of social cognition and behavior. In A. W. Kruglanski & E. T. Higgins (Eds.), *Social psychology: Handbook of basic principles* (2nd ed., pp. 176–200). New York: Guilford.

Fiedler, K., Schmid, J., & Stahl, T. (2002). What is the current truth about polygraph lie detection? *Basic and Applied Social Psychology, 24*, 313–324.

Field, A. P., & Nightengale, Z. C. (2009). What if Little Albert had escaped? *Clinical Child Psychology and Psychiatry, 14*, 311–319.

Fields, R. D. (2005, February). Making memories stick. *Scientific American*, 75–81.

Fields, R. D. (2009). *The other brain*. New York: Simon & Schuster.

Fink, P., Hansen, M. S., & Oxhoj, M. (2004). The prevalence of somatoform disorders among internal medical inpatients. *Journal of Psychosomatic Research, 56*, 413–418.

Finke, R. A. (1993). Mental imagery and creative discovery. In B. Roskos-Ewoldsen, M. J. Intons-Peterson, & Anderson, R. E. (Eds.), *Imagery, creativity, and discovery: A cognitive perspective*. Amsterdam: North-Holland.

Finney, M. L. (2003, March). Cited in D. Smith, Angry thoughts, at-risk hearts. *Monitor on Psychology*, 46–47.

First, M. B. (2007, January 24). *A research agenda for DSM-V: Summary of the DSM-V preplanning white papers published in May 2002*. Retrieved from http://www.dsm5.org/whitepapers.cfm

Fischer, J. S. (1999, September 13). From Romania, a lesson in resilience. *U.S. News & World Report*.

Fischman, J. (2006, December 11). Alzheimer's today. *U.S. News & World Report*, 70–78.

Fiske, S. (2006, January 2). Cited in Don't race to judgment. *U.S. News & World Report*, 90–91.

Fiske, S. T. (2008). Core social motivations. In J. Y. Shah & W. L. Gardner (Eds.), *Handbook of motivation science* (pp. 3–22). New York: Guilford.

Flagg, S. (2008, December 8). For drivers, text messaging is becoming most dangerous distraction. *Columbia Missourian*.

Fletcher, G. J. O., & Simpson, J. A. (2000). Ideal standards in close relationships: Their structure and functions. *Directions in Psychological Science, 9*, 102–105.

Foer, J. (2006, April). How to win the world memory championship. *Discover*, 62–66.

Folkman, S., & Moskowitz, J. T. (2000). Stress, positive emotion, and coping. *Current Directions in Psychological Science, 9*, 115–118.

Food and Drug Administration. (2006, June 8). *FDA licenses new vaccine for prevention of cervical cancer and other diseases in females caused by human papillomavirus*. Retrieved from http://www.fda.gov/bbs/ topics/NEWS/2006/NEW01385.html

Fotopoulou, A. (2006, April/May). Cited in M. Solms, Freud returns. *Scientific American Mind*, 28–34.

Fox, M. J. (2002). *Lucky man: A memoir*. New York: Hyperion.

Frank, D. A., Augustyn, M., Knight, W. G., Pell, T., & Zuckerman, B. (2001). Growth, development, and behavior in early childhood following prenatal cocaine exposure. *Journal of the American Medical Association, 285*, 1613–1625.

Frank, M. G. (2006). The function of sleep. In T. L. Lee-Chiong (Ed.), *Sleep: A comprehensive handbook* (pp. 45–48). Hoboken, NJ: John Wiley & Sons.

Franks, C. M. (1994). Behavioral model. In V. B. Van Hasselt & M. Hersen (Eds.), *Advanced abnormal psychology*. New York: Plenum Press.

Franz, V. H., Gegenfurtner, K. R., Bulthoff, H. H., & Fahle, M. (2000). Grasping visual illusions: No evidence for a dissociation between perception and action. *Psychological Science, 11*, 20–25.

Freed, C. (2008, February/March). Cited in N. Branan, Stem cells for memory. *Scientific American Mind*, 13.

Freud, S. (1900; reprinted 1980). *The interpretation of dreams* (J. Strachey, Ed. and Trans.). New York: Avon.

Freud, S. (1901; reprinted 1960). The psychopathology of everyday life. In J. Strachey (Ed. and Trans.), *The standard edition of the complete psychological works of Sigmund Freud* (Vol. 6). London: Hogarth.

Freud, S. (1909; reprinted 1949). Notes upon a case of obsessional neurosis. In *Collected papers* (Vol. 3), (Alix and James Strachey, Trans.). London: Hogarth.

Freud, S. (1924). *A general introduction to psychoanalysis*. New York: Boni & Liveright.

Freud, S. (1940; reprinted 1961). An outline of psychoanalysis. In J. Strachey (Ed. and Trans.), *The standard edition of the complete psychological works of Sigmund Freud* (Vol. 23). London: Hogarth.

Frey, B. S. (2011). Happy people live longer. *Science, 331*.

Freyd, J. J. (1994). Circling creativity. *Psychological Science, 5*, 122–126.

Fried, S. (2008, October 9). Cited in N. Hellmich, Think fat just hangs around, does nothing? *USA Today*, p. 6D.

Friedman, J. H., & Chou, K. L. (2007). Mood, emotion, and thought. In C. G. Goetz (Ed.), *Textbook of clinical neurology* (3rd ed., pp. 35–54). Philadelphia: Saunders Elsevier.

Friedman, M., & Rosenman, R. (1974). *Type A behavior and your heart*. New York: Knopf.

Frieswick, K. (2004, July 1). Casting to type. *CFO Magazine*.

Frijda, N. (2008). The psychologists' point of view. Cited in M. Lewis, J. M. Haviland-Jones, & L. F. Barrett (Eds.), Handbook of emotions (3rd ed., pp. 68–87). New York: Guilford.

Fritz, C., & Sonnentag, S. (2006). Recovery, well-being, and performance-related outcomes: The role of workload and vacation experiences. *Journal of Applied Psychology, 91,* 936–945.

Fryer, R. (2005, November 29). Cited in J. Tierney, Got each other's backs, or holding each other back? *The New York Times,* A27.

Fryer, S. L., McGee, C. L., Matt, G. E., Riley, E. P., & Mattson, S. N. (2007). Evaluation of psychopathological conditions in children with heavy prenatal alcohol exposure. *Pediatrics, 119,* e733–741.

Funder, D. C. (2008). Persons, situations, and person-situation interactions. Cited in O. P. John, R. W. Robins & L. A. Pervin (Eds.), *Handbook of personality* (pp. 568–580). New York: Guilford.

Fuster, J. (2008). The prefrontal cortex (4th ed.). London: Academic Press.

Gale, C. R., Batty, D., & Deary, I. J. (2008). Locus of control at age 10 years and health outcomes and behaviors at age 30 years: The 1970 British cohort study. *Psychosomatic Medicine, 70,* 397–403.

Galovski, T. E., Malta, L. S., & Blanchard, E. B. (2006). *Road rage: Assessment and treatment of the angry, aggressive driver.* Washington, DC: American Psychological Association.

Galton, F. (1888). Head growth in students at the University of Cambridge. *Nature, 38,* 14–15.

Gamer, M., Bauermann, T., Stoeter, P., & Vossel, G. (2007). Covariations among fMRI, skin conductance, and behavioral data during processing of concealed information. *Human Brain Mapping, 28,* 1287–1301.

Garbarini, N. (2005, December). Blinking turns off the brain. *Scientific American Mind.*

Gardner, B. T., & Gardner, R. A. (1975). Evidence for sentence constituents in the early utterances of child and chimpanzee. *Journal of Experimental Psychology: General, 104,* 244–267.

Gardner, H. (1993). *Creating minds.* New York: Basic Books.

Gardner, H. (1999). *Intelligence reframed.* New York: Basic Books.

Gardner, H. (2006a). *Changing minds.* Boston: Harvard Business School Publishing.

Gardner, H. (2006b). *Multiple intelligences: New horizons.* New York: Basic Books.

Garfield, S. L., & Bergin, A. E. (1994). Introduction and historical overview. In A. E. Bergin & S. L. Garfield (Eds.), *Handbook of psychotherapy and behavior change* (4th ed.). New York: Wiley.

Gazzaniga, M. S. (1998, July). The split brain revisited. *Scientific American,* 50–55.

Gazzaniga, M. S. (2005). Forty-five years of split-brain research and still going strong. *Nature Review Neuroscience, 6,* 653–659.

Gazzaniga, M. S. (2008a). *Human: The science behind what makes us unique.* New York: Harper Collins.

Gazzaniga, M. S. (2008b, June/July). Spheres of influence. *Scientific American Mind,* 32–39.

Geeraerts, D. (2006). Prospects and problems of prototype theory. In D. Geeraerts (Ed.), *Cognitive linguistics: Basic readings* (pp. 141–167). New York: Mouton de Gruyter.

Geiger, D. (2002). Cited in K. Cobb, Sleepy heads. *Science News, 162,* 38.

Gelbard-Sagiv, H., Mukamel, R., Harel, M., Malach, R., & Fried, I. (2008). Internally generates reactivation of single neurons in human hippocampus during free recall. *Science, 322,* 96–101.

Geliebter, A., Ladell, T., Logan, M., Schweider, T., Sharafi, M., & Hirsch, J. (2006). Responsivity to food stimuli in obese and lean binge eaters using functional MRI. *Appetite, 46,* 31–35.

Gelles, K. (2009, March 9). Drinking patterns: Where do you fit? *USA Today,* p. 5D.

George, M. (2009, August). The brain: Magnetic depression treatment. *U.S. News & World Report,* 40–43.

Gerl, E. J., & Morris, M. R. (2008). The causes and consequences of color vision. *Evolution: Education and Outreach, 1,* 476–486.

Gibbs, N. (1995, October 2). The EQ factor. *Time,* 60–68.

Gibson, E. J., & Walk, R. (1960). The visual "cliff." *Scientific American, 202,* 64–71.

Gigone, D., & Hastie, R. (1997). Proper analysis of the accuracy of group judgments. *Psychological Bulletin, 121,* 149–167.

Gilbert, A. (2008). *What the nose knows: The science of scent in everyday life.* New York: Crown.

Gillman, M. (2007, July 28). Cited in B. Bower, Weighting for friends. Science News, 172, 51.

Giorgi, A. (2005). Remaining challenges for humanistic psychology. *Journal of Humanistic Psychology, 45,* 204–216.

Gitlin, M. J. (2009). Pharmacotherapy and other somatic treatment for depression. In I. H. Gotlib & C. L. Hammen (Eds.), *Handbook of depression* (2nd ed., pp. 554–585). New York: Guilford.

Gladwell, M. (2004, September 20). Personality plus. *The New Yorker,* 42–48.

Gladwell, M. (2008). *Outliers: The story of success.* New York: Little, Brown and Company.

Glanzer, M., & Cunitz, A. R. (1966). Two storage mechanisms in free recall. *Journal of Verbal Learning and Verbal Behavior, 5,* 351–360.

Glass, R. M. (2001). Electroconvulsive therapy. *Journal of the American Medical Association, 285,* 1346–1348.

Gleick, E., Alexander, B., Eskin, L., Pick, G., Skolnik, S., Dodd, J., & Sugden, J. (1994, December 12). The final victim. *People.*

Goddard, A. W., Ball, S. G., Martinez, J., Robinson, M. J., Yang, C. R., Russell, J. M., & Shekhar, A. (2010). Current perspectives of the roles of the central norepinephrine system in anxiety and depression. *Depression and Anxiety, 27,* 339-50.

Godlasky, A. (2008, October 16). MP3 players can damage hearing. *USA Today,* p. 4D.

Goldberg, C. (2003, July 15). *Inside the psychopath: Moving ahead on diagnosis and possible treatment.* Retrieved from http://hubel.sfasu. edu/courseinfo/articles/ physio–psychopathology.html

Goldberg, R. (2010). *Drugs across the spectrum* (6th ed.). Belmont, CA: Wadsworth Cengage.

Goldberger, L., & Breznitz, S. (Eds.). (1993). *Handbook of stress: Theoretical and clinical aspects.* New York: Free Press.

Goldfried, M. R., & Davison, G. C. (1976). *Clinical behavior therapy.* New York: Holt, Rinehart and Winston.

Goldsmith, H. H. (2003). Introduction: Genetics and development. In R. J. Davidson, K. B. Scherer & H. H. Goldsmith (Eds.), Handbook of affective sciences. New York: Oxford University Press.

Goldstein, E. B. (2008). *Cognitive psychology* (2nd ed.). Belmont, CA: Thomson Wadsworth.

Goldstein, E. B. (2010). *Sensation and perception* (8th ed.). Belmont, CA: Wadsworth.

Goleman, D. (1995). *Emotional intelligence: Why it can matter more than IQ.* New York: Bantam Books.

Goleman, D. (2005). *Emotional intelligence. The tenth anniversary edition.* New York: Bantam Dell.

Goode, E. (2002, March 12). The uneasy fit of the precocious and the average. *The New York Times,* p. D1.

Goodwin, F. K. (2003). Rationale for long-term treatment of bipolar disorder and evidence for long-term lithium treatment. *Journal of Clinical Psychiatry, 64*(Suppl. 6), 5–12.

Goodwin, J. (2006, June). Forget me not. *Reader's Digest,* 124–131.

Gostout, B. (2007, January 22). *Cervical cancer vaccine: Who needs it, how it works.* Retrieved from http://www.mayoclinic.com/print/ cervical-cancer-vaccine/WO00120

Gottesman, I. I. (2001). Psychopathology through a lifespan-genetic prism. *American Psychologist, 56,* 867–877.

Gottman, J. M. (1999). *Seven principles for making marriage work.* New York: Three Rivers Press.

Gottman, J. M. (2000. September 14). Cited in K. S. Peterson, "Hot" and "cool" phases could predict divorce. *USA Today,* p. 9D.

Gottman, J. M. (2003, May 1). Cited in B. Carey, For better or worse: Marriage by the numbers. *Los Angeles Times,* p. F1.

Gould, S. J. (1996). *The mismeasure of man* (revised and expanded). New York: Norton.

Graham, L. O. (1995). *Member of the club.* New York: HarperCollins.

Grandin, T. (1992). Calming effects of deep touch pressure in patients with autistic disorder, college students, and animals. *Journal of Child and Adolescent Psychopharmacology, 2,* 63–72.

Grandin, T. (2002, May 6). Myself. *Time,* 56.

Grandin, T. (2009). *Animals make us human.* Boston: Houghton Mifflin Harcourt.

Grant, P., Young, P., & DeRubeis, R. (2005). Cognitive behavioral therapy. In G. O. Gabbard, J. S. Beck & J. Holmes (Eds.), *Oxford textbook of psychotherapy.* New York: Oxford University Press.

Gravetter, F. J., & Forzano, L. B. (2009). *Research methods for the behavioral sciences* (3rd ed.). Belmont, CA: Wadsworth Cengage.

Gray, K., & Wegner, D. M. (2008). The sting of intentional pain. *Psychological Science, 19,* 1260–1262.

Greatley, A. (2004, June 13). Cited in BBC News, *Bid to end mental health stigma.* Retrieved from http://news.bbc.co.uk/go/pr/-/2/hi/health/3798593.stm

Greenberg, R., & Perlman, C. A. (1999). The interpretation of dreams: A classic revisited. *Psychoanalytic Dialogues, 9,* 749–765.

Griffiths, R. (2006, October/November). Cited in J. Talan, Visions for psychedelics. *Scientific American Mind, 7.*

Griffiths, R. (2008, October 22). Cited in W. Weise, Petition calls for FDA to regulate energy drinks. *USA Today,* p. 6D.

Grimaldi, J. V. (1986, April 16). "The mole" evicted from sewer. *San Diego Tribune.*

Grinker, R. (2007). *Unstrange minds: Remapping the world of autism.* Philadelphia: Basic Books.

Grogan, B., Shaw, B., Ridenhour, R., Fine, A., & Eftimiades, M. (1993, May). Their brothers' keepers? *People.*

Grossman, L. (2008, November 24). Wise guy. *Time,* 48–49.

Groth-Marnat, G. (2009). *Handbook of psychological assessment* (5th ed.). Hoboken, NJ: John Wiley & Sons.

Grunbaum, A. (1993). *Validation in the clinical theory of psychoanalysis.* Madison, CT: International Universities Press.

Grunbaum, A. (2006). Is Sigmund Freud's psychoanalytic edifice relevant to the 21st century? *Psychoanalytic Psychology, 23,* 257–284.

Guilford, J. P. (1967). *The nature of human intelligence.* New York: McGraw-Hill.

Gunn, E. P. (2006, October 16). It is in your head. *U.S. News & World Report,* EE8–9.

Gupta, S. (2006, March 13). Sleep deprived. *Time.*

Gupta, S. (2007, October 1). The caffeine habit. *Time,* 62.

Gura, T. (1997). Obesity sheds its secrets. Science, 275, 751–753.

Gutierrez, D. (2009, March 15). Scientists developing memory-erasing drug. *NaturalNews.* Retrieved from http://www.naturalnews.com/026282.html

Gwyer, P., & Clifford, B. R. (1997). The effects of the cognitive interview on recall, identification, confidence, and the confidence/accuracy relationship. *Applied Cognitive Psychology, 11,* 121–145.

Hadders-Algra, M. (2002). Variability in infant motor behavior: A hallmark of the healthy nervous system. *Infant Behavior & Development, 2,* 433–451.

Haggard, T. (2006a, November 5). Ted Haggard's letter to New Life Church. *Colorado Springs Gazette.*

Haggard, T. (2006b, November 19). Cited in L. Goodstein, Minister's own rules sealed his fate. *The New York Times,* p. 22.

Haglund, K. (2008, January 28). Cited in New Miss America once battled anorexia. ChinaDaily [Online]. Retrieved from http://www.chinadaily.com/cn/entertainment/2008-01/28/content_6425452.htm

Hales, D. (2008, February). The ways to happiness. *Reader's Digest,* 98–103.

Halpern, S. (2008, May 19). Forgetting is the new normal. *Time,* 42–45.

Hamann, S. B., Ely, T. D., Hoffman, J. M., & Kilts, C. D. (2002). Ecstasy and agony: Activation of the human amygdala in positive and negative emotions. *Psychological Science, 13,* 135–141.

Hamer, D. (2002). Rethinking behavior genetics. Science, 298, 71–72.

Hamilton, B. (2004). *Soul surfer.* New York: Pocket Books.

Han, S., & Humphreys, G. W. (1999). Interactions between perceptual organization based on Gestalt laws and those based on hierarchical processing. *Perception & Psychophysics, 61,* 1287–1298.

Hancock, L. (1996, March 18). Mother's little helper. *Newsweek.*

Hanson, G. R., Venturelli, P. J., & Fleckenstein, A. E. (2002). *Drugs and society* (7th ed.). Boston: Jones and Bartlett.

Hareli, S., & Weiner, B. (2002). Social emotions and personality inferences: A scaffold for a new direction in the study of achievement motivation. *Educational Psychologist, 37,* 183–193.

Harmon-Jones, E., & Harmon Jones, C. (2002). Testing the action-based model of cognitive dissonance: The effect of action orientation on postdecisional attitudes. *Personality and Social Psychology Bulletin, 28,* 711–723.

Harris, J. C. (1995). *Developmental neuropsychiatry* (Vol. 1). New York: Oxford University Press.

Harris, J. C. (2003). Pinel orders the chains removed from the insane at Bicetre. *Archives of General Psychiatry, 60,* 442.

Harris, J. M., & Dean, P. J. A. (2003). Accuracy and precision of binocular 3-D motion perception. *Journal of Experimental Psychology, 29,* 869–881.

Harris, J. R. (1998). *The nurture assumption: Why children turn out the way they do.* New York: Free Press.

Harris, J. R. (2006). *No two alike: Human nature and human individuality.* New York: W. W. Norton.

Harris, J. R. (2007, August 9). Do pals matter more than parents? *The Times.*

Harris, J. R. (2009a, July/August). Cited in J. Lehrer, Do parent matter? *Scientific American Mind,* 61–63.

Harris, J. R. (2009b). *The nurture assumption: Why children turn out the way they do* (revised and updated). New York: Free Press.

Hart, F., & Risley, T. (1996). Cited in B. Bower, Talkative parents make kids smarter. *Science News, 150,* 150.

Harvey, G. A., Bryant, R. A., & Tarrier, N. (2003). Cognitive behaviour therapy for posttraumatic stress disorder. *Clinical Psychology Review, 23,* 501–522.

Harzem, P. (2004). Behaviorism for new psychology: What was wrong with behaviorism and what is wrong with it now? *Behavior and Philosophy, 32,* 5–12.

Haseltine, E. (2008, August). Cited in S. Kruglinski, How to spot the truth. *Discover*, 44–45.

Hatfield, J., & Murphy, S. (2006). The effects of mobile phone use on pedestrian crossing behaviour at signalized and unsignalised intersections. *Accident Analysis & Prevention, 39,* 197–205.

Hathaway, W. (2006, April 13). Teens lose out on ample hours of precious sleep. *Northwest Herald.*

Hauser, M. (2003, July 15). Cited in N. Wade, Early voices: The leap to language. *The New York Times*, p. D1.

Hawk, T. (2002). *Tony Hawk: Professional skateboarder.* New York: HarperCollins.

Healy, B. (2006, September 4). Obesity gets an early start. *U.S. News & World Report*, 79.

Healy, B. (2007, July 16). Stop the decibel damage. *U.S. News & World Report,* 58.

Heider, F. (1958). The psychology of interpersonal relations. New York: Wiley.

Heilman, K. M. (2000). Emotional experience: A neurological model. In R. D. Lane & L. Nadel (Eds.), *Cognitive neuroscience of emotion.* New York: Oxford University Press.

Heiman, J. R. (2002). Sexual dysfunction: Overview of prevalence, etiological factors, and treatments. *The Journal of Sex Research*, 39, 73–78.

Hellmich, N. (2005, October 20). Bigger portions will get eaten. *USA Today*, p. 9D.

Hellmich, N. (2008, October. 29). Bad habits contribute to weight gain throughout college. *USA Today*, p. 5D.

Hendy, H. M., Williams, K. E., & Camise, T. S. (2005). "Kids Choice" school lunch program increases children's fruit and vegetable acceptance. *Appetite, 49,* 683–686.

Hendy, H. M., Williams, K. E., Camise, T. S., Alderman, S., Ivy, J., & Reed, J. (2007). Overweight and average-weight children equally responsive to "Kids Choice Program" to increase fruit and vegetable consumption. *Appetite, 49,* 250–263.

Hergenhahn, B. R. (2009). *An introduction to the history of psychology* (6th ed.). Belmont, CA: Wadsworth.

Herman, W. E. (1990). Fear of failure as a distinctive personality trait measure of test anxiety. *Journal of Research and Development in Education, 23,* 180–185.

Hersen, M., & Thomas, J. C. (Eds.). (2006). *Comprehensive handbook of personality and psychopathology: Adult psychopathology* (Vol. 2). Hoboken, NJ: John Wiley & Sons.

Hersen, M., & Thomas, J. C. (Eds.). (2007). *Handbook of clinical interviewing with adults.* Thousand Oaks, CA: Sage.

Hettema, J. M., Prescott, C. A., Myers, J. M., Neale, M. C., & Kendler, K. S. (2005). The structure of genetic and environmental risk factors for anxiety disorders in men and women. *Archives of General Psychiatry, 62,* 182-89.

Heussler, H. S. (2005). Common causes of sleep disruption and daytime sleepiness: Childhood sleep disorders II. *Medical Journal of Australia, 182,* 484–489.

Hickey, E. W. (2006). *Serial murderers and their victims* (4th ed.). Belmont, CA: Thomson Wadsworth.

Hidalgo, R. B., & Davidson, J. R. T. (2000). Post-traumatic stress disorder: Epidemiology and health-related considerations. *Journal of Clinical Psychiatry, 61*(Suppl. 7), 5–13.

Higbee, K. L. (2001). *Your memory: How it works and how to improve it* (2nd ed.). New York: Marlowe & Company.

Higgins, D. M., Peterson, J. B., Pihl, R. O., & Less, A. G. M. (2007). Prefrontal cognitive ability, intelligence, big five personality, and the prediction of advanced academic and workplace performance. *Journal of Personality and Social Psychology, 93,* 298–319.

Higgins, E. S. (2008, June/July). The new genetics of mental illness. *Scientific American Mind,* 40–47.

Higgins, E. T., & Scholer, A. A. (2008). When is personality revealed: A motivated cognition approach. Cited in O. P. John, R. W. Robins, & L. A. Pervin (Eds.), *Handbook of personality* (pp. 182–207). New York: Guilford.

Hilbert, A., Saelens, B. E., Stein, R. I., Mockus, D. S., Welch, R. R., Matt, G. E., & Wilfley, D. E. (2007). Pretreatment and process predictors of outcome in interpersonal and cognitive behavioral psychotherapy for binge eating disorder. *Journal of Consulting and Clinical Psychology, 75,* 645–651.

Hill, C. E., & Nakayama, E. Y. (2000). Client-centered therapy: Where has it been and where is it going? A comment on Hathaway (1948). *Journal of Clinical Psychology, 56,* 861–875.

Hill, J. O., Wyatt, H. R., Reed, G. W., & Peters, J. C. (2003). Obesity and the environment: Where do we go from here? *Science, 299,* 853–855.

Hilts, P. H. (1995). *Memory's ghost: The strange tale of Mr. M and the nature of memory.* New York: Simon & Schuster.

Hinshaw, S. (2010, June 1). Cited in K. Ellison, Seeking an objective test for attention disorder. *The New York Times,* D5.

Hinson, J. P., Raven, P., & Chew, S. L. (2010). *The endocrine system: Systems of the body series* (2nd ed.). Philadelphia: Elsevier.

Hirshey, G. (2003, April). Songs from the heart. *Ladies Home Journal,* 122–123.

Hitti, M. (2006a, June 8). What you need to know about Gardasil, the newly approved cervical cancer vaccine. *WebMD.* Retrieved from http://www.webmd.com/content/Article/123/115100.htm

Hitti, M. (2006b, November 22). Eat your words? Some can taste them. *WebMD.* Retrieved from http://www.webmd.com/content/article/130/117619?printing=true

Hobson, J. A. (2002). *Making sense of dreaming.* New York: Oxford University Press.

Hoff, E. (2009). *Language development* (4th ed.). Belmont, CA: Wadsworth Cengage Learning.

Hoge, C. W., Terhakopian, A., Castro, C. A., Messer, S. C., & Engel, C. C. (2007). Association of posttraumatic stress disorder with somatic symptoms, health care visits, and absenteeism among Iraq war veterans. *The American Journal of Psychiatry, 164,* 150–153.

Honey, R. C. (2000). Associative priming in Pavlovian conditioning. *The Quarterly Journal of Experimental Psychology, 53B,* 1–23.

Honts, C. R. (1994). Psychophysiological detection of deception. *Current Directions in Psychological Science, 3,* 77–82.

Honts, C. R., Raskin, D. C., & Kircher, J. C. (1994). Mental and physical countermeasures reduce the accuracy of polygraph tests. *Journal of Applied Psychology, 79,* 252–259.

Hoover, N. C., & Pollard, N. J. (2000). *Initiation rites in American high schools: A national survey.* Retrieved from http://www.alfred.edu/news/html/hazing_study.html

Howard, M. S., & Medway, F. (2004). Adolescents' attachment and coping with stress. *Psychology in the Schools, 41,* 391–402.

Howard Hughes Medical Institute. (2008). *Color blindness: More prevalent among males.* Retrieved from http://www.hhmi.org/senses/b130.html

Hsu, C. (2006, January 14). Put down that fork. *Science News, 169,* 21.

Hubbard, E. M., & Ramachandran, V. S. (2005). Neurocognitive mechanisms of synesthesia. *Neuron, 48,* 509–520.

Human Rights Watch. (2008). *A violent education: Corporal punishment of children in U.S. public schools.* New York: Author.

Humphreys, G. W., & Forde, E. M. E. (2001). Category specificity in mind and brain. *Behavioral and Brain Sciences, 243,* 497–509.

Humphreys, G. W., & Muller, H. (2000). A search asymmetry reversed by figure-ground assignment. *Psychological Science,* 11, 196–210.

Husain, M. M., Rush, A. J., Fink, M., Knapp, R., Petrides, G., Rummans, T., ... Kellner, C. H. (2004). Speed of response and remission in major depressive disorder with acute electroconvulsive (ECT): A Consortium for Research in ECT (CORE) report. *Journal of Clinical Psychiatry, 65,* 485–491.

Huskinson, T. L. H., & Haddock, G. (2006). Individual differences in attitude structure and the accessibility of the affective and cognitive components of attitude. *Social Cognition, 24,* 453–468.

Hutchinson, C. (2009, July/August). Live strong and prosper. *Psychology Today,* 11.

Iacoboni, M. (2008a). *Mirroring people.* New York: Farrar, Strauss & Giroux.

Iacoboni, M. (2008b, July). The mirror neuron revolution: Explaining what makes humans social. *Scientific American.*

Iacoboni, M., & Mazziotta, J. C. (2007). Mirror neuron system: Basic findings and clinical applications. *Annals of Neurology, 62,* 213–218.

Ingram, J. A. (2006, November 3). Cited in C. Woodward, Amnesiac can't return to his past to go into future. *The San Diego Union-Tribune,* p. A4.

Innes, S. I. (2005). Psychosocial factors and their role in chronic pain: A brief review of development and current status. *Chiropractic & Osteopathy, 13,* 6.

Irwin, M. R., Wang, M., Ribeiro, D., Cho, H. J., Olmstead, R., Breen, E. C., ... Cole, S. (2008). Sleep loss activates cellular inflammatory signaling. *Biological Psychiatry, 64,* 538–540.

ISC (International Schizophrenia Consortium). (2009). Common polygenic variation contributes to risk of schizophrenia and bipolar disorder. *Nature, 460,* 748–752.

Iversen, L. L. (2000). *The science of marijuana.* New York: Oxford University Press.

Iversen, L. L. (2008). *Speed, ecstasy, Ritalin: The science of amphetamines.* New York: Oxford University Press.

Izard, C. E. (1993). Four systems for emotion activation: Cognitive and noncognitive processes. *Psychological Review, 100,* 68–90.

Jackendoff, R. (1994). *Patterns in the mind: Language and human nature.* New York: Basic Books.

Jacks, J. Z., & Cameron, K. A. (2003). Strategies for resisting persuasion. *Basic and Applied Social Psychology, 25,* 145–161.

Jackson, R. L. (1994, May 4). A false sense of sincerity: Some cases belie polygraph results. *Los Angeles Times.*

Jackson, S. J. (2009). *Research methods and statistics* (3rd ed.). Belmont, CA: Wadsworth Cengage.

James, W. (1884; reprinted 1969). What is an emotion? In *William James: Collected essays and reviews.* New York: Russell & Russell.

Jang, K. L. (2005). *The behavioral genetics of psychopathology: A clinical guide.* Mahwah, NJ: Lawrence Erlbaum.

Jang, K. L., Livesley, W. J., Ando, J., Yamagata, S., Suzuki, A., Angleitner, A., ...Spinath, F. (2006). Behavioral genetics of the higher-order factors of the Big Five. *Personality and Individual Differences, 41,* 261–272.

Janis, I. L. (1989). *Crucial decisions: Leadership in policy-making and crisis management.* New York: Free Press.

Japenga, A. (1994, June 5). Rewriting the dictionary of madness. *Los Angeles Times Magazine.*

Jardin, X. (2005, August 19). Virtual reality therapy for combat stress. *NPR.* Retrieved from http://www.npr.org/templates/story/story.php?storyId=4806921

Jarrett, C. (2006, March 3). Food, glorious food - Czech eating habits after 1989. Radio Prague. Retrieved from http://www.radio.cz/en/article/77368

Jarriel, T., & Sawyer, D. (1997, January 16). Romania: What happened to the children? *Turning point.* New York: ABC News.

Jayson, S. (2005, July 18). Cohabitation is replacing dating. *USA Today,* p. 6D.

Jayson, S. (2009a, February 11). Science asks: What's the attraction? *USA Today,* p. D1.

Jefferson, D. J. (2005, August 8). America's most dangerous drug. *Newsweek,* 40–48.

Jenson, A. R. (2005). Mental chronometry and the unification of differential psychology. In R. J. Sternberg & J. E. Pretz (Eds.), *Cognition and intelligence* (pp. 26–50). New York: Cambridge University Press.

Johnson, J. G., Cohen, P., Smailes, E. M., Kasen, S., & Brook, J. S. (2002). Television viewing and aggressive behavior during adolescence and adulthood. *Science, 295,* 2468–2471.

Johnson, N. (2006, September 30). *Supporters: Med marijuana bill needed.* Retrieved from http://www.yankton.net/stories/093006/community_20060930030.shtml

Johnston, J. C., & McClelland, J. L. (1974). Perception of letters in words: Seek not and ye shall find. *Science, 184,* 1192–1194.

Johnston, V. (2000, February). Cited in B. Lemley, Isn't she lovely. *Discover,* 43–49.

Jones, S. R., & Fernyhough, C. (2007). A new look at the neural diathesis-stress model of schizo-phrenia: The primacy of social-evaluative and uncontrollable situations. *Schizophrenia Bulletin, 33,* 1171–1177.

Joseph, S., Manafi, E., Iakovaki, A. M., & Cooper, R. (2003). Personality, smoking motivation, and self-efficacy to quit. *Personality and Individual Differences, 34,* 749–758.

Judge, T. A., Hurst, C., & Simon, L. S. (2009). Does it pay to be smart, attractive, or confident (or all three)? Relationships among general mental ability, physical attractiveness, core self-evaluations, and income. *Journal of Applied Psychology, 94,* 742–755.

Julien, R. M. (2005). *A primer of drug action: A comprehensive guide to the actions, uses, and side effects* (10th ed.). New York: Worth.

Junod, R. E. V., DuPaul, G. J., Jitendra, A. K., Volpe, R. J., & Cleary, K. S. (2006). Classroom observations of students with and without ADHD: Differences across types of engagement. *Journal of School Psychology, 44,* 87–104.

Kalat, J. W. (2009). *Biological psychology* (10th ed.). Belmont, CA: Wadsworth Cengage Learning.

Kalat, J. W., & Shiota, M. N. (2007). *Emotion.* Belmont, CA: Thomson/Wadsworth.

Kalb, C. (2009, April 27). To pluck a rooted sorrow. *Newsweek,* 52–54.

Kalimo, R., Tenkanen, L., Harma, M., Poppius, E., & Heinsalmi, P. (2000). Job stress and sleep disorders: Findings from the Helsinki heart study. *Stress Medicine, 16,* 65–75.

Kantowitz, B. H., Roediger, H. L., III, & Elemes, D. G. (2009). *Experimental psychology* (9th ed.). Belmont, CA: Wadsworth/Cengage Learning.

Kaplan, R. M., & Saccuzzo, K. P. (2009). *Psychological testing: Principles, applications, and issues* (7th ed.). Belmont, CA: Wadsworth Cengage.

Karussis, D., & Kassis, I. (2007). Use of stem cells for treatment of multiple sclerosis. *Expert Review of Neurotherapies, 7,* 1189–1201.

Kaufman, A. S. (2000). Tests of intelligence. In R. J. Sternberg (Ed.), *Handbook of intelligence.* New York: Cambridge University Press.

Kaufman, A. S., Reynolds, C. R., & McLean J. E. (1989). Age and WAIS-R intelligence in a national sample of adults in the 20 to 74 age range: A cross-sectional analysis with educational level controlled. *Intelligence, 13,* 235–253.

Kaufman, L. (2000). Cited in B. Bower, The moon also rises—and assumes new sizes. *Science News, 157,* 22.

Kaufman, M. (2006b, June 9). FDA approves vaccine that should prevent most cervical cancers. *Washington Post*, p. A1.

Kaye, W. (2008, June 9). Cited in S. Gupta, Taking on the thin ideal. *Time*, 50.

Kazdin, A. (2008, October). Trauma in children: How we can communicate what we know? *Monitor on Psychology*, 5.

Keisler, B. D., & Armsey, T. D., II. (2006). Caffeine as an ergogenic acid. *Current Sports Medicine Reports, 5*, 215–219.

Kelly, D., & Tangney, B. (2006). Adapting to intelligence profile in an adaptive educational system. *Human Factors in Personalised Systems and Services, 18*, 385–409.

Keltner, D., & Ekman, P. (2000). Facial expression of emotion: Cognitive and social construction in emotions. In M. Lewis & J. M. Haviland-Jones (Eds.), *Handbook of emotions* (2nd ed.). New York: Guilford Press.

Kemeny, M. C. (2003). The psychobiology of stress. *Current Directions in Psychological Science, 12*, 125–129.

Kendler, K. S., Kuhn, J., & Prescott, C. A. (2004). The interrelationship of neuroticism, sex, and stressful life events in the prediction of episodes of major depression. *American Journal of Psychiatry, 161*, 631–636.

Kerns, R. (2006, December 22). Cited in Psychological treatments improve outcomes for back pain sufferers. *Science Daily*. Retrieved from http://www.sciencedaily.com/releases/2006/12/06122090925.htm

Kerns, R. (2007, January 2). Cited in J. Fischman, Psychological treatments are a balm for back pain. *U.S. News & World Report*.

Kershaw, S. (2010, July 27). Following a script to escape a nightmare. *The New York Times*, p. D1.

Kershaw, T. C., & Ohlsson, S. (2004). Multiple causes of difficulty in insight: The case of the nine-dot problem. *Journal of Experimental Psychology: Learning, Memory, and Cognition, 30*, 3–13.

Kessler, R. C., Berglund, P., Demler, O., Jim, R., Merikangas, K. R., & Walters, E. E. (2005). Lifetime prevalence and age-of-onset distributions of DSM-IV disorders in the national co-morbidity survey replication. *Archives of General Psychiatry, 62*, 593–602.

Khawam, E. A., Laurencic, G., & Malone, D. A. (2006). Side effects of antidepressants: An overview. *Cleveland Clinical Journal of Medicine, 73*, 351–361.

Kiecolt-Glaser, J. (2008, October). Cited in S. F. Dingfelder, An insidious enemy. *Monitor on Psychology*, 22–23.

Kiecolt-Glaser, J. K., McGuire, L., Robles, T. F., & Glaser, R. (2002). Emotions, morbidity, and mortality: New perspectives from psychoneuroimmunology. *Annual Review of Psychology, 53*, 83–107.

Kiernan, J. A. (2008). *Barr's the human nervous system: An anatomical viewpoint* (9th ed.). Philadelphia: Lippincott Williams & Wilkins.

Kiernan, J. A. (2009). *Barr's the human nervous system: An anatomical viewpoint* (9th ed.). Baltimore: Lippincott, Williams, & Wilkins.

Kihlstrom, J. F., Glisky, M. L., & Angiulo, M. J. (1994). Dissociative tendencies and dissociative disorders. *Journal of Abnormal Psychology, 103*, 117–124.

Kindt, M., Soeter, M., & Vervliet, B. (2009). Beyond extinction: Erasing human fear responses and preventing the return of fear. *Nature Neuroscience, 12*, 256–258.

King, S. (1991, August 25). From hard time to prime time. *Los Angeles Times/Calendar*, p. 3.

Kinsbourne, M. (1994). Sugar and the hyperactive child. *New England Journal of Medicine, 330*, 355–356.

Kirsch, I., & Braffman, W. (2001). Imaginative suggestibility and hypnotizability. *Current Directions in Psychological Sciences, 10*, 57–61.

Kirschenbaum, H., & Jourdan, A. (2005). The current status of Carl Rogers and the person-centered approach. *Psychotherapy: Theory, Research, Practice, Training, 42*, 37–51.

Kirtland, C. (2009, May/June). Driving distractions. *AAA Living*, 18–21.

Klein, C. T. F., & Helweg-Larsen, M. (2002). Perceived control and the optimistic bias: A meta-analytic review. *Psychology and Health, 17*, 437–446.

Klein, D. N., Durbin, C. E., Shankman, S. A., & Santiago, N. J. (2002). Depression and personality. In I. H. Gotlib & C. L. Hammen (Eds.), *Handbook of depression*. New York: Guilford Press.

Klein, S. B. (2009). *Learning: Principles and application*. Thousand Oaks, CA: Sage.

Klinger, E. (1987, October). The power of daydreams. *Psychology Today*.

Klomegah, R. Y. (2007, June). Predictors of academic performance of university students: An application of the goal efficacy model. *College Student Journal*.

Kluger, J. (2003, January 20). Masters of denial. *Time*.

Kluger, J. (2007, June 11). The science of appetite. *Time*, 48–58.

Kluger, J. (2007b, September 10). Rewiring the brain. *Time*, 46–47.

Kluger, J., & Masters, C. (2006, August 28). How to spot a liar. *Time*, 46–48.

Koenigs, M., Young, L., Adolphs, R., Tranel, D., Cushman, F., Hauser, M., & Damasio, A. (2007). Damage to the prefrontal cortex increases utilitarian moral judgements. *Nature, 446*, 908–911.

Kohlberg, L. (1984). *The psychology of moral development: Essays on moral development* (Vol. 11). San Francisco: Harper & Row.

Köhler, W. (1917; reprinted 1925). *The mentality of apes* (E. Winter, Trans.). New York: Harcourt Brace & World.

Kolata, G. (2000b, October 17). How the body knows when to gain or lose. *The New York Times*, p. D1.

Kolb, B., & Taylor, L. (2000). Facial expression, emotion and hemispheric organization. In R. D. Lane & L. Nadel (Eds.), *Cognitive neuroscience of emotion*. New York: Oxford University Press.

Kopp, C. B., & Neufeld, S. J. (2003). Emotional development during infancy. In R. J. Davidson, K. R. Scherer, & H. H. Goldsmith (Eds.), *Handbook of affective sciences*. New York: Oxford University Press.

Koren, G. (2007). Special aspects of perinatal and pediatric pharmacology. In B. G. Katzung (Ed.), *Basic and clinical pharmacology* (10th ed., pp. 971–982). New York: McGraw-Hill.

Kornack, D. R., & Rakic, P. (2001). Cell proliferation without neurogenesis in adult primate neocortex. *Science, 29*, 2127–2130.

Kotulak, R. (2006, June 22). Hormone that may launch puberty is discovered. *The San Diego Union-Tribune*, p. E1.

Kotz, D. (2007c, October 29). What to do about HPV? *U.S. News & World Report*, 53.

Kozel, F., Johnson, K., Mu, Q., Grenesko, E., Laken, S., & George, M. (2005). Detecting deception using functional magnetic resonance imaging. *Biological Psychiatry, 58*, 605–613.

Kraft, U. (2007, June/July). Rhythm and blues. *Scientific American Mind*, 62–65.

Kramer, M. (2006b). Psychology of dreaming. In T. L. Lee-Chiong (Ed.), *Sleep: A comprehensive handbook* (pp. 37–43). Hoboken, NJ: John Wiley & Sons.

Kringelbach, M. L., & Aziz, T. Z. (2008). Sparking recovery with brain "pacemakers." *Scientific American Mind*, 36–43.

Kübler-Ross, E. (1969). *On death and dying*. New York: MacMillan.

Kübler-Ross, E. (1974). *Questions and answers on death and dying*. New York: MacMillan.

Lalwani, A. K., & Snow, J. G., Jr. (2006). Disorders of smell, taste, and hearing. In S. L. Hauser (Ed.). *Harrison's neurology in clinical medicine*. New York: McGraw-Hill.

Lamberg, L. (2004). Road to recovery for cocaine users can start in primary care setting. *Journal of the American Medical Association, 292,* 1807–1809.

Lambert, M. J., Bergin, A. E., & Garfield, S. L. (2004). Introduction and historical overview. In M. J. Lambert (Ed.), *Bergin and Garfield's handbook of psychotherapy and behavior change*. New York: Wiley.

Langlois, J. (2009, January 17). Cited in E. Quill, It's written all over your face. *Science News,* 24–28.

Langlois, J. H., Kalakanis, L., Rubenstein, A. J., Larson, A., Hallam, M., & Smoot, M. (2000). Maxims or myths of beauty? A meta-analysis and theoretical review. *Psychological Bulletin, 136,* 390–423.

Langlois, J. H., Roggman, L. A., & Musselman, L. (1994). What is average and what is not average about attractive faces? *Psychological Science, 5,* 214–220.

Langdridge, D., & Butt, T. (2004). The fundamental attribution error: A phenomenological critique. *British Journal of Social Psychology, 43,* 357–369.

Lanyado, M., & Horne, A. (Eds.). (1999). *The handbook of child and adolescent psychotherapy*. New York: Routledge.

Largo-Wight, E., Peterson, P. M., & Chen, W. W. (2005). Perceived problem solving, stress, and health among college students. *American Journal of Health Behavior, 29,* 360–370.

Larson, C. (2008, February 11). Attacking Alzheimer's. *U.S. News & World Report,* 48.

Larson, E. (2009, March 12). Cited in J. D. Bedrossian, Intel Science Talent Search crowns 10 promising young scientists. *USA Today,* p. 7D.

Larsson, H., Andershed, H., & Lichtenstein, P. (2006). A genetic factor explains most of the variation in the psychopathic personality. *Journal of Abnormal Psychology, 115,* 221–230.

Latané, B. (1981). The psychology of social impact. *American Psychologist, 36,* 343–356.

Latané, B., & Darley, J. M. (1970). The unresponsive bystander. Why doesn't he help? New York: Appleton-Century-Crofts.

Latané, B., & Nida, S. (1981). Ten years of research on group size and helping. *Psychological Bulletin, 89,* 308–324.

Laws, K. R., & Kokkalis, J. (2007). Ecstasy (MDMA) and memory function: A meta-analytic update. *Human Psychopharmacology: Clinical and Experimental, 22,* 381–388.

Lazar, S. W., Kerr, C. E., Wasserman, R. H., Gray, J. R., Greve, D. N., Treadway, M. T., ... Fischi, B. (2005). Meditation experience is associated with increased cortical thickness. *Neuroreport, 16,* 1893–1897.

Lazarus, R. S. (1999). *Stress and emotion*. New York: Springer.

Lazarus, R. S. (2000). Evolution of a model of stress, coping and discrete emotions. In V. R. Rice (Ed.), *Handbook of stress, coping and health*. Thousand Oaks, CA: Sage.

Lazarus, R. S. (2006). *Stress and emotion: A new synthesis*. New York: Springer.

Leckman, J. F., & Kim, Y. S. (2006). A primary candidate gene for obsessive-compulsive disorder. *Archives of General Psychiatry, 63,* 717–20.

Lee-Chiong, T. (2008). *Sleep medicine: Essentials and review*. New York: Oxford University Press.

Lee, C. W., Taylor, G., & Drummond, P. D. (2006). The active ingredient in EMDR: Is it traditional exposure or dual focus of attention? *Clinical Psychology and Psychotherapy, 13,* 97–107.

Leedham, B., Meyerowitz, B. E., Muirhead, J., & Frist, W. H. (1995). Positive expectations predict health after heart transplantation. *Health Psychology, 14,* 74–79.

Lehrer, J. (2009). *How we decide*. New York: Houghton Mifflin Harcourt.

Leibel, R. L., Rosenbaum, M., & Hirsch, J. (1995). Changes in energy expenditure resulting from altered body weight. *New England Journal of Medicine, 332,* 621–628.

Leippe, M. R., & Eisenstadt, D. (1994). Generalization of dissonance reduction: Decreasing prejudice through induced compliance. *Journal of Personality and Social Psychology, 67,* 395–413.

Leming, T. (2008, July 7). omg. almost caused fendr bendr, lol! *Time,* 53.

Lemley, B. (1999, December). Do you see what they see? *Discover*.

Lemley, B. (2006, August). Shiny happy people: Can you reach nirvana with the aid of science? *Discover, 27,* 62–77.

Lemonick, M. D. (2007, July 16). The science of addiction. *Time,* 42–48.

Lemonick, M. D. (2007a, January 29). The flavor of memories. *Time,* 100–102.

Leo, J. (1987, January 12). Exploring the traits of twins. *Time*.

Lessmoellmann, A. (2006, October). Don't count on it. *Scientific American Mind*.

Leventhal, H., & Patrick-Miller, L. (2000). Emotions and physical illness: Causes and indicators of vulnerability. In M. Lewis & J. M. Haviland-Jones (Eds.), *Handbook of emotions* (2nd ed.). New York: Guilford.

Levine, J. M., & Kerr, N. L. (2007). Inclusion and exclusion: Implications for group processes. In A. W. Kruglanski & E. T. Higgins (Eds.), *Social psychology: Handbook of basic principles* (2nd ed., pp. 759–784). New York: Guilford.

Levinson, D. F. (2009). Genetics of major depression. In I. H. Gotlib & C. L. Hammen (Eds.), *Handbook of depression* (2nd ed., pp. 165–186). New York: Guilford.

Levitan, I. B., & Kaczmarek, L. K. (2002). *The neuron: Cell and molecular biology*. New York: Oxford University Press.

Levy, D. (1997). *Tools of critical thinking*. New York: Allyn & Bacon.

Levy, J., & Trevarthen, C. (1976). Metacontrol of hemispheric function in human split-brain patients. *Journal of Experimental Psychology: Human Perception and Performance, 2,* 299–312.

Lewis, A. (2001, March 26). Snakes scarier than public speaking. *USA Today,* p. A1.

Lewis, A. J., Dennerstein, M., & Biggs, P. M. (2008). Short-term psychodynamic psychotherapy: Review of recent process and outcome studies. *Australian and New Zealand Journal of Psychiatry, 42,* 445–455.

Lewis, M, Haviland-Jones, J. M., & Barrett, F. (Eds.), *Handbook of Emotions* (3rd ed., pp. 533–547). New York: Guilford.

Lie, H. (2009, January 17). Cited in E. Quill, It's written all over your face. *Science News,* 24–28.

Lieberman, D. A. (2004). *Learning and memory*. Belmont, CA: Wadsworth/Thomson Learning.

Liebert, R. M., & Spiegler, M. D. (1994). *Personality: Strategies and issues* (7th ed.). Pacific Grove, CA: Brooks/Cole.

Lilienfeld, S. O., & Arkowitz, H. (2006, December/2007, January). Taking a closer look: Can moving your eyes back and forth help to ease anxiety? *Scientific American Mind,* 80–81.

Lilienfeld, S. O., & Arkowitz, H. (2007, December/2008, January). What "psychopath" means. *Scientific American Mind,* 80–81.

Lilienfeld, S. O., Kirsch, I., Sarbin, T. R., Lynn, S. J., Chaves, J. F., Ganaway, G. K., & Powell, R. A. (1999). Dissociative identity disorder and the sociocognitive model: Recalling the lessons of the past. *Psychological Bulletin, 125,* 507–523.

Lindsay, J. J., & Anderson, C. A. (2000). From antecedent conditions to violent actions: A general affective aggression model. *Personality and Social Psychological Bulletin, 26,* 533–547.

Lindstrom, M. (2005). *Brand sense: Build powerful brands through touch, taste, smell, sight, and sound.* New York: Free Press.

Linnenbrink-Garcia, L., & Fredricks, J. A. (2008). Developmental perspectives on achievement motivation. In J. Y. Shah & W. L. Gardner (Eds.), *Handbook of motivation science* (pp. 448–464). New York: Guilford.

Lipkins, S. (2006). *Preventing hazing: How parents, teachers, and coaches can stop the violence, harassment, and humiliation.* San Francisco: Jossey-Bass.

Lipton, F. R., Siegel, C., Hannigan, A., Samuels, J., & Baker, S. (2000). Tenure in supportive housing for homeless persons with severe mental illness. *Psychiatric Services, 51,* 479–486.

Lipton, S. D. (1983). A critique of so-called standard psychoanalytic technique. *Contemporary Psychoanalysis, 19,* 35–52.

Lithwick, D. (2009, March 23). When our eyes deceive use. *Newsweek,* 17.

Livneh, H., Lott, S. M., & Antonak, R. F. (2004). Patterns of psychosocial adaptation to chronic illness and disability: A cluster analytic approach. *Psychology, Health, and Medicine, 9,* 411–430.

Loehlin, J. C., Neiderhiser, J. M., & Reiss, D. (2003). The behavior genetics of personality and the NEAD study. *Journal of Research in Personality, 37,* 373–387.

Loftus, E. F. (1975). Leading questions and the eyewitness report. *Cognitive Psychology, 7,* 560–572.

Loftus, E. F. (1979). The malleability of memory. *American Scientist, 67,* 312–320.

Loftus, E. F. (1997a, September). Creating false memories. *Scientific American,* 70–75.

Loftus, E. F. (1999). Repressed memories. *Forensic Psychiatry, 22,* 61–69.

Loftus, E. F. (2000, April 25). Cited in J. E. Brody, Memories of things that never were. *The New York Times,* p. D8.

Loftus, E. F. (2003a, February 17). Cited in J. Gottlieb, Memories made to order at UCI. *Los Angeles Times,* p. 81.

Loftus, E. F. (2005b). Planting misinformation in the human mind: A 30-year investigation of the malleability of memory. *Learning & Memory, 12,* 361–366.

Loftus, E. F., & Davis, D. (2006). Recovered memories. *Annual Review of Clinical Psychology, 2,* 469–498.

Loftus, E. F., & Hoffman, H. G. (1989). Misinformation and memory: The creation of new memories. *Journal of Experimental Psychology: General, 118,* 409–420.

Loftus, E. F., Miller, D. G., & Burns, H. J. (1978). Semantic integration of verbal information into a visual memory. *Journal of Experimental Psychology: Human Learning and Memory, 4,* 19–31.

Lohman, D. F. (2000). Complex information processing and intelligence. In R. J. Sternberg (Ed.), *Handbook of intelligence.* New York: Cambridge University Press.

Lonsway, K., Moore, M., Harrington, C. P., Smeal, E., & Spillar, K. (2003, Spring). Hiring & retaining more women: The advantages to law enforcement agencies. *National Center for Women & Policing,* 1–16.

Lopes, P. N., Salovey, P., & Straus, R. (2003). Emotional intelligence, personality, and the perceived quality of social relationships. *Personality and Individual Differences, 35,* 641–658.

Lothane, Z. (2006a). Freud's legacy—Is it still with us? *Psychoanalytic Psychology, 23,* 285–301.

Lothane, Z. (2006b). Reciprocal free association. *Psychoanalytic Psychology, 23,* 711–727.

Lovaas, O. I. (1993). The development of a treatment-research project for developmentally disabled autistic children. *Journal of Applied Behavior Analysis, 26,* 617–630.

Luan, P. K., Fitzgerald, D. A., Nathan, P. J., & Tancer, M. E. (2006). Association between amygdala hyperactivity to harsh faces and severity of social anxiety in generalized social phobia. *Biological Psychiatry, 59,* 424–429.

Luborsky, E. B., O'Reilly-Landry, M., & Arlow, J. A. (2008). Psychoanalysis. In R. J. Corsini & Wedding, D. (Eds.), *Current psychotherapies* (8th ed., pp. 15–62). Belmont, CA: Thomson Brooks/Cole.

Luborsky, L., & Barrett, M. S. (2006). The history of empirical status of key psychoanalytic concepts. *Annual Review of Clinical Psychology, 2,* 1–19.

Luborsky, L., Rosenthal, R., Diguer, L., Andrusyna, T. P., Berman, J. S., Levitt, J. T., ... Krause, E. D. (2002). The dodo bird verdict is alive and well—mostly. *Clinical Psychology: Science and Practice, 9,* 2–12.

Luna, B. (2006, August/September). Cited in L. Sabbagh, Hard at work no, really. *Scientific American Mind,* 20–25.

Lupart, J. L., & Pyryt, M. C. (1996). Hidden gifted students: Underachiever prevalence and profile. *Journal for the Education of the Gifted, 20,* 36–53

Luszczynska, A., & Sutton, S. (2006). Physical activity after cardiac rehabilitation: Evidence that different types of self-efficacy are important in maintainers and relapsers. *Rehabilitation Psychology, 51,* 314–321.

Lykken, D. T. (2003). Cited in D. Watson, Happiness is in your jeans. *Contemporary Psychology, 48,* 242–243.

Lynn, S. J. (2007). Hypnosis reconsidered. *American Journal of Clinical Hypnosis, 49,* 195–197.

Lynn, S. J., Kirsch, I., Knox, J., Fassler, O., & Lilienfeld, S. O. (2007a). Hypnosis and neuroscience: Implications for the altered state debate. In G. Jamieson (Ed.), *Hypnosis and conscious states: The cognitive neuroscience perspective* (pp. 146–166). New York: Oxford University Press.

Lynn, S. J., Loftus, E. F., Lilienfeld, S. O., & Lock, T. (2003, July/August). Memory recovery techniques in psychotherapy. *Skeptical Inquirer,* 40–46.

Maathai, W. (2006). *Unbowed.* New York: Alfred A. Knopf.

Macfarlane, A. J. (1975). Olfaction in the development of social preferences in the human neonate. *CIBA Foundation Symposium, 33,* 103–117.

Macht, M. (2007, October/November). Feeding the psyche. *Scientific American Mind,* 64–69.

Maciejewski, P. K., Prigerson, H. G., & Mazure, C. M. (2000). Self-efficacy as a mediator between stressful life events and depressive symptoms: Differences based on history of prior depression. *British Journal of Psychiatry, 176,* 373-78.

Maddi, S. R. (2008, September). The courage and strategies of hardiness as helpful in growing despite major, disruptive stresses. *American Psychologist,* 563.

Madeley, G. (2007, October 19). £20,000 payout for woman who falsely accused her father of rape after "recovered memory" therapy. *MailOnline.* Retrieved from http://www.dailymail.co.uk/news/article-488623/20-000-payout-woman-falsely-accused-father-rape-recovered-memory-therapy.html

Maio, G. R., & Haddock, G. (2007). Attitude change. In A. W. Kruglanski & E. T. Higgins (Eds.), *Social psychology: Handbook of basic principles* (2nd ed., pp. 565–586). New York: Guilford.

Maio, G. R., Olson, J. M., Bernard, M. M., & Luke, M. A. (2006). Ideologies, values, attitudes, and behavior. In J. Delamater (Ed.), *Handbook of social psychology* (pp. 283–308). New York: Springer.

Malle, B. F. (2006). The actor-observer assymmetry in attribution: A (surprising) meta-analysis. *Psychological Bulletin, 132,* 895–919.

Mansvelder, D. D., De Rover, M., McGehee, D. S., & Brussaard, A. B. (2003). Cholinergic modulation of dopaminergic reward areas: Upstream and downstream targets of nicotine addiction. *European Journal of Pharmacology, 480,* 117–123.

Marchetti, S., & Bunte, K. (2006). Retailers and banks leverage fundraising power, raising more than $139 million for hurricane relief. *Press room: American Red Cross.* Retrieved from http://redcross.org/pressrelease/0,1077,0_314_5172,00.htm

Marcus, D. K., & Miller, R. W. (2003). Sex differences in judgments of physical attractiveness: A social relations analysis. *Personality and Social Psychology Bulletin, 29,* 325–335.

"Mariah in hospital with 'exhaustion.'" (2001, July 27). *BBC News.*

Marschall, J. (2007, February/March). Seduced by sleep. *Scientific American Mind,* 52–57.

Marshall, G. N., Schell, T. L., Glynn, S. M., & Shetty, V. (2006). The role of hyperarousal in the manifestation of posttraumatic psychological distress following injury. *Journal of Abnormal Psychology, 115,* 624–628.

Martens, W. H. J. (2002, January). The hidden suffering of the psychopath. *Psychiatric Times, 19.*

Martin, C. L. (2000). Cognitive theories of gender development. In T. Eckes & H. M. Trautner (Eds.), *The developmental social psychology of gender.* Mahwah, NJ: Lawrence Erlbaum.

Martin, C. L., Ruble, D. N., & Szrkrybalo, J. (2002). Cognitive theories of early gender development. *Psychological Bulletin, 128,* 903–933.

Martin, J. K., Pescosolido, B. A., & Tuch, S. A. (2000). Of fear and loathing: The role of "disturbing behavior," labels, and causal attributions in shaping public attitudes toward people with mental illness. *Journal of Health and Social Behavior, 41,* 208–223.

Maslach, C. (2003). Job burnout: New directions in research and intervention. *Current Directions in Psychological Science, 12,* 189–192.

Maslow, A. H. (1968). *Toward a psychology of being* (2nd ed.). New York: Van Nostrand.

Maslow, A. H. (1970). *Motivation and personality.* New York: Harper & Row.

Maslow, A. H. (1971). *The farther reaches of human nature.* New York: Viking Press.

Masters, W. H., & Johnson, V. E. (1966). *Human sexual response.* Boston: Little, Brown.

Masters, W. H., & Johnson, V. E. (1970). *Human sexual inadequacy.* Boston: Little, Brown.

Masters, W. H., & Johnson, V. E. (1981). Sex and the aging process. *Journal of the American Geriatrics Society, 19,* 385–389.

Mather, M., & Carstensen, L. L. (2005). Aging and motivated cognition: The positivity effect in attention and memory. *Trends in Cognitive Sciences, 9,* 496–502.

Matsumoto, D., & Juang, L. (2008). *Culture and psychology* (4th ed). Belmont, CA: Wadsworth.

Matsumoto, D., Keltner, D., Shiota, M. N., O'Sullivan, M., & Frank, M. (2008). Facial expressions of emotion. Cited in M. Lewis, J. M. Haviland-Jones, & L. F. Barrett (Eds.), *Handbook of emotions* (3rd ed., pp. 211–234). New York: Guilford.

Matsumoto, D., & Willingham, B. (2009). Spontaneous facial expression of emotion of congenitally and noncongenitally blind individuals. *Journal of Personality and Social Psychology, 96,* 1–10.

Mauss, I. (2005). Control your anger! *Scientific American Mind, 16,* 64–71.

Mayer, J. D., Salovey, P., & Caruso, D. (2000). Models of emotional intelligence. In R. J. Sternberg (Ed.), *Handbook of intelligence.* New York: Cambridge University Press.

Mayford, M., & Korzus, E. (2002). Genetics of memory in the mouse. In L. R. Squire & D. L. Schacter (Eds.), *Neuropsychology of memory* (3rd ed.). New York: Guilford.

Mayo Clinic. (2006a). Cited in Eating disorders. CNN.com. Retrieved from http://www.cnn.com/HEALTH/library/DS/00194.html

Mayo Foundation for Medical Education and Research. (2005, August 8). *Adolescent sleep problems: Why is your teen so tired?* Retrieved from http://www.mayoclinic.com/health/teens-health/CC00019

Mayr, E. (2000, July). Darwin's influence on modern thought. *Scientific American,* 79–83.

Mazure, C. M., Brude, M. L., Maciejewski, P. K., & Jacobs, S. C. (2000). Adverse life events and cognitive-personality characteristics in the prediction of major depression and antidepressant response. *American Journal of Psychiatry, 157,* 896–903.

Mcallister, H. A., Baker, J. D., Mannes, C., Stewart, H., & Sutherland, A. (2002). The optimal margin of illusion hypothesis: Evidence from self-serving bias and personality disorders. *Journal of Social and Clinical Psychology, 21,* 414–426.

McAuliffe, K. (2008, September 28). Mental fitness. *Discover,* 56–60.

McCall, R. B. (1994). Academic underachievers. *Current Directions in Psychological Science, 3,* 15–19.

McCarthy, T. (2005, October 24). Getting inside your head. *Time,* 95–97.

McClain, D. L. (2005, June 29). Machine clobbers man. *The New York Times,* p. B2.

McClearn, G. E., Johansson, B., Berg, S., Pedersen, N. L., Ahern, F., Petrill, S. A., & Plomin, R. (1997). Substantial genetic influence on cognitive abilities in twins 80 or more years old. *Science, 276,* 1560–1563.

McClelland, D. C. (1985). *Human motivation.* Glenview, IL: Scott, Foresman.

McCrae, R. R., & Costa, P. T., Jr. (Eds.). (2003). *Personality in adulthood* (2nd ed.). New York: Guilford.

McDaniel, M. A. (2005). Big-brained people are smarter: A meta-analysis of the relationship between in vivo brain volume and intelligence. *Intelligence, 33,* 337–346.

McDaniel, M. A., & Einstein, G. O. (1986). Bizarre imagery as an effective memory aid: The importance of distinctiveness. *Journal of Experimental Psychology: Learning, Memory and Cognition, 12,* 54–65.

McDougall, W. (1908). *Social psychology.* New York: Putnam.

McElrath, D. (1997). The Minnesota model. *Journal of Psychoactive Drugs, 29,* 141–144.

McEwen, B. S. (2002, December 17). Cited in E. Goode, The heavy cost of stress. *The New York Times,* p. D1.

McGowan, K. (2009, July/August). Out of the past. *Discover,* 30–37.

McIntosh, V. V. W., Jordan, J., Carter, F. A., Luty, S. E., McKenzie, J. M., Bulik, C. M., Frampton, C. M. A., & Joyce, P. R. (2005). Three psychotherapies for anorexia nervosa: A randomized, controlled trial. *The American Journal of Psychiatry, 162,* 741–747.

Megargee, E. I. (1997). Internal inhibitions and controls. In R. Hogan, J. Johnson, & S. Briggs (Eds.), *Handbook of personality psychology.* New York: Academic Press.

Melamed, S., Shirom, A., Toker, S., Berliner, S., & Shapira, I. (2006). Burnout and risk of cardiovascular disease: Evidence, possible causal paths, and promising research directions. *Psychological Bulletin, 132,* 327–353.

Melzack, R., & Katz, J. (2004). *The gate control theory: Reaching for the brain.* Mahwah, NJ: Lawrence Erlbaum.

Mendelson, J. H., Mello, N. K., Schuckit, M. A., & Segal, D. S. (2006). Cocaine, opioids, and other commonly abused drugs. In S. L. Hauser (Ed.), *Harrison's neurology in clinical medicine* (pp. 625–632). New York: McGraw-Hill.

Messager, S. (2006). Kisspeptin and its receptors: New gatekeepers of puberty. *British Society for Neuroendocrinology, 24.*

Mestel, R. (2003b, May 19). Rorschach tested. *Los Angeles Times,* p. F1.

Meyer-Lindenberg, A. (2006, May 27). Cited in B. Bower, Violent developments. Disruptive kids grow into their behavior. *Science News, 169,* 328–329.

Meyer-Lindenberg, A. (2009, April/May). Perturbed personalities. Scientific American Mind, 40–43.

Michels, S. (2008, September 24). Doctors warn of dangers of texting and walking. *ABC News.*

Milgram, S. (1963). Behavioral study of obedience. *Journal of Abnormal and Social Psychology, 67,* 371–378.

Milgram, S. (1974). *Obedience to authority.* New York: Harper & Row.

Milham, M. P., Erickson, K. I., Banich, M. T., Kramer, A. F., Webb, A., Wszalek, T., & Cohen, H. J. (2002). Attentional control in the aging brain: Insights from an fMRI study of the Stroop task. *Brain and Cognition, 49,* 277–296.

Miller, A. (Ed.). (2005). The social psychology of good and evil. New York: Guilford.

Miller, G. (1956). The magical number seven, plus or minus two: Some limits on our capacity for information processing. *Psychological Review, 48,* 337–442.

Miller, G. (2009, March 20). Rewiring faulty circuits in the brain. *Science, 323,* 1554–1556.

Miller, K. (2007, November). Class act. *Reader's Digest,* 114–119.

Miller, M. A., & Rahe, R. H. (1997). Life changes scaling for the 1990s. *Journal of Psychosomatic Research, 43,* 279–292.

Miller, M. C. (2005, October 3). The dangers of chronic disease. *Newsweek,* 58–59.

Miller M. C. (2007, December 10). Diagnosis: Same as it never was. *Newsweek,* 86.

Miller, R. (2003, November). Cited in K. Wright, Staying alive. *Discover,* 64–70.

Milrod, B., Leon, A. C., Busch, F., Gudden, M., Schwalberg, M., Clarkin, J., ... Shear, M. K. (2007). A randomized controlled clinical trial of psychoanalytic psychotherapy for panic disorder. *American Journal of Psychiatry, 164,* 265–272.

Miltenberger, R. G. (2007). *Behavioral modification: Principles and procedures* (4th ed.). Belmont, CA: Wadsworth Cengage.

Mirsky, A. F., & Quinn, O. W. (1988). The Genain quadruplets. *Schizophrenia Bulletin, 14,* 595–612.

Mitchell, J. E., Agras, S., & Wonderlich, S. (2007). Treatment of bulimia nervosa: Where are we and where are we going? *International Journal of Eating Disorders, 40,* 95–101.

Money, J. (1987). Sin, sickness or status? *American Psychologist, 42,* 384–399.

Montgomery, G. H., & Bovbjerg, D. H. (1997). The development of anticipatory nausea in patients receiving adjuvant chemotherapy for breast cancer. *Physiology & Behavior, 61,* 737–741.

Moore, D. W. (2005, June 16). Three in four Americans believe in paranormal. *Gallup Poll News Service.*

Morey, L. C. (1997). Personality diagnosis and personality disorders. In R. Hogan, J. Johnson & S. Briggs (Eds.), *Handbook of personality psychology.* New York: Academic Press.

Morgan, A. B., & Lilienfeld, S. O. (2000). A meta-analytic review of the relation between antisocial behavior and neuropsychological measures of executive function. *Clinical Psychology Review, 20,* 113–136.

Morrison, A. (1993). Cited in H. Herzog, Animal rights and wrongs. *Science, 262,* 1906–1908.

Mortensen, E. L., Michaelsen, K. F., Sanders, S. A., & Reinisch, J. M. (2002). The association between duration of breastfeeding and adult intelligence. *The Journal of the American Medical Association, 287,* 2365–2371.

Morton, S. (2004, November 1). Rare disease makes girl unable to feel pain. *Associated Press.*

Moscovitch, D. A., Antony, M. A., & Swinson, R. P. (2008). Exposure-based treatments for anxiety disorders: Theory and process. In M. M. Antony & M. B. Stein (Eds.), *Oxford handbook of anxiety and related disorders* (pp. 461–475). New York: Oxford University Press.

Mosher, W. D., Chandra, A., & Jones, J. (2005, September 15). Sexual behavior and selected health measures: Men and women 15–44 years of age, United States, 2002. *Centers for Disease Control and Prevention: Advance data from vital and health statistics,* 362.

Mosing, M. A., Gordon, S. D., Medland, S. E., Statham, D. J., Nelson, E. C., Heath, A. C., ... Wray, N. R. (2009). Genetic and environmental influences on the comorbidity between depression, panic disorder, agoraphobia, and social phobia. A twin study. *Depression and Anxiety, 26,* 1004-11.

MSNBC. (2006, June 19). *Parents split on STD shot for preteens.* Retrieved from http://www.msnbc .com/id/12956410/

Mullin, B. C., & Hinshaw, S. P. (2007). Emotion regulation and externalizing disorders in children and adolescents. In J. J. Gross (Ed.), *Handbook of emotion regulation* (pp. 523–541). New York: Guilford.

Mullins, L. (2008, August 18/August 25). Tapping the brain for growth. *U.S. News & World Report,* 51–54.

Mumford, M. D., Connelly, M. S., Helton, W. B., Strange, J. M., & Osburn, H. K. (2001). On the construct validity of integrity tests: Individual and situational factors as predictors of test performance. *International Journal of Selection and Assessment, 9,* 240–257.

Mungadze, J. (2008, April 14). Cited in B. Woodruff, J. Hennessey, & J. Hill. Herschel Walker: "Tell the world my truth." *ABC News.*

Munoz, H. (2003, May 30). Working to get more female police officers. *Los Angeles Times,* p. B2.

Munsey, C. (2008a, February). Prescriptive authority in the states. *Monitor on Psychology,* 60.

Munsey, C. (2008b, December). Success on the state level. *Monitor on Psychology,* 18–19.

Munsey, C. (2010, April). RxP moves ahead in Oregon. *Monitor on Psychology,* 12.

Murray, H. (1943). *Thematic Apperception Test manual.* Cambridge, MA: Harvard University Press.

Mydans, S. (2003, March 11). Clustering in cities, Asians are becoming obese. *The New York Times,* p. A3.

Myrtek, M. (1995). Type A behavior pattern, personality factors, disease, and physiological reactivity: A metaanalytic update. *Personality and Individual Differences, 18,* 491–502.

Nagtegaal, J. E., Laurant, M. W., Kerkof, G. A., Smits, M. G., van der Meer, Y. G., & Coenen, A. M. L. (2000). Effects of melatonin on the quality of life in patients with delayed sleep phase syndrome. *Journal of Psychosomatic Research, 48,* 45–50.

Naish, P. L. N. (2006). Time to explain the nature of hypnosis? *Contemporary Hypnosis, 23,* 33–46.

Nash, M. R. (2001, July). The truth and the hype of hypnosis. *Scientific American,* 47–55.

Nathan, L., & Judd, H. L. (2007). Menopause and postmenopause. In A. H. DeCherney, L. Nathan, T. M. Goodwin & N. Laufer (Eds.), *Current diagnosis & treatment obstetrics & gynecology* (10th ed.). New York: McGraw-Hill.

Nathan, P. E., Stuart, S. P., & Dolan, S. L. (2000). Research of psychotherapy efficacy and effectiveness: Between Scylla and Charybdis. *Psychological Bulletin, 126,* 964–981.

National Highway Traffic Safety Administration. (2008, September 28). Cited in M. vos Savant, Ask Marilyn. *Parade,* 30.

National Institute of Mental Health (2008b). *The numbers count: Mental disorders in America.* Retrieved from http://www.nimh.nih.gov/health/publications/the-numbers-count-mental-disorders-in-america/index.shtml

National Institute of Mental Health. (2009a). Cited in APA, Finding help: How to choose a psychotherapist. *American Psychological Association Help Center.* Retrieved from http://www.apahelpcenter.org/articles/article.php?id=51

National Institute on Drug Abuse. (2006a). Crack and cocaine. *NIDA InfoFacts.* Retrieved from http://www.drugabuse.gov

National Institute on Drug Abuse. (2006c, July). *Tobacco addiction.* NIH Publication 06-4342.

National Institutes of Health. (2005). *Alzheimer's disease: Fact sheet* (NIH Publication 03-3431). Washington, DC: U.S. Government Printing Office.

National Institutes of Health. (2008). *Alzheimer's disease: Fact sheet.* NIH Publication 08-6423. Washington, DC: U.S. Government Printing Office.

National Sleep Foundation. (2003). *2003 Sleep in America poll.* Washington, DC: Author.

National Sleep Foundation. (2005). *2005 Sleep in America poll.* Washington, DC: Author.

National Sleep Foundation. (2008). *2008 Sleep in America poll.* Washington, DC: Author.

National Sleep Foundation. (2010). *Sleep talking.* Washington, DC: Author.

Neath, I., & Suprenant, A. M. (2003). Human memory (2nd ed.). Belmont, CA: Wadsworth/Thomson Learning.

Neisser, U., Boodoo, G., Bourchard, T. J., Jr., Boykin, A. W., Brody, N., Ceci, S. J., ... Urbina, S. (1996). Intelligence: Knowns and unknowns. *American Psychologist, 51,* 77–101.

Neisser, U., & Libby, L. K. (2005). Remembering life experiences. In E. Tulving & F. M. Craik (Eds.), *The Oxford handbook of memory.* New York: Oxford University Press.

Nelson, D. L. (2004). 5-HT5 receptors. *Current Drug Targets. CNS Neurological Disorders, 3,* 53–58.

Nemeroff, C. G. (2007). The burden of severe depression: A review of diagnostic challenges and treatment alternatives. *Journal of Psychiatric Research, 41,* 189–206.

Nes, L. S., & Segerstrom, S. C. (2006). Dispositional optimism and coping: A meta-analytic review. *Personality and Social Psychology Review, 10,* 235–251.

Nesse, R. M. (2005). Evolutionary psychology and mental health. In D. M. Buss (Ed.), *The handbook of evolutionary psychology* (pp. 903–927). New York: Wiley.

Neugarten, B. (1994, May). Cited in B. Azar, Women are barraged by media on "the change." *APA Monitor.*

Newman, L. S. (2001). A cornerstone for the science of interpersonal behavior? Person perception and person memory, past, present, and future. In G. B. Moskowitz (Ed.), *Cognitive social psychology.* Mahwah, NJ: Lawrence Erlbaum.

Newsweek. (2006, September 18). "I feel good, I feel alive," 62–63.

Nicholson, K., & Martelli, M. F. (2004). The problem of pain. *The Journal of Head Trauma Rehabilitation, 19,* 2–9.

Nicosia, N., Pacula, R. L., Kilmer, B., Lundberg, R., Chiesa, J. (2009). *The economic costs of methamphetamine use in the United States, 2005.* Santa Monica, CA: RAND.

Nisbett, R. E. (2009). *Intelligence and how to get it.* New York: W. W. Norton & Co.

Niznikiewicz, M. A., Kubicki, M., & Shenton, M. E. (2003). Recent structural and functional imaging findings in schizophrenia. *Current Opinion in Psychiatry, 16,* 123–147.

Noback, C. R., Ruggiero, D. A., Demarest, R. J., & Strominger, N. L. (2005). *The human nervous system: Structure and function* (6th ed.). Clifton, NJ: Humana Press.

Noonan, D., & Cowley, G. (2002, July 15). Prozac vs. placebos. *Newsweek,* 48–49.

Norman, D. A. (1982). *Learning and memory.* New York: Freeman.

Nosofsky, R. M., & Zaki, S. R. (2002). Exemplar and prototype models revisited: Response strategies, selective attention, and stimulus generalization. *Journal of Experimental Psychology: Learning, Memory and Cognition, 28,* 924–940.

Novotney, A. (2009, February). Dangerous distraction. *Monitor on Psychology,* 32–36.

Nowak, R. (1994). Chronobiologists out of sync over light therapy patents. *Science, 263,* 1217–1218.

Nunn, J. A., Gregory, L. J., Brammer, M., Williams, S. C. R., Parslow, D. M., Morgan, M. J., ... Gray, J. A. (2002). Functional magnetic resonance imaging of synesthesia: Activation of V4/V8 by spoken words. *Nature Neuroscience, 5,* 371–375.

Nyberg, L., & Cabeza, R. (2005). Brain imaging of memory. In E. Tulving & F. M. Craik (Eds.), *The Oxford handbook of memory.* New York: Oxford University Press.

O'Driscoll, P. (2005, February 28). Wichita cheers arrest in "BTK" killings. *USA Today,* p. 3A.

OECD (Organization for Economic Cooperation and Development). (2009, May 27). Cited in A. R. Carey & A. Gonzalez, Nations' obesity rates. *USA Today,* p. 1A.

Office of Animal Care and Use. (2010). Retrieved from http://oacu.od.nih.gov/index.htm

Ogloff, J. R. P. (2006). Psychopathy/antisocial personality disorder continuum. *Australian and New Zealand Journal of Psychiatry, 40,* 519–528.

Ohayon, M. M., & Guilleminault, C. (2006). Epidemiology of sleep disorders. In T. L. Lee-Chiong (Ed.), *Sleep: A comprehensive handbook* (pp. 73–82). Hoboken, NJ: John Wiley & Sons.

Ohayon, M. M., Lemine, P., Arnaud-Briant, V., & Dreyfus, M. (2002). Prevalence and consequences of sleep disorders in a shift worker population. *Journal of Psychosomatic Research, 53,* 577–583.

Ohman, A. (2002). Automaticity and the amygdala: Nonconscious responses to emotional faces. *Current Directions in Psychological Science, 11,* 62–66.

Olfson, M., & Marcus, S. C. (2009). National patterns in antidepressant medication treatment. *Archives of General Psychiatry, 66,* 848–856.

Olshansky, J. (2003, November). Cited in K. Wright, Staying alive. *Discover,* 64–70.

Olshansky, J., Hayflick, L., & Carnes, B. A. (2002, June). No truth to the fountain of youth. *Scientific American,* 92–95.

Olsson, H., Wennerholm, P., & Lyxzen, U. (2004). Exemplars, prototypes, and the flexibility of classification models. *Journal of Experimental Psychology, 30,* 936–941.

O'Neil, J. (2006, June 28). A warning on hazards of smoke secondhand. *The New York Times,* p. A14.

O'Reardon, J. P., Solvason, H. B., Janicak, P. G., Sampson, S., Isenberg, K. E., Nahas, Z., ... Sackeim, H. A. (2007). Efficacy and safety of transcranial magnetic stimulation in the acute treatment of major depression: A multistate randomized controlled trial. *Biological Psychiatry, 62,* 1208–1216.

O'Regan, J. K., Deubel, H., Clark, J. J., & Rensink, R. A. (2000). Picture changes during blinks: Looking without seeing and seeing without looking. *Visual Cognition, 7,* 191–211.

Ortiz, B. (2005, December 12). BTK thought police wouldn't lie to him. *Herald-Leader.*

Osborne, B. J., Lio, G. T., & Newman, N. J. (2007). Cranial nerve II and afferent visual pathways.

In C. G. Goetz (Ed.), *Textbook of clinical neurology* (3rd ed., pp. 113–132). Philadelphia: Saunders Elsevier.

Osborne, L. (2002, December 15). The year in ideas: Virtual-reality therapy. *The New York Times.*

Osofsky, J. D. (1995). The effects of exposure to violence on young children. *American Psychologist, 50,* 782–788.

Ost, L., Helstrom, K., & Kaver, A. (1992). One versus five sessions of exposure in the treatment of injection phobia. *Behavior Therapy, 23,* 263–282.

Owen, P. (2003). *Minnesota model: Description of counseling approach.* Retrieved from http://www.nida.nih.gov

Ozer, E. J., Best, S. R., Lipsey, T. L., & Weiss, D. S. (2003). Predictors of posttraumatic stress disorder and symptoms in adults: A meta-analysis. *Psychological Bulletin, 129,* 52–71.

Pahwa, R., & Lyons, K. E. (2003). Essential tremor: Differential diagnosis and current therapy. *The American Journal of Medicine, 115,* 134–142.

Panksepp, J. (2008). The affective brain and core consciousness: How does neural activity generate emotional feelings? In M. Lewis, J. M. Haviland-Jones, & L. F. Barrett (Eds.), *Handbook of emotions* (3rd ed., pp. 47–67). New York: Guilford.

Parens, E., Chapman, A. R., & Press, N. (Eds.). (2006). *Wrestling with behavioral genetics: Science, ethics, and public conversation.* Baltimore: Johns Hopkins University Press.

Pascalis, O., de Haan, M., & Nelson, C. A. (2002). Is face processing species-specific during the first year of life? *Science, 296,* 1321–1323.

Patterson, D. R., & Jensen, M. P. (2003). Hypnosis and clinical pain. *Psychological Bulletin, 129,* 495–521.

Paul, S. M., Extein, I., Calil, H. M., Potter, W. Z., Chodoff, P., & Goodwin, F. K. (1981). Use of ECT with treatment-resistant depressed patients at the National Institute of Mental Health. *American Journal of Psychiatry, 138,* 486–489.

Paulozzi, L. J. (2006). Opioid analgesic involvement in drug abuse deaths in American metropolitan areas. *American Journal of Public Health, 96,* 1755–1757.

Pelham, W. E., Manos, M. J., Ezzell, C. A., Tresco, K. T., Gnagy, E. M., Hoffman, M. T ... Morse, G. (2005). A dose-ranging study of a methylphenidate transdermal system in children with ADHD. *Journal of the American Academy of Child and Adolescent Psychiatry, 44,* 522–529.

Pelle, A. J., van den Broek, K. C., Szabó, B., & Kupper, N. (2009, May 22). The relationship between Type D personality and chronic heart failure is not confounded by disease severity as assessed by BNP. *International Journal of Cardiology.*

Peltzer, D. (1995). *A child called "it."* Deerfield Beach, FL: Health Communications.

Peltzer, D. (1997). *The lost boy: A foster child's search for the love of a family.* Deerfield Beach, FL: Health Communications.

Peltzer, D. (1999). *A man named Dave: A story of triumph and forgiveness.* New York: Penguin.

Peltzer, D. (2000). *Help yourself: Celebrating the rewards of resilience and gratitude.* New York: Penguin.

Peltzer, D. (2003). Cited in M. Peltzer, *The self-made man behind the marvel.* Retrieved from http://www.bookbrowse.com/author_interviews/full/index.cfm?author_number=145

Peltzer, D. (2009). *About Dave.* Retrieved from www.davepeltzer.com

Peng, T. (2008a, March 24). No Buddha required. *Newsweek,* 71.

Peng, T. (2008b, August 18). A summer caffeine rush. *Newsweek,* 63.

Penley, J. A., Tomaka, J., & Wiebe, J. S. (2002). The association of coping to physical and psychological health outcomes: A meta-analytic review. *Journal of Behavioral Medicine, 25,* 551–603.

Penn, H. E. (2006). Neurobiological correlates of autism: A review of recent research. *Child Neuropsychology, 12,* 57–59.

Persons, J. B. (1997). Dissemination of effective methods: Behavior therapy's next challenge. *Behavior Therapy, 28,* 465–471.

Pert, C. B., Snowman, A. M., & Snyder, S. H. (1974). Localization of opiate receptor binding in presynaptic membranes of rat brain. *Brain Research, 70,* 184–188.

Pesant, N., & Zadra, A. (2006). Dream content and psychological well-being: A longitudinal study of the continuity hypothesis. *Journal of Clinical Psychology, 62,* 111–121.

Peterson, L. A. (2007, February 3). Texas gov. orders anti-cancer vaccine. *Yahoo! News.*

Peterson, L. R., & Peterson, M. J. (1950). Short-term retention of individual verbal terms. *Journal of Experimental Psychology, 58,* 193–198.

Peterson, M. A., Gillam, B., & Sedgwick, H. A. (2007). *In the mind's eye: Julian Hockberg on the perception of pictures, films, and the world.* New York: Oxford University Press.

Petitto, L. A. (1997, December 11). Cited in R. L. Hotz, The brain: Designed to speak the mind. *Los Angeles Times.*

Petri, H. L., & Govern, J. M. (2004). *Motivation* (5th ed.). Belmont, CA: Wadsworth.

Petrides, K. V., Furnham, A., & Martin, G. N. (2004). Estimates of emotional and psychometric intelligence: Evidence for gender-based stereotypes. *The Journal of Social Psychology, 144,* 149–162.

Petrovic, P., Kalso, E., Petersson, K. M., & Ingvar, M. (2002). Placebo and opioid analgesia—imaging a shared neuronal network. *Science, 295,* 1737–1740.

Petty, R. E., & Cacioppo, J. T. (1986). *Attitudes and persuasion: Classic and contemporary approaches.* Dubuque, IA: William C. Brown.

Petty, R. E., Wegener, D. T., & Fabrigar, L. R. (1997). Attitudes and attitude change. *Annual Review of Psychology, 46,* 609–647.

Phelps, E. A. (2004). The human amygdala and awareness: Interactions between emotion and cognition. In M. S. Gazzaniga (Ed.), *The cognitive neurosciences III* (pp. 1005–1030). Cambridge, MA: MIT Press.

Picchioni, D., Goeltzenleucher, B., Green, D. N., Convento, M. J., Crittenden, R., Hallgren, M., & Hicks, R. A. (2002). Nightmares as a coping mechanism for stress. *Dreaming, 12,* 155–169.

Piliavin, J. A., Dovidio, J. F., Gaertner, S. L., & Clark, R. D. (1982). Responsive bystanders: The process of intervention. In V. J. Derlega & J. Grzelak (Eds.), *Cooperation and helping behavior.* Orlando, FL: Academic Press.

Pillemer, D. B. (1984). Flashbulb memories of the assassination attempt on President Reagan. *Cognition, 16,* 63–80.

Pincus, T., & Morley, S. (2001). Cognitive-processing bias in chronic pain: A review and integration. *Psychological Bulletin, 127,* 599–617.

Pingitore, R., Dugoni, B. L., Tindale, R. S., & Spring, B. (1994). Bias against overweight job applicants in a simulated employment interview. *Journal of Applied Psychology, 79,* 909–917.

Pinker, S. (1994). *The language instinct.* New York: William Morrow.

Pinker, S. (1995). Introduction. In M. S. Gazzaniga (Ed.), *The cognitive neurosciences.* Cambridge, MA: MIT Press.

Pinker, S. (2002). *The blank slate: The modern denial of human nature.* New York: Penguin.

Pinker, S. (2008, January 13). The moral instinct. *The New York Times.*

Piomelli, D. (1999). Cited in J. Travis, Marijuana mimic reveals brain role. *Science News, 155,* 215.

Pirko, I., & Noseworthy, J. H. (2007). Demyelinating disorders of the central nervous system. In C. G. Goetx (Ed.), *Textbook of clinical neurology* (3rd ed.). Philadelphia: Saunders Elsevier.

Pi-Sunyer, X. (2003). A clinical view of the obesity problem. *Science, 299,* 859–860.

Plante, T. (2005). *Contemporary clinical psychology.* Hoboken, NJ: John Wiley & Sons.

Pleuvry, B. J. (2005). Opioid mechanisms and opioid drugs. *Anaesthesia and Intensive Care Medicine, 6,* 30–34.

Ploghaus, A., Becerra, L., Borras, C., & Borsook, D. (2003). Neural circuitry underlying pain modulation: Expectation, hypnosis, placebo. *Trends in Cognitive Science, 7,* 197–200.

Plomin, R., & Petrill, S. A. (1997). Genetics and intelligence: What's new? *Intelligence, 24,* 53–77.

Plomin, R., & Spinath, F. M. (2004). Intelligence: Genetics, genes, and genomics. *Journal of Personality and Social Psychology, 86,* 112–129.

Plummer, W., & Ridenhour, R. (1995, August 28). Saving grace. *People.*

Politi, P., Minoretti, P., Falcone, C., Martinelli, V., & Emanuele, E. (2006). Association analysis of the functional Ala111Glu polymorphism of the glyoxalase I gene in panic disorder. *Neuroscience Letter, 396,* 163-66.

Polivy, J., & Herman, C. P. (2002). Causes of eating disorders. *Annual Review of Psychology, 53,* 187–213.

Post, S. (2005). Altruism, happiness, and health: It's good to be good. *International Journal of Behavioral Medicine, 2,* 66–77.

Potter, J. (2006). Female sexuality: Assessing satisfaction and addressing problems. In D. C. Dale & D. D. Federman (Eds.), *ACP medicine.* New York: WebMD Professional Publishing.

Preston, R. (2008, January 22). Meet the smartest man in America. *KMOV.* Retrieved from http://www.kmov.com/featuredstories/stories/kmov_localnews_061115_genius.3f6953ad.html

Price, M. (2008a, April). Caffeine's wake-up call. *Monitor on Psychology, 26*–27.

Price, M. (2008c[G55], November). Against doctors' orders. *Monitor on Psychology, 34*–36.

Priester, J. R., & Petty, R. E. (1995). Source attributions and persuasion: Perceived honesty as a determinant of message scrutiny. *Personality and Social Psychological Bulletin, 21,* 637–654.

Prochaska, J. O., & Norcross, J. C. (2010). *Systems of psychotherapy* (7th ed.). Belmont, CA: Brooks/Cole.

Pruitt, D. G. (1971). Choice shifts in group discussion: An introductory review. *Journal of Personality and Social Psychology, 20,* 339–360.

Purves, D., Augustine, G. J., Fitzpatrick, D., Hall, W. C., LaMantia, A., McNamara, J. O., & White, L. E. (2008). *Neuroscience* (4th ed.). Sunderland, MA: Sinauer Associates.

Quill, E. (2009, January 17). It's written all over your face. *Science News,* 24–28.

Quirk, G. J. (2007). Prefrontal-amygdala interactions in the regulation of fear. In J. J. Gross (Ed.), *Handbook of emotion regulation* (pp. 27–46). New York: Guilford.

Rabasca, L. (2000a, March). Humanistic psychologists look to revamp their image. *Monitor on Psychology,* 54–55.

Raine, A. (2002). Biosocial studies of antisocial and violent behavior in children and adults: A review. *Journal of Abnormal Child Psychology, 30,* 311–326.

Raine, A., Ishikawa, S. S., Arce, E., Lencz, T., Knuth, K. H., Bihrie, S., ... Colletti, P. (2004). Hippocampal structural asymmetry in unsuccessful psychopaths. *Biological Psychiatry, 55,* 185–191.

Raine, A., Lencz, T., Bihrle, S., LaCasse, L., & Colletti, P. (2000). Reduced prefrontal gray matter volume and reduced autonomic activity in antisocial personality disorder. *Archives of General Psychiatry, 57,* 119–127.

Ramachandran, V. S. (2006, April/May). Cited in M. Solms, Freud returns. *Scientific American Mind,* 28–34.

Ramachandran, V. S., & Anstis, S. M. (1986). The perception of apparent motion. *Scientific American, 254,* 102–109.

Ramachandran, V. S., & Oberman, L. M. (2006, November). Broken mirrors: A theory of autism. *Scientific American,* 63–69.

Ramachandran, V. S., & Rogers-Ramachandran, D. (2007, February/March). A moving experience. *Scientific American Mind,* 14–16.

Randi, J. (2005). 'Twas brillig ...: Million dollar excuses, Dutch psychic caught cheating, Sylvia Browne and the Virginia miners, from the JREF museum. *Skeptic.*

Randi, J. (2009). 'Twas brillig ...: Prayer and pregnancy; shooting UFO photos. *Skeptic, 14.*

Rapoport, J. L. (1988). The neurobiology of obsessive-compulsive disorder. *Journal of the American Medical Association, 260,* 2888–2890.

Rapson, E., & Hatfield, R. L. (2005). *Love and sex: Cross-cultural perspectives.* Lanham, MD: University Press of America.

Raskin, N. J., Rogers, C. R., & Witty, M. C. (2008). Client-centered therapy. In R. J. Corsini &

Wedding, D. (Eds.), *Current psychotherapies* (8th ed., pp. 141–186). Belmont, CA: Thomson Brooks/Cole.

Rasmussen, K. G. (2003). Clinical applications of recent research on electroconvulsive therapy. *Bulletin of the Menninger Clinic, 67,* 18–31.

Ray, L. A., & Hutchinson, K. E. (2007). Effects of naltrexone on alcohol sensitivity and genetic moderators of medication response: A double-blind-placebo-controlled study. *Archives of General Psychiatry, 64,* 1067–1077.

Reed, S., & Breu, G. (1995, June 6). The wild ones. *People.*

Reed, S., & Cook, D. (1993, April 19). Realm of the senses. *People.*

Reed, S., & Free, C. (1995, October 16). The big payoff. *People.*

Reed, S., & Stambler, L. (1992, May 25). The umpire strikes back. *People,* 87–88.

Reed, S. D., & Sutton, E. L. (2006). Menopause. In D. C. Dale & D. D. Federman (Eds.), *ACP Medicine.* New York: WebMD Professional Publishing.

Reilly, S., & Schachtman, T. R. (2009). *Conditioned taste aversion: Neural and behavioral processes.* New York: Oxford University Press.

Reitman, V. (1999, February 22). Learning to grin—and bear it. *Los Angeles Times,* p. A1.

Resick, P. A., Monson, C. M., & Rizvi, S. L. (2008). Posttraumatic stress disorder. In D. H. Barlow (Ed.), *Clinical handbook of psychological disorders* (4th ed., pp. 65–122). New York: Guilford.

Rey, G. (1983). Concepts and stereotypes. *Cognition, 15,* 237–262.

Rhee, S. H., & Waldman, I. D. (2002). Genetic and environmental influences on antisocial behavior: A meta-analysis of twin and adoption studies. *Psychological Bulletin, 128,* 490–529.

Ridderinkhof, K. R., de Vlugt, Y., Bramlage, A., Spaan, M., Elton, M., Snel, J., & Band, G. P. H. (2002). Alcohol consumption impairs detection of performance errors in mediofrontal cortex. *Science, 298,* 2209–2211.

Riley, E. P., & McGee, C. L. (2005). Fetal alcohol spectrum disorders: An overview with emphasis on changes in brain and behavior. *Experimental Biology and Medicine, 230,* 357–365.

Rizzo, A., Reger, G., Gahm, G., Difede, J., & Rothbaum, B. O. (2009). Virtual reality exposure therapy for combat-related PTSD. In P. J. Shiromani, T. M. Keane, & J. E. LeDoux (Eds.), *Post-traumatic stress disorder: Basic science and clinical practice.* New York: Humana Press.

Rizzo, S. (2008, October). In K. McAuliffe, Interview: Virtual therapist. *Discover,* 58.

Roa, J., Aguilar, E., Dieguez, C., Pinilla, L., & Tena-Sempere, M. (2008). New frontiers in kisspeptin/GPR54 physiology as fundamental gatekeepers of reproductive function. *Frontiers in Neuroendocrinology, 29,* 48–69.

Robertson, D. (Ed.). (2005). *Primer on the autonomic nervous system* (2nd ed.). New York: Academic Press.

Robinson-Riegler, B., & McDaniel, M. A. (1994). Further constraints on the bizarreness effect: Elaboration at encoding. *Memory and Cognition, 22,* 702–712.

Rochlen, A. B., Zack, J. S., & Speyer, C. (2004). Online therapy: Review of relevant definitions, debates, and current empirical support. *Journal of Clinical Psychology, 60,* 269–283.

Rodafinos, A., Vucevic, A., & Sideridis, G. D. (2005). The effectiveness of compliance techniques: Foot in the door versus door in the face. *The Journal of Social Psychology, 145,* 237–239.

Rodgers, J. E. (1982). The malleable memory of eyewitnesses. *Science.*

Roediger, H. L., & McDermott, K. B. (2005). Distortions of memory. In E. Tulving & F. M. Craik (Eds.), *The Oxford handbook of memory.* New York: Oxford University Press.

Rogers, C. R. (1951). *Client-centered therapy: Its current practice, implications, and theory.* Boston: Houghton Mifflin.

Rogers, C. R. (1980). *A way of being.* Boston: Houghton Mifflin.

Rogers, C. R. (1986). Client-centered therapy. In I. L. Kutash & A. Wolf (Eds.), *Psychotherapists' casebook.* San Francisco: Jossey-Bass.

Rogers, C. R. (1989). Cited in N. J. Raskin & C. R. Rogers, Person-centered therapy. In R. J. Corsini & D. Wedding (Eds.), *Current psychotherapies* (4th ed.). Itasca, IL: F. E. Peacock.

Rogers, M. A., Yamasue, H., Abe, O., Yamada, H., Ohtani, T., Iwanami, A., ... Kasai, K. (2009). Smaller amygdala volume and reduced anterior cingulated gray matter density associated with history of post-traumatic stress disorder. *Psychiatry Research, 174,* 210-16.

Rogers, P., & Morehouse, W., III. (1999, April 12). She's got it. *People,* 89.

Root, R. W., II, & Resnick, R. J. (2003). An update on the diagnosis and treatment of attention-deficit/hyperactivity disorders in children. *Professional Psychology: Research Practice, 34,* 34–41.

Ropper, A., & Samuels, M. (2009). *Adam's and Victor's principles of neurology* (9th ed.). New York: McGraw-Hill.

Rorschach, R. (1921; reprinted 1942). *Psychodiagnostics.* Bern, Switzerland: Hans Huber.

Rosch, E. (1978). Principles of categorization. In E. Rosch & B. B. Lloyd (Eds.), Cognition and categorization. Hillsdale, NJ: Lawrence Erlbaum.

Rosenberg, J. (2006). *Community mental health: Challenges for the 21st century.* New York: Routledge.

Rosenthal, L. (2006). Physiologic processes during sleep. In T. L. Lee-Chiong (Ed.), *Sleep: A comprehensive handbook* (pp. 19–23). Hoboken, NJ: John Wiley & Sons.

Rosenthal, R. (2003). Covert communication in laboratories, classrooms, and the truly real world. *Current Directions in Psychological Science, 12,* 151–154.

Rosenthal, Z. (2007, November 5). In Virtual reality game helps drug addicts recover. *ABC News.* Retrieved from http://abcmews.go.com/print?id=3819621

Ross, P. E. (2006, August). The expert mind. *Scientific American,* 64–71.

Rothbaum, B. O. (2009). Using virtual reality to help our patients in the real world. *Depression and Anxiety, 26,* 209–211.

Rotter, J. B. (1990). Internal versus external control of reinforcement: A case history of a variable. *American Psychologist, 45,* 489–493.

Routh, D. K. (1994). *The founding of clinical psychology (1896) and some important early developments: Introduction.* New York: Plenum Publishing.

Rouw, R., & Scholte, H. S. (2007). Increased structural connectivity in grapheme-color synesthesia. *Nature Neuroscience, 10,* 792–797.

Rowe, M. L., & Goldin-Meadow, S. (2009). Differences in early gesture explain SES disparities in child vocabulary size at school entry. *Science, 323,* 951–953.

Rozin, P. (2003). Introduction: Evolutionary and cultural perspectives on affect. In R. D. Lane & L. Nadel (Eds.), *Cognitive neuroscience of emotion.* New York: Oxford University Press.

Ruben, R. J. (2007). Hearing loss and deafness. Cited in *The Merck manual online medical library: Home edition.* Retrieved from http://www.merck.com/mmhe

Rubin, R. (2007, February 20). Merck drops its push for vaccine mandate. *USA Today.*

Ruble, D. N., Martin, C. L., & Berenbaum, S. A. (2006). Gender development. In N. Eisenberg, W. Damon & R. M. Lerner (Eds.), *Handbook of child psychology* (6th ed., pp. 858–932). Hoboken, NJ: John Wiley & Sons.

Rudman, L. A., & Glick, P. (2008). *The social psychology of gender.* New York: Guilford.

Rui, L. (2005, August 21). Leptin-signaling protein maintains normal body weight and energy balance in mice. *Science Daily.*

Ruibal, S. (2006, February 12). White a gold winner in halfpipe, Kass is second. *USA Today.*

Ruiter, R. A. C., Abraham, C., & Kok, G. (2001). Scary warnings and rational precautions: A review of the psychology of fear appeals. *Psychology and Health, 16,* 613–630.

Ruiz-Bueno, J. B. (2000). Locus of control, perceived control, and learned helplessness. In V. R. Rice (Ed.), *Handbook of stress, coping and health.* Thousand Oaks, CA: Sage.

Runco, M. A. (2004). Creativity. *Annual Review of Psychology, 55,* 657–687.

Rupke, S. J., Blecke, D., & Renfrow, M. (2006). Cognitive therapy for depression. *American Family Physician, 73,* 83–86.

Russell, R., Duchaine, B., & Nakayama, K. (2009). Super-recognizers: People with extraordinary face recognition ability. *Psychonomic Bulletin & Review, 16,* 252–257.

Russell, S. (2005, March 23). The Terri Schiavo case: Her condition: Doctor explains the "persistent vegetative state." *San Francisco Chronicle.*

Rutter, M., & Silberg, J. (2002). Gene-environment interplay in relation to emotional and behavioral disturbance. *Annual Review of Psychology, 53,* 463–490.

Ryan, R. M., & Deci, E. L. (2000). Self-determination theory and the facilitation of intrinsic motivation, social development, and well-being. *American Psychologist, 55,* 68–78.

Sackeim, H. A., Prudic, J., Devanand, D. P., Nobler, M. S., Lisanby, S., Peyser, S., ... Clark, J. (2000). A prospective, randomized, double blind comparison of bilateral and right unilateral electroconvulsive therapy at different stimulus intensities. *Archives of General Psychiatry, 57,* 425–434.

Sackeim, H. A., & Stern, Y. (1997). Neuropsychiatric aspects of memory and amnesia. In S. C. Yudofsky & R. E. Hales (Eds.), *The American Psychiatric Press textbook of neuropsychiatry* (3rd ed.). Washington, DC: American Psychiatric Press.

Sacks, O. (2008, January). Cited in S. Kruglinski, The *Discover* interview. *Discover,* 72–78.

Saey, T. H. (2008a, August 2). Astrocytes are rising stars of the brain. *Science News,* 5.

Saey, T. H. (2008a, May 24). Epic genetics. *Science News,* 14–19.

Saey, T. H. (2008b, September 27). Creating new nerve cells makes sense for the brain. *Science News,* 5–6.

Saladin, M. E., Brady, K. T., Graap, K., & Rothbaum, B. O. (2006). A preliminary report on the use of virtual reality technology to elicit craving and cue reactivity in cocaine dependent individuals. *Addictive Behaviors, 31,* 1881–1894.

Saletan, W. (2006, March 5). Irreconcilable differences. *The New York Times.*

Salovey, P., Detweiler-Bedell, B. T., Detweiler-Bedell, J. B., & Mayer, J. D. (2008). Emotional intelligence. In M. Lewis, J. M. Haviland-Jones, & Feldman Barrett, L. (Eds.), Handbook of emotions (3rd edition, pp. 533–547). New York: Guilford.

Salovey, P., & Mayer, J. D. (1990). Emotional intelligence. *Imagination, Cognition, and Personality, 9,* 185–211.

Salovey, P., & Pizarro, D. A. (2003). In R. J. Sternberg, J. Lautrey & T. I. Lubart (Eds.), *Models of intelligence.* Washington, DC: American Psychological Association.

Salzman, C. (2008, September 22). How to help anxious minds. *Newsweek,* 69.

Samelson, F. (1980). J. B. Watson's little Albert, Cyril Burt's twins, and the need for a critical science. *American Psychologist, 35,* 619–625.

Samuel, D. (1996). Cited in N. Williams, How the ancient Egyptians brewed beer. *Science, 273,* 432.

San Diego Union-Tribune. (1994, June 17). Author.

Sapolsky, R. M. (2002, December 17). Cited in E. Goode, The heavy cost of stress. *The New York Times,* p. D1.

Savage-Rumbaugh, S. (1998, January 19). Cited in S. Begley, Aping language. *Newsweek.*

Savage-Rumbaugh, S., & Lewin, R. (1994). *Kanzi.* New York: Wiley.

Sax, L. J. (2002, September 11). Cited in M. Duenwald, Students find another staple of campus life: Stress. *The New York Times,* p. D5.

Saxe, L. (1994). Detection of deception: Polygraph and integrity tests. *Current Directions in Psychological Science, 3,* 69–73.

Scarr, S., & Weinberg, R. A. (1976). IQ test performance of black children adopted by white families. *American Psychologist, 31,* 726–739.

Schachter, S., & Singer, J. (1962). Cognitive, social and physiological determinants of emotional state. *Psychological Review, 69,* 379–399.

Schacter, D. L. (1996). *Searching for memory.* New York: Basic Books.

Schacter, D. L. (2001). *The seven sins of memory: How the mind forgets and remembers.* New York: Houghton Mifflin.

Scheck, B. (2008, August 10). Cited in M. Sherman, Race sometimes a problem in eyewitness IDs. *MSNBC.* Retrieved from http://www.msnbc .msn.com/id/26123421/wid/17621070/

Schenck, C. H. (2003, January 7). Cited in E. Goode, When the brain disrupts the night. *The New York Times,* p. D1.

Schiff, N. D., Giacino, J. T., Kalmar, K., Victor, J. D., Baker, K., Gerber, M., ... Rezai, A. R. (2007). Behavioural improvements with thalamic stimulation after traumatic brain injury. *Nature, 448,* 600–603.

Schilt, T., de Win, M. M. L., Koeter, M., Jager, G., Korf, D. J., van den Brink, W., & Schmand, B. (2007). Cognition in novice ecstasy users with minimal exposure to other drugs. *Archives of General Psychiatry, 64,* 728–736.

Schlaggar, B. L., Brown, T. T., Lugar, H. M., Visscher, K. M., Miezin, F. M., & Petersen, S. E. (2002). Functional neuroanatomical differences between adults and school-age children in the processing of single words. *Science, 296,* 1476–1479.

Schmitt, D. R., Allik, J., McCrae, R. R., & Benet-Martinez, V. (2007). The geographic distribution of big five personality traits. *Journal of Cross-Cultural Psychology, 38,* 173–212.

Schneider, M. (2007, October 10). Dutton back in biz at HBO. *Daily Variety.*

Schnurr, P. P., Friedman, M. J., & Bernardy, N. C. (2002). Research on posttraumatic stress disorder: Epidemiology, pathophysiology, and assessment. *Journal of Clinical Psychology/In Session: Psychotherapy in Practice, 58,* 877–889.

Schorn, D. (2007, January 28). Brain man: One man's gift may be the key to better understanding the brain. *CBS News: 60 Minutes.*

Schrock, K. (2007, April/May). Freeing a locked-in mind. *Scientific American Mind,* 40–45.

Schroeder, D. A., Penner, L. A., Dovidio, J. F., & Piliavin, J. A. (1995). *The psychology of helping and altruism: Problems and puzzles.* New York: McGraw-Hill.

Schuckit, M. (2000). *Drug and alcohol abuse* (5th ed.). New York: Kluwer Academic.

Schuckit, M. (2006). Alcohol and alcoholism. In S. L. Hauser (Ed.), *Harrison's neurology in clinical medicine* (pp. 617–624). New York: McGraw-Hill.

Schulman, K. A., Berlin, J. A., Harless, W., Kerner, J. F., Sistrunk, S., Gersh, B. J., ... Escarce, J. J. (1999). The effect of race and sex on physicians' recommendations for cardiac catheterization. *The New England Journal of Medicine, 340,* 618–626.

Schultz, D. P., & Schultz, S. E. (2008). *A history of modern psychology* (9th ed.). Belmont, CA: Wadsworth.

Schwartz, B. L. (1999). Sparkling at the end of the tongue: The etiology of tip-of-the-tongue phenomenology. *Psychonomic Bulletin & Review, 6,* 379–393.

Schwartz, M. S., & Andrasik, F. (2005). *Biofeedback: A practitioner's guide* (3rd ed.). New York: Guilford.

Schwartz, N. (1999). Self-reports: How the questions shape the answers. *American Psychologist, 54,* 93–105.

ScienceDaily. (2009b, May 20). Some people really 'never forget a face': Understanding extraordinary face recognition ability. Retrieved from http://www.sciencedaily.com/releases/2009/05/090519712204.htm

Scott, D. J., Stohler, C. S., Egnatuk, C. M., Wang, H., Koeppe, R. A., & Zubieta, J. K. (2007). Individual differences in reward processing explain placebo-induced expectations and effects. *Neuron, 55,* 325–336.

Searles, J. (1998, September). Write on! Learn to read his handwriting and read his mind. *Cosmopolitan,* 310–311.

Segerstrom, S. C., & Miller, G. E. (2004). Psychological stress and the human immune system: A meta-analytic study of 30 years of inquiry. *Psychological Bulletin, 130,* 601–630.

Seligman, M. E. P. (2002, December 9). Cited in M. Elias, What makes people happy psychologists now know. *USA Today,* p. A1.

Seligman, M. E. P. (2003). The past and future of positive psychology. In C. L. M. Keyes & J. Daidt (Eds.), *Flourishing: Positive psychology and the life well-lived.* Washington, DC: American Psychological Association.

Seligman, M. E. P., & Csikszentmihalyi, M. (2000). Positive psychology: An introduction. *American Psychologist, 55,* 5–14.

Selye, H. (1993). History of the stress concept. In L. Goldberger & S. Breznitz (Eds.), *Handbook of stress: Theoretical and clinical aspects* (2nd ed.). New York: Free Press.

Seppa, N. (2009, January 17). Disorder of REM sleep may signal high risk of Parkinson's, dementia. *Science News,* 9.

Shafer, V. L., & Garrido-Nag, K. (2007). The neurodevelopmental bases of language. In E. Hoff & M. Shatz (Eds.), *Blackwell handbook of lan-*

guage development (pp. 21–45). Malden, MA: Blackwell Publishing.

Shanker, S. G., Savage-Rumbaugh, E. S., & Taylor, T. J. (1999). Kanzi: A new beginning. *Animal Learning & Behavior, 27,* 24–25.

Shannon, C. (1994). Stress management. In D. K. Granvold (Ed.), *Cognitive and behavioral treatment.* Pacific Grove, CA: Brooks/Cole.

Shapiro, F. (2002). EMDR 12 years after its introduction: Past and future research. *Journal of Clinical Psychology, 58,* 1–22.

Shapiro, J. P. (1996, May 27). Beyond the rain man. *U.S. News & World Report,* 78–79.

Shapiro, S. L., Shapiro, D. E., & Schwartz, G. E. R. (2000). Stress management in medical education: A review of the literature. *Academic Medicine, 75,* 748–759.

"Shaun White." (2006). Retrieved from http://www.nbcolympics.com/athletes/5058606/detail.html

Shaw, G. M., Carmichael, S. L., Vollset, S. E., Yang, W., Finnell, R. H., Blom, H., Midttun, O., & Ueland, P. M. (2009). Mid-pregnancy cotinine and risks of orofacial clefts and neural tube defects. *The Journal of Pediatrics, 154,* 17–19.

Shaywitz, B. A., Sullivan, C. M., Anderson, G. M., Gillespie, S. M., Sullivan, B., & Shaywitz, S. E. (1994). Aspartame, behavior, and cognitive function in children with attention deficit disorder. *Pediatrics, 93,* 70–75.

Sher, L. (2004). Type D personality, cortisol and cardiac disease. *Australian & New Zealand Journal of Psychiatry, 38,* 652–653.

Shermer, M. (2002, December). Mesmerized by magnetism. *Scientific American,* 41.

Shimizu, M., & Pelham, B. W. (2004). The unconscious cost of good fortune: Implicit and explicit self-esteem, positive life events, and health. *Health Psychology, 23,* 101–105.

Shiraev, E., & Levy, D. (2009). *Cross-cultural psychology: Critical thinking and contemporary applications* (4th ed.). Boston: Allyn & Bacon.

Shute, N. (2009, February). The amazing teen brain. *U.S. News & World Report,* 36–39.

Sidtis, J. J., Volpe, B. T., Wilson, D. H., Rayport, M., & Gazzaniga, M. S. (1981). Variability in right hemisphere language function after callosal section: Evidence for a continuum of generative capacity. *Journal of Neuroscience, 1,* 323–331.

Siegal, M. (2005). Can we cure fear? *Scientific American Mind, 16,* 45–49.

Sigelman, C. K., & Rider, E. A. (2006). *Life-span human development* (5th ed.). Belmont, CA: Wadsworth/Thomson.

Silbernagl, S., & Despopoulos, A. (2008). *Color atlas of physiology* (6th ed.). New York: Thieme Medical.

Silke, A. (2003). Deindividuation, anonymity, and violence: Findings from Northern Ireland. *Journal of Social Psychology, 143,* 493–499.

Silver, J., & Miller, J. H. (2004). Regeneration beyond the glial scar. *Nature Reviews Neuroscience, 5,* 146–156.

Simon, B., & Sturmer, S. (2003). Respect for group members: Intragroup determinants of collective identification and group-serving behavior. *Personality and Social Psychology Bulletin, 29,* 183–193.

Singer, T., Seymour, B., O'Doherty, J., Kaube, H., Dolan, R. J., & Frith, C. (2004). Empathy for pain involves the affective but not sensory components of pain. *Science, 303,* 1157–1162.

Singular, S. (2006). *Unholy messenger: The life and crimes of the BTK serial killer.* New York: Scribner.

Skinner, B. F. (1938). *The behavior of organisms.* New York: Appleton-Century-Crofts.

Skinner, B. F. (1953). *Science and human behavior.* New York: Macmillan.

Slade, B. A., Leidel, L., Vellozzi, C., Woo, E. J., Hua, W., Sutherland, A., ... Iskander, J. (2009). Postlicensure safety surveillance for quadrivalent human papillomavirus recombinant vaccine. *Journal of the American Medical Association, 302,* 750–757.

Sloman, S. A. (1996). The empirical case for two systems of reasoning. *Psychological Bulletin, 119,* 3-22.

Smith, C. (1997, February 9). Companies using personality tests for making hires that fit. *The Los Angeles Times.*

Smith, D. (2002, June). Where are recent grads getting jobs? *Monitor on Psychology,* 28–32.

Smith, D. (2003, March). Angry thoughts, at-risk hearts. *Monitor on Psychology,* 46–47.

Smith, E. E. (2000). Neural bases of human working memory. *Current Directions in Psychological Science, 9,* 45–49.

Smith, N. T. (2002). A review of the published literature into cannabis withdrawal symptoms in human users. *Addiction, 97,* 621–632.

Smoller, J. W., Paulus, M. P., Fagerness, J. A., Purcell, S., Yamaki, L. H., Hirshfeld-Becker, D., ... Stein, M. B. (2008). Influence of RGS2 on anxiety-related temperament, personality, and brain function. *Archives of General Psychiatry, 65,* 298-308.

Society for Neuroscience. (2007, November 5). New clinical trials could open 'golden era' in spinal cord injury and ALS research. Retrieved from http://www.sfn.org/index.cfm?pagename=news_110507c&print=on

Society for Personality Assessment. (2005). The status of the Rorschach in clinical and forensic practice: An official statement by the Board of Trustees of the Society for Personality Assessment. *Journal of Personality Assessment, 85,* 219–237.

Solms, M. (2006, April/May). Freud returns. *Scientific American Mind,* 28–34.

Solomon, P. R., Adams, F., Silver, A., Zimmer, J., & DeVeaux, R. (2002). Ginkgo for memory enhancement. *Journal of the American Medical Association, 288,* 835–840.

Song, S. (2006a, March 27). Mind over medicine. *Time,* 13.

Sotsky, S. M., Glass, D. R., Shea, T., Pilkonis, P. A., Collins, F., Elkin, I., ... Oliveri, M. E. (2006, April). Patient predictors of response to psychotherapy and pharmacotherapy: Findings in the NIMH treatment of depression collaborative research program. *Focus, 4,* 278.

Soyez, V., & Broekaert, E. (2005). Therapeutic communities, family therapy, and humanistic psychology: History and current examples. *Journal of Humanistic Psychology, 45,* 302–332.

Spalding, K. L., Arner, E., Westermark, P. O., Bernard, S., Buchholz, B. A., Bergmann, O., ... Arner, P. (2008, June). Dynamics of fat cell turnover in humans. *Nature,* 453.

Spanos, N. P. (1994). Multiple identity enactments and multiple personality disorder: A sociocognitive perspective. *Psychological Bulletin, 116,* 143–165.

Spearman, C. (1904). "General intelligence" objectively determined and measured. *American Journal of Psychology, 15,* 201–293.

Spector, P. E., Cooper, C. L., Sanchez, J. I., O'Driscoll, M., Sparks, K., Bernin, P., ... Yu, A. S. (2001). Do national levels of individualism and internal locus of control relate to well-being: An ecological level international study. *Journal of Organizational Behavior, 22,* 815–832.

Spector, P. E., Fox, S., Penney, L. M., Bruursema, K., Goh, A., & Kessler, S. (2006). The dimensionality of counterproductivity: Are all counterproductive behaviors created equal? *Journal of Vocational Behavior, 68,* 446–460.

Sperry, R. W. (1974). Lateral specialization in the surgically separated hemisphere. In R. O. Schmitt & F. G. Worden (Eds.), *The neurosciences: Third study program.* Cambridge, MA: MIT Press.

Spiegal, D. (2005, November 22). Cited in S. Blakeslee, This is your brain under hypnosis. *The New York Times,* pp. D1, D4.

Spiegler, M. D., & Guevremont, D. C. (2003). *Contemporary behavior therapy* (4th ed.). Belmont, CA: Wadsworth/Thomson Learning.

Spiegler, M. D., & Guevremont, D. C. (2009). *Contemporary behavior therapy* (5th ed.). Belmont, CA: Wadsworth Cengage.

Spillar, K., & Harrington, P. (2000, February, 18). This is what you get when men rule the roost. *Los Angeles Times,* p. B7.

Spitzer, R. L., Gibbon, M., Skodol, A. E., Williams, J. B. W., & First, M. B. (Eds.). (1994). *DSM-IV casebook.* Washington, DC: American Psychiatric Association.

Spitzer, R. L., Terman, M., Williams, J. B., Terman, J. S., Malt, U. F., Singer, F., & Lewy, A. J. (1999). Jet lag. *American Journal of Psychiatry, 156,* 1392–1396.

Squire, L. R., Clark, R. E., & Bayley, P. J. (2004). Medial temporal lobe function and memory. In M. S. Gazzaniga (Ed.), *The cognitive neurosciences III.* Cambridge, MA: MIT Press.

Squire, L. R., & Kandel, E. R. (2009). *Memory: From mind to molecules.* Greenwood Village, CO: Roberts and Company Publishers.

Stahl, L. (2009, March 8). Eyewitness: How accurate is visual memory? *60 Minutes* [television series]. Retrieved from http://www.cbsnews.com/stories/2009/03/06/60minutes/main4848039.shtml

Stasser, G., & Dietz-Uhler, B. (2003). Collective choice, judgment, and problem solving. In M. A. Hogg & S. Tindale (Eds.), *Blackwell handbook of social psychology: Group processes* (pp. 31–55). Malden, MA: Blackwell Publishing.

Stein, J. (2003, August 4). Just say Om. *Time,* 50–55.

Stein, L. M., & Memon, A. (2006). Testing the efficacy of the cognitive interview in a developing country. *Applied Cognitive Psychology, 20,* 597–605.

Stein, M., & Perrin, J. M. (2003). Diagnosis and treatment of ADHD school-age children in primary care settings. *Pediatrics in Review, 24,* 92–98.

Stein, M. T. (2004). When parents and teachers disagree about a child's behavior: An opportunity for further evaluations. *Journal of Developmental & Behavioral Pediatrics, 25,* 50–51.

Stein, R. (2005a, October 9). Scientists finding out what losing sleep does to a body. *Washington Post,* p. A1.

Stein, R. (2005b, October 31). Cervical cancer vaccine gets injected with a social issue. *Washington Post,* p. A3.

Steiner, R. (1989). Live TV special explores, tests psychic powers. *Skeptical Inquirer, 14,* 2–6.

Sternberg, R. J. (1999). *Cupid's arrow: The course of love through time.* New York: Cambridge University Press.

Sternberg, R. J. (2001). What is the common thread of creativity? *American Psychologist, 56,* 360–362.

Sternberg, R. J. (2003a). Our research program validating the triarchic theory of successful intelligence: Reply to Gottfredson. *Intelligence, 31,* 399–413.

Sternberg, R. J., & O'Hara, L. A. (2000). Intelligence and creativity. In R. J. Sternberg (Ed.), *Handbook of intelligence.* New York: Cambridge University Press.

Sternberg, R. J., & Pretz, J. E. (2005). *Cognition and intelligence: Identifying the mechanisms of the mind.* New York: Cambridge University Press.

Sternberg, S. (2009, September 1). Adoption of HPV vaccine slow going. *USA Today,* p. 6D.

Stice, E. (2002). Risk and maintenance factors for eating pathology: A meta-analytic review. *Psychological Bulletin, 128,* 825–848.

Stickgold, R. (2000, March 7). Cited in S. Blakeslee, For better learning, researchers endorse "sleep on it" adage. *The New York Times,* p. D2.

Stickgold, R. (2005). Sleep-dependent memory consolidation. *Nature, 437,* 1272–1278.

Stickgold, R., & Ellenbogen, J. M. (2008, August/September). Quiet! Sleeping brain at work. *Scientific American Mind,* 22–29.

Story, M., Kaphingst, K. M., Robinson-O'Brien, R., & Glanz, K. (2008). Creating healthy food and eating environments: Policy and environmental approaches. *Annual Review of Public Health, 29,* 253–272.

Strain, E. C., Mumford, G. K., Silverman, K., & Griffiths, R. R. (1994). Caffeine dependence syndrome. *Journal of the American Medical Association, 272,* 1043–1048.

Streissguth, A. P., Barr, H. M., Bookstein, F. L., Sampson, P. D., & Olson, H. C. (1999). The long-term neurocognitive consequences of prenatal alcohol exposure: A 14-year study. *Psychological Science, 10,* 186–190.

Stromeyer, C. F., III. (1970, November). Eidetikers. *Psychology Today.*

Stutts, J. C., Wilkins, J. W., Osberg, J. S., & Vaughn, B. V. (2002). Driver risk factors for sleep-related crashes. *Accident Analysis & Prevention, 841,* 1–11.

Substance Abuse and Mental Health Services Administration. (2008). *Results from the 2007 national survey on drug use and health: National findings.* NSDUH Series H-34, DHHS Publication SMA 08-4343. Rockville, MD: Author.

Substance Abuse and Mental Health Services Administration. (2009). *Results from the 2008 national survey on drug use and health: National findings.* NSDUH Series H-36, DHHS Publication SMA 09-4434. Rockville, MD: Author.

Sue, D., Sue, D. W., & Sue, S. (2010). *Understanding abnormal behavior* (9th ed.). Boston: Wadsworth.

Swim, J. K., Aikin, K. J., Hall, W. S., & Hunter, B. A. (1995). Sexism and racism: Old-fashioned and modern principles. *Journal of Personality and Social Psychology, 68,* 199–214.

Talan, J. (2006b, October/November). Visions for psychedelics. *Scientific American Mind, 7.*

Talarico, J. M., & Rubin, D. C. (2003). Confidence, not consistency, characterizes flashbulb memories. *Psychological Science, 14,* 455–461.

Tammet, D. (2007). *Born on a blue day: Inside the extraordinary mind of an autistic savant.* New York: Free Press.

Tammet, D. (2009, April/May). Think better: Tips from a savant. *Scientific American Mind,* 60–64.

Tanouye, E. (1997, July 7). Got a big public speaking phobia? *San Diego Union-Tribune.*

Taylor, B. E. S. (2007). *ADHD & me: What I learned from lighting fires at the dinner table.* Oakland, CA: New Harbinger.

Taylor, B. E. S. (2008). Student writes personal account of ADHD. Cited in A. Hollyfield, *ABC News.* Retrieved from http://abclocal.go.com/kgo/story/?section=news/local&id=5921407&pt=print

Taylor, S. E., Kemeny, M. E., Reed, G. M., Bower, J. E., & Gruenewald, T. L. (2000). Psychological resources, positive illusions, and health. *American Psychologist, 55,* 99–109.

Taylor-Barnes, N. (2008, February 15). Teen addresses hyperactivity in own terms. Cited in C. Cadelago, *San Francisco Gate.*

Terman, L. M. (1916). *The measurement of intelligence.* Boston: Houghton Mifflin.

Terrace, H. S. (1981). A report to an academy, 1980. *Annals of the New York Academy of Sciences, 364,* 94–114.

Thapar, A., & McGuffin, P. (1993). Is personality disorder inherited? An overview of the evidence. *Journal of Psychopathology and Behavioral Assessment, 15,* 325–345.

Thase, M. E. (2006). Major depressive disorder. In M. Hersen & J. C. Thomas (Eds.), *Comprehensive handbook of personality and psychopathology: Adult psychopathology* (Vol. 2, pp. 207–230). Hoboken, NJ: John Wiley & Sons.

Thase, M. E. (2009). Neurobiological aspects of depression. In I. H. Gotlib & C. L. Hammen (Eds.), *Handbook of depression* (2nd ed., pp. 187–217). New York: Guilford.

Thelen, E. (1995). Motor development. *American Psychologist, 50,* 79–95.

Thomas, A., & Chess, S. (1977). *Temperament and development.* New York: Brunner/Mazel.

Thorpe, G. L., & Sigman, S. T. (2008). Behavior therapy. In I. Marini & M. A. Stebnicki (Eds.), *The professional counselor's desk reference* (pp. 337–344). New York: Springer Publishing.

Thraenhardt, B. (2006, December/2007, January). Hearing voices. *Scientific American Mind,* 74–79.

Time. (2007a, July 16). Opiates for the masses, 14.

Time. (2007b, November 19). Milestones.

Time. (2007c, December 3). The year in medicine: From A to Z, 63–86.

Time. (2008, July 18). The world: Numbers, 14–15.

Tisak, M. S., Tisak, J., & Goldstein, S. E. (2006). Aggression, delinquency, and morality: A social-cognitive perspective. In M. Killen & J. Smetana (Eds.), *Handbook of moral development* (pp. 611–629). Mahwah, NJ: Lawrence Erlbaum.

Tolman, E. C. (1948). Cognitive maps in rats and men. *Psychological Review, 55,* 189–208.

Tompkins, J. (2003a, June 16). A night owl resets his body clock. *Los Angeles Times,* F1.

Tompkins, J. (2003b, June 16). How light became a therapy. *Los Angeles Times,* F1.

Tonegawa, S., & Wilson, M. (1997). Cited in W. Roush, New knockout mice point to molecular basis of memory. *Science, 275,* 32–33.

Toner, M. (2006, January 29). Chimpanzees closer to humans than to other apes, study confirms. *The Sunday Times,* p. A10.

Torrey, F. E., Bowler, A. E., Taylor, E. H., & Gottesman, I. I. (1994). *Schizophrenia and manic-depressive disorder.* New York: Basic Books.

Touchthetop. (2009). Erik Weihenmayer. Retrieved from http://www.touchthetop.com

Toufexis, A., Cronin, M., & Lafferty, E. (2989, June 5). The times of your life. *Time.*

Towle, L. H. (1995, July 31). Elegy for lost boys. *Time.*

Tresniowski, A., Harmel, K., & Matsushita, N. (2005, January 24). The girl who can't feel pain. *People,* 99–101.

Tripician, R. J. (2000, January/February). Confessions of a (former) graphologist. *Skeptical Inquirer,* 44–47.

Trump, D. J (2007, May 14). Wesley Autrey: From New York, NY subway rider to all-American hero. *Time,* 101.

Tsien, J. Z. (2000). Building a brainier mouse. *Scientific American,* 62–68.

Tulving, E., & Craik, F. M. (Eds.). (2005). *The Oxford handbook of memory.* New York: Oxford University Press.

Turnbull, B. (2008, September 17). India's first female officer had tough job. *The Star.* Retrieved from http://www.thestar.com/printArticle/500506

Tyre, P. (2005, December 5). Fighting anorexia. No one to blame. *Newsweek,* 50–59.

Underwood, A. (2006, October 23). How to read a face. *Newsweek,* 65.

United Press International. (2006, November 24). Chinese learn to smile for 2008 Olympics. *Science Daily.*

U.S. Census Bureau. (2008). Cited in M. B. Marcus, People 65 and up will soon outnumber tots. *USA Today,* p. 5D.

U.S. Census Bureau. (2009a). Facts for features: Older Americans month May 2009. *U.S. Census Bureau News,* p. CB09-FF.07.

U.S. Census Bureau. (2009b, July 9). Cited in S. Jayson, Couples study debunks 'trial marriage' notion. *USA Today,* p. 7D.

U.S. Drug Enforcement Agency. (2009). *National statistics: DEA drug seizures.* Washington, DC: Author.

USA Today. (2005, August 18). Race disparities in health care persist, p. 5D.

Uys, J. D., & LaLumiere, R. T. (2008). Glutamate: The new frontier in pharmacotherapy for cocaine addiction. *CNS & Neurological Disorders—Drug Targets, 7,* 482–491.

Vahtera, J., Kivimaki, M., Uutela, A., & Pentti, J. (2000). Hostility and ill health: Role of psychosocial resources in two contexts of working life. *Journal of Psychosomatic Research, 48,* 89–98.

Valdes, L. (2006, October 16). Cited in E. P. Gunn, It is in your head. *U.S. News & World Report,* EE8–9.

Vallacher, R. R., & Nowak, A. (2007). Dynamical social psychology: Finding order in the flow of human experience. In A. W. Kruglanski & E. T. Higgins (Eds.), *Social psychology: Handbook of basic principles* (2nd ed., pp. 734–758). New York: Guilford.

Van Manen, K., & Whitbourne, S. K. (1997). Psychosocial development and life experiences in adulthood: A 22-year sequential study. *Psychology and Aging, 12,* 239–246.

van Rossum, E. F. C., Koper, J. W., Huizenga, N. A. T. M., Uitterlnden, A. G., Janssen, J. A. J. L., Brinkman, A. O., ... Lamberts, S. W. J. (2002). A polymorphism in the glucocorticoid receptor gene, which decreases sensitivity to glucocorticoids in vivo, is associated with low insulin and cholesterol levels. *Diabetes, 51,* 3128–3134.

Vargha-Khadem, F. (2000, November 20). Cited in J. Fischman, Seeds of a sociopath. *U.S. News & World Report,* 82.

Verkhratsky, A., & Butt, A. (2007). *Glial neurobiology.* West Sussex, UK: John Wiley & Sons.

Vernon, P. A., Wickett, J. C., Bazana, G. P., & Stelmack, R. M. (2000). The neuropsychology of human intelligence. In R. J. Sternberg (Ed.), *Handbook of intelligence.* New York: Cambridge University Press.

Villarreal, Y. (2008, May 18). Not even sleep can stop us texting. *The Atlanta Journal Constitution.*

Vocci, F. J., Acri, J., & Elkashef, A. (2005). Medication development for addictive disorders: The state of the science. *American Journal of Psychiatry, 162,* 1432–1440.

Vogele, C., Coles, J., Wardle, J., & Steptoe, A. (2003). Psychophysiologic effects of applied tension on the emotional fainting response to blood and injury. *Behaviour Research and Therapy, 41,* 139–155.

Volkow, N. D. (2007, March 1). *Fiscal year 2008 budget request—Testimony before the house subcommittee on labor-HHS-education appropriations.* Retrieved from http://www.nida.nih–.org

Vredenburgh, J. (2007). Cited in Big Brothers Big Sisters, *Our impact.* Retrieved from http://www.bbbs.org

Walker, H. (2008). *Breaking free.* New York: Touchstone/Howard.

Wallisch, P. (2008, February/March). An odd sense of timing. *Scientific American Mind,* 37–43.

Walsh, B. T., Kaplan, A. S., Attia, E., Olmsted, M., Parides, M., Carter, J. C., ... Rockert, W. (2006, June 14). Fluoxetine after weight restoration in anorexia nervosa. *The Journal of the American Medical Association, 295,* 2605–2612.

Walsh, T., McClellan, J. M., McCarthy, S. E., Addington, A. M., Pierce, S. B., Cooper, G. M., ... Sebat, J. (2008). Rare structural variants disrupt multiple genes in neurodevelopmental pathways in schizophrenia. *Science, 320,* 539–543.

Wansink, B., Payne, C. R., & Chandon, P. (2007). Internal and external cues of meal cessation: The French paradox redux? *Obesity, 15,* 2920–2924.

Ward, A., Tiller, J., Treasure, J., & Russell, G. (2000). Eating disorders: Psyche or soma? *International Journal of Eating Disorders, 27,* 279–287.

Ward, J., Hall, K., & Haslam, C. (2006). Patterns of memory dysfunction in current and 2-year abstinent MDMA users. *Journal of Clinical and Experimental Neuropsychology, 28,* 306–324.

Watson, J. B. (1924). *Behaviorism.* Chicago: University of Chicago Press.

Watson, J. B., & Rayner, R. (1920). Conditioned emotional reactions. *Journal of Experimental Psychology, 3,* 1–14.

Weaver, F. M., Follett, K., Stern, M., Hur, K., Harris, C., Marks, W. J., Jr., ... Huang, G. D. (2009). Bilateral deep brain stimulation vs. best medical therapy for patients with advanced Parkinson disease. *The Journal of the American Medical Association, 201,* 63–73.

Webb, W. B. (1992). *Sleep: The gentle tyrant* (2nd ed.). Bolton, MA: Anker.

Weihenmayer, E. (1999). Cited in Erik Weihenmayer, *Everest News.* Retrieved from http://www.k2news.com/erik/htm

Weinberg, R. A., Scarr, S., & Waldman, I. D. (1992). The Minnesota transracial adoption study: A follow-up of IQ test performance at adolescence. *Intelligence, 16,* 117–135.

Weiner, B. (1991). Metaphors in motivation and attribution. *American Psychologist, 46,* 921–930.

Weiner, I. B., & Meyer, G. J. (2009). Personality assessment with the Rorschach inkblot method. In J. N. Butcher (Ed.), *Oxford handbook of personality assessment* (pp. 277–298). New York: Oxford University Press.

Weir, K. (2009, March/April). Taste the rainbow. *Psychology Today,* 26.

Weissman, M. M., Verdeli, H., Gameroff, M. J., Bledsoe, S. E., Betts, K., Mufson, L., ... Wickramaratne, P. (2006). National survey of psychotherapy training in psychiatry, psychology, and social work. *Archives of General Psychiatry, 63,* 925–934.

Weitzenhoffer, A. M. (2002). Scales, scales, and more scales. *American Journal of Clinical Hypnosis, 44,* 209–219.

Wells, G. (2009, March 11). Cited in S. Finkelstein, Eyewitness: Anatomy of a story. *60 Minutes* [television program]. Retrieved from http://www.cbsnews.com/stories/2009/03/11/60minutes/main4859708.shtml

Wells, G. L., & Olson, E. A. (2003). Eyewitness testimony. *Annual Review of Psychology, 54,* 277–295.

Wenner, M. (2008a, April/May). Infected with insanity. *Scientific American Mind,* 40–47.

Werner, E. E., & Smith, R. S. (2001). *Journeys from childhood to midlife: Risk, resilience and recovery.* Ithaca, NY: Cornell University Press.

Wessel, H. (2003, February 17). Big employers increasingly using personality tests before they hire. *The Milwaukee Journal Sentinel.*

Westen, D. (2007, June 9). Cited in B. Bower, Past impressions. *Science News,* 363–365.

Westen, D., & Gabbard, G. O. (1999). Psychoanalytic approaches to personality. In L. A. Pervin & O. P. John (Eds.), *Handbook of personality* (2nd ed.), New York: Guilford.

Westen, D., Gabbard, G. O., & Ortigo, K. M. (2008). Psychoanalytic approaches to personality. Cited in O. P. John, R. W. Robins & L. A. Pervin (Eds.), *Handbook of personality* (pp. 61–113). New York: Guilford.

Westly, E. (2008, December/2009, January). Psychiatry in flux. *Scientific American Mind,* 14.

Whalen, P. J., & Phelps, E. A. (Eds.). (2009). *The human amygdala.* New York: Guilford.

White, J. M., & Porth, C. M. (2000). Evolution of a model of stress, coping and discrete emotions. In V. R. Rice (Ed.), *Handbook of stress, coping and health.* Thousand Oaks, CA: Sage.

Whitlock, G., Lewington, S., Sherliker, P., & Peto, R. (2009). Body-mass index and mortality: authors' reply. *The Lancet, 374,* 114.

Whittle, S., Yap, M. B. H., Yucel, M., Fornito, A., Simmons, J. G., Barrett, A., Sheeber, L., & Allen, N. B. (2008). Prefrontal and amygdala volumes are related to adolescents' affective behaviors during parent-adolescent interactions. *Proceedings of the National Academy of Sciences, 105,* 9.

Whorf, B. L. (1956). *Language, thought, and reality.* New York: Wiley.

Widiger, T. A., & Clark, L. A. (2000). Toward DSM-V and the classification of psychopathology. *Psychological Bulletin, 126,* 946–963.

Wiech, K., Farias, M., Kahane, G., Shackel, N., Tiede, W., & Tracey, I. (2008). An fMRI study measuring analgesia enhanced by religion as a belief system. *Pain, 139,* 467–476.

Wieloch, T., & Nikolich, K. (2006). Mechanism of neural plasticity following brain injury. *Current Opinion in Neurobiology, 16,* 258–264.

Wilgoren, J. (2005, August 19). 10 life terms for B.T.K. strangler as anguished families condemn him in court. *The New York Times,* p. A13.

Wilkins, K. (2009, March 16). There she is, strong and healthy: Miss America 2008 speaks out on eating disorders. *Detroit Free Press.*

Williams, D. (1992). *Nobody nowhere.* New York: Times Books.

Williams, D. (1994). *Somebody somewhere.* New York: Times Books.

Williams, D. (2009). *Donna Williams.* Retrieved from http://www.donnawilliams.net

Williams, J. (2009). Treat arachnophobia with virtual reality therapy. *Associated Content.*

Williams, L., O'Connor, R. C., Howard, S., Hughes, B. M., Johnston, D. W., Hay, J. L., ... O'Carroll, R. E. (2008). Type-D personality mechanisms of effect: The role of health-related behavior and social support. *Journal of Psychosomatic Research, 64,* 63–69.

Williams, M. A., & Gross, A. M. (1994). Behavior therapy. In V. B. Hasselt & M. Hersen (Eds.), *Advanced abnormal psychology.* New York: Plenum Press.

Williams, M. A., & Mattingley, J. B. (2006, June 6). Do angry men get noticed? *Current Biology, 16,* R402.

Williams, W. (2009, April 20). Cited in S. Begley, Sex, race, and IQ: Off limits? *Newsweek,* 53.

Wilson, G. T. (2005). Behavior therapy. In R. J. Corsini & D. Wedding, *Current psychotherapies* (7th ed., pp. 202–237). Belmont, CA: Brooks/Cole–Thomson Learning.

Wilson, G. T., Fairburn, C. C., Agras, W. S., Walsh, B. T., & Kramer, H. (2002). Cognitive-behavioral therapy for bulimia nervosa: Time course and mechanisms of change. *Journal of Consulting and Clinical Psychology, 20,* 267–274.

Winerman, L. (2005, October). The mind's mirror. *Monitor on Psychology, 36,* 48.

Wingert, P., & Brant, M. (2005, August 15). Reading your baby's mind. *Newsweek,* 32–39.

Winner, E. (2000). The origins and ends of giftedness. *American Psychologist, 55,* 159–169.

Wise, T. N., & Birket-Smith, M. (2002). The somatoform disorders for DSM-V: The need for changes in process and content. *Psychosomatics 43,* 437–440.

Wolf, T. H. (1973). *Alfred Binet.* Chicago: University of Chicago Press.

Wolfing, K., Flor, H., & Grusser, S. M. (2008). Psychophysiological responses to drug-associated stimuli in chronic heavy cannabis use. *European Journal of Neuroscience, 27,* 976–983.

Wolpe, J. (1958). *Psychotherapy by reciprocal inhibition.* Stanford, CA: Stanford University Press.

Wolpe, J. (1990). *The practice of behavior therapy* (4th ed.). London: Pergamon Press.

Wolpe, J., & Lazarus, A. A. (1966). *Behavior therapy techniques.* London: Pergamon Press.

Women's Sexual Health Foundation. (2008, September 15/September 22). Cited in D. Kotz, Sex, health & happiness. *U.S. News & World Report, 50–53.*

Wong, A. M., Hodges, H., & Horsburg, K. (2005). Neural stem cell grafts reduce the extent of neuronal damage in a mouse model of global ischaemia. *Brain Research, 1063,* 140–150.

Wong, P. T. P. (2006). Existential and humanistic theories. In J. C. Thomas & D. L. Segal (Eds.), *Comprehensive handbook of personality and psychopathology.* New York: Wiley.

Wood, J. M., Garb, H. N., Lilienfeld, S. O., & Nezworski, M. T. (2002). Clinical assessment. *Annual Review of Psychology, 53,* 519–543.

Wood, J. M., Nezworski, M. T., Garb, H. N., & Lilienfeld, S. O. (2006, Spring). The controversy over Exner's comprehensive system for the Rorschach: The critics speak. *Independent Practitioner.*

Wood, J. M., Nezworski, M. T., Lilienfeld, S. O., & Garb, H. N. (2003). *What's wrong with the Rorschach?* San Francisco: Jossey-Bass.

Wood, W., Christensen, P. N., Hebl, M. R., & Rothgerber, H. (1997). Conformity to sex-typed norms, affect and the self-concept. *Journal of Personality and Social Psychology, 73,* 523–535.

Woodruff, B., Hennessey, J., & Hill, J. (2008, April 14). Herschel Walker: "Tell the world my truth." *ABC News.*

Woods, S. C., Schwartz, M. W., Baskin, D. G., & Seeley, R. J. (2000). Food intake and the regulation of body weight. *Annual Review of Psychology, 51,* 255–277.

Woodward, C. (2006, November 3). Amnesiac can't return to his past to go into future. *The San Diego Union-Tribune,* p. A4.

World Health Organization. (2009). Cited in A. R. Carey & J. Snider, Life expectancies. *USA Today,* p. A1.

Wright, I. C., Rabe-Hesketh, S., Woodruff, P. W. R., David, A. S., Murray, R. M., & Bullmore, E. T. (2000). Meta-analysis of regional brain volumes in schizophrenia. *American Journal of Psychiatry, 157,* 16–25.

Wright, K. (2002, September). Times of our lives. *Scientific American,* 59–65.

Wright, K. (2003, November). Staying alive. *Discover,* 64–70.

Yamagata, S., Suzuki, A., Ando, J., Ono, Y., Kijima, N., Yoshimura, K., ... Jang, K. L. (2006). Is the genetic structure of human personality universal? A cross-cultural twin study from North America, Europe, and Asia. *Journal of Personality and Social Psychology, 90,* 987–998.

Yang, Y., Raine, A., Lencz, T., Bihrle, S., Lacasse, L., & Colletti, P. (2005a). Prefrontal white matter in pathological liars. *British Journal of Psychiatry, 187,* 320–325.

Ybarra, M. J. (1991, September 13). The psychic and the skeptic. *Los Angeles Times.*

Yoo, S., Gujar, N., Hu, P., Jolesz, F. A., & Walker, M. P. (2007). The human emotional brain without sleep—A prefrontal amygdala disconnect. *Current Biology, 17,* 877–878.

Young, M. W. (2000, March). The tick-tock of the biological clock. *Scientific American,* 64–71.

Yule, W., & Fernando, P. (1980). Blood phobia: Beware. *Behavior Research and Therapy, 18,* 587–590.

Zack, J., Kraus, R., & Stricker, G. (2004). *Online counseling: A handbook for mental health professionals.* San Diego, CA: Elsevier.

Zeineh, M. M., Engel, S. A., Thompson, P. M., & Bookheimer, S. Y. (2003). Dynamics of the hippocampus during encoding and retrieval of face-name pairs. *Science, 299,* 577–580.

Zillmer, E. A., Spiers, M. V., & Culbertson, W. C. (2008). *Principles of neuropsychology* (2nd ed.). Belmont, CA: Thomson Wadsworth.

Zimbardo, P. G. (1970). The human choice: Individuation, reason and order versus deindividuation, impulse and chaos. In W. J. Arnold & D. Levine (Eds.), *Nebraska symposium on motivation.* Lincoln, NE: University of Nebraska Press.

Zimmer, C. (2009a, February 23). Evolving Darwin. *Time,* 50–52.

Zimmer, C. (2009b, May). The brain. *Discover,* 28-29.

Zimmerman, B. J. (2000). Self-efficacy: An essential motive to learn. *Contemporary Educational Psychology, 25,* 82–91.

Zimmerman, M. A., Copeland, L. A., Shope, J. T., & Gielman, T. E. (1997). A longitudinal study of self-esteem: Implications for adolescent development. *Journal of Youth and Adolescence, 26,* 117–141.

Zola, S. M., & Squire, L. R. (2005). The medial temporal lobe and the hippocampus. In E. Tulving & F. M. Craik (Eds.), *The Oxford handbook of memory.* New York: Oxford University Press.

Zubieta, J., Bueller, J. A., Jackson, L. R., Scott, D. J., Xu, Y., Koeppe, R. A., ... Stohler, C. S. (2005). Placebo effects mediated by endogenous opioid activity on u-opioid receptors. *The Journal of Neuroscience, 25,* 7754–7762.

Zubieta, J. K. (2007, Summer). Cited in CAM (Center for Complementary and Alternative Medicine), Placebos: Sugar, shams, therapies, or all of the above. *CAM at the NIH: Focus on Complementary and Alternative Medicine,* 14.

Zucker, K. J. (1990). Gender identity disorders in children: Clinical descriptions and natural history. In R. Blanchard & B. W. Steiner (Eds.), *Clinical management of gender identity disorders in children and adults.* Washington, DC: American Psychiatric Press.

Name Index

Horney, K., 515
Horsburg, K., 71
Howard Hughes Medical Institute, 113
Howard, M. S., 371
Howard, S., 665
HRW, 228
Hsu, C., 414
Hu, L., 527
Hu, P., 173
Huang, G. D., 629
Hubbard, E. M., 103
Huesmann, L. R., 486
Hughes, B. M., 665
Huizenga, N. A. T. M., 655
Humphreys, G. W., 132–133, 325
Hunter, B. A., 463
Hur, K., 77, 629
Hurst, C., 463
Husain, M. M., 631
Huskinson, T. L., 466
Huston, J. P., 272
Hutchinson, C., 675
Hutchinson, K. E., 195

Iacoboni, M., 12, 93
Iakovaski, A. M., 663
Ingram, J., 581
Ingvar, M., 126
Innes, S. I., 126
International Schizophrenia Consortium, 578
Irwin, M. R., 173
Ishikawa, S. S., 591
Ito, T. A., 436
Iversen, L. L., 187
Ivy, J., 230
Iwanami, A., 571
Izard, C. E., 445

Jackendoff, R., 342
Jacks, J. Z., 471
Jackson, R. L., 442
Jackson, S. J., 25
Jacobs, S. C., 575
Jager, G., 193
Jahr, E., 7
James, W., 9, 436
Jang, K. L., 523, 533
Janis, I. L., 483
Jansse, J. A. J. L., 655
Japenga, A., 565
Jardin, X., 633
Jarrett, C., 421
Jarriel, T., 356
Jayson, S., 395, 461
Jefferson, D. J., 187
Jensen, M. P., 183
Jenson, A. R., 307

Jim, R., 566
Jitendra, A. K., 28
Joffee, J. M., 565
Johansson, B., 523
Johnson, J. G., 486
Johnson, K., 443
Johnson, N., 192
Johnson, S. C., 565
Johnson, V. E., 429
Johnston, D. W., 665
Johnston, J. C., 131
Johnston, V., 461
Jolesz, F. A., 173
Jones, J., 428
Jones, S. R., 578
Jones, W. H., 464
Jordan, J., 423
Joseph, S., 663
Jourdan, A., 615
Joyce, J. A., 187
Joynce, P. R., 423
Juan-Espinosa, M., 306
Juang, L., 14
Judd, H. L., 391
Judge, T. A., 463
Jung, C., 514
Junod, R. E. V., 28

Kaczmarek, L. K., 61, 63, 65
Kahane, G., 126
Kahn, R. S., 361
Kalakanis, L., 461
Kalat, J., 484
Kalat, J. W., 410
Kalb, C., 295
Kalimo, R., 176
Kalmar, K., 77, 629
Kalso, E., 126
Kandel, E. R., 256, 269, 273, 283
Kantowitz, B. H., 107
Kaplan, A. S., 423
Kaplan, R. M., 538–539, 541
Karau, S. J., 379
Karlsson, H., 578
Karussis, D., 71
Kasai, K., 571
Kasen, S., 486
Kassis, I., 71
Katz, J., 127
Kaube, H., 93
Kaufman, A. S., 317
Kaufman, L., 231
Kaufman, M., 493
Kaye, W., 422
Keisler, B. D., 189
Kellner, C. H., 631
Kelly, D., 311

Keltner, D., 437
Kemeny, M. C., 654, 662
Kendler, K. S., 418, 571, 575
Kerkof, G. A., 165
Kerner, J. F., 462
Kerns, R., 126
Kerr, C. E., 671
Kerr, N. L., 472
Kershaw, S., 178
Kershaw, T. C., 328
Kessler, R. C., 566, 644
Khatri, N., 617, 624
Khawam, E. A., 626
Kiernan, J. A., 71, 85
Kihlstrom, J. F., 580
Kilmer, B., 187
Kim, Y. S., 571
Kim-Cohen, J., 31
Kindt, M., 295
King, L. A., 446, 672
King, S., 516
Kinsbourne, M., 27, 32
Kirsch, I., 181–182, 583
Kirschenbaum, M. L., 615
Kirtland, C., 158
Kirtley, L. G., 659
Kitts, C. D., 283
Klecolt-Glaser, J. K., 655, 658–659
Klein, C. T. F., 662
Klein, D. N., 575
Klein, S. B., 230
Kleitman, N., 168
Klerman, E. B., 165
Klinger, E., 159
Klomegah, R. Y., 319
Kluger, J., 77, 416–417, 419, 443, 586, 629
Knapp, R., 631
Knight, W. G., 361
Knox, J., 182
Knuth, K. H., 591
Koch, C., 580
Koenings, M., 334
Koeppe, R. A., 126
Koestner, R., 432–433
Koeter, M., 193
Koffka, K., 10–11
Koh, M. T., 220
Kohlberg, L., 384–385
Köhler, W., 10–11, 242–243
Kok, G., 471
Kokkalis, J., 193
Kolata, G., 414
Kolb, B., 437
Koning, P., 326
Koper, J. W., 655
Kopp, C. B., 445
Koren, G., 360

Masters, C., 443
Masters, W. H., 429
Mather, M., 265
Matsumoto, D., 14, 437, 445
Matsushita, N., 146–147
Matt, G. E., 361, 423
Mattingley, J. B., 440
Mattson, S. N., 361
Mauss, I., 449
Mayer, J. D., 306, 310–311
Mayford, M., 285
Mayo Clinic, 421
Mayo Foundation for Medical Education and
    Research, 172
Mayr, E., 56
Mazure, C. M., 575, 663
Mazziotta, J., 93
Mcallister, H. A., 465
McAuliffe, K., 393
McCall, R. B., 431
McCarthy, T., 75
McClain, D. L., 326
McClearn, G. E., 523
McClelland, D. C., 430
McClelland, J. L., 131
McCrae, R. R., 533, 536
McDaniel, M. A., 275, 278, 312
McDermott, K. B., 276, 281, 291
McDougall, W., 410
McElrath, D., 195
McEwen, B. S., 654
McFarlane, W. R., 577
McGee, C. L., 361
McGehee, D. S., 189
McGowan, K., 295
McGue, M., 418
McGuffin, P., 589
McGuire, L., 655, 658–659
McIntosh, V. V. W., 423
McKenzie, J. M., 423
McLean, J. E., 317
McManus, F., 617
McNamara, J. O., 75, 85, 163
Medland, S. E., 571
Medway, F., 371
Megargee, E. I., 521
Meijer, C. J. L. M., 493
Melamed, S., 647
Mello, N. K., 186, 188, 190
Melzack, R., 127
Memon, A., 291
Mendelson, J. H., 186, 188, 190
Merikangas, K. R., 566
Mervielde, I., 535
Mesmer, A., 180
Messager, S., 380
Messer, S. C., 657
Mestel, R., 539

Meyer-Lindenberg, A., 485, 587
Meyerowitz, B. E., 662
Mezworski, M. T., 539
Michaelsen, K. F., 31
Michels, S., 197
Midtun, O., 361
Miezin, F. M., 339
Milgram, S., 475–477
Milham, M. P., 393
Miller, A., 475, 659
Miller, D. G., 290
Miller, G. E., 77, 261–262, 629
Miller, J. H., 59
Miller, M. A., 645
Miller, M. C., 560, 642, 665
Miller, R., 388
Miller, R. W., 461
Milne, B. J., 31
Milrod, B., 613
Miltenberger, R. G., 234
Minoretti, P., 571
Mirsky, A. F., 578
Mitchell, J. E., 423
Mitchell, P. B., 617
Mockus, D. S., 423
Moffitt, T. E., 31
Moller, A. C., 433
Money, J., 428
Monson, C. M., 557, 646
Montgomery, G. H., 218
Moore, D. W., 144
Moore, M., 530
Morehouse, W., III, 292
Morell, D., 577
Morey, L. C., 589
Morgan, A. B., 589
Morgan, M. J., 103
Morley, S., 127
Morris, M. R., 113
Morrison, A., 41
Morse, G., 35
Mortensen, E. L., 31
Morton, S., 146–147
Mosher, W. D., 428
Mosing, M. A., 571
Moskowitz, G. B., 462, 468
Moskowitz, J. T., 662
MSNBC, 493
Mu, Q., 443
Mufson K., 606
Muirhead, J., 662
Mukamel, R., 283
Müller, H. J., 133
Mullin, B. C., 485
Mullins, L., 77, 629
Mumford, G. K., 189
Mumford, M. D., 540
Mungadze, J., 583

Munoz, H., 530
Munoz, N., 493
Munsey, C., 16
Murphy, S., 197
Murray, H., 538
Murray, R. M., 578
Mydans, S., 421
Myers, J. M., 571
Myers, M., 577
Myrtek, M., 664

Nadel, L., 272
Nagtegaal, J. E., 165
Naish, P. L. N., 182
Nakayama, E. Y., 615
Nakayama, K., 293
Nash, M. R., 181–182
Nathan, L., 391
Nathan, P. E., 607
Nathan, P. J., 556
National Highway Traffic Safety Administra-
    tion, 158
National Institute of Mental Health, 604, 606
National Institute on Drug Abuse, 188–189
National Institutes of Health, 53
National Sleep Foundation, 172, 179
Neal, R. J., 326
Neale, J. M., 566, 602
Neale, M. C., 571
Neath, I., 266
Neiderhiser, J. M., 529
Neisser, U., 290, 319
Nelson, C. A., 363
Nelson, D. L., 191
Nelson, E. C., 571
Nemeroff, C. G., 631
Nes, L. S., 662
Nesse, R. M., 57
Neufeld, S. J., 445
Neugarten, B., 391
Newman, L. S., 460
Newman, N. J., 85
Newsweek magazine, 631
Nicholson, K., 126
Nicosia, N., 187
Nida, S., 481
Nightengale, Z. C., 213
Nikolich, K., 59
Nisbett, R. E., 311
Niznikiewicz, M. A., 578
Noback, C. R., 69
Norcross, J. C., 613, 615
Norman, D. A., 259
Nosek, B. A., 462, 468
Noseworthy, J. H., 70
Nosofsky, R. M., 322
Novotney, A., 197
Nowak, A., 483

Motivation (*continued*)
theories of, 410–413
types of, 411
Motor system
cortex, 82
development of, 364–365
disordered, 577
neurons of, 69
Movement information, 69
MRI (magnetic resonance imaging), 74
Müller-Lyer illusion, 143
Multiple personality disorder, Dissociative
identity disorder
Multiple-intelligence theory, 308
Murray, Henry, 539
Myelin, 61
Myelin sheath, 65
Myers-Briggs, 542

Narcolepsy, 177
Nash, Michael, 182
Naturalistic observation, 28–29
Nature-nurture continuum
aggression and, 484–485
intelligence and, 320–321
social development and, 356–357
Needs
achievement, 430–433
biological, 412
hierarchy of, 412–413
hunger, 414–423
sexual, 424–429
social, 412, 430
Negative affectivity, 665
Negative cognitive style, 575
Negative punishment, 231
Negative reinforcement, 229
Negative symptoms, 577
Neo-Freudians, 514–515
Nerves
characterization of, 71
deafness and, 121
impulse of, 64–65
impulses, 110
Nervous system
major divisions of, 70–73
postnatal development of, 365
psychoactive drugs effects, 186
Neuroleptic drugs, 628
Neurological factors. See Brain
Neurons
characterization of, 59
communication of, 62–63
efferent, 69
function of, 60–61
growth and repair of, 59–60
mirror, 12, 93, 491
motor, 69

reflex responses, 68–69
repair capacity of, 70–71
structure of, 60–61
transmitters for, 66
Neuropeptide Y, 419
Neuroses, 610
Neurotransmitters
end bulbs and, 65
function of, 61
psychoactive drugs and, 186
types of, 67–68
Neutral stimulus
defined, 210–211
dental fear experiment, 214–215
response to, 236
Watson's experiment, 212
Nicotine
characterization of, 189
prenatal development and, 361
Night terrors, 178
Nightmares, 178
Nim, the chimp, 345
No-single-category babies, 370
Non-REM sleep, 166–167, 179
Nonassociative learning, 208
Nondeclarative memory. See Procedural memory
Nonverbal skills, 89
Normal aging, 388
Norms
developmental, 365
deviation from, 555
group, 478
Nucleus accumbens, 410

Obama, Barack, 470
Obedience
defined, 475
Milgram's experiment, 475–477
Obesity
defined, 414
social-cultural factors in, 421
Object permanence, 367
Objective personality tests, 540–541
Observational learning, 240
Obsessive-compulsive disorder, 570
Occipital lobe, 80, 85
OCEAN, 532, 536
Olfactory cells, 123
Online activities
adolescent development, 355, 402–403
adult development, 355, 402–403
behavior, 51, 95, 97
childhood development, 355, 401
consciousness, 155, 199, 201
emotion, 407, 451, 453
intelligence, 303, 349, 351
learning, 205, 247
memory, 249, 253, 297, 299

mental disorders, 593, 595
motivation, 407, 451, 453
perceptions, 101, 149, 151
personality, 501, 545, 547
psychological disorders, 551
psychology overview, 47–49
psychotherapies, 599
sensations, 101, 151, 159
social psychology, 457, 495, 497
stress, 641, 677, 679
therapies, 635, 637
Operant conditioning
behavior modification in, 234–235
characterization of, 209
classical conditioning vs., 236–237
consequences in, 228–233
defined, 222
discrimination in, 227
extinction in, 227
generalization in, 226
history of, 222–223
for killer whale training, 244–245
law of effect in, 222
reinforcement in, 229–233
responses in, 236
Skinner box procedure, 224–225
Operant response, 223
Operations state, 326
Opiates, 190
Opium, 190
Opponent-process theory, 112
Optimal weight, 414
Optimism, 662
Oral stage, 373, 512
Organic mental disorder, 561
Organic sexual response factors, 429
Organisms, 7
Organization
information, 325
perceptions, 132–133
rules of, 132–133
Ossicles, 119
Outer ear, 118
Overgeneralization, 341
Overweight
defined, 414
social-cultural factors in, 421
Ovulation, 358

Pacinian corpuscle, 125
Pagano, Fr. Bernard, 289
Pain
characterization of, 126
gate control theory of, 127
insensitivity to, 146–147
Panic disorder, 567
Paradoxical sleep, 168
Paranoid schizophrenia, 576